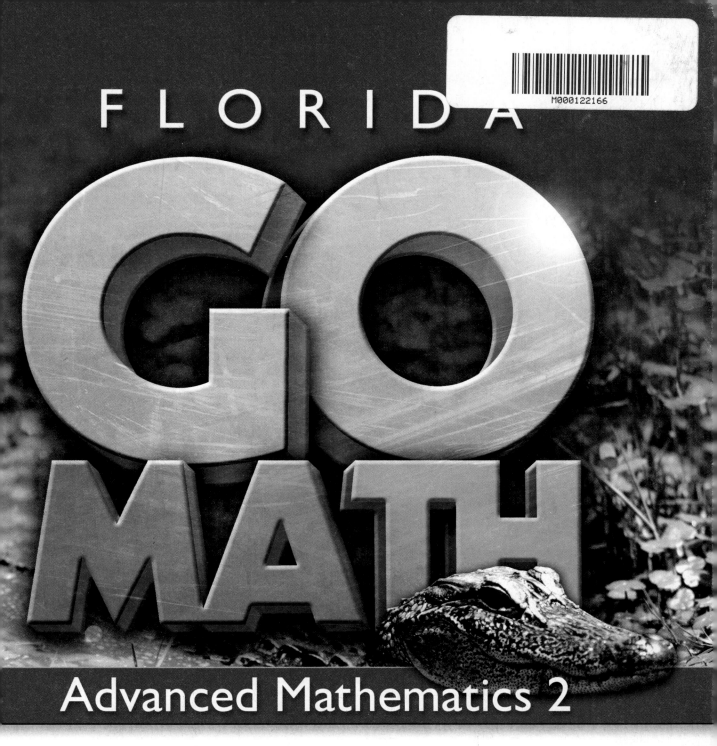

FLORIDA

GO MATH

Advanced Mathematics 2

Edward B. Burger

Juli K. Dixon

Timothy D. Kanold

Matthew R. Larson

Steven J. Leinwand

Martha E. Sandoval-Martinez

Special thanks to the students, teachers, staff, and principal Cheri Godek at Gotha Middle School, Windermere, FL.

Cover Image Credits: © C. McIntyre/PhotoLink/Getty Images

Edward B. Burger, Ph.D., is the president of Southwestern University, a former Francis Christopher Oakley Third Century Professor of Mathematics at Williams College, and a former vice provost at Baylor University. He has authored or coauthored more than sixty-five articles, books, and video series; delivered over five hundred addresses and workshops throughout the world; and made more than fifty radio and television appearances. He is a Fellow of the American Mathematical Society as well as having earned many national honors, including the Robert Foster Cherry Award for Great Teaching in 2010. In 2012, Microsoft Education named him a "Global Hero in Education."

Juli K. Dixon, Ph.D., is a Professor of Mathematics Education at the University of Central Florida. She has taught mathematics in urban schools at the elementary, middle, secondary, and post-secondary levels. She is an active researcher and speaker with numerous publications and conference presentations. Key areas of focus are deepening teachers' content knowledge and communicating and justifying mathematical ideas. She is a past chair of the NCTM Student Explorations in Mathematics Editorial Panel and member of the Board of Directors for the Association of Mathematics Teacher Educators.

Timothy D. Kanold, Ph.D., is an award-winning international educator, author, and consultant. He is a former superintendent and director of mathematics and science at Adlai E. Stevenson High School District 125 in Lincolnshire, Illinois. He is a past president of the National Council of Supervisors of Mathematics (NCSM) and the Council for the Presidential Awardees of Mathematics (CPAM). He has served on several writing and leadership commissions for NCTM during the past decade. He presents motivational professional development seminars with a focus on developing professional learning communities (PLC's) to improve the teaching, assessing, and learning of students. He has recently authored nationally recognized articles, books, and textbooks for mathematics education and school leadership, including *What Every Principal Needs to Know about the Teaching and Learning of Mathematics*.

Matthew R. Larson, Ph.D., is the K-12 mathematics curriculum specialist for the Lincoln Public Schools and served on the Board of Directors for the National Council of Teachers of Mathematics from 2010-2013. He is a past chair of NCTM's Research Committee and was a member of NCTM's Task Force on Linking Research and Practice. He is the author of several books on implementing the Common Core Standards for Mathematics. He has taught mathematics at the secondary and college levels and held an appointment as an honorary visiting associate professor at Teachers College, Columbia University.

Steven J. Leinwand is a Principal Research Analyst at the American Institutes for Research (AIR) in Washington, D.C., and has over 30 years in leadership positions in mathematics education. He is past president of the National Council of Supervisors of Mathematics and served on the NCTM Board of Directors. He is the author of numerous articles, books, and textbooks and has made countless presentations with topics including student achievement, reasoning, effective assessment, and successful implementation of standards.

Martha E. Sandoval-Martinez is a mathematics instructor at El Camino College in Torrance, California. She was previously a Math Specialist at the University of California at Davis and former instructor at Santa Ana College, Marymount College, and California State University, Long Beach. In her current and former positions, she has worked extensively to improve fundamental pre-algebra and algebra skills in students who have historically struggled with mathematics.

Florida Reviewers

Richard Austin
University of South Florida, Retired
Tampa, Florida

Lori Bartholomew
Girls Preparatory Academy
School District of
Hillsborough County
Tampa, Florida

Sharon Brown
Instructional Staff Developer
Pinellas County Schools
St. Petersburg, Florida

Jackie Cruse
Math Coach
Ferrell GPA
Tampa, Florida

Princess Hemingway
Mathematics Instructor
Clearwater High School
Clearwater, Florida

Donald Hoessler
Math Teacher
Discovery Middle School
Orlando, Florida

Becky (Rebecca) Jones, M.Ed.
NBCT EA-Math
Orange County Public Schools
Orlando, Florida

Danon Noga
Adams Middle School
Tampa, Florida

Debbi Petrone-Cosme
Buchanan Middle School
School District of Hillsborough County
Tampa, Florida

Bennie Royal Smith
Bay Point Middle School
Pinellas County Schools
St. Petersburg, Florida

Jean Sterner
Thurgood Marshall Fundamental
Middle School
Pinellas County Schools
St. Petersburg, Florida

UNIT 1

Expressions, Equations, and Inequalities

MODULE 1

Expressions and Equations

MODULE 2

Inequalities

UNIT 2 Geometry

MODULE 3 Modeling Geometric Figures

MODULE 4 Circumference, Area, and Volume

UNIT 3 Statistics and Sampling

MODULE 5 Random Samples and Populations

MODULE 6 Analyzing and Comparing Data

UNIT 4 Probability

MODULE 7 Experimental Probability

FL

MODULE 8 Theoretical Probability and Simulations

FL

UNIT 5 Real Numbers, Exponents, and Scientific Notation

MODULE 9 Real Numbers

FL

MODULE 10 Exponents and Scientific Notation

FL

UNIT 6 Proportional and Nonproportional Relationships and Function

MODULE 11 Proportional Relationships

MODULE 12 Nonproportional Relationships

MODULE 13 Writing Linear Equations

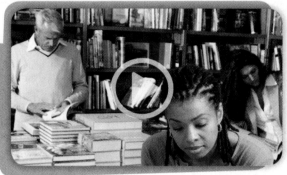

FL

MODULE 14 Functions

FL

UNIT 7 Solving Equations and Systems of Equations

MODULE 15 Solving Linear Equations

FL

MODULE 16 Solving Systems of Linear Equations

FL

UNIT 8 Transformational Geometry

MODULE 17 Transformations and Congruence

MODULE 18 Transformations and Similarity

UNIT 9 Measurement Geometry

MODULE 19 Angle Relationships in Parallel Lines and Triangles

FL

MODULE 20 The Pythagorean Theorem

FL

MODULE 21 Volume

FL

UNIT 10 Statistics: Bivariate D

MODULE 22 Scatter Plots

MODULE 23 Two-Way Tables

Florida Standards for Mathematics

Correlations for *HMH Florida Go Math* Advanced Mathematics 2

Standard	Descriptor	Citations
MAFS.7.EE.2	**Solve real-life and mathematical problems using numerical and algebraic expressions and equations.**	
MAFS.7.EE.2.3	Solve multi-step real-life and mathematical problems posed with positive and negative rational numbers in any form (whole numbers, fractions, and decimals), using tools strategically. Apply properties of operations to calculate with numbers in any form; convert between forms as appropriate; and assess the reasonableness of answers using mental computation and estimation strategies.	Develop Conceptual Understanding: SE: 25, 27, 51, 52, 53, 271–274, 304, 305, 309, 310, 311, 315, 316, 317 Fluency: SE: 25, 26, 28, 29, 30, 54, 55, 56, 272, 273, 274, 277, 278, 304, 305, 306, 307, 308, 310, 311–314, 316–320 Application: SE: 26, 30, 31, 32, 54, 56, 57, 58, 278, 291, 292, 305, 306, 308, 314, 316, 318, 320, 321, 322
MAFS.7.EE.2.4	Use variables to represent quantities in a real-world or mathematical problem, and construct simple equations and inequalities to solve problems by reasoning about the quantities.	Develop Conceptual Understanding: SE: 13, 14, 15, 19, 20, 21, 25, 41, 45, 46, 47 Fluency: SE: 13–18, 21–25, 28–30, 41, 42, 43, 44, 46, 47, 48, 49, 50 Application: SE: 14, 16, 18, 19, 20, 22, 24, 28, 30, 31, 32, 42, 44, 45, 48, 50, 57, 58
MAFS.7.EE.2.4a	Solve word problems leading to equations of the form $px + q = r$ and $p(x + q) = r$, where p, q, and r are specific rational numbers. Solve equations of these forms fluently. Compare an algebraic solution to an arithmetic solution, identifying the sequence of the operations used in each approach.	Develop Conceptual Understanding: SE: 25, 26, 27, 475 Fluency: SE: 12, 25, 26, 28, 29, 30, 471, 472, 475, 482 Application: SE: 12, 26, 28, 30, 58, 60, 63, 64, 471, 472, 475, 482
MAFS.7.EE.2.4b	Solve word problems leading to inequalities of the form $px + q > r$ or $px + q < r$, where p, q, and r are specific rational numbers. Graph the solution set of the inequality and interpret it in the context of the problem.	Develop Conceptual Understanding: SE: 37, 38, 39, 41, 51, 52, 53 Fluency: SE: 39, 40, 41, 42, 43, 44, 52, 54, 55, 56 Application: SE: 37, 38, 42, 44, 54, 56
MAFS.7.G.1	**Draw, construct, and describe geometrical figures and describe the relationships between them.**	
FS.7.G.1.1	Solve problems involving scale drawings of geometric figures, including computing actual lengths and areas from a scale drawing and reproducing a scale drawing at a different scale.	Develop Conceptual Understanding: SE: 70, 71, 72, 131 Fluency: SE: 73, 74, 75, 76 Application: SE: 71, 72, 73, 74, 75, 76, 80, 131, 132, 136

Standard	Descriptor	Citations
MAFS.7.G.1.2	Draw (freehand, with ruler and protractor, and with technology) geometric shapes with given conditions. Focus on constructing triangles from three measures of angles or sides, noticing when the conditions determine a unique triangle, more than one triangle, or no triangle.	Develop Conceptual Understanding: SE: 77, 78 Fluency: SE: 79, 80 Application: SE: 79, 80
MAFS.7.G.1.3	Describe the two-dimensional figures that result from slicing three-dimensional figures, as in plane sections of right rectangular prisms and right rectangular pyramids.	Develop Conceptual Understanding: SE: 82 Fluency: SE: 83, 84 Application: SE: 82, 83, 84, 93, 94, 132, 137, 188, 258
MAFS.7.G.2 Solve real-life and mathematical problems involving angle measure, area, surface area, and volume.		
MAFS.7.G.2.4	Know the formulas for the area and circumference of a circle and use them to solve problems; give an informal derivation of the relationship between the circumference and area of a circle.	Develop Conceptual Understanding: SE: 99, 100, 101, 105, 106, 107 Fluency: SE: 100, 101, 102, 103, 104, 106, 108, 109, 110 Application: SE: 99, 100, 101, 102, 104, 105, 106, 108, 110
MAFS.7.G.2.5	Use facts about supplementary, complementary, vertical, and adjacent angles in a multi-step problem to write and solve simple equations for an unknown angle in a figure.	Develop Conceptual Understanding: SE: 70, 85, 86, 88, 613, 614, 621 Fluency: SE: 87, 89, 90, 91, 92, 614, 615, 616, 621, 622 Application: SE: 85, 87, 90, 92, 93, 94, 614, 616, 622, 633, 634
MAFS.7.G.2.6	Solve real-world and mathematical problems involving area, volume and surface area of two- and three-dimensional objects composed of triangles, quadrilaterals, polygons, cubes, and right prisms.	Develop Conceptual Understanding: SE: 111–113, 117–119, 123–125 Fluency: SE: 113–116, 118, 120–128 Application: SE: 111, 114, 116, 117, 120, 122–130
MAFS.7.SP.1 Use random sampling to draw inferences about a population.		
MAFS.7.SP.1.1	Understand that statistics can be used to gain information about a population by examining a sample of the population; generalizations about a population from a sample are valid only if the sample is representative of that population. Understand that random sampling tends to produce representative samples and support valid inferences.	Develop Conceptual Understanding: SE: 145, 146, 147, 151, 152, 153 Fluency: SE: 147, 148, 149, 150, 153, 154, 155, 156 Application: SE: 146, 148, 150, 151, 152, 153, 154, 156, 163, 164
MAFS.7.SP.1.2	Use data from a random sample to draw inferences about a population with an unknown characteristic of interest. Generate multiple samples (or simulated samples) of the same size to gauge the variation in estimates or predictions.	Develop Conceptual Understanding: SE: 151, 153, 157, 158 Fluency: SE: 153–156, 160–162 Application: SE: 151, 152, 153, 1 156, 158, 160, 162–164

Standard	Descriptor	Citations
MAFS.7.SP.2 Draw informal comparative inferences about two populations.		
MAFS.7.SP.2.3	Informally assess the degree of visual overlap of two numerical data distributions with similar variabilities, measuring the difference between the centers by expressing it as a multiple of a measure of variability.	Develop Conceptual Understanding: SE: 170, 176, 181, 182, 183 Fluency: SE: 170, 172, 173, 174, 178, 179, 180, 182, 184, 185, 186 Application: SE: 172, 174, 176, 178, 180, 184, 186, 187, 188
MAFS.7.SP.2.4	Use measures of center and measures of variability for numerical data from random samples to draw informal comparative inferences about two populations.	Develop Conceptual Understanding: SE: 183 Fluency: SE: 172, 173, 174, 178, 179, 180, 184, 185, 186 Application: SE: 172, 174, 178, 180, 184, 186, 187, 188
MAFS.7.SP.3 Investigate chance processes and develop, use, and evaluate probability models.		
MAFS.7.SP.3.5	Understand that the probability of a chance event is a number between 0 and 1 that expresses the likelihood of the event occurring. Larger numbers indicate greater likelihood. A probability near 0 indicates an unlikely event, a probability around $\frac{1}{2}$ indicates an event that is neither unlikely nor likely, and a probability near 1 indicates a likely event.	Develop Conceptual Understanding: SE: 201, 202, 203, 204, 211, 215, 216 Fluency: SE: 203, 204, 205, 206, 207, 208, 211, 212, 213, 214, 216, 219, 220, 237, 238 Application: SE: 201, 202, 205, 206, 208, 212, 214, 220, 227, 228, 237, 238
MAFS.7.SP.3.6	Approximate the probability of a chance event by collecting data on the chance process that produces it and observing its long-run relative frequency, and predict the approximate relative frequency given the probability.	Develop Conceptual Understanding: SE: 209, 211, 221, 222, 223, 235, 245, 246, 247 Fluency: SE: 211, 212, 213, 214, 221, 222, 224, 225, 226, 236, 246, 247, 248, 249, 250 Application: SE: 209, 212, 214, 222, 224, 226, 236, 248, 250
MAFS.7.SP.3.7	Develop a probability model and use it to find probabilities of events. Compare probabilities from a model to observed frequencies; if the agreement is not good, explain possible sources of the discrepancy.	Develop Conceptual Understanding: SE: 202, 204, 215, 216, 235 Fluency: SE: 204, 206, 207, 208, 216, 218, 219, 220, 236, 237, 238 Application: SE: 202, 205, 206, 208, 218, 220, 236, 237, 238
MAFS.7.SP.3.7a	Develop a uniform probability model by assigning equal probability to all outcomes, and use the model to determine probabilities of events.	Develop Conceptual Understanding: SE: 203, 204, 233, 234, 247 Fluency: SE: 203–208, 234, 237, 238, 247, 248, 249, 250 Application: SE: 205, 206, 208, 227, 228, 233, 237, 238, 248, 250, 257, 258

Standard	Descriptor	Citations
MAFS.7.SP.3.7b	Develop a probability model (which may not be uniform) by observing frequencies in data generated from a chance process.	Develop Conceptual Understanding: SE: 209, 211, 233, 234, 235 Fluency: SE: 211–214, 234, 236, 237, 238, 249, 250, 255, 256 Application: SE: 209, 212, 214, 227, 228, 233, 236, 237, 238, 250, 256, 258, 263, 264
MAFS.7.SP.3.8	Find probabilities of compound events using organized lists, tables, tree diagrams, and simulation.	Develop Conceptual Understanding: SE: 215, 216, 239, 240, 241, 251, 252 Fluency: SE: 216, 218, 219, 220, 240–244, 252–256 Application: SE: 218, 220, 227, 228, 239, 242, 244, 254, 256, 257, 258
MAFS.7.SP.3.8a	Understand that, just as with simple events, the probability of a compound event is the fraction of outcomes in the sample space for which the compound event occurs.	Develop Conceptual Understanding: SE: 215, 216, 239 Fluency: SE: 216, 218, 219, 220, 242, 243, 244 Application: SE: 218, 220, 227, 228, 239, 242, 244, 257, 258
MAFS.7.SP.3.8b	Represent sample spaces for compound events using methods such as organized lists, tables and tree diagrams. For an event described in everyday language (e.g., "rolling double sixes"), identify the outcomes in the sample space which compose the event.	Develop Conceptual Understanding: SE: 215, 216, 240, 241 Fluency: SE: 216, 218, 219, 220, 240, 241, 242, 243, 244 Application: SE: 218, 220, 227, 228, 242, 244
MAFS.7.SP.3.8c	Design and use a simulation to generate frequencies for compound events.	Develop Conceptual Understanding: SE: 251, 252 Fluency: SE: 218, 220, 252, 253, 254, 255, 256 Application: SE: 218, 220, 254, 256, 257, 258
MAFS.8.EE.1 Work with radicals and integer exponents.		
MAFS.8.EE.1.1	Know and apply the properties of integer exponents to generate equivalent numerical expressions.	Develop Conceptual Understanding: SE: 297, 299 Fluency: SE: 298, 299, 300, 301, 302 Application: SE: 297, 299, 300, 302, 321, 322
MAFS.8.EE.1.2	Use square root and cube root symbols to represent solutions to equations of the form $x^2 = p$ and $x^3 = p$, where p is a positive rational number. Evaluate square roots of small perfect squares and cube roots of small perfect cubes. Know that $\sqrt{2}$ is irrational.	Develop Conceptual Understanding: SE: 273, 274 Fluency: SE: 273, 274, 276, 277, 278 Application: SE: 275, 276, 277, 278, 291, 292
MAFS.8.EE.1.3	Use numbers expressed in the form of a single digit times an integer power of 10 to estimate very large or very small quantities, and to express how many times as much one is than the other.	Develop Conceptual Understanding: SE: 303, 304, 305, 309, 311 Fluency: SE: 304–308, 311–314 Application: SE: 303, 305, 306, 308, 309, 311, 312, 314, 321, 322

Standard	Descriptor	Citations
MAFS.8.EE.1.4	Perform operations with numbers expressed in scientific notation, including problems where both decimal and scientific notation are used. Use scientific notation and choose units of appropriate size for measurements of very large or very small quantities (e.g., use millimeters per year for seafloor spreading). Interpret scientific notation that has been generated by technology.	Develop Conceptual Understanding: 　SE: 315, 317 Fluency: SE: 316, 317, 318, 319, 320 Application: SE: 316, 318, 319, 320
MAFS.8.EE.2　Understand the connections between proportional relationships, lines, and linear equations.		
MAFS.8.EE.2.5	Graph proportional relationships, interpreting the unit rate as the slope of the graph. Compare two different proportional relationships represented in different ways.	Develop Conceptual Understanding: 　SE: 347, 348, 349, 432 Fluency: SE: 348, 349, 350, 351, 352, 434, 435, 436 Application: SE: 348, 349, 350, 352, 353, 354, 432, 434, 436
MAFS.8.EE.2.6	Use similar triangles to explain why the slope m is the same between any two distinct points on a non-vertical line in the coordinate plane; derive the equation $y = mx$ for a line through the origin and the equation $y = mx + b$ for a line intercepting the vertical axis at b.	Develop Conceptual Understanding: 　SE: 335, 336, 337, 365, 367, 628 Fluency: SE: 336, 337, 338, 339, 340, 368, 370, 628, 629, 632 Application: SE: 335, 338, 340, 353, 354, 367, 368, 370, 385, 386, 629, 632
MAFS.8.EE.3　Analyze and solve linear equations and pairs of simultaneous linear equations.		
MAFS.8.EE.3.7	Solve linear equations in one variable.	Develop Conceptual Understanding: SE: 461, 462, 463, 467, 468, 469, 619, 627, 628 Fluency: SE: 463, 464, 465, 466, 468, 469, 470, 471, 472, 619, 622, 628, 630, 631, 632 Application: SE: 461, 464, 466, 467, 470, 472, 485, 486, 619, 627, 632
MAFS.8.EE.3.7a	Give examples of linear equations in one variable with one solution, infinitely many solutions, or no solutions. Show which of these possibilities is the case by successively transforming the given equation into simpler forms, until an equivalent equation of the form $x = a$, $a = a$, or $a = b$ results (where a and b are different numbers).	Develop Conceptual Understanding: 　SE: 479, 480 Fluency: SE: 480, 481, 482, 483, 484 Application: SE: 481, 482, 484, 485, 486
MAFS.8.EE.3.7b	Solve linear equations with rational number coefficients, including equations whose solutions require expanding expressions using the distributive property and collecting like terms.	Develop Conceptual Understanding: SE: 461, 462, 463, 467, 468, 469, 473, 474, 475 Fluency: SE: 463, 464, 465, 466, 468, 469, 470, 471, 472, 474, 475, 476, 477, 478, 623, 624 Application: SE: 461, 464, 466, 467, 470, 472, 475, 476, 478, 485, 486, 622, 624

Standard	Descriptor	Citations
MAFS.8.EE.3.8	Analyze and solve pairs of simultaneous linear equations.	Develop Conceptual Understanding: SE: 491, 494, 499, 500, 501, 502, 507, 508, 509, 510, 515, 516, 517, 518, 523, 524 Fluency: SE: 496, 497, 498, 500, 502, 504, 505, 506, 508, 510, 512, 513, 516, 518, 520, 521, 522, 525, 526, 527, 528 Application: SE: 496, 497, 498, 500, 504, 506, 508, 509, 512, 514, 522, 523, 525, 526, 528, 529, 530
MAFS.8.EE.3.8a	Understand that solutions to a system of two linear equations in two variables correspond to points of intersection of their graphs, because points of intersection satisfy both equations simultaneously.	Develop Conceptual Understanding: SE: 491 Fluency: SE: 496, 497, 498 Application: SE: 496, 497, 498, 529, 530
MAFS.8.EE.3.8b	Solve systems of two linear equations in two variables algebraically, and estimate solutions by graphing the equations. Solve simple cases by inspection.	Develop Conceptual Understanding: SE: 499, 500, 501, 502, 507, 508, 509, 510, 515, 516, 517, 518, 523, 524 Fluency: SE: 500, 502, 504, 505, 506, 508, 510, 512, 513, 516, 518, 520, 521, 522, 525, 526, 527, 528 Application: SE: 500, 504, 506, 508, 509, 514, 522, 523, 525, 526, 529, 530
MAFS.8.EE.3.8c	Solve real-world and mathematical problems leading to two linear equations in two variables.	Develop Conceptual Understanding: SE: 494, 502, 510, 518 Fluency: SE: 496, 497, 498, 502, 504, 505, 506, 510, 512, 513, 518, 520, 521, 522, 528 Application: SE: 496, 497, 498, 504, 506, 512, 514, 522, 528, 529, 530
MAFS.8.F.1 Define, evaluate, and compare functions.		
MAFS.8.F.1.1	Understand that a function is a rule that assigns to each input exactly one output. The graph of a function is the set of ordered pairs consisting of an input and the corresponding output.	Develop Conceptual Understanding: SE: 417, 418, 419, 421 Fluency: SE: 419, 420, 421, 422, 423, 424, 429, 430 Application: SE: 418, 419, 420, 421, 422, 424, 425, 430, 443, 444
MAFS.8.F.1.2	Compare properties of two functions each represented in a different way (algebraically, graphically, numerically in tables, or by verbal descriptions).	Develop Conceptual Understanding: SE: 349, 380, 431, 433 Fluency: SE: 349, 350, 351, 352, 381, 382, 432, 434, 435, 436 Application: SE: 349, 350, 352, 382, 385, 386, 432, 434, 436
MAFS.8.F.1.3	Interpret the equation $y = mx + b$ as defining a linear function, whose graph is a straight line; give examples of functions that are not linear.	Develop Conceptual Understanding: SE: 359, 360, 361, 371, 372, 425, 426, 427 Fluency: SE: 359, 361, 362, 363, 364, 372, 374, 375, 376, 383, 426, 427, 428, 429, 430 Application: SE: 360, 362, 364, 372, 374, 376, 385, 386, 425, 428, 430

Standard	Descriptor	Citations
MAFS.8.F.2 Use functions to model relationships between quantities.		
MAFS.8.F.2.4	Construct a function to model a linear relationship between two quantities. Determine the rate of change and initial value of the function from a description of a relationship or from two (*x, y*) values, including reading these from a table or from a graph. Interpret the rate of change and initial value of a linear function in terms of the situation it models, and in terms of its graph or a table of values.	Develop Conceptual Understanding: SE: 341, 343, 347, 366, 372, 378, 379, 391, 392, 393, 397, 398, 431, 432, 433 Fluency: SE: 340, 341, 343, 344, 345, 346, 350, 351, 366, 368, 369, 370, 372, 374, 375, 376, 378, 379, 382, 383, 384, 392, 394, 395, 396, 398, 399, 400, 401, 402, 432, 434, 435, 436 Application: SE: 340, 342, 344, 346, 350, 353, 354, 368, 370, 372, 374, 376, 378, 382, 384, 385, 386, 392, 393, 394, 396, 399, 400, 402, 432, 434, 436
MAFS.8.F.2.5	Describe qualitatively the functional relationship between two quantities by analyzing a graph (e.g., where the function is increasing or decreasing, linear or nonlinear). Sketch a graph that exhibits the qualitative features of a function that has been described verbally.	Develop Conceptual Understanding: SE: 437, 438 Fluency: SE: 440, 441, 442 Application: SE: 437, 438, 439, 440, 442, 443, 444
MAFS.8.G.1 Understand congruence and similarity using physical models, transparencies, or geometry software.		
MAFS.8.G.1.1a	Verify experimentally the properties of rotations, reflections, and translations: lines are taken to lines, and line segments to line segments of the same length.	Develop Conceptual Understanding: SE: 543, 544, 545, 549, 550, 551, 555, 556, 557 Fluency: SE: 546, 547, 548, 552, 553, 554, 558, 559, 560 Application: SE: 543, 545, 546, 548, 549, 551, 552, 554, 555, 557, 558, 560, 573, 574
MAFS.8.G.1.1b	Verify experimentally the properties of rotations, reflections, and translations: angles are taken to angles of the same measure.	Develop Conceptual Understanding: SE: 543, 544, 545, 549, 550, 551, 555, 556, 557 Fluency: SE: 546, 548, 552, 553, 554, 558, 559, 560 Application: SE: 543, 545, 546, 548, 549, 551, 552, 554, 555, 557, 558, 560, 573, 574
MAFS.8.G.1.1c	Verify experimentally the properties of rotations, reflections, and translations: parallel lines are taken to parallel lines.	Develop Conceptual Understanding: SE: 543, 544, 545, 549, 550, 551, 555, 556, 557 Fluency: SE: 546, 548, 552, 553, 554, 558, 559, 560 Application: SE: 543, 545, 546, 548, 549, 551, 552, 554, 555, 557, 558, 560, 573, 574
MAFS.8.G.1.2	Understand that a two-dimensional figure is congruent to another if the second can be obtained from the first by a sequence of rotations, reflections, and translations; given two congruent figures, describe a sequence that exhibits the congruence between them.	Develop Conceptual Understanding: SE: 567, 568 Fluency: SE: 569, 570, 571, 572 Application: SE: 567, 570, 572, 573, 574

Standard	Descriptor	Citations
MAFS.8.G.1.3	Describe the effect of dilations, translations, rotations, and reflections on two-dimensional figures using coordinates.	Develop Conceptual Understanding: SE: 545, 551, 557, 561, 562, 563, 579, 580, 581, 585, 586, 587 Fluency: SE: 546, 548, 552, 553, 554, 558, 559, 560, 562, 563, 564, 565, 566, 582, 583, 584, 587, 588, 589, 590 Application: SE: 545, 546, 548, 551, 552, 554, 557, 558, 560, 564, 566, 580, 581, 582, 584, 586, 588, 590, 597, 598
MAFS.8.G.1.4	Understand that a two-dimensional figure is similar to another if the second can be obtained from the first by a sequence of rotations, reflections, translations, and dilations; given two similar two-dimensional figures, describe a sequence that exhibits the similarity between them.	Develop Conceptual Understanding: SE: 579, 580, 581, 591, 592 Fluency: SE: 582, 583, 584, 593, 594, 595, 596 Application: SE: 580, 581, 582, 584, 594, 596, 597, 598
MAFS.8.G.1.5	Use informal arguments to establish facts about the angle sum and exterior angle of triangles, about the angles created when parallel lines are cut by a transversal, and the angle-angle criterion for similarity of triangles.	Develop Conceptual Understanding: SE: 611, 613, 617, 618, 619, 620, 621, 625, 626 Fluency: SE: 614, 615, 616, 619, 621, 622, 623, 624, 626, 631, 632 Application: SE: 612, 614, 616, 617, 619, 620, 622, 624, 625, 632, 633, 634
MAFS.8.G.2 Understand and apply the Pythagorean Theorem.		
MAFS.8.G.2.6	Explain a proof of the Pythagorean Theorem and its converse.	Develop Conceptual Understanding: SE: 639, 640, 645, 646, 647 Fluency: SE: 646, 647, 648, 649, 650 Application: SE: 640, 644, 645, 648, 650
MAFS.8.G.2.7	Apply the Pythagorean Theorem to determine unknown side lengths in right triangles in real-world and mathematical problems in two and three dimensions.	Develop Conceptual Understanding: SE: 639, 640, 641 Fluency: SE: 641, 642, 643, 644 Application: SE: 640, 642, 644, 685, 686
MAFS.8.G.2.8	Apply the Pythagorean Theorem to find the distance between two points in a coordinate system.	Develop Conceptual Understanding: SE: 651, 652, 653 Fluency: SE: 651, 654, 655, 656 Application: SE: 652, 654, 656, 657, 658, 686, 688
MAFS.8.G.3 Solve real-world and mathematical problems involving volume of cylinders, cones, and spheres.		
MAFS.8.G.3.9	Know the formulas for the volumes of cones, cylinders, and spheres and use them to solve real-world and mathematical problems.	Develop Conceptual Understanding: SE: 663, 664, 665, 669, 670, 671, 675, 676, 677 Fluency: SE: 665, 666, 667, 668, 671, 672, 673, 674, 676, 677, 678, 679, 680 Application: SE: 663, 664, 666, 668, 669, 670, 672, 674, 675, 677, 678, 680, 681, 682

MAFS.8.NS.1 Know that there are numbers that are not rational, and approximate them by rational numbers.

Standard	Descriptor	Citations
MAFS.8.NS.1.1	Know that numbers that are not rational are called irrational. Understand informally that every number has a decimal expansion; for rational numbers show that the decimal expansion repeats eventually, and convert a decimal expansion which repeats eventually into a rational number.	Develop Conceptual Understanding: SE: 271, 272, 273, 279, 280, 281 Fluency: SE: 272, 273, 276, 277, 278, 280, 281, 282, 283, 284 Application: SE: 276, 278, 282, 284
MAFS.8.NS.1.2	Use rational approximations of irrational numbers to compare the size of irrational numbers, locate them approximately on a number line diagram, and estimate the value of expressions (e.g., π^2).	Develop Conceptual Understanding: SE: 274, 285, 286, 287 Fluency: SE: 274, 285, 286, 287, 288, 289, 290 Application: SE: 275, 276, 278, 288, 290

MAFS.8.SP.1 Investigate patterns of association in bivariate data.

Standard	Descriptor	Citations
MAFS.8.SP.1.1	Construct and interpret scatter plots for bivariate measurement data to investigate patterns of association between two quantities. Describe patterns such as clustering, outliers, positive or negative association, linear association, and nonlinear association.	Develop Conceptual Understanding: SE: 406, 697, 699, 703, 704 Fluency: SE: 408, 409, 410, 699, 700, 701, 702, 706, 707, 708 Application: SE: 408, 410, 697, 698, 699, 700, 702, 703, 708
MAFS.8.SP.1.2	Know that straight lines are widely used to model relationships between two quantitative variables. For scatter plots that suggest a linear association, informally fit a straight line, and informally assess the model fit by judging the closeness of the data points to the line.	Develop Conceptual Understanding: SE: 403, 404, 703, 704 Fluency: SE: 404, 408, 409, 410, 705, 706, 707, 708 Application: SE: 408, 410, 703, 708
MAFS.8.SP.1.3	Use the equation of a linear model to solve problems in the context of bivariate measurement data, interpreting the slope and intercept.	Develop Conceptual Understanding: SE: 404, 703, 704, 705 Fluency: SE: 404, 405, 408, 409, 410, 705, 706, 707, 708 Application: SE: 405, 408, 410, 703, 705, 706, 708, 709, 710
MAFS.8.SP.1.4	Understand that patterns of association can also be seen in bivariate categorical data by displaying frequencies and relative frequencies in a two-way table. Construct and interpret a two-way table summarizing data on two categorical variables collected from the same subjects. Use relative frequencies calculated for rows or columns to describe possible association between the two variables.	Develop Conceptual Understanding: SE: 715, 716, 721, 722, 723, 724, 725 Fluency: SE: 717, 718, 719, 720, 724, 725, 726, 727 Application: SE: 716, 718, 720, 721, 724, 726, 728, 729, 730

Standard	Descriptor	Citations
MP Mathematical Practices Standards		*The mathematical practices standards are integrated throughout the book. See, for example, the citations below.*
MAFS.K12.MP.1.1	**Make sense of problems and persevere in solving them.** Mathematically proficient students start by explaining to themselves the meaning of a problem and looking for entry points to its solution. They analyze givens, constraints, relationships, and goals. They make conjectures about the form and meaning of the solution and plan a solution pathway rather than simply jumping into a solution attempt. They consider analogous problems, and try special cases and simpler forms of the original problem in order to gain insight into its solution. They monitor and evaluate their progress and change course if necessary. Older students might, depending on the context of the problem, transform algebraic expressions or change the viewing window on their graphing calculator to get the information they need. Mathematically proficient students can explain correspondences between equations, verbal descriptions, tables, and graphs or draw diagrams of important features and relationships, graph data, and search for regularity or trends. Younger students might rely on using concrete objects or pictures to help conceptualize and solve a problem. Mathematically proficient students check their answers to problems using a different method, and they continually ask themselves, "Does this make sense?" They can understand the approaches of others to solving complex problems and identify correspondences between different approaches.	SE: 11–12, 17–18, 19–22, 23–24 29–30, 37–42, 43–44, 49–50, 55–56, 75–76, 79–80, 83–84, 91–92, 109–110, 115–116, 121–122, 127–128, 149–150, 155–156, 161–162, 173–174, 179–180, 185–186, 207–208, 213–214, 219–220, 225–226, 237–238, 243–244, 249–250, 255–256, 277–278, 283–284, 289–290, 301–302, 307–308, 313–314, 316–318, 319–320, 339–340, 345–346, 351–352, 363–364, 369–370, 375–376, 383–384, 395–396, 401–402, 409–410, 423–424, 429–430, 435–436, 441–442, 465–466, 471–472, 474–476, 477–478, 483–484, 497–498, 505–506, 508–512, 513–514, 521–522, 527–528, 547–548, 553–554, 559–560, 565–566, 571–572, 583–584, 589–590, 595–596, 615–616, 623–624, 631–632, 643–644, 649–650, 655–656, 667–668, 673–674, 679–680, 701–702, 707–708, 719–720, 727–728
MAFS.K12.MP.2.1	**Reason abstractly and quantitatively.** Mathematically proficient students make sense of quantities and their relationships in problem situations. They bring two complementary abilities to bear on problems involving quantitative relationships: the ability to decontextualize—to abstract a given situation and represent it symbolically and manipulate the representing symbols as if they have a life of their own, without necessarily attending to their referents—and the ability to contextualize, to pause as needed during the manipulation process in order to probe into the referents for the symbols involved. Quantitative reasoning entails habits of creating a coherent representation of the problem at hand; considering the units involved; attending to the meaning of quantities, not just how to compute them; and knowing and flexibly using different properties of operations and objects.	SE: 11, 12, 30, 43, 45–48, 50, 52, 76, 85–90, 103, 107, 111–113, 122, 127, 128, 155, 156, 161, 175–178, 181–182, 185, 213, 215–218, 219, 220, 225, 239–242, 243, 249, 250, 255, 278, 284, 289, 302, 309–312, 313, 346, 352, 367, 375, 376, 383, 384, 391, 394, 396, 401, 409, 410, 417–418, 424, 429, 430, 436, 441, 442, 465, 466, 472, 477, 483, 497, 513, 514, 518–519, 521, 523–526, 527, 553, 555–558, 559, 560, 566, 572, 583, 584, 589, 590, 595, 615, 616, 618–619, 624, 631, 632, 649, 650, 651–654, 656, 673, 674, 680, 720, 728

Standard	Descriptor	Citations
MAFS.K12.MP.3.1	**Construct viable arguments and critique the reasoning of others.** Mathematically proficient students understand and use stated assumptions, definitions, and previously established results in constructing arguments. They make conjectures and build a logical progression of statements to explore the truth of their conjectures. They are able to analyze situations by breaking them into cases, and can recognize and use counterexamples. They justify their conclusions, communicate them to others, and respond to the arguments of others. They reason inductively about data, making plausible arguments that take into account the context from which the data arose. Mathematically proficient students are also able to compare the effectiveness of two plausible arguments, distinguish correct logic or reasoning from that which is flawed, and—if there is a flaw in an argument—explain what it is. Elementary students can construct arguments using concrete referents such as objects, drawings, diagrams, and actions. Such arguments can make sense and be correct, even though they are not generalized or made formal until later grades. Later, students learn to determine domains to which an argument applies. Students at all grades can listen or read the arguments of others, decide whether they make sense, and ask useful questions to clarify or improve the arguments.	SE: 8, 11, 12, 18, 30, 44, 50, 56, 79, 80, 91, 92, 104, 109, 110, 116, 121, 127, 150, 155, 156, 161, 162, 174, 179, 180, 185, 186, 213, 214, 226, 237, 238, 243, 244, 249, 250, 256, 278, 283, 284, 290, 301, 302, 307, 308, 313–314, 320, 340, 345, 346, 352, 364, 370, 376, 384, 396, 402, 410, 423, 424, 429, 430, 431–434, 435, 436, 442, 466, 472, 477, 478, 483, 491–496, 498, 505, 514, 521, 522, 527, 528, 548, 553, 554, 560, 561–564, 566, 572, 584, 590, 595, 615, 616, 624, 632, 644, 650, 663–666, 668, 674, 680, 702, 708, 728
MAFS.K12.MP.4.1	**Model with mathematics.** Mathematically proficient students can apply the mathematics they know to solve problems arising in everyday life, society, and the workplace. In early grades, this might be as simple as writing an addition equation to describe a situation. In middle grades, a student might apply proportional reasoning to plan a school event or analyze a problem in the community. By high school, a student might use geometry to solve a design problem or use a function to describe how one quantity of interest depends on another. Mathematically proficient students who can apply what they know are comfortable making assumptions and approximations to simplify a complicated situation, realizing that these may need revision later. They are able to identify important quantities in a practical situation and map their relationships using such tools as diagrams, two-way tables, graphs, flowcharts and formulas. They can analyze those relationships mathematically to draw conclusions. They routinely interpret their mathematical results in the context of the situation and reflect on whether the results make sense, possibly improving the model if it has not served its purpose.	SE: 7–10, 16, 17, 18, 23, 24, 25–28, 29, 37, 41, 42, 43, 44, 49, 71–74, 75, 76, 79, 81–83, 84, 103, 104, 105–108, 109, 110, 115, 117–120, 121, 122, 127, 128, 145–148, 149, 151–154, 155, 156, 162, 173, 179, 185, 186, 207, 209–212, 213, 214, 219, 220, 221–224, 225, 226, 237, 243, 244, 245–248, 249, 255, 256, 277, 278, 285–288, 290, 301, 303–306, 307, 308, 313–314, 319, 335–338, 339, 340, 345, 347–350, 351, 352, 359–362, 363, 375, 383, 393–394, 395, 397–400, 401, 402, 409, 417–422, 423, 435, 436, 437–440, 441, 442, 461–464, 465, 468–469, 471, 477, 478, 483, 484, 498, 505, 506, 513, 521, 522, 528, 548, 560, 571, 585–588, 589, 595, 596, 625–630, 643, 644, 649, 655, 656, 667, 669–672, 673, 679, 680, 707, 719, 727

Standard	Descriptor	Citations
MAFS.K12.MP.5.1	**Use appropriate tools strategically.** Mathematically proficient students consider the available tools when solving a mathematical problem. These tools might include pencil and paper, concrete models, a ruler, a protractor, a calculator, a spreadsheet, a computer algebra system, a statistical package, or dynamic geometry software. Proficient students are sufficiently familiar with tools appropriate for their grade or course to make sound decisions about when each of these tools might be helpful, recognizing both the insight to be gained and their limitations. For example, mathematically proficient high school students analyze graphs of functions and solutions generated using a graphing calculator. They detect possible errors by strategically using estimation and other mathematical knowledge. When making mathematical models, they know that technology can enable them to visualize the results of varying assumptions, explore consequences, and compare predictions with data. Mathematically proficient students at various grade levels are able to identify relevant external mathematical resources, such as digital content located on a website, and use them to pose or solve problems. They are able to use technological tools to explore and deepen their understanding of concepts.	SE: 9, 19, 22, 23, 25, 28, 29, 45, 48, 51–54, 55, 77–80, 85–86, 92, 99, 105, 111–114, 115, 116, 122, 157–160, 173, 189, 212, 217, 220, 251–254, 256, 284, 286, 289, 301, 314, 317, 319, 342, 345, 348, 375, 402, 405, 428, 430, 461, 464, 466, 472, 491–495, 501, 505, 540, 544, 549–552, 556, 579–582, 584, 590, 616–622, 623, 625, 639–642, 643, 645, 648, 649, 655, 667, 679, 726
MAFS.K12.MP.6.1	**Attend to precision.** Mathematically proficient students try to communicate precisely to others. They try to use clear definitions in discussion with others and in their own reasoning. They state the meaning of the symbols they choose, including using the equal sign consistently and appropriately. They are careful about specifying units of measure, and labeling axes to clarify the correspondence with quantities in a problem. They calculate accurately and efficiently, express numerical answers with a degree of precision appropriate for the problem context. In the elementary grades, students give carefully formulated explanations to each other. By the time they reach high school they have learned to examine claims and make explicit use of definitions.	SE: 5, 23, 24, 29, 35, 69, 84, 97, 100, 124, 125, 143, 145–148, 167, 181–184, 199, 201–206, 207, 208, 214, 231, 269, 271–276, 283, 289, 295, 319, 320, 333, 357, 369, 370, 371–374, 377–382, 383, 384, 389, 395, 403–408, 407, 415, 424, 425–428, 441, 459, 467–470, 478, 489, 497, 499–504, 506, 518, 541, 543–546, 547, 548, 553, 554, 565, 566, 567–570, 577, 583, 591–594, 609, 611–614, 615, 624, 632, 637, 650, 661, 668, 675–678, 695, 702, 703–706, 713, 715–718, 728

Standard	Descriptor	Citations
MAFS.K12.MP.7.1	**Look for and make use of structure.** Mathematically proficient students look closely to discern a pattern or structure. Young students, for example, might notice that three and seven more is the same amount as seven and three more, or they may sort a collection of shapes according to how many sides the shapes have. Later, students will see 7×8 equals the well remembered $7 \times 5 + 7 \times 3$, in preparation for learning about the distributive property. In the expression $x^2 + 9x + 14$, older students can see the 14 as 2×7 and the 9 as $2 + 7$. They recognize the significance of an existing line in a geometric figure and can use the strategy of drawing an auxiliary line for solving problems. They also can step back for an overview and shift perspective. They can see complicated things, such as some algebraic expressions, as single objects or as being composed of several objects. For example, they can see $5 - 3(x - y)^2$ as 5 minus a positive number times a square and use that to realize that its value cannot be more than 5 for any real numbers x and y.	SE: 9, 12, 14–16, 18, 24, 30, 49, 50, 56, 75, 80, 84, 99–102, 110, 115, 116, 117–118, 121, 122, 123–126, 128, 149, 156, 169–172, 180, 183, 185, 226, 233–236, 244, 255, 256, 274–275, 278, 279–282, 283, 284, 297–299, 301, 302, 307, 308, 340, 341–344, 345, 346, 364, 365–368, 397–399, 417–418, 472, 506, 522, 528, 547, 561–564, 565, 645–648, 680, 697–700, 701, 702, 727
MAFS.K12.MP.8.1	**Look for and express regularity in repeated reasoning.** Mathematically proficient students notice if calculations are repeated, and look both for general methods and for shortcuts. Upper elementary students might notice when dividing 25 by 11 that they are repeating the same calculations over and over again, and conclude they have a repeating decimal. By paying attention to the calculation of slope as they repeatedly check whether points are on the line through (1, 2) with slope 3, middle school students might abstract the equation $\frac{(y - 2)}{(x - 1)} = 3$. Noticing the regularity in the way terms cancel when expanding $(x - 1)(x + 1)$, $(x - 1)(x^2 + x + 1)$, and $(x - 1)(x^3 + x^2 + x + 1)$ might lead them to the general formula for the sum of a geometric series. As they work to solve a problem, mathematically proficient students maintain oversight of the process, while attending to the details. They continually evaluate the reasonableness of their intermediate results.	SE: 24, 37–38, 44, 75, 78, 80, 84, 85, 91, 92, 99, 124, 156, 173, 174, 179, 185, 208, 219, 220, 237, 238, 241, 249, 250, 272, 278, 284, 297–300, 309, 313–314, 340, 342, 364, 371, 376, 410, 461, 472, 478, 479–482, 499, 507, 515, 522, 545, 547, 548, 551, 554, 557, 561–564, 566, 567, 584, 616, 624, 625, 650, 652, 656, 663, 674, 722–726

Florida English Language Arts Standards

HMH Florida Go Math supports English language learners at all proficiency levels. The *HMH Florida Go Math Student Edition* provides integrated resources to assist all levels of learners, as shown in the correlation tables provided below.

In addition, students at various levels may benefit from additional program support:

Beginning—Students at a Beginning level are supported by *Spanish Student Edition, Spanish Assessment Resources*, Success for Every Learner and Leveled Practice A worksheets in *Differentiated Instruction, Math On the Spot* videos with Spanish closed captioning, and the *Multilingual Glossary*.

Intermediate—Students at the Intermediate level may use any of the resources above, and may also use Reading Strategies in *Differentiated Instruction*.

Advanced and Advanced High—Students at these levels will be successful as the *Student Edition* promotes vocabulary development through visual and context clues. The *Multilingual Glossary* may also be helpful.

English Language Arts Standard	Student Edition Citations
LAFS.68.WHST.1.1 Write arguments focused on *discipline-specific content*. **a.** Introduce claim(s) about a topic or issue, acknowledge and distinguish the claim(s) from alternate or opposing claims, and organize the reasons and evidence logically. **b.** Support claim(s) with logical reasoning and relevant, accurate data and evidence that demonstrate an understanding of the topic or text, using credible sources. **c.** Use words, phrases, and clauses to create cohesion and clarify the relationships among claim(s), counterclaims, reasons, and evidence. **d.** Establish and maintain a formal style. **e.** Provide a concluding statement or section that follows from and supports the argument presented.	Develop Conceptual Understanding: SE: 14, 71, 145, 146, 545, 567, 587, 611, 645, 675, 697 Fluency: SE: 12, 14, 71, 80, 146, 179, 180, 205, 238, 297, 299, 320, 360, 370, 407, 442, 545, 554, 567, 587, 612, 644, 645, 674, 675, 697, 708 Application: SE: 12, 14, 71, 80, 146, 180, 238, 297, 299, 320, 360, 370, 407, 442, 545, 554, 567, 612, 644, 645, 674, 675, 697, 708
LAFS.68.WHST.2.4 Produce clear and coherent writing in which the development, organization, and style are appropriate to task, purpose, and audience.	Develop Conceptual Understanding: SE: 45, 159 Fluency: SE: 50, 110, 160, 238, 320, 410, 478, 548, 590, 668, 708 Application: SE: 50, 110, 160, 238, 320, 410, 478, 548, 590, 668, 708

English Language Arts Standard	Student Edition Citations
LAFS.7.SL.1.1 Engage effectively in a range of collaborative discussions (one-on-one, in groups, and teacher-led) with diverse partners on grade 7 topics, texts, and issues, building on others' ideas and expressing their own clearly. **a.** Come to discussions prepared, having read or researched material under study; explicitly draw on that preparation by referring to evidence on the topic, text, or issue to probe and reflect on ideas under discussion. **b.** Follow rules for collegial discussions, track progress toward specific goals and deadlines, and define individual roles as needed. **c.** Pose questions that elicit elaboration and respond to others' questions and comments with relevant observations and ideas that bring the discussion back on topic as needed. **d.** Acknowledge new information expressed by others and, when warranted, modify their own views.	Develop Conceptual Understanding: SE: 14, 19, 51, 85, 105, 113, 151, 157–158, 160, 202, 235, 236, 273, 309, 342, 360, 379, 407, 417, 426, 433, 439, 474, 491, 493, 501, 544, 550, 551, 556, 568, 580, 611–612, 621, 629, 653, 698, 706 Application: SE: 379, 417, 433, 653
LAFS.7.SL.1.2 Analyze the main ideas and supporting details presented in diverse media and formats (e.g., visually, quantitatively, orally) and explain how the ideas clarify a topic, text, or issue under study.	Develop Conceptual Understanding: SE: 5, 53, 69, 100, 143, 153, 158, 199, 210, 269, 299, 361, 389, 459, 463, 561, 577, 653, 704, 713 Fluency: SE: 23, 115, 313, 384, 423, 572, 702 Application: SE: 572
LAFS.7.SL.1.3 Delineate a speaker's argument and specific claims, evaluating the soundness of the reasoning and the relevance and sufficiency of the evidence.	Develop Conceptual Understanding: SE: 27, 153, 211, 241, 371, 475, 518 Fluency: SE: 30, 127, 156, 214, 243, 284, 308, 320, 376, 410, 466, 472, 478, 514, 521, 522 Application: SE: 30, 127, 156, 214, 243, 284, 308, 320, 376, 410, 466, 472, 478, 514, 521, 522
LAFS.7.SL.2.4 Present claims and findings, emphasizing salient points in a focused, coherent manner with pertinent descriptions, facts, details, and examples; use appropriate eye contact, adequate volume, and clear pronunciation.	Develop Conceptual Understanding: SE: 14, 37–38, 45, 46, 71, 72, 101, 111, 124, 146, 151, 158, 175, 201, 205, 298, 335, 347, 348, 367, 399, 425, 437, 438, 439, 461, 462, 502, 525, 581, 586, 591, 617, 640, 652, 663, 698, 704, 716, 721, 723, 724 Fluency: SE: 275 Application: SE: 425, 437, 439, 462, 581, 716, 722–723
LAFS.68.RST.1.3 Follow precisely a multistep procedure when carrying out experiments, taking measurements, or performing technical tasks.	Develop Conceptual Understanding: SE: 9, 77, 88–89, 152, 153, 211, 215, 274–275, 365, 461, 462, 567, 628–629, 715 Fluency: SE: 15, 16, 162, 277, 369, 505, 548, 596, 631, 679, 720 Application: SE: 211, 369, 462, 505, 595, 631, 719
LAFS.68.RST.2.4 Determine the meaning of symbols, key terms, and other domain-specific words and phrases as they are used in a specific scientific or technical context relevant to grades 6–8 texts and topics.	Develop Conceptual Understanding: SE: 5, 6, 97, 98, 143, 144, 231, 232, 269, 270, 389, 390, 459, 460, 577, 578, 637, 638, 713, 714 Fluency: SE: 338, 351, 497, 546, 552, 558, 570, 666, 678 Application: SE: 337, 351
LAFS.68.RST.3.7 Integrate quantitative or technical information expressed in words in a text with a version of that information expressed visually (e.g., in a flowchart, diagram, model, graph, or table).	Develop Conceptual Understanding: SE: 5, 69, 143, 199, 269, 389, 459, 577, 637, 713 Fluency: SE: 22, 115, 158, 313, 384, 423, 572, 702 Application: SE: 313, 314, 384, 572, 701

Succeeding with HMH Florida Go Math

Actively participate in your learning with your write-in Student Edition. Explore concepts, take notes, answer questions, and complete your homework right in your textbook!

LESSON 11.3 Interpreting the Unit Rate as Slope

FL 8.EE.2.5

Graph proportional relationships, interpreting the unit rate as the slope of the graph. Compare two different proportional relationships represented in different ways. Also 8.F.1.2, 8.F.2.4

? ESSENTIAL QUESTION
How do you interpret the unit rate as slope?

EXPLORE ACTIVITY Real World   FL 8.EE.2.5, 8.F.2.4

Relating the Unit Rate to Slope
A rate is a comparison of two quantities that have different units, such as miles and hours. A **unit rate** is a rate in which the second quantity in the comparison is one unit.

A storm is raging on Misty Mountain. The graph shows the constant rate of change of the snow level on the mountain.

Misty Mountain Storm

A Find the slope of the graph using the points (1, 2) and (5, 10). Remember that the slope is the constant rate of change.

B Find the unit rate of snowfall in inches per hour. Explain your method.

C Compare the slope of the graph and the unit rate of change in the snow level. What do you notice?

D Which unique point on this graph gives you the slope of the graph and the unit rate of change in the snow level? Explain how you found the point.

LESSON 12.1 Representing Linear Nonproportional Relationships

FL 8.F.1.3

Interpret the equation $y = mx + b$ as defining a linear function, whose graph is a straight line; ...

? ESSENTIAL QUESTION
How can you use tables, graphs, and equations to represent linear nonproportional situations?

Representing Linear Relationships Using Tables
You can use an equation to describe the relationship between two quantities in a real-world situation. You can use a table to show some values that make the equation true.

EXAMPLE 1 Real World   FL Prep for 8.F.1.3

The equation $y = 3x + 2$ gives the total charge, y, for one person to rent a pair of shoes and bowl x games at Baxter Bowling Lanes based on the prices shown. Make a table of values for this situation.

STEP 1 Choose several values for x that make sense in context.

x (number of games)	1	2	3	4
y (total cost in dollars)				

STEP 2 Use the equation $y = 3x + 2$ to find y for each value of x.

x (number of games)	1	2	3	4
y (total cost in dollars)	5	8	11	14

Substitute 1 for x
$y = 3(1) + 2 = 5.$

BAXTER bowling lanes
$3 per game
$2 shoe rental

YOUR TURN

1. Francisco makes $12 per hour doing part-time work on Saturdays. He spends $4 on transportation to and from work. The equation $y = 12x - 4$ gives his earnings y, ... a table of values for t...

x (number of hours)			
y (earnings in dollars			

EXPLORE ACTIVITY Real World

Explore Activities help you develop a deeper understanding of math concepts.

Math On the Spot
my.hrw.com

Scan QR codes with your smart phone to watch Math On the Spot tutorial videos for every example in the book!

YOUR TURN
Your Turn exercises check your understanding of new concepts.

UNIT 1 MIXED REVIEW
Assessment Readiness

Check your mastery of concepts through review and practice for high-stakes tests.

Enhance Your Learning!

The Interactive Student Edition provides additional videos, activities, tools, and learning aids to support you as you study!

Practice skills and complete your homework online with the Personal Math Trainer. Your Personal Math Trainer provides a variety of learning aids that develop and improve your understanding of math concepts including videos, guided examples, and step-by-step solutions.

Personal Math Trainer
Online Assessment and Intervention
⏻ my.hrw.com

Math On the Spot
⏻ my.hrw.com

Math On the Spot video tutorials provide step-by-step instruction of the math concepts covered in each example.

Animated Math activities let you interactively explore and practice key math concepts and skills.

Animated Math
⏻ my.hrw.com

Standards for Mathematical Practice

The topics described in the Standards for Mathematical Content will vary from year to year. However, the *way* in which you learn, study, and think about mathematics will not. The Standards for Mathematical Practice describe skills that you will use in all of your math courses. These pages show some features of your book that will help you gain these skills and use them to master this year's topics.

MP.1.1 Make sense of problems and persevere in solving them.

Mathematically proficient students start by explaining to themselves the meaning of a problem… They analyze givens, constraints, relationships, and goals. They make conjectures about the form… of the solution and plan a solution pathway…

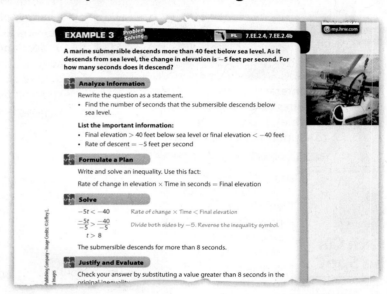

Problem-solving examples and exercises lead students through problem solving steps.

MP.2.1 Reason abstractly and quantitatively.

Mathematically proficient students… bring two complementary abilities to bear on problems…: the ability to decontextualize— to abstract a given situation and represent it symbolically… and the ability to contextualize, to pause… in order to probe into the referents for the symbols involved.

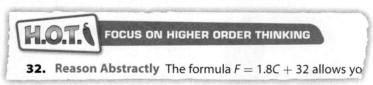

32. Reason Abstractly The formula $F = 1.8C + 32$ allows yo

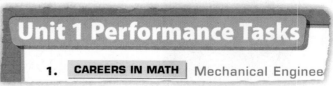

1. CAREERS IN MATH Mechanical Enginee

Focus on Higher Order Thinking exercises in every lesson and **Performance Tasks** in every unit require you to use logical reasoning, represent situations symbolically, use mathematical models to solve problems, and state your answers in terms of a problem context.

MP.3.1 Construct viable arguments and critique the reasoning of others.

Mathematically proficient students... justify their conclusions, [and]... distinguish correct... reasoning from that which is flawed.

Reflect
2. **Make a Conjecture** Use your results from parts **E**, **H**, and a conjecture about translations.

ESSENTIAL QUESTION CHECK-IN

Essential Question Check-in and **Reflect** in every lesson ask you to evaluate statements, explain relationships, apply mathematical principles, make conjectures, construct arguments, and justify your reasoning.

MP.4.1 Model with mathematics.

Mathematically proficient students can apply... mathematics... to... problems... in everyday life, society, and the workplace.

Real-world examples and **mathematical modeling** apply mathematics to other disciplines and real-world contexts such as science and business.

MP.5.1 Use appropriate tools strategically.

Mathematically proficient students consider the available tools when solving a... problem... [and] are... able to use technological tools to explore and deepen their understanding...

Exploration Activities in lessons use concrete and technological tools, such as manipulatives or graphing calculators, to explore mathematical concepts.

MP.6.1 Attend to precision.

Mathematically proficient students... communicate precisely... with others and in their own reasoning... [They] give carefully formulated explanations...

19. Communicate Mathematical Ideas Explain how you can fir height of a cylinder if you know the diameter and the volum an example with your explana

Key Vocabulary

slope *(pendiente)*
A measure of the steepness of a line on a graph; the rise divided by the run.

Precision refers not only to the correctness of calculations but also to the proper use of mathematical language and symbols. **Communicate Mathematical Ideas** exercises and **Key Vocabulary** highlighted for each module and unit help you learn and use the language of math to communicate mathematics precisely.

MP.7.1 Look for and make use of structure.

Mathematically proficient students... look closely to discern a pattern or structure... They can also step back for an overview and shift perspectives.

Follow the steps to informally prove the Triangle Sum Theorem. You should draw each step on your own paper. The figures below are provided for you to check your work.

A Draw a triangle and label the angles as ∠1, ∠2, and ∠3 as shown.

B Draw line *a* through the base of the triangle.

C The Parallel Postulate states that through a point not on a line ℓ, there is exactly one line parallel to line ℓ. Draw line *b* parallel to line *a*, through the vertex opposite the base of the triangle.

D Extend each of the non-base sides of the triangle to form transversal *s* and transversal *t*. Transversals *s* and *t* intersect parallel lines *a* and *b*.

E Label the angles formed by line *b* and the transversals as ∠4 and ∠5.

F Because ∠4 and _____ are alternate interior

Throughout the lessons, you will observe regularity in mathematical structures in order to make generalizations and make connections between related problems. For example, you can apply your knowledge of geometric theorems to determine when an auxiliary line would be helpful.

MP.8.1 Look for and express regularity in repeated reasoning.

Mathematically proficient students... look both for general methods and for shortcuts... [and] maintain oversight of the process, while attending to the details.

Use your pattern to complete this equation: $(7^2)^4 = 7^{\boxed{}}$.

B Describe any patterns you see. Use your pattern to dete of 1 pencil.

20. Look for a Pattern Describe the pattern in the equation. The equation.

$$0.3x + 0.03x + 0.003x + 0.0003x + \dots = 3$$

You will look for repeated calculations and mathematical patterns in examples and exercises. Recognizing patterns can help you make generalizations and obtain a better understanding of the underlying mathematics.

ADVANCED MATHEMATICS 1 **PART 1**

Review Test

Personal
Math Trainer

Online
Assessment and
Intervention

my.hrw.com

Selected Response

1. Suppose you have developed a scale that indicates the brightness of sunlight. Each category in the table is 5 times brighter than the category above it. For example, a day that is dazzling is 5 times brighter than a day that is radiant. How many times brighter is a dazzling day than a dim day?

Sunlight Intensity	
Category	**Brightness**
Dim	2
Illuminated	3
Radiant	4
Dazzling	5

(A) 125 times brighter

(B) 625 times brighter

(C) 3 times brighter

(D) 25 times brighter

2. Patricia paid $584 for 8 nights at a hotel. Find the unit rate.

(A) $\frac{\$146}{1 \text{ night}}$

(C) $\frac{\$37}{1 \text{ night}}$

(B) $\frac{\$584}{1 \text{ night}}$

(D) $\frac{\$73}{1 \text{ night}}$

3. Valerie sold 6 tickets to the school play and Mark sold 16 tickets. What is the ratio of the number of tickets Valerie sold to the number of tickets Mark sold?

(A) 16 to 6

(C) 2 to 8

(B) 2 to 3

(D) 3 to 8

4. Grant and Pedro are comparing their stocks for the week. On Monday, their results were opposites. Explain how you would graph their results for Monday if Grant lost $4.

(A) Grant's point is 4 units to the right of 0 on a number line, and Pedro's point is 4 units to the left of 0.

(B) Grant's point is 4 units to the right of 0 on a number line, and Pedro's point is the same point.

(C) Grant's loss is a point 4 units to the left of 0 on a number line, and Pedro's point is 4 units to the right of 0.

(D) Grant's loss is a point 4 units to the left of 0 on a number line, and Pedro's point is the same point because it's already negative.

5. The fuel for a chain saw is a mix of oil and gasoline. The label says to mix 5 ounces of oil with 15 gallons of gasoline. How much oil would you use if you had 45 gallons of gasoline?

(A) 21 ounces

(C) 15 ounces

(B) 1.67 ounces

(D) 135 ounces

6. A stack of blocks is 12.3 inches tall. If there are 10 blocks stacked one on top of the other, how tall is each block?

(A) 1.33 inches

(C) 2.3 inches

(B) 1.13 inches

(D) 1.23 inches

7. Which temperature is warmest?

(A) 16 °F

(C) −21 °F

(B) −16 °F

(D) 21 °F

8. Each student needs a pencil and an eraser to take a test. If pencils come 8 in a box and erasers come 12 in a bag, what is the least number of boxes and bags needed for 24 students to each have a pencil and an eraser?

(A) 3 boxes of pencils, 2 bags of erasers

(B) 1 box of pencils, 1 bag of erasers

(C) 8 boxes of pencils, 12 bags of erasers

(D) 2 boxes of pencils, 3 bags of erasers

9. Find the quotient $7\frac{1}{6} \div \frac{5}{9}$.

(A) 12

(C) $12\frac{9}{10}$

(B) $13\frac{1}{2}$

(D) $1\frac{13}{30}$

10. Find the product 4.7×4.75.

(A) 223.25

(C) 22.325

(B) 9.45

(D) 2.2325

11. Carla is building a table out of boards that are 4.25 inches wide. She wants the table to be at least 36 inches wide. What is the least number of boards she can use?

(A) 8

(C) 9.5

(B) 9

(D) 153

12. How many centimeters are there in 740.2 millimeters?

(A) 7402 cm

(C) 7.402 cm

(B) 74.02 cm

(D) 0.7402 cm

Mini-Tasks

13. Jada is making lasagna and pizzas for a large party. Her lasagna recipe calls for $1\frac{1}{4}$ cups of tomato paste, and her pizza recipe uses $\frac{1}{2}$ cup of tomato paste per pizza. She will double her lasagna recipe and make 5 pizzas. Write and evaluate an expression for how many $\frac{3}{4}$-cup cans of tomato paste she will need in all.

_____

14. Explain how you can use multiplication to find the quotient $\frac{3}{5} \div \frac{3}{15}$. Then evaluate the expression.

_____

_____

15. You are working as an assistant to a chef. The chef has 8 cups of berries and will use $\frac{2}{3}$ cup of berries for each dessert he makes. How many desserts can he make?

_____

_____

Performance Task

16. School A has 216 students and 12 classrooms. School B has 104 students and 4 classrooms.

Part A: What is the ratio of students to classrooms at School A?

Part B: What is the ratio of students to classrooms at School B?

Part C: How many students would have to transfer from School B to School A for the ratios of students to classrooms at both schools to be the same? Explain your reasoning.

_____

_____

_____

_____

_____

_____

_____

_____

_____

_____

Selected Response

1. Kahlil is recording a beat for a song that he is working on. He wants the length of the beat to be more than 17 seconds long. His friend tells him the beat needs to be 9 seconds longer than that to match the lyrics he has written.

Write an inequality to represent the beat's length. Give three possible beat lengths that satisfy the inequality.

(A) $t < 17$
   8, 6, 5

(B) $t > 26$
   27, 35, 33

(C) $t > 8$
   27, 35, 33

(D) $t < 26$
   8, 6, 5

2. Write an expression for the missing value in the table.

Tom's Age	Kim's Age
11	14
12	15
13	16
a	?

(A) $a + 16$
(B) $a + 11$
(C) $a + 1$
(D) $a + 3$

3. A plant's height is 1.6 times its age. Write an equation for the situation. Tell what each variable you use represents.

(A) h = plant's height; y = plant's age;
   $1.6 = hy$

(B) h = plant's height; y = plant's age;
   $y = 1.6h$

(C) h = plant's age; y = plant's height;
   $h = 1.6y$

(D) h = plant's height; y = plant's age;
   $h = 1.6y$

4. A driveway is 162 feet long, 6 feet wide, and 4 inches deep. How many cubic feet of concrete will be required for the driveway?

(A) 355 ft³
(B) 324 ft³
(C) 3,888 ft³
(D) 254 ft³

5. Write the phrase as an algebraic expression.
   6 less than a number times 11

(A) $6y - 11y$
(B) $11 \div y$
(C) $11y - 6$
(D) $11 + y$

6. Wilson bought gift cards for some lawyers and their assistants. Each lawyer got a gift card worth \$$\ell$. Each assistant got a gift card worth \$$a$. There are 14 lawyers. Each lawyer has 3 assistants. The expression for the total cost of the gift cards is $14\ell + 42a$. Write an expression that is equivalent to the given expression.

(A) $14(\ell + 2a)$
(B) $14(\ell + 3a)$
(C) $14(\ell + 42a)$
(D) $42(\ell + 3a)$

7. At the beginning of the year, Jason had \$80 in his savings account. Each month, he added \$15 to his account. Write an expression for the amount of money in Jason's savings account each month. Then use the expression to find the amount of money in his account at the end of the year.

Month	January	February	March	m
Amount	\$95	\$110	\$125	\$?

(A) $95 + 15m$; \$275
(B) $95 + m$; \$107
(C) $80 + 12m$; \$224
(D) $15m + 80$; \$260

8. In a fish tank, $\frac{6}{7}$ of the fish have a red stripe on them. If 18 of the fish have red stripes, how many total fish are in the tank?

Ⓐ 26 fish   Ⓒ 23 fish

Ⓑ 21 fish   Ⓓ 25 fish

9. Solve the equation $s + 2.8 = 6.59$.

Ⓐ $s = 4.13$ Ⓒ $s = 9.39$

Ⓑ $s = 3.79$ Ⓓ $s = 3$

10. Which question is a statistical question?

Ⓐ How long is lunch period at your school?

Ⓑ How old is the oldest student in your class?

Ⓒ How many classrooms are there in your school?

Ⓓ What are the ages of all the people in your class?

11. In a box-and-whisker plot, the *interquartile range* is a measure of the spread of the middle half of the data. Find the interquartile range for the data set: 10, 3, 7, 6, 9, 12, 13.

Ⓐ 12   Ⓒ 6

Ⓑ 7   Ⓓ 8

12. Mike was in charge of collecting contributions for the Food Bank. He received contributions of $50, $80, $60, $50, and $90. Find the mean and median of the contributions.

Ⓐ mean: $66   Ⓒ mean: $50
    median: $60   median: $60

Ⓑ mean: $50   Ⓓ mean: $60
    median: $66   median: $66

13. Which expression is NOT equivalent to this expression? $11y - 5$

Ⓐ $88y - 40$ Ⓒ $19y - 3$

Ⓑ $5y - 11$ Ⓓ $22y - 10$

Mini-Tasks

14. It costs $9 to go to Pete's Pottery Place to make your own bowls for $3 per bowl. Natalie goes to Pete's Pottery Place and makes b bowls. She decides to make bowls 5 days this month so she can sell them at a crafts fair.

Part A: Write an expression that will represent Natalie's total cost for this month.

Part B: If she makes 4 bowls each time she goes to Pete's Pottery Place, what will her total cost be?

_____

_____

15. To find the mileage, or how many miles per gallon a car can travel, you can use the expression $\frac{m}{g}$, where m is the distance in miles and g is the number of gallons of gas used. Find the mileage for a car that travels 576 miles on 18 gallons of gas.

_____

Performance Task

16. **Part A:** Is $x = 6$ a solution of the equation $8x + 8 = 56$? Explain.
Part B: Suppose the solution $x = 6$ increases to $x = 9$, and the left side of the equation stays the same. How would the right side need to change if the solution is now $x = 9$?

_____

_____

_____

_____

_____

_____

_____

_____

Benchmark Test

Personal Math Trainer

my.hrw.com

Online Assessment and Intervention

Selected Response

1. What are the actual dimensions of the Check-out Area?

Floor plan of library

2 cm — 3 cm

4 cm

Study area

Books

7 cm

Check-out area

Scale: 1 cm : 5 m

(A) 25 m × 15 m   (C) 15 m × 35 m

(B) 15 m × 20 m   (D) 2 m × 4 m

2. For a history fair, a school is building a circular wooden stage that will stand 2 feet off the ground. Find the area of the stage if the radius of the stage is 19 feet. Use 3.14 for π.

(A) 1,133.54 ft²   (C) 2,267.08 ft²

(B) 119.32 ft²   (D) 4534.16 ft²

3. Find the area of the circle to the nearest tenth. Use 3.14 for π.

4.4 mm

(A) 47.7 mm²   (C) 60.8 mm²

(B) 15.2 mm²   (D) 13.8 mm²

4. What is the solution of the inequality $-0.4x - 1.2 > 0.8$?

(A) $x < -5$ (C) $x < -0.8$

(B) $x < -1$ (D) $x > 5$

5. Find m∠LMN.

L $x°$

$(3x-70)°$ N

M

(A) m∠LMN = 40°   (C) m∠LMN = 35°

(B) m∠LMN = 45°   (D) m∠LMN = 50°

6. Ralph is an electrician. He charges an initial fee of $32, plus $33 per hour. If Ralph earned $197 on a job, how long did the job take?

(A) 5.1 hours   (C) 5 hours

(B) 132 hours   (D) 4 hours

7. Find the volume of the cylinder. Use 3.14 for π. Round your answer to the nearest tenth.

3.9 m

15 m

(A) 183.7 m³   (C) 2,865.6 m³

(B) 716.4 m³   (D) 2,755.4 m³

8. Which is the least valid way to simulate how many boys and girls are in a random sample of 20 students from a school population that is half boys and half girls?

(A) Flip a coin 20 times, assigning one outcome to boys and the other to girls.

(B) Drop 20 coins at once and count the number of each outcome.

(C) Count how many boys and girls are in your math class and use a proportion.

(D) Have a calculator generate 20 random integers and count the number of even and odd integers.

9. Roberto plays on the school baseball team. In the last 9 games, Roberto was at bat 32 times and got 11 hits. What is the experimental probability that Roberto will get a hit during his next time at bat? Express your answer as a fraction in simplest form.

Ⓐ $\frac{32}{11}$ Ⓒ $\frac{21}{32}$

Ⓑ $\frac{11}{32}$ Ⓓ $\frac{11}{21}$

10. A coin-operated machine sells plastic rings. It contains 14 pink rings, 10 green rings, 9 purple rings, and 13 black rings. Sarah puts a coin into the machine. Find the theoretical probability she gets a pink ring. Express your answer as a decimal. If necessary, round your answer to the nearest thousandth.

Ⓐ 3.286   Ⓒ 4.6

Ⓑ 0.304   Ⓓ 0.217

11. A manufacturer inspects a sample of 400 personal video players and finds that 399 of them have no defects. The manufacturer sent a shipment of 2000 video players to a distributor. Predict the number of players in the shipment that are likely to have no defects.

Ⓐ 5   Ⓒ 399

Ⓑ 1995   Ⓓ 1950

12. An experiment consists of rolling two fair number cubes. What is the probability that the sum of the two numbers will be 8? Express your answer as a fraction in simplest form.

Ⓐ $\frac{5}{36}$ Ⓒ $\frac{36}{5}$

Ⓑ $\frac{1}{9}$ Ⓓ $\frac{31}{36}$

Mini-Tasks

13. A map of Australia has a scale of 1 cm : 110 km. If the distance between Darwin and Alice Springs is 1444 kilometers, how far apart are they on the map, to the nearest tenth of a centimeter?

_____

14. The student council president wants to find out the opinion of the students on the issue of school lunch options. The president sends out a survey to a random sample of students in the school. What type of sample is this? Explain.

_____

_____

_____

_____

15. Using the following data, state the errors in the box-and-whisker plot.

33, 27, 6, 34, 31, 59, 26, 1, 30

_____

_____

Performance Task

16. The number of goals scored by a hockey team in each of its first 10 games is 2, 4, 0, 3, 4, 1, 3, 1, 1, and 5.

a. Find the mean number of goals scored.

_____

b. Find the mean absolute deviation (MAD) of the number of goals scored.

_____

c. A second team in the same division scores a mean of 4.5 goals in its first 10 games, with the same MAD as the team above. Compare the difference in the teams' mean number of goals with the MAD in the number of goals scored.

_____

_____

Selected Response

1. Multiply. Write the product as one power.
$a^8 \cdot a^5$

Ⓐ a^{13} 　　Ⓒ a^{40}

Ⓑ a^3 　　Ⓓ Cannot combine

2. Simplify $(6^{-4})^6$.

Ⓐ -24^6 　　Ⓒ 6^2

Ⓑ $\frac{1}{6^{24}}$ 　　Ⓓ $\frac{1}{6^{10}}$

3. A square mosaic is made of small glass squares. If there are 196 small squares in the mosaic, how many are along an edge?

Ⓐ 98 squares 　　Ⓒ 14 squares

Ⓑ 49 squares 　　Ⓓ 16 squares

4. Simplify $2\sqrt{-19 + 44}$.

Ⓐ 13.3 　　Ⓒ 10

Ⓑ 44 　　Ⓓ 27

5. A passenger plane travels at about 7.97×10^2 feet per second. The plane takes 1.11×10^4 seconds to reach its destination.

About how far must the plane travel to reach its destination? Write your answer in scientific notation.

Ⓐ 8.85×10^8 feet 　　Ⓒ 8.85×10^6 feet

Ⓑ 9.08×10^6 feet 　　Ⓓ 9.08×10^8 feet

6. Approximate $\sqrt{158}$ to the nearest hundredth.

Ⓐ 12.57 　　Ⓒ 16.57

Ⓑ 16.62 　　Ⓓ 8.52

7. Write a rule for the linear function.

x	y
−3	12
−2	10
3	0
5	−4

Ⓐ $y = -2x - 6$ 　　Ⓒ $y = \frac{1}{2}x + 6$

Ⓑ $y = -2x + 6$ 　　Ⓓ $y = \frac{1}{2}x - 6$

8. A remote-control airplane descends at a rate of 2 feet per second. After 3 seconds it is 67 feet above the ground. Write the equation in point-slope form that models the situation. Then, find the height of the plane after 8 seconds.

Ⓐ $y - 67 = -2(x - 3)$; 57 feet

Ⓑ $y - 67 = -3(x - 2)$; 49 feet

Ⓒ $y - 3 = -2(x - 67)$; 121 feet

Ⓓ $y - 2 = 67(x - 3)$; 337 feet

9. A bicyclist heads east at 19 km/h. After she has traveled 24.2 kilometers, another cyclist sets out in the same direction going 30 km/h. About how long will it take the second cyclist to catch up to the first cyclist?

Ⓐ It will take the second cyclist 3.2 hours to catch up to the first cyclist.

Ⓑ It will take the second cyclist 3.7 hours to catch up to the first cyclist.

Ⓒ It will take the second cyclist 2.2 hours to catch up to the first cyclist.

Ⓓ It will take the second cyclist 1.7 hours to catch up to the first cyclist.

10. What is the equation of the graph in slope-intercept form?

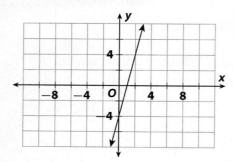

- Ⓐ $y = -4x - 4$
- Ⓒ $y = -5x - 4$
- Ⓑ $y = 4x - 4$
- Ⓓ $y = 5x - 4$

11. Solve $-2z + 3 + 7z = -12$.

- Ⓐ $z = -3$
- Ⓒ $z = 1$
- Ⓑ $z = -15$
- Ⓓ $z = -1.8$

12. Which equation has only one solution?

- Ⓐ $c + 2 = c + 2$
- Ⓒ $c + 2 = c - 2$
- Ⓑ $c = -c + 2$
- Ⓓ $c - c = 2$

13. Which ordered pair is a solution of the system of equations?
$y = 3x + 1$
$y = 5x - 1$

- Ⓐ $(2, 3)$
- Ⓒ $(1, 2)$
- Ⓑ $(0, 1)$
- Ⓓ $(1, 4)$

14. Which of these functions is *not* linear?

- Ⓐ $y = x^2 - x$
- Ⓒ $y = \frac{x}{3}$
- Ⓑ $y = 1 - x$
- Ⓓ $y = \frac{2}{3}x - 2x$

15. Which function has the greatest rate of change?

- Ⓐ $y = -5x$
- Ⓑ $\{(-1, -2), (1, 2), (3, 6), (5, 10), (7, 14)\}$
- Ⓒ A fitness club charges a $200 membership fee plus monthly fees of $25.
- Ⓓ $y = 3x - 16$

Mini-Tasks

16. The graph below shows an airplane's speed over a period of time. Describe the events.

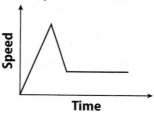

_____

_____

_____

_____

17. Identify $\sqrt{\frac{169}{64}}$ as *rational* or *irrational*. Explain your reasoning.

_____

Performance Task

18. Ashley reads 2 pages/minute for 10 minutes, takes a 10 minute break, and then reads at the same rate for 10 more minutes. Adam reads at the same rate the entire time. The equation for the number of pages he reads is $y = 1.2x$. How are these functions similar? How are they different?

_____

_____

_____

_____

_____

_____

_____

Selected Response

1. In the gift shop of the History of Flight museum, Elisa bought a kit to make a model of a jet airplane. The actual plane is 21 feet long with a wingspan of 17.5 feet. If the finished model will be 12 inches long, what will the wingspan be?

(A) 30.6 in.

(C) 14.4 in.

(B) 10 in.

(D) 5 in.

2. Find the angle measures in the isosceles triangle.

(A) $f = 18°$

(C) $f = 68°$

(B) $f = 118°$

(D) $f = 11.7°$

3. Which ordered pair is a solution of the system of equations?

$y = 3x - 1$
$y = 5x + 1$

(A) $(4, 1)$

(C) $(-4, -1)$

(B) $(1, 4)$

(D) $(-1, -4)$

4. Melanie is making a piece of jewelry that is in the shape of a right triangle. The two shorter sides of the piece of jewelry are 9 mm and 12 mm. Find the perimeter of the piece of jewelry.

(A) 32 mm

(C) 30 mm

(B) 36 mm

(D) 34 mm

5. Find the distance, to the nearest tenth, from $T(4, -2)$ to $U(-2, 3)$.

(A) -1.0 units

(C) 0.0 units

(B) 3.4 units

(D) 7.8 units

6. Which of the following is *not* a congruence transformation?

(A) A reflection over the *x*-axis.

(B) A dilation with scale factor 0.5.

(C) A translation 1 unit left.

(D) A dilation with scale factor 1.

7. Harry and Selma start driving from the same location. Harry drives 42 miles north while Selma drives 144 miles east. How far apart are Harry and Selma when they stop?

(A) 1,764 miles

(C) 22,500 miles

(B) 150 miles

(D) 20,736 miles

8. Which triangle with side lengths given below is a right triangle?

(A) 10, 15, 20

(C) 9, 40, 41

(B) 10, 24, 25

(D) 16, 20, 25

9. Angles *B* and *F* are corresponding angles formed by a transversal intersecting two parallel lines. Angle *B* has a measure of 44°. What is the measure of Angle *F*?

(A) 44°

(C) 90°

(B) 46°

(D) 136°

10. Which transformation below preserves similarity between the preimage and image, but does not preserve congruence?

(A) reflections

(C) translations

(B) rotations

(D) dilations

11. An artist is creating a large conical sculpture for a park. The cone has a height of 16 m and a diameter of 25 m. Find the volume of the sculpture to the nearest hundredth.

Ⓐ 833.33 m³   Ⓒ 2,616.67 m³

Ⓑ 7,850 m³   Ⓓ 209.33 m³

12. A cylindrical barrel has a radius of 7.6 ft and a height of 10.8 ft. Tripling which dimension(s) will triple the volume of the barrel?

Ⓐ height

Ⓑ radius

Ⓒ both height and radius

Ⓓ neither height nor radius

13. Which linear equation approximates the best fit to the data?

Ⓐ $y = -2x + 65$ Ⓒ $y = -x + 68$

Ⓑ $y = -5x + 100$ Ⓓ $y = -0.5x + 55$

Mini-Tasks

14. On Monday, a work group eats at Ava's café, where a lunch special is $8 and a dessert is $2. The total is $108. On Friday, the group eats at Bo's café, where a lunch special is $6 and a dessert is $3. The total is $90. Each time, the group orders the same number of lunches and the same number of desserts. How many lunches and desserts are ordered?

_____

15. Dilate the figure by a scale factor of 0.5 with the origin as the center of dilation.

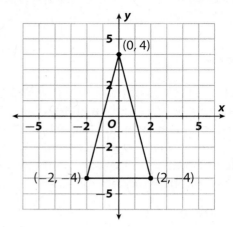

Performance Task

16. In a drought, many trees on a plot of land died. The table shows how many oak trees and pine trees survived or died.

Survived/Died	Survived	Died	Total
Oak	60	20	80
Pine	72	48	120
Total	0	68	200

a. Create a two-way relative frequency table using decimals.

b. As a percent, what was the joint relative frequency of pine trees that died?

_____

c. Compare the conditional relative frequencies, in percent form, that a tree survived given that it was an oak and that it survived given that it was a pine.

_____

Expressions, Equations, and Inequalities

MODULE 1
Expressions and Equations
FL 7.EE.1.1, 7.EE.1.2, 7.EE.2.3, 7.EE.2.4, 7.EE.2.4a

MODULE 2
Inequalities
FL 7.EE.2.3, 7.EE.2.4, 7.EE.2.4b

CAREERS IN MATH

Mechanical Engineer A mechanical engineer designs, develops, and manufactures mechanical devices and technological systems. Mechanical engineers use math to solve diverse problems, from calculating the strength of materials to determining energy consumption of a device.

If you are interested in a career in mechanical engineering, you should study these mathematical subjects:

- Algebra
- Geometry
- Trigonometry
- Statistics
- Calculus

Research other careers that require the daily use of mathematics to solve problems.

Unit 1 Performance Task

At the end of the unit, check out how **mechanical engineers** use math.

Use the puzzle to preview key vocabulary from this unit. Unscramble the circled letters to answer the riddle at the bottom of the page.

An expression that contains at least one variable. (Lesson 1.1)

___ ___ ___◯___ ___ ___ ___

___ ___ ___ ___ ___ ___◯___ ___

An equation with more than one operation. (Lesson 1.3)

___ ___ ___ ___ ___ ___ ___◯___ ___ ___ ___ ___◯

A variable whose value is less than zero. (Lesson 1.3)

___◯___ ___ ___ ___ ___ ___ ___ ___ ___ ___◯

A variable whose value is greater than zero. (Lesson 1.3)

___◯___ ___ ___◯___ ___ ___ ___◯___ ___ ___

A mathematical sentence that shows the relationship between quantities that are not equivalent. (Lesson 2.1)

___◯___ ___ ___ ___◯___ ___

Q: Why does the sum of −4 and 3 complain more than the sum of −3 and 5?

A: It's the ___ ___ ___ ___ ___ ___ ___ ___ ___ ___ ___!

Expressions and Equations

ESSENTIAL QUESTION

How can you use algebraic expressions and equations to solve real-world problems?

Real-World Video

When you take a taxi, you will be charged an initial fee plus a charge per mile. To describe situations like this, you can write a two-step equation.

my.hrw.com

GO DIGITAL
my.hrw.com

my.hrw.com

Go digital with your write-in student edition, accessible on any device.

Math On the Spot

Scan with your smart phone to jump directly to the online edition, video tutor, and more.

Animated Math

Interactively explore key concepts to see how math works.

Personal Math Trainer

Get immediate feedback and help as you work through practice sets.

Are YOU Ready?

Complete these exercises to review skills you will need for this chapter.

Personal Math Trainer

Online Assessment and Intervention

my.hrw.com

Words for Operations

EXAMPLE

the difference of 2 and b Difference means subtraction.

$2 - b$

the product of -8 and a number   Product means multiplication.

$(-8)x$ or $-8x$ Let x represent the unknown number.

Write an algebraic expression for each word expression.

1. the sum of 5 and a number x _____

2. 11 decreased by n _____

3. the quotient of -9 and y _____

4. twice a number, minus 13 _____

Evaluate Expressions

EXAMPLE Evaluate $3x - 5$ for $x = -2$.

$3x - 5 = 3(-2) - 5$ Substitute the given value of x for x.

$= -6 - 5$ Multiply.

$= -11$ Subtract.

Evaluate each expression for the given value of x.

5. $2x + 3$ for $x = 3$ _____

6. $-4x + 7$ for $x = -1$ ___

7. $1.5x - 2.5$ for $x = 3$ ____

8. $0.4x + 6.1$ for $x = -5$ ___

9. $\frac{2}{3}x - 12$ for $x = 18$ ____

10. $-\frac{5}{8}x + 10$ for $x = -8$ ___

Operations with Fractions

EXAMPLE $\frac{2}{5} \div \frac{7}{10}$ $\frac{2}{5} \div \frac{7}{10} = \frac{2}{5} \times \frac{10}{7}$ Multiply by the reciprocal of the divisor.

$= \frac{2}{{}_1\cancel{5}} \times \frac{\cancel{10}^2}{7}$ Divide by the common factors.

$= \frac{4}{7}$ Simplify.

Divide.

11. $\frac{1}{2} \div \frac{1}{4}$ _____

12. $\frac{3}{8} \div \frac{13}{16}$ _____

13. $\frac{2}{5} \div \frac{14}{15}$ _____

14. $\frac{4}{9} \div \frac{16}{27}$ _____

Reading Start-Up

Visualize Vocabulary

Use the ✔ words to complete the graphic. You may put more than one word in each box.

<table>
<tr><td>

Identify the operation performed on the variable in the equation.

↓

Apply the inverse _____ to both sides

of the _____.

↓

The _____ in the equation is alone, and set

equal to the _____.

</td><td>

$x - 5.5 = 3$
$\underline{+5.5 \quad +5.5}$
$x \quad\quad = \quad 8.5$

Add 5.5 to both sides.
The solution is $x = 8.5$.

</td></tr>
</table>

Vocabulary

Review Words

algebraic expression
(expresión algebraica)
Distributive Property
(Propiedad distributiva)
✔ equation *(ecuación)*
factor *(factor)*
✔ operation *(operación)*
✔ solution *(solución)*
✔ variable *(variable)*

Understand Vocabulary

Complete the sentences using the review words.

1. A(n) _____ contains at least one variable.

2. A mathematical sentence that shows that two expressions are equivalent

   is called a(n) _____.

Active Reading

Tri-Fold Before beginning the module, create a tri-fold to help you learn the concepts and vocabulary in this module. Fold the paper into three sections. Label the columns "What I Know," "What I Need to Know," and "What I Learned." Complete the first two columns before you read. After studying the module, complete the third column.

Unpacking the Standards

Understanding the standards and the vocabulary terms in the standards will help you know exactly what you are expected to learn in this module.

 FL 7.EE.1.1

Apply properties of operations as strategies to add, subtract, factor, and expand linear expressions with rational coefficients.

Key Vocabulary

coefficient *(coeficiente)*
The number that is multiplied by the variable in an algebraic expression.

rational number *(número racional)* Any number that can be expressed as a ratio of two integers.

What It Means to You

You will use your knowledge of properties of operations to write equivalent expressions.

UNPACKING EXAMPLE 7.EE.1.1

Expand the expression $2(a + 7)$ using the distributive property.

$$2(a + 7) = 2 \cdot a + 2 \cdot 7 \qquad \text{Multiply each term in parentheses by 2.}$$
$$= 2a + 14$$

 FL 7.EE.2.4a

Solve word problems leading to equations of the form $px + q = r$ and $p(x + q) = r$, where p, q, and r are specific rational numbers. Solve equations of these forms fluently.

Key Vocabulary

equation *(ecuación)*
A mathematical sentence that shows that two expressions are equivalent.

solution *(solución)*
The value for the variable that makes the equation true.

What It Means to You

You will write and solve real-world equations that require two steps.

UNPACKING EXAMPLE 7.EE.2.4a

Jai and Lúpe plan to rent a kayak. The rental is $12 for the first hour and $9 for each hour after that. If they have $50, for how long can they rent the kayak?

Rental Charge $= 12 + 9x$, where x is the number of hours after the first hour.

$$50 = 12 + 9x$$
$$50 - 12 = 12 - 12 + 9x \qquad \text{Subtract 12 from both sides.}$$
$$38 = 9x$$
$$\frac{38}{9} = x, \text{ or } x \approx 4.2 \qquad \text{Divide both sides by 9.}$$

They can rent the kayak for 4 hours.

Visit **my.hrw.com** to see all **Florida Math Standards** unpacked.

my.hrw.com

LESSON 1.1 Algebraic Expressions

FL 7.EE.1.1

Apply properties of operations as strategies to add, subtract, factor, and expand linear expressions with rational coefficients. *Also 7.EE.1.2*

? **ESSENTIAL QUESTION**

How do you add, subtract, factor, and multiply algebraic expressions?

Adding and Subtracting Expressions

You can use the properties of addition along with the Distributive Property to add and subtract algebraic expressions.

Math On the Spot
⊙ my.hrw.com

EXAMPLE 1

FL 7.EE.1.1, 7.EE.1.2

Jill and Kyle get paid per project. Jill is paid a project fee of $25 plus $10 per hour. Kyle is paid a project fee of $18 plus $14 per hour. Write an expression to represent how much a company will pay to hire both to work the same number of hours on a project.

STEP 1 Write expressions for how much the company will pay each person. Let h represent the number of hours they will work on the project.

Jill: $\$25 + \$10h$ Kyle: $\$18 + \$14h$

Fee + Hourly rate × Hours   Fee + Hourly rate × Hours

STEP 2 Add the expressions to represent the amount the company will pay to hire both.

$25 + 10h + 18 + 14h$ *Combine their pay.*

$= 25 + 18 + 10h + 14h$ *Use the Commutative Property.*

$= 43 + 24h$ *Combine like terms.*

The company will pay $43 + 24h$ dollars to hire both Jill and Kyle.

Reflect

1. **Critical Thinking** What can you read directly from the expression $43 + 24h$ that you cannot read directly from the equivalent expression $25 + 10h + 18 + 14h$?

_____

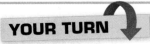
YOUR TURN

Simplify each expression.

2. $\left(3x + \frac{1}{2}\right) + \left(7x - 4\frac{1}{2}\right)$ **3.** $(-0.25x - 3) - (1.5x + 1.4)$

_____   _____

Personal Math Trainer

Online Assessment and Intervention

⊙ my.hrw.com

Using the Distributive Property

You can use the Distributive Property to remove the parentheses from an algebraic expression like $3(x + 5)$. Sometimes this is called "simplifying" or "expanding" the expression. Multiply the quantity in front of parentheses by each term within parentheses: $3(x + 5) = 3 \cdot x + 3 \cdot 5 = 3x + 15$.

EXAMPLE 2

 FL 7.EE.1.1, 7.EE.1.2

Marc is selling tickets for a high school band concert. The band gets to keep 25% of the money he collects from ticket sales to put toward new uniforms. Write an expression to represent how much the band gets to keep.

Let a represent the number of adult tickets he sells.

Let y represent the number of youth tickets he sells.

The expression $16.60a + 12.20y$ represents the amount of money Marc collects from ticket sales.

Write 25% as a decimal: 0.25

Write an expression to represent 25% of the money he collects:

0.25	×	(16.60a	+	12.20y)
25%	of	adult ticket sales	and	youth ticket sales

Use the Distributive Property to simplify the expression.

$0.25(16.60a) + 0.25(12.20y) = 4.15a + 3.05y$

Math Talk
Mathematical Practices

How much does the band get to keep if Marc sells 20 adult tickets and 40 youth tickets?

Reflect

4. **Analyze Relationships** Instead of using the Distributive Property to expand $0.25 \times (16.60a + 12.20y)$, could you have first found the sum $16.60a + 12.20y$? Explain.

_____

_____

YOUR TURN

Simplify each expression.

5. $7(9k + 6m)$

6. $0.2(3b - 15c)$

7. $\frac{2}{3}(6e + 9f - 21g)$

_____ _____ _____

Factoring Expressions

A factor is a number that is multiplied by another number to get a product.
To **factor** is to write a number or an algebraic expression as a product.

Factor 4x + 8.

A Model the expression with algebra tiles.

Use _____ positive x tiles and _____ +1-tiles.

B Arrange the tiles to form a rectangle. The total area represents 4x + 8.

C Since the length multiplied by the width equals the area, the
length and the width of the rectangle are the factors of 4x + 8.
Find the length and width.

The length is
__ x tile and
__ +1-tiles, or
_____.

× ← The width is __ +1-tiles,
or __.

D Use the expressions for the length and width of the rectangle

to write the area of the rectangle, 4x + 8, in factored form. _____

Reflect

8. **Communicate Mathematical Ideas** How could you use the
Distributive Property to check your factoring?

_____

Factor each expression.

9. 2x + 2   **10.** 3x + 9   **11.** 5x + 15   **12.** 4x + 16

_____   _____   _____   _____

**Personal
Math Trainer**

Online Assessment
and Intervention

my.hrw.com

1. The manager of a summer camp has 14 baseballs and 23 tennis balls. The manager buys some boxes of baseballs with 12 baseballs to a box and an equal number of boxes of tennis balls with 16 tennis balls to a box. Write an expression to represent the total number of balls. (Example 1)

STEP 1 Write expressions for the total number of baseballs and tennis balls. Let n represent the number of boxes of each type.

baseballs: _____ + (_____)n tennis balls: _____ + (_____)n

STEP 2 Find an expression for the total number of balls.

_____ + _____ + _____ + _____   Combine the two expressions.

_____ + _____ + _____ + _____   Use the Commutative Property.

_____ + _____   Combine like terms.

So, the total number of baseballs and tennis balls is _____ + _____.

2. Use the expression you found above to find the total number of baseballs and tennis balls if the manager bought 9 boxes of each type. (Example 1) _____

Use the Distributive Property to expand each expression. (Example 2)

3. $0.5(12m - 22n)$

$0.5(12m - 22n) = 0.5($_____$) - 0.5($_____$)$ Distribute 0.5 to both terms in parentheses.

$=$ _____ $-$ _____   Multiply.

4. $\frac{2}{3}(18x + 6z)$

$\frac{2}{3}($_____$) + \frac{2}{3}($_____$) =$ _____ $+$ _____

Factor each expression. (Example 3)

5. $2x + 12$ **6.** $12x + 24$ **7.** $7x + 35$

_____   _____   _____

? **ESSENTIAL QUESTION CHECK-IN**

8. What is the relationship between multiplying and factoring?

_____

_____

_____

1.1 Independent Practice

 FL 7.EE.1.1, 7.EE.1.2

Write and simplify an expression for each situation.

9. A company rents out 15 food booths and 20 game booths at the county fair. The fee for a food booth is $100 plus $5 per day. The fee for a game booth is $50 plus $7 per day. The fair lasts for d days, and all the booths are rented for the entire time. Write and simplify an expression for the amount in dollars that the company is paid.

_____

10. A rug maker is using a pattern that is a rectangle with a length of 96 inches and a width of 60 inches. The rug maker wants to increase each dimension by a different amount. Let ℓ and w be the increases in inches of the length and width. Write and simplify an expression for the perimeter of the new pattern.

_____

In 11–12, identify the two factors that were multiplied together to form the array of tiles. Then identify the product of the two factors.

11.   _____

12.   _____

13. Explain how the figure illustrates that $6(9) = 6(5) + 6(4)$.

In 14–15, the perimeter of the figure is given. Find the length of the indicated side.

14.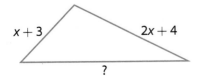

$x + 3$ $2x + 4$

$?$

Perimeter $= 6x$ _____

15.

$?$

$3x - 3$

Perimeter $= 10x + 6$ _____

16. Persevere in Problem Solving The figures show the dimensions of a tennis court and a basketball court given in terms of the width x in feet of the tennis court.

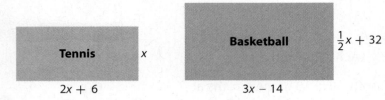

a. Write an expression for the perimeter of each court. _____

b. Write an expression that describes how much greater the perimeter of the basketball court is than the perimeter of the

tennis court. _____

c. Suppose the tennis court is 36 feet wide. Find all dimensions of the

two courts. _____

  FOCUS ON HIGHER ORDER THINKING

Work Area

17. Draw Conclusions Use the figure to find the product $(x + 3)(x + 2)$. (*Hint*: Find the area of each small square or rectangle, then add.)

$(x + 3)(x + 2) =$ _____

	x	1	1	1
x				
1				
1				

18. Communicate Mathematical Ideas Desmond claims that the product shown at the right illustrates the Distributive Property. Do you agree? Explain why or why not.

```
    58
  × 23
   174
  1160
 1,334
```

_____

_____

_____

_____

19. Justify Reasoning Describe two different ways that you could find the product 8×997 using mental math. Find the product and explain why your methods work.

_____

_____

_____

_____

One-Step Equations with Rational Coefficients

 FL 7.EE.2.4

Use variables to represent quantities in a real-world or mathematical problem, and construct simple equations ... to solve problems by reasoning about the quantities.

ESSENTIAL QUESTION

How do you use one-step equations with rational coefficients to solve problems?

One-Step Equations

You have written and solved one-step equations involving whole numbers. Now you will learn to work with equations containing negative numbers.

Math On the Spot
my.hrw.com

EXAMPLE 1 FL 7.EE.2.4

Use inverse operations to solve each equation.

A $x + 3.2 = -8.5$

$$x + 3.2 = -8.5$$
$$\underline{-3.2 \qquad -3.2}$$
$$x = -11.7$$

Subtract 3.2 from both sides.

B $-\frac{2}{3} + y = 8$

$$-\frac{2}{3} + y = 8$$
$$\underline{+\frac{2}{3} \qquad\quad +\frac{2}{3}}$$
$$y = 8\frac{2}{3}$$

Add $\frac{2}{3}$ to both sides.

$-7.5 = -1.5n$

C $30 = -0.5a$

$$\frac{30}{-0.5} = \frac{-0.5a}{-0.5}$$

Divide both sides by -0.5.

$$-60 = a$$

D $-\frac{q}{3.5} = 9.2$

$$-\frac{q}{3.5}(-3.5) = 9.2\,(-3.5)$$

Multiply both sides by -3.5.

$$q = -32.2$$

YOUR TURN

Use inverse operations to solve each equation.

1. $4.9 + z = -9$ _____

2. $r - 17.1 = -4.8$ _____

3. $-3c = 36$ _____

Personal Math Trainer

Online Assessment and Intervention

my.hrw.com

Writing and Solving One-Step Addition and Subtraction Equations

Negative numbers often appear in real-world situations. For example, elevations below sea level are represented by negative numbers. When you increase your elevation, you are moving in a positive direction. When you decrease your elevation, you are moving in a negative direction.

EXAMPLE 2

FL 7.EE.2.4

A scuba diver is exploring at an elevation of −12.2 meters. As the diver rises to the surface, she plans to stop and rest briefly at a reef that has an elevation of −4.55 meters. Find the vertical distance that the diver will travel.

— 0 m

— −4.55 m

— −12.2 m

STEP 1 Write an equation. Let x represent the vertical distance between her initial elevation and the elevation of the reef.

$$-12.2 + x = -4.55$$

STEP 2 Solve the equation using an inverse operation.

$$\begin{array}{rl} -12.2 + x &= -4.55 \\ +12.2 \qquad &+12.2 \\ \hline x &= 7.65 \end{array}$$ *Add 12.2 to both sides.*

The diver will travel a vertical distance of 7.65 meters.

Reflect

4. **Make a Prediction** Explain how you know whether the diver is moving in a positive or a negative direction before you solve the equation.

_____

_____

_____

YOUR TURN

5. An airplane descends 1.5 miles to an elevation of 5.25 miles. Find the elevation of the plane before its descent.

_____

_____

Writing and Solving One-Step Multiplication and Division Problems

Temperatures can be both positive and negative, and they can increase or decrease during a given period of time. A decrease in temperature is represented by a negative number. An increase in temperature is represented by a positive number.

Math On the Spot

⊙ my.hrw.com

EXAMPLE 3   **FL** 7.EE.2.4

Between the hours of 10 P.M. and 6 A.M., the temperature decreases an average of $\frac{3}{4}$ of a degree per hour. How many minutes will it take for the temperature to decrease by 5 °F?

STEP 1 Write an equation. Let x represent the number of hours it takes for the temperature to decrease by 5 °F.

$$-\frac{3}{4}x = -5$$

STEP 2 Solve the equation using an inverse operation.

$$-\frac{3}{4}x = -5$$

$$-\frac{4}{3}\left(-\frac{3}{4}x\right) = -\frac{4}{3}(-5) \qquad \text{Multiply both sides by } -\frac{4}{3}.$$

$$x = \frac{20}{3}$$

STEP 3 Convert the number of hours to minutes.

$$\frac{20}{3} \text{ hours} \times \frac{60 \text{ minutes}}{1 \text{ hour}} = 400 \text{ minutes}$$

It takes 400 minutes for the temperature to decrease by 5 °F.

Math Talk
Mathematical Practices

Why is multiplying by $-\frac{4}{3}$ the inverse of multiplying by $-\frac{3}{4}$?

YOUR TURN

6. The value of a share of stock decreases in value at a rate of $1.20 per hour during the first 3.5 hours of trading. Write and solve an equation to find the decrease in the value of the share of stock during that time.

_____

7. After a power failure, the temperature in a freezer increased at an average rate of 2.5 °F per hour. The total increase was 7.5 °F. Write and solve an equation to find the number of hours until the power was restored.

_____

Personal Math Trainer

Online Assessment and Intervention

⊙ my.hrw.com

The table shows the average temperature in Barrow, Alaska, for three months during one year.

Month	Average Temperature (°F)
January	−13.4
June	34.0
November	−1.7

1. How many degrees warmer is the average temperature in November than in January? (Examples 1 and 2)

STEP 1 Write an equation. Let x represent _____

_____.

$x +$ _____ $=$ _____ , or $x -$ _____ $=$ _____

STEP 2 Solve the equation. Show your work.

The average temperature in November

is _____ warmer.

2. Suppose that during one period of extreme cold, the average daily temperature decreased $1\frac{1}{2}$ °F each day. How many days did it take for the temperature to decrease by 9 °F? (Examples 1 and 3)

STEP 1 Write an equation. Let x represent _____

_____.

_____ $x =$ _____

STEP 2 Solve the equation. Show your work.

It took _____ days for the temperature to decrease by 9 °F.

Use inverse operations to solve each equation. (Example 1)

3. $-2x = 34$

4. $y - 3.5 = -2.1$

5. $\frac{2}{3}z = -6$

_____   _____   _____

? ESSENTIAL QUESTION CHECK-IN

6. How does writing an equation help you solve a problem?

_____

_____

1.2 Independent Practice

FL 7.EE.2.4

Personal Math Trainer

Online Assessment and Intervention

my.hrw.com

The table shows the elevation in feet at the peaks of several mountains. Use the table for 7–9.

Mountain	Elevation (feet)
Mt. McKinley	20,321.5
K2	28,251.31
Tupungato	22,309.71
Dom	14,911.42

7. Mt. Everest is 8,707.37 feet higher than Mt. McKinley. What is the elevation of Mt. Everest?

_____

8. Liam descended from the summit of K2 to an elevation of 23,201.06 feet. How many feet did Liam descend? What was his change in elevation?

_____

9. K2 is 11,194.21 feet higher than Mt. Kenya. Write and solve an equation to find the elevation of Mt. Kenya.

_____

_____

10. A hot air balloon begins its descent at a rate of $22\frac{1}{2}$ feet per minute. How long will it take for the balloon's elevation to change by −315 feet?

_____

11. During another part of its flight, the balloon in Exercise 10 had a change in elevation of −901 feet. What was its rate of descent?

_____

The table shows the average temperatures in several states from January through March. Use the table for 12–14.

State	Average Temperature (°C)
Florida	18.1
Minnesota	−2.5
Montana	−0.7
Texas	12.5

12. Write and solve an equation to find how much warmer Montana's average 3-month temperature is than Minnesota's.

_____

13. How much warmer is Florida's average 3-month temperature than Montana's?

_____

14. How would the average temperature in Texas have to change to match the average temperature in Florida?

_____

15. A football team has a net yardage of $-26\frac{1}{3}$ yards on a series of plays. The team needs a net yardage of 10 yards to get a first down. How many yards do they have to get on their next play to get a first down?

_____

16. A diver begins at sea level and descends vertically at a rate of $2\frac{1}{2}$ feet per second. How long does the diver take to reach

−15.6 feet? _____

17. Analyze Relationships In Exercise 16, what is the relationship between the rate at which the diver descends, the elevation he reaches, and the time it takes to reach that elevation?

_____

18. Check for Reasonableness Jane withdrew money from her savings account in each of 5 months. The average amount she withdrew per month was $45.50. How much did she withdraw in all during the 5 months? Show that your answer is reasonable.

_____

_____

H.O.T. FOCUS ON HIGHER ORDER THINKING

19. Justify Reasoning Consider the two problems below. Which values in the problems are represented by negative numbers? Explain why.

(1) A diver below sea level ascends 25 feet to a reef at −35.5 feet. What was the elevation of the diver before she ascended to the reef?

(2) A plane descends 1.5 miles to an elevation of 3.75 miles. What was the elevation of the plane before its descent?

_____

_____

_____

20. Analyze Relationships How is solving $-4x = -4.8$ different from solving $-\frac{1}{4}x = -4.8$? How are the solutions related?

_____

_____

_____

21. Communicate Mathematical Ideas Flynn opens a savings account. In one 3-month period, he makes deposits of $75.50 and $55.25. He makes withdrawals of $25.15 and $18.65. His balance at the end of the 3-month period is $210.85. Explain how you can find his initial deposit amount.

_____

_____

_____

LESSON 1.3 Writing Two-Step Equations

FL 7.EE.2.4

Use variables to represent quantities in a real-world or mathematical problem, and construct simple equations... to solve problems by reasoning about the quantities.

ESSENTIAL QUESTION

How do you write a two-step equation?

EXPLORE ACTIVITY **FL** Prep for 7.EE.2.4

Modeling Two-Step Equations

You can use algebra tiles to model two-step equations.

KEY

| + | = positive variable |
| − | = negative variable |

$\boxed{+} = 1 \quad \boxed{-} = -1$

Use algebra tiles to model $3x - 4 = 5$.

A How can you model the left side of the equation?

_____

B How can you model the right side of the equation?

_____

C Use algebra tiles or draw them to model the equation on the mat.

Math Talk
Mathematical Practices

Why is the mat divided into two equal halves with a line?

Reflect

1. What If? How would you change the equation in the Explore Activity to model $-3x + 4 = 5$?

_____

_____

_____

Writing Two-Step Equations

You can write two-step equations to represent real-world problems by translating the words of the problems into numbers, variables, and operations.

EXAMPLE 1 FL 7.EE.2.4

A one-year membership to Metro Gym costs $460. There is a fee of $40 when you join, and the rest is paid monthly. Write an equation to represent what you will pay monthly for the yearlong membership. Write an equation that would help members find how much they pay per month.

STEP 1 Identify what you are trying to find. This will be the variable in the equation.

Let m represent the amount of money members pay per month.

STEP 2 Identify important information in the problem that can be used to help write an equation.

one-time joining fee: **$40**
fee charged for 1 year: **$12 \cdot m$**
total cost for the year: **$460**

> Convert 1 year into 12 months to find how much members pay per month.

STEP 3 Use words in the problem to tie the information together and write an equation.

One-time joining fee	plus	12	times	monthly cost	equals	$460
↓	↓	↓	↓	↓	↓	↓
$40	+	12	·	m	=	$460

The equation $40 + 12m = 460$ can help members find out their monthly fee.

Reflect

2. Multiple Representations Why would this equation for finding the monthly fee be difficult to model with algebra tiles?

_____

3. Can you rewrite the equation in the form $52m = 460$? Explain.

_____

_____

YOUR TURN

4. Billy has a gift card with a $150 balance. He buys several video games that cost $35 each. After the purchases, his gift card balance is $45. Write an equation to help find out how many video games Billy bought.

_____

Personal Math Trainer
Online Assessment and Intervention
my.hrw.com

Math On the Spot
my.hrw.com

Writing a Verbal Description of a Two-Step Equation

You can also write a verbal description to fit a two-step equation.

EXAMPLE 2   FL 7.EE.2.4

Write a corresponding real-world problem to represent $5x + 50 = 120$.

STEP 1 Analyze what each part of the equation means mathematically.

x is the solution of the problem, the quantity you are looking for.

$5x$ means that, for a reason given in the problem, the quantity you are looking for is multiplied by 5.

$+ 50$ means that, for a reason given in the problem, 50 is added to $5x$.

$= 120$ means that after multiplying the solution x by 5 and adding 50 to it, the result is 120.

STEP 2 Think of some different situations in which a quantity x might be multiplied by 5.

You have x number of books, each weighing 5 pounds, and you want to know their total weight.	You save $5 each week for x weeks and want to know the total amount you have saved.

STEP 3 Build on the situation and adjust it to create a verbal description that takes all of the information of the equation into account.

- A publisher ships a package of x number of books each weighing 5 pounds, plus a second package weighing 50 pounds. The total weight of both packages is 120 pounds. How many books are being shipped?

- Leon receives a birthday gift of $50 from his parents and decides to save it. Each week he adds $5 to his savings. How many weeks will it take for him to save $120?

My Notes

Lesson 1.3 **21**

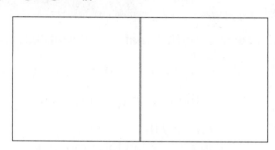

YOUR TURN

5. Write a real-world problem that can be represented by $10x + 40 = 100$.

_____

_____

Guided Practice

Draw algebra tiles to model the given two-step equation. (Explore Activity)

1. $2x + 5 = 7$

2. $-3 = 5 - 4x$

3. A group of adults plus one child attend a movie at Cineplex 15. Tickets cost $9 for adults and $6 for children. The total cost for the movie is $78. Write an equation to find the number of adults in the group. (Example 1) _____

4. Break down the equation $2x + 10 = 16$ to analyze each part. (Example 2)

x is _____ of the problem.

2x is the quantity you are looking for _____.

+ 10 means 10 is _____. **= 16** means the _____ is 16.

5. Write a corresponding real-world problem to represent $2x - 125 = 400$.

(Example 2) _____

_____

? ESSENTIAL QUESTION CHECK-IN

6. Describe the steps you would follow to write a two-step equation you can use to solve a real-world problem.

_____

_____

_____

Solving Two-Step Equations

FL   7.EE.2.4a

Solve word problems leading to equations of the form $px + q = r$ and $p(x + q) = r$ ...
Compare an algebraic solution to an arithmetic solution ...
Also 7.EE.2.3, 7.EE.2.4

ESSENTIAL QUESTION

How do you solve a two-step equation?

Modeling and Solving Two-Step Equations

You can solve two-step equations using algebra tiles.

Math On the Spot

my.hrw.com

EXAMPLE 1

FL   7.EE.2.4

Use algebra tiles to model and solve $3n + 2 = 11$.

STEP 1   Model the equation.

STEP 2   Remove 2 +1-tiles from each side of the mat.

Since there are +1-tiles on both sides of the equation, you can remove, or subtract, 2 +1-tiles from each side to help isolate the variable.

STEP 3   Divide each side into 3 equal groups.

STEP 4   The solution is $n = 3$.

YOUR TURN

Use algebra tiles to model and solve each equation.

1. $2x + 5 = 11$ _____

2. $3n - 1 = 8$ _____

3. $2a - 3 = -5$ _____

4. $-4y + 2 = -2$ _____

Personal Math Trainer

Online Assessment and Intervention

my.hrw.com

Solving Two-Step Equations

You can use inverse operations to solve equations with more than one operation.

EXAMPLE 2   **FL** **7.EE.2.4a**

A dog sled driver added more gear to the sled, doubling its weight. This felt too heavy, so the driver removed 20 pounds to reach the final weight of 180 pounds. Write and solve an equation to find the sled's original weight.

STEP 1 Write an equation. Let w represent the original weight of the sled.

$2w - 20 = 180$.

STEP 2 Solve the equation.

$$2w - 20 = 180$$
$$\underline{+\ 20\quad +\ 20} \qquad \text{Add 20 to both sides.}$$
$$2w\qquad\ = 200$$
$$\frac{2w}{2} = \frac{200}{2} \qquad \text{Divide both sides by 2.}$$
$$w = 100$$

The sled's original weight was 100 pounds.

Reflect

5. **Analyze Relationships** Describe how you could find the original weight of the sled using only arithmetic. Compare this method with the method shown in Example 2.

_____

_____

_____

_____

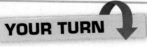

YOUR TURN

Solve each problem by writing and solving an equation.

6. The Wilsons have triplets and another child who is ten years old. The sum of the ages of their children is 37. How old are the triplets?

_____

7. Five less than the quotient of a number and 4 is 15. What is the number?

_____

Two-Step Equations with Negative Numbers

Many real-world quantities such as altitude or temperature involve negative numbers. You solve equations with negative numbers just as you did equations with positive numbers.

Math On the Spot
my.hrw.com

EXAMPLE 3   FL 7.EE.2.4a

A To convert a temperature from degrees Fahrenheit to degrees Celsius, first subtract 32. Then multiply the result by $\frac{5}{9}$. An outdoor thermometer showed a temperature of $-10\ °C$. What was the temperature in degrees Fahrenheit?

STEP 1 Write an equation. Let x represent the temperature in degrees Fahrenheit.

$$-10 = \frac{5}{9}(x - 32)$$

STEP 2 Solve the equation.

$$\frac{9}{5}(-10) = \frac{9}{5}\left(\frac{5}{9}(x-32)\right)$$ Multiply both sides by $\frac{9}{5}$.

$$-18 = x - 32$$

$$\underline{+32 \qquad +32}$$ Add 32 to both sides.

$$14 = x$$

The temperature was 14 degrees Fahrenheit.

> **Math Talk**
> **Mathematical Practices**
> How can you check the solution?

B An airplane flies at an altitude of 38,000 feet. As it nears the airport, the plane begins to descend at a rate of 600 feet per minute. At this rate, how many minutes will the plane take to descend to 18,800 feet?

STEP 1 Write an equation. Let m represent the number of minutes.

$$38{,}000 - 600m = 18{,}800$$

STEP 2 Solve the equation. Start by isolating the term that contains the variable.

$$38{,}000 - 600m = 18{,}800$$

$$\underline{-38{,}000 \qquad\qquad -38{,}000}$$ Subtract 38,000 from both sides.

$$-600m = -19{,}200$$

$$\frac{-600m}{-600} = \frac{-19{,}200}{-600}$$ Divide both sides by -600.

$$m = 32$$

The plane will take 32 minutes to descend to 18,800 feet.

Animated Math
my.hrw.com

Personal Math Trainer

Online Assessment and Intervention

🔘 my.hrw.com

Solve each problem by writing and solving an equation.

8. What is the temperature in degrees Fahrenheit of a freezer kept at −20 °C?

_____

9. Jenny earned 92 of a possible 120 points on a test. She lost 4 points for each incorrect answer. How many incorrect answers did she have?

_____

Guided Practice

The equation $2x + 1 = 9$ is modeled below. (Example 1)

1. To solve the equation with algebra tiles, first remove _____ .

   Then divide each side into _____ .

2. The solution is $x =$ _____ .

Solve each problem by writing and solving an equation.

3. A rectangular picture frame has a perimeter of 58 inches. The height of the frame is 18 inches. What is the width of the frame? (Example 2)

_____

4. A school store has 1200 pencils in stock, and sells an average of 24 pencils per day. The manager reorders when the number of pencils in stock is 500. In how many days will the manager have to reorder? (Example 3)

_____

? ESSENTIAL QUESTION CHECK-IN

5. How can you decide which operations to use to solve a two-step equation?

_____

_____

_____

Inequalities

ESSENTIAL QUESTION

How can you use inequalities to solve real-world problems?

Real-World Video

Many school groups and other organizations hold events to raise money. Members can write and solve inequalities to represent the financial goals they are trying to achieve.

ⓘ my.hrw.com

GO DIGITAL

my.hrw.com

my.hrw.com

Go digital with your write-in student edition, accessible on any device.

Math On the Spot

Scan with your smart phone to jump directly to the online edition, video tutor, and more.

Animated Math

Interactively explore key concepts to see how math works.

Personal Math Trainer

Get immediate feedback and help as you work through practice sets.

Are YOU Ready?

Complete these exercises to review skills you will need for this module.

Personal Math Trainer

Online Assessment and Intervention

my.hrw.com

Inverse Operations

EXAMPLE

$3x = 24$ x is multiplied by 3.

$\dfrac{3x}{3} = \dfrac{24}{3}$ Use the inverse operation, division.
Divide both sides by 3.

$x = 8$

$z + 6 = 4$ 6 is added to z.

$\underline{-6 = -6}$ Use the inverse operation, subtraction.

$z = -2$ Subtract 6 from both sides.

Solve each equation, using inverse operations.

1. $9w = -54$ _____

2. $b - 12 = 3$ _____

3. $\frac{n}{4} = -11$ _____

Locate Points on a Number Line

EXAMPLE

Graph $+2$ by starting at 0 and counting 2 units to the *right*.

Graph -4 by starting at 0 and counting 4 units to the *left*.

Graph each number on the number line.

```
←—+—+—+—+—+—+—+—+—+—+—+—+—+—+—+—+—+—+—+—+—→
  -10         -5          0          5          10
```

4. 3   **5.** -9 **6.** 7   **7.** -3

Integer Operations

EXAMPLE

$-7 - (-4) = -7 + 4$ To subtract an integer, add its opposite.

$= |-7| - |4|$ The signs are different, so find the difference of the absolute values.

$= 7 - 4,$ or 3

$= -3$ Use the sign of the number with the greater absolute value.

8. $3 - (-5)$ _____   **9.** $-4 - 5$ _____   **10.** $6 - 10$ _____   **11.** $-5 - (-3)$ _____

12. $8 - (-8)$ _____   **13.** $9 - 5$ _____   **14.** $-3 - 9$ _____   **15.** $0 - (-6)$ _____

Reading Start-Up

Visualize Vocabulary

Use the ✔ words to complete the graphic. You may put more than one word in each box.

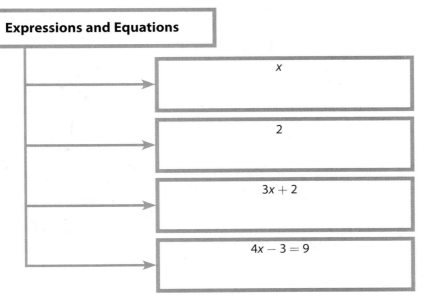

Expressions and Equations

x

2

$3x + 2$

$4x - 3 = 9$

Understand Vocabulary

Complete each sentence, using the review words.

1. A value of the variable that makes the equation true is a _____.

2. The set of all whole numbers and their opposites are _____.

3. An _____ is an expression that contains at least one variable.

Active Reading

Layered Book Before beginning the module, create a layered book to help you learn the concepts in this module. At the top of the first flap, write the title of the module, "Inequalities." Then label each flap with one of the lesson titles in this module. As you study each lesson, write important ideas, such as vocabulary and processes, under the appropriate flap.

Unpacking the Standards

Understanding the standards and the vocabulary terms in the standards will help you know exactly what you are expected to learn in this module.

FL 7.EE.2.4

Use variables to represent quantities in a real-world or mathematical problem, and construct simple equations and inequalities to solve problems by reasoning about the quantities.

Key Vocabulary

inequality *(desigualdad)*
A mathematical sentence that shows that two quantities are not equal.

What It Means to You

You will write an inequality to solve a real-world problem.

UNPACKING EXAMPLE 7.EE.2.4

To rent a certain car for a day costs $39 plus $0.29 for every mile the car is driven. Write an inequality to show the maximum number of miles you can drive and keep the rental cost under $100.

The expression for the cost of the rental is $39 + 0.29m$. The total cost of the rental must be under $100. So the inequality is as shown.

$$39 + 0.29m < 100$$

FL 7.EE.2.4b

Solve word problems leading to inequalities of the form $px + q > r$ or $px + q < r$, where p, q, and r are specific rational numbers. Graph the solution set of the inequality and interpret it in the context of the problem.

Key Vocabulary

solution *(solución)*
The value(s) for the variable that makes the inequality true.

What It Means to You

You will solve inequalities that involve two steps and interpret the solutions.

UNPACKING EXAMPLE 7.EE.2.4b

Solve and graph the solution of $-3x + 7 > -8$.

$$-3x + 7 > -8$$

$-3x > -7 -8$	Subtract 7 from both sides.
$-3x > -15$	Simplify.
$x < 5$	Divide both sided by -5, and reverse the inequality.

All numbers less than 5 are solutions for this inequality.

Visit **my.hrw.com** to see all **Florida Math Standards** unpacked.

my.hrw.com

LESSON 2.1 Writing and Solving One-Step Inequalities

FL 7.EE.2.4b

Use variables to represent quantities in a real-world or mathematical problem, and construct simple ... inequalities to solve problems by reasoning about the quantities.

ESSENTIAL QUESTION

How do you write and solve one-step inequalities?

EXPLORE ACTIVITY **FL** Prep. for 7.EE.2.4b

Investigating Inequalities

You know that when you perform any of the four basic operations on both sides of an equation, the resulting equation is still true. What effect does performing these operations on both sides of an *inequality* have?

A Complete the table.

Inequality	Add to both sides:	New Inequality	Is new inequality true or false?
$2 \geq -3$	3		
$-1 \leq 6$	-1		
$-8 > -10$	-8		

Reflect

1. Make a Conjecture When you add the same number to both sides of an inequality, is the inequality still true? Explain how you know that your conjecture holds for *subtracting* the same number.

_____

B Complete the table.

Inequality	Divide both sides by:	New Inequality	Is new inequality true or false?
$4 < 8$	4		
$12 \geq -15$	3		
$-16 \leq 12$	-4		
$15 > 5$	-5		

What do you notice when you divide both sides of an inequality by the same negative number?

_____

Reflect

2. Make a Conjecture What could you do to make the inequalities that are not true into true statements?

_____

3. Communicate Mathematical Ideas Explain how you know that your conjecture holds for multiplying both sides of an inequality by a negative number.

_____

Solving Inequalities Involving Addition and Subtraction

You can use properties of inequality to solve inequalities involving addition and subtraction with rational numbers.

Addition and Subtraction Properties of Inequality	
Addition Property of Inequality	**Subtraction Property of Inequality**
You can add the same number to both sides of an inequality and the inequality will remain true.	You can subtract the same number from both sides of an inequality and the inequality will remain true.

EXAMPLE 1

  FL 7.EE.2.4b

Solve each inequality. Graph and check the solution.

A $x + 5 < -12$

STEP 1 Solve the inequality.

$x + 5 < -12$ Use the Subtraction Property of Inequality.

$\dfrac{-5 \quad\quad -5}{x \quad < \quad -17}$ Subtract 5 from both sides.

STEP 2 Graph the solution.

$$-20\ -19\ -18\ -17\ -16\ -15\ -14\ -13\ -12\ -11\ -10$$

STEP 3 Check the solution. Substitute a solution from the shaded part of your number line into the original inequality.

$-18 + 5 \overset{?}{<} -12$ Substitute −18 for x into $x + 5 < -12$.

$-13 < -12$ The inequality is true.

B $8 \le y - 3$

STEP 1 Solve the inequality.

$\quad\quad 8 \le y - 3$ Use the Addition Property of Inequality.

$\quad\quad \underline{+\,3 \quad +\,3}$ Add 3 to both sides.

$\quad\quad 11 \le y$ You can rewrite $11 \le y$ as $y \ge 11$.

STEP 2 Graph the solution.

5 6 7 8 9 10 11 12 13 14 15

STEP 3 Check the solution. Substitute a solution from the shaded part of your number line into the original inequality.

$\quad\quad 8 \overset{?}{\le} 12 - 3$ Substitute 12 for y in $8 \le y - 3$.

$\quad\quad 8 \le 9$ The inequality is true.

Math Talk

Mathematical Practices

How does the true inequality you found by substituting 12 into the original inequality help you check the solution?

YOUR TURN

Solve each inequality. Graph and check the solution.

4. $y - 5 \ge -7$

−5 −4 −3 −2 −1 0 1 2 3 4 5

5. $21 > 12 + x$

0 1 2 3 4 5 6 7 8 9 10

Personal Math Trainer

Online Assessment and Intervention

my.hrw.com

Solving Inequalities Involving Multiplication and Division

You can use properties of inequality to solve inequalities involving multiplication and division with rational numbers.

Math On the Spot

my.hrw.com

Multiplication and Division Properties of Inequality

- You can multiply or divide both sides of an inequality by the same positive number and the inequality will remain true.

- If you multiply or divide both sides of an inequality by the same negative number, you must reverse the inequality symbol for the statement to still be true.

EXAMPLE 2   FL   7.EE.2.4b

Solve each inequality. Graph and check the solution.

A $\frac{y}{3} \geq 5$

STEP 1   Solve the inequality.

$3\left(\frac{y}{3}\right) \geq 3(5)$ Multiply both sides by 3.

$y \geq 15$

> Use a closed circle to show that 15 is a solution.

STEP 2   Graph the solution.

STEP 3   Check the solution by substituting a solution from the shaded part of the graph into the original inequality. For convenience, choose a multiple of 3.

$\frac{18}{3} \overset{?}{\geq} 5$ Substitute 18 for x in the original inequality.

$6 \geq 5$ The inequality is true.

B $-4x > 52$

STEP 1   Solve the inequality.

$-4x > 52$

$\frac{-4x}{-4} < \frac{52}{-4}$ Divide both sides by -4.
Reverse the inequality symbol.

$x < -13$

STEP 2   Graph the solution.

STEP 3   Check your answer using substitution.

$-4(-15) \overset{?}{>} 52$ Substitute -15 for x in $-4x > 52$.

$60 > 52$ The statement is true.

YOUR TURN

Solve each inequality. Graph and check the solution.

6. $-10y < 60$ _____

7. $7 \geq -\frac{t}{6}$ _____

My Notes

Personal Math Trainer

Online Assessment and Intervention

⊙ my.hrw.com

Solving a Real-World Problem

Although elevations below sea level are represented by negative numbers, we often use absolute values to describe these elevations. For example, −50 feet relative to sea level might be described as 50 feet below sea level.

EXAMPLE 3 Problem Solving   **FL**   7.EE.2.4, 7.EE.2.4b

A marine submersible descends more than 40 feet below sea level. As it descends from sea level, the change in elevation is −5 feet per second. For how many seconds does it descend?

 Analyze Information

Rewrite the question as a statement.
- Find the number of seconds that the submersible descends below sea level.

List the important information:
- Final elevation > 40 feet below sea level or final elevation < −40 feet
- Rate of descent = −5 feet per second

 Formulate a Plan

Write and solve an inequality. Use this fact:

Rate of change in elevation × Time in seconds = Final elevation

 Solve

$-5t < -40$ Rate of change × Time < Final elevation

$\dfrac{-5t}{-5} > \dfrac{-40}{-5}$ Divide both sides by −5. Reverse the inequality symbol.

$t > 8$

The submersible descends for more than 8 seconds.

 Justify and Evaluate

Check your answer by substituting a value greater than 8 seconds in the original inequality.

$-5(9) \overset{?}{<} -40$ Substitute 9 for t in the inequality $-5t < -40$.

$-45 < -40$ The statement is true.

YOUR TURN

8. Every month, $35 is withdrawn from Tony's savings account to pay for his gym membership. He has enough savings to withdraw no more than $315. For how many months can Tony pay for his gym membership?

_____

_____

Personal Math Trainer

Online Assessment and Intervention

 my.hrw.com

Guided Practice

Write the resulting inequality. (Explore Activity)

1. $-5 \leq -2$; Add 7 to both sides _____

2. $-6 < -3$; Divide both sides by -3 _____

3. $7 > -4$; Subtract 7 from both sides _____

4. $-1 \geq -8$; Multiply both sides by -2 _____

Solve each inequality. Graph and check the solution. (Examples 1 and 2)

5. $n - 5 \geq -2$ _____

6. $3 + x < 7$ _____

7. $-7y \leq 14$ _____

8. $\frac{b}{5} > -1$ _____

9. For a scientific experiment, a physicist must make sure that the temperature of a metal at 0 °C gets no colder than -80 °C. The physicist changes the metal's temperature at a steady rate of -4 °C per hour. For how long can the physicist change the temperature? (Example 3)

   a. Let t represent temperature in degrees Celsius. Write an inequality. Use the fact that the rate of change in temperature times the number of hours equals the final temperature.

   _____

   b. Solve the inequality in part **a**. How long can the physicist change the temperature of the metal?

   _____

   c. The physicist has to repeat the experiment if the metal gets cooler than -80 °C. How many hours would the physicist have to cool the metal for this to happen?

   _____

? ESSENTIAL QUESTION CHECK-IN

10. Suppose you are solving an inequality. Under what circumstances do you reverse the inequality symbol?

   _____

2.1 Independent Practice

 FL 7.EE.2.4, 7.EE.2.4b

Personal Math Trainer

Online Assessment and Intervention

my.hrw.com

In 11–16, solve each inequality. Graph and check the solution.

11. $x - 35 > 15$ _____

0 10 20 30 40 50 60 70 80 90 100

12. $193 + y \geq 201$ _____

0 1 2 3 4 5 6 7 8 9 10

13. $-\dfrac{q}{7} \geq -1$ _____

0 1 2 3 4 5 6 7 8 9 10

14. $-12x < 60$ _____

$-10\ -9\ -8\ -7\ -6\ -5\ -4\ -3\ -2\ -1\ \ 0$

15. $5 > z - 3$ _____

0 1 2 3 4 5 6 7 8 9 10

16. $0.5 \leq \dfrac{y}{8}$ _____

0 1 2 3 4 5 6 7 8 9 10

17. The vet says that Lena's puppy will grow to be at most 28 inches tall. Lena's puppy is currently 1 foot tall. How many more inches will the puppy grow?

_____

18. In a litter of 7 kittens, each kitten weighs less than 3.5 ounces. Find all the possible values of the combined weights of the kittens.

_____

19. **Geometry** The sides of the hexagon shown are equal in length. The perimeter of the hexagon is at most 42 inches. Find the possible side lengths of the hexagon.

_____

20. To get a free meal at his favorite restaurant, Tom needs to spend $50 or more at the restaurant. He has already spent $30.25. How much more does Tom need to spend to get his free meal?

_____

21. To cover a rectangular region of her yard, Penny needs at least 170.5 square feet of sod. The length of the region is 15.5 feet. What are the possible widths of the region?

_____

22. **Draw Conclusions** A submarine descends from sea level to the entrance of an underwater cave. The elevation of the entrance is -120 feet. The rate of change in the submarine's elevation is no greater than -12 feet per second. Can the submarine reach the entrance to the cave in less than 10 seconds? Explain.

_____

_____

_____

_____

The sign shows some prices at a produce stand.

23. Selena has $10. What is the greatest amount of spinach she can buy?

_____

Produce	Price per Pound
Onions	$1.25
Yellow Squash	$0.99
Spinach	$3.00
Potatoes	$0.50

24. Gary has enough money to buy at most 5.5 pounds of potatoes. How much money does Gary have?

_____

25. Florence wants to spend no more than $3 on onions. Will she be able to buy 2.5 pounds of onions? Explain.

_____

_____

H.O.T. **FOCUS ON HIGHER ORDER THINKING**

Work Area

26. **Counterexamples** John says that if one side of an inequality is 0, you don't have to reverse the inequality symbol when you multiply or divide both sides by a negative number. Find an inequality that you can use to disprove John's statement. Explain your thinking.

_____

_____

_____

_____

27. **Look for a Pattern** Solve $x + 1 > 10$, $x + 11 > 20$, and $x + 21 > 30$. Describe a pattern. Then use the pattern to predict the solution of $x + 9{,}991 > 10{,}000$.

_____

_____

_____

28. **Persevere in Problem Solving** The base of a rectangular prism has a length of 13 inches and a width of $\frac{1}{2}$ inch. The volume of the prism is less than 65 cubic inches. Find all possible heights of the prism. Show your work.

_____

_____

_____

LESSON 2.2 Writing Two-Step Inequalities

FL 7.EE.2.4

Use variables to represent quantities in a real-world or mathematical problem, and construct simple... inequalities...

ESSENTIAL QUESTION

How do you write a two-step inequality?

EXPLORE ACTIVITY   **FL**   Prep for 7.EE.2.4

Modeling Two-Step Inequalities

You can use algebra tiles to model two-step inequalities.

Use algebra tiles to model $2k + 5 \geq -3$.

A Using the line on the mat, draw in the inequality symbol shown in the inequality.

B How can you model the left side of the inequality?

_____

C How can you model the right side of the inequality?

_____

D Use algebra tiles or draw them to model the inequality on the mat.

Reflect

1. **Multiple Representations** How does your model differ from the one you would draw to model the equation $2k + 5 = -3$?

_____

_____

_____

2. Why might you need to change the inequality sign when you solve an inequality using algebra tiles?

_____

_____

_____

Math On the Spot

my.hrw.com

Writing Two-Step Inequalities

You can write two-step inequalities to represent real-world problems by translating the words of the problems into numbers, variables, and operations.

EXAMPLE 1 Real World

FL 7.EE.2.4

A mountain climbing team is camped at an altitude of 18,460 feet on Mount Everest. The team wants to reach the 29,029-foot summit within 6 days. Write an inequality to find the average number of feet per day the team must climb to accomplish its objective.

STEP 1 Identify what you are trying to find. This will be the variable in the inequality.

Let d represent the average altitude the team must gain each day.

STEP 2 Identify important information in the problem that you can use to write an inequality.

starting altitude: **18,460 ft**   target altitude: **29,029 ft**
number of days times altitude gained to reach target altitude: $6 \cdot d$

STEP 3 Use words in the problem to tie the information together and write an inequality.

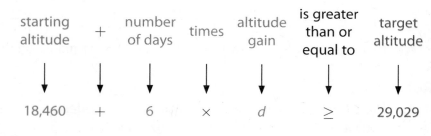

starting altitude	+	number of days	times	altitude gain	is greater than or equal to	target altitude
↓	↓	↓	↓	↓	↓	↓
18,460	+	6	×	d	≥	29,029

$18,460 + 6d \geq 29,029$

Math Talk
Mathematical Practices

Why is the inequality sign $\geq$ used, rather than an equal sign?

YOUR TURN

3. The 45 members of the glee club are trying to raise $6,000 so they can compete in the state championship. They already have $1,240. What inequality can you write to find the amount each member must raise, on average, to meet the goal? _____

4. Ella has $40 to spend at the State Fair. Admission is $6 and each ride costs $3. Write an inequality to find the greatest number of rides she can go on.

_____

Personal Math Trainer

Online Assessment and Intervention

my.hrw.com

Writing a Verbal Description of a Two-Step Inequality

You can also write a verbal description to fit a two-step inequality.

Math On the Spot

⏻ my.hrw.com

EXAMPLE 2   **FL** 7.EE.2.4

Write a corresponding real-world problem to represent $2x + 20 \leq 50$.

My Notes

STEP 1 Analyze what each part of the inequality means mathematically.

x is the solution of the problem, the quantity you are looking for.

$2x$ means that, for a reason given in the problem, the quantity you are looking for is multiplied by 2.

$+ 20$ means that, for a reason given in the problem, 20 is added to $2x$.

≤ 50 means that after multiplying the solution x by 2 and adding 20 to it, the result can be no greater than 50.

STEP 2 Think of some different situations in which a quantity x is multiplied by 2.

You run x miles per day for 2 days. So, $2x$ is the total distance run.	You buy 2 items each costing x dollars. So, $2x$ is the total cost.

STEP 3 Build on the situation and adjust it to create a verbal description that takes all of the information into account.

- Tomas has run 20 miles so far this week. If he intends to run 50 miles or less, how many miles on average should he run on each of the 2 days remaining in the week?

- Manny buys 2 work shirts that are each the same price. After using a $20 gift card, he can spend no more than $50. What is the maximum amount he can spend on each shirt?

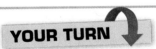

Write a real-world problem for each inequality.

5. $3x + 10 > 30$

_____

_____

_____

_____

6. $5x - 50 \leq 100$

_____

_____

_____

_____

Personal Math Trainer

Online Assessment and Intervention

⏻ my.hrw.com

Draw algebra tiles to model each two-step inequality. (Explore Activity)

1. $4x - 5 < 7$

2. $-3x + 6 > 9$

3. The booster club needs to raise at least $7,000 for new football uniforms. So far, they have raised $1,250. Write an inequality to find the average amounts each of the 92 members can raise to meet the club's objective. (Example 1)

Let a represent the amount each member must raise.

amount to be raised: _____

amount already raised: _____

number of members: _____

Use clues in the problem to write an equation.

The inequality that represents the situation is _____.

4. Analyze what each part of $7x - 18 \leq 32$ means mathematically. (Example 2)

x is _____. $7x$ is _____.

-18 means that _____.

≤ 32 means that _____

5. Write a real-world problem to represent $7x - 18 \leq 32$.

_____

? ESSENTIAL QUESTION CHECK-IN

6. Describe the steps you would follow to write a two-step inequality you can use to solve a real-world problem.

_____

_____

Solving Two-Step Inequalities

FL 7.EE.2.4b

Solve...inequalities of the form $px + q > r$ or $px + q < r$, where p, q, and r are specific rational numbers. Graph the solution set...and interpret it in the context of the problem. *Also 7.EE.2.3*

ESSENTIAL QUESTION

How do you solve a two-step inequality?

Modeling and Solving Two-Step Inequalities

You can solve two-step inequalities using algebra tiles. The method is similar to the one you used to solve two-step equations.

Math On the Spot

my.hrw.com

EXAMPLE 1

FL Prep for 7.EE.2.4b

Use algebra tiles to model and solve $4d - 3 \geq 9$.

STEP 1 Model the inequality. Use a "$\geq$" symbol between the mats.

STEP 2 Add three $+1$ tiles to both sides of the mat.

Math Talk
Mathematical Practices

Why are three $+1$-tiles added to both sides of the mat in Step 3?

STEP 3 Remove zero pairs from the left side of the mat.

STEP 4 Divide each side into 4 equal groups.

STEP 5 The solution is $d \geq 3$.

Use algebra tiles to model and solve each inequality.

1. $2x + 7 > 11$ _____

2. $5h - 4 \geq 11$ _____

Solving and Interpreting Solutions

You can apply what you know about solving two-step equations and one-step inequalities to solving two-step inequalities.

EXAMPLE 2 FL 7.EE.2.4b

Serena wants to complete the first 3 miles of a 10-mile run in 45 minutes or less running at a steady pace. The inequality $10 - 0.75p \leq 7$ can be used to find p, the pace, in miles per hour, she can run to reach her goal. Solve the inequality. Then graph and interpret the solution.

STEP 1 Use inverse operations to solve the inequality.

$$10 - 0.75p \leq 7$$ Subtract 10 from both sides.

$$\underline{-10 \qquad\qquad -10}$$

$$-0.75p \leq -3$$

$$\frac{-0.75p}{-0.75} \geq \frac{-3}{-0.75}$$ Divide both sides by -0.75. Reverse the inequality symbol.

$$n \geq 4$$

STEP 2 Graph the inequality and interpret the circle and the arrow.

Serena can meet her goal by running at a pace of 4 miles per hour.

Serena can run at paces faster than 4 miles per hour and reach her goal.

Serena has to run at a steady pace of at least 4 miles per hour.

3. Joshua wants to complete the first mile of a 5-mile run in 10 minutes or less running at a steady pace. The inequality $5 - \frac{p}{6} \leq 4$ can be used to find p, the pace, in miles per hour, he can run to reach his goal. Solve the inequality. Then graph and interpret the solution.

Determining if a Given Value Makes the Inequality True

You can use substitution to decide whether a given value is the solution of an inequality.

Math On the Spot
my.hrw.com

EXAMPLE 3

FL 7.EE.2.4b

At Gas 'n' Wash, gasoline sells for $4.00 a gallon and a car wash costs $12. Harika wants to have her car washed and keep her total purchase under $60. The inequality $4g + 12 < 60$ can be used to find g, the number of gallons of gas she can buy. Determine which, if any, of these values is a solution: $g = 10$; $g = 11$; $g = 12$.

STEP 1 Substitute each value for g in the inequality $4g + 12 < 60$.

$g = 10$	$g = 11$	$g = 12$
$4(10) + 12 < 60$	$4(11) + 12 < 60$	$4(12) + 12 < 60$

STEP 2 Evaluate each expression to see if a true inequality results.

$4(10) + 12 \overset{?}{<} 60$	$4(11) + 12 \overset{?}{<} 60$	$4(12) + 12 \overset{?}{<} 60$
$40 + 12 \overset{?}{<} 60$	$44 + 12 \overset{?}{<} 60$	$48 + 12 \overset{?}{<} 60$
$52 \overset{?}{<} 60$	$56 \overset{?}{<} 60$	$60 \overset{?}{<} 60$
true ✓	true ✓	*not* true ✗

So, Harika can buy 10 or 11 gallons of gas but not 12 gallons.

Check: Solve and graph the inequality.

$4g + 12 < 60$

$4g < 48$

$g < 12$

The closed circle at zero represents the minimum amount she can buy, zero gallons. She cannot buy a negative number of gallons. The open circle at 12 means that she can buy any amount up to but not including 12 gallons.

Math Talk
Mathematical Practices

In Example 2, how will the graph change if Serena's maximum pace is 12 miles per hour?

YOUR TURN

Circle any given values that make the inequality true.

4. $3v - 8 > 22$

$v = 9; v = 10; v = 11$

5. $5h + 12 \leq -3$

$h = -3; h = -4; h = -5$

Guided Practice

1. Describe how to solve the inequality $3x + 4 < 13$ using algebra tiles. (Example 1)

_____

_____

Solve each inequality. Graph and check the solution. (Example 2)

2. $5d - 13 < 32$ _____

3. $-4b + 9 \leq -7$ _____

Circle any given values that make the inequality true. (Example 3)

4. $2m + 18 > -4$

$m = -12; m = -11; m = -10$

5. $-6y + 3 \geq 0$

$y = 1; \ y = \frac{1}{2}; y = 0$

6. Lizzy has 6.5 hours to tutor 4 students and spend 1.5 hours in a lab. She plans to tutor each student the same amount of time. The inequality $6.5 - 4t \geq 1.5$ can be used to find t, the amount of time in hours Lizzy could spend with each student. Solve the inequality. Graph and interpret the solution. Can Lizzy tutor each student for 1.5 hours? Explain. (Examples 2 and 3)

_____

_____

❓ ESSENTIAL QUESTION CHECK-IN

7. How do you solve a two-step inequality?

_____

_____

_____

2.3 Independent Practice

Personal Math Trainer

Online Assessment and Intervention

my.hrw.com

FL 7.EE.2.3, 7.EE.2.4b

Solve each inequality. Graph and check the solution.

8. $2s + 5 \geq 49$ _____

10 12 14 16 18 20 22 24 26 28 30

9. $-3t + 9 \geq -21$ _____

−10 −8 −6 −4 −2 0 2 4 6 8 10

10. $55 > -7v + 6$ _____

−10 −9 −8 −7 −6 −5 −4 −3 −2 −1 0

11. $41 > 6m - 7$ _____

0 1 2 3 4 5 6 7 8 9 10

12. $\dfrac{a}{-8} + 15 > 23$ _____

−70 −69 −68 −67 −66 −65 −64 −63 −62 −61 −60

13. $\dfrac{f}{2} - 22 < 48$ _____

100 105 110 115 120 125 130 135 140 145 150

14. $-25 + \dfrac{t}{2} \geq 50$ _____

130 135 140 145 150 155 160 165 170 175 180

15. $10 + \dfrac{g}{-9} > 12$ _____

−20 −19 −18 −17 −16 −15 −14 −13 −12 −11 −10

16. $25.2 \leq -1.5y + 1.2$ _____

−20 −19 −18 −17 −16 −15 −14 −13 −12 −11 −10

17. $-3.6 \geq -0.3a + 1.2$ _____

10 11 12 13 14 15 16 17 18 19 20

18. **What If?** The perimeter of a rectangle is at most 80 inches. The length of the rectangle is 25 inches. The inequality $80 - 2w \geq 50$ can be used to find w, the width of the rectangle in inches. Solve the inequality and interpret the solution. How will the solution change if the width must be at least 10 inches and a whole number?

_____

_____

_____

19. **Interpret the Answer** Grace earns $7 for each car she washes. She always saves $25 of her weekly earnings. This week, she wants to have at least $65 in spending money. How many cars must she wash? Write and solve an inequality to represent this situation. Interpret the solution in context.

_____

_____

H.O.T. | **FOCUS ON HIGHER ORDER THINKING**

Work Area

20. **Critical Thinking** Is there any value of x with the property that $x < x - 1$? Explain your reasoning.

_____

_____

_____

21. **Analyze Relationships** A *compound inequality* consists of two simple equalities joined by the word "*and*" or "*or*." Graph the solution sets of each of these compound inequalities.

a. $x > 2$ and $x < 7$

b. $x < 2$ or $x > 7$

```
←+—+—+—+—+—+—+—+—+—+—+→
  0  1  2  3  4  5  6  7  8  9 10
```

c. Describe the solution set of the compound inequality $x < 2$ and $x > 7$.

_____

d. Describe the solution set of the compound inequality $x > 2$ or $x < 7$.

_____

22. **Communicate Mathematical Ideas** Joseph used the problem-solving strategy Work Backward to solve the inequality $2n + 5 < 13$. Shawnee solved the inequality using the algebraic method you used in this lesson. Compare the two methods.

_____

_____

_____

_____

_____

_____

Study Guide Review

Expressions and Equations

Key Vocabulary
algebraic expression
  (expresión algebraica)
equation *(ecuación)*

ESSENTIAL QUESTION

How can you use equations to solve real-world problems?

EXAMPLE 1

Huang and Belita both repair computers. Huang makes $50 a day plus $25 per repair. Belita makes $20 a day plus $35 per repair. Write an expression for Huang and Belita's total daily earnings if they make the same number of repairs _r_.

Huang: $50 + 25r$

Belita: $20 + 35r$

Together: $(50 + 25r) + (20 + 35r) = 50 + 20 + 25r + 35r$

$$= 70 + 60r$$

Huang and Belita earn $70 + 60r$ together.

EXAMPLE 2

A skydiver's parachute opens at a height of 2,790 feet. He then falls at a rate of $-15\frac{1}{2}$ feet per second. How long will it take the skydiver to reach the ground?

Let x represent the number of seconds it takes to reach the ground.

$$-15\frac{1}{2}x = -2{,}790$$

$$-\frac{31}{2}x = -2{,}790 \qquad \text{Write as a fraction.}$$

$$\left(-\frac{2}{31}\right)\left(-\frac{31}{2}x\right) = \left(-\frac{2}{31}\right)(-2{,}790) \qquad \text{Multiply both sides by the reciprocal.}$$

$$x = 180$$

It takes 180 seconds for the skydiver to reach the ground.

EXAMPLE 3

A clothing store sells clothing for 2 times the wholesale cost plus $10. The store sells a pair of pants for $48. How much did the store pay for the pants? Represent the solution on a number line.

Let w represent the wholesale cost of the pants, or the price paid by the store.

$2w + 10 = 48$

$\quad 2w = 38$ *Subtract 10 from both sides.*

$\quad\ w = 19$ *Divide both sides by 2.*

The store paid $19 for the pants.

EXERCISES

Simplify each expression. (Lesson 1.1)

1. $(2x + 3\frac{2}{5}) + (5x - \frac{4}{5})$ _____

2. $(-0.5x - 4) - (1.5x + 2.3)$ _____

3. $9(3t + 4b)$ _____

4. $0.7(5a - 13p)$ _____

Factor each expression. (Lesson 1.1)

5. $8x + 56$ _____

6. $3x + 57$ _____

Use inverse operations to solve each equation. (Lesson 1.2)

7. $1.6 + y = -7.3$ _____

8. $-\frac{2}{3}n = 12$ _____

9. The cost of a ticket to an amusement park is $42 per person. For groups of up to 8 people, the cost per ticket decreases by $3 for each person in the group. Marcos's ticket cost $30. Write and solve an equation to find the number of people in Marcos's group. (Lesson 1.3, 1.4)

_____

Solve each equation. Graph the solution on a number line. (Lesson 1.4)

10. $8x - 28 = 44$

_____

11. $-5z + 4 = 34$

_____

? **ESSENTIAL QUESTION**

How can you use inequalities to solve real-world problems?

EXAMPLE 1

Amy is having her birthday party at a roller skating rink. The rink charges a fee of $50 plus $8 per person. If Amy wants to spend at most $170 for the party at the rink, how many people can she invite to her party?

Let p represent the number of people skating at the party.

$50 + 8p \leq 170$

$\quad\quad 8p \leq 120$ *Subtract 50 from both sides.*

$\quad\quad \dfrac{8p}{8} \leq \dfrac{120}{8}$ *Divide both sides by 8.*

$\quad\quad\quad p \leq 15$

Up to 15 people can skate, so Amy can invite up to 14 people to her party.

EXAMPLE 2

Determine which, if any, of these values makes the inequality $-7x + 42 \leq 28$ true: $x = -1, x = 2, x = 5$.

$-7(-1) + 42 \leq 28 \quad\quad -7(2) + 42 \leq 28 \quad\quad -7(5) + 42 \leq 28$

$x = 2$ and $x = 5$

Substitute each value for x in the inequality and evaluate the expression to see if a true inequality results.

EXERCISES

1. Prudie needs $90 or more to be able to take her family out to dinner. She has already saved $30 and wants to take her family out to eat in 4 days. (Lesson 2.2)

   a. Suppose that Prudie earns the same each day. Write an inequality to find how much she needs to earn each day.

   _____

   b. Suppose that Prudie earns $18 each day. Will she have enough money to take her family to dinner in 4 days? Explain.

   _____

Solve each inequality. Graph and check the solution. (Lesson 2.3)

2. $11 - 5y < -19$

3. $7x - 2 \leq 61$

Unit 1 Performance Tasks

1. **CAREERS IN MATH** Mechanical Engineer A mechanical engineer is testing how different springs stretch for a given force. Force is measured in units called *Newtons*, abbreviated N. A spring stretches 2.5 millimeters for each 1-N force applied.

   a. Write an expression for the stretch of this spring in millimeters for a given force x in Newtons. Use your expression to find how much the spring stretches for a 6-N force.

   _____

   b. Write an expression for the stretch of this spring in *centimeters* for a given force x in Newtons. Use your expression to find how much the spring stretches for a 6-N force. Does the spring stretch the same length as in part a? Explain.

   _____

   _____

   c. The spring is 4 cm long when unloaded. Write and solve an equation for the force needed to stretch the spring to a length of 7 cm. Include a description of the variable.

   _____

   _____

   The amount a spring stretches for a 1-N force is called the *spring constant*, and depends on the spring's construction and material. The spring constant applies when the spring is compressed, which reduces its length, as well as when it is stretched.

   d. Write an expression for the 4-centimeter spring under a compressive force c. Then find the length of the spring under a 6-N compressive force.

   _____

   _____

2. Yolanda saves money to buy a $200 cell phone. She has $70, and saves $25 each week.

   a. Write and solve an inequality to find out how many full weeks Yolanda must save to have at least enough money to buy the cell phone.

   _____

   b. Yolanda buys her phone when she has enough money saved. Will she also have enough to buy a $35 protective case? Explain.

   _____

UNIT 1 MIXED REVIEW

Assessment Readiness

Personal
Math Trainer

Online
Assessment and
Intervention

my.hrw.com

Selected Response

1. Which expression is equivalent to $(9x - 3\frac{1}{8}) - (7x + 1\frac{3}{8})$?

(A) $2x - 4\frac{1}{2}$ (C) $2x - 1\frac{3}{4}$

(B) $16x - 4\frac{1}{2}$ (D) $16x - 1\frac{3}{4}$

2. Timothy began the week with $35. He bought lunch at school, paying $2.25 for each meal. Let x be the number of meals he bought at school and y be the amount of money he had left at the end of the week. Which equation represents the relationship in the situation?

(A) $y = 2.25x + 35$

(B) $y = 35 - 2.25x$

(C) $x = 35 - 2.25y$

(D) $y = 2.25x - 35$

3. Which expression factors to $8(x + 2)$?

(A) $8x + 2$ (C) $16x$

(B) $8x + 10$ (D) $8x + 16$

4. Ramón's toll pass account has a value of $32. Each time he uses the toll road, $1.25 is deducted from the account. When the value drops below $10, he must add value to the toll pass. Which inequality represents how many times Ramón can use the toll road without having to add value to the toll pass?

(A) $10 - 1.25t \geq 0$

(B) $-1.25t + 32 < 10$

(C) $32 - 1.25t \geq 10$

(D) $32 - 10t \geq 1.25$

5. A taxi costs $1.65 for the first mile and $0.85 for each additional mile. Which equation could be solved to find the number x of additional miles traveled in a taxi given that the total cost of the trip is $20?

(A) $1.65x + 0.85 = 20$

(B) $0.85x + 1.65 = 20$

(C) $1.65x - 0.85 = 20$

(D) $0.85x - 1.65 = 20$

6. A sales tax of 6% is added to the price of an item. If Marisa buys an item, which expression indicates how much she will pay in all?

(A) $n + 0.06$ (C) $n + 0.06n$

(B) $0.06n$ (D) $0.06 + 0.06n$

7. Which equation has the solution $x = 12$?

(A) $4x + 3 = 45$

(B) $3x + 6 = 42$

(C) $2x - 5 = 29$

(D) $5x - 8 = 68$

8. The 23 members of the school jazz band are trying to raise at least $1,800 to cover the cost of traveling to a competition. The members have already raised $750. Which inequality could you solve to find the amount that each member should raise to meet the goal?

(A) $23x + 750 > 1,800$

(B) $23x + 750 \geq 1,800$

(C) $23x + 750 < 1,800$

(D) $23x + 750 \leq 1,800$

9. What is the solution of the inequality
$2x - 9 < 7$?

Ⓐ $x < 8$

Ⓑ $x \leq 8$

Ⓒ $x > 8$

Ⓓ $x \geq 8$

10. Which inequality has the solution $n < 5$?

Ⓐ $4n + 11 > -9$

Ⓑ $4n + 11 < -9$

Ⓒ $-4n + 11 < -9$

Ⓓ $-4n + 11 > -9$

11. Which inequality has the solution shown?

Ⓐ $3x + 5 < 2$

Ⓑ $4x + 12 < 4$

Ⓒ $2x + 5 \leq 1$

Ⓓ $3x + 6 \leq 3$

12. A bike rental costs $8 plus $3 per hour. Ravi spent a total of $29 for a bike rental. For how many hours did he rent the bike?

Ⓐ 3 hours

Ⓑ 7 hours

Ⓒ 8 hours

Ⓓ 29 hours

13. Which equation has the solution $x = -5$?

Ⓐ $3x - 5 = -10$

Ⓑ $6x + 2 = 32$

Ⓒ $-2x + 3 = 13$

Ⓓ $-4x - 8 = -28$

14. What is the solution of the inequality
$-4z < -20$?

Ⓐ $z < 5$　　　　Ⓒ $z > 5$

Ⓑ $z < -5$　　　Ⓓ $z > -5$

Mini-Task

15. Max wants to buy some shorts that are priced at $8 each. He decided to buy a pair of sneakers for $39, but the total cost of the shorts and the sneakers must be less than $75.

a. Write an inequality to find out how many pairs of shorts Max can buy.

_____

b. Suppose that Max wants to buy 6 pairs of shorts. Will he have enough money? Explain.

_____

_____

_____

_____

_____

c. Solve the inequality to find the greatest number of pairs of shorts that Max can buy. Show your work.

_____

_____

_____

_____

_____

_____

Geometry

 MODULE **3**

Modeling Geometric Figures

FL   7.G.1.1, 7.G.1.2, 7.G.1.3, 7.G.2.5

 MODULE **4**

Circumference, Area, and Volume

FL   7.G.2.4, 7.G.2.6

CAREERS IN MATH

Product Design Engineer A product design engineer works to design and develop manufactured products and equipment. A product design engineer uses math to design and modify models, and to calculate costs in producing their designs.

If you are interested in a career in product design engineering, you should study these mathematical subjects:
- Algebra
- Geometry
- Trigonometry
- Statistics
- Calculus

Research other careers that require the use of mathematics to design and modify products.

Unit 2 Performance Task

At the end of the unit, check out how **product design engineers** use math.

Vocabulary Preview

Use the puzzle to preview key vocabulary from this unit. Unscramble the circled letters to answer the riddle at the bottom of the page.

1. NEONGTURC LANSEG

2. LEOTECRAYMPMN SEGLAN

3. RIMEUCEEFNRCC

4. LEARATL ERAA

5. PIECOTMOS GUISEFR

1. Angles that have the same measure. (Lesson 3.4)
2. Two angles whose measures have a sum of 90 degrees. (Lesson 3.4)
3. The distance around a circle. (Lesson 4.1)
4. The sum of the areas of the lateral faces of a prism. (Lesson 4.4)
5. A two-dimensional figure made from two or more geometric figures. (Lesson 4.3)

Q: What do you say when you see an empty parrot cage?

A: _ _ _ _ _ _ _ _ _ _!

Modeling Geometric Figures

MODULE

? ESSENTIAL QUESTION

How can you use proportions to solve real-world geometry problems?

Real-World Video

Architects make blueprints and models of their designs to show clients and contractors. These scale drawings and scale models have measurements in proportion to those of the project when built.

⏱ my.hrw.com

GO DIGITAL
my.hrw.com

my.hrw.com
Go digital with your write-in student edition, accessible on any device.

Math On the Spot
Scan with your smart phone to jump directly to the online edition, video tutor, and more.

Animated Math
Interactively explore key concepts to see how math works.

Personal Math Trainer
Get immediate feedback and help as you work through practice sets.

67

Are YOU Ready?

Complete these exercises to review skills you will need for this module.

Personal Math Trainer

Online Assessment and Intervention

my.hrw.com

Solve Two-Step Equations

EXAMPLE

$$5x + 3 = -7$$
$$5x + 3 - 3 = -7 - 3 \qquad \text{Subtract 3 from both sides.}$$
$$5x = -10 \qquad \text{Simplify.}$$
$$\frac{5x}{5} = \frac{-10}{5} \qquad \text{Divide both sides by 5.}$$
$$x = -2$$

Solve.

1. $3x + 4 = 10$

2. $5x - 11 = 34$

3. $-2x + 5 = -9$

4. $-11 = 8x + 13$

5. $4x - 7 = -27$

6. $\frac{1}{2}x + 16 = 39$

7. $12 = 2x - 16$

8. $5x - 15 = -65$

Solve Proportions

EXAMPLE

$$\frac{a}{4} = \frac{27}{18}$$
$$a \times 18 = 4 \times 27 \qquad \text{Write the cross products.}$$
$$18a = 108 \qquad \text{Simplify.}$$
$$\frac{18a}{18} = \frac{108}{18} \qquad \text{Divide both sides by 18.}$$
$$a = 6$$

Solve for x.

9. $\frac{x}{5} = \frac{18}{30}$

10. $\frac{x}{12} = \frac{24}{36}$

11. $\frac{3}{9} = \frac{x}{3}$

12. $\frac{14}{15} = \frac{x}{75}$

13. $\frac{8}{x} = \frac{14}{7}$

14. $\frac{14}{x} = \frac{2}{5}$

15. $\frac{5}{6} = \frac{x}{15}$

16. $\frac{81}{33} = \frac{x}{5.5}$

Reading Start-Up

Visualize Vocabulary

Use the ✔ words to complete the graphic. You may put more than one word on each line.

two lines joining at one point

a shape made of straight lines

2D-Shapes

unit measured by a protractor

dimensions of two-dimensional shapes

Vocabulary

Review Words
- ✔ angle (*ángulo*)
- ✔ degree (*grado*)
- dimension (*dimensión*)
- ✔ length (*longitud*)
- proportion (*proporción*)
- ✔ polygon (*polígono*)
- ratio (*razón*)
- ✔ width (*ancho*)

Preview Words
- adjacent angles (*ángulos adyacentes*)
- complementary angles (*ángulos complementarios*)
- congruent angles (*ángulos congruentes*)
- cross section (*sección transversal*)
- intersection (*intersección*)
- scale (*escala*)
- scale drawing (*dibujo a escala*)
- supplementary angles (*ángulos suplementarios*)
- vertical angles (*ángulos verticales*)

Understand Vocabulary

Complete each sentence using a preview word.

1. What is a proportional two-dimensional drawing of an object?

   _____

2. _____ are angles that have the same measure.

3. _____ are angles whose measures have a sum of 90°.

Active Reading

Key-Term Fold Before beginning the module, create a key-term fold to help you learn the vocabulary in this module. Write each highlighted vocabulary word on one side of a flap. Write the definition for each word on the other side of the flap. Use the key-term fold to quiz yourself on the definitions in this module.

MODULE 3
Unpacking the Standards

Understanding the standards and the vocabulary terms in the standards will help you know exactly what you are expected to learn in this module.

 FL 7.G.1.1

Solve problems involving scale drawings of geometric figures, including computing actual lengths and areas from a scale drawing and reproducing a scale drawing at a different scale.

Key Vocabulary

scale *(escala)*
The ratio between two sets of measurements.

What It Means to You

You will learn how to calculate actual measurements from a scale drawing.

UNPACKING EXAMPLE 7.G.1.1

A photograph of a painting has dimensions 5.4 cm and 4 cm. The scale factor is $\frac{1}{15}$. Find the length and width of the actual painting.

$$\frac{1}{15} = \frac{5.4}{\ell} \qquad\qquad \frac{1}{15} = \frac{4}{w}$$

$$\frac{1 \times 5.4}{15 \times 5.4} = \frac{5.4}{\ell} \qquad\qquad \frac{1 \times 4}{15 \times 4} = \frac{4}{w}$$

$$15 \times 5.4 = \ell \qquad\qquad 15 \times 4 = w$$

$$81 = \ell \qquad\qquad 60 = w$$

The painting is 81 cm long and 60 cm wide.

 FL 7.G.2.5

Use facts about supplementary, complementary, vertical, and adjacent angles in a multi-step problem to write and solve simple equations for an unknown angle in a figure.

Key Vocabulary

supplementary angles
(ángulos suplementarios)
Two angles whose measures have a sum of 180°.

What It Means to You

You will learn about supplementary, complementary, vertical, and adjacent angles. You will solve simple equations to find the measure of an unknown angle in a figure.

UNPACKING EXAMPLE 7.G.2.5

Suppose $m\angle 1 = 55°$.

Adjacent angles formed by two intersecting lines are supplementary.

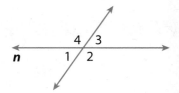

$$m\angle 1 + m\angle 2 = 180°$$

$$55° + m\angle 2 = 180° \qquad \textit{Substitute.}$$

$$m\angle 2 = 180° - 55°$$

$$= 125°$$

LESSON 3.1 Similar Shapes and Scale Drawings

FL 7.G.1.1
Solve problems involving scale drawings of geometric figures, including computing actual lengths and areas from a scale drawing and reproducing a scale drawing at a different scale.

ESSENTIAL QUESTION

How can you use scale drawings to solve problems?

EXPLORE ACTIVITY 1   FL 7.G.1.1

Finding Dimensions

Scale drawings and scale models are used in mapmaking, construction, and other trades.

A blueprint is a technical drawing that usually displays architectural plans. Pete's blueprint shows a layout of a house. Every 4 inches in the blueprint represents 3 feet of the actual house. One of the walls in the blueprint is 24 inches long. What is the actual length of the wall?

A Complete the table to find the actual length of the wall.

Blueprint length (in.)	4	8	12	16	20	24
Actual length (ft)	3	6				

Reflect

1. In Pete's blueprint the length of a side wall is 16 inches. Find the actual length of the wall.

_____

2. The back wall of the house is 33 feet long. What is the length of the back wall in the blueprint?

_____

3. **Check for Reasonableness** How do you know your answer to **2** is reasonable?

_____

_____

_____

_____

Using a Scale Drawing to Find Area

A **scale drawing** is a proportional two-dimensional drawing of an object. Scale drawings can represent objects that are smaller or larger than the actual object.

A **scale** is a ratio between 2 sets of measurements. It shows how a dimension in a scale drawing is related to the actual object. Scales are usually shown as two numbers separated by a colon such as 1:20 or 1 cm:1 m. Scales can be shown in the same unit or in different units.

You can solve scale-drawing problems by using proportional reasoning.

My Notes

EXAMPLE 1

FL   7.G.1.1

The art class is planning to paint a mural on an outside wall. This figure is a scale drawing of the wall. What is the area of the actual wall?

28 in.

11 in.

2 in.:3 ft

STEP 1 Find the number of feet represented by 1 inch in the drawing.

$$\frac{2 \text{ in.} \div 2}{3 \text{ ft} \div 2} = \frac{1 \text{ in.}}{1.5 \text{ ft}}$$

1 inch in this drawing equals 1.5 feet on the actual wall.

STEP 2 Find the height of the actual wall labeled 11 inches in the drawing.

$$\frac{1 \text{ in.} \times 11}{1.5 \text{ ft} \times 11} = \frac{11 \text{ in.}}{16.5 \text{ ft}}$$

The height of the actual wall labeled 11 in. is 16.5 ft.

STEP 3 Find the length of the actual wall labeled 28 inches in the drawing.

$$\frac{1 \text{ in.} \times 28}{1.5 \text{ ft} \times 28} = \frac{28 \text{ in.}}{42 \text{ ft}}$$

The length of the actual wall is 42 ft.

STEP 4 Since area is length times width, the area of the actual wall is 16.5 ft × 42 ft = 693 ft².

Math Talk

Mathematical Practices

How can use a scale to determine whether the drawing or the object is larger?

Reflect

4.   **Analyze Relationships** How could you solve the example without having to determine the number of feet represented by 1 inch?

_____

_____

_____

_____

5. Find the length and width of the actual room, shown in the scale drawing. Then find the area of the actual room. Round your answer to the nearest tenth.

6.5 in.

5 in.

3 in.:8 ft

_____

_____

6. The drawing plan for an art studio shows a rectangle that is 13.2 inches by 6 inches. The scale in the plan is 3 in.:5 ft. Find the length and width of the actual studio. Then find the area of the actual studio.

_____

_____

EXPLORE ACTIVITY 2 Real World   FL 7.G.1.1

Drawing in Different Scales

A A scale drawing of a meeting hall is drawn on centimeter grid paper as shown. The scale is 1 cm:3 m.

Suppose you redraw the rectangle on centimeter grid paper using a scale of 1 cm:6 m. In the new scale, 1 cm

represents **more than/less** than 1 cm in the old scale.

The measurement of each side of the new drawing will

be **twice/half** as long as the measurement of the original drawing.

B Draw the rectangle for the new scale 1 cm:6 m.

Reflect

7. Find the actual length of each side of the hall using the original drawing. Then find the actual length of each side of the hall using the your new drawing and the new scale. How do you know your answers are correct?

_____

_____

_____

_____

1. The scale of a room in a blueprint is 3 in : 5 ft. A wall in the same blueprint is 18 in. Complete the table. (Explore Activity 1)

Blueprint length (in.)	3				
Actual length (ft)					

   a. How long is the actual wall? _____

   b. A window in the room has an actual width of 2.5 feet. Find the width of the window in the blueprint. _____

2. The scale in the drawing is 2 in. : 4 ft. What are the length and width of the actual room? Find the area of the actual room. (Example 1)

   14 in.

   7 in.

   _____

   _____

3. The scale in the drawing is 2 cm : 5 m. What are the length and width of the actual room? Find the area of the actual room. (Example 1)

   10 cm

   6 cm

   _____

4. A scale drawing of a cafeteria is drawn on centimeter grid paper as shown. The scale is 1 cm : 4 m. (Explore Activity 2)

   a. Redraw the rectangle on centimeter grid paper using a scale of 1 cm:6 m.

   b. What is the actual length and width of the cafeteria using the original scale? What are the actual dimensions of the cafeteria using the new scale?

   _____

? ESSENTIAL QUESTION CHECK-IN

5. If you have an accurate, complete scale drawing and the scale, which measurements of the object of the drawing can you find?

   _____

   _____

3.1 Independent Practice

 FL 7.G.1.1

Personal
Math Trainer

Online
Assessment and
Intervention

my.hrw.com

6. Art Marie has a small copy of Rene Magritte's famous painting, *The Schoolmaster*. Her copy has dimensions 2 inches by 1.5 inches. The scale of the copy is 1 in.:40 cm.

a. Find the dimensions of the original painting.

_____

b. Find the area of the original painting.

_____

c. Since 1 inch is 2.54 centimeters, find the dimensions of the original painting in inches.

_____

d. Find the area of the original painting in square inches.

_____

7. A game room has a floor that is 120 feet by 75 feet. A scale drawing of the floor on grid paper uses a scale of 1 unit:5 feet. What are the dimensions of the scale drawing?

_____

8. Multiple Representations The length of a table is 6 feet. On a scale drawing, the length is 2 inches. Write three possible scales for the drawing.

_____

9. Analyze Relationships A scale for a scale drawing is 10 cm:1 mm. Which is larger, the actual object or the scale drawing? Explain.

_____

_____

10. Architecture The scale model of a building is 5.4 feet tall.

a. If the original building is 810 meters tall, what was the scale used to make the model?

_____

b. If the model is made out of tiny bricks each measuring 0.4 inch in height, how many bricks tall is the model?

_____

11. You have been asked to build a scale model of your school out of toothpicks. Imagine your school is 30 feet tall. Your scale is 1 ft:1.26 cm.

    a. If a toothpick is 6.3 cm tall, how many toothpicks tall will your model be?

_____

    b. Your mother is out of toothpicks, and suggests you use cotton swabs instead. You measure them, and they are 7.6 cm tall. How many cotton swabs tall will your model be?

_____

H.O.T. FOCUS ON HIGHER ORDER THINKING

Work Area

12. Draw Conclusions The area of a square floor on a scale drawing is 100 square centimeters, and the scale of the drawing is 1 cm : 2 ft. What is the area of the actual floor? What is the ratio of the area in the drawing to the actual area?

_____

13. Multiple Representations Describe how to redraw a scale drawing with a new scale.

_____

_____

_____

_____

_____

_____

14. Represent Real-World Problems Describe how several jobs or professions might use scale drawings at work.

_____

_____

_____

_____

_____

_____

_____

LESSON
3.2 Geometric Drawings

FL 7.G.1.2
Draw... geometric shapes with given conditions. Focus on constructing triangles...

ESSENTIAL QUESTION
How can you draw shapes that satisfy given conditions?

EXPLORE ACTIVITY 1 FL 7.G.1.2

Drawing Three Sides

Use geometry software to draw a triangle whose sides have the following lengths: 2 units, 3 units, and 4 units.

A Draw the segments.

B Let $\overline{AB}$ be the base of the triangle. Place point C on top of point B and point E on top of point A.

C Using the points C and E as fixed vertices, rotate points F and D to see if they will meet in a single point.

Note that the line segments form a triangle.

D Repeat **A** and **B**, but use a different segment as the base. Do the segments form a triangle? If so, is it the same as the original triangle?

_____

E Use geometry software to draw a triangle with sides of length 2, 3, and 6 units, and one with sides of length 2, 3, and 5 units. Do the line segments form triangles? How does the sum of the lengths of the two shorter sides of each triangle compare to the length of the third side?

Animated Math

⏻ my.hrw.com

_____

Reflect

1. **Conjecture** Do two segments of lengths a and b units and a longer segment of length c units form one triangle, more than one, or none?

_____

EXPLORE ACTIVITY 2   FL   7.G.1.2

Two Angles and Their Included Side

Use a ruler and a protractor to draw each triangle.

Triangle 1	Triangle 2
Angles: 30° and 80°	Angles: 55° and 50°
Length of included side: 2 inches	Length of included side: 1 inch

A Draw Triangle 1.

STEP 1 Use a ruler to draw a line that is 2 inches long. This will be the included side.

STEP 2 Place the center of the protractor on the left end of the 2-in. line. Then make a 30°-angle mark.

STEP 4 Repeat Step 2 on the right side of the triangle to construct the 80° angle.

STEP 3 Draw a line connecting the left side of the 2-in. line and the 30°-angle mark. This will be the 30° angle.

STEP 5 The side of the 80° angle and the side of the 30° angle will intersect. This is Triangle 1 with angles of 30° and 80° and an included side of 2 inches.

B Use the steps in A to draw Triangle 2.

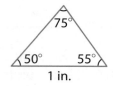

Reflect

2. **Conjecture** When you are given two angle measures and the length of the included side, do you get a unique triangle?

_____

_____

Guided Practice

Tell whether each figure creates the conditions to form a unique triangle, more than one triangle, or no triangle. (Explore Activities 1 and 2)

1.

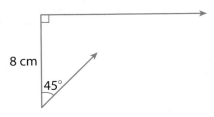

8 cm

45°

_____

2.

4 cm   3 cm

11 cm

_____

3.

40°   30°

7 cm

_____

4.   6 cm
_____

12 cm
_____

7 cm
_____

_____

 ESSENTIAL QUESTION CHECK-IN

5. Describe lengths of three segments that could **not** be used to form a triangle.

_____

3.2 Independent Practice

FL 7.G.1.2

Personal Math Trainer

Online Assessment and Intervention

my.hrw.com

6. On a separate piece of paper, try to draw a triangle with side lengths of 3 centimeters and 6 centimeters, and an included angle of 120°. Determine whether the given segments and angle produce a unique triangle, more than one triangle, or no triangle.

_____

7. A landscape architect submitted a design for a triangle-shaped flower garden with side lengths of 21 feet, 37 feet, and 15 feet to a customer. Explain why the architect was not hired to create the flower garden.

_____

_____

8. **Make a Conjecture** The angles in an actual triangle-shaped traffic sign all have measures of 60°. The angles in a scale drawing of the sign all have measures of 60°. Explain how you can use this information to decide whether three given angle measures can be used to form a unique triangle or more than one triangle.

_____

_____

H.O.T. **FOCUS ON HIGHER ORDER THINKING**

Work Area

9. **Communicate Mathematical Ideas** The figure on the left shows a line segment 2 inches long forming a 45° angle with a dashed line whose length is not given. The figure on the right shows a compass set at a width of $1\frac{1}{2}$ inches with its point on the top end of the 2-inch segment. An arc is drawn intersecting the dashed line twice.

Explain how you can use this figure to decide whether two sides and an angle **not** included between them can be used to form a unique triangle, more than one triangle, or no triangle.

_____

_____

_____

_____

_____

_____

10. **Critical Thinking** Two sides of an isosceles triangle have lengths of 6 inches and 15 inches, respectively. Find the length of the third side. Explain your reasoning.

_____

_____

_____

_____

LESSON
3.3 Cross Sections

FL 7.G.1.3
Describe the two-dimensional figures that result from slicing three-dimensional figures ...

EXPLORE ACTIVITY 1 FL 7.G.1.3

Cross Sections of a Right Rectangular Prism

An **intersection** is a point or set of points common to two or more geometric figures. A **cross section** is the intersection of a three-dimensional figure and a plane. Imagine a plane slicing through the pyramid shown, or through a cone or a prism.

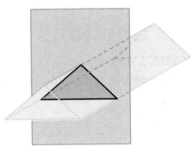

This figure shows the intersection of the cone and a plane. The cross section is a circle.

This figure shows the intersection of a triangular prism and a plane. The cross section is a triangle.

A three-dimensional figure can have several different cross sections depending on the position and the direction of the slice. For example, if the intersection of the plane and cone were vertical, the cross section would form a triangle.

Describe each cross section of the right rectangular prism with the name of its shape. (In a *right* prism, all the sides connecting the bases are rectangles at right angles with the base.)

A

B

_____   _____

C   **D**

_____   _____

Reflect

1. **Conjecture** Is it possible to have a circular cross section in a right rectangular prism?

_____

EXPLORE ACTIVITY 2 🏴 FL 7.G.1.3

Describing Cross Sections

A right rectangular pyramid with a non-square base is shown. (In a *right* pyramid, the point where the triangular sides meet is centered over the base.)

A The shape of the base is a _____

The shape of each side is a _____

B Is it possible for a cross section of the pyramid to have each shape?

square   rectangle   triangle   circle   trapezoid

_____   _____   _____   _____   _____

C Sketch the cross sections of the right rectangular pyramid below.

Reflect

2. **What If?** Suppose the figure in **B** had a square base. Would your answers in **B** be the same? Explain.

_____

_____

> **Math Talk**
> **Mathematical Practices**
>
> Describe and compare the cross sections created when two horizontal planes intersect a right rectangular pyramid.

Name_____ Class_____ Date_____

Describe each cross section.

1.

(Explore Activity 1)

_____

2.

(Explore Activity 2)

_____

3.

h

(Explore Activity 2)

_____

4.

(Explore Activity 2)

_____

ESSENTIAL QUESTION CHECK-IN

5. What is the first step in describing what figure results when a given plane intersects a given three-dimensional figure?

_____

3.3 Independent Practice

Personal Math Trainer

Online Assessment and Intervention

my.hrw.com

FL 7.G.1.3

6. Describe different ways in which a plane might intersect the cylinder, and the cross section that results.

_____

_____

_____

7. Make a Conjecture What cross sections might you see when a plane intersects a cone that you would **not** see when a plane intersects a pyramid or a prism? _____

FOCUS ON HIGHER ORDER THINKING

8. Critical Thinking The two figures on the left below show that you can form a cross section of a cube that is a pentagon. Think of a plane cutting the cube at an angle in such a way as to slice through five of the cube's six faces. Draw dotted lines on the third cube to show how to form a cross section that is a hexagon.

9. Analyze Relationships A sphere has a radius of 12 inches. A horizontal plane passes through the center of the sphere.

  a. Describe the cross section formed by the plane and the sphere.

  _____

  b. Describe the cross sections formed as the plane intersects the interior of the sphere but moves away from the center.

  _____

  _____

  _____

10. Communicate Mathematical Ideas A right rectangular prism is intersected by a horizontal plane and a vertical plane. The cross section formed by the horizontal plane and the prism is a rectangle with dimensions 8 in. and 12 in. The cross section formed by the vertical plane and the prism is a rectangle with dimensions 5 in. and 8 in. Describe the faces of the prism, including their dimensions. Then find its volume.

  _____

  _____

11. Represent Real-World Problems Describe a real-world situation that could be represented by planes slicing a three-dimensional figure to form cross sections.

  _____

  _____

  _____

3.4 Angle Relationships

FL 7.G.2.5

Use facts about supplementary, complementary, vertical, and adjacent angles in a multi-step problem to write and solve simple equations for an unknown angle in a figure.

ESSENTIAL QUESTION

How can you use angle relationships to solve problems?

EXPLORE ACTIVITY FL Prep. for 7.G.2.5

Measuring Angles

It is useful to work with pairs of angles and to understand how pairs of angles relate to each other. **Congruent angles** are angles that have the same measure.

STEP 1 Using a ruler, draw a pair of intersecting lines. Label each angle from 1 to 4.

STEP 2 Use a protractor to help you complete the chart.

Angle	Measure of Angle
m∠1	
m∠2	
m∠3	
m∠4	
m∠1 + m∠2	
m∠2 + m∠3	
m∠3 + m∠4	
m∠4 + m∠1	

Reflect

1. **Make a Conjecture** Share your results with other students. Make a conjecture about pairs of angles that are opposite each other.

_____

_____

2. **Make a Conjecture** When two lines intersect to form two angles, what conjecture can you make about the pairs of angles that are next to each other?

_____

_____

Angle Pairs and One-Step Equations

Vertical angles are the opposite angles formed by two intersecting lines. Vertical angles are congruent because the angles have the same measure.

Adjacent angles are pairs of angles that share a vertex and one side but do not overlap.

Complementary angles are two angles whose measures have a sum of 90°.

Supplementary angles are two angles whose measures have a sum of 180°. You discovered in the Explore Activity that adjacent angles formed by two intersecting lines are supplementary.

EXAMPLE 1

  FL 7.G.2.5

Use the diagram.

A **Name a pair of vertical angles.**

Vertical angles are opposite angles formed by intersecting lines.

∠AFB and ∠DFE are vertical angles.

B **Name a pair of adjacent angles.**

Adjacent angles share a vertex and a side but do not overlap.

∠AFB and ∠BFD are adjacent angles.

C **Name a pair of supplementary angles.**

Adjacent angles formed by intersecting lines are supplementary.

∠AFB and ∠BFD are supplementary angles.

D **Name two pairs of supplementary angles that include ∠DFE.**

Any angle that forms a line with ∠DFE is a supplementary angle to ∠DFE.

∠DFE and ∠EFA are supplementary angles, as are ∠DFE and ∠DFB.

D **Find the measure of ∠AFB.**

Use the fact that ∠AFB and ∠BFD in the diagram are supplementary angles to find m∠AFB.

m∠AFB + m∠BFD = 180°   They are supplementary angles.

$$x + 140° = 180°$$ m∠BFD = 50° + 90° = 140°

$$\underline{-140°\quad -140°}$$ Subtract 140 from both sides.

$$x = 40°$$

The measure of ∠AFB is 40°.

Reflect

3. **Analyze Relationships** What is the relationship between ∠AFB and ∠BFC? Explain.

_____

_____

4. **Draw Conclusions** Are ∠AFC and ∠BFC adjacent angles? Why or why not?

_____

_____

YOUR TURN

Use the diagram.

5. Name a pair of supplementary angles.

_____

6. Name a pair of vertical angles.

_____

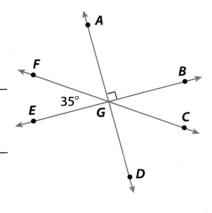

7. Name a pair of adjacent angles.

_____

8. Name a pair of complementary angles.

_____

9. Find the measure of ∠CGD. _____

Personal
Math Trainer

Online Assessment
and Intervention

my.hrw.com

Angle Pairs and Two-Step Equations

Sometimes solving an equation is only the first step in using an angle relationship to solve a problem.

My Notes

EXAMPLE 2

 FL 7.G.2.5

A Find the measure of ∠EHF.

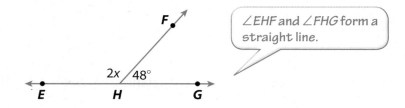

∠EHF and ∠FHG form a straight line.

STEP 1 Identify the relationship between ∠EHF and ∠FHG.

Since angles ∠EHF and ∠FHG form a straight line, the sum of the measures of the angles is 180°.

∠EHF and ∠FHG are supplementary angles.

STEP 2 Write and solve an equation to find x.

$\text{m}\angle EHF + \text{m}\angle FHG = 180°$ *The sum of the measures of supplementary angles is 180°.*

$2x + 48° = 180°$

$\underline{\;-48°\quad -48°}$ *Subtract 48 from both sides.*

$2x = 132°$ *Divide both sides by 2.*

$x = 66°$

STEP 3 Find the measure of ∠EHF.

$\text{m}\angle EHF = 2x$

$= 2(66°)$ *Substitute 66° for x.*

$= 132°$ *Multiply.*

The measure of ∠EHF is 132°.

Check Confirm that ∠EHF and ∠FHG are supplementary.

$\text{m}\angle EHF + \text{m}\angle FHG \overset{?}{=} 180°$

$132° + 48° \overset{?}{=} 180°$

$180° = 180°$

Circumference, Area, and Volume

ESSENTIAL QUESTION

How can you apply geometry concepts to solve real-world problems?

Real-World Video

A 16-inch pizza has a diameter of 16 inches. You can use the diameter to find circumference and area of the pizza. You can also determine how much pizza in one slice of different sizes of pizzas.

my.hrw.com

GO DIGITAL
my.hrw.com

my.hrw.com

Go digital with your write-in student edition, accessible on any device.

Math On the Spot

Scan with your smart phone to jump directly to the online edition, video tutor, and more.

Animated Math

Interactively explore key concepts to see how math works.

Personal Math Trainer

Get immediate feedback and help as you work through practice sets.

Are YOU Ready?

Complete these exercises to review skills you will need for this module.

Multiply with Fractions and Decimals

EXAMPLE		
	7.3	Multiply as you would with whole numbers.
	× 2.4	Count the total number of decimal places in the two factors.
	2 9 2	
	+ 1 4 6	Place the decimal point in the product so that there are the
	1 7.5 2	same number of digits after the decimal point.

Multiply.

1. 4.16
      × 13

2. 6.47
      × 0.4

3. 7.05
      × 9.4

4. 25.6
      × 0.49

Area of Squares, Rectangles, and Triangles

EXAMPLE

2.8 cm

7.8 cm

$A = \frac{1}{2}bh$ Use the formula for area of a triangle.

$= \frac{1}{2}(7.8)(2.8)$ Substitute for each variable.

$= 10.92 \text{ cm}^2$ Multiply.

Find the area of each figure.

5. triangle with base 14 in. and height 10 in. _____

6. square with sides of 3.5 ft _____

7. rectangle with length $8\frac{1}{2}$ in. and width 6 in. _____

8. triangle with base 12.5 m and height 2.4 m _____

Reading Start-Up

Visualize Vocabulary

Use the ✔ words to complete the graphic. You will put one word in each oval. Then write examples of formulas in each rectangle.

Measuring Geometric Figures

Distance around a two-dimensional figure

Square units covered by a two-dimensional figure

Capacity of a three-dimensional figure

Distance around a _____ is
$P = 2l + 2w$.

Square units covered by a _____ is
$A = \frac{1}{2} bh$.

Space taken up by a rectangular prism is
$V = lwh$.

Vocabulary

Review Words
✔ area (*área*)
parallelogram (*paralelogramo*)
✔ perimeter (*perímetro*)
prism (*prisma*)
rectangle (*rectángulo*)
square (*cuadrado*)
trapezoid (*trapecio*)
triangle (*triángulo*)
✔ volume (*volumen*)

Preview Words
circumference (*circunferencia*)
composite figure (*figura compuesta*)
diameter (*diámetro*)
radius (*radio*)

Understand Vocabulary

Match the term on the left to the correct expression on the right.

1. ____ circumference
2. ____ diameter
3. ____ radius

A. A line segment that passes through the center of a circle and has endpoints on the circle, or the length of that segment.

B. A line segment with one endpoint at the center of the circle and the other on the circle, or the length of that segment.

C. The distance around a circle.

Active Reading

Four-Corner Fold Before beginning the module, create a four-corner fold to help you organize what you learn. As you study this module, note important ideas, such as vocabulary, properties, and formulas, on the flaps. Use one flap each for circumference, area, surface area, and volume. You can use your FoldNote later to study for tests and complete assignments.

Unpacking the Standards

Understanding the standards and the vocabulary terms in the standards will help you know exactly what you are expected to learn in this module.

 FL 7.G.2.4

Know the formulas for the area and circumference of a circle and use them to solve problems; give an informal derivation of the relationship between the circumference and area of a circle.

Key Vocabulary

circumference *(circunferencia)*
The distance around a circle.

What It Means to You

You will use formulas to solve problems involving the area and circumference of circles.

UNPACKING EXAMPLE 7.G.2.4

Lily is drawing plans for a circular fountain. The diameter of the fountain is 20 feet. What is the approximate circumference?

$$C = \pi d$$
$$C \approx 3.14 \cdot 20 \quad \text{Substitute.}$$
$$C \approx 62.8$$

The circumference of the fountain is about 62.8 feet.

 FL 7.G.2.6

Solve real-world and mathematical problems involving area, volume and surface area of two- and three-dimensional objects composed of triangles, quadrilaterals, polygons, cubes, and right prisms.

Key Vocabulary

volume *(volumen)*
The number of cubic units inside a three-dimensional solid.

surface area *(área total)*
The sum of the areas of all the surfaces of a three-dimensional solid.

What It Means to You

You will find area, volume and surface area of real-world objects.

UNPACKING EXAMPLE 7.G.2.6

Find the volume and the surface area of a tissue box before the hole is cut in the top.

The tissue box is a right rectangular prism. The base is $4\frac{3}{8}$ in. by $4\frac{3}{8}$ in. and the height is 5 in.

Use the volume and surface area formulas:

B is the area of the base, h is the height of the box, and P is the perimeter of the base.

$$V = Bh \qquad\qquad\qquad S = 2B + Ph$$
$$= \left(4\tfrac{3}{8} \cdot 4\tfrac{3}{8}\right)5 \qquad\qquad = 2\left(4\tfrac{3}{8} \cdot 4\tfrac{3}{8}\right) + \left(4 \cdot 4\tfrac{3}{8}\right)5$$
$$= 95\tfrac{45}{64}\ \text{in}^3 \qquad\qquad = 125\tfrac{25}{32}\ \text{in}^2$$

The volume is $95\frac{45}{64}$ in³ and the surface area is $125\frac{25}{32}$ in².

Visit **my.hrw.com** to see all **Florida Math Standards** unpacked.

my.hrw.com

LESSON
4.1 Circumference

FL 7.G.2.4
Know the formulas for the
area and circumference of a
circle and use them to solve
problems . . .

ESSENTIAL QUESTION

How do you find and use the circumference of a circle?

EXPLORE ACTIVITY FL 7.G.2.4

Exploring Circumference

A circle is a set of points in a plane that are a fixed distance from
the center.

A **radius** is a line segment with one endpoint at the center of the
circle and the other endpoint on the circle. The length of a radius
is called the radius of the circle.

A **diameter** of a circle is a line segment that passes
through the center of the circle and whose endpoints lie on the
circle. The length of the diameter is twice the length of the radius.
The length of a diameter is called the diameter of the circle.

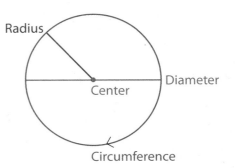

The **circumference** of a circle is the distance around the circle.

A Use a measuring tape to find the circumference of five circular
objects. Then measure the distance across each item to find its
diameter. Record the measurements of each object in the table
below.

Object	Circumference C	Diameter d	$\frac{C}{d}$

B Divide the circumference of each object by its diameter. Record
your answer, rounded to the nearest hundredth, in the table above.

Reflect

1. **Make a Conjecture** Describe what you notice about the ratio $\frac{C}{d}$ in
your table.

_____

Finding Circumference

The ratio of the circumference to the diameter $\frac{C}{d}$ is the same for all circles. This ratio is called π or *pi*, and you can approximate it as 3.14 or as $\frac{22}{7}$. You can use π to find a formula for circumference.

For any circle, $\frac{C}{d} = \pi$. Solve the equation for C to give an equation for the circumference of a circle in terms of the diameter.

$\frac{C}{d} = \pi$ *The ratio of the circumference to the diameter is π.*

$\frac{C}{d} \times d = \pi \times d$ *Multiply both sides by d.*

$C = \pi d$ *Simplify.*

The diameter of a circle is twice the radius. You can use the equation $C = \pi d$ to find a formula for the circumference C in terms of the radius r.

$C = \pi d = \pi(2r) = 2\pi r$

The two equivalent formulas for circumference are $C = \pi d$ and $C = 2\pi r$.

EXAMPLE 1

 FL   7.G.2.4

An irrigation sprinkler waters a circular region with a radius of 14 feet. Find the circumference of the region watered by the sprinkler. Use $\frac{22}{7}$ for π.

Use the formula.

$C = 2\pi r$ | The radius is 14 feet. |

$C = 2\pi(14)$ *Substitute 14 for r.*

$C \approx 2\left(\frac{22}{7}\right)(14)$ *Substitute $\frac{22}{7}$ for π.*

$C \approx 88$ *Multiply.*

14 ft

The circumference of the region watered by the sprinkler is about 88 feet.

Reflect

2. **Analyze Relationships** When is it logical to use $\frac{22}{7}$ instead of 3.14 for π?

_____

YOUR TURN

3. Find the circumference of the circle to the nearest hundredth.

11 cm

_____

Using Circumference

Given the circumference of a circle, you can use the appropriate circumference formula to find the radius or the diameter of the circle. You can use that information to solve problems.

EXAMPLE 2   **FL** 7.G.2.4

A circular pond has a circumference of 628 feet. A model boat is moving directly across the pond, along a radius, at a rate of 5 feet per second. How long does it take the boat to get from the edge of the pond to the center?

My Notes

STEP 1 Find the radius of the pond.

$C = 2\pi r$ Use the circumference formula.

$628 \approx 2(3.14)r$ Substitute for the circumference and for π.

$\dfrac{628}{6.28} \approx \dfrac{6.28r}{6.28}$ Divide both sides by 6.28.

$100 \approx r$ Simplify.

C = 628 ft
r = ? ft

The radius is about 100 feet.

STEP 2 Find the time it takes the boat to get from the edge of the pond to the center along the radius. Divide the radius of the pond by the speed of the model boat.

$$100 \div 5 = 20$$

It takes the boat about 20 seconds to get to the center of the pond.

Reflect

4. **Analyze Relationships** Dante checks the answer to Step 1 by multiplying it by 6 and comparing it with the given circumference. Explain why Dante's estimation method works. Use it to check Step 1.

_____

Math Talk
Mathematical Practices
Would it be reasonable to solve Example 2 using $\frac{22}{7}$ for π? Explain.

5. **What If?** Suppose the model boat were traveling at a rate of 4 feet per second. How long would it take the model boat to get from the edge of the pond to the center? _____

YOUR TURN

6. A circular garden has a circumference of 44 yards. Lars is digging a straight line along a diameter of the garden at a rate of 7 yards per hour. How many hours will it take him to dig across the garden?

_____

Personal Math Trainer
Online Assessment and Intervention
⏻ my.hrw.com

Guided Practice

Find the circumference of each circle. (Example 1)

1. $C = \pi d$

$C \approx$ _____

$C \approx$ _____ inches

9 in.

2. $C = 2\pi r$

$C \approx 2\left(\frac{22}{7}\right)$ (_____)

$C \approx$ _____ cm

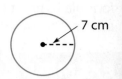
7 cm

Find the circumference of each circle. Use 3.14 or $\frac{22}{7}$ for π. Round to the nearest hundredth, if necessary. (Example 1)

3.

25 m

_____

4.

4.8 yd

_____

5.

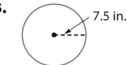
7.5 in.

_____

6. A round swimming pool has a circumference of 66 feet. Carlos wants to buy a rope to put across the diameter of the pool. The rope costs $0.45 per foot, and Carlos needs 4 feet more than the diameter of the pool. How much will Carlos pay for the rope? (Example 2)

Find the diameter.

$C = \pi d$

_____ $\approx 3.14d$

$\dfrac{\boxed{}}{3.14} \approx \dfrac{3.14d}{3.14}$

_____ $\approx d$

Find the cost.

Carlos needs _____ feet of rope.

_____ $\times$ \$0.45 $=$ _____

Carlos will pay _____ for the rope.

Find each missing measurement to the nearest hundredth. Use 3.14 for π. (Examples 1 and 2)

7. $r =$ _____

$d =$ _____

$C = \pi$ yd

8. $r \approx$ _____

$d \approx$ _____

$C = 78.8$ ft

9. $r \approx$ _____

$d \approx 3.4$ in.

$C =$ _____

? ESSENTIAL QUESTION CHECK-IN

10. Norah knows that the diameter of a circle is 13 meters. How would you tell her to find the circumference?

_____

_____

4.1 Independent Practice

 FL 7.G.2.4

Personal Math Trainer
Online Assessment and Intervention
my.hrw.com

For 11–13, find the circumference of each circle. Use 3.14 or $\frac{22}{7}$ for π. Round to the nearest hundredth, if necessary.

11.

5.9 ft

_____

12.

56 cm

_____

13.

35 in.

_____

14. In Exercises 11–13, for which problems did you use $\frac{22}{7}$ for π? Explain your choice.

_____

_____

_____

15. A circular fountain has a radius of 9.4 feet. Find its diameter and circumference to the nearest tenth.

_____

16. Find the radius and circumference of a CD with a diameter of 4.75 inches.

_____

17. A dartboard has a diameter of 18 inches. What are its radius and circumference?

_____

18. **Multistep** Randy's circular garden has a radius of 1.5 feet. He wants to enclose the garden with edging that costs $0.75 per foot. About how much will the edging cost? Explain.

_____

_____

19. **Represent Real-World Problems** The Ferris wheel shown makes 12 revolutions per ride. How far would someone travel during one ride?

diameter 63 feet

_____

20. The diameter of a bicycle wheel is 2 feet. About how many revolutions does the wheel make to travel 2 kilometers? Explain. Hint: 1 km ≈ 3,280 ft

_____

_____

21. **Multistep** A map of a public park shows a circular pond. There is a bridge along a diameter of the pond that is 0.25 mi long. You walk across the bridge, while your friend walks halfway around the pond to meet you at the other side of the bridge. How much farther does your friend walk?

_____

22. Architecture The Capitol Rotunda connects the House and the Senate sides of the U.S. Capitol. Complete the table. Round your answers to the nearest foot.

Capitol Rotunda Dimensions	
Height	180 ft
Circumference	301.5 ft
Radius	
Diameter	

 FOCUS ON HIGHER ORDER THINKING

Work Area

23. Multistep A museum groundskeeper is creating a semicircular statuary garden with a diameter of 30 feet. There will be a fence around the garden. The fencing costs $9.25 per linear foot. About how much will the fencing cost altogether?

_____

24. Critical Thinking Sam is placing rope lights around the edge of a circular patio with a diameter of 18 feet. The lights come in lengths of 54 inches. How many strands of lights does he need to surround the patio edge?

_____

25. Represent Real-World Problems A circular path 2 feet wide has an inner diameter of 150 feet. How much farther is it around the outer edge of the path than around the inner edge?

_____

26. Critique Reasoning A gear on a bicycle has the shape of a circle. One gear has a diameter of 4 inches, and a smaller one has a diameter of 2 inches. Justin says that the circumference of the larger gear is 2 inches more than the circumference of the smaller gear. Do you agree? Explain your answer.

_____

_____

_____

_____

27. Persevere in Problem Solving Consider two circular swimming pools. Pool A has a radius of 12 feet, and Pool B has a diameter of 7.5 meters. Which pool has a greater circumference? How much greater? Justify your answers.

_____

_____

_____

_____

LESSON
4.2 Area of Circles

FL 7.G.2.4

Know the formulas for the area and circumference of a circle and use them to solve problems; give an informal derivation of the relationship between the circumference and area of a circle.

ESSENTIAL QUESTION

How do you find the area of a circle?

EXPLORE ACTIVITY 1   FL 7.G.2.4

Exploring Area of Circles

You can use what you know about circles and π to help find the formula for the area of a circle.

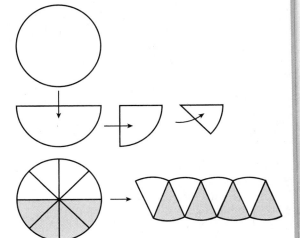

STEP 1 Use a compass to draw a circle and cut it out.

STEP 2 Fold the circle three times as shown to get equal wedges.

STEP 3 Unfold and shade one-half of the circle.

STEP 4 Cut out the wedges, and fit the pieces together to form a figure that looks like a parallelogram.

The base and height of the parallelogram relate to the parts of the circle.

Radius

Half the circumference

base $b = \dfrac{\Box}{\Box}$ the circumference of the circle, or _____

height $h =$ the _____ of the circle, or _____

To find the area of a parallelogram, the equation is $A =$ _____.

To find the area of the circle, substitute for b and h in the area formula.

$A = bh$

$A = \boxed{}\, h$ Substitute for b.

$A = \pi r \boxed{}$ Substitute for h.

$A = \pi \boxed{}$ Write using an exponent.

Reflect

1. How can you make the wedges look more like a parallelogram?

_____

_____

_____

Finding the Area of a Circle

Area of a Circle

The area of a circle is equal to π times the radius squared.

$$A = \pi r^2$$

Remember that area is given in square units.

EXAMPLE 1   **FL** 7.G.2.4

A biscuit recipe calls for the dough to be rolled out and circles to be cut from the dough. The biscuit cutter has a radius of 4 cm. Find the area of the top of the biscuit once it is cut. Use 3.14 for π.

$A = \pi r^2$	Use the formula.
$A = \pi(4)^2$	Substitute. Use 4 for r.
$A \approx 3.14 \times 4^2$	Substitute. Use 3.14 for π.
$A \approx 3.14 \times 16$	Evaluate the power.
$A \approx 50.24$	Multiply.

If the radius increases by 1 centimeter, how does the area of the top of the biscuit change?

The area of the biscuit is about 50.24 cm².

Reflect

2. Compare finding the area of a circle when given the radius with finding the area when given the diameter.

_____

_____

_____

3. Why do you evaluate the power in the equation before multiplying by π?

_____

_____

Personal Math Trainer

Online Assessment and Intervention

my.hrw.com

YOUR TURN

4. A circular pool has a radius of 10 feet. What is the area of the *surface* of the water in the pool? Use 3.14 for π. _____

Finding the Relationship between Circumference and Area

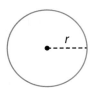

You can use what you know about circumference and area of circles to find a relationship between them.

Find the relationship between the circumference and area of a circle.

Start with a circle that has radius r.

Solve the equation $C = 2\pi r$ for r.

$$r = \frac{\boxed{}}{\boxed{}}$$

Substitute your expression for r in the formula for area of a circle.

$$A = \pi \left(\frac{\boxed{}}{\boxed{}} \right)^2$$

> Remember: Because the exponent is outside the parentheses, you must apply it to the numerator and to each factor of the denominator.

Square the term in the parentheses.

$$A = \pi \left(\frac{\boxed{}^2}{\boxed{}^2 \cdot \boxed{}^2} \right)$$

Evaluate the power.

$$A = \frac{\boxed{} \cdot \boxed{}^2}{\boxed{} \cdot \boxed{}^2}$$

Simplify.

$$A = \frac{\boxed{}^2}{\boxed{} \cdot \boxed{}}$$

Solve for C^2.

$$C^2 = 4 \boxed{} \boxed{}$$

The circumference of the circle squared is equal to

_____.

Reflect

5. Does this formula work for a circle with a radius of 3 inches? Show your work.

Guided Practice

Find the area of each circle. Round to the nearest tenth if necessary. Use 3.14 for π.
(Explore Activity 1)

1.

14 m _____

2.

12 mm _____

3.

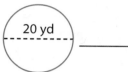

20 yd _____

Solve. Use 3.14 for π. (Example 1)

4. A clock face has a radius of 8 inches. What is the area of the clock face? Round your answer to the nearest hundredth.

_____

5. A DVD has a diameter of 12 centimeters. What is the area of the DVD? Round your answer to the nearest hundredth.

_____

6. A company makes steel lids that have a diameter of 13 inches. What is the area of each lid? Round your answer to the nearest hundredth.

_____

Find the area of each circle. Give your answers in terms of π.
(Explore Activity 2)

7. $C = 4\pi$

$A =$ _____

8. $C = 12\pi$

$A =$ _____

9. $C = \frac{\pi}{2}$

$A =$ _____

10. A circular pen has an area of 64π square yards. What is the circumference of the pen? Give your answer in terms of π.
    (Explore Activity 2)

    _____

 ESSENTIAL QUESTION CHECK-IN

11. What is the formula for the area *A* of a circle in terms of the radius *r*? _____

4.2 Independent Practice

 FL 7.G.2.4

 Personal Math Trainer

Online Assessment and Intervention

⏻ my.hrw.com

12. The most popular pizza at Pavone's Pizza is the 10-inch personal pizza with one topping. What is the area of a pizza with a diameter of 10 inches? Round your answer to the nearest hundredth.

_____

13. A hubcap has a radius of 16 centimeters. What is the area of the hubcap? Round your answer to the nearest hundredth.

16 cm

_____

14. A stained glass window is shaped like a semicircle. The bottom edge of the window is 36 inches long. What is the area of the stained glass window? Round your answer to the nearest hundredth.

_____

15. Analyze Relationships The point (3, 0) lies on a circle with the center at the origin. What is the area of the circle to the nearest hundredth?

_____

16. Multistep A radio station broadcasts a signal over an area with a radius of 50 miles. The station can relay the signal and broadcast over an area with a radius of 75 miles. How much greater is the area of the broadcast region when the signal is relayed? Round your answer to the nearest square mile.

_____

17. Multistep The sides of a square field are 12 meters. A sprinkler in the center of the field sprays a circular area with a diameter that corresponds to a side of the field. How much of the field is **not** reached by the sprinkler? Round your answer to the nearest hundredth.

_____

18. Justify Reasoning A small silver dollar pancake served at a restaurant has a circumference of 2π inches. A regular pancake has a circumference of 4π inches. Is the area of the regular pancake twice the area of the silver dollar pancake? Explain.

_____

_____

_____

_____

_____

_____

19. Analyze Relationships A bakery offers a small circular cake with a diameter of 8 inches. It also offers a large circular cake with a diameter of 24 inches. Does the top of the large cake have three times the area of that of the small cake? If not, how much greater is its area? Explain.

_____

_____

_____

_____

_____

20. Communicate Mathematical Ideas You can use the formula $A = \frac{C^2}{4\pi}$ to find the area of a circle given the circumference. Describe another way to find the area of a circle when given the circumference.

_____

_____

_____

21. Draw Conclusions Mark wants to order a pizza. Which is the better deal? Explain.

Donnie's Pizza Palace		
Diameter (in.)	12	18
Cost ($)	10	20

_____

_____

_____

22. Multistep A bear was seen near a campground. Searchers were dispatched to the region to find the bear.

a. Assume the bear can walk in any direction at a rate of 2 miles per hour. Suppose the bear was last seen 4 hours ago. How large an area must the searchers cover? Use 3.14 for π. Round your answer to the

nearest square mile. _____

b. What If? How much additional area would the searchers have to

cover if the bear were last seen 5 hours ago? _____

H.O.T. **FOCUS ON HIGHER ORDER THINKING**

Work Area

23. Analyze Relationships Two circles have the same radius. Is the combined area of the two circles the same as the area of a circle with twice the radius? Explain.

_____

_____

24. Look for a Pattern How does the area of a circle change if the radius is multiplied by a factor of n, where n is a whole number?

_____

25. Represent Real World Problems The bull's-eye on a target has a diameter of 3 inches. The whole target has a diameter of 15 inches. What part of the whole target is the bull's-eye? Explain.

_____

LESSON 4.3 Area of Composite Figures

 FL 7.G.2.6

Solve real-world and mathematical problems involving area, . . . of . . . objects composed of triangles, quadrilaterals, polygons, ...

ESSENTIAL QUESTION

How do you find the area of composite figures?

EXPLORE ACTIVITY   FL 7.G.2.6

Exploring Areas of Composite Figures

Aaron was plotting the shape of his garden on grid paper. While it was an irregular shape, it was perfect for his yard. Each square on the grid represents 1 square meter.

A Describe one way you can find the area of this garden.

_____

_____

_____

B The area of the garden is _____ square meters.

C Compare your results with other students. What other methods were used to find the area?

_____

_____

_____

D How does the area you found compare with the area found using different methods?

_____

Reflect

1. Use dotted lines to show two different ways Aaron's garden could be divided up into simple geometric figures.

Finding the Area of a Composite Figure

A composite figure is made up of simple geometric shapes. To find the area of a composite figure or other irregular-shaped figure, divide it into simple, nonoverlapping figures. Find the area of each simpler figure, and then add the areas together to find the total area of the composite figure.

Use the chart below to review some common area formulas.

Shape	Area Formula
triangle	$A = \frac{1}{2}bh$
square	$A = s^2$
rectangle	$A = \ell w$
parallelogram	$A = bh$
trapezoid	$A = \frac{1}{2}h(b_1 + b_2)$

Animated Math
my.hrw.com

EXAMPLE 1 FL 7.G.2.6

Find the area of the figure.

STEP 1 Separate the figure into smaller, familiar figures: a parallelogram and a trapezoid.

10 cm · 3 cm · 1.5 cm · 4 cm · 1.5 cm · 2 cm · 7 cm

STEP 2 Find the area of each shape.

Area of the Parallelogram

base = 10 cm

height = 1.5 cm

Use the formula.

$A = bh$

$A = 10 \cdot 1.5$

$A = 15$

The area of the parallelogram is 15 cm².

Area of the Trapezoid

base₁ = 7 cm   base₂ = 10 cm

height 1.5 cm

Use the formula.

$A = \frac{1}{2}h(b_1 + b_2)$

$A = \frac{1}{2}(1.5)(7 + 10)$

$A = \frac{1}{2}(1.5)(17) = 12.75$

> The top base of the trapezoid is 10 cm since it is the same length as the base of the parallelogram.

The area of the trapezoid is 12.75 cm².

STEP 3 Add the areas to find the total area.

$A = 15 + 12.75 = 27.75$ cm²

The area of the figure is 27.75 cm².

Find the area of each figure. Use 3.14 for π.

2.

3.

_____   _____

Using Area to Solve Problems

EXAMPLE 2   Real World   FL 7.G.2.6

A banquet room is being carpeted. A floor plan of the room is shown at right. Each unit represents 1 yard. The carpet costs $23.50 per square yard. How much will it cost to carpet the room?

STEP 1 Separate the composite figure into simpler shapes as shown by the dashed lines: a parallelogram, a rectangle, and a triangle.

STEP 2 Find the area of the simpler figures. Count units to find the dimensions.

Parallelogram	Rectangle	Triangle
$A = bh$	$A = \ell w$	$A = \frac{1}{2}bh$
$A = 4 \cdot 2$	$A = 6 \cdot 4$	$A = \frac{1}{2}(1)(2)$
$A = 8 \text{ yd}^2$	$A = 24 \text{ yd}^2$	$A = 1 \text{ yd}^2$

Math Talk
Mathematical Practices

Describe how you can estimate the cost to carpet the room.

STEP 3 Find the area of the composite figure.

$A = 8 + 24 + 1 = 33$ square yards

STEP 4 Calculate the cost to carpet the room.

Area · Cost per yard = Total cost

33 · $23.50 = $775.50

The cost to carpet the banquet room is $775.50.

YOUR TURN

4. A window is being replaced with tinted glass. The plan at the right shows the design of the window. Each unit length represents 1 foot. The glass costs $28 per square foot. How much will it cost to replace the glass? Use 3.14 for π.

_____

Guided Practice

1. A tile installer plots an irregular shape on grid paper. Each square on the grid represents 1 square centimeter. What is the area of the irregular shape? (Explore Activity, Example 2)

   STEP 1   Separate the figure into a triangle, a _____, and a parallelogram.

   STEP 2   Find the area of each figure.

   triangle: _____ cm²; rectangle: _____ cm²; parallelogram: _____ cm²

   STEP 3   Find the area of the composite figure: ____ + ____ + ____ = ____ cm²

   The area of the irregular shape is _____ cm².

2. Show two different ways to divide the composite figure. Find the area both ways. Show your work below. (Example 1)

3. Sal is tiling his entryway. The floor plan is drawn on a unit grid. Each unit length represents 1 foot. Tile costs $2.25 per square foot. How much will Sal pay to tile his entryway? (Example 2)

_____

? ESSENTIAL QUESTION CHECK-IN

4. What is the first step in finding the area of a composite figure?

_____

4.3 Independent Practice

FL 7.G.2.6

5. A banner is made of a square and a semicircle. The square has side lengths of 26 inches. One side of the square is also the diameter of the semicircle. What is the total area of the banner? Use 3.14 for π.

_____

6. Multistep Erin wants to carpet the floor of her closet. A floor plan of the closet is shown.

10 ft

4 ft

3 ft

6 ft

a. How much carpet does Erin need?

_____

b. The carpet Erin has chosen costs $2.50 per square foot. How much will it cost her to carpet the floor?

_____

7. Multiple Representations Hexagon *ABCDEF* has vertices $A(-2, 4)$, $B(0, 4)$, $C(2, 1)$, $D(5, 1)$, $E(5, -2)$, and $F(-2, -2)$. Sketch the figure on a coordinate plane. What is the area of the hexagon?

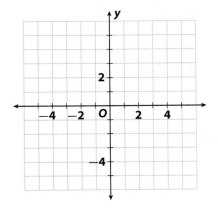

8. A field is shaped like the figure shown. What is the area of the field? Use 3.14 for π.

8 m

8 m

8 m

_____

9. A bookmark is shaped like a rectangle with a semicircle attached at both ends. The rectangle is 12 cm long and 4 cm wide. The diameter of each semicircle is the width of the rectangle. What is the area of the bookmark? Use 3.14 for π.

_____

10. Multistep Alex is making 12 pennants for the school fair. The pattern he is using to make the pennants is shown in the figure. The fabric for the pennants costs $1.25 per square foot. How much will it cost Alex to make 12 pennants?

1 ft

3 ft

1 ft

_____

11. Reasoning A composite figure is formed by combining a square and a triangle. Its total area is 32.5 ft². The area of the triangle is 7.5 ft². What is the length of each side of the square? Explain.

_____

_____

_____

_____

Work Area

12. Represent Real-World Problems Christina plotted the shape of her garden on graph paper. She estimates that she will get about 15 carrots from each square unit. She plans to use the entire garden for carrots. About how many carrots can she expect to grow? Explain.

_____

_____

_____

13. Analyze Relationships The figure shown is made up of a triangle and a square. The perimeter of the figure is 56 inches. What is the area of the figure? Explain.

_____

_____

_____

_____

14. Critical Thinking The pattern for a scarf is shown at right. What is the area of the scarf? Use 3.14 for π.

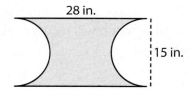

_____

15. Persevere in Problem Solving The design for the palladium window shown includes a semicircular shape at the top. The bottom is formed by squares of equal size. A shade for the window will extend 4 inches beyond the perimeter of the window, shown by the dashed line around the window. Each square in the window has an area of 100 in².

a. What is the area of the window? Use 3.14 for π.

_____

b. What is the area of the shade? Round your answer to the nearest whole number.

_____

Solving Surface Area Problems

FL 7.G.2.6
Solve real-world and mathematical problems involving ... surface area of ... three-dimensional objects composed of ... cubes and right prisms.

ESSENTIAL QUESTION How can you find the surface area of a figure made up of cubes and prisms?

EXPLORE ACTIVITY FL 7.G.2.6

Modeling Surface Area of a Prism

The surface area of a three-dimensional figure is the sum of the areas of all its surfaces. You know how to use the net of a figure to find its surface area. Now you will discover a formula that you can use.

A The lateral area L of a prism is the area of all faces except the bases.

$L = 2(\underline{\hspace{3cm}}) + 2(\underline{\hspace{3cm}}) = \underline{\hspace{2.5cm}}$.

B The area B of each base is \underline{\hspace{3cm}}.

C The surface area S of the prism is the sum of the lateral area L and the

total area of the bases, or \underline{\hspace{3cm}}.

Reflect

1. **Analyze Relationships** Use the net above to answer this question: How does the product of the perimeter P of the base of the prism and the height h of the prism compare to the lateral area L? \underline{\hspace{3cm}}

2. **Critical Thinking** How can you express the surface area S of the prism in terms of P, h, and B? Use your answer to Question 1. \underline{\hspace{3cm}}

Finding the Surface Area of a Prism

Given a prism's dimensions, you can use a formula to find the surface area.

Surface Area of a Prism

The surface area S of a prism with base perimeter P, height h, and base area B is $S = Ph + 2B$.

My Notes

EXAMPLE 1 Real World

FL 7.G.2.6

Erin is making a jewelry box of wood in the shape of a rectangular prism. The jewelry box will have the dimensions shown. She plans to spray paint the exterior of the box. How many square inches will she have to paint?

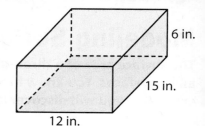

6 in.

15 in.

12 in.

STEP 1 Make a sketch of the box. Drawing a diagram helps you understand and solve the problem.

STEP 2 Identify a base, and find its area and perimeter.

Any pair of opposite faces can be the bases. For example, you can choose the bottom and top of the box as the bases.

$B = \ell \times w$ $P = 2(12) + 2(15)$

$= 12 \times 15$ $= 24 + 30$

$= 180$ square inches $= 54$ inches

STEP 3 Identify the height, and find the surface area.

The height h of the prism is 6 inches. Use the formula to find the surface area.

$S = Ph + 2B$

$S = 54(6) + 2(180) = 684$ square inches

Erin will have to spray paint 684 square inches of wood.

Math Talk
Mathematical Practices

How can you express the formula for the surface area S of a rectangular prism in terms of its dimensions ℓ, w, and h?

YOUR TURN

3. A brand of uncooked spaghetti comes in a box that is a rectangular prism with a length of 9 inches, a width of 2 inches, and a height of $1\frac{1}{2}$ inches.

What is the surface area of the box? _____

Finding the Surface Area of a Composite Solid

A composite solid is made up of two or more solid figures. To find the surface area of a composite solid, find the surface area of each figure. Subtract any area not on the surface.

Math On the Spot

my.hrw.com

EXAMPLE 2 Problem Solving

FL 7.G.2.6

Daniel built the birdhouse shown. What was the surface area of the birdhouse before the hole was drilled?

17 cm
8 cm
18 cm
24 cm
30 cm

Analyze Information

Identify the important information.
- The top is a triangular prism with $h = 24$ cm. The base is a triangle with height 8 cm and base 30 cm.
- The bottom is a rectangular prism with $h = 18$ cm. The base is a 30 cm by 24 cm rectangle.
- One face of each prism is not on the surface of the figure.

Formulate a Plan

Find the surface area of each prism.

Add the areas. Subtract the areas of the parts not on the surface.

Solve

Find the area of the triangular prism.

Perimeter $= 17 + 17 + 30 = 64$ cm; Base area $= \frac{1}{2}(30)(8) = 120$ cm^2

Surface area $= Ph + 2B$

$= 64(24) + 2(120) = 1,776$ cm^2

Find the area of the rectangular prism.

Perimeter $= 2(30) + 2(24) = 108$ cm; Base area $= 30(24) = 720$ cm^2

Surface area $= Ph + 2B$

$= 108(18) + 2(720) = 3,384$ cm^2

Add. Then subtract twice the areas of the parts not on the surface.

Surface area $= 1,776 + 3,384 - 2(720) = 3,720$ cm^2

The surface area before the hole was drilled was 3,720 cm^2.

Justify and Evaluate

You can check your work by using a net to find the surface areas.

Math Talk
Mathematical Practices

How could you find the surface area by letting the front and back of the prism be the bases?

4. Dara is building a plant stand. She wants to stain the plant stand, except for the bottom of the larger prism. Find the surface area of the part of the plant stand she will stain. _____

8 in.

8 in.

8 in.

12 in.

12 in.

12 in.

Guided Practice

Find the surface area of each solid figure. (Examples 1 and 2)

1.

5 ft   5 ft

3 ft   7 ft

8 ft

Perimeter of base = _____

Height = _____

Base area = _____

Surface area:

$S = ($ _____ $)($ _____ $) + 2($ _____ $)$

= _____

2.

2.5 m   2.5 m

2.5 m

7 m   9 m

11 m

Surface area of cube:

$S = $ _____

Surface area of rectangular prism:

$S = $ _____

Overlapping area: $A = $ _____

Surface area of composite figure:

= _____ + _____ − 2(_____) =

_____ m²

? ESSENTIAL QUESTION CHECK-IN

3. How can you find the surface area of a composite solid made up of prisms?

_____

_____

_____

4.4 Independent Practice

FL 7.G.2.6

Personal Math Trainer

Online Assessment and Intervention

my.hrw.com

4. Carla is wrapping a present in the box shown. How much wrapping paper does she need, not including overlap?

4 in.
3 in.
10 in.

_____

5. Dmitri wants to cover the top and sides of the box shown with glass tiles that are 5 mm square. How many tiles does he need?

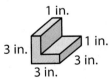

9 cm
20 cm
15 cm

_____

6. Shera is building a cabinet. She is making wooden braces for the corners of the cabinet. Find the surface area of each brace.

1 in.
3 in.
1 in.
3 in.
3 in.

_____

7. The doghouse shown has a floor, but no windows. Find the total surface area of the doghouse, including the door.

2 ft
2.5 ft
2.5 ft
2 ft
4 ft
3 ft

Eddie built the ramp shown to train his puppy to do tricks. Use the figure for 8–9.

12 in.
20 in.
20 in.
24 in.
16 in. 16 in. 16 in.

8. **Analyze Relationships** Describe two ways to find the surface area of the ramp.

_____

_____

_____

_____

9. What is the surface area of the ramp?

_____

Marco and Elaine are building a stand like the one shown to display trophies. Use the figure for 10–11.

1 ft
3 ft
3 ft
3 ft
2 ft
7 ft
1 ft

10. What is the surface area of the stand?

_____

11. **Critique Reasoning** Marco and Elaine want to paint the entire stand silver. A can of paint covers 25 square feet and costs $6.79. They set aside $15 for paint. Is that enough? Explain.

_____

_____

12. Henry wants to cover the box shown with paper without any overlap. How many square centimeters will be covered with paper?

10 cm 24 cm 27 cm

_____

13. **What If?** Suppose the length and width of the box in Exercise 12 double. Does the surface area *S* double? Explain.

_____

 FOCUS ON HIGHER ORDER THINKING

 Work Area

14. **Persevere in Problem Solving** Enya is building a storage cupboard in the shape of a rectangular prism. The rectangular prism has a square base with side lengths of 2.5 feet and a height of 3.5 feet. Compare the amount of paint she would use to paint all but the bottom surface of the prism to the amount she would use to paint the entire prism.

_____

_____

_____

15. **Interpret the Answer** The oatmeal box shown is shaped like a cylinder. Use a net to find the surface area *S* of the oatmeal box to the nearest tenth. Then find the number of square feet of cardboard needed for 1,500 oatmeal boxes. Round your answer to the nearest whole number.

2 in.
Oatmeal 9 in.

_____

_____

16. **Analyze Relationships** A prism is made of centimeter cubes. How can you find the surface area of the prism in Figure 1 without using a net or a formula? How does the surface area change in Figures 2, 3, and 4? Explain.

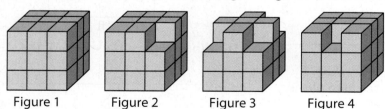

Figure 1   Figure 2   Figure 3   Figure 4

_____

_____

_____

_____

_____

Solving Volume Problems

FL 7.G.2.6

Solve real-world and mathematical problems involving . . . volume of . . . three-dimensional objects composed of . . . cubes, and right prisms.

ESSENTIAL QUESTION How do you find the volume of a figure made of cubes and prisms?

Volume of a Triangular Prism

The formula for the volume of a rectangular prism can be used for *any* prism.

Volume of a Prism

The volume V of a prism is the area of its base B times its height h.
$$V = Bh$$

Math On the Spot
my.hrw.com

EXAMPLE 1 FL 7.G.2.6

Bradley's tent is in the shape of a triangular prism. How many cubic feet of space are in his tent?

4 ft
5 ft
9 ft
6 ft

STEP 1 Find the base area B of the triangular prism.

$B = \frac{1}{2}bh$ Area of a triangle with base length b and height h

$= \frac{1}{2}(6)(4)$ Substitute 6 for b and 4 for h.

$= 12 \text{ ft}^2$

STEP 2 Find the volume of the prism.

$V = Bh$ Volume of a prism with base area B and height h

$= (12)(9)$ Substitute 12 for B and 9 for h.

$= 108 \text{ ft}^3$

The volume of Bradley's tent is 108 ft³.

Reflect

1. **Analyze Relationships** For a prism that is **not** a rectangular prism, how do you determine which sides are the bases?

_____

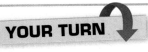 **YOUR TURN**

2. Find the volume of the prism.

_____

7 m
22 m
24 m

Personal Math Trainer

Online Assessment and Intervention

my.hrw.com

Volume of a Trapezoidal Prism

Prisms are named for the polygons that form their bases. In this lesson, you will focus on prisms whose bases are either triangles or quadrilaterals other than squares and rectangles.

EXAMPLE 2   FL 7.G.2.6

Cherise is setting up her tent. Her tent is in the shape of a trapezoidal prism. How many cubic feet of space are in her tent?

STEP 1 Find the base area B of the trapezoidal prism.

$B = \frac{1}{2}(b_1 + b_2)h$ — Area of a trapezoid with bases of lengths b_1 and b_2 and height h

$= \frac{1}{2}(6 + 4)4$ — Substitute 6 for b_1, 4 for b_2, and 4 for h.

$= \frac{1}{2}(10)4 = 20$ ft

STEP 2 Find the volume of the prism.

$V = Bh$ — Volume of a prism with base area B and height h

$= (20)(9)$ — Substitute 20 for B and 9 for h.

$= 180$ ft³

The volume of Cherise's tent is 180 ft³.

Reflect

3. **Look for a Pattern** How could you double the volume of the tent by doubling just one of its dimensions?

_____

_____

4. **What If?** How would doubling *all* the dimensions of the prism affect the volume of the tent?

_____

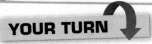

5. Find the volume of the prism.

_____

Volume of a Composite Solid

You can use the formula for the volume of a prism to find the volume of a composite figure that is made up of prisms.

EXAMPLE 3   **FL** 7.G.2.6

Allie has two aquariums connected by a small square prism. Find the volume of the double aquarium.

 STEP 1 Find the volume of each of the larger aquariums.

$V = Bh$ *Volume of a prism*

$= (12)(3)$ *Substitute $3 \times 4 = 12$ for B and 3 for h.*

$= 36 \text{ ft}^3$

STEP 2 Find the volume of the connecting prism.

$V = Bh$ *Volume of a prism*

$= (1)(2)$ *Substitute $1 \times 1 = 1$ for B and 2 for h.*

$= 2 \text{ ft}^3$

STEP 3 Add the volumes of the three parts of the aquarium.

$V = 36 + 36 + 2 = 74 \text{ ft}^3$

The volume of the aquarium is 74 ft³.

My Notes

Reflect

6. **What If?** Find the volume of one of the large aquariums on either end using another pair of opposite sides as the bases. Do you still get the same volume? Explain.

_____

_____

7. The figure is composed of a rectangular prism and a triangular prism. Find the volume of the figure.

_____

1. Find the volume of the triangular prism. (*Example 1*)

$B = \frac{1}{2}bh = \frac{1}{2}(8)(3) = 12$ ft $\square$

$V = Bh = \left(\boxed{} \times \boxed{}\right)$ ft $^{\boxed{}} = \boxed{}$ ft^3

2. Find the volume of the trapezoidal prism. (*Example 2*)

$B = \frac{1}{2}(b_1 + b_2)h = \frac{1}{2}(15 + 5)(3) = 30$ m $\square$

$V = Bh = \left(\boxed{} \times \boxed{}\right)$ m $^{\boxed{}} = \boxed{}$ m^3

3. Find the volume of the composite figure. (*Example 3*)

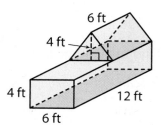

Volume of rectangular prism = _____

Volume of triangular prism = _____

Volume of composite figure = _____

Find the volume of each figure. (*Examples 2 and 3*)

4. The figure shows a barn that Mr. Fowler is building for his farm.

_____

5. The figure shows a container, in the shape of a trapezoidal prism, that Pete filled with sand.

_____

6. How do you find the volume of a composite solid formed by two or more prisms?

_____

_____

4.5 Independent Practice

 FL 7.G.2.6

Personal
Math Trainer

Online
Assessment and
my.hrw.com   Intervention

7. A trap for insects is in the shape of a triangular prism. The area of the base is 3.5 in² and the height of the prism is 5 in. What is the volume of this trap?

_____

8. Arletta built a cardboard ramp for her little brothers' toy cars. Identify the shape of the ramp. Then find its volume.

6 in.

25 in.

7 in

_____

9. Alex made a sketch for a homemade soccer goal he plans to build. The goal will be in the shape of a triangular prism. The legs of the right triangles at the sides of his goal measure 4 ft and 8 ft, and the opening along the front is 24 ft. How much space is contained within this goal?

_____

10. A gift box is in the shape of a trapezoidal prism with base lengths of 7 inches and 5 inches and a height of 4 inches. The height of the gift box is 8 inches. What is the volume of the gift box?

_____

11. **Explain the Error** A student wrote this statement: "A triangular prism has a height of 15 inches and a base area of 20 square inches. The volume of the prism is 300 square inches." Identify and correct the error.

_____

Find the volume of each figure. Round to the nearest hundredth if necessary.

12. B ≈ 23.4 in²

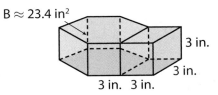

3 in.

3 in.

3 in. 3 in.

13.

7.5 m

7.5 m

3.75 m

3.75 m

15 m

_____   _____

14. **Multi-Step** Josie has 260 cubic centimeters of candle wax. She wants to make a hexagonal prism candle with a base area of 21 square centimeters and a height of 8 centimeters. She also wants to make a triangular prism candle with a height of 14 centimeters. Can the base area of the triangular prism candle be 7 square centimeters? Explain.

_____

15. A movie theater offers popcorn in two different containers for the same price. One container is a trapezoidal prism with a base area of 36 square inches and a height of 5 inches. The other container is a triangular prism with a base area of 32 square inches and a height of 6 inches. Which container is the better deal? Explain.

_____

_____

 FOCUS ON HIGHER ORDER THINKING

Work Area

16. Critical Thinking The wading pool shown is a trapezoidal prism with a total volume of 286 cubic feet. What is the missing dimension?

_____

17. Persevere in Problem Solving Lynette has a metal doorstop with the dimensions shown. Each cubic centimeter of the metal in the doorstop has a mass of about 8.6 grams. Find the volume of the metal in the doorstop. Then find the mass of the doorstop.

_____

_____

18. Analyze Relationships What effect would tripling all the dimensions of a triangular prism have on the volume of the prism? Explain your reasoning.

_____

_____

_____

_____

19. Persevere in Problem Solving Each of two trapezoidal prisms has a volume of 120 cubic centimeters. The prisms have no dimensions in common. Give possible dimensions for each prism.

_____

_____

_____

_____

Ready to Go On?

Personal Math Trainer

Online Assessment and Intervention

my.hrw.com

4.1, 4.2 Circumference and Area of Circles

Find the circumference and area of each circle. Use 3.14 for π. Round to the nearest hundredth if necessary.

1.

7 m

_____

2.

12 ft

_____

4.3 Area of Composite Figures

Find the area of each figure. Use 3.14 for π.

3.

10 m

16 m

_____

4.

4.5 cm

5.5 cm

20 cm

_____

4.4, 4.5 Solving Surface Area and Volume Problems

Find the surface area and volume of each figure.

5.

5 cm

10 cm

3 cm

4 cm

_____

6.

2.5 yd

1.5 yd

2 yd

2.5 yd

4 yd

_____

? ESSENTIAL QUESTION

7. How can you use geometry figures to solve real-world problems?

_____

_____

Assessment Readiness

Selected Response

1. What is the circumference of the circle?

11 m

- Ⓐ 34.54 m
- Ⓑ 69.08 m
- Ⓒ 379.94 m
- Ⓓ 1,519.76 m

2. What is the area of the circle?

15 m

- Ⓐ 23.55 m²
- Ⓒ 176.625 m²
- Ⓑ 47.1 m²
- Ⓓ 706.5 m²

3. What is the area of the figure?

6 m

6 m

- Ⓐ 28.26 m²
- Ⓒ 64.26 m²
- Ⓑ 36 m²
- Ⓓ 92.52 m²

4. A one-year membership to a health club costs $480. This includes a $150 fee for new members that is paid when joining. Which equation represents the monthly cost x in dollars for a new member?

- Ⓐ $12x + 150 = 480$
- Ⓑ $\frac{x}{12} + 150 = 480$
- Ⓒ $12x + 480 = 150$
- Ⓓ $\frac{x}{12} + 480 = 150$

5. What is the volume of the prism?

2 ft

12 ft

8 ft

- Ⓐ 192 ft³
- Ⓑ 48 ft³
- Ⓒ 69 ft³
- Ⓓ 96 ft³

6. The price of mailing a small package is $0.32 for the first ounce and $0.21 for each additional ounce. Sandra paid $1.16 to mail her package. How much did it weigh?

- Ⓐ 4 ounces
- Ⓑ 5 ounces
- Ⓒ 6 ounces
- Ⓓ 7 ounces

Mini-Task

7. Each dimension of the smaller prism is half the corresponding dimension of the larger prism.

8 in.

10 in.

16 in.

a. What is the surface area of the figure?

_____

b. What is the volume of the figure?

_____

Modeling Geometric Figures

Key Vocabulary
adjacent angles *(ángulos adyacentes)*
complementary angles *(ángulos complementarios)*
congruent angles *(ángulos congruentes)*
cross section *(sección transversal)*
intersection *(intersección)*
scale *(escala)*
scale drawing *(dibujo a escala)*
supplementary angles *(ángulos suplementarios)*
vertical angles *(ángulos opuestos por el vértice)*

ESSENTIAL QUESTION

How can you apply geometry concepts to solve real-world problems?

EXAMPLE 1

Use the scale drawing to find the perimeter of Tim's yard.

15 cm

4 cm

2 cm : 14 ft

$\dfrac{2\text{ cm}}{14\text{ ft}} = \dfrac{1\text{ cm}}{7\text{ ft}}$ 1 cm in the drawing equals 7 feet in the actual yard.

$\dfrac{1\text{ cm} \times 15}{7\text{ ft} \times 15} = \dfrac{15\text{ cm}}{105\text{ ft}}$ 15 cm in the drawing equals 105 feet in the actual yard. Tim's yard is 105 feet long.

$\dfrac{1\text{ cm} \times 4}{7\text{ ft} \times 4} = \dfrac{4\text{ cm}}{28\text{ ft}}$ 4 cm in the drawing equals 7 feet in the actual yard. Tim's yard is 28 feet wide.

Perimeter is twice the sum of the length and the width. So the perimeter of Tim's yard is $2(105 + 28) = 2(133)$, or 266 feet.

EXAMPLE 2

Find (a) the value of x and (b) the measure of $\angle APY$.

a. $\angle XPB$ and $\angle YPB$ are supplementary.

$3x + 78° = 180°$

$3x = 102°$

$x = 34°$

b. $\angle APY$ and $\angle XPB$ are vertical angles.

$m\angle APY = m\angle XPB = 3x = 102°$

EXERCISES

1. In the scale drawing of a park, the scale is
   1 cm: 10 m. Find the area of the actual park.

   (Lesson 3.1) _____

3 cm

1.5 cm

1 cm : 10 m

2. Find the value of *y* and the measure of ∠*YPS* (Lesson 3.4)

   y = _____

   m ∠*YPS* = _____

3. Kanye wants to make a triangular flower bed using logs with the
   lengths shown below to form the border. Can Kanye form a triangle
   with the logs without cutting any of them? Explain. (Lesson 3.2)

   3 ft

   4 ft

   8 ft

   _____

   _____

   _____

4. In shop class, Adriana makes a pyramid with a 4-inch square base
   and a height of 6 inches. She then cuts the pyramid vertically in half
   as shown. What is the area of each cut surface? (Lesson 3.3)

   _____

Circumference, Area, and Volume

 ESSENTIAL QUESTION

How can you use geometry concepts to solve real-world problems?

EXAMPLE 1

Find the area of the composite figure. It consists of a semicircle and a rectangle.

10 cm

6 cm

Area of semicircle $= 0.5(\pi r^2)$

$\approx 0.5(3.14)25$

≈ 39.25 cm^2

Area of rectangle $= \ell w$

$= 10(6)$

$= 60$ cm^2

The area of the composite figure is approximately 99.25 square centimeters.

EXAMPLE 2

Find the volume and surface area of the regular hexagonal prism hat box shown. Each side of the hexagonal base is 20 inches.

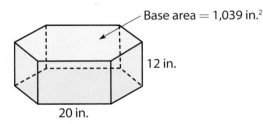

Base area $= 1{,}039$ in.^{2}

12 in.

20 in.

Use the formulas for volume and surface area of a prism.

$V = Bh$

$= 1{,}039(12)$

$= 12{,}468$ in^3

$S = Ph + 2B$

$= 120(12) + 2(1{,}039)$

$= 1{,}440 + 2{,}078$

$= 3{,}518$ in^2

Perimeter $= 6(20) = 120$ in.

EXERCISES

Find the circumference and area of each circle. Round to the nearest hundredth. (Lessons 4.1, 4.2)

1.

22 in.

_____

2.

4.5 m

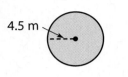

_____

Find the area of each composite figure. Round to the nearest hundredth if necessary. (Lesson 4.3)

3.

9 in.

9 in.

13 in.

Area _____

4.

20 cm

16 cm

Area _____

5. Find the volume of each figure. (Lesson 4.5)

12 in.

5 in.

7 in.

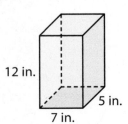

_____

6. The volume of a triangular prism is 264 cubic feet. The area of a base of the prism is 48 square feet. Find the height of the prism.

(Lesson 4.5) _____

A glass paperweight has a composite shape: a square pyramid fitting exactly on top of an 8 centimeter cube. The pyramid has a height of 3 cm. Each triangular face has a height of 5 centimeters. (Lessons 4.4, 4.5)

5 cm
3 cm
8 cm
8 cm
8 cm

7. What is the volume of the paperweight? _____

8. What is the total surface area of the paperweight? _____

Unit 2 Performance Tasks

1. **CAREERS IN MATH** **Product Design Engineer** Miranda is a product design engineer working for a sporting goods company. She designs a tent in the shape of a triangular prism. The approximate dimensions of the tent are shown in the diagram.

$7\frac{1}{4}$ ft

6 ft

$9\frac{1}{2}$ ft

8 ft

a. How many square feet of material does Miranda need to make the tent (including the floor)? Show your work.

_____

_____

b. What is the volume of the tent? Show your work.

_____

c. Suppose Miranda wants to increase the volume of the tent by 10%. The specifications for the height (6 feet) and the width (8 feet) must stay the same. How can Miranda meet this new requirement? Explain.

_____

_____

2. Li is making a stand to display a sculpture made in art class. The stand will be 45 centimeters wide, 25 centimeters long, and 1.2 meters high.

a. What is the volume of the stand? Write your answer in cubic centimeters.

_____

_____

b. Li needs to fill the stand with sand so that it is heavy and stable. Each piece of wood is 1 centimeter thick. The boards are put together as shown in the figure, which is not drawn to scale. How many cubic centimeters of sand does she need to fill the stand? Explain how you found your answer.

_____

_____

_____

_____

_____

_____

3. Lucia is designing her dream house. The plans shown represent the dimensions of the house's exterior. They are drawn to a scale of 1 cm = 5 ft.

a. What is the area of house? Use 3.14 for π.

_____

b. Lucia wants to change the scale of the plans so that they are larger. She is considering using a scale of 2 cm = 12 ft. Will this scale produce a larger set of plans? Justify your answer.

_____

_____

_____

Selected Response

1. A school flag is in the shape of a rectangle with a triangle removed as shown.

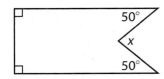

What is the measure of angle x?

Ⓐ 50°   Ⓒ 90°

Ⓑ 80°   Ⓓ 100°

2. On a map with a scale of 2 cm = 1 km, the distance from Beau's house to the beach is 4.6 centimeters. What is the actual distance?

Ⓐ 2.3 km   Ⓒ 6.5 km

Ⓑ 4.6 km   Ⓓ 9.2 km

3. Lalasa and Yasmin are designing a triangular banner to hang in the school gymnasium. They first draw the design on paper. The triangle has a base of 5 inches and a height of 7 inches. If 1 inch on the drawing is equivalent to 1.5 feet on the actual banner, what will the area of the actual banner be?

Ⓐ 17.5 ft²   Ⓒ 39.375 ft²

Ⓑ 52.5 ft²   Ⓓ 78.75 ft²

4. Which has the same solution as $4x + 5 = -11$?

Ⓐ $-5x = 25$

Ⓑ $x + 6 = 2$

Ⓒ $7 - x = -2$

Ⓓ $\frac{x}{3} = 2$

5. A one-topping pizza costs $15.00. Each additional topping costs $1.25. Let x be the number of additional toppings. You have $20 to spend. Which equation can you solve to find the number of additional toppings you can get on your pizza?

Ⓐ $15x + 1.25 = 20$

Ⓑ $1.25x + 15 = 20$

Ⓒ $15x - 1.25 = 20$

Ⓓ $1.25x - 15 = 20$

6. Which inequality can be used to find how many $1.25 snack packs can be purchased for $10.00?

Ⓐ $1.25s \geq 10.00$ Ⓒ $\frac{s}{1.25} \geq 10.00$

Ⓑ $1.25s \leq 10.00$ Ⓓ $\frac{s}{1.25} \leq 10.00$

7. What is the volume of a triangular prism that is 75 centimeters long and that has a base with an area of 30 square centimeters?

Ⓐ 2.5 cubic centimeters

Ⓑ 750 cubic centimeters

Ⓒ 1,125 cubic centimeters

Ⓓ 2,250 cubic centimeters

8. Consider the right circular cone shown.

If a vertical plane slices through the cone to create two identical half cones, what is the shape of the cross section?

Ⓐ a rectangle   Ⓒ a triangle

Ⓑ a square   Ⓓ a circle

9. The radius of the circle is given in meters. What is the circumference of the circle? Use 3.14 for π.

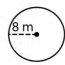

Ⓐ 25.12 meters

Ⓑ 50.24 meters

Ⓒ 200.96 meters

Ⓓ 803.84 meters

10. The dimensions of the figure are given in millimeters. What is the area of the two-dimensional figure?

Ⓐ 39 square millimeters

Ⓑ 169 square millimeters

Ⓒ 208 square millimeters

Ⓓ 247 square millimeters

11. A forest ranger wants to determine the radius of the trunk of a tree. She measures the circumference to be 8.6 feet. What is the trunk's radius to the nearest tenth of a foot?

Ⓐ 1.4 ft   Ⓑ 4.3 ft

Ⓒ 2.7 ft   Ⓓ 17.2 ft

It is helpful to draw or redraw a figure. Answers to geometry problems may become clearer as you redraw the figure.

12. What is the measure in degrees of an angle that is supplementary to a 74° angle?

Ⓐ 16°

Ⓑ 74°

Ⓒ 90°

Ⓓ 106°

13. What is the volume in cubic centimeters of a rectangular prism that has a length of 6.2 centimeters, a width of 3.5 centimeters, and a height of 10 centimeters?

Ⓐ 19.7 cm³

Ⓑ 108.5 cm³

Ⓒ 217.0 cm³

Ⓓ 237.4 cm³

14. A patio is the shape of a circle with diameter shown.

What is the area of the patio? Use 3.14 for π.

Ⓐ 9.00 m²

Ⓑ 28.26 m²

Ⓒ 254.34 m²

Ⓓ 1,017.36 m²

Mini-Task

15. Petra fills a small cardboard box with sand. The dimensions of the box are 3 inches by 4 inches by 2 inches.

a. What is the volume of the box?

_____

b. Petra decides to cover the box by gluing on wrapping paper. How much wrapping paper does she need to cover all six sides of the box?

_____

c. Petra has a second, larger box that is 6 inches by 8 inches by 4 inches. How many times larger is the volume of this second box? The surface area?

_____

_____

Statistics and Sampling

Random Samples and Populations

 FL 7.RP.1.2c, 7.SP.1.1, 7.SP.1.2

MODULE **6**

Analyzing and Comparing Data

 FL 7.SP.2.3, 7.SP.2.4

CAREERS IN MATH

Entomologist An entomologist is a biologist who studies insects. These scientists analyze data and use mathematical models to understand and predict the behavior of insect populations.

If you are interested in a career in entomology, you should study these mathematical subjects:
- Algebra
- Trigonometry
- Probability and Statistics
- Calculus

Research other careers that require the analysis of data and use of mathematical models.

Unit 3 Performance Task

At the end of the unit, check out how **entomologists** use math.

Vocabulary Preview

Use the puzzle to preview key vocabulary from this unit. Unscramble the circled letters to answer the riddle at the bottom of the page.

Across

2. A sample in which every person, object, or event has an equal chance of being selected (2 words). (Lesson 5.1)

4. Part of a population chosen to represent the entire group. (Lesson 5.1)

5. A display in which each piece of data is represented by a dot above a number line (2 words). (Lesson 6.2)

6. An integer generated by chance, such as by rolling a number cube or using a graphing calculator. (Lesson 5.1)

Down

1. The entire group of objects, individuals, or events in a set of data. (Lesson 5.1)

3. A display that shows how the values in a data set are distributed (2 words). (Lesson 6.3)

Q: Where do cowboys who love statistics live?

A: on the ___ ___ ___ ___ ___!

Random Samples and Populations

ESSENTIAL QUESTION

How can you use random samples and populations to solve real-world problems?

Real-World Video

Scientists study animals like dolphins to learn more about characteristics such as behavior, diet, and communication. Acoustical data (recordings of dolphin sounds) can reveal the species that made the sound.

my.hrw.com

GO DIGITAL
my.hrw.com

my.hrw.com

Go digital with your write-in student edition, accessible on any device.

Math On the Spot

Scan with your smart phone to jump directly to the online edition, video tutor, and more.

Animated Math

Interactively explore key concepts to see how math works.

Personal Math Trainer

Get immediate feedback and help as you work through practice sets.

Are YOU Ready?

Complete these exercises to review skills you will need for this module.

Personal Math Trainer

Online Assessment and Intervention

⚫ my.hrw.com

Solve Proportions

EXAMPLE

$$\frac{a}{1} = \frac{30}{1.5}$$

$a \times 1.5 = 1 \times 30$ Write the cross products.

$1.5a = 30$ Simplify.

$\frac{1.5a}{1.5} = \frac{30}{1.5}$ Divide both sides by 1.5.

$a = 20$

Solve for x.

1. $\frac{x}{16} = \frac{45}{40}$ _____
2. $\frac{x}{5} = \frac{1}{4}$ _____
3. $\frac{2.5}{10} = \frac{x}{50}$ _____
4. $\frac{x}{6} = \frac{2}{9}$ _____

Find the Range

EXAMPLE

29, 26, 21, 30, 32, 19   Order the data from least to greatest.
19, 21, 26, 29, 30, 32

range = 32 − 19   The range is the difference between the
= 13   greatest and the least data items.

Find the range of the data.

5. 52, 48, 57, 47, 49, 60, 59, 51 _____
6. 5, 9, 13, 6, 4, 5, 8, 12, 12, 6 _____

7. 97, 106, 99, 97, 115, 95, 108, 100 _____
8. 27, 13, 35, 19, 71, 12, 66, 47, 39 _____

Find the Mean

EXAMPLE

21, 15, 26, 19, 25, 14

mean = $\frac{21 + 15 + 26 + 19 + 25 + 14}{6}$ The mean is the sum of the data items divided by the number of items.

= $\frac{120}{6}$

= 20

Find the mean of each set of data.

9. 3, 5, 7, 3, 6, 4, 8, 6, 9, 5 _____
10. 8.1, 9.4, 11.3, 6.7, 6.2, 7.5 _____

Reading Start-Up

Visualize Vocabulary

Use the ✔ words to complete the right column of the chart.

Box Plots to Display Data	
Definition	**Review Word**
A display that uses values from a data set to show how the values are spread out.	
The middle value of a data set.	
The median of the lower half of the data.	
The median of the upper half of the data.	

Understand Vocabulary

Complete each sentence, using the preview words.

1. An entire group of objects, individuals, or events is a

   _____.

2. A _____ is part of the population chosen to represent the entire group.

3. A sample that does not accurately represent the population is a

   _____.

Vocabulary

Review Words

✔ box plot *(diagrama de caja)*

data *(datos)*

dot plot *(diagrama de puntos)*

interquartile range *(rango entre cuartiles)*

✔ lower quartile *(cuartil inferior)*

✔ median *(mediana)*

spread *(dispersión)*

survey *(estudio)*

✔ upper quartile *(cuartil superior)*

Preview Words

biased sample *(muestra sesgada)*

population *(población)*

random sample *(muestra aleatoria)*

sample *(muestra)*

Active Reading

Tri-Fold Before beginning the module, create a tri-fold to help you learn the concepts and vocabulary in this module. Fold the paper into three sections. Label the columns "What I Know," "What I Need to Know," and "What I Learned." Complete the first two columns before you read. After studying the module, complete the third column.

Unpacking the Standards

Understanding the standards and the vocabulary terms in the standards will help you know exactly what you are expected to learn in this module.

 FL 7.SP.1.1

Understand that statistics can be used to gain information about a population by examining a sample of the population; generalizations about a population from a sample are valid only if the sample is representative of that population. Understand that random sampling tends to produce representative samples and support valid inferences.

What It Means to You

You will learn how a random sample can be representative of a population.

UNPACKING EXAMPLE 7.SP.1.1

Avery wants to survey residents who live in an apartment building. She writes down all of the apartment numbers on slips of paper, and draws slips from a box without looking to decide who to survey. Will this produce a random sample?

The population is all of the residents or people who live in the apartment building. The sample is a valid random sample because every apartment number has the same chance of being selected.

 FL 7.SP.1.2

Use data from a random sample to draw inferences about a population with an unknown characteristic of interest. Generate multiple samples (or simulated samples) of the same size to gauge the variation in estimates or predictions.

Key Vocabulary

population (*población*)
The entire group of objects or individuals considered for a survey.

sample (*muestra*)
A part of the population.

What It Means to You

You will use data collected from a random sample to make inferences about a population.

UNPACKING EXAMPLE 7.SP.1.2

Alexi surveys a random sample of 80 students at his school and finds that 22 of them usually walk to school. There are 1,760 students at the school. Predict the number of students who usually walk to school.

$$\frac{\text{number in sample who walk}}{\text{size of sample}} = \frac{\text{number in population who walk}}{\text{size of population}}$$

$$\frac{22}{80} = \frac{x}{1,760}$$

$$x = \frac{22}{80} \cdot 1,760$$

$$x = \frac{38,720}{80} = 484$$

Approximately 484 students usually walk to school.

Visit **my.hrw.com** to see all **Florida Math Standards** unpacked.

my.hrw.com

Populations and Samples

FL 7.SP.1.1

...Understand that random sampling tends to produce representative samples and support valid inferences.

ESSENTIAL QUESTION

How can you use a sample to gain information about a population?

EXPLORE ACTIVITY   FL 7.SP.1.1

Random and Non-Random Sampling

When information is being gathered about a group, the entire group of objects, individuals, or events is called the **population**. A **sample** is part of the population that is chosen to represent the entire group.

A vegetable garden has 36 tomato plants arranged in a 6-by-6 array. The gardener wants to know the average number of tomatoes on the plants. Each white cell in the table represents a plant. The number in the cell tells how many tomatoes are on that particular plant.

Because counting the number of tomatoes on all of the plants is too time-consuming, the gardener decides to choose plants at random to find the average number of tomatoes on them.

To simulate the random selection, roll two number cubes 10 times. Find the cell in the table identified by the first and second number cubes. Record the number in each randomly selected cell.

						First Number Cube
8	9	13	18	24	15	**1**
34	42	46	20	13	41	**2**
29	21	14	45	27	43	**3**
22	45	46	41	22	33	**4**
12	42	44	17	42	11	**5**
18	26	43	32	33	26	**6**
Second Number Cube						
1	2	3	4	5	6	

A What is the average number of tomatoes on the 10 plants that were randomly selected?

_____

B Alternately, the gardener decides to choose the plants in the first row. What is the average number of tomatoes on these plants?

_____

Math Talk
Mathematical Practices

How do the averages you got with each sampling method compare?

Reflect

1. How do the averages you got with each sampling method compare to the average for the entire population, which is 28.25?

_____

_____

2. Why might the first method give a closer average than the second method?

_____

_____

Math On the Spot

my.hrw.com

Random Samples and Biased Samples

A sample in which every person, object, or event has an equal chance of being selected is called a **random sample**. A random sample is more likely to be representative of the entire population than other sampling methods. When a sample does not accurately represent the population, it is called a **biased sample**.

EXAMPLE 1

FL 7.SP.1.1

Identify the population. Determine whether each sample is a random sample or a biased sample. Explain your reasoning.

Math Talk

Mathematical Practices

Why do you think samples are used? Why not survey each member of the population?

A Roberto wants to know the favorite sport of adults in his hometown. He surveys 50 adults at a baseball game.

The population is adults in Roberto's hometown.

Think: People who don't like baseball will not be represented in this sample.

The sample is biased.

B Paula wants to know the favorite type of music for students in her class. She puts the names of all students in a hat, draws 8 names, and surveys those students.

The population is students in Paula's class.

Think: Each student has an equal chance of being selected.

The sample is random.

Reflect

3. How might you choose a sample of size 20 to determine the preferred practice day of all the players in a soccer league?

_____

_____

YOUR TURN

4. For a survey, a company manager assigned a number to each of the company's 500 employees, and put the numbers in a bag. The manager chose 20 numbers and surveyed the employees with those numbers. Did the manager choose a random sample?

_____

_____

Bias in Survey Questions

Once you have selected a representative sample of the population, be sure that the data is gathered without bias. Make sure that the survey questions themselves do not sway people to respond a certain way.

EXAMPLE 2   **FL** 7.SP.1.1

In Madison County, residents were surveyed about a new skateboard park. Determine whether each survey question may be biased. Explain.

A Would you like to waste the taxpayers' money to build a frivolous skateboard park?

This question is biased. It discourages residents from saying yes to a new skateboard park by implying it is a waste of money.

B Do you favor a new skateboard park?

This question is not biased. It does not include an opinion on the skateboard park.

C Studies have shown that having a safe place to go keeps kids out of trouble. Would you like to invest taxpayers' money to build a skateboard park?

This question is biased. It leads people to say yes because it mentions having a safe place for kids to go and to stay out of trouble.

YOUR TURN

Determine whether each question may be biased. Explain.

5. When it comes to pets, do you prefer cats?

_____

6. What is your favorite season?

_____

_____

1. Follow each method described below to collect data to estimate the average shoe size of seventh grade boys. (Explore Activity)

   Method 1

   A Randomly select 6 seventh grade boys and ask each his shoe size. Record your results in a table like the one shown.

   _____

Random Sample of Seventh Grade Male Students	
Student	Shoe Size

   B Find the mean of this data. Mean:

   _____

   Method 2

   A Find the 6 boys in your math class with the largest shoes and ask their shoe size. Record your results in a table like the one shown in Method 1.

   _____

   B Find the mean of this data. Mean: _____

2. Method 1 produces results that are **more / less** representative of the entire student population because it is a **random / biased** sample. (Example 1)

3. Method 2 produces results that are **more / less** representative of the entire student population because it is a **random / biased** sample. (Example 1)

4. Heidi decides to use a random sample to determine her classmates' favorite color. She asks, "Is green your favorite color?" Is Heidi's question biased? If so, give an example of an unbiased question that would serve Heidi better. (Example 2)

   _____

   _____

? ESSENTIAL QUESTION CHECK-IN

5. How can you select a sample so that the information gained represents the entire population?

   _____

   _____

Making Inferences from a Random Sample

FL 7.SP.1.2
Use data from a random sample to draw inferences about a population with an unknown characteristic of interest ... Also 7.RP.1.2c, 7.SP.1.1

ESSENTIAL QUESTION

How can you use a sample to gain information about a population?

EXPLORE ACTIVITY 1   FL 7.SP.1.2, 7.SP.1.1

Using Dot Plots to Make Inferences

After obtaining a random sample of a population, you can make inferences about the population. Random samples are usually representative and support valid inferences.

Rosee asked students on the lunch line how many books they had in their backpacks. She recorded the data as a list: 2, 6, 1, 0, 4, 1, 4, 2, 2. Make a dot plot for the books carried by this sample of students.

STEP 1 Order the data from least to greatest. Find the least and greatest values in the data set.

STEP 2 Draw a number line from 0 to 6. Place a dot above each number on the number line for each time it appears in the data set.

Notice that the dot plot puts the data values in order.

Math Talk
Mathematical Practices
No students in Rosee's sample carry 3 books. Do you think this is true of all the students at the school? Explain.

Reflect

1. **Critical Thinking** How are the number of dots you plotted related to the number of data values?

_____

2. **Draw Conclusions** Complete each qualitative inference about the population.

Most students have _____ 1 book in their backpacks.

Most students have fewer than _____ books in their backpacks.

Most students have between _____ books in their backpacks.

3. **Analyze Relationships** What could Rosee do to improve the quality of her data?

_____

Using Box Plots to Make Inferences

You can also analyze box plots to make inferences about a population.

The number of pets owned by a random sample of students at Park Middle school is shown below. Use the data to make a box plot.

9, 2, 0, 4, 6, 3, 3, 2, 5

STEP 1 Order the data from least to greatest. Then find the least and greatest values, the median, and the lower and upper quartiles.

STEP 2 The lower and upper quartiles can be calculated by finding the medians of each "half" of the number line that includes all the data.

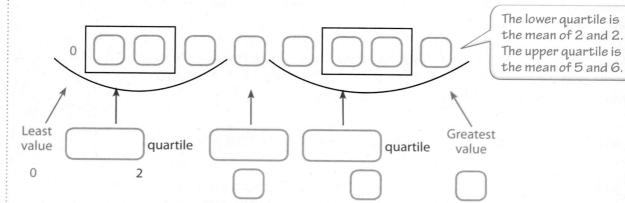

> The lower quartile is the mean of 2 and 2. The upper quartile is the mean of 5 and 6.

Draw a number line that includes all the data values.

Plot a point for each of the values found in Step 1.

STEP 3 Draw a box from the lower to upper quartile. Inside the box, draw a vertical line through the median. Finally, draw the whiskers by connecting the least and greatest values to the box.

Reflect

4. Draw Conclusions Complete each qualitative inference about the population.

A good measure for the most likely number of pets is _____.

50% of the students have between _____ and 3 pets.

Almost every student in Parkview has at least _____ pet.

Math Talk
Mathematical Practices

What can you see from a box plot that is not readily apparent in a dot plot?

Using Proportions to Make Inferences

You can use data based on a random sample, along with proportional reasoning, to make inferences or predictions about the population.

Math On the Spot
my.hrw.com

EXAMPLE 1   FL 7.SP.1.2, 7.RP.1.2c

A shipment to a warehouse consists of 3,500 MP3 players. The manager chooses a random sample of 50 MP3 players and finds that 3 are defective. How many MP3 players in the shipment are likely to be defective?

It is reasonable to make a prediction about the population because this sample is random.

STEP 1 Set up a proportion.

$$\frac{\text{defective MP3s in sample}}{\text{size of sample}} = \frac{\text{defective MP3s in population}}{\text{size of population}}$$

STEP 2 Substitute values into the proportion.

$$\frac{3}{50} = \frac{x}{3{,}500}$$ *Substitute known values. Let x be the number of defective MP3 players in the population.*

$$\frac{3 \cdot 70}{50 \cdot 70} = \frac{x}{3{,}500}$$ *50 · 70 = 3,500, so multiply the numerator and denominator by 70.*

$$\frac{210}{3{,}500} = \frac{x}{3{,}500}$$

$$210 = x$$

Based on the sample, you can predict that 210 MP3 players in the shipment would be defective.

Animated Math
my.hrw.com

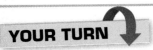

5. **What If?** How many MP3 players in the shipment would you predict to be damaged if 6 MP3s in the sample had been damaged?

_____

Reflect

6. **Check for Reasonableness** How could you use estimation to check if your answer is reasonable?

_____

_____

Personal Math Trainer
Online Assessment and Intervention
my.hrw.com

Patrons in the children's section of a local branch library were randomly selected and asked their ages. The librarian wants to use the data to infer the ages of all patrons of the children's section so he can select age appropriate activities. In 3–6, complete each inference. (Explore Activity 1 and 2)

7, 4, 7, 5, 4, 10, 11, 6, 7, 4

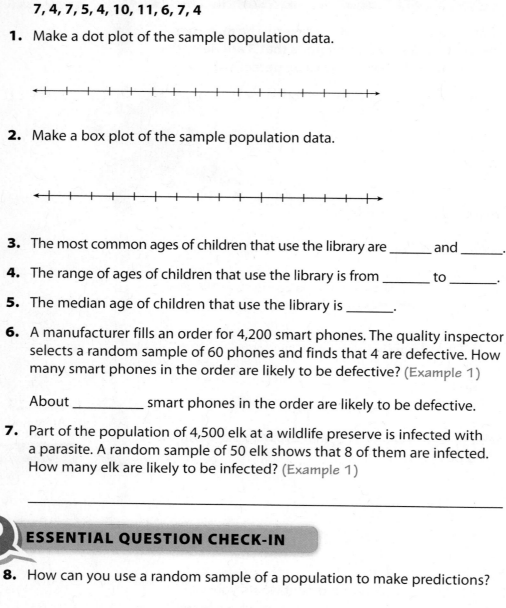

1. Make a dot plot of the sample population data.

←|—|—|—|—|—|—|—|—|—|—|—|—|—|—|—|→

2. Make a box plot of the sample population data.

←|—|—|—|—|—|—|—|—|—|—|—|—|—|—|→

3. The most common ages of children that use the library are _____ and _____.

4. The range of ages of children that use the library is from _____ to _____.

5. The median age of children that use the library is _____.

6. A manufacturer fills an order for 4,200 smart phones. The quality inspector selects a random sample of 60 phones and finds that 4 are defective. How many smart phones in the order are likely to be defective? (Example 1)

About _____ smart phones in the order are likely to be defective.

7. Part of the population of 4,500 elk at a wildlife preserve is infected with a parasite. A random sample of 50 elk shows that 8 of them are infected. How many elk are likely to be infected? (Example 1)

_____

? ESSENTIAL QUESTION CHECK-IN

8. How can you use a random sample of a population to make predictions?

_____

_____

_____

_____

_____

LESSON 5.3
Generating Random Samples

FL 7.SP.1.2

Use data from a random sample ... Generate multiple samples (or simulated samples) of the same size to gauge the variation in estimates or predictions.

> **ESSENTIAL QUESTION**
> How can you generate and use random samples to represent a population?

EXPLORE ACTIVITY 1 **FL** 7.SP.1.2

Generating a Random Sample Using Technology

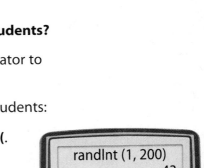

In an earlier lesson, you generated random samples by rolling number cubes. You can also generate random samples by using technology. In Explore Activity 1, you will generate samples using a graphing calculator.

Each of the 200 students in a school will have a chance to vote on one of two names, Tigers or Bears, for the school's athletic teams. A group of students decides to select a random sample of 20 students and ask them for which name they intend to vote. How can the group choose a random sample to represent the entire population of 200 students?

A One way to identify a random sample is to use a graphing calculator to generate random integers.

To simulate choosing 20 students at random from among 200 students:

• Press **MATH**, scroll right and select **PRB**, then select **5: randInt(**.

• Enter the least value, comma, greatest possible value.

In this specific case, the students will enter **randInt** $\left(\bigcirc , \bigcirc\right)$

because there are _____ students in school.

randInt (1, 200)
| 43 |
| 93 |
| 75 |
| 178 |

• Hit **ENTER** _____ times to generate _____ random numbers.

The group gets a list of all the students in the school and assigns a number to each one. The group surveys the students with the given numbers.

Of the 20 students surveyed, 9 chose Tigers. The percent choosing

Tigers was _____. What might the group infer?

_____

_____

B You can simulate multiple random samples to see how much statistical measures vary for different samples of size 20.

Assume that the 200 students are evenly divided among those voting for Tigers and those voting for Bears. You can generate random numbers and let each number represent a vote. Let numbers from 1 to 100 represent votes for Tigers, and numbers from 101 to 200 represent votes for Bears. For each simulated sample, use randInt(1, 200) and generate 20 numbers.

Perform the simulation 10 times and record how many numbers from 1 to 100 are generated. How many of the samples indicated that there were 9 or fewer votes for Tigers?

_____

Combine your results with those of your classmates. Make a dot plot showing the number of numbers from 1 to 100 generated in each simulation.

_____

Reflect

1. **Communicate Mathematical Reasoning** Assume that it was accurate to say that the 200 students are evenly divided among those voting for Tigers and those voting for Bears. Based on your results, does it seem likely that in a sample of size 20, there would be 9 or fewer votes for Tigers?

_____

2. **Make a Prediction** Based on your answers, do you think it is likely that Tigers will win? Explain.

_____

3. **Multiple Representations** Suppose you wanted to simulate a random sample for the situation in Explore Activity 1 without using technology. One way would be to use marbles of two different colors to represent students choosing the different names. Describe how you could perform a simulation.

_____

_____

_____

_____

_____

_____

Generating a Random Sample without Technology

A tree farm has a 100 acre square field arranged in a 10-by-10 array. The farmer wants to know the average number of trees per acre. Each cell in the table represents an acre. The number in each cell represents the number of trees on that acre.

22	24	27	29	31	24	27	29	30	25
37	22	60	53	62	42	64	53	41	62
61	54	57	34	44	66	39	60	65	40
45	33	64	36	33	51	62	66	42	42
37	34	57	33	47	43	66	33	61	66
66	45	46	67	60	59	51	46	67	48
53	46	35	35	55	56	61	46	38	64
55	51	54	62	55	58	51	45	41	53
61	38	48	48	43	59	64	48	49	47
41	53	53	59	58	48	62	53	45	59

The farmer decides to choose a random sample of 10 of the acres.

A To simulate the random selection, number the table columns 1–10 from left to right, and the rows 1–10 from top to bottom. Write the numbers 1–10 on identical pieces of paper. Place the pieces into a bag. Draw one at random, replace it, and draw another. Let the first number represent a table column, and the second represent a row. For instance, a draw of 2 and then 3 represents the cell in the second column and third row of the table, an acre containing 54 trees. Repeat this process 9 more times.

B Based on your sample, predict the average number of trees per acre. How does your answer compare with the actual mean number, 48.4?

_____

_____

C Compare your answer to **B** with several of your classmates' answers. Do they vary a lot? Is it likely that you can make a valid prediction about the average number of trees per acre? Explain.

_____

Reflect

4. **Communicate Mathematical Ideas** Suppose that you use the method
    in Ⓐ to collect a random sample of 25 acres. Do you think any resulting
    prediction would be more or less reliable than your original one? Explain.

    _____

    _____

5. **Multiple Representations** How could you use technology to select the
    acres for your sample?

    _____

    _____

Guided Practice

**A manufacturer gets a shipment of 600 batteries of which 50 are defective.
The store manager wants to be able to test random samples in future
shipments. She tests a random sample of 20 batteries in this shipment to
see whether a sample of that size produces a reasonable inference about
the entire shipment.** (Explore Activities 1 and 2)

1. The manager selects a random sample using the formula

    randInt $\left(\boxed{},\boxed{}\right)$ to generate _____ random numbers.

2. She lets numbers from 1 to _____ represent defective batteries, and

    _____ to _____ represent working batteries. She generates this list: 120,
    413, 472, 564, 38, 266, 344, 476, 486, 177, 26, 331, 358, 131, 352, 227, 31,
    253, 31, 277.

3. Does the sample produce a reasonable inference?

    _____

    _____

? ESSENTIAL QUESTION CHECK-IN

4. What can happen if a sample is too small or is not random?

    _____

    _____

Name_____ Class_____ Date_____

5.3 Independent Practice

FL 7.SP.1.2

Personal Math Trainer

Online Assessment and Intervention

my.hrw.com

Maureen owns three bagel shops. Each shop sells 500 bagels per day. Maureen asks her store managers to use a random sample to see how many whole-wheat bagels are sold at each store each day. The results are shown in the table. Use the table for 5–7.

	Total bagels in sample	Whole-wheat bagels
Shop A	50	10
Shop B	100	23
Shop C	25	7

5. If you assume the samples are representative, how many whole-wheat bagels might you infer are sold at each store?

_____

6. Rank the samples for the shops in terms of how representative they are likely to be. Explain your rankings.

_____

_____

7. Which sample or samples should Maureen use to tell her managers how many whole-wheat bagels to make each day? Explain.

_____

_____

_____

8. In a shipment of 1,000 T-shirts, 75 do not meet quality standards. The table below simulates a manager's random sample of 20 T-shirts to inspect. For the simulation, the integers 1 to 75 represent the below-standard shirts.

124	876	76	79	12	878	86	912	435	91
340	213	45	678	544	271	714	777	812	80

In the sample, how many of the shirts are below quality standards? _____

If someone used the sample to predict the number of below standard shirts in the shipment, how far off would the prediction be?

_____

_____

9. Multistep A 64-acre coconut farm is arranged in an 8-by-8 array. Mika wants to know the average number of coconut palms on each acre. Each cell in the table represents an acre of land. The number in each cell tells how many coconut palms grow on that particular acre.

56	54	40	34	44	66	43	65
66	33	42	36	33	51	62	63
33	34	66	33	47	43	66	61
46	35	48	67	60	59	52	67
46	32	64	35	55	47	61	38
45	51	53	62	55	58	51	41
48	38	47	48	43	59	64	54
53	67	59	59	58	48	62	45

a. The numbers in green represent Mika's random sample of 10 acres. What is the average number of coconut palms on the randomly selected acres?

_____

b. Project the number of palms on the entire farm.

_____

H.O.T. **FOCUS ON HIGHER ORDER THINKING**

Work Area

10. Draw Conclusions A random sample of 15 of the 78 competitors at a middle school gymnastics competition are asked their height. The data set lists the heights in inches: 55, 57, 57, 58, 59, 59, 59, 59, 59, 61, 62, 62, 63, 64, 66. What is the mean height of the sample? Do you think this is a reasonable prediction of the mean height of all competitors? Explain.

_____

_____

_____

11. Critical Thinking The six-by-six grid contains the ages of actors in a youth Shakespeare festival. Describe a method for randomly selecting 8 cells by using number cubes. Then calculate the average of the 8 values you found.

12	15	16	9	21	11
9	10	14	10	13	12
16	21	14	12	8	14
16	20	9	16	19	18
17	14	12	15	10	15
12	20	14	10	12	9

_____

_____

_____

_____

_____

_____

12. Communicating Mathematical Ideas Describe how the size of a random sample affects how well it represents a population as a whole.

_____

_____

Ready to Go On?

Personal Math Trainer

Online Assessment and Intervention

my.hrw.com

5.1 Populations and Samples

1. A company uses a computer to identify their 600 most loyal customers from its database and then surveys those customers to find out how they like their service. Identify the population and determine whether the sample is random or biased.

_____

_____

5.2 Making Inferences from a Random Sample

2. A university has 30,330 students. In a random sample of 270 students, 18 speak three or more languages. Predict the number of students at the university who speak three or more languages.

_____

5.3 Generating Random Samples

A store receives a shipment of 5,000 MP3 players. In a previous shipment of 5,000 MP3 players, 300 were defective. A store clerk generates random numbers to simulate a random sample of this shipment. The clerk lets the numbers 1 through 300 represent defective MP3 players, and the numbers 301 through 5,000 represent working MP3 players. The results are given.

13   2,195   3,873   525   900   167   1,094   1,472   709   5,000

3. Based on the sample, how many of the MP3 players might the clerk predict would be defective?

_____

4. Can the manufacturer assume the prediction is valid? Explain.

_____

? ESSENTIAL QUESTION

5. How can you use random samples to solve real-world problems?

_____

_____

MODULE 5 MIXED REVIEW
Assessment Readiness

Personal
Math Trainer

Online
Assessment and
Intervention

my.hrw.com

Selected Response

1. A farmer is using a random sample to predict the number of broken eggs in a shipment of 3,000 eggs. Using a calculator, the farmer generates the following random numbers. The numbers 1–250 represent broken eggs.

| 477 | 2,116 | 1,044 | 81 | 619 | 755 |
| 2,704 | 900 | 238 | 1,672 | 187 | 1,509 |

Based on this sample, how many broken eggs might the farmer expect?

Ⓐ 250 broken eggs

Ⓑ 375 broken eggs

Ⓒ 750 broken eggs

Ⓓ 900 broken eggs

2. A middle school has 490 students. Mae surveys a random sample of 60 students and finds that 24 of them have pet dogs. How many students are likely to have pet dogs?

Ⓐ 98

Ⓑ 196

Ⓒ 245

Ⓓ 294

3. A circular garden has a diameter of 18 meters. What is the circumference of the garden?

Ⓐ 28.26 meters

Ⓑ 56.52 meters

Ⓒ 254.34 meters

Ⓓ 1,017.36 meters

4. Which of the following is a random sample?

Ⓐ A radio DJ asks the first 10 listeners who call in if they liked the last song.

Ⓑ 20 customers at a chicken restaurant are surveyed on their favorite food.

Ⓒ A polling organization numbers all registered voters, then generates 800 random integers. The polling organization interviews the 800 voters assigned those numbers.

Ⓓ Rebecca used an email poll to survey 100 students about how often they use the internet.

Mini-Task

5. Each cell in the table represents the number of people who work in one 25-square-block section of the town of Middleton. The mayor uses a random sample to estimate the average number of workers per block.

47	61	56	48	ⓢ56
ⓢ60	39	63	· 60	46
51	58	49	63	45
55	58	ⓢ50	ⓢ43	48
ⓢ62	ⓢ53	44	66	55

a. The circled numbers represent the mayor's random sample. What is the mean number of workers in this sample?

_____

b. Predict the number of workers in the entire 25-block section of Middleton.

_____

Analyzing and Comparing Data

? ESSENTIAL QUESTION

How can you use solve real-world problems by analyzing and comparing data?

Real-World Video

Scientists place radio frequency tags on some animals within a population of that species. Then they track data, such as migration patterns, about the animals.

⏻ my.hrw.com

GO DIGITAL

my.hrw.com

my.hrw.com

Go digital with your write-in student edition, accessible on any device.

Math On the Spot

Scan with your smart phone to jump directly to the online edition, video tutor, and more.

Animated Math

Interactively explore key concepts to see how math works.

Personal Math Trainer

Get immediate feedback and help as you work through practice sets.

Are YOU Ready?

Complete these exercises to review skills you will need for this module.

Personal Math Trainer

Online Assessment and Intervention

⊙ my.hrw.com

Fractions, Decimals, and Percents

EXAMPLE Write $\frac{13}{20}$ as a decimal and a percent.

$$\begin{array}{r} 0.65 \\ 20\overline{)13.00} \\ -12\,0 \\ \hline 1\,00 \\ -1\,00 \\ \hline 0 \end{array}$$

$0.65 = 65\%$

Write the fraction as a division problem.
Write a decimal point and zeros in the dividend.
Place a decimal point in the quotient.

Write the decimal as a percent.

Write each fraction as a decimal and a percent.

1. $\frac{7}{8}$ _____   **2.** $\frac{4}{5}$ _____   **3.** $\frac{1}{4}$ _____   **4.** $\frac{3}{10}$ _____

5. $\frac{19}{20}$ _____   **6.** $\frac{7}{25}$ _____   **7.** $\frac{37}{50}$ _____   **8.** $\frac{29}{100}$ _____

Find the Median and Mode

EXAMPLE 17, 14, 13, 16, 13, 11
11, 13, 13, 14, 16, 17

$\text{median} = \frac{13 + 14}{2} = 13.5$

$\text{mode} = 13$

Order the data from least to greatest.

The median is the middle item or the average of the two middle items.

The mode is the item that appears most frequently in the data.

Find the median and the mode of the data.

9. 11, 17, 7, 6, 7, 4, 15, 9 _____   **10.** 43, 37, 49, 51, 56, 40, 44, 50, 36 _____

Find the Mean

EXAMPLE 17, 14, 13, 16, 13, 11

$\text{mean} = \frac{17 + 14 + 13 + 16 + 13 + 11}{6}$

$= \frac{84}{6}$

$= 14$

The mean is the sum of the data items divided by the number of items.

Find the mean of the data.

11. 9, 16, 13, 14, 10, 16, 17, 9 _____   **12.** 108, 95, 104, 96, 97, 106, 94 _____

Reading Start-Up

Visualize Vocabulary

Use the ✔ words to complete the right column of the chart.

Statistical Data		
Definition	**Example**	**Review Word**
A group of facts.	Grades on history exams: 85, 85, 90, 92, 94	
The middle value of a data set.	85, 85, 90, 92, 94	
A value that summarizes a set of values, found through addition and division.	Results of the survey show that students typically spend 5 hours a week studying.	

Understand Vocabulary

Complete each sentence using the preview words.

1. A display that uses values from a data set to show how the

values are spread out is a _____.

2. A _____ uses a number line to display data.

Vocabulary

Review Words

✔ data *(datos)*
  interquartile range *(rango entre cuartiles)*
✔ mean *(media)*
  measure of center *(medida central)*
  measure of spread *(medida de dispersión)*
✔ median *(mediana)*
  survey *(encuesta)*

Preview Words

  box plot *(diagrama de caja)*
  dot plot *(diagrama de puntos)*
  mean absolute deviation (MAD) *(desviación absoluta media, (DAM))*

Active Reading

Layered Book Before beginning the module, create a layered book to help you learn the concepts in this module. Label the first flap with the module title. Label the remaining flaps with the lesson titles. As you study each lesson, write important ideas, such as vocabulary and formulas, under the appropriate flap. Refer to your finished layered book as you work on exercises from this module.

MODULE 6
Unpacking the Standards

Understanding the standards and the vocabulary terms in the standards will help you know exactly what you are expected to learn in this module.

 FL 7.SP.2.3

Informally assess the degree of visual overlap of two numerical data distributions with similar variabilities, measuring the difference between the centers by expressing it as a multiple of a measure of variability.

Key Vocabulary

measure of center *(medida de centro)*
A measure used to describe the middle of a data set; the mean and median are measures of center.

What It Means to You

You will compare two populations based on random samples.

UNPACKING EXAMPLE 7.SP.2.3

Melinda surveys a random sample of 16 students from two college dorms to find the average number of hours of sleep they get. Use the results shown in the dot plots to compare the two populations.

Average Daily Hours of Sleep

Anderson Hall

Jones Hall

Students in Jones Hall tend to sleep more than students in Anderson Hall, but the variation in the data sets is similar.

 FL 7.SP.2.3

Informally assess… distributions with similar variabilities, measuring the difference between the centers by expressing it as a multiple of a measure of variability.

Key Vocabulary

measure of spread *(medida de la dispersión)*
A measure used to describe how much a data set varies; the range, IQR, and mean absolute deviation are measures of spread.

What It Means to You

You will compare two groups of data by comparing the difference in the means to the variability.

UNPACKING EXAMPLE 7.SP.2.3

The tables show the number of items that students in a class answered correctly on two different math tests. How does the difference in the means of the data sets compare to the variability?

Items Correct on Test 1
20, 13, 18, 19, 15, 18, 20, 20, 15, 15, 19, 18

Mean: 17.5; Mean absolute deviation: 2

Items Correct on Test 2
8, 12, 12, 8, 15, 16, 14, 12, 13, 9, 14, 11

Mean: 12; Mean absolute deviation: 2

The means of the two data sets differ by $\frac{17.5-12}{2}=2.75$ times the variability of the data sets.

LESSON
6.1

Comparing Data Displayed in Dot Plots

FL 7.SP.2.4

Use measures of center and measures of variability . . . to draw informal comparative inferences about two populations. *Also 7.SP.2.3*

ESSENTIAL QUESTION

How do you compare two sets of data displayed in dot plots?

EXPLORE ACTIVITY FL 7.SP.2.4

Analyzing Dot Plots

You can use dot plots to analyze a data set, especially with respect to its center and spread.

People once used body parts for measurements. For example, an inch was the width of a man's thumb. In the 12th century, King Henry I of England stated that a yard was the distance from his nose to his outstretched arm's thumb. The dot plot shows the different lengths, in inches, of the "yards" for students in a 7th grade class.

Length from Nose to Thumb (in.)

A Describe the shape of the dot plot. Are the dots evenly distributed or grouped on one side?

_____

B Describe the center of the dot plot. What single dot would best represent the data?

_____

_____

C Describe the spread of the dot plot. Are there any outliers?

_____

_____

Reflect

1. Calculate the mean, median, and range of the data in the dot plot.

_____

Comparing Dot Plots Visually

You can compare dot plots visually using various characteristics, such as center, spread, and shape.

EXAMPLE 1 **FL 7.SP.2.3**

The dot plots show the heights of 15 high school basketball players and the heights of 15 high school softball players.

Softball Players' Heights

Basketball Players' Heights

A Visually compare the shapes of the dot plots.

Softball: All the data is 5'6" or less.
Basketball: Most of the data is 5'8" or greater.
As a group, the softball players are shorter than the basketball players.

B Visually compare the centers of the dot plots.

Softball: The data is centered around 5'4".
Basketball: The data is centered around 5'8".
This means that the most common height for the softball players is 5 feet 4 inches, and for the basketball players 5 feet 8 inches.

C Visually compare the spreads of the dot plots.

Softball: The spread is from 4'11" to 5'6".
Basketball: The spread is from 5'2" to 6'0".
There is a greater spread in heights for the basketball players.

YOUR TURN

2. Visually compare the dot plot of heights of field hockey players to the dot plots for softball and basketball players.

Field Hockey Players' Heights

Shape: _____

_____

Center: _____

_____

Spread: _____

_____

Comparing Data Displayed in Box Plots

 FL 7.SP.2.3

Informally assess the degree of visual overlap of two numerical data distributions with similar variabilities, ...
Also 7.SP.2.4

ESSENTIAL QUESTION

How do you compare two sets of data displayed in box plots?

EXPLORE ACTIVITY FL 7.SP.2.4

Analyzing Box Plots

Box plots show five key values to represent a set of data, the least and greatest values, the lower and upper quartile, and the median. To create a box plot, arrange the data in order, and divide them into four equal-size parts or quarters. Then draw the box and the whiskers as shown.

The number of points a high school basketball player scored during the games he played this season are organized in the box plot shown.

Points Scored

A Find the least and greatest values.

Least value: _____   Greatest value: _____

B Find the median and describe what it means for the data.

_____

_____

_____

C Find and describe the lower and upper quartiles.

_____

_____

_____

Math Talk
Mathematical Practices

How do the lengths of the whiskers compare? Explain what this means.

D The interquartile range is the difference between the lower and upper quartiles, which is represented by the length of the box. Find the interquartile range.

$Q_3 - Q_1 =$ _____ $-$ _____ $=$ _____

Reflect

1. Why is one-half of the box wider than the other half of the box?

_____

_____

Box Plots with Similar Variability

You can compare two box plots numerically according to their centers, or medians, and their spreads, or variability. Range and interquartile range (IQR) are both measures of spread. Box plots with similar variability should have similar boxes and whiskers.

EXAMPLE 1 FL 7.SP.2.3

My Notes

The box plots show the distribution of times spent shopping by two different groups.

Group A
Group B

Shopping Time (min)

A Compare the shapes of the box plots.

The positions and lengths of the boxes and whiskers appear to be very similar. In both plots, the right whisker is shorter than the left whisker.

B Compare the centers of the box plots.

Group A's median, 47.5, is greater than Group B's, 40. This means that the median shopping time for Group A is 7.5 minutes more.

C Compare the spreads of the box plots.

The box shows the interquartile range. The boxes are similar.

Group A: $55 - 30 = 25$ min   Group B: About $59 - 32 = 26$ min

The whiskers have similar lengths, with Group A's slightly shorter than Group B's.

Math Talk
Mathematical Practices

Which store has the shopper who shops longest? Explain how you know.

Reflect

2. Which group has the greater variability in the bottom 50% of shopping times? The top 50% of shopping times? Explain how you know.

_____

_____

LESSON 6.3
Using Statistical Measures to Compare Populations

FL 7.SP.2.3

Informally assess ... two numerical data distributions ... measuring the difference between the centers by expressing it as a multiple of a measure of variability. *Also 7.SP.2.4*

💬 **ESSENTIAL QUESTION**

How can you use statistical measures to compare populations?

Comparing Differences in Centers to Variability

Recall that to find the mean absolute deviation (MAD) of a data set, first find the mean of the data. Next, take the absolute value of the difference between the mean and each data point. Finally, find the mean of those absolute values.

Math On the Spot
⟳ my.hrw.com

EXAMPLE 1 Real World   FL 7.SP.2.3

The tables show the number of minutes per day students in a class spend exercising and playing video games. What is the difference of the means as a multiple of the mean absolute deviations?

Minutes Per Day Exercising
0, 7, 7, 18, 20, 38, 33, 24, 22, 18, 11, 6

Minutes Per Day Playing Video Games
13, 18, 19, 30, 32, 46, 50, 34, 36, 30, 23, 19

STEP 1 Calculate the mean number of minutes per day exercising.

$$0 + 7 + 7 + 18 + 20 + 38 + 33 + 24 + 22 + 18 + 11 + 6 = 204$$

$204 \div 12 = 17$ *Divide the sum by the number of students.*

STEP 2 Calculate the mean absolute deviation for the number of minutes exercising.

$|0-17| = 17$	$|7-17| = 10$	$|7-17| = 10$	$|18-17| = 1$
$|20-17| = 3$	$|38-17| = 21$	$|33-17| = 16$	$|24-17| = 7$
$|22-17| = 5$	$|18-17| = 1$	$|11-17| = 6$	$|6-17| = 11$

Find the mean of the absolute values.

$$17 + 10 + 10 + 1 + 3 + 21 + 16 + 7 + 5 + 1 + 6 + 11 = 108$$

$108 \div 12 = 9$ *Divide the sum by the number of students.*

STEP 3 Calculate the mean number of minutes per day playing video games. Round to the nearest tenth.

$$13 + 18 + 19 + 30 + 32 + 46 + 50 + 34 + 36 + 30 + 23 + 19 = 350$$

$350 \div 12 \approx 29.2$ *Divide the sum by the number of students.*

STEP 4 Calculate the mean absolute deviation for the numbers of minutes playing video games.

$|13-29.2| = 16.2$	$|18-29.2| = 11.2$	$|19-29.2| = 10.2$
$|30-29.2| = 0.8$	$|32-29.2| = 2.8$	$|46-29.2| = 16.8$
$|50-29.2| = 20.8$	$|34-29.2| = 4.8$	$|36-29.2| = 6.8$
$|30-29.2| = 0.8$	$|23-29.2| = 6.2$	$|19-29.2| = 10.2$

Find the mean of the absolute values. Round to the nearest tenth.

$$16.2 + 11.2 + 10.2 + 0.8 + 2.8 + 16.8 + 20.8 + 4.8 + 6.8 + 0.8 + 6.2 + 10.2 = 107.6$$

$107.6 \div 12 \approx 9$ *Divide the sum by the number of students.*

STEP 5 Find the difference in the means.

$29.2 - 17 = 12.2$ *Subtract the lesser mean from the greater mean.*

STEP 6 Write the difference of the means as a multiple of the mean absolute deviations, which are similar but not identical.

$12.2 \div 9 \approx 1.36$ *Divide the difference of the means by the MAD.*

The means of the two data sets differ by about 1.4 times the variability of the two data sets.

YOUR TURN

1. The high jumps in inches of the students on two intramural track and field teams are shown below. What is the difference of the means as a multiple of the mean absolute deviations?

High Jumps for Students on Team 1 (in.)
44, 47, 67, 89, 55, 76, 85, 80, 87, 69, 47, 58

High Jumps for Students on Team 2 (in.)
40, 32, 52, 75, 65, 70, 72, 61, 54, 43, 29, 32

Personal
Math Trainer

Online Assessment
and Intervention

⏻ my.hrw.com

Using Multiple Samples to Compare Populations

Many different random samples are possible for any given population, and their measures of center can vary. Using multiple samples can give us an idea of how reliable any inferences or predictions we make are.

EXAMPLE 2 FL 7.SP.2.4

A group of about 250 students in grade 7 and about 250 students in grade 11 were asked, "How many hours per month do you volunteer?" Responses from one random sample of 10 students in grade 7 and one random sample of 10 students in grade 11 are summarized in the box plots.

Two Random Samples of Size 10

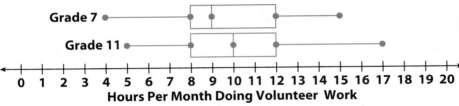

Hours Per Month Doing Volunteer Work

How can we tell if the grade 11 students do more volunteer work than the grade 7 students?

STEP 1 The median is higher for the students in grade 11. But there is a great deal of variation. To make an inference for the entire population, it is helpful to consider how the medians vary among multiple samples.

STEP 2 The box plots below show how the medians from 10 different random samples for each group vary.

Distribution of Medians from 10 Random Samples of Size 10

Medians

The medians vary less than the actual data. Half of the grade 7 medians are within 1 hour of 9. Half of the grade 11 medians are within 1 or 2 hours of 11. Although the distributions overlap, the middle halves of the data barely overlap. This is fairly convincing evidence that the grade 11 students volunteer more than the grade 7 students.

> **Math Talk**
> **Mathematical Practices**
>
> Why doesn't the first box plot establish that students in grade 11 volunteer more than students in grade 7?

YOUR TURN

2. The box plots show the variation in the means for 10 different random samples for the groups in the example. Why do these data give less convincing evidence that the grade 11 students volunteer more?

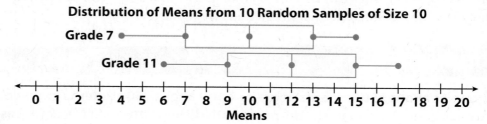

Distribution of Means from 10 Random Samples of Size 10

_____

Guided Practice

The tables show the numbers of miles run by the students in two classes. Use the tables in 1–2. (Example 1)

Miles Run by Class 1 Students
12, 1, 6, 10, 1, 2, 3, 10, 3, 8, 3, 9, 8, 6, 8

Miles Run by Class 2 Students
11, 14, 11, 13, 6, 7, 8, 6, 8, 13, 8, 15, 13, 17, 15

1. For each class, what is the mean? What is the mean absolute deviation?

_____

2. The difference of the means is about _____ times the mean absolute deviations.

3. Mark took 10 random samples of 10 students from two schools. He asked how many minutes they spend per day going to and from school. The tables show the medians and the means of the samples. Compare the travel times using distributions of the medians and means. (Example 2)

School A
Medians: 28, 22, 25, 10, 40, 36, 30, 14, 20, 25
Means: 27, 24, 27, 15, 42, 36, 32, 18, 22, 29

School B
Medians: 22, 25, 20, 14, 20, 18, 21, 18, 26, 19
Means: 24, 30, 22, 15, 20, 17, 22, 15, 36, 27

_____

_____

? ESSENTIAL QUESTION CHECK-IN

4. Why is it a good idea to use multiple random samples when making comparative inferences about two populations?

_____

6.3 Independent Practice

  7.SP.2.3, 7.SP.2.4

Personal Math Trainer

Online Assessment and Intervention

my.hrw.com

Josie recorded the average monthly temperatures for two cities in the state where she lives. Use the data for 5–7.

Average Monthly Temperatures for City 1 (°F)
23, 38, 39, 48, 55, 56, 71, 86, 57, 53, 43, 31

Average Monthly Temperatures for City 2 (°F)
8, 23, 24, 33, 40, 41, 56, 71, 42, 38, 28, 16

5. For City 1, what is the mean of the average monthly temperatures? What is the mean absolute deviation of the average monthly temperatures?

_____

6. What is the difference between each average monthly temperature for

City 1 and the corresponding temperature for City 2? _____

7. **Draw Conclusions** Based on your answers to Exercises 5 and 6, what do you think the mean of the average monthly temperatures for City 2 is? What do you think the mean absolute deviation of the average monthly temperatures for City 2 is? Give your answers without actually calculating the mean and the mean absolute deviation. Explain your reasoning.

_____

_____

8. What is the difference in the means as a multiple of the mean absolute

deviations? _____

9. **Make a Conjecture** The box plots show the distributions of mean weights of 10 samples of 10 football players from each of two leagues, A and B. What can you say about any comparison of the weights of the two populations? Explain.

Distribution of Means from 10 Random Samples of Size 10

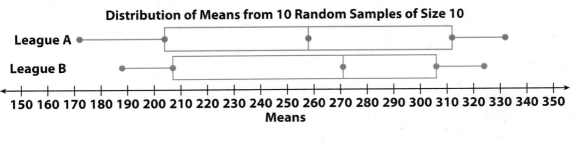

_____

_____

10. Justify Reasoning Statistical measures are shown for the ages of middle school and high school teachers in two states.

State A: Mean age of middle school teachers = 38, mean age of high school teachers = 48, mean absolute deviation for both = 6

State B: Mean age of middle school teachers = 42, mean age of high school teachers = 50, mean absolute deviation for both = 4

In which state is the difference in ages between members of the two groups more significant? Support your answer.

_____

_____

11. Analyze Relationships The tables show the heights in inches of all the adult grandchildren of two sets of grandparents, the Smiths and the Thompsons. What is the difference in the medians as a multiple of the ranges?

Heights of the Smiths' Adult Grandchildren (in.)
64, 65, 68, 66, 65, 68, 69, 66, 70, 67

Heights of the Thompsons' Adult Grandchildren (in.)
75, 80, 78, 77, 79, 76, 75, 79, 77, 74

_____

 FOCUS ON HIGHER ORDER THINKING

Work Area

12. Critical Thinking Jill took many samples of 10 tosses of a standard number cube. What might she reasonably expect the median of the medians of the samples to be? Why?

_____

_____

13. Analyze Relationships Elly and Ramon are both conducting surveys to compare the average numbers of hours per month that men and women spend shopping. Elly plans to take many samples of size 10 from both populations and compare the distributions of both the medians and the means. Ramon will do the same, but will use a sample size of 100. Whose results will probably produce more reliable inferences? Explain.

_____

_____

14. Counterexamples Seth believes that it is always possible to compare two populations of numerical values by finding the difference in the means of the populations as a multiple of the mean absolute deviations. Describe a situation that explains why Seth is incorrect.

_____

_____

Random Samples and Populations

 ESSENTIAL QUESTION

How can you use random samples and populations to solve real-world problems?

EXAMPLE 1

An engineer at a lightbulb factory chooses a random sample of 100 lightbulbs from a shipment of 2,500 and finds that 2 of them are defective. How many lightbulbs in the shipment are likely to be defective?

$$\frac{\text{defective lightbulbs}}{\text{size of sample}} = \frac{\text{defective lightbulbs in population}}{\text{size of population}}$$

$$\frac{2}{100} = \frac{x}{2,500}$$

$$\frac{2 \cdot 25}{100 \cdot 25} = \frac{x}{2,500}$$

$$x = 50$$

In a shipment of 2,500 lightbulbs, 50 are likely to be defective.

EXAMPLE 2

The 300 students in a school are about to vote for student body president. There are two candidates, Jay and Serena, and each candidate has about the same amount of support. Use a simulation to generate a random sample. Interpret the results.

Step 1: Write the digits 0 through 9 on 10 index cards, one digit per card. Draw and replace a card three times to form a 3-digit number. For example, if you draw 0-4-9, the number is 49. If you draw 1-0-8, the number is 108. Repeat this process until you have a sample of 30 3-digit numbers.

Step 2: Let the numbers from 1 to 150 represent votes for Jay and the numbers from 151 to 300 represent votes for Serena. For example:

Jay: 83, 37, 16, 4, 127, 93, 9, 62, 91, 75, 13, 35, 94, 26, 60, 120, 36, 73

Serena: 217, 292, 252, 186, 296, 218, 284, 278, 209, 296, 190, 300

Step 3: Notice that 18 of the 30 numbers represent votes for Jay. The results suggest that Jay will receive $\frac{18}{30} = 60\%$ of the 300 votes, or 180 votes.

Step 4: Based on this one sample, Jay will win the election. The results of samples can vary. Repeating the simulation many times and looking at the pattern across the different samples will produce more reliable results.

EXERCISES

1. Molly uses the school directory to select, at random, 25 students from her school for a survey on which sports people like to watch on television. She calls the students and asks them, "Do you think basketball is the best sport to watch on television?" (Lesson 5.1)

   a. Did Molly survey a random sample or a biased sample of the students at her school?

   _____

   b. Was the question she asked an unbiased question? Explain your answer.

   _____

   _____

2. There are 2,300 licensed dogs in Clarkson. A random sample of 50 of the dogs in Clarkson shows that 8 have ID microchips implanted. How many dogs in Clarkson are likely to have ID microchips implanted? (Lesson 5.2)

   _____

3. A store gets a shipment of 500 MP3 players. Twenty-five of the players are defective, and the rest are working. A graphing calculator is used to generate 20 random numbers to simulate a random sample of the players. (Lesson 5.3)

   A list of 20 randomly generated numbers representing MP3 players is:

474	77	101	156	378	188	116	458	230	333
78	19	67	5	191	124	226	496	481	161

   a. Let numbers 1 to 25 represent players that are _____.

   b. Let numbers 21 to 500 represent players that are _____.

   c. How many players in this sample are expected to be

      defective? _____

   d. If 300 players are chosen at random from the shipment, how many are expected to be defective based on the sample? Does the sample provide a reasonable inference? Explain.

   _____

   _____

   _____

Analyzing and Comparing Data

Key Vocabulary
mean absolute deviation
(MAD) *(desviación
absoluta media, (DAM))*

ESSENTIAL QUESTION

How can you solve real-world problems by analyzing
and comparing data?

EXAMPLE

**The box plots show amounts donated
to two charities at a fundraising drive.
Compare the shapes, centers and
spreads of the box plots.**

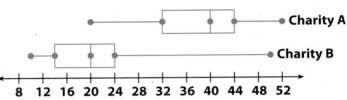

Shapes: The lengths of the boxes and
overall plot lengths are fairly similar, but while the whiskers for Charity A are similar
in length, Charity B has a very short whisker and a very long whisker.

Centers: The median for Charity A is $40, and for Charity B is $20.

Spreads: The interquartile range for Charity A is $44 - 32 = 12$. The interquartile
range for Charity B is slightly less, $24 - 14 = 10$.

The donations varied more for Charity B and were lower overall.

EXERCISES

**The dot plots show the number
of hours a group of students
spends online each week, and
how many hours they spend
reading. Compare the dot
plots visually.** (Lesson 6.1)

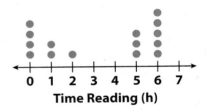

1. Compare the shapes, centers, and spreads of the dot plots.

   Shape: _____

   _____

   Center: _____

   _____

   Spread: _____

   _____

2. Calculate the medians of the dot plots. _____

3. Calculate the ranges of the dot plots. _____

4. The average times (in minutes) a group of students spends studying and watching TV per school day are given. (*Lesson 6.3*)

Studying: 25, 30, 35, 45, 60, 60, 70, 75
Watching TV: 0, 35, 35, 45, 50, 50, 70, 75

   a. Find the mean times for studying and for watching TV.

   _____

   b. Find the mean absolute deviations (MADs) for each data set.

   _____

   c. Find the difference of the means as a multiple of the MAD, to two decimal places.

   _____

Unit 3 Performance Tasks

1. **CAREERS IN MATH** Entomologist An entomologist is studying how two different types of flowers appeal to butterflies. The box-and-whisker plots show the number of butterflies that visited one of two different types of flowers in a field. The data were collected over a two-week period, for one hour each day.

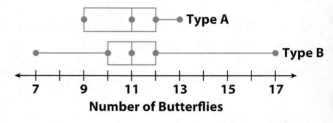

   a. Find the median, range, and interquartile range for each data set.

   _____

   _____

   b. Which measure makes it appear that flower type A had a more consistent number of butterfly visits? Which measure makes it appear that flower type B did? If you had to choose one flower as having the more consistent visits, which would you choose? Explain your reasoning.

   _____

   _____

   _____

   _____

Assessment Readiness

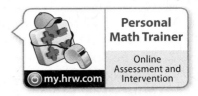

Personal Math Trainer

my.hrw.com · Online Assessment and Intervention

Selected Response

1. Which is a true statement based on the dot plots below?

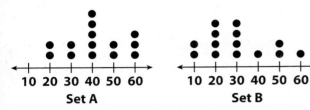

Set A

Set B

- Ⓐ Set B has the greater range.
- Ⓑ Set B has the greater median.
- Ⓒ Set B has the greater mean.
- Ⓓ Set A is less symmetric than Set B.

2. Which is a solution to the equation $7g - 2 = 47$?

- Ⓐ $g = 5$
- Ⓑ $g = 6$
- Ⓒ $g = 7$
- Ⓓ $g = 8$

3. Which is a true statement based on the box plots below?

Team A

Team B

- Ⓐ The data for Team B have the greater range.
- Ⓑ The data for Team A are more symmetric.
- Ⓒ The data for Team B have the greater interquartile range.
- Ⓓ The data for Team A have the greater median.

4. Which is the best way to choose a random sample of people from a sold-out movie audience for a survey?

- Ⓐ Survey all audience members who visit the restroom during the movie.
- Ⓑ Assign each seat a number, write each number on a slip of paper, and then draw several slips from a hat. Survey the people in those seats.
- Ⓒ Survey all of the audience members who sit in the first or last row of seats in the movie theater.
- Ⓓ Before the movie begins, ask for volunteers to participate in a survey. Survey the first twenty people who volunteer.

5. What is the solution of $-3x + 2 < 11$?

- Ⓐ $x < 3$
- Ⓒ $x > 3$
- Ⓑ $x < -3$
- Ⓓ $x > -3$

6. A survey asked 100 students in a school to name the temperature at which they feel most comfortable. The box plot below shows the results for temperatures in degrees Fahrenheit. Which could you infer based on the box plot below?

- Ⓐ Most students prefer a temperature less than 65 degrees.
- Ⓑ Most students prefer a temperature of at least 70 degrees.
- Ⓒ Almost no students prefer a temperature of less than 75 degrees.
- Ⓓ Almost no students prefer a temperature of more than 65 degrees.

7. The box plots below show data from a survey of students under 14 years old. They were asked on how many days in a month they read and draw. Based on the box plots, which is a true statement about students?

Read

Draw

0 6 12 18 24 30

Ⓐ Most students draw at least 12 days a month.

Ⓑ Most students read less than 12 days a month.

Ⓒ Most students read more often than they draw.

Ⓓ Most students draw more often than they read.

Use logic to eliminate answer choices that are incorrect. This will help you to make an educated guess if you are having trouble with the question.

8. Which describes the relationship between ∠NOM and ∠JOK in the diagram?

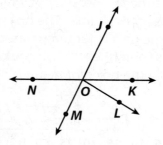

Ⓐ adjacent angles

Ⓑ complementary angles

Ⓒ supplementary angles

Ⓓ vertical angles

Mini-Task

9. The tables show the typical number of minutes spent exercising each week for a group of fourth-grade students and a group of seventh-grade students.

Weekly Exercising (minutes), 4th Grade
120, 75, 30, 30, 240, 90, 100, 180, 125, 300

Weekly Exercising (minutes), 7th Grade
410, 145, 240, 250, 125, 95, 210, 190, 245, 300

a. What is the mean number of minutes spent exercising for fourth graders? For seventh graders?

_____

b. What is the mean absolute deviation of each data set?

_____

c. Compare the two data sets with respect to their measures of center and their measures of variability.

_____

_____

_____

_____

d. How many times the MADs is the difference between the means, to the nearest tenth?

_____

_____

_____

Probability

CAREERS IN MATH

Meteorologist Meteorologists use scientific principles to explain, understand, observe, and forecast atmospheric phenomena and how the atmosphere affects us. They use math in many ways, such as calculating wind velocities, computing the probabilities of weather conditions, and creating and using mathematical models to predict weather patterns. If you are interested in a career as a meteorologist, you should study these mathematical subjects:

- Algebra
- Geometry
- Trigonometry
- Calculus
- Probability and Statistics

Research other careers that require computing probabilities and using mathematical models.

Unit 4 Performance Task

At the end of the unit, check out how **meteorologists** use math.

Use the puzzle to preview key vocabulary from this unit. Unscramble the circled letters within found words to answer the riddle at the bottom of the page.

```
Y  R  F  S  P  D  A  U  L  B  S  T  Y  C  P
T  N  U  E  A  G  V  V  X  I  Y  R  C  A  R
N  N  B  A  H  M  C  P  M  F  U  I  Y  H  O
R  E  E  X  C  K  P  P  L  O  O  A  A  X  B
K  V  H  M  H  O  L  L  D  G  H  L  T  O  A
Q  L  R  B  I  E  W  V  E  Z  V  I  W  S  B
L  F  E  B  E  R  X  E  X  S  I  F  Y  I  I
Q  V  I  V  T  N  E  M  E  L  P  M  O  C  L
Q  O  E  S  H  J  R  P  S  R  K  A  L  E  I
A  N  H  C  J  D  D  O  X  H  P  F  C  X  T
T  P  Z  K  V  Z  V  F  N  E  P  F  U  E  Y
U  V  K  S  I  M  U  L  A  T  I  O  N  P  J
K  X  O  L  P  M  O  M  S  U  Z  J  W  A  P
R  O  C  P  T  U  N  D  N  V  E  R  T  U  A
U  W  O  G  L  B  U  H  K  E  S  F  A  P  B
```

- An activity based on chance in which results are observed. (Lesson 7.1)
- The set of all outcomes that are not included in the event. (Lesson 7.1)
- Each observation of an experiment. (Lesson 7.1)
- A model of an experiment that would be difficult or too time-consuming to perform. (Lesson 7.2)
- Measures the likelihood that the event will occur. (Lesson 7.1)
- An event with only one outcome (2 words). (Lesson 7.2)
- A set of all possible outcomes for an event (2 words). (Lesson 7.1)

Q: Why was there little chance of success for the clumsy thieves?

A: Because they had low ___ ___ ___ – ___ ___ ___ ___ ___ ___ ___!

Experimental Probability

ESSENTIAL QUESTION

How can you use experimental probability to solve real-world problems?

Real-World Video

Meteorologists use sophisticated equipment to gather data about the weather. Then they use experimental probability to forecast, or predict, what the weather conditions will be.

my.hrw.com

GO DIGITAL

my.hrw.com

my.hrw.com

Go digital with your write-in student edition, accessible on any device.

Math On the Spot

Scan with your smart phone to jump directly to the online edition, video tutor, and more.

Animated Math

Interactively explore key concepts to see how math works.

Personal Math Trainer

Get immediate feedback and help as you work through practice sets.

Are YOU Ready?

Complete these exercises to review skills you will need for this module.

Simplify Fractions

EXAMPLE Simplify $\frac{12}{21}$.

12: 1, 2, ③, 4, 6, 12   List all the factors of the numerator and denominator.
21: 1, ③, 7, 21   Circle the greatest common factor (GCF).

$\frac{12 \div 3}{21 \div 3} = \frac{4}{7}$ Divide the numerator and denominator by the GCF.

Write each fraction in simplest form.

1. $\frac{6}{10}$ _____

2. $\frac{9}{15}$ _____

3. $\frac{16}{24}$ _____

4. $\frac{9}{36}$ _____

5. $\frac{45}{54}$ _____

6. $\frac{30}{42}$ _____

7. $\frac{36}{60}$ _____

8. $\frac{14}{42}$ _____

Write Fractions as Decimals

EXAMPLE $\frac{13}{25} \rightarrow$

$$25\overline{)13.00} \\ \quad \underline{-12.5} \\ \quad\quad 50 \\ \quad\quad \underline{-50} \\ \quad\quad\quad 0$$

with quotient 0.52

Write the fraction as a division problem.
Write a decimal point and a zero in the dividend.
Place a decimal point in the quotient.
Write more zeros in the dividend if necessary.

Write each fraction as a decimal.

9. $\frac{3}{4}$ _____

10. $\frac{7}{8}$ _____

11. $\frac{3}{20}$ _____

12. $\frac{19}{50}$ _____

Percents and Decimals

EXAMPLE $109\% = 100\% + 9\%$
$= \frac{100}{100} + \frac{9}{100}$
$= 1 + 0.09$
$= 1.09$

Write the percent as the sum of 1 whole and a percent remainder.
Write the percents as fractions.
Write the fractions as decimals.
Simplify.

Write each percent as a decimal.

13. 67% _____

14. 31% _____

15. 7% _____

16. 146% _____

Write each decimal as a percent.

17. 0.13 _____

18. 0.55 _____

19. 0.08 _____

20. 1.16 _____

Reading Start-Up

Visualize Vocabulary

Use the ✔ words to complete the graphic. You can put more than one word in each box.

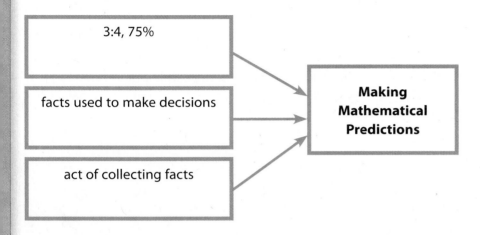

3:4, 75%	
facts used to make decisions	→ **Making Mathematical Predictions**
act of collecting facts	

Vocabulary

Review Words
✔ data *(datos)*
✔ observation *(observación)*
✔ percent *(porcentaje)*
✔ ratio *(razón)*

Preview Words
complement *(complemento)*
compound event *(suceso compuesto)*
event *(suceso)*
experiment *(experimento)*
experimental probability *(probabilidad experimental)*
outcome *(resultado)*
probability *(probabilidad)*
simple event *(suceso simple)*
simulation *(simulación)*
trial *(prueba)*

Understand Vocabulary

Match the term on the left to the definition on the right.

1. probability   **A.** Measures the likelihood that the event will occur.

2. trial   **B.** A set of one or more outcomes.

3. event   **C.** Each observation of an experiment.

Active Reading

Pyramid Before beginning the module, create a rectangular pyramid to help you organize what you learn. Label each side with one of the lesson titles from this module. As you study each lesson, write important ideas, such as vocabulary, properties, and formulas, on the appropriate side.

Unpacking the Standards

Understanding the standards and the vocabulary terms in the standards will help you know exactly what you are expected to learn in this module.

 FL 7.SP.3.6

Approximate the probability of a chance event by collecting data on the chance process that produces it and observing its long-run relative frequency, and predict the approximate relative frequency given the probability.

Key Vocabulary

simple event *(suceso simple)*
An event consisting of only one outcome.

experimental probability *(probabilidad experimental)*
The ratio of the number of times an event occurs to the total number of trials, or times that the activity is performed.

What It Means to You

You will use experimental probabilities to make predictions and solve problems.

UNPACKING EXAMPLE 7.SP.3.6

Caitlyn finds that the experimental probability of her making a goal in hockey is 30%. Out of 500 attempts to make a goal, about how many could she predict she would make?

$$\frac{3}{10} \cdot 500 = x$$

$$150 = x$$

Caitlyn can predict that she will make about 150 of the 500 goals that she attempts.

 FL 7.SP.3.7b

Develop a probability model (which may not be uniform) by observing frequencies in data generated from a chance process.

Key Vocabulary

sample space *(espacio muestral)*
All possible outcomes of an experiment.

What It Means to You

You will use data to determine experimental probabilities.

UNPACKING EXAMPLE 7.SP.3.7b

Anders buys a novelty coin that is weighted more heavily on one side. He flips the coin 60 times and a head comes up 36 times. Based on his results, what is the experimental probability of flipping a head?

$$\text{experimental probability} = \frac{\text{number of times event occurs}}{\text{total number of trials}}$$

$$= \frac{36}{60} = \frac{3}{5}$$

The experimental probability of flipping a head is $\frac{3}{5}$.

LESSON
7.1 Probability

FL 7.SP.3.5

Understand that the probability of a chance event is a number between 0 and 1 that expresses the likelihood of the event occurring. Larger numbers indicate greater likelihood. ... *Also 7.SP.3.7a*

ESSENTIAL QUESTION

How can you describe the likelihood of an event?

EXPLORE ACTIVITY FL 7.SP.3.5

Finding the Likelihood of an Event

Each time you roll a number cube, a number from 1 to 6 lands face up. This is called an *event*.

Work with a partner to decide how many of the six possible results of rolling a number cube match the described event.

Then order the events from least likely (1) to most likely (9) by writing a number in each box to the right.

Rolling a number less than 7 _____ ☐

Rolling an 8 _____ ☐

Rolling a number greater than 4 _____ ☐

Rolling a 5 _____ ☐

Rolling a number other than 6 _____ ☐

Rolling an even number _____ ☐

Rolling a number less than 5 _____ ☐

Rolling an odd number _____ ☐

Rolling a number divisible by 3 _____ ☐

Reflect

1. Are any of the events impossible? _____

_____

Describing Events

An **experiment** is an activity involving chance in which results are observed. Each observation of an experiment is a **trial**, and each result is an **outcome**. A set of one or more outcomes is an **event**.

The **probability** of an event, written P(event), measures the likelihood that the event will occur. Probability is a measure between 0 and 1 as shown on the number line, and can be written as a fraction, a decimal, or a percent.

If the event is not likely to occur, the probability of the event is close to 0. If an event is likely to occur, the event's probability is closer to 1.

Impossible	Unlikely	As likely as not	Likely	Certain

0		$\frac{1}{2}$		1
0		0.5		1.0
0%		50%		100%

EXAMPLE 1

 FL 7.SP.3.5

Tell whether each event is impossible, unlikely, as likely as not, likely, or certain. Then, tell whether the probability is 0, close to 0, $\frac{1}{2}$, close to 1, or 1.

A You roll a six-sided number cube and the number is 1 or greater.

> Because you can roll the numbers 1, 2, 3, 4, 5, and 6 on a number cube, there are 6 possible outcomes.

This event is certain to happen. Its probability is 1.

B You roll two number cubes and the sum of the numbers is 3.

This event is unlikely to happen. Its probability is close to 0.

C A bowl contains disks marked with the numbers 1 through 10. You close your eyes and select a disk at random. You pick an odd number.

This event is as likely as not. The probability is $\frac{1}{2}$.

D A spinner has 8 equal sections marked 0 through 7. You spin and land on a prime number.

> Remember that a prime number is a whole number greater than 1 and has exactly 2 divisors, 1 and itself.

This event is as likely as not. The probability is $\frac{1}{2}$.

Math Talk
Mathematical Practices

Is an event that is *not* certain an impossible event? Explain.

Reflect

2. The probability of event A is $\frac{1}{3}$. The probability of event B is $\frac{1}{4}$. What can you conclude about the two events?

_____

_____

3. A hat contains pieces of paper marked with the numbers 1 through 16. Tell whether picking an even number is impossible, unlikely, as likely as not, likely, or certain. Tell whether the probability is 0, close to 0, $\frac{1}{2}$, close to 1, or 1.

_____

Personal Math Trainer
Online Assessment and Intervention

⊙ my.hrw.com

Finding Probability

The **sample space** is a set of all possible outcomes for an event. A sample space can be small, such as the 2 outcomes when a coin is flipped. Or a sample space can be large, such as the possible number of Texas Classic automobile license plates. Identifying the sample space can help you calculate the probability of an event.

Math On the Spot
⊙ my.hrw.com

Probability of An Event

$$P(\text{event}) = \frac{\text{number of times the event occurs}}{\text{total number of equally likely possible outcomes}}$$

EXAMPLE 2

FL 7.SP.3.7a

What is the probability of rolling an even number on a standard number cube?

STEP 1 Find the sample space for a standard number cube.

{1, 2, 3, 4, 5, 6}   *There are 6 possible outcomes.*

STEP 2 Find the number of ways to roll an even number.

2, 4, 6   *The event can occur 3 ways.*

STEP 3 Find the probability of rolling an even number.

$$P(\text{even}) = \frac{\text{number of ways to roll an even number}}{\text{number of faces on a number cube}}$$

$$= \frac{3}{6} = \frac{1}{2}$$ *Substitute values and simplify.*

The probability of rolling an even number is $\frac{1}{2}$.

YOUR TURN

Find each probability. Write your answer in simplest form.

4. Picking a purple marble from a jar with 10 green and 10 purple marbles. _____

5. Rolling a number greater than 4 on a standard number cube.

_____

Using the Complement of an Event

The **complement** of an event is the set of all outcomes in the sample space that are *not* included in the event. For example, in the event of rolling a 3 on a number cube, the complement is rolling any number other than 3, which means the complement is rolling a 1, 2, 4, 5, or 6.

> ## An Event and Its Complement
>
> The sum of the probabilities of an event and its complement equals 1.
> $$P(\text{event}) + P(\text{complement}) = 1$$

You can apply probabilities to situations involving random selection, such as drawing a card out of a shuffled deck or pulling a marble out of a closed bag.

EXAMPLE 3

There are 2 red jacks in a standard deck of 52 cards. What is the probability of not getting a red jack if you select one card at random?

$$P(\text{event}) + P(\text{complement}) = 1$$

$P(\text{red jack}) + P(\text{not a red jack}) = 1$ *The probability of getting a red jack is $\frac{2}{52}$.*

$\frac{2}{52} + P(\text{not a red jack}) = 1$ *Substitute $\frac{2}{52}$ for $P(\text{red jack})$.*

$\frac{2}{52} + P(\text{not a red jack}) = \frac{52}{52}$ *Subtract $\frac{2}{52}$ from both sides.*

$$\underline{-\frac{2}{52} \qquad\qquad\qquad\qquad -\frac{2}{52}}$$

$$P(\text{not a red jack}) = \frac{50}{52}$$

$P(\text{not a red jack}) = \frac{25}{26}$ *Simplify.*

The probability that you will not draw a red jack is $\frac{25}{26}$. It is likely that you will not select a red jack.

Reflect

6. Why do the probability of an event and the probability of its complement add up to 1?

_____

_____

_____

_____

_____

7. A jar contains 8 marbles marked with the numbers 1 through 8. You pick a marble at random. What is the probability of not picking the marble marked with the number 5? _____

8. You roll a standard number cube. Use the probability of rolling an even number to find the probability of rolling an odd number. _____

Guided Practice

1. In a hat, you have index cards with the numbers 1 through 10 written on them. Order the events from least likely to happen (1) to most likely to happen (8) when you pick one card at random. In the boxes, write a number from 1 to 8 to order the eight different events. *(Explore Activity)*

You pick a number greater than 0. ☐

You pick an even number. ☐

You pick a number that is at least 2. ☐

You pick a number that is at most 0. ☐

You pick a number divisible by 3. ☐

You pick a number divisible by 5. ☐

You pick a prime number. ☐

You pick a number less than the greatest prime number. ☐

Determine whether each event is impossible, unlikely, as likely as not, likely, or certain. Then, tell whether the probability is 0, close to 0, $\frac{1}{2}$, close to 1, or 1. (Example 1)

2. randomly picking a green card from a standard deck of playing cards

_____

3. randomly picking a red card from a standard deck of playing cards

_____

4. picking a number less than 15 from a jar with papers labeled from 1 to 12

_____

5. picking a number that is divisible by 5 from a jar with papers labeled from 1 to 12

_____

Find each probability. Write your answer in simplest form. (Example 2)

6. spinning a spinner that has 5 equal sections marked 1 through 5 and landing on an even number

_____

7. picking a diamond from a standard deck of playing cards which has 13 cards in each of four suits: spades, hearts, diamonds and clubs

_____

Use the complement to find each probability. (Example 3)

8. What is the probability of not rolling a 5 on a standard number cube?

_____

9. A spinner has 3 equal sections that are red, white, and blue. What is the probability of not landing on blue?

_____

10. A spinner has 5 equal sections marked 1 through 5. What is the probability of not landing on 4?

_____

11. There are 4 queens in a standard deck of 52 cards. You pick one card at random. What is the probability of not picking a queen?

_____

? ESSENTIAL QUESTION CHECK-IN

12. Describe an event that has a probability of 0% and an event that has a probability of 100%.

_____

_____

_____

7.1 Independent Practice

 FL 7.SP.3.5, 7.SP.3.7a

Personal Math Trainer

Online Assessment and Intervention

my.hrw.com

13. There are 4 aces and 4 kings in a standard deck of 52 cards. You pick one card at random. What is the probability of selecting an ace or a king? Explain your reasoning.

_____

_____

14. There are 12 pieces of fruit in a bowl. Seven of the pieces are apples and two are peaches. What is the probability that a randomly selected piece of fruit will not be an apple or a peach? Justify your answer.

_____

_____

15. Critique Reasoning For breakfast, Clarissa can choose from oatmeal, cereal, French toast, or scrambled eggs. She thinks that if she selects a breakfast at random, it is likely that it will be oatmeal. Is she correct? Explain your reasoning.

_____

_____

_____

16. Draw Conclusions A researcher's garden contains 90 sweet pea plants, which have either white or purple flowers. About 70 of the plants have purple flowers, and about 20 have white flowers. Would you expect that one plant randomly selected from the garden will have purple or white flowers? Explain.

_____

_____

_____

17. The power goes out as Sandra is trying to get dressed. If she has 4 white T-shirts and 10 colored T-shirts in her drawer, is it likely that she will pick a colored T-shirt in the dark? What is the probability she will pick a colored T-shirt? Explain your answers.

_____

_____

18. James counts the hair colors of the 22 people in his class, including himself. He finds that there are 4 people with blonde hair, 8 people with brown hair, and 10 people with black hair. What is the probability that a randomly chosen student in the class does not have red hair? Explain.

_____

_____

19. Persevere in Problem Solving A bag contains 8 blue coins and 6 red coins. A coin is removed at random and replaced by three of the other color.

   a. What is the probability that the removed coin is blue?

   _____

   b. If the coin removed is blue, what is the probability of drawing a red coin after three red coins are put in the bag to replace the blue one?

   _____

   c. If the coin removed is red, what is the probability of drawing a red coin after three blue coins are put in the bag to replace the red one?

   _____

H.O.T.   **FOCUS ON HIGHER ORDER THINKING**

Work Area

20. Draw Conclusions Give an example of an event in which all of the outcomes are not equally likely. Explain.

_____

_____

_____

21. Critique Reasoning A box contains 150 black pens and 50 red pens. Jose said the sum of the probability that a randomly selected pen will not be black and the probability that the pen will not be red is 1. Explain whether you agree.

_____

_____

_____

22. Communicate Mathematical Ideas A spinner has 7 identical sections. Two sections are blue, 1 is red, and 4 of the sections are green. Suppose the probability of an event happening is $\frac{2}{7}$. What does each number in the ratio represent? What outcome matches this probability?

_____

_____

Experimental Probability of Simple Events

 FL 7.SP.3.6

Approximate the probability of a chance event by collecting data on the chance process that produces it and observing its long-run relative frequency ... *Also 7.SP.3.7b*

ESSENTIAL QUESTION

How do you find the experimental probability of a simple event?

EXPLORE ACTIVITY

 FL 7.SP.3.6, 7.SP.3.7b

Finding Experimental Probability

You can toss a paper cup to demonstrate *experimental probability*.

A Consider tossing a paper cup. Fill in the Outcome column of the table with the three different ways the cup could land.

B Toss a paper cup twenty times. Record your observations in the table.

Outcome	Number of Times

Reflect

1. Do the outcomes appear to be equally likely? _____

2. Describe the three outcomes using the words *likely* and *unlikely*.

_____

_____

3. Use the number of times each event occurred to approximate the probability of each event.

4. **Make a Prediction** What do you think would happen if you performed more trials?

_____

_____

_____

5. What is the sum of the probabilities in 3?

_____

Outcome	Experimental Probability
Open-end up	$\dfrac{\text{open-end up}}{20} = \dfrac{\boxed{}}{20}$
Open-end down	$\dfrac{\text{open-end down}}{20} = \dfrac{\boxed{}}{20}$
On its side	$\dfrac{\text{on its side}}{20} = \dfrac{\boxed{}}{20}$

Calculating Experimental Probability

You can use *experimental probability* to approximate the probability of an event. An **experimental probability** of an event is found by comparing the number of times the event occurs to the total number of trials. When there is only one outcome for an event, it is called a **simple event**.

Experimental Probability

For a given experiment:

$$\text{Experimental probability} = \frac{\text{number of times the event occurs}}{\text{total number of trials}}$$

EXAMPLE 1

FL 7.SP.3.7b

Martin has a bag of marbles. He removed one marble at random, recorded the color and then placed it back in the bag. He repeated this process several times and recorded his results in the table. Find the experimental probability of drawing each color.

Color	Frequency
Red	12
Blue	10
Green	15
Yellow	13

STEP 1 Identify the number of trials: $12 + 10 + 15 + 13 = 50$

STEP 2 Complete the table of experimental probabilities. Write each answer as a fraction in simplest form.

Color	Experimental Probability
Red	$\dfrac{\text{frequency of the event}}{\text{total number of trials}} = \dfrac{12}{50} = \dfrac{6}{25}$
Blue	$\dfrac{\text{frequency of the event}}{\text{total number of trials}} = \dfrac{10}{50} = \dfrac{1}{5}$
Green	$\dfrac{\text{frequency of the event}}{\text{total number of trials}} = \dfrac{15}{50} = \dfrac{3}{10}$
Yellow	$\dfrac{\text{frequency of the event}}{\text{total number of trials}} = \dfrac{13}{50}$

> Substitute the results recorded in the table. You can also write each probability as a decimal or as a percent.

Reflect

6. **Communicate Mathematical Ideas** What are two different ways you could find the experimental probability of the event that Martin does **not** draw a red marble?

_____

_____

_____

_____

YOUR TURN

7. A spinner has three unequal sections: red, yellow, and blue. The table shows the results of Nolan's spins. Find the experimental probability of landing on each color. Write your answers in simplest form.

Color	Frequency
Red	10
Yellow	14
Blue	6

Math Talk
Mathematical Practices
Will everyone who does this experiment get the same results?

_____

Making Predictions with Experimental Probability

A **simulation** is a model of an experiment that would be difficult or inconvenient to actually perform. You can use a simulation to find an experimental probability and make a prediction.

Math On the Spot
my.hrw.com

EXAMPLE 2 Real World   FL   7.SP.3.6

A baseball team has a batting average of 0.250 so far this season. This means that the team's players get hits in 25% of their chances at bat. Use a simulation to predict the number of hits the team's players will have in their next 34 chances at bat.

My Notes

STEP 1 Choose a model.

Batting average $= 0.250 = \frac{250}{1,000} = \frac{1}{4}$

A standard deck of cards has four suits, hearts, diamonds, spades, and clubs. Since $\frac{1}{4}$ of the cards are hearts, you can let hearts represent a "hit." Diamonds, clubs, and spades then represent "no hit."

STEP 2 Perform the simulation.

Draw a card at random from the deck, record the result, and put the card back into the deck. Continue until you have drawn and replaced 34 cards in all.

> Since the team has 34 chances at bat, you must draw a card 34 times.

(H = heart, D = diamond, C = club, S = spade)

```
H  D  D  S  H  C  H  S  D  H  C  D  C  C  D  H  H
S  D  D  H  C  C  H  C  H  H  D  S  S  S  C  H  D
```

STEP 3 Make a prediction.

Count the number of hearts in the simulation.

Since there are 11 hearts, you can predict that the team will have 11 hits in its next 34 chances at bat.

Personal Math Trainer

Online Assessment and Intervention

ⓞ **my.hrw.com**

YOUR TURN

8. A toy machine has equal numbers of red, white, and blue foam balls which it releases at random. Ross wonders which color ball will be released next. Describe how you could use a standard number cube to predict the answer.

_____

_____

_____

_____

_____

Guided Practice

1. A spinner has four sections lettered A, B, C, and D. The table shows the results of several spins. Find the experimental probability of spinning each letter as a fraction in simplest form, a decimal, and a percent. (Explore Activity and Example 1)

Letter	A	B	C	D
Frequency	14	7	11	8

A: _____   B: _____

C: _____   D: _____

2. Rachel's free-throw average for basketball is 60%. She wants to predict how many times in the next 50 tries she will make a free throw. Describe how she could use 10 index cards to predict the answer. (Example 2)

_____

_____

_____

? ESSENTIAL QUESTION CHECK-IN

3. **Essential Question Follow Up** How do you find an experimental probability of a simple event?

_____

_____

212 Unit 4

7.2 Independent Practice

FL 7.SP.3.6, 7.SP.3.7b

Personal Math Trainer

Online Assessment and Intervention

my.hrw.com

4. Dree rolls a strike in 6 out of the 10 frames of bowling. What is the experimental probability that Dree will roll a strike in the first frame of the next game? Explain why a number cube would not be a good way to simulate this situation.

_____

_____

_____

5. To play a game, you spin a spinner like the one shown. You win if the arrow lands in one of the areas marked "WIN". Lee played this game many times and recorded her results. She won 8 times and lost 40 times. Use Lee's data to explain how to find the experimental probability of winning this game.

_____

_____

6. The names of the students in Mr. Hayes' math class are written on the board. Mr. Hayes writes each name on an index card and shuffles the cards. Each day he randomly draws a card, and the chosen student explains a math problem at the board. What is the probability that Ryan is chosen today? What is the probability that Ryan is **not** chosen today?

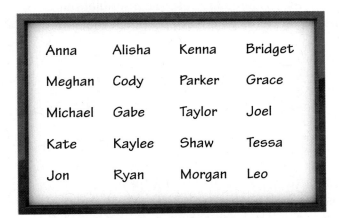

Anna	Alisha	Kenna	Bridget
Meghan	Cody	Parker	Grace
Michael	Gabe	Taylor	Joel
Kate	Kaylee	Shaw	Tessa
Jon	Ryan	Morgan	Leo

_____

7. **Critique Reasoning** A meteorologist reports an 80% chance of precipitation. Is this an example of experimental probability, written as a percent? Explain your reasoning.

_____

8. Mica and Joan are on the same softball team. Mica got 8 hits out of 48 times at bat, while Joan got 12 hits out of 40 times at bat. Who do you think is more likely to get a hit her next time at bat? Explain.

_____

_____

9. Make a Prediction In tennis, Gabby serves an ace, a ball that can't be returned, 4 out of the 10 times she serves. What is the experimental probability that Gabby will serve an ace in the first match of the next game? Make a prediction about how many aces Gabby will have for the next 40 serves. Justify your reasoning.

_____

10. Represent Real-World Problems Patricia finds that the experimental probability that her dog will want to go outside between 4 P.M. and 5 P.M. is $\frac{7}{12}$. About what percent of the time does her dog **not** want to go out between 4 P.M. and 5 P.M.?

_____

H.O.T. ‖ **FOCUS ON HIGHER ORDER THINKING**

Work Area

11. Explain the Error Talia tossed a penny many times. She got 40 heads and 60 tails. She said the experimental probability of getting heads was $\frac{40}{60}$. Explain and correct her error.

_____

12. Communicate Mathematical Ideas A high school has 438 students, with about the same number of males as females. Describe a simulation to predict how many of the first 50 students who leave school at the end of the day are female.

_____

_____

_____

13. Critical Thinking For a scavenger hunt, Chessa put one coin in each of 10 small boxes. Four coins are quarters, 4 are dimes, and 2 are nickels. How could you simulate choosing one box at random? Would you use the same simulation if you planned to put these coins in your pocket and choose one? Explain your reasoning.

_____

_____

_____

_____

Experimental Probability of Compound Events

FL 7.SP.3.8
Find probabilities of compound events using... tables, ..., and simulation. *Also* 7.SP.3.8a, 7.SP.3.8b, 7.SP.3.8c

ESSENTIAL QUESTION

How do you find the experimental probability of a compound event?

EXPLORE ACTIVITY   FL 7.SP.3.8a, 7.SP.3.8b

Exploring Compound Probability

A **compound event** is an event that includes two or more simple events, such as flipping a coin *and* rolling a number cube. A compound event can include events that depend on each other or are independent. Events are independent if the occurrence of one event does not affect the probability of the other event, such as flipping a coin and rolling a number cube.

A What are the possible outcomes of flipping a coin once?   _____

B What are the possible outcomes of rolling a standard number cube once?   _____

C Complete the list for all possible outcomes for flipping a coin *and* rolling a number cube.

H1, H2, _____, _____, _____, _____, T1, _____, _____, _____, _____, _____

There are _____ possible outcomes for this compound event.

> H1 would mean the coin landed on heads, and the number cube showed a 1.

D Flip a coin and roll a number cube 50 times. Use tally marks to record your results in the table.

	1	2	3	4	5	6
H						
T						

E Based on your data, which compound event had the greatest experimental probability and what was it? The least experimental

probability? _____

F **Draw Conclusions** Did you expect to have the same probability for each possible combination of flips and rolls? Why or why not?

_____

_____

Calculating Experimental Probability of Compound Events

The experimental probability of a compound event can be found using recorded data.

EXAMPLE 1 FL 7.SP.3.8, 7.SP.3.8a

A food trailer serves chicken and records the order size and sides on their orders, as show in the table. What is the experimental probability that the next order is for 3-pieces with cole slaw?

	Green Salad	Macaroni & Cheese	French Fries	Cole Slaw
2 pieces	33	22	52	35
3 pieces	13	55	65	55

STEP 1 Find the total number of trials, or orders.

$$33 + 22 + 52 + 35 + 13 + 55 + 65 + 55 = 330$$

STEP 2 Find the number of orders that are for 3 pieces with cole slaw: 55.

STEP 3 Find the experimental probability.

$$P(\text{3 piece} + \text{slaw}) = \frac{\text{number of 3 piece} + \text{slaw}}{\text{total number of orders}}$$

$$= \frac{55}{330} \quad \text{Substitute the values.}$$

$$= \frac{1}{6} \quad \text{Simplify.}$$

The experimental probability that the next order is for 3 pieces of chicken with cole slaw is $\frac{1}{6}$.

Math Talk

Mathematical Practices

Javier said the total number of orders is 8 and not 330. Is he correct? Explain.

YOUR TURN

1. Drink sales for an afternoon at the school carnival were recorded in the table. What is the experimental probability that the next drink is a small cocoa?

	Soda	Water	Cocoa
Small	77	98	60
Large	68	45	52

_____

Using a Simulation to Make a Prediction

You can use a simulation or model of an experiment to find the experimental probability of compound events.

EXAMPLE 2   FL 7.SP.3.8c

At a street intersection, a vehicle is classified either as a *car* or a *truck*, and it can turn *left*, *right*, or go *straight*. About an equal number of cars and trucks go through the intersection and turn in each direction. Use a simulation to find the experimental probability that the next vehicle will be a car that turns right.

My Notes

STEP 1 Choose a model.
Use a coin toss to model the two vehicle types.
Let Heads = **C**ar and Tails = **T**ruck

Use a spinner divided into 3 equal sectors to represent the *three* directions as shown.

STEP 2 Find the sample space for the compound event.

There are 6 possible outcomes: **C**L, **C**R, **C**S, **T**L, **T**R, **T**S

STEP 3 Perform the simulation.

A coin was tossed and a spinner spun 50 times.
The results are shown in the table.

	Car	Truck
Left	8	9
Right	6	11
Straight	9	7

STEP 4 Find the experimental probability that a car turns right.

$$P(\text{Car turns right}) = \frac{\text{frequency of compound event}}{\text{total number of trials}}$$

$$= \frac{6}{50} \quad \textit{Substitute the values.}$$

$$= \frac{3}{25} \quad \textit{Simplify.}$$

Based on the simulation, the experimental probability is $\frac{3}{25}$ that the next vehicle will be a car that turns right.

Reflect

2. **Make a Prediction** Predict the number of cars that turn right out of 100 vehicles that enter the intersection. Explain your reasoning.

_____

_____

YOUR TURN

3. A jeweler sells necklaces made in three sizes and two different metals. Use the data from a simulation to find the experimental probability that the next necklace sold is a 20-inch gold necklace.

	Silver	Gold
12 in.	12	22
16 in.	16	8
20 in.	5	12

_____

Guided Practice

1. A dentist has 400 male and female patients that range in ages from 10 years old to 50 years old and up as shown in the table. What is the experimental probability that the next patient will be female and in the age range 22–39? (Explore Activity and Example 1)

	Range: 10–21	Range: 22–39	Range: 40–50	Range: 50+
Male	44	66	32	53
Female	36	50	45	74

_____

2. At a car wash, customers can choose the type of wash and whether to use the interior vacuum. Customers are equally likely to choose each type of wash and whether to use the vacuum. Use a simulation to find the experimental probability that the next customer purchases a deluxe wash and no interior vacuum. Describe your simulation. (Example 2)

_____

_____

_____

? **ESSENTIAL QUESTION CHECK-IN**

3. How do you find the experimental probability of a compound event?

_____

_____

7.3 Independent Practice

FL 7.SP.3.8, 7.SP.3.8a, 7.SP.3.8b, 7.SP.3.8c

Personal Math Trainer

Online Assessment and Intervention

my.hrw.com

4. Represent Real-World Problems For the same food trailer mentioned in Example 1, explain how to find the experimental probability that the next order is two pieces of chicken with a green salad.

_____

_____

The school store sells spiral notebooks in four colors and three different sizes. The table shows the sales by size and color for 400 notebooks.

	Red	Green	Blue	Yellow
100 Pages	55	37	26	12
150 Pages	60	44	57	27
200 Pages	23	19	21	19

5. What is the experimental probability that the next customer buys a red notebook with 150 pages?

_____

6. What is the experimental probability that the next customer buys any red notebooks?

_____

7. Analyze Relationships How many possible combined page count and color choices are possible? How does this number relate to the number of page size choices and to the number of color choices?

_____

_____

A middle school English teacher polled random students about how many pages of a book they read per week.

	6th	7th	8th
75 Pages	24	18	22
100 Pages	22	32	24
150 Pages	30	53	25

8. Critique Reasoning Jennie says the experimental probability that a 7th grade student reads at least 100 pages per week is $\frac{16}{125}$. What is her error and the correct experimental probability?

_____

9. Analyze Relationships Based on the data, which group(s) of students should be encouraged to read more? Explain your reasoning.

_____

_____

FOCUS ON HIGHER ORDER THINKING

10. Make a Conjecture Would you expect the probability for the simple event "rolling a 6" to be greater than or less than the probability of the compound event "rolling a 6 and getting heads on a coin"? Explain.

_____

_____

11. Critique Reasoning Donald says he uses a standard number cube for simulations that involve 2, 3, or 6 equal outcomes. Explain how Donald can do this.

_____

_____

_____

12. Draw Conclusions Data collected in a mall recorded the shoe styles worn by 150 male and for 150 female customers. What is the probability that the next customer is male and has an open-toe

	Male	**Female**
Open toe	11	92
Closed toe	139	58

shoe (such as a sandal)? What is the probability that the next male customer has an open-toe shoe? Are the two probabilities the same? Explain.

_____

_____

_____

13. What If? Suppose you wanted to perform a simulation to model the shoe style data shown in the table. Could you use two coins? Explain.

_____

_____

14. Represent Real-World Problems A middle school is made up of grades 6, 7, and 8, and has about the same number of male and female students in each grade. Explain how to use a simulation to find the experimental probability that the first 50 students who arrive at school are male and 7th graders.

_____

_____

_____

_____

Making Predictions with Experimental Probability

FL 7.SP.3.6
Approximate the probability of a chance event by collecting data on the chance process that produces it..., and predict the approximate relative frequency given the probability.

ESSENTIAL QUESTION

How do you make predictions using experimental probability?

Using Experimental Probability to Make a Prediction

Scientists study data to make predictions. You can use probabilities to make predictions in your daily life.

Math On the Spot
my.hrw.com

EXAMPLE 1

FL 7.SP.3.6

Danae found that the experimental probability of her making a bull's-eye when throwing darts is $\frac{2}{10}$, or 20%. Out of 75 throws, about how many bull's-eyes could she predict she would make?

Method 1: Use a proportion.

$\frac{2}{10} = \frac{x}{75}$ Write a proportion. 2 out of 10 is how many out of 75?

$\frac{2}{10} = \frac{x}{75}$
$\times 7.5$

$\frac{2}{10} = \frac{15}{75}$ Since 10 times 7.5 is 75, multiply 2 times 7.5 to find the value of x.
$\times 7.5$

$x = 15$

Method 2: Use a percent equation.

$0.20 \cdot 75 = x$ Find 20% of 75.

$15 = x$

> You can write probabilities as ratios, decimals, or percents.

Danae can predict that she will make about 15 bull's-eye throws out of 75.

YOUR TURN

1. A car rental company sells accident insurance to 24% of its customers. Out of 550 customers, about how many customers are predicted to

   purchase insurance? _____

Personal Math Trainer

Online Assessment and Intervention

my.hrw.com

Using Experimental Probability to Make a Qualitative Prediction

A prediction is something you reasonably expect to happen in the future. A qualitative prediction helps you decide which situation is more likely in general.

EXAMPLE 2

 FL 7.SP.3.6

A doctor's office records data and concludes that, on average, 11% of patients call to reschedule their appointments per week. The office manager predicts that 23 appointments will be rescheduled out of the 240 total appointments during next week. Explain whether the prediction is reasonable.

Method 1: Use a proportion.

$$\frac{11}{100} = \frac{x}{240}$$

Write a proportion. 11 out of 100 is how many out of 240?

$$\frac{11}{100} = \frac{x}{240}$$
$\times 2.4$

> 26.4 is the average number of patients that would call to reschedule.

$\times 2.4$
$$\frac{11}{100} = \frac{26.4}{240}$$
$\times 2.4$

Since 100 times 2.4 is 240, multiply 11 times 2.4 to find the value of x.

$$x = 26.4$$

Method 2: Use a percent equation.

$$0.11 \cdot 240 = x$$ Find 11% of 240.

$$26.4 = x$$ Solve for x.

The prediction of 23 is reasonable but a little low, because 23 is a little less than 26.4.

Reflect

2. Does 26.4 make sense for the number of patients?

_____

_____

YOUR TURN

3. In emails to monthly readers of a newsletter 3% of the emails come back undelivered. The editor predicts that if he sends out 12,372 emails, he will receive 437 notices for undelivered email. Do you agree with his prediction?

Explain. _____

_____

Making a Quantitative Prediction

You can use proportional reasoning to make quantitative predictions and compare options in real-world situations.

Math On the Spot
ⓞ my.hrw.com

EXAMPLE 3 Problem Solving

 FL 7.SP.3.6

An online poll for a movie site shows its polling results for a new movie. If a newspaper surveys 150 people leaving the movie, how many people can it predict will like the movie based on the online poll? Is the movie site's claim accurate if the newspaper has 104 people say they like the movie?

My Notes

Analyze Information

The **answer** is a prediction for how many people out of 150 will like the movie based on the online poll. Also tell whether the 104 people that say they like the movie is enough to support the movie site's claim.

List the important information:
- The online poll says 72% of movie goers like the new movie.
- A newspaper surveys 150 people.

Formulate a Plan

Use a proportion to calculate 72% of the 150 people surveyed.

Solve

$\frac{72}{100} = \frac{x}{150}$ Set up a proportion. 72 out of 100 is how many out of 150?

$\frac{72}{100} = \frac{x}{150}$
   $\times 1.5$

   $\times 1.5$
$\frac{72}{100} = \frac{108}{150}$ Since 100 times 1.5 is 150, multiply 72 times 1.5 to find the value of x.
   $\times 1.5$

$x = 108$

The newspaper can predict that 108 out of 150 people will say they like the movie, based on the online poll.

Justify and Evaluate

Since 108 is close to 104, the newspaper survey and the online poll show that about the same percent of people like the movie.

YOUR TURN

4. On average, 24% of customers who buy shoes in a particular store buy two or more pairs. One weekend, 350 customers purchased shoes. How many can be predicted to buy two or more pairs? If 107 customers buy more than two pairs, did more customers than normal buy two or more pairs?

_____

_____

Guided Practice

1. A baseball player reaches first base 30% of the times he is at bat. Out of 50 times at bat, about how many times will the player reach first base? (Example 1)

_____

2. The experimental probability that it will rain on any given day in Houston, Texas, is about 15%. Out of 365 days, about how many days can residents predict rain? (Example 1)

_____

3. A catalog store has 6% of its orders returned for a refund. The owner predicts that a new candle will have 812 returns out of the 16,824 sold. Do you agree with this prediction? Explain. (Example 2)

_____

_____

4. On a toy assembly line, 3% of the toys are found to be defective. The quality control officer predicts that 872 toys will be found defective out of 24,850 toys made. Do you agree with this prediction? Explain. (Example 2)

_____

_____

5. A light-rail service claims to be on time 98% of the time. Jeanette takes the light-rail 40 times one month, how many times can she predict she will be on time? Is the light-rail's claim accurate if she is late 6 times? (Example 3)

_____

_____

6. On average, a college claims to accept 18% of its applicants. If the college has 5,000 applicants, predict how many will be accepted. If 885 applicants are accepted, is the college's claim accurate? (Example 3)

_____

_____

? ESSENTIAL QUESTION CHECK-IN

7. How do you make predictions using experimental probability?

_____

_____

_____

7.4 Independent Practice

FL 7.SP.3.6

Personal Math Trainer

Online Assessment and Intervention

my.hrw.com

The table shows the number of students in a middle school at the beginning of the year and the percentage that can be expected to move out of the area by the end of the year.

	6th	7th	8th
Number of Students	250	200	150
% Moves	2%	4%	8%

8. How many 7th grade students are expected to move by the end of the year? If 12 students actually moved, did more or fewer 7th grade students move than expected? Justify your answer.

_____

_____

9. **Critique Reasoning** The middle school will lose some of its funding if 50 or more students move away in any year. The principal claims he only loses about 30 students a year. Do the values in the table support his claim? Explain.

_____

_____

_____

10. **Represent Real-World Problems** An airline knows that, on average, the probability that a passenger will not show up for a flight is 6%. If an airplane is fully booked and holds 300 passengers, how many seats are expected to be empty? If the airline overbooked the flight by 10 passengers, about how many passengers are expected to show up for the flight? Justify your answer.

_____

_____

_____

_____

11. **Draw Conclusions** In a doctor's office, an average of 94% of the clients pay on the day of the appointment. If the office has 600 clients per month, how many are expected not to pay on the day of the appointment? If 40 clients do not pay on the day of their appointment in a month, did more or fewer than the average not pay?

_____

12. Counterexamples The soccer coach claimed that, on average, only 80% of the team come to practice each day. The table shows the number of students that came to practice for 8 days. If the team has 20 members, how many team members should come to practice to uphold the coach's claim? Was the coach's claim accurate? Explain your reasoning.

	1	2	3	4	5	6	7	8
Number of Students	18	15	18	17	17	19	20	20

_____

_____

13. What's the Error? Ronnie misses the school bus 1 out of every 30 school days. He sets up the proportion $\frac{1}{30} = \frac{180}{x}$ to predict how many days he will miss the bus in the 180-day school year. What is Ronnie's error?

_____

 FOCUS ON HIGHER ORDER THINKING

Work Area

14. Persevere in Problem Solving A gas pump machine rejects 12% of credit card transactions. If this is twice the normal rejection rate for a normal gas pump, how many out of 500 credit cards transactions would a

normal gas pump machine reject? _____

15. Make Predictions An airline's weekly flight data showed a 98% probability of being on time. If this airline has 15,000 flights in a year, how many flights would you predict to arrive on time? Explain whether you can use the data to predict whether a specific flight with this airline will be on time.

_____

_____

_____

_____

16. Draw Conclusions An average response rate for a marketing letter is 4%, meaning that 4% of the people who receive the letter respond to it. A company writes a new type of marketing letter, sends out 2,400 of them, and gets 65 responses. Explain whether the new type of letter would be considered to be a success.

_____

_____

_____

Ready to Go On?

Personal Math Trainer

Online Assessment and Intervention

⏻ my.hrw.com

7.1 Probability

1. Josue tosses a coin and spins the spinner at the right. What are all the possible outcomes?

_____

7.2 Experimental Probability of Simple Events

2. While bowling with friends, Brandy rolls a strike in 6 out of 10 frames. What is the experimental probability that Brandy will roll

a strike in the first frame of the next game? _____

3. Ben is greeting customers at a music store. Of the first 20 people he sees enter the store, 13 are wearing jackets and 7 are not. What is the experimental probability that the next person to enter the store will be wearing a jacket? _____

7.3 Experimental Probability of Compound Events

4. Auden rolled two number cubes and recorded the results.

Roll #1	Roll #2	Roll #3	Roll #4	Roll #5	Roll #6	Roll #7
2, 1	4, 5	3, 2	2, 2	1, 3	6, 2	5, 3

What is the experimental probability that the sum of the next two numbers rolled is greater than 5? _____

7.4 Making Predictions with Experimental Probability

5. A player on a school baseball team reaches first base $\frac{3}{10}$ of the time he is at bat. Out of 80 times at bat, about how many times would you predict he will reach first base? _____

? **ESSENTIAL QUESTION**

6. How is experimental probability used to make predictions?

_____

_____

_____

Selected Response

1. A frozen yogurt shop offers scoops in cake cones, waffle cones, or cups. You can get vanilla, chocolate, strawberry, pistachio, or coffee flavored frozen yogurt. If you order a single scoop, how many outcomes are in the sample space?

   (A) 3   (C) 8
   (B) 5   (D) 15

2. A bag contains 7 purple beads, 4 blue beads, and 4 pink beads. What is the probability of **not** drawing a pink bead?

   (A) $\frac{4}{15}$ (C) $\frac{8}{15}$
   (B) $\frac{7}{15}$ (D) $\frac{11}{15}$

3. During the month of June, Ava kept track of the number of days she saw birds in her garden. She saw birds on 18 days of the month. What is the experimental probability that she will see birds in her garden on July 1?

   (A) $\frac{1}{18}$ (C) $\frac{1}{2}$
   (B) $\frac{2}{5}$ (D) $\frac{3}{5}$

4. A rectangle has a width of 4 inches and a length of 6 inches. A similar rectangle has a width of 12 inches. What is the length of the similar rectangle?

   (A) 8 inches   (C) 14 inches
   (B) 12 inches   (D) 18 inches

5. The experimental probability of hearing thunder on any given day in Ohio is 30%. Out of 600 days, on about how many days can Ohioans expect to hear thunder?

   (A) 90 days   (C) 210 days
   (B) 180 days   (D) 420 days

6. Isidro tossed two coins several times and then recorded the results in the table below.

Toss 1	Toss 2	Toss 3	Toss 4	Toss 5
H; T	T; T	T; H	H; T	H; H

   What is the experimental probability that both coins will land on the same side on Isidro's next toss?

   (A) $\frac{1}{5}$ (C) $\frac{3}{5}$
   (B) $\frac{2}{5}$ (D) $\frac{4}{5}$

Mini-Task

7. Magdalena had a spinner that was evenly divided into sections of red, blue, and green. She spun the spinner and tossed a coin several times. The table below shows the results.

Trial 1	Trial 2	Trial 3	Trial 4	Trial 5
blue; T	green; T	green; H	red; T	blue; H

   a. What are all the possible outcomes?

   _____

   _____

   b. What experimental probability did Magdalena find for spinning blue? Give your answer as a fraction in simplest form, as a decimal, and as a percent.

   _____

   c. Out of 90 trials, how many times should Magdalena predict she will spin green while tossing tails?

   _____

Theoretical Probability and Simulations

? **ESSENTIAL QUESTION**

How can you use theoretical probability to solve real-world problems?

Real-World Video

my.hrw.com

Many carnival games rely on theoretical probability to set the chance of winning fairly low. Understanding how the game is set up might help you be more likely to win.

GO DIGITAL
my.hrw.com

my.hrw.com

Go digital with your write-in student edition, accessible on any device.

Math On the Spot

Scan with your smart phone to jump directly to the online edition, video tutor, and more.

X²

Animated Math

Interactively explore key concepts to see how math works.

Personal Math Trainer

Get immediate feedback and help as you work through practice sets.

Are YOU Ready?

Complete these exercises to review skills you will need for this module.

Fractions, Decimals, and Percents

EXAMPLE   Write $\frac{3}{8}$ as a decimal and a percent.

$$\begin{array}{r} 0.375 \\ 8\overline{)3.000} \\ -2\,4 \\ \hline 60 \\ -56 \\ \hline 40 \\ -40 \\ \hline 0 \end{array}$$

Write the fraction as a division problem. Write a decimal point and zeros in the dividend.
Place a decimal point in the quotient.
Divide as with whole numbers.

$0.375 = 37.5\%.$ Write the decimal as a percent.

Write each fraction as a decimal and a percent.

1. $\frac{3}{4}$ _____

2. $\frac{2}{5}$ _____

3. $\frac{9}{10}$ _____

4. $\frac{7}{20}$ _____

5. $\frac{7}{8}$ _____

6. $\frac{1}{20}$ _____

7. $\frac{19}{25}$ _____

8. $\frac{23}{50}$ _____

Operations with Fractions

EXAMPLE

$$1 - \frac{7}{12} = \frac{12}{12} - \frac{7}{12}$$

Use the denominator of the fraction to write 1 as a fraction.

$$= \frac{12 - 7}{12}$$

Subtract the numerators.

$$= \frac{5}{12}$$

Simplify.

Find each difference.

9. $1 - \frac{1}{5}$ _____

10. $1 - \frac{2}{9}$ _____

11. $1 - \frac{8}{13}$ _____

12. $1 - \frac{3}{20}$ _____

Multiply Fractions

EXAMPLE

$$\frac{4}{15} \times \frac{5}{6} = \frac{\cancel{4}^{2}}{\cancel{15}_{3}} \times \frac{\cancel{5}^{1}}{\cancel{6}_{3}}$$

Divide by the common factors.

$$= \frac{2}{9}$$

Simplify.

Multiply. Write each product in simplest form.

13. $\frac{8}{15} \times \frac{5}{8}$ _____

14. $\frac{2}{9} \times \frac{3}{4}$ _____

15. $\frac{9}{16} \times \frac{12}{13}$ _____

16. $\frac{7}{10} \times \frac{5}{28}$ _____

Reading Start-Up

Visualize Vocabulary

Use the ✔ words to complete the graphic.

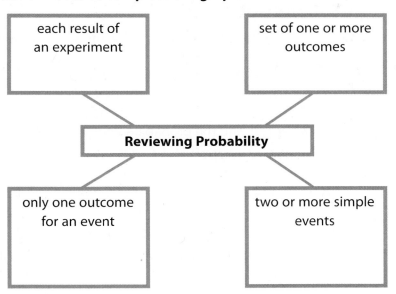

each result of
an experiment

set of one or more
outcomes

Reviewing Probability

only one outcome
for an event

two or more simple
events

Vocabulary

Review Words
  complement
  (complemento)
✔ compound event *(suceso
  compuesto)*
✔ event *(suceso)*
  experiment *(experimento)*
✔ outcome *(resultado)*
✔ simple event *(suceso
  simple)*
  probability *(probabilidad)*

Preview Words
  theoretical probability
  (probabilidad teórica)

Understand Vocabulary

Match the term on the left to the correct expression on the right.

1. compound
   event

2. theoretical
   probability

3. complement

A. The set of all outcomes that are not
the desired event.

B. An event made of two or more
simple events.

C. The ratio of the number of equally
likely outcomes in an event to the
total number of possible outcomes.

Active Reading

Two-Panel Flip Chart Create a two-panel flip
chart, to help you understand the concepts
in this module. Label one flap "Simple Events"
and the other flap "Compound Events." As you
study each lesson, write important ideas under
the appropriate flap. Include information that
will help you remember the concepts later
when you look back at your notes.

Unpacking the Standards

Understanding the standards and the vocabulary terms in the standards will help you know exactly what you are expected to learn in this module.

FL 7.SP.3.7a

Develop a uniform probability model by assigning equal probability to all outcomes, and use the model to determine probabilities of events.

What It Means to You

You will find the probabilities of a simple event and its complement.

UNPACKING EXAMPLE 7.SP.3.7A

Tara has a bag that contains 8 white marbles, 10 green marbles, and 7 red marbles. She selects a marble at random. Find the probability that the marble is red, and the probability that it is **not** red.

$$P(\text{red}) = \frac{\text{number of red marbles}}{\text{total number of marbles}}$$

$$= \frac{7}{25}$$

$$P(\text{not red}) = 1 - P(\text{red}) = 1 - \frac{7}{25} = \frac{25}{25} - \frac{7}{25} = \frac{18}{25}$$

The probability that the marble is red is $\frac{7}{25}$, and the probability that it is not red is $\frac{18}{25}$.

FL 7.SP.3.8b

Represent sample spaces for compound events using methods such as organized lists, tables and tree diagrams. For an event described in everyday language (e.g., "rolling double sixes"), identify the outcomes in the sample space which compose the event.

Key Vocabulary

compound event *(suceso compuesto)*
An event made of two or more simple events.

What It Means to You

You will identify the outcomes in the sample space of a compound event.

UNPACKING EXAMPLE 7.SP.3.8B

Identify the sample space for flipping a coin and rolling a number cube.

Make a table to organize the information.

		Number Cube Outcomes					
		1	2	3	4	5	6
C O I N	H	H1	H2	H3	H4	H5	H6
	T	T1	T2	T3	T4	T5	T6

The sample space includes 12 possible outcomes: H1, H2, H3, H4, H5, H6, T1, T2, T3, T4, T5, and T6.

Theoretical Probability of Simple Events

FL 7.SP.3.7a

Develop a uniform probability model by assigning equal probability to all outcomes, and use the model to determine probabilities of events. *Also 7.SP.3.6, 7.SP.3.7*

ESSENTIAL QUESTION

How can you find the theoretical probability of a simple event?

EXPLORE ACTIVITY 1 **FL** 7.SP.3.7a

Finding Theoretical Probability

In previous lessons, you found probabilities based on observing data, or experimental probabilities. In this lesson, you will find *theoretical probabilities*.

At a school fair, you have a choice of spinning Spinner A or Spinner B. You win an MP3 player if the spinner lands on a section with a star in it. Which spinner should you choose if you want a better chance of winning?

A Complete the table.

Spinner A

	Spinner A	**Spinner B**
Total number of outcomes		
Number of sections with stars		
$P(\text{winning MP3})$ $= \dfrac{\text{number of sections with stars}}{\text{total number of outcomes}}$		

Spinner B

B Compare the ratios for Spinner A and Spinner B.

The ratio for Spinner _____ is greater than the ratio for Spinner _____.

I should choose _____ for a better chance of winning.

Reflect

1. *Theoretical probability* is a way to describe how you found the chance of winning an MP3 player in the scenario above. Using the spinner example to help you, explain in your own words how to find the theoretical probability of an event.

_____

_____

_____

Math Talk
Mathematical Practices

Describe a way to change Spinner B to make your chances of winning equal to your chances of not winning. Explain.

Math On the Spot

my.hrw.com

Calculating Theoretical Probability of Simple Events

Theoretical probability is the probability that an event occurs when all of the outcomes of the experiment are equally likely.

> **Theoretical Probability**
>
> $$P(\text{event}) = \frac{\text{number of ways the event can occur}}{\text{total number of equally likely outcomes}}$$

Probability can be written as a fraction, a decimal, or a percent. For example, the probability you win with Spinner B is $\frac{5}{16}$. You can also write that as 0.3125 or as 31.25%.

EXAMPLE 1

 FL 7.SP.3.7a

A bag contains 6 red marbles and 12 blue ones. You select one marble at random from the bag. What is the probability that you select a red marble? Write your answer in simplest form.

STEP 1 Find the number of ways the event can occur, that is, the number of red marbles: 6

STEP 2 Add to find the total number of equally likely outcomes.

number of red marbles	+	number of blue marbles	=	total number of marbles
6	+	12	=	**18**

There are 18 possible outcomes in the sample space.

STEP 3 Find the probability of selecting a red marble.

$$P(\text{red marble}) = \frac{\text{number of red marbles}}{\text{total number of marbles}} = \frac{6}{18}$$

The probability that you select a red marble is $\frac{6}{18}$, or $\frac{1}{3}$.

Math Talk
Mathematical Practices

Describe a situation that has a theoretical probability of $\frac{1}{4}$.

YOUR TURN

2. You roll a number cube one time. What is the probability that you roll a 3 or 4? Write your answer in simplest form.

$$P(\text{rolling a 3 or 4}) = \frac{\quad}{\quad} = \frac{\ }{\ } = \frac{\ }{\ }$$

3. How is the sample space for an event related to the formula for theoretical probability? _____

_____

Personal Math Trainer

Online Assessment and Intervention

 my.hrw.com

Comparing Theoretical and Experimental Probability

Now that you have calculated theoretical probabilities, you may wonder how theoretical and experimental probabilities compare.

Six students are performing in a talent contest. You roll a number cube to determine the order of the performances.

STEP 1 You roll the number cube once. Complete the table of theoretical probabilities for the different outcomes.

Number	1	2	3	4	5	6
Theoretical probability						

STEP 2 Predict the number of times each number will be rolled out of 30 total rolls.

1: ☐ times   3: ☐ times   5: ☐ times

2: ☐ times   4: ☐ times   6: ☐ times

STEP 3 Roll a number cube 30 times. Complete the table for the frequency of each number and then find its experimental probability.

Number	1	2	3	4	5	6
Frequency						
Experimental probability						

STEP 4 Look at the tables you completed. How do the experimental probabilities compare with the theoretical probabilities?

_____

_____

STEP 5 **Conjecture** By performing more trials, you tend to get experimental results that are closer to the theoretical probabilities. Combine your table from **Step 3** with those of your classmates to make one table for the class. How do the class experimental probabilities compare with the theoretical probabilities?

_____

_____

Reflect

4. Could the experimental probabilities ever be exactly equal to the theoretical probability? If so, how likely is it? If not, why not?

_____

_____

Guided Practice

At a school fair, you have a choice of randomly picking a ball from Basket A or Basket B. Basket A has 5 green balls, 3 red balls, and 8 yellow balls. Basket B has 7 green balls, 4 red balls, and 9 yellow balls. You can win a digital book reader if you pick a red ball. (Explore Activity 1)

	Basket A	Basket B
Total number of outcomes		
Number of red balls		
$P(\textbf{win}) =$ $\dfrac{\text{number of red balls}}{\text{total number of outcomes}}$		

1. Complete the chart. Write each answer in simplest form.

2. Which basket should you choose if you want the better chance of winning? _____

A spinner has 11 equal-sized sections marked 1 through 11. Find each probability. (Example 1)

3. You spin once and land on an odd number.

$P(\text{odd}) = \dfrac{\text{number of} \quad \text{sections}}{\text{total number of}} = \dfrac{\boxed{}}{\boxed{}}$

4. You spin once and land on an even number.

$P(\text{even}) = \dfrac{\text{number of} \quad \text{sections}}{\text{total number of}} = \dfrac{\boxed{}}{\boxed{}}$

You roll a number cube once.

5. What is the theoretical probability that you roll a 3 or 4? (Example 1) _____

6. Suppose you rolled the number cube 199 more times. Would you expect the experimental probability of rolling a 3 or 4 to be the same as your answer to Exercise 5? (Explore Activity 2)

_____

? ESSENTIAL QUESTION CHECK-IN

7. How can you find the probability of a simple event if the total number of equally likely outcomes is 20?

_____

8.1 Independent Practice

 FL 7.SP.3.7, 7.SP.3.7a

Personal Math Trainer

Online Assessment and Intervention

my.hrw.com

Find the probability of each event. Write each answer as a fraction in simplest form, as a decimal to the nearest hundredth, and as a percent to the nearest whole number.

8. You spin the spinner shown. The spinner lands on yellow.

_____

9. You spin the spinner shown. The spinner lands on blue or green.

_____

10. A jar contains 4 cherry cough drops and 10 honey cough drops. You choose one cough drop without looking. The cough drop is cherry.

_____

11. You pick one card at random from a standard deck of 52 playing cards. You pick a black card.

_____

12. There are 12 pieces of fruit in a bowl. Five are lemons and the rest are limes. You choose a piece of fruit without looking. The piece of fruit is a lime.

_____

13. You choose a movie CD at random from a case containing 8 comedy CDs, 5 science fiction CDs, and 7 adventure CDs. The CD is **not** a comedy.

_____

14. You roll a number cube. You roll a number that is greater than 2 and less than 5.

_____

15. Communicate Mathematical Ideas The theoretical probability of a given event is $\frac{9}{13}$. Explain what each number represents.

_____

_____

_____

16. Leona has 4 nickels, 6 pennies, 4 dimes, and 2 quarters in a change purse. Leona lets her little sister Daisy pick a coin at random. If Daisy is equally likely to pick each type of coin, what is the probability that her coin is worth more than five cents? Explain.

_____

_____

_____

Work Area

17. Critique Reasoning A bowl of flower seeds contains 5 petunia seeds and 15 begonia seeds. Riley calculated the probability that a randomly selected seed is a petunia seed as $\frac{1}{3}$. Describe and correct Riley's error.

_____

_____

_____

18. There are 20 seventh graders and 15 eighth graders in a club. A club president will be chosen at random.

a. Analyze Relationships Compare the probabilities of choosing a seventh grader or an eighth grader.

_____

_____

b. Critical Thinking If a student from one grade is more likely to be chosen than a student from the other, is the method unfair? Explain.

_____

_____

A jar contains 8 red marbles, 10 blue ones, and 2 yellow ones. One marble is chosen at random. The color is recorded in the table, and then it is returned to the jar. This is repeated 40 times.

Red	Blue	Yellow
14	16	10

19. Communicate Mathematical Ideas Use proportional reasoning to explain how you know that for each color, the theoretical and experimental probabilities are not the same.

_____

_____

_____

_____

20. Persevere in Problem Solving For which color marble is the experimental probability closest to the theoretical probability? Explain.

_____

_____

LESSON 8.2 Theoretical Probability of Compound Events

FL 7.SP.3.8

Find probabilities of compound events using organized lists, tables, tree diagrams, ... *7.SP.3.8a, 7.SP.3.8b*

ESSENTIAL QUESTION

How do you find the probability of a compound event?

EXPLORE ACTIVITY FL 7.SP.3.8, 7.SP.3.8a, 7.SP.3.8b

Finding Probability Using a Table

Recall that a compound event consists of two or more simple events. To find the probability of a compound event, you write a ratio of the number of ways the compound event can happen to the total number of equally likely possible outcomes.

Jacob rolls two fair number cubes. Find the probability that the sum of the numbers he rolls is 8.

STEP 1 Use the table to find the sample space for rolling a particular sum on two number cubes. Each cell is the sum of the first number in that row and column.

STEP 2 How many possible outcomes are in the sample space? _____

STEP 3 Circle the outcomes that give the sum of 8.

STEP 4 How many ways are there to roll a sum of 8? _____

STEP 5 What is the probability of rolling a sum of 8? _____

	1	2	3	4	5	6
1						
2						
3						
4						
5						
6						

Reflect

1. Give an example of an event that is more likely than rolling a sum of 8.

_____

2. Give an example of an event that is less likely than rolling a sum of 8.

_____

Finding Probability Using a Tree Diagram

You can also use a tree diagram to calculate theoretical probabilities of compound events.

A deli prepares sandwiches with one type of bread (white or wheat), one type of meat (ham, turkey, or chicken), and one type of cheese (cheddar or Swiss). Each combination is equally likely. Find the probability of choosing a sandwich at random and getting turkey and Swiss on wheat bread.

STEP 1 Make a tree diagram to find the sample space for the compound event.

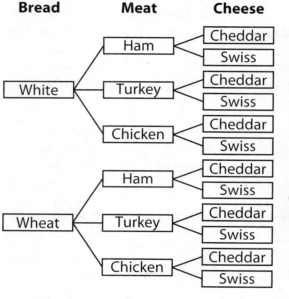

Math Talk

Mathematical Practices

How many sandwich combinations are possible if one of the meat options is unavailable?

STEP 2 Find the number of possible outcomes in the sample space: **12**

STEP 3 Find the probability of choosing turkey and Swiss on wheat bread at random: $\frac{1}{12}$

Personal Math Trainer

Online Assessment and Intervention

⏻ my.hrw.com

YOUR TURN

Use the diagram from Example 1 to find the given probabilities.

3. ham sandwich _____

4. sandwich containing Swiss cheese _____

Finding Probability Using a List

One way to provide security for a locker or personal account is to assign it an access code number known only to the owner.

EXAMPLE 2   **FL** 7.SP.3.8, 7.SP.3.8b

The combination for Khiem's locker is a 3-digit code that uses the numbers 1, 2, and 3. Any of these numbers may be repeated. Find the probability that Khiem's randomly-assigned number is 222.

My Notes

Make an organized list to find the sample space.

STEP 1 List all the codes that start with 1 and have 1 as a second digit.

1	1	1
1	1	2
1	1	3

STEP 2 List all the codes that start with 1 and have 2 as a second digit.

1	2	1
1	2	2
1	2	3

STEP 3 List all the codes that start with 1 and have 3 as a second digit.

1	3	1
1	3	2
1	3	3

STEP 4 You have now listed all the codes that start with 1. Repeat Steps 1–3 for codes that start with 2, and then for codes that start with 3.

2	1	1
2	1	2
2	1	3

2	2	1
2	2	2
2	2	3

2	3	1
2	3	2
2	3	3

3	1	1
3	1	2
3	1	3

3	2	1
3	2	2
3	2	3

3	3	1
3	3	2
3	3	3

> Notice that there are 3 possible first numbers, 3 possible second numbers, and 3 possible third numbers, or $3 \times 3 \times 3 = 27$ numbers in all.

STEP 5 Find the number of outcomes in the sample space by counting all the possible codes. There are **27** such codes.

STEP 6 Find the probability that Khiem's locker code is 222.

$$P(\text{Code } 222) = \frac{\text{number of favorable outcomes}}{\text{total number of possible outcomes}} = \frac{1}{27}$$

Math Talk
Mathematical Practices

How could you find the probability that Khiem's locker code includes exactly two 1s?

YOUR TURN

5. Martha types a 4-digit code into a keypad to unlock her car doors. The code uses the numbers 1 and 0. If the digits are selected at random, what is the probability of getting a code with exactly two 0s? _____

Personal Math Trainer
Online Assessment and Intervention
my.hrw.com

Drake rolls two fair number cubes. (Explore Activity)

1. Complete the table to find the sample space for rolling a particular product on two number cubes.

	1	2	3	4	5	6
1						
2						
3						
4						
5						
6						

2. What is the probability that the product of the two numbers Drake rolls is a multiple of 4?_____

3. What is the probability that the product of the two numbers Drake rolls is less than 13? _____

You flip three coins and want to explore probabilities of certain events. (Examples 1 and 2)

4. Complete the tree diagram and make a list to find the sample space.

List: HHH   HHT ____ ____   T___ T___ ____ ____

5. How many outcomes are in the sample space? _____

6. List all the ways to get three tails. _____

7. Complete the expression to find the probability of getting three tails.

$P = \dfrac{\text{number of outcomes with } \boxed{}}{\text{total number of possible outcomes}} = \dfrac{\boxed{}}{\boxed{}}$

The probability of getting three tails when three coins are flipped is _____.

8. What is the probability of getting exactly two heads?

There are _____ way(s) to obtain exactly two heads: HHT, _____

$P = \dfrac{\text{number of outcomes with } \boxed{}}{\text{total number of possible outcomes}} = \dfrac{\boxed{}}{\boxed{}}$

? ESSENTIAL QUESTION CHECK-IN

9. There are 6 ways a given compound event can occur. What else do you need to know to find the theoretical probability of the event?

_____

8.2 Independent Practice

FL 7.SP.3.8, 7.SP.3.8a, 7.SP.3.8b

Personal Math Trainer

Online Assessment and Intervention

my.hrw.com

In Exercises 10–12, use the following information. Mattias gets dressed in the dark one morning and chooses his clothes at random. He chooses a shirt (green, red, or yellow), a pair of pants (black or blue), and a pair of shoes (checkered or red).

10. Use the space below to make a tree diagram to find the sample space.

11. What is the probability that Mattias picks an outfit at random that includes red shoes? _____

12. What is the probability that no part of Mattias's outfit is red? _____

13. Rhee and Pamela are two of the five members of a band. Every week, the band picks two members at random to play on their own for five minutes. What is the probability that Rhee and Pamela are chosen this week? _____

14. Ben rolls two number cubes. What is the probability that the sum of the numbers he rolls is less than 6? _____

15. Nhan is getting dressed. He considers two different shirts, three pairs of pants, and three pairs of shoes. He chooses one of each of the articles at random. What is the probability that he will wear his jeans but not his sneakers?

Shirt	Pants	Shoes
collared	khakis	sneakers
T-shirt	jeans	flip-flops
	shorts	sandals

_____

16. **Communicate Mathematical Ideas** A ski resort has 3 chair lifts, each with access to 6 ski trails. Explain how you can find the number of possible outcomes when choosing a chair lift and a ski trail without making a list, a tree diagram, or table.

_____
_____
_____
_____

17. **Explain the Error** For breakfast, Sarah can choose eggs, granola or oatmeal as a main course, and orange juice or milk for a drink. Sarah says that the sample space for choosing one of each contains $3^2 = 9$ outcomes. What is her error? Explain.

_____
_____
_____

18. Represent Real-World Problems A new shoe comes in two colors, black or red, and in sizes from 5 to 12, including half sizes. If a pair of the shoes is chosen at random for a store display, what is the probability it will be

red and size 9 or larger? _____

H.O.T. FOCUS ON HIGHER ORDER THINKING

Work Area

19. Analyze Relationships At a diner, Sondra tells the server, "Give me one item from each column." Gretchen says, "Give me one main dish and a vegetable." Who has a greater probability of getting a meal that includes salmon? Explain.

Main Dish	Vegetable	Side
Pasta	Carrots	Tomato soup
Salmon	Peas	Tossed salad
Beef	Asparagus	
Pork	Sweet potato	

_____

_____

20. The digits 1 through 5 are used for a set of locker codes.

a. Look for a Pattern Suppose the digits cannot repeat. Find the number of possible two-digit codes and three-digit codes. Describe any pattern and use it to predict the number of possible five-digit codes.

_____

_____

_____

b. Look for a Pattern Repeat part **a**, but allow digits to repeat.

_____

_____

_____

c. Justify Reasoning Suppose that a gym plans to issue numbered locker codes by choosing the digits at random. Should the gym use codes in which the digits can repeat or not? Justify your reasoning.

_____

_____

_____

244 Unit 4

Making Predictions with Theoretical Probability

FL 7.SP.3.6

... predict the approximate relative frequency given the probability. *Also 7.SP.3.7a*

ESSENTIAL QUESTION

How do you make predictions using theoretical probability?

Using Theoretical Probability to Make a Quantitative Prediction

You can make quantitative predictions based on theoretical probability just as you did with experimental probability earlier.

Math On the Spot

⏻ my.hrw.com

EXAMPLE 1   FL 7.SP.3.6

My Notes

A **You roll a standard number cube 150 times. Predict how many times you will roll a 3 or a 4.**

The probability of rolling a 3 or a 4 is $\frac{2}{6} = \frac{1}{3}$.

Method 1: Set up a proportion.

$$\frac{1}{3} = \frac{x}{150}$$ Write a proportion. 1 out of 3 is how many out of 150?

$$\frac{1}{3} = \frac{x}{150}$$
$\times 50$

$\times 50$
$$\frac{1}{3} = \frac{50}{150}$$ Since 3 times 50 is 150, multiply 1 times 50 to find the value of x.

$$x = 50$$

Method 2: Set up an equation and solve.

p(rolling a 3 or 4) · Number of events = Prediction

$$\frac{1}{3} \cdot 150 = x$$ Multiply the probability by the total number of rolls.

$$50 = x$$ Solve for x.

You can expect to roll a 3 or a 4 about 50 times out of 150.

B Celia volunteers at her local animal shelter. She has an equally likely chance to be assigned to the dog, cat, bird, or reptile section. If she volunteers 24 times, about how many times should she expect to be assigned to the dog section?

Set up a proportion. The probability of being assigned to the dog section is $\frac{1}{4}$.

$$\frac{1}{4} = \frac{x}{24}$$ *Write a proportion. 1 out of 4 is how many out of 24?*

$$\frac{1}{4} = \frac{x}{24}$$
$$\searrow \times 6 \nearrow$$

$$\nearrow \times 6 \searrow$$
$$\frac{1}{4} = \frac{x}{24}$$ *Since 4 times 6 is 24, multiply 1 times 6 to find the value of x.*

$$x = 6$$

Celia can expect to be assigned to the dog section about 6 times out of 24.

YOUR TURN

1. Predict how many times you will roll a number less than 5 if you roll a standard number cube 250 times.

_____

2. You flip a fair coin 18 times. About how many times would you expect heads to appear?

_____

Using Theoretical Probability to Make a Qualitative Prediction

Earlier, you learned how to make predictions using experimental probability. You can use theoretical probabilities in the same way to help you predict or compare how likely events are.

EXAMPLE 2 **Real World**   FL   7.SP.3.6, 7.SP.3.7a

A Herschel pulls a sock out of his drawer without looking and puts it on. The sock is black. There are 7 black socks, 8 white socks, and 5 striped socks left in the drawer. He pulls out a second sock without looking. Is it likely that he will be wearing matching socks to school?

Find the theoretical probability that Herschel picks a matching sock and the probability that he picks one that does not match.

$P(\text{matching}) = \frac{7}{20}$ $P(\text{not matching}) = 1 - \frac{7}{20} = \frac{13}{20}$

> $P(\text{not matching}) = 1 - P(\text{matching})$

The probability that Herschel picks a matching sock is about half the probability that he picks one that does not match. It is likely that he will **not** be wearing matching socks to school.

B All 2,000 customers at a gym are randomly assigned a 3-digit security code that they use to access their online accounts. The codes are made up of the digits 0 through 4, and the digits can be repeated. Is it likely that fewer than 10 of the customers are issued the code 103?

Set up a proportion. The probability of the code 103 is $\frac{1}{125}$.

$\frac{1}{125} = \frac{x}{2,000}$

Write a proportion. 1 out of 125 is how many out of 2,000?

$\frac{1}{125} = \frac{16}{2,000}$ (×16)

Since 125 times 16 is 2,000, multiply 1 times 16 to find the value of x.

> There are 5 possible first numbers, 5 possible second numbers, and 5 possible third numbers. So, the probability of any one code is $\frac{1}{5} \cdot \frac{1}{5} \cdot \frac{1}{5} = \frac{1}{125}$.

It is **not** likely that fewer than 10 of the customers get the same code. It is more likely that 16 members get the code 103.

YOUR TURN

3. A bag of marbles contains 8 red marbles, 4 blue marbles, and 5 white marbles. Tom picks a marble at random. Is it more likely that he picks a red marble or a marble of another color?

_____

4. At a fundraiser, a school group charges $6 for tickets for a "grab bag." You choose one bill at random from a bag that contains 40 $1 bills, 20 $5 bills, 5 $10 bills, 5 $20 bills, and 1 $100 bill. Is it likely that you will win enough to pay for your ticket? Justify your answer.

_____

_____

_____

Personal Math Trainer

Online Assessment and Intervention

⊙ my.hrw.com

1. Bob works at a construction company. He has an equally likely chance to be assigned to work different crews every day. He can be assigned to work on crews building apartments, condominiums, or houses. If he works 18 days a month, about how many times should he expect to be assigned to the house crew? (Example 1)

STEP 1 Find the probabilities of being assigned to each crew.

Apartment ☐   Condo ☐   House ☐

The probability of being assigned to the house crew is _____

STEP 2 Set up and solve a proportion.

$$\frac{\boxed{}}{\boxed{}} = \frac{x}{\boxed{}} \quad x = \underline{\quad\quad}$$

Bob can expect to be assigned to the house crew about

_____ times out of 18.

2. During a raffle drawing, half of the ticket holders will receive a prize. The winners are equally likely to win one of three prizes: a book, a gift certificate to a restaurant, or a movie ticket. If there are 300 ticket holders, predict the

number of people who will win a movie ticket. (Example 1) _____

3. In Mr. Jawarani's first period math class, there are 9 students with hazel eyes, 10 students with brown eyes, 7 students with blue eyes, and 2 students with green eyes. Mr. Jawarani picks a student at random. Which color eyes is the student most likely to have? Explain. (Example 2)

_____

_____

_____

? ESSENTIAL QUESTION CHECK-IN

4. How do you make predictions using theoretical probability?

_____

_____

_____

8.3 Independent Practice

 FL 7.SP.3.6, 7.SP.3.7a

Personal Math Trainer

Online Assessment and Intervention

my.hrw.com

5. A bag contains 6 red marbles, 2 white marbles, and 1 gray marble. You randomly pick out a marble, record its color, and put it back in the bag. You repeat this process 45 times. How many white or gray marbles do you expect to get?

_____

6. Using the blank circle below, draw a spinner with 8 equal sections and 3 colors—red, green, and yellow. The spinner should be such that you are equally likely to land on green or yellow, but more likely to land on red than either on green or yellow.

Use the following for Exercises 7–9. In a standard 52-card deck, half of the cards are red and half are black. The 52 cards are divided evenly into 4 suits: spades, hearts, diamonds, and clubs. Each suit has three face cards (jack, queen, king), and an ace. Each suit also has 9 cards numbered from 2 to 10.

7. Dawn draws 1 card, replaces it, and draws another card. Is it more likely that she draws 2 red cards or 2 face cards?

_____

_____

8. Luis draws 1 card from a deck, 39 times. Predict how many times he draws an ace.

_____

9. Suppose a solitaire player has played 1,000 games. Predict how many times the player turned over a red card as the first card.

_____

10. John and O'Neal are playing a board game in which they roll two number cubes. John needs to get a sum of 8 on the number cubes to win. O'Neal needs a sum of 11. If they take turns rolling the number cube, who is more likely to win? Explain.

_____

_____

_____

11. Every day, Navya's teacher randomly picks a number from 1 to 20 to be the number of the day. The number of the day can be repeated. There are 180 days in the school year. Predict how many days the number of

the day will be greater than 15. _____

12. Eben rolls two standard number cubes 36 times. Predict how many times he will

roll a sum of 4. _____

13. **Communicate Mathematical Ideas** Can you always show that a prediction based on theoretical probability is true by performing the event often enough? If so, explain why. If not, describe a situation that justifies your response.

_____

_____

_____

_____

_____

14. Represent Real-World Problems Give a real-world example of an experiment in which all of the outcomes are not equally likely. Can you make a prediction for this experiment, using theoretical probability?

_____

_____

_____

_____

_____

H.O.T. FOCUS ON HIGHER ORDER THINKING

15. Critical Thinking Pierre asks Sherry a question involving the theoretical probability of a compound event in which you flip a coin and draw a marble from a bag of marbles. The bag of marbles contains 3 white marbles, 8 green marbles, and 9 black marbles. Sherry's answer, which is correct, is $\frac{12}{40}$. What was Pierre's question?

_____

_____

_____

16. Make a Prediction Horace is going to roll a standard number cube and flip a coin. He wonders if it is more likely that he rolls a 5 **and** the coin lands on heads, or that he rolls a 5 **or** the coin lands on heads. Which event do you think is more likely to happen? Find the probability of both events to justify or reject your initial prediction.

_____

_____

_____

_____

17. Communicate Mathematical Ideas Cecil solved a theoretical prediction problem and got this answer: "The spinner will land on the red section 4.5 times." Is it possible to have a prediction that is not a whole number? If so, give an example.

_____

_____

_____

_____

Using Technology to Conduct a Simulation

FL 7.SP.3.8c
Design and use a simulation to generate frequencies for compound events. *Also* 7.SP.3.8

ESSENTIAL QUESTION

How can you use technology simulations to estimate probabilities?

Designing and Conducting a Simulation for a Simple Event

You can use a graphing calculator or computer to generate random numbers and conduct a simulation.

Math On the Spot
my.hrw.com

EXAMPLE 1 FL 7.SP.3.8c

A cereal company is having a contest. There are codes for winning prizes in 30% of its cereal boxes. Find an experimental probability that you have to buy *exactly* 3 boxes of cereal before you find a winning code.

STEP 1 Choose a model.

The probability of finding a winning code is $30\% = \frac{3}{10}$.

Use whole numbers from 1 to 10.
Let three numbers represent buying a box with a winning code.

Winning code: 1, 2, 3   Nonwinning code: 4, 5, 6, 7, 8, 9, 10

STEP 2 Generate random numbers from 1 to 10 until you get one that represents a box with a winning code. Record how many boxes you bought before finding a winning code.

5 numbers generated: 9, 6, 7, 8, 1 1 represents a box with a winning code.

STEP 3 Perform multiple trials by repeating Step 2.

STEP 4 Find the experimental probability.

In 1 of 10 trials, you bought exactly 3 boxes of cereal before finding a winning code. The experimental probability is $\frac{1}{10}$, or 10%.

Trial	Numbers generated	Boxes bought
1	9, 6, 7, 8, 1	5
2	2	1
3	10, 4, 8, 1	4
4	4, 10, 7, 1	4
5	2	1
6	4, 3	2
7	3	1
8	7, 5, 2	3
9	8, 5, 4, 8, 10, 3	6
10	9, 1	2

Animated Math
my.hrw.com

Trial 8 represents a winning code after buying 3 boxes.

Math Talk

Mathematical Practices

Could you generate random numbers from a list of more than 2 numbers? Explain.

1. An elephant has a 50% chance of giving birth to a male or a female calf. Use a simulation to find an experimental probability that the elephant gives birth to 3 male calves before having a female calf. (*Hint:* Use 0s and 1s. Let 0 represent a male calf, and 1 represent a female calf. Generate random numbers until you get a 1.)

Trial	Numbers generated	3 Males first	Trial	Numbers generated	3 Males first
1			6		
2			7		
3			8		
4			9		
5			10		

Designing and Conducting a Simulation for a Compound Event

You can use random numbers to simulate compound events as well as simple events.

EXAMPLE 2 FL 7.SP.3.8c, 7.SP.3.8

Suppose that there is a 20% chance that a particular volcano will erupt in any given decade. Find an experimental probability that the volcano will erupt in at least 1 of the next 5 decades.

STEP 1 Choose a model.

The probability of an eruption is $20\% = \frac{1}{5}$. Use whole numbers from 1 to 5.

Let 1 represent a decade with an eruption.

Let 2, 3, 4, and 5 represent a decade without an eruption.

STEP 2 Generate 5 random numbers from 1 to 5. Record the number of decades with an eruption.

5 numbers generated: 3, 1, 3, 4, 2   Eruption decades: 1

STEP 3 Perform multiple trials by repeating Step 2. Calculate the percent of trials in which there was an eruption in at least 1 of the 5 decades.

Trial	Numbers generated	Eruption decades
1	3, 1, 3, 4, 2	1
2	3, 2, 2, 4, 5	0
3	1, 3, 3, 2, 5	1
4	5, 3, 4, 5, 4	0
5	5, 5, 3, 2, 4	0

Trial	Numbers generated	Eruption decades
6	2, 3, 3, 4, 2	0
7	1, 2, 4, 1, 4	2
8	1, 3, 2, 1, 5	2
9	1, 2, 4, 2, 5	1
10	5, 5, 3, 2, 4	0

In 5 out of the 10 trials, there was an eruption in at least 1 of the 5 decades. The experimental probability of an eruption in at least 1 of the next 5 decades is $\frac{5}{10} = 50\%$.

YOUR TURN

2. Matt guesses the answers on a quiz with 5 true-false questions. The probability of guessing a correct answer on each question is 50%. Use a simulation to find an experimental probability that he gets at least 2 questions right. (*Hint:* Use 0s and 1s. Let 0s represent incorrect answers, and 1s represent correct answers. Perform 10 trials, generating 5 random numbers in each, and count the number of 1s.)

Trial	Numbers generated	Correct answers
1		
2		
3		
4		
5		

Trial	Numbers generated	Correct answers
6		
7		
8		
9		
10		

Personal Math Trainer

Online Assessment and Intervention

my.hrw.com

There is a 30% chance that T'Shana's county will have a drought during any given year. She performs a simulation to find the experimental probability of a drought in at least 1 of the next 4 years. (Examples 1 and 2)

1. T'Shana's model involves the whole numbers from 1 to 10. Complete the description of her model.

   Let the numbers 1 to 3 represent [   ]

   and the numbers 4 to 10 represent [   ]

   Perform multiple trials, generating [   ] random numbers each time.

2. Suppose T'Shana used the model described in Exercise 1 and got the results shown in the table. Complete the table.

Trial	Numbers generated	Drought years
1	10, 3, 5, 1	
2	10, 4, 6, 5	
3	3, 2, 10, 3	
4	2, 10, 4, 4	
5	7, 3, 6, 3	

Trial	Numbers generated	Drought years
6	8, 4, 8, 5	
7	6, 2, 2, 8	
8	6, 5, 2, 4	
9	2, 2, 3, 2	
10	6, 3, 1, 5	

3. According to the simulation, what is the experimental probability that there will be a drought in the county in at least 1 of the next 4 years? _____

? ESSENTIAL QUESTION CHECK-IN

4. You want to generate random numbers to simulate an event with a 75% chance of occurring. Describe a model you could use.

   _____

   _____

   _____

   _____

8.4 Independent Practice

 FL 7.SP.3.8, 7.SP.3.8c

Personal
Math Trainer

Online
Assessment and
Intervention

my.hrw.com

Every contestant on a game show has a 40% chance of winning. In the simulation below, the numbers 1–4 represent a winner, and the numbers 5–10 represent a nonwinner. Numbers were generated until one that represented a winner was produced.

Trial	Numbers generated
1	7, 4
2	6, 5, 2
3	1
4	9, 1
5	3

Trial	Numbers generated
6	8, 8, 6, 2
7	2
8	5, 9, 4
9	10, 3
10	1

5. In how many of the trials did it take exactly 4 contestants to get a winner? _____

6. Based on the simulation, what is the experimental probability that it will take exactly 4 contestants to get a winner? _____

Over a 100-year period, the probability that a hurricane struck Rob's city in any given year was 20%. Rob performed a simulation to find an experimental probability that a hurricane would strike the city in at least 4 of the next 10 years. In Rob's simulation, 1 represents a year with a hurricane.

Trial	Numbers generated
1	2, 5, 3, 2, 5, 5, 1, 4, 5, 2
2	1, 1, 5, 2, 2, 1, 3, 1, 1, 5
3	4, 5, 4, 5, 5, 4, 3, 5, 1, 1
4	1, 5, 5, 5, 1, 2, 2, 3, 5, 3
5	5, 1, 5, 3, 5, 3, 4, 5, 3, 2

Trial	Numbers generated
6	1, 1, 5, 5, 1, 4, 2, 2, 3, 4
7	2, 1, 5, 3, 1, 5, 1, 2, 1, 4
8	2, 4, 3, 2, 4, 4, 2, 1, 3, 1
9	3, 2, 1, 4, 5, 3, 5, 5, 1, 2
10	3, 4, 2, 4, 3, 5, 2, 3, 5, 1

7. According to Rob's simulation, what was the experimental probability that a hurricane would strike the city in at least 4 of the next 10 years? _____

8. **Analyze Relationships** Suppose that over the 10 years following Rob's simulation, there was actually 1 year in which a hurricane struck. How did this compare to the results of Rob's simulation?

_____

_____

9. **Communicate Mathematical Ideas** You generate three random whole numbers from 1 to 10. Do you think that it is unlikely or even impossible that all of the numbers could be 10? Explain?

_____

_____

_____

_____

_____

10. Erika collects baseball cards, and 60% of the packs contain a player from her favorite team. Use a simulation to find an experimental probability that she has to buy exactly 2 packs before she gets a player from her favorite team.

_____

_____

H.O.T. FOCUS ON HIGHER ORDER THINKING

Work Area

11. **Represent Real-World Problems** When Kate plays basketball, she usually makes 37.5% of her shots. Design and conduct a simulation to find the experimental probability that she makes at least 3 of her next 10 shots. Justify the model for your simulation.

_____

_____

_____

_____

_____

_____

12. **Justify Reasoning** George and Susannah used a simulation to simulate the flipping of 8 coins 50 times. In all of the trials, at least 5 heads came up. What can you say about their simulation? Explain.

_____

_____

_____

_____

Ready to Go On?

Personal Math Trainer

Online Assessment and Intervention

my.hrw.com

8.1, 8.2 Theoretical Probability of Simple and Compound Events

Find the probability of each event. Write your answer as a fraction, as a decimal, and as a percent.

1. You choose a marble at random from a bag containing 12 red, 12 blue, 15 green, 9 yellow, and 12 black marbles. The marble is red. _____

2. You draw a card at random from a shuffled deck of 52 cards. The deck has four 13-card suits (diamonds, hearts, clubs, spades). The card is a diamond or a spade. _____

8.3 Making Predictions with Theoretical Probability

3. A bag contains 23 red marbles, 25 green marbles, and 18 blue marbles. You choose a marble at random from the bag. What color marble will you most likely choose? _____

8.4 Using Technology to Conduct a Simulation

4. Bay City has a 25% chance of having a flood in any given decade. The table shows the results of a simulation using random numbers to find the experimental probability that there will be a flood in Bay City in at least 1 of the next 5 decades. In the table, the number 1 represents a decade with a flood. The numbers 2 through 5 represent a decade without a flood.

Trial	Numbers generated	Trial	Numbers generated
1	2, 2, 5, 5, 5	6	4, 2, 2, 5, 4
2	3, 2, 3, 5, 4	7	1, 3, 2, 4, 4
3	5, 5, 5, 4, 3	8	3, 5, 5, 2, 1
4	5, 1, 3, 3, 5	9	4, 3, 3, 2, 5
5	4, 5, 5, 3, 2	10	5, 4, 1, 2, 1

According to the simulation, what is the experimental probability of a flood in Bay City in at least 1 of the next 5 decades? _____

? ESSENTIAL QUESTION

5. How can you use theoretical probability to make predictions in real-world situations?

_____

_____

MODULE 8 **MIXED REVIEW**

Assessment Readiness

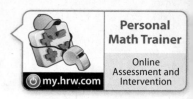

Personal
Math Trainer

Online
Assessment and
Intervention

my.hrw.com

Selected Response

1. What is the probability of flipping two fair coins and having both show tails?

(A) $\frac{1}{8}$ (C) $\frac{1}{3}$

(B) $\frac{1}{4}$ (D) $\frac{1}{2}$

2. A bag contains 8 white marbles and 2 black marbles. You pick out a marble, record its color, and put the marble back in the bag. If you repeat this process 45 times, how many times would you expect to remove a white marble from the bag?

(A) 9   (C) 36

(B) 32   (D) 40

3. Philip rolls a standard number cube 24 times. Which is the best prediction for the number of times he will roll a number that is even and less than 4?

(A) 2   (C) 4

(B) 3   (D) 6

4. A set of cards includes 24 yellow cards, 18 green cards, and 18 blue cards. What is the probability that a card chosen at random is **not** green?

(A) $\frac{3}{10}$ (C) $\frac{3}{5}$

(B) $\frac{4}{10}$ (D) $\frac{7}{10}$

5. A rectangle made of square tiles measures 10 tiles long and 8 tiles wide. What is the width of a similar rectangle whose length is 15 tiles?

(A) 3 tiles   (C) 13 tiles

(B) 12 tiles   (D) 18.75 tiles

6. Which of the following could NOT be a cross section of a rectangular prism?

(A) rectangle   (C) parallelogram

(B) circle   (D) triangle

7. There are 20 tennis balls in a bag. Five are orange, 7 are white, 2 are yellow, and 6 are green. You choose one at random. Which color ball are you **least** likely to choose?

(A) green   (C) white

(B) orange   (D) yellow

Mini-Task

8. Center County has had a 1 in 6 (or about 16.7%) chance of a tornado in any given decade. In a simulation to consider the probability of tornadoes in the next 5 decades, Ava rolled a number cube. She let a 1 represent a decade with a tornado, and 2–6 represent decades without tornadoes. What experimental probability did Ava find for each event?

Trial	Numbers Generated	Trial	Numbers Generated
1	2, 2, 3, 1, 5	6	4, 5, 2, 2, 4
2	3, 5, 6, 4, 5	7	5, 1, 6, 3, 1
3	1, 3, 3, 2, 2	8	1, 2, 1, 2, 4
4	6, 3, 3, 5, 4	9	1, 4, 4, 1, 4
5	4, 1, 4, 4, 4	10	3, 6, 5, 3, 6

a. Center County has a tornado in at least one of the next five decades.

_____

b. Center County has a tornado in exactly one of the next five decades.

_____

Study Guide Review

MODULE 7 Experimental Probability

Key Vocabulary

complement *(complemento)*
compound event *(suceso compuesto)*
event *(suceso)*
experiment *(experimento)*
experimental probability *(probabilidad experimental)*
outcome *(resultado)*
probability *(probabilidad)*
sample space *(espacio muestral)*
simple event *(suceso simple)*
simulation *(simulación)*
trial *(prueba)*

? ESSENTIAL QUESTION

How can you use experimental probability to solve real-world problems?

EXAMPLE 1

What is the probability of picking a red marble from a jar with 5 green marbles and 2 red marbles?

$P(\text{picking a red marble}) = \dfrac{\text{number of red marbles}}{\text{number of total marbles}}$

$= \dfrac{2}{7}$ There are 2 red marbles.
The total number of marbles is $2 + 5 = 7$.

EXAMPLE 2

For one month, a doctor recorded information about new patients as shown in the table.

	Senior	Adult	Young adult	Child
Female	5	8	2	14
Male	3	10	1	17

What is the experimental probability that his next new patient is a female adult?

$P\left(\begin{array}{c}\text{new patient is a}\\ \text{female adult}\end{array}\right) = \dfrac{\text{number of female adults}}{\text{total number of patients}}$

$P = \dfrac{8}{60} = \dfrac{2}{15}$

What is the experimental probability that his next new patient is a child?

$P\left(\begin{array}{c}\text{new patient is}\\ \text{a child}\end{array}\right) = \dfrac{\text{number of children}}{\text{total number of patients}}$

$P = \dfrac{31}{60}$

EXERCISES

Find the probability of each event. (Lesson 7.1)

1. Rolling a 5 on a fair number cube.

_____

2. Picking a 7 from a standard deck of 52 cards. A standard deck includes 4 cards of each number from 2 to 10.

_____

3. Picking a blue marble from a bag of 4 red marbles, 6 blue marbles, and 1 white marble.

_____

4. Rolling a number greater than 7 on a 12-sided number cube.

_____

5. Christopher picked coins randomly from his piggy bank and got the numbers of coins shown in the table. Find each experimental probability. (Lessons 7.2, 7.3)

Penny	Nickel	Dime	Quarter
7	2	8	6

    a. The next coin that Christopher picks is a quarter. _____

    b. The next coin that Christopher picks is not a quarter. _____

    c. The next coin that Christopher picks is a penny or a nickel. _____

6. A grocery store manager found that 54% of customers usually bring their own bags. In one afternoon, 82 out of 124 customers brought their own grocery bags. Did a greater or lesser number of people than usual bring their own bags? (Lesson 7.4)

MODULE **8** # Theoretical Probability

Key Vocabulary
theoretical probability
(probabilidad teórica)

? ESSENTIAL QUESTION

How can you use theoretical probability to solve real-world problems?

EXAMPLE 1

A. Lola rolls two fair number cubes. What is the probability that the two numbers Lola rolls include at least one 4 and have a product of at least 16?

There are 5 pairs of numbers that include a 4 and have a product of at least 16:

(4, 4), (4, 5), (4, 6), (5, 4), (6, 4)

Find the probability.

$$P = \frac{\text{number of possible ways}}{\text{total number of possible outcomes}} = \frac{5}{36}$$

	1	2	3	4	5	6
1	1	2	3	4	5	6
2	2	4	6	8	10	12
3	3	6	9	12	15	18
4	4	8	12	16	20	24
5	5	10	15	20	25	30
6	6	12	18	24	30	36

B. Suppose Lola rolls the two number cubes 180 times. Predict how many times she will roll two numbers that include a pair of numbers like the ones described above.

One way to answer is to write and solve an equation.

$\frac{5}{36} \times 180 = x$ Multiply the probability by the total number of rolls.

      $25 = x$ Solve for x.

Lola can expect to roll two numbers that include at least one 4 and have a product of 16 or more about 25 times.

EXAMPLE 2

A store has a sale bin of soup cans. There are 6 cans of chicken noodle soup, 8 cans of split pea soup, 8 cans of minestrone, and 13 cans of vegetable soup. Find the probability of picking each type of soup at random. Then predict what kind of soup a customer is most likely to pick.

$P(\text{chicken noodle}) = \frac{6}{35}$ $\qquad\qquad$ $P(\text{split pea}) = \frac{8}{35}$

$P(\text{minestrone}) = \frac{8}{35}$ $\qquad\qquad$ $P(\text{vegetable}) = \frac{13}{35}$

The customer is most likely to pick vegetable soup. That is the event that has the greatest probability.

EXERCISES

Find the probability of each event. (Lessons 8.1, 8.2)

1. Graciela picks a white mouse at random from a bin of 8 white mice, 2 gray mice, and 2 brown mice.

   _____

2. Theo spins a spinner that has 12 equal sections marked 1 through 12. It does **not** land on 1.

   _____

3. Tania flips a coin three times. The coin lands on heads twice and on tails once, not necessarily in that order.

   _____

4. Students are randomly assigned two-digit codes. Each digit is either 1, 2, 3, or 4. Guy is given the number 11.

   _____

5. Patty tosses a coin and rolls a number cube. (Lesson 8.3)

   a. Find the probability that the coin lands on heads and the cube lands on an even number.

   _____

   b. Patty tosses the coin and rolls the number cube 60 times. Predict how many times the coin will land on heads and the cube will land on an even number.

   _____

6. Rajan's school is having a raffle. The school sold raffle tickets with 3-digit numbers. Each digit is either 1, 2, or 3. The school also sold 2 tickets with the number 000. Which number is more likely to be picked, 123 or 000? (Lesson 8.3)

   _____

7. Suppose you know that over the last 10 years, the probability that your town would have at least one major storm was 40%. Describe a simulation that you could use to find the experimental probability that your town will have at least one major storm in at least 3 of the next 5 years. (*Lesson 8.4*)

_____

_____

_____

_____

Unit 4 Performance Tasks

1. **CAREERS IN MATH**   Meteorologist   A meteorologist predicts a 20% chance of rain for the next two nights, and a 75% chance of rain on the third night.

   a. On which night is it most likely to rain? On that night, is it *likely* to rain or *unlikely* to rain?

   _____

   b. Tara would like to go camping for the next 3 nights, but will not go if it is likely to rain on all 3 nights. Should she go? Use probability to justify your answer.

   _____

   _____

2. Sinead tossed 4 coins at the same time. She did this 50 times, and 6 of those times, all 4 coins showed the same result (heads or tails).

   a. Find the experimental probability that all 4 coins show the same result when tossed.

   _____

   b. Can you determine the experimental probability that **no** coin shows heads? Explain.

   _____

   c. Suppose Sinead tosses the coins 125 more times. Use experimental probability to predict the number of times that all 4 coins will show heads or tails. Show your work.

   _____

Selected Response

1. A pizza parlor offers thin, thick, and traditional style pizza crusts. You can get pepperoni, beef, mushrooms, olives, or peppers for toppings. You order a one-topping pizza. How many outcomes are in the sample space?

(A) 3   (C) 8

(B) 5   (D) 15

2. A bag contains 9 purple marbles, 2 blue marbles, and 4 pink marbles. The probability of randomly drawing a blue marble is $\frac{2}{15}$. What is the probability of **not** drawing a blue marble?

(A) $\frac{2}{15}$ (C) $\frac{11}{15}$

(B) $\frac{4}{15}$ (D) $\frac{13}{15}$

3. During the month of April, Dora kept track of the bugs she saw in her garden. She saw a ladybug on 23 days of the month. What is the experimental probability that she will see a ladybug on May 1?

(A) $\frac{1}{23}$ (C) $\frac{1}{2}$

(B) $\frac{7}{30}$ (D) $\frac{23}{30}$

4. Ryan flips a coin 8 times and gets tails all 8 times. What is the experimental probability that Ryan will get heads the next time he flips the coin?

(A) 1   (C) $\frac{1}{8}$

(B) $\frac{1}{2}$ (D) 0

5. Angle D is a vertical angle to $\angle F$. The measure of $\angle D$ is 53°. What is the measure of $\angle F$?

(A) 3°   (C) 43°

(B) 37°   (D) 53°

6. Jay tossed two coins several times and then recorded the results in the table below.

Coin Toss Results				
Toss 1	Toss 2	Toss 3	Toss 4	Toss 5
H; H	H; T	T; H	T; T	T; H

What is the experimental probability that the coins will land on different sides on his next toss?

(A) $\frac{1}{5}$ (C) $\frac{3}{5}$

(B) $\frac{2}{5}$ (D) $\frac{4}{5}$

7. What is the probability of tossing two fair coins and having exactly one land tails side up?

(A) $\frac{1}{8}$ (C) $\frac{1}{3}$

(B) $\frac{1}{4}$ (D) $\frac{1}{2}$

8. Which inequality can be used to find how many $0.35 pencils can be purchased for $5.00?

(A) $0.35p \geq 5$ (C) $5p \geq 0.25$

(B) $0.35p \leq 5$ (D) $5p \leq 0.35$

9. A bag contains 6 white beads and 4 black beads. You pick out a bead, record its color, and put the bead back in the bag. You repeat this process 35 times. Which is the best prediction of how many times you would expect to remove a white bead from the bag?

(A) 6   (C) 18

(B) 10   (D) 21

10. A set of cards includes 20 yellow cards, 16 green cards, and 24 blue cards. What is the probability that a blue card is chosen at random?

(A) 0.04   (C) 0.4

(B) 0.24   (D) 0.66

11. Jason, Erik, and Jamie are friends in art class. The teacher randomly chooses 2 of the 21 students in the class to work together on a project. What is the probability that two of these three friends will be chosen?

Ⓐ $\frac{1}{105}$

Ⓑ $\frac{1}{70}$

Ⓒ $\frac{34}{140}$

Ⓓ $\frac{4}{50}$

12. Philip rolls a number cube 12 times. Which is the best prediction for the number of times that he will roll a number that is odd and less than 5?

Ⓐ 2   Ⓒ 4

Ⓑ 3   Ⓓ 6

Estimate your answer before solving the problem. Use your estimate to check the reasonableness of your answer.

13. A survey reveals that one airline's flights have a 92% probability of being on time. Based on this, out of 4000 flights in a year, how many flights would you predict will arrive on time?

Ⓐ 368   Ⓒ 3,680

Ⓑ 386   Ⓓ 3,860

14. Matt's house number is a two-digit number. Neither of the digits is 0 and the house number is even. What is the probability that Matt's house number is 18?

Ⓐ $\frac{1}{45}$ Ⓒ $\frac{1}{18}$

Ⓑ $\frac{1}{36}$ Ⓓ $\frac{1}{16}$

Mini-Tasks

15. Laura picked a crayon randomly from a box, recorded the color, and then placed it back in the box. She repeated the process and recorded the results in the table.

Red	Blue	Yellow	Green
5	6	7	2

Find each experimental probability. Write your answers in simplest form.

a. The next crayon Laura picks is red.

_____

b. The next crayon Laura picks is **not** red.

_____

16. For breakfast, Trevor has a choice of 3 types of bagels (plain, sesame, or multigrain), 2 types of eggs (scrambled or poached), and 2 juices (orange or apple).

a. Use the space below to make a tree diagram to find the sample space.

b. If he chooses at random, what is the probability that Trevor eats a breakfast that has orange juice?

_____

Real Numbers, Exponents, and Scientific Notation

MODULE 9

Real Numbers

FL 8.NS.1.1, 8.NS.1.2, 8.EE.1.2

MODULE 10

Exponents and Scientific Notation

FL 8.EE.1.1, 8.EE.1.3, 8.EE.1.4

CAREERS IN MATH

Astronomer An astronomer is a scientist who studies and tries to interpret the universe beyond Earth. Astronomers use math to calculate distances to celestial objects and to create mathematical models to help them understand the dynamics of systems from stars and planets to black holes. If you are interested in a career as an astronomer, you should study the following mathematical subjects:

- Algebra
- Geometry
- Trigonometry
- Calculus

Research other careers that require creating mathematical models to understand physical phenomena.

Unit 5 Performance Task

At the end of the unit, check out how **astronomers** use math.

Vocabulary Preview

Use the puzzle to preview key vocabulary from this unit. Unscramble the circled letters to answer the riddle at the bottom of the page.

1. **TCREEFP SEAQUR**

2. **NOLRATAI RUNMEB**

3. **PERTIANEG MALCEDI**

4. **LAER SEBMNUR**

5. **NIISICFTCE OITANTON**

1. Has integers as its square roots. (Lesson 9.1)
2. Any number that can be written as a ratio of two integers. (Lesson 9.1)
3. A decimal in which one or more digits repeat infinitely. (Lesson 9.1)
4. The set of rational and irrational numbers. (Lesson 9.2)
5. A method of writing very large or very small numbers by using powers of 10. (Lesson 10.2)

Q: What keeps a square from moving?

A: ___ ___ ___ ___ ___ ___ ___ ___   ___ ___ ___ ___ ___ ___!

Real Numbers

? ESSENTIAL QUESTION

How can you use real numbers to solve real-world problems?

Real-World Video

Living creatures can be classified into groups. The sea otter belongs to the kingdom Animalia and class Mammalia. Numbers can also be classified into groups such as rational numbers and integers.

my.hrw.com

GO DIGITAL

my.hrw.com

my.hrw.com

Go digital with your write-in student edition, accessible on any device.

Math On the Spot

Scan with your smart phone to jump directly to the online edition, video tutor, and more.

Animated Math

Interactively explore key concepts to see how math works.

Personal Math Trainer

Get immediate feedback and help as you work through practice sets.

Are YOU Ready?

Complete these exercises to review skills you will need for this module.

Find the Square of a Number

EXAMPLE   Find the square of $\frac{2}{3}$.

$\frac{2}{3} \times \frac{2}{3} = \frac{2 \times 2}{3 \times 3}$ Multiply the number by itself.

$= \frac{4}{9}$ Simplify.

Find the square of each number.

1. 7 _____   **2.** 21 _____   **3.** −3 _____   **4.** $\frac{4}{5}$ _____

5. 2.7 _____   **6.** $-\frac{1}{4}$ _____   **7.** −5.7 _____   **8.** $1\frac{2}{5}$ _____

Exponents

EXAMPLE $5^3 = 5 \times 5 \times 5$ Use the base, 5, as a factor 3 times.

$= 25 \times 5$ Multiply from left to right.

$= 125$

Simplify each exponential expression.

9. 9^2 _____   **10.** 2^4 _____   **11.** $\left(\frac{1}{3}\right)^2$ _____   **12.** $(-7)^2$ _____

13. 4^3 _____   **14.** $(-1)^5$ _____   **15.** 4.5^2 _____   **16.** 10^5 _____

Write a Mixed Number as an Improper Fraction

EXAMPLE $2\frac{2}{5} = 2 + \frac{2}{5}$ Write the mixed number as a sum of a whole number and a fraction.

$= \frac{10}{5} + \frac{2}{5}$ Write the whole number as an equivalent fraction with the same denominator as the fraction in the mixed number.

$= \frac{12}{5}$ Add the numerators.

Write each mixed number as an improper fraction.

17. $3\frac{1}{3}$ _____   **18.** $1\frac{5}{8}$ _____   **19.** $2\frac{3}{7}$ _____   **20.** $5\frac{5}{6}$ _____

Reading Start-Up

Visualize Vocabulary

Use the ✔ words to complete the graphic. You can put more than one word in each section of the triangle.

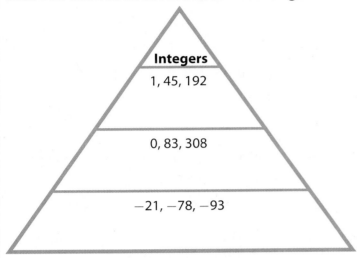

| Integers |
| 1, 45, 192 |

| 0, 83, 308 |

| −21, −78, −93 |

Understand Vocabulary

Complete the sentences using the preview words.

1. One of the two equal factors of a number is a _____.

2. A _____ has integers as its square roots.

3. The _____ is the nonnegative square root of a number.

Active Reading

Layered Book Before beginning the lessons in this module, create a layered book to help you learn the concepts in this module. Label the flaps "Rational Numbers," "Irrational Numbers," "Square Roots," and "Real Numbers." As you study each lesson, write important ideas such as vocabulary, models, and sample problems under the appropriate flap.

MODULE 9

Unpacking the Standards

Understanding the standards and the vocabulary terms in the standards will help you know exactly what you are expected to learn in this module.

 FL 8.NS.1.1

Know that numbers that are not rational are called irrational. Understand informally that every number has a decimal expansion; for rational numbers show that the decimal expansion repeats eventually, and convert a decimal expansion which repeats eventually into a rational number.

Key Vocabulary

rational number *(número racional)*
   A number that can be expressed as a ratio of two integers.

irrational number *(número irracional)*
   A number that cannot be expressed as a ratio of two integers or as a repeating or terminating decimal.

What It Means to You

You will recognize a number as rational or irrational by looking at its fraction or decimal form.

UNPACKING EXAMPLE 8.NS.1.1

Classify each number as rational or irrational.

$0.\overline{3} = \frac{1}{3}$ $\qquad\qquad\qquad\qquad$ $0.25 = \frac{1}{4}$

These numbers are rational because they can be written as ratios of integers or as repeating or terminating decimals.

$\pi \approx 3.141592654\ldots$ $\qquad\qquad$ $\sqrt{5} \approx 2.236067977\ldots$

These numbers are irrational because they cannot be written as ratios of integers or as repeating or terminating decimals.

 FL 8.NS.1.2

Use rational approximations of irrational numbers to compare the size of irrational numbers, locate them approximately on a number line diagram, and estimate the value of expressions (e.g., π^2).

Visit **my.hrw.com** to see all **Florida Math Standards** unpacked.

my.hrw.com

What It Means to You

You will learn to estimate the values of irrational numbers.

UNPACKING EXAMPLE 8.NS.1.2

Estimate the value of $\sqrt{8}$.
8 is not a perfect square. Find the two perfect squares closest to 8.

8 is between the perfect squares 4 and 9.
So $\sqrt{8}$ is between $\sqrt{4}$ and $\sqrt{9}$.
   $\sqrt{8}$ is between 2 and 3.

8 is close to 9, so $\sqrt{8}$ is close to 3.
$2.8^2 = 7.84$ $\qquad$ $2.85^2 = 8.1225$ $\qquad$ $2.9^2 = 8.41$
$\sqrt{8}$ is between 2.8 and 2.9, but closer to 2.8.
A good estimate for $\sqrt{8}$ is 2.8.

Rational and Irrational Numbers

FL 8.NS.1.1

Know that numbers that are not rational are called irrational. Understand informally that every number has a decimal expansion; ...
Also 8.NS.1.2, 8.EE.1.2

ESSENTIAL QUESTION

How do you rewrite rational numbers and decimals, take square roots and cube roots, and approximate irrational numbers?

Expressing Rational Numbers as Decimals

A **rational number** is any number that can be written as a ratio in the form $\frac{a}{b}$, where a and b are integers and b is not 0. Examples of rational numbers are 6 and 0.5.

Math On the Spot
⏻ my.hrw.com

6 can be written as $\frac{6}{1}$.   0.5 can be written as $\frac{1}{2}$.

Every rational number can be written as a terminating decimal or a repeating decimal. A **terminating decimal**, such as 0.5, has a finite number of digits. A **repeating decimal** has a block of one or more digits that repeat indefinitely.

EXAMPLE 1   **FL** 8.NS.1.1

Write each fraction as a decimal.

My Notes

A $\frac{1}{4}$

$$
\begin{array}{r}
0.25 \\
4\overline{)1.00} \\
-8 \\
\hline
20 \\
-20 \\
\hline
0
\end{array}
$$

$\frac{1}{4} = 0.25$

Remember that the fraction bar means "divided by." Divide the numerator by the denominator.

Divide until the remainder is zero, adding zeros after the decimal point in the dividend as needed.

$\frac{1}{3} = 0.3333333333333...$

B $\frac{1}{3}$

$$
\begin{array}{r}
0.333 \\
3\overline{)1.000} \\
-9 \\
\hline
10 \\
-9 \\
\hline
10 \\
-9 \\
\hline
1
\end{array}
$$

$\frac{1}{3} = 0.\overline{3}$

Divide until the remainder is zero or until the digits in the quotient begin to repeat.

Add zeros after the decimal point in the dividend as needed.

When a decimal has one or more digits that repeat indefinitely, write the decimal with a bar over the repeating digit(s).

YOUR TURN

Write each fraction as a decimal.

1. $\frac{5}{11}$ _____

2. $\frac{1}{8}$ _____

3. $2\frac{1}{3}$ _____

My Notes

Expressing Decimals as Rational Numbers

You can express terminating and repeating decimals as rational numbers.

EXAMPLE 2　　　　　　　　　　　　　　FL　8.NS.1.1

Write each decimal as a fraction in simplest form.

A 0.825

The decimal 0.825 means "825 thousandths." Write this as a fraction.

$\frac{825}{1000}$　　　　　　To write "825 thousandths", put 825 over 1000.

Then simplify the fraction.

$\frac{825 \div 25}{1000 \div 25} = \frac{33}{40}$　　　Divide both the numerator and the denominator by 25.

$0.825 = \frac{33}{40}$

B $0.\overline{37}$

Let $x = 0.\overline{37}$. The number $0.\overline{37}$ has 2 repeating digits, so multiply each side of the equation $x = 0.\overline{37}$ by 10^2, or 100.

$x = 0.\overline{37}$

$(100)x = 100(0.\overline{37})$

$100x = 37.\overline{37}$　　　100 times $0.\overline{37}$ is $37.\overline{37}$.

Because $x = 0.\overline{37}$, you can subtract x from one side and $0.\overline{37}$ from the other.

$100x = 37.\overline{37}$

$\underline{-x \qquad -0.\overline{37}}$

$99x = 37$　　　　　$37.\overline{37}$ minus $0.\overline{37}$ is 37.

Now solve the equation for x. Simplify if necessary.

$\frac{99x}{99} = \frac{37}{99}$　　　Divide both sides of the equation by 99.

$x = \frac{37}{99}$

Write each decimal as a fraction in simplest form.

4. 0.12 _____

5. $0.\overline{57}$ _____

6. 1.4 _____

Finding Square Roots and Cube Roots

The **square root** of a positive number p is x if $x^2 = p$. There are two square roots for every positive number. For example, the square roots of 36 are 6 and −6 because $6^2 = 36$ and $(-6)^2 = 36$. The square roots of $\frac{1}{25}$ are $\frac{1}{5}$ and $-\frac{1}{5}$. You can write the square roots of $\frac{1}{25}$ as $\pm\frac{1}{5}$. The symbol $\sqrt{}$ indicates the positive, or **principal square root**.

A number that is a **perfect square** has square roots that are integers. The number 81 is a perfect square because its square roots are 9 and −9.

The **cube root** of a positive number p is x if $x^3 = p$. There is one cube root for every positive number. For example, the cube root of 8 is 2 because $2^3 = 8$. The cube root of $\frac{1}{27}$ is $\frac{1}{3}$ because $\left(\frac{1}{3}\right)^3 = \frac{1}{27}$. The symbol $\sqrt[3]{}$ indicates the cube root.

A number that is a **perfect cube** has a cube root that is an integer. The number 125 is a perfect cube because its cube root is 5.

EXAMPLE 3   FL 8.EE.1.2

Solve each equation for x.

A $x^2 = 121$

$x^2 = 121$ *Solve for x by taking the square root of both sides.*

$x = \pm\sqrt{121}$ *Apply the definition of square root.*

$x = \pm 11$ *Think: What numbers squared equal 121?*

The solutions are 11 and −11.

B $x^2 = \frac{16}{169}$

$x^2 = \frac{16}{169}$ *Solve for x by taking the square root of both sides.*

$x = \pm\sqrt{\frac{16}{169}}$ *Apply the definition of square root.*

$x = \pm\frac{4}{13}$ *Think: What numbers squared equal $\frac{16}{169}$?*

The solutions are $\frac{4}{13}$ and $-\frac{4}{13}$.

Math Talk
Mathematical Practices

Can you square an integer and get a negative number? What does this indicate about whether negative numbers have square roots?

C $729 = x^3$

$\sqrt[3]{729} = \sqrt[3]{x^3}$ Solve for x by taking the cube root of both sides.

$\sqrt[3]{729} = x$ Apply the definition of cube root.

$9 = x$ Think: What number cubed equals 729?

The solution is 9.

D $x^3 = \frac{8}{125}$

$\sqrt[3]{x^3} = \sqrt[3]{\frac{8}{125}}$ Solve for x by taking the cube root of both sides.

$x = \sqrt[3]{\frac{8}{125}}$ Apply the definition of cube root.

$x = \frac{2}{5}$ Think: What number cubed equals $\frac{8}{125}$?

The solution is $\frac{2}{5}$.

YOUR TURN

Solve each equation for x.

7. $x^2 = 196$ _____

8. $x^2 = \frac{9}{256}$ _____

9. $x^3 = 512$ _____

10. $x^3 = \frac{64}{343}$ _____

EXPLORE ACTIVITY FL 8.NS.1.2, 8.EE.1.2

Estimating Irrational Numbers

Irrational numbers are numbers that are not rational. In other words, they cannot be written in the form $\frac{a}{b}$, where a and b are integers and b is not 0. Square roots of perfect squares are rational numbers. Square roots of numbers that are not perfect squares are irrational. The number $\sqrt{3}$ is irrational because 3 is not a perfect square of any rational number.

Estimate the value of $\sqrt{2}$.

A Since 2 is not a perfect square, $\sqrt{2}$ is irrational.

B To estimate $\sqrt{2}$, first find two consecutive perfect squares that 2 is between. Complete the inequality by writing these perfect squares in the boxes.

C Now take the square root of each number.

D Simplify the square roots of perfect squares.

$\sqrt{2}$ is between _____ and _____.

$\boxed{} < 2 < \boxed{}$

$\sqrt{\boxed{}} < \sqrt{2} < \sqrt{\boxed{}}$

$\boxed{} < \sqrt{2} < \boxed{}$

E Estimate that $\sqrt{2} \approx 1.5$.

$$\sqrt{2} \approx 1.5$$

F To find a better estimate, first choose some numbers between 1 and 2 and square them. For example, choose 1.3, 1.4, and 1.5.

$1.3^2 = $ _____ $1.4^2 = $ _____ $1.5^2 = $ _____

Is $\sqrt{2}$ between 1.3 and 1.4? How do you know?

_____

_____

Is $\sqrt{2}$ between 1.4 and 1.5? How do you know?

_____

_____

$\sqrt{2}$ is between _____ and _____, so $\sqrt{2} \approx$ _____.

G Locate and label this value on the number line.

Reflect

11. How could you find an even better estimate of $\sqrt{2}$?

_____

_____

12. Find a better estimate of $\sqrt{2}$. Draw a number line and locate and label your estimate.

$\sqrt{2}$ is between _____ and _____, so $\sqrt{2} \approx$ _____.

13. Estimate the value of $\sqrt{7}$ to two decimal places. Draw a number line and locate and label your estimate.

$\sqrt{7}$ is between _____ and _____, so $\sqrt{7} \approx$ _____.

Write each fraction or mixed number as a decimal. (Example 1)

1. $\frac{2}{5}$ _____

2. $\frac{8}{9}$ _____

3. $3\frac{3}{4}$ _____

4. $\frac{7}{10}$ _____

5. $2\frac{3}{8}$ _____

6. $\frac{5}{6}$ _____

Write each decimal as a fraction or mixed number in simplest form. (Example 2)

7. 0.675 _____

8. 5.6 _____

9. 0.44 _____

10. $0.\overline{4}$

$$10x = \boxed{}$$

$$-x \quad -\boxed{}$$

$$\boxed{}x = \boxed{}$$

$$x = \text{_____}$$

11. $0.\overline{26}$

$$100x = \boxed{}$$

$$-x \quad -\boxed{}$$

$$\boxed{}x = \boxed{}$$

$$x = \text{_____}$$

12. $0.\overline{325}$

$$1000x = \boxed{}$$

$$-x \quad -\boxed{}$$

$$\boxed{}x = \boxed{}$$

$$x = \text{_____}$$

Solve each equation for x. (Example 3)

13. $x^2 = 144$

$$x = \pm\sqrt{\boxed{}} = \pm\boxed{}$$

14. $x^2 = \frac{25}{289}$

$$x = \pm\sqrt{\frac{\boxed{}}{\boxed{}}} = \pm\frac{\boxed{}}{\boxed{}}$$

15. $x^3 = 216$

$$x = \sqrt[3]{\boxed{}} = \boxed{}$$

Approximate each irrational number to two decimal places without a calculator.
(Explore Activity)

16. $\sqrt{5} \approx \boxed{}$

17. $\sqrt{3} \approx \boxed{}$

18. $\sqrt{10} \approx \boxed{}$

? ESSENTIAL QUESTION CHECK-IN

19. What is the difference between rational and irrational numbers?

_____

_____

9.1 Independent Practice

 FL 8.NS.1.1, 8.NS.1.2, 8.EE.1.2

Personal
Math Trainer

Online
Assessment and
Intervention

my.hrw.com

20. A $\frac{7}{16}$-inch-long bolt is used in a machine. What is the length of the bolt written as a decimal?

_____

21. The weight of an object on the moon is $\frac{1}{6}$ its weight on Earth. Write $\frac{1}{6}$ as a decimal.

_____

22. The distance to the nearest gas station is $2\frac{4}{5}$ kilometers. What is this distance written as a decimal?

_____

23. A baseball pitcher has pitched $98\frac{2}{3}$ innings. What is the number of innings written as a decimal?

_____

24. A heartbeat takes 0.8 second. How many seconds is this written as a fraction?

_____

25. There are 26.2 miles in a marathon. Write the number of miles using a fraction.

_____

26. The average score on a biology test was $72.\overline{1}$. Write the average score using a fraction.

_____

27. The metal in a penny is worth about 0.505 cent. How many cents is this written as a fraction?

_____

28. Multistep An artist wants to frame a square painting with an area of 400 square inches. She wants to know the length of the wood trim that is needed to go around the painting.

a. If x is the length of one side of the painting, what equation can you set up to find the length of a side? _____

b. Solve the equation you wrote in part a. How many solutions does the equation have?

_____

_____

c. Do all of the solutions that you found in part b make sense in the context of the problem? Explain.

_____

_____

_____

d. What is the length of the wood trim needed to go around the painting?

_____

29. Analyze Relationships To find $\sqrt{15}$, Beau found $3^2 = 9$ and $4^2 = 16$. He said that since 15 is between 9 and 16, $\sqrt{15}$ must be between 3 and 4. He thinks a good estimate for $\sqrt{15}$ is $\frac{3+4}{2} = 3.5$. Is Beau's estimate high, low, or correct? Explain.

_____

_____

_____

30. Justify Reasoning What is a good estimate for the solution to the equation $x^3 = 95$? How did you come up with your estimate?

_____

_____

_____

31. The volume of a sphere is 36π ft³. What is the radius of the sphere? Use the formula $V = \frac{4}{3}\pi r^3$ to find your answer.

_____

H.O.T. FOCUS ON HIGHER ORDER THINKING

32. Draw Conclusions Can you find the cube root of a negative number? If so, is it positive or negative? Explain your reasoning.

_____

_____

_____

33. Make a Conjecture Evaluate and compare the following expressions.

$$\sqrt{\frac{4}{25}} \text{ and } \frac{\sqrt{4}}{\sqrt{25}} \qquad \sqrt{\frac{16}{81}} \text{ and } \frac{\sqrt{16}}{\sqrt{81}} \qquad \sqrt{\frac{36}{49}} \text{ and } \frac{\sqrt{36}}{\sqrt{49}}$$

Use your results to make a conjecture about a division rule for square roots. Since division is multiplication by the reciprocal, make a conjecture about a multiplication rule for square roots.

_____

_____

34. Persevere in Problem Solving The difference between the solutions to the equation $x^2 = a$ is 30. What is a? Show that your answer is correct.

_____

_____

LESSON
9.2 Sets of Real Numbers

FL 8.NS.1.1

Know that numbers that are not rational are called irrational. ...

ESSENTIAL QUESTION

How can you describe relationships between sets of real numbers?

Classifying Real Numbers

Biologists classify animals based on shared characteristics. A cardinal is an animal, a vertebrate, a bird, and a passerine.

Animals
Vertebrates
Birds
Passerines

Math On the Spot
my.hrw.com

You already know that the set of rational numbers consists of whole numbers, integers, and fractions. The set of **real numbers** consists of the set of rational numbers and the set of irrational numbers.

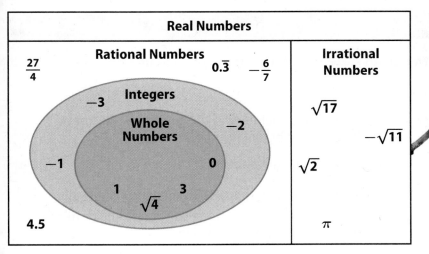

Real Numbers

Rational Numbers

$\frac{27}{4}$ $0.\overline{3}$ $-\frac{6}{7}$

Integers
-3 -2

Whole Numbers
-1 0 1 3 $\sqrt{4}$

4.5

Irrational Numbers
$\sqrt{17}$
$-\sqrt{11}$
$\sqrt{2}$
π

Passerines, such as the cardinal, are also called "perching birds."

EXAMPLE 1

FL 8.NS.1.1

Write all names that apply to each number.

A $\sqrt{5}$ *5 is a whole number that is not a perfect square.*
irrational, real

B -17.84 *-17.84 is a terminating decimal.*
rational, real

C $\frac{\sqrt{81}}{9}$ $\frac{\sqrt{81}}{9} = \frac{9}{9} = 1$
whole, integer, rational, real

Animated Math
my.hrw.com

Math Talk
Mathematical Practices

What types of numbers are between 3.1 and 3.9 on a number line?

Write all names that apply to each number.

1. A baseball pitcher has pitched $12\frac{2}{3}$ innings.

    _____

2. The length of the side of a square that has an

    area of 10 square yards. _____

Understanding Sets and Subsets of Real Numbers

By understanding which sets are subsets of types of numbers, you can verify whether statements about the relationships between sets are true or false.

EXAMPLE 2

FL 8.NS.1.1

Tell whether the given statement is true or false. Explain your choice.

A All irrational numbers are real numbers.

True. Every irrational number is included in the set of real numbers. Irrational numbers are a subset of real numbers.

B No rational numbers are whole numbers.

False. A whole number can be written as a fraction with a denominator of 1, so every whole number is included in the set of rational numbers. Whole numbers are a subset of rational numbers.

Math Talk

Mathematical Practices

Give an example of a rational number that is a whole number. Show that the number is both whole and rational.

YOUR TURN

Tell whether the given statement is true or false. Explain your choice.

3. All rational numbers are integers.

    _____

    _____

    _____

4. Some irrational numbers are integers.

    _____

    _____

Identifying Sets for Real-World Situations

Real numbers can be used to represent real-world quantities. Highways have posted speed limit signs that are represented by natural numbers such as 55 mph. Integers appear on thermometers. Rational numbers are used in many daily activities, including cooking. For example, ingredients in a recipe are often given in fractional amounts such as $\frac{2}{3}$ cup flour.

Math On the Spot

my.hrw.com

EXAMPLE 3   **FL 8.NS.1.1**

Identify the set of numbers that best describes each situation. Explain your choice.

A the number of people wearing glasses in a room

The set of whole numbers best describes the situation. The number of people wearing glasses may be 0 or a counting number.

B the circumference of a flying disk has a diameter of 8, 9, 10, 11, or 14 inches

The set of irrational numbers best describes the situation. Each circumference would be a product of π and the diameter, and any multiple of π is irrational.

My Notes

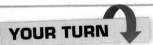

Identify the set of numbers that best describes the situation. Explain your choice.

5. the amount of water in a glass as it evaporates

_____

_____

_____

6. the number of seconds remaining when a song is playing, displayed as a negative number

_____

_____

_____

Personal Math Trainer

Online Assessment and Intervention

my.hrw.com

Write all names that apply to each number. (Example 1)

1. $\frac{7}{8}$

_____

2. $\sqrt{36}$

_____

3. $\sqrt{24}$

_____

4. 0.75

_____

5. 0

_____

6. $-\sqrt{100}$

_____

7. $5.\overline{45}$

_____

8. $-\frac{18}{6}$

_____

Tell whether the given statement is true or false. Explain your choice.
(Example 2)

9. All whole numbers are rational numbers.

_____

_____

10. No irrational numbers are whole numbers.

_____

Identify the set of numbers that best describes each situation. Explain your choice. (Example 3)

11. the change in the value of an account when given to the nearest dollar

_____

_____

12. the markings on a standard ruler

_____

$\frac{1}{16}$ inch

IN.   1

ESSENTIAL QUESTION CHECK-IN

13. What are some ways to describe the relationships between sets of numbers?

_____

_____

9.2 Independent Practice

FL 8.NS.1.1

Personal Math Trainer

Online Assessment and Intervention

my.hrw.com

Write all names that apply to each number. Then place the numbers in the correct location on the Venn diagram.

14. $\sqrt{9}$ _____

15. 257 _____

16. $\sqrt{50}$ _____

17. $8\frac{1}{2}$ _____

18. 16.6 _____

19. $\sqrt{16}$ _____

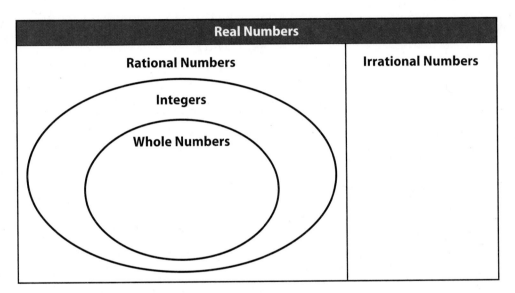

Identify the set of numbers that best describes each situation. Explain your choice.

20. the height of an airplane as it descends to an airport runway

_____

21. the score with respect to par of several golfers: 2, −3, 5, 0, −1

_____

_____

22. Critique Reasoning Ronald states that the number $\frac{1}{11}$ is not rational because, when converted into a decimal, it does not terminate. Nathaniel says it is rational because it is a fraction. Which boy is correct? Explain.

_____

_____

23. Critique Reasoning The circumference of a circular region is shown. What type of number best describes the diameter of the circle? Explain your answer. _____

π mi

24. Critical Thinking A number is not an integer. What type of number can it be?

_____

25. A grocery store has a shelf with half-gallon containers of milk. What type of number best represents the total number of gallons?

_____

H.O.T. FOCUS ON HIGHER ORDER THINKING

Work Area

26. Explain the Error Katie said, "Negative numbers are integers." What was her error?

_____

_____

27. Justify Reasoning Can you ever use a calculator to determine if a number is rational or irrational? Explain.

_____

_____

_____

_____

_____

_____

28. Draw Conclusions The decimal $0.\overline{3}$ represents $\frac{1}{3}$. What type of number best describes $0.\overline{9}$, which is $3 \cdot 0.\overline{3}$? Explain.

_____

29. Communicate Mathematical Ideas Irrational numbers can never be precisely represented in decimal form. Why is this?

_____

_____

_____

_____

Ordering Real Numbers

FL 8.NS.1.2

Use rational approximations of irrational numbers to compare the size of irrational numbers, locate them approximately on a number line diagram, and estimate the value of expressions (e.g., π^2).

ESSENTIAL QUESTION

How do you order a set of real numbers?

Comparing Irrational Numbers

Between any two real numbers is another real number. To compare and order real numbers, you can approximate irrational numbers as decimals.

Math On the Spot
⊙ my.hrw.com

EXAMPLE 1

FL 8.NS.1.2

Compare $\sqrt{3} + 5$ $3 + \sqrt{5}$. **Write** $<$, $>$, or $=$.

My Notes

STEP 1 First approximate $\sqrt{3}$.

$\sqrt{3}$ is between 1 and 2.

Next approximate $\sqrt{5}$.

$\sqrt{5}$ is between 2 and 3.

> Use perfect squares to estimate square roots.
> $1^2 = 1$ $2^2 = 4$ $3^2 = 9$

STEP 2 Then use your approximations to simplify the expressions.

$\sqrt{3} + 5$ is between 6 and 7.

$3 + \sqrt{5}$ is between 5 and 6.

So, $\sqrt{3} + 5 > 3 + \sqrt{5}$.

Reflect

1. If $7 + \sqrt{5}$ is equal to $\sqrt{5}$ plus a number, what do you know about the number? Why?

_____

2. What are the closest two integers that $\sqrt{300}$ is between?

_____

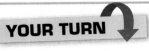
YOUR TURN

Compare. Write $<$, $>$, or $=$.

3. $\sqrt{2} + 4$ ◯ $2 + \sqrt{4}$

4. $\sqrt{12} + 6$ ◯ $12 + \sqrt{6}$

Personal Math Trainer
Online Assessment and Intervention
⊙ my.hrw.com

Math On the Spot

my.hrw.com

My Notes

Ordering Real Numbers

You can compare and order real numbers and list them from least to greatest.

EXAMPLE 2

 FL 8.NS.1.2

Order $\sqrt{22}$, $\pi + 1$, and $4\frac{1}{2}$ from least to greatest.

STEP 1 First approximate $\sqrt{22}$.

$\sqrt{22}$ is between 4 and 5. Since you don't know where it falls between 4 and 5, you need to find a better estimate for $\sqrt{22}$ so you can compare it to $4\frac{1}{2}$.

Since 22 is closer to 25 than 16, use squares of numbers between 4.5 and 5 to find a better estimate of $\sqrt{22}$.

$4.5^2 = 20.25$ $4.6^2 = 21.16$ $4.7^2 = 22.09$ $4.8^2 = 23.04$

Since $4.7^2 = 22.09$, an approximate value for $\sqrt{22}$ is 4.7.

An approximate value of π is 3.14. So an approximate value of $\pi + 1$ is 4.14.

STEP 2 Plot $\sqrt{22}$, $\pi + 1$, and $4\frac{1}{2}$ on a number line.

Read the numbers from left to right to place them in order from least to greatest.

From least to greatest, the numbers are $\pi + 1$, $4\frac{1}{2}$, and $\sqrt{22}$.

YOUR TURN

Order the numbers from least to greatest. Then graph them on the number line.

5. $\sqrt{5}$, 2.5, $\sqrt{3}$ _____

6. π^2, 10, $\sqrt{75}$ _____

Math Talk
Mathematical Practices

If real numbers a, b, and c are in order from least to greatest, what is the order of their opposites from least to greatest? Explain.

Personal Math Trainer

Online Assessment and Intervention

my.hrw.com

Ordering Real Numbers in a Real-World Context

Calculations and estimations in the real world may differ. It can be important to know not only which are the most accurate but which give the greatest or least values, depending upon the context.

Math On the Spot
⊙ my.hrw.com

EXAMPLE 3   **FL** **8.NS.1.2**

Four people have found the distance in kilometers across a canyon using different methods. Their results are given in the table. Order the distances from greatest to least.

Distance Across Quarry Canyon (km)			
Juana	**Lee Ann**	**Ryne**	**Jackson**
$\sqrt{28}$	$\frac{23}{4}$	$5.\overline{5}$	$5\frac{1}{2}$

STEP 1 Write each value as a decimal.

$\sqrt{28}$ is between 5.2 and 5.3. Since $5.3^2 = 28.09$, an approximate value for $\sqrt{28}$ is 5.3.

$\frac{23}{4} = 5.75$

$5.\overline{5}$ is 5.555…, so $5.\overline{5}$ to the nearest hundredth is 5.56.

$5\frac{1}{2} = 5.5$

STEP 2 Plot $\sqrt{28}$, $\frac{23}{4}$, $5.\overline{5}$, and $5\frac{1}{2}$ on a number line.

From greatest to least, the distances are:

$\frac{23}{4}$ km, $5.\overline{5}$ km, $5\frac{1}{2}$ km, $\sqrt{28}$ km.

YOUR TURN

7. Four people have found the distance in miles across a crater using different methods. Their results are given below.

   Jonathan: $\frac{10}{3}$, Elaine: $3.\overline{45}$, José: $3\frac{1}{2}$, Lashonda: $\sqrt{10}$

   Order the distances from greatest to least.

   _____

Personal Math Trainer

Online Assessment and Intervention

⊙ my.hrw.com

Guided Practice

Compare. Write <, >, or =. (Example 1)

1. $\sqrt{3} + 2$ ◯ $\sqrt{3} + 3$

2. $\sqrt{11} + 15$ ◯ $\sqrt{8} + 15$

3. $\sqrt{6} + 5$ ◯ $6 + \sqrt{5}$

4. $\sqrt{9} + 3$ ◯ $9 + \sqrt{3}$

5. $\sqrt{17} - 3$ ◯ $-2 + \sqrt{5}$

6. $10 - \sqrt{8}$ ◯ $12 - \sqrt{2}$

7. $\sqrt{7} + 2$ ◯ $\sqrt{10} - 1$

8. $\sqrt{17} + 3$ ◯ $3 + \sqrt{11}$

9. Order $\sqrt{3}$, 2π, and 1.5 from least to greatest. Then graph them on the number line. (Example 2)

$\sqrt{3}$ is between _____ and _____, so $\sqrt{3} \approx$ _____.

$\pi \approx 3.14$, so $2\pi \approx$ _____.

From least to greatest, the numbers are _____, _____,

_____.

10. Four people have found the perimeter of a forest using different methods. Their results are given in the table. Order their calculations from greatest to least. (Example 3)

_____

_____

Forest Perimeter (km)			
Leon	**Mika**	**Jason**	**Ashley**
$\sqrt{17} - 2$	$1 + \dfrac{\pi}{2}$	$\dfrac{12}{5}$	2.5

? **ESSENTIAL QUESTION CHECK-IN**

11. Explain how to order a set of real numbers.

_____

_____

_____

_____

_____

9.3 Independent Practice

FL 8.NS.1.2

Order the numbers from least to greatest.

12. $\sqrt{7}, 2, \frac{\sqrt{8}}{2}$

_____

13. $\sqrt{10}, \pi, 3.5$

_____

14. $\sqrt{220}, -10, \sqrt{100}, 11.5$

_____

15. $\sqrt{8}, -3.75, 3, \frac{9}{4}$

_____

16. Your sister is considering two different shapes for her garden. One is a square with side lengths of 3.5 meters, and the other is a circle with a diameter of 4 meters.

a. Find the area of the square. _____

b. Find the area of the circle. _____

c. Compare your answers from parts **a** and **b**. Which garden would give your sister the most space to plant?

_____

_____

17. Winnie measured the length of her father's ranch four times and got four different distances. Her measurements are shown in the table.

a. To estimate the actual length, Winnie first approximated each distance to the nearest hundredth. Then she averaged the four numbers. Using a calculator, find Winnie's estimate.

Distance Across Father's Ranch (km)			
1	2	3	4
$\sqrt{60}$	$\frac{58}{8}$	$7.\overline{3}$	$7\frac{3}{5}$

_____

_____

b. Winnie's father estimated the distance across his ranch to be $\sqrt{56}$ km. How does this distance compare to Winnie's estimate?

_____

Give an example of each type of number.

18. a real number between $\sqrt{13}$ and $\sqrt{14}$ _____

19. an irrational number between 5 and 7 _____

20. A teacher asks his students to write the numbers shown in order from least to greatest. Paul thinks the numbers are already in order. Sandra thinks the order should be reversed. Who is right?

$\sqrt{115}$, $\frac{115}{11}$, and

_____

_____

21. Math History There is a famous irrational number called Euler's number, symbolized with an *e*. Like π, its decimal form never ends or repeats. The first few digits of *e* are 2.7182818284.

a. Between which two square roots of integers could you find this number?

_____

b. Between which two square roots of integers can you find π?

_____

 FOCUS ON HIGHER ORDER THINKING

22. Analyze Relationships There are several approximations used for π, including 3.14 and $\frac{22}{7}$. π is approximately 3.14159265358979...

a. Label π and the two approximations on the number line.

3.140   3.141   3.142   3.143

b. Which of the two approximations is a better estimate for π? Explain.

_____

c. Find a whole number *x* in $\frac{x}{113}$ so that the ratio is a better estimate for

π than the two given approximations. _____

23. Communicate Mathematical Ideas If a set of six numbers that include both rational and irrational numbers is graphed on a number line, what is the fewest number of distinct points that need to be graphed? Explain.

_____

_____

_____

24. Critique Reasoning Jill says that $12.\overline{6}$ is less than 12.63. Explain her error.

_____

Ready to Go On?

Personal
Math Trainer

Online Assessment
and Intervention

my.hrw.com

9.1 Rational and Irrational Numbers

Write each fraction as a decimal or each decimal as a fraction.

1. $\frac{7}{20}$ _____

2. $1.\overline{27}$ _____

3. $1\frac{7}{8}$ _____

Solve each equation for x.

4. $x^2 = 81$ _____

5. $x^3 = 343$ _____

6. $x^2 = \frac{1}{100}$ _____

7. A square patio has an area of 200 square feet. How long is each side

of the patio to the nearest 0.05? _____

9.2 Sets of Real Numbers

Write all names that apply to each number.

8. $\frac{121}{\sqrt{121}}$ _____

9. $\frac{\pi}{2}$ _____

10. Tell whether the statement "All integers are rational numbers" is true
or false. Explain your choice.

_____

_____

9.3 Ordering Real Numbers

Compare. Write $<$, $>$, or $=$.

11. $\sqrt{8} + 3$ ◯ $8 + \sqrt{3}$

12. $\sqrt{5} + 11$ ◯ $5 + \sqrt{11}$

Order the numbers from least to greatest.

13. $\sqrt{99}, \pi^2, 9.\overline{8}$ _____

14. $\sqrt{\frac{1}{25}}, \frac{1}{4}, 0.\overline{2}$ _____

? ESSENTIAL QUESTION

15. How are real numbers used to describe real-world situations?

_____

_____

MODULE 9 MIXED REVIEW

Assessment Readiness

Personal
Math Trainer

Online
Assessment and
Intervention

my.hrw.com

Selected Response

1. The square root of a number is 9. What is the other square root?

Ⓐ -9 Ⓒ 3

Ⓑ -3 Ⓓ 81

2. A square acre of land is 4,840 square yards. Between which two integers is the length of one side?

Ⓐ between 24 and 25 yards

Ⓑ between 69 and 70 yards

Ⓒ between 242 and 243 yards

Ⓓ between 695 and 696 yards

3. Which of the following is an integer but not a whole number?

Ⓐ -9.6 Ⓒ 0

Ⓑ -4 Ⓓ 3.7

4. Which statement is false?

Ⓐ No integers are irrational numbers.

Ⓑ All whole numbers are integers.

Ⓒ No real numbers are irrational numbers.

Ⓓ All integers greater than 0 are whole numbers.

5. An eighth-grade class has 120 students. Gavin surveys a random sample of 30 students and finds that 17 of them have brown eyes. How many students in the class are likely to have brown eyes?

Ⓐ 17 Ⓒ 52

Ⓑ 30 Ⓓ 68

6. Which of the following is <u>not</u> true?

Ⓐ $\pi^2 < 2\pi + 4$ Ⓒ $\sqrt{27} + 3 > \frac{17}{2}$

Ⓑ $3\pi > 9$ Ⓓ $5 - \sqrt{24} < 1$

7. Which number is between $\sqrt{21}$ and $\frac{3\pi}{2}$?

Ⓐ $\frac{14}{3}$ Ⓒ 5

Ⓑ $2\sqrt{6}$ Ⓓ $\pi + 1$

8. What number is shown on the graph?

Ⓐ $\pi + 3$ Ⓒ $\sqrt{20} + 2$

Ⓑ $\sqrt{4} + 2.5$ Ⓓ $6.\overline{14}$

9. Which is in order from least to greatest?

Ⓐ $3.3, \frac{10}{3}, \pi, \frac{11}{4}$ Ⓒ $\pi, \frac{10}{3}, \frac{11}{4}, 3.3$

Ⓑ $\frac{10}{3}, 3.3, \frac{11}{4}, \pi$ Ⓓ $\frac{11}{4}, \pi, 3.3, \frac{10}{3}$

Mini-Task

10. The volume of a cube is given by $V = x^3$, where x is the length of an edge of the cube. The area of a square is given by $A = x^2$, where x is the length of a side of the square. A given cube has a volume of 1,728 cubic inches.

a. Find the length of an edge.

_____

b. Find the area of one side of the cube.

_____

c. Find the surface area of the cube.

_____

d. What is the surface area in square feet?

_____

Exponents and Scientific Notation

ESSENTIAL QUESTION

How can you use scientific notation to solve real-world problems?

Real-World Video

The distance from Earth to other planets, moons, and stars is a very great number of kilometers. To make it easier to write very large and very small numbers, we use scientific notation.

my.hrw.com

GO DIGITAL
my.hrw.com

my.hrw.com
Go digital with your write-in student edition, accessible on any device.

Math On the Spot
Scan with your smart phone to jump directly to the online edition, video tutor, and more.

Animated Math
Interactively explore key concepts to see how math works.

Personal Math Trainer
Get immediate feedback and help as you work through practice sets.

Are YOU Ready?

Complete these exercises to review skills you will need for this module.

Exponents

EXAMPLE $10^4 = 10 \times 10 \times 10 \times 10$

$= 10,000$

Write the exponential expression as a product.
Simplify.

Write each exponential expression as a decimal.

1. 10^2 _____

2. 10^3 _____

3. 10^5 _____

4. 10^7 _____

Multiply and Divide by Powers of 10

EXAMPLE $0.0478 \times 10^5 = 0.0478 \times 100,000$

$= 4,780$

Identify the number of zeros in the power of 10.
When multiplying, move the decimal point to the *right* the same number of places as the number of zeros.

$37.9 \div 10^4 = 37.9 \div 10,000$

$= 0.00379$

Identify the number of zeros in the power of 10.
When dividing, move the decimal point to the *left* the same number of places as the number of zeros.

Find each product or quotient.

5. 45.3×10^3

_____

6. $7.08 \div 10^2$

_____

7. 0.00235×10^6

_____

8. $3,600 \div 10^4$

_____

9. 0.5×10^2

_____

10. $67.7 \div 10^5$

_____

11. 0.0057×10^4

_____

12. $195 \div 10^6$

_____

Reading Start-Up

Visualize Vocabulary

Use the ✔ words to complete the Venn diagram. You can put more than one word in each section of the diagram.

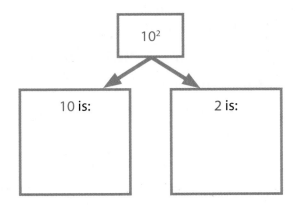

10²

10 is:

2 is:

Understand Vocabulary

Complete the sentences using the preview words.

1. A number produced by raising a base to an exponent

   is a _____.

2. _____ is a method of writing very large or very small numbers by using powers of 10.

3. A _____ is any number that can be expressed as a ratio of two integers.

Vocabulary

Review Words
✔ base *(base)*
✔ exponent *(exponente)*
   integers *(entero)*
✔ positive number *(número positivo)*
   standard notation *(notación estándar)*

Preview Words
   power *(potencia)*
   rational number *(número racional)*
   real numbers *(número real)*
   scientific notation *(notación científica)*
   whole number *(número entero)*

Active Reading

Two-Panel Flip Chart Create a two-panel flip chart to help you understand the concepts in this module. Label one flap "Positive Powers of 10" and the other flap "Negative Powers of 10." As you study each lesson, write important ideas under the appropriate flap. Include sample problems that will help you remember the concepts later when you look back at your notes.

Unpacking the Standards

Understanding the standards and the vocabulary terms in the standards will help you know exactly what you are expected to learn in this module.

 FL 8.EE.1.1

Know and apply the properties of integer exponents to generate equivalent numerical expressions.

Key Vocabulary

integer *(entero)*
The set of whole numbers and their opposites

exponent *(exponente)*
The number that indicates how many times the base is used as a factor.

What It Means to You

You will use the properties of integer exponents to find equivalent expressions.

UNPACKING EXAMPLE 8.EE.1.1

Evaluate two different ways.

$\dfrac{8^3}{8^5}$ $\dfrac{8^3}{8^5} = \dfrac{8 \cdot 8 \cdot 8}{8 \cdot 8 \cdot 8 \cdot 8 \cdot 8} = \dfrac{1}{8 \cdot 8} = \dfrac{1}{64}$

$\dfrac{8^3}{8^5} = 8^{(3-5)} = 8^{-2} = \dfrac{1}{8^2} = \dfrac{1}{8 \cdot 8} = \dfrac{1}{64}$

$(3^2)^4$ $(3^2)^4 = (3^2)(3^2)(3^2)(3^2) = 3^{2+2+2+2} = 3^8 = 6{,}561$

$(3^2)^4 = 3^{(2 \cdot 4)} = 3^8 = 6{,}561$

 FL 8.EE.1.3

Use numbers expressed in the form of a single digit times an integer power of 10 to estimate very large or very small quantities, and to express how many times as much one is than the other.

Key Vocabulary

scientific notation *(notación científica)*
A method of writing very large or very small numbers by using powers of 10.

What It Means to You

You will convert very large numbers to scientific notation.

UNPACKING EXAMPLE 8.EE.1.3

There are about 55,000,000,000 cells in an average-sized adult. Write this number in scientific notation.

Move the decimal point to the left until you have a number that is greater than or equal to 1 and less than 10.

5.5 0 0 0 0 0 0 0 0 0   *Move the decimal point 10 places to the left.*

5.5   *Remove the extra zeros.*

You would have to multiply 5.5 by 10^{10} to get 55,000,000,000.

$55{,}000{,}000{,}000 = 5.5 \times 10^{10}$

Visit **my.hrw.com** to see all **Florida Math Standards** unpacked.

my.hrw.com

10.1 Integer Exponents

FL 8.EE.1.1
Know and apply the properties of integer exponents to generate equivalent numerical expressions.

ESSENTIAL QUESTION How can you develop and use the properties of integer exponents?

EXPLORE ACTIVITY 1 FL 8.EE.1.1

Using Patterns of Integer Exponents

The table below shows powers of 5, 4, and 3.

$5^4 = 625$	$5^3 = 125$	$5^2 = 25$	$5^1 = 5$	$5^0 = \boxed{}$	$5^{-1} = \boxed{}$	$5^{-2} = \boxed{}$
$4^4 = 256$	$4^3 = 64$	$4^2 = 16$	$4^1 = 4$	$4^0 = \boxed{}$	$4^{-1} = \boxed{}$	$4^{-2} = \boxed{}$
$3^4 = 81$	$3^3 = 27$	$3^2 = 9$	$3^1 = 3$	$3^0 = \boxed{}$	$3^{-1} = \boxed{}$	$3^{-2} = \boxed{}$

A What pattern do you see in the powers of 5?

_____

_____

B What pattern do you see in the powers of 4?

_____

_____

C What pattern do you see in the powers of 3?

_____

_____

D Complete the table for the values of $5^0, 5^{-1}, 5^{-2}$.

E Complete the table for the values of $4^0, 4^{-1}, 4^{-2}$.

F Complete the table for the values of $3^0, 3^{-1}, 3^{-2}$.

Reflect

1. Make a Conjecture Write a general rule for the value of a^0. _____

2. Make a Conjecture Write a general rule for the value of a^{-n}. _____

Exploring Properties of Integer Exponents

A Complete the following equations.

$3 \cdot 3 \cdot 3 \cdot 3 \cdot 3 = 3^{\boxed{}}$

$(3 \cdot 3 \cdot 3 \cdot 3) \cdot 3 = 3^{\boxed{}} \cdot 3^{\boxed{}} = 3^{\boxed{}}$

$(3 \cdot 3 \cdot 3) \cdot (3 \cdot 3) = 3^{\boxed{}} \cdot 3^{\boxed{}} = 3^{\boxed{}}$

What pattern do you see when multiplying two powers with the same base?

_____

_____

Use your pattern to complete this equation: $5^2 \cdot 5^5 = 5^{\boxed{}}$.

B Complete the following equation:

$$\frac{4^5}{4^3} = \frac{4 \cdot 4 \cdot 4 \cdot 4 \cdot 4}{4 \cdot 4 \cdot 4} = \frac{{}^1\!\!\!\!\diagup\!\!4 \cdot {}^1\!\!\!\!\diagup\!\!4 \cdot {}^1\!\!\!\!\diagup\!\!4 \cdot 4 \cdot 4}{\diagdown\!\!4_1 \cdot \diagdown\!\!4_1 \cdot \diagdown\!\!4_1} = 4 \cdot 4 = 4^{\boxed{}}$$

What pattern do you see when dividing two powers with the same base?

_____

_____

_____

Use your pattern to complete this equation: $\dfrac{6^8}{6^3} = 6^{\boxed{}}$.

C Complete the following equations:

$(5^3)^2 = (5 \cdot 5 \cdot 5)^{\boxed{}} = (5 \cdot 5 \cdot 5) \cdot (5 \cdot 5 \cdot 5) = 5^{\boxed{}}$

What pattern do you see when raising a power to a power?

_____

_____

Use your pattern to complete this equation: $(7^2)^4 = 7^{\boxed{}}$.

Math Talk
Mathematical Practices

Do the patterns you found in parts A–C apply if the exponents are negative? If so, give an example of each.

Reflect

Let _m_ and _n_ be integers.

3. **Make a Conjecture** Write a general rule for the value of $a^m \cdot a^n$. _____

4. **Make a Conjecture** Write a general rule for the value of $\frac{a^m}{a^n}$, $a \neq 0$. _____

5. **Make a Conjecture** Write a general rule for the value of $(a^m)^n$. _____

Applying Properties of Integer Exponents

You can use the general rules you found in the Explore Activities to simplify more complicated expressions.

Math On the Spot
my.hrw.com

EXAMPLE 1   FL 8.EE.1.1

My Notes

Simplify each expression.

A $(5 - 2)^5 \cdot 3^{-8} + (5 + 2)^0$

$(3)^5 \cdot 3^{-8} + (7)^0$ Simplify within parentheses.

$3^{5 + (-8)} + 1$ Use properties of exponents.

$3^{-3} + 1$ Simplify.

$\frac{1}{27} + 1 = 1\frac{1}{27}$ Apply the rule for negative exponents and add.

B $\dfrac{\left[(3 + 1)^2\right]^3}{(7 - 3)^2}$

$\dfrac{(4^2)^3}{4^2}$ Simplify within parentheses.

$\dfrac{4^6}{4^2}$ Use properties of exponents.

4^{6-2} Use properties of exponents.

$4^4 = 256$ Simplify.

Simplify each expression.

6. $\dfrac{\left[(6 - 1)^2\right]^2}{(3 + 2)^3}$

7. $(2^2)^3 - (10 - 6)^3 \cdot 4^{-5}$

_____   _____

Personal Math Trainer

Online Assessment and Intervention

my.hrw.com

Guided Practice

Find the value of each power. (Explore Activity 1)

1. $8^{-1} =$ _____

2. $6^{-2} =$ _____

3. $256^0 =$ _____

4. $10^2 =$ _____

5. $5^4 =$ _____

6. $2^{-5} =$ _____

7. $4^{-5} =$ _____

8. $89^0 =$ _____

9. $11^{-3} =$ _____

Use properties of exponents to write an equivalent expression. (Explore Activity 2)

10. $4 \cdot 4 \cdot 4 = 4^{\boxed{}}$

11. $(2 \cdot 2) \cdot (2 \cdot 2 \cdot 2) = 2^{\boxed{}} \cdot 2^{\boxed{}} = 2^{\boxed{}}$

12. $\dfrac{6^7}{6^5} = \dfrac{6 \cdot 6 \cdot 6 \cdot 6 \cdot 6 \cdot 6 \cdot 6}{6 \cdot 6 \cdot 6 \cdot 6 \cdot 6} = \boxed{}^{\boxed{}}$

13. $\dfrac{8^{12}}{8^9} = 8^{\boxed{} - \boxed{}} = \boxed{}^{\boxed{}}$

14. $5^{10} \cdot 5 \cdot 5 = 5^{\boxed{}}$

15. $7^8 \cdot 7^5 = \boxed{}^{\boxed{}}$

16. $(6^2)^4 = (6 \cdot 6)^{\boxed{}}$

$= (6 \cdot 6) \cdot (6 \cdot 6) \cdot \left(\boxed{} \cdot \boxed{} \right) \cdot$ _____

$= \boxed{}^{\boxed{}}$

17. $(3^3)^3 = (3 \cdot 3 \cdot 3)^3$

$= (3 \cdot 3 \cdot 3) \cdot \left(\boxed{} \cdot \boxed{} \cdot \boxed{} \right)$ _____

$= \boxed{}^{\boxed{}}$

Simplify each expression. (Example 1)

18. $(10 - 6)^3 \cdot 4^2 + (10 + 2)^2$ _____

19. $\dfrac{(12 - 5)^7}{\left[(3 + 4)^2 \right]^2}$ _____

? ESSENTIAL QUESTION CHECK-IN

20. Summarize the rules for multiplying powers with the same base, dividing powers with the same base, and raising a power to a power.

_____

_____

_____

_____

10.1 Independent Practice

  FL 8.EE.1.1

21. Explain why the exponents cannot be added in the product $12^3 \cdot 11^3$.

_____

22. List three ways to express 3^5 as a product of powers.

_____

23. **Astronomy** The distance from Earth to the moon is about 22^4 miles. The distance from Earth to Neptune is about 22^7 miles. Which distance is the greater distance and about how many times greater is it?

_____

24. **Critique Reasoning** A student claims that $8^3 \cdot 8^{-5}$ is greater than 1. Explain whether the student is correct or not.

_____

_____

Find the missing exponent.

25. $(b^2)^{\boxed{}} = b^{-6}$

26. $x^{\boxed{}} \cdot x^6 = x^9$

27. $\dfrac{y^{25}}{y^{\boxed{}}} = y^6$

28. **Communicate Mathematical Ideas** Why do you subtract exponents when dividing powers with the same base?

_____

_____

_____

29. **Astronomy** The mass of the Sun is about 2×10^{27} metric tons, or 2×10^{30} kilograms. How many kilograms are in one metric ton?

_____

30. **Represent Real-World Problems** In computer technology, a kilobyte is 2^{10} bytes in size. A gigabyte is 2^{30} bytes in size. The size of a terabyte is the product of the size of a kilobyte and the size of a gigabyte. What is the size of a terabyte?

_____

31. Write equivalent expressions for $x^7 \cdot x^{-2}$ and $\frac{x^7}{x^2}$. What do you notice? Explain how your results relate to the properties of integer exponents.

_____

_____

_____

_____

A toy store is creating a large window display of different colored cubes stacked in a triangle shape. The table shows the number of cubes in each row of the triangle, starting with the top row.

Row	1	2	3	4
Number of cubes in each row	3	3^2	3^3	3^4

32. Look for a Pattern Describe any pattern you see in the table.

_____

33. Using exponents, how many cubes will be in Row 6? How many times as many cubes will be in Row 6 than in Row 3?

_____

34. Justify Reasoning If there are 6 rows in the triangle, what is the total number of cubes in the triangle? Explain how you found your answer.

_____

 FOCUS ON HIGHER ORDER THINKING

Work Area

35. Critique Reasoning A student simplified the expression $\frac{6^2}{36^2}$ as $\frac{1}{3}$. Do you agree with this student? Explain why or why not.

_____

36. Draw Conclusions Evaluate $-a^n$ when $a = 3$ and $n = 2, 3, 4,$ and 5. Now evaluate $(-a)^n$ when $a = 3$ and $n = 2, 3, 4,$ and 5. Based on this sample, does it appear that $-a^n = (-a)^n$? If not, state the relationships, if any, between $-a^n$ and $(-a)^n$.

_____

_____

_____

_____

37. Persevere in Problem Solving A number to the 12th power divided by the same number to the 9th power equals 125. What is the number?

_____

Scientific Notation with Positive Powers of 10

FL 8.EE.1.3
Use numbers expressed in the form of a single digit times an integer power of 10 to estimate very large or very small quantities, ...

ESSENTIAL QUESTION

How can you use scientific notation to express very large quantities?

EXPLORE ACTIVITY (Real World) FL 8.EE.1.3

Using Scientific Notation

Scientific notation is a method of expressing very large and very small numbers as a product of a number greater than or equal to 1 and less than 10, and a power of 10.

The weights of various sea creatures are shown in the table. Write the weight of the blue whale in scientific notation.

Sea Creature	Blue whale	Gray whale	Whale shark
Weight (lb)	250,000	68,000	41,200

A Move the decimal point in 250,000 to the left as many places as necessary to find a number that is greater than or equal to 1 and less than 10.

What number did you find? _____

B Divide 250,000 by your answer to **A**. Write your answer as a power of 10.

_____

C Combine your answers to **A** and **B** to represent 250,000.

$250,000 = \boxed{} \times 10^{\boxed{}}$

Repeat steps **A** through **C** to write the weight of the whale shark in scientific notation.

$41,200 = \boxed{} \times 10^{\boxed{}}$

Reflect

1. How many places to the left did you move the decimal point to write 41,200 in scientific notation? _____

2. What is the exponent on 10 when you write 41,200 in scientific notation?

_____

Writing a Number in Scientific Notation

To translate between standard notation and scientific notation, you can count the number of places the decimal point moves.

Writing Large Quantities in Scientific Notation		
When the number is greater than or equal to 10, use a positive exponent.	$84{,}000 = 8.4 \times 10^4$	*The decimal point moves 4 places to the left.*

EXAMPLE 1

 FL 8.EE.1.3

The distance from Earth to the Sun is about 93,000,000 miles. Write this distance in scientific notation.

STEP 1 Move the decimal point in 93,000,000 to the left until you have a number that is greater than or equal to 1 and less than 10.

9.3 0 0 0 0 0 0.   *Move the decimal point 7 places to the left.*

9.3   *Remove extra zeros.*

STEP 2 Divide the original number by the result from Step 1.

10,000,000   *Divide 93,000,000 by 9.3.*

10^7 *Write your answer as a power of 10.*

STEP 3 Write the product of the results from Steps 1 and 2.

$93{,}000{,}000 = 9.3 \times 10^7$ miles   *Write a product to represent 93,000,000 in scientific notation.*

Math Talk
Mathematical Practices

Is 12×10^7 written in scientific notation? Explain.

YOUR TURN

Write each number in scientific notation.

3. 6,400

_____

4. 570,000,000,000

_____

5. A light-year is the distance that light travels in a year and is equivalent to 9,461,000,000,000 km. Write this distance in scientific notation.

_____

Writing a Number in Standard Notation

To translate between scientific notation and standard notation, move the decimal point the number of places indicated by the exponent in the power of 10. When the exponent is positive, move the decimal point to the right and add placeholder zeros as needed.

Math On the Spot
⏻ my.hrw.com

EXAMPLE 2 **FL** 8.EE.1.3

My Notes

Write 3.5×10^6 in standard notation.

STEP 1 Use the exponent of the power of 10 to see how many places to move the decimal point.

6 places

STEP 2 Place the decimal point. Since you are going to write a number greater than 3.5, move the decimal point to the *right*. Add placeholder zeros if necessary.

3 5 0 0 0 0 0.

The number 3.5×10^6 written in standard notation is 3,500,000.

Reflect

6. Explain why the exponent in 3.5×10^6 is 6, while there are only 5 zeros in 3,500,000.

_____

_____

_____

7. What is the exponent on 10 when you write 5.3 in scientific notation?

_____

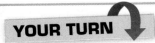

Write each number in standard notation.

8. 7.034×10^9

9. 2.36×10^5

_____   _____

10. The mass of one roosting colony of Monarch butterflies in Mexico was estimated at 5×10^6 grams. Write this mass in standard notation.

_____

Personal Math Trainer

Online Assessment and Intervention

⏻ my.hrw.com

Write each number in scientific notation. (Explore Activity and Example 1)

1. 58,927
Hint: Move the decimal left 4 places.

_____

2. 1,304,000,000
Hint: Move the decimal left 9 places.

_____

3. 6,730,000

_____

4. 13,300

_____

5. An ordinary quarter contains about 97,700,000,000,000,000,000,000 atoms.

_____

6. The distance from Earth to the Moon is about 384,000 kilometers.

_____

Write each number in standard notation. (Example 2)

7. 4×10^5
Hint: Move the decimal right 5 places.

_____

8. 1.8499×10^9
Hint: Move the decimal right 9 places.

_____

9. 6.41×10^3

_____

10. 8.456×10^7

_____

11. 8×10^5

_____

12. 9×10^{10}

_____

13. Diana calculated that she spent about 5.4×10^4 seconds doing her math homework during October. Write this time in standard notation. (Example 2)

_____

14. The town recycled 7.6×10^6 cans this year. Write the number of cans in standard notation. (Example 2)

_____

? **ESSENTIAL QUESTION CHECK-IN**

15. Describe how to write 3,482,000,000 in scientific notation.

_____

_____

_____

_____

10.2 Independent Practice

FL 8.EE.1.3

Personal Math Trainer

Online Assessment and Intervention

my.hrw.com

Paleontology Use the table for problems 16–21. Write the estimated weight of each dinosaur in scientific notation.

Estimated Weight of Dinosaurs	
Name	**Pounds**
Argentinosaurus	220,000
Brachiosaurus	100,000
Apatosaurus	66,000
Diplodocus	50,000
Camarasaurus	40,000
Cetiosauriscus	19,850

16. Apatosaurus _____

17. Argentinosaurus _____

18. Brachiosaurus _____

19. Camarasaurus _____

20. Cetiosauriscus _____

21. Diplodocus _____

22. A single little brown bat can eat up to 1,000 mosquitoes in a single hour. Express in scientific notation how many mosquitoes a little brown bat might eat in 10.5 hours.

_____

23. **Multistep** Samuel can type nearly 40 words per minute. Use this information to find the number of hours it would take him to type 2.6×10^5 words.

_____

_____

24. **Entomology** A tropical species of mite named *Archegozetes longisetosus* is the record holder for the strongest insect in the world. It can lift up to 1.182×10^3 times its own weight.

a. If you were as strong as this insect, explain how you could find how many pounds you could lift.

_____

_____

_____

b. Complete the calculation to find how much you could lift, in pounds, if you were as strong as an *Archegozetes longisetosus* mite. Express your answer in both scientific notation and standard notation.

_____

_____

25. During a discussion in science class, Sharon learns that at birth an elephant weighs around 230 pounds. In four herds of elephants tracked by conservationists, about 20 calves were born during the summer. In scientific notation, express approximately how much the calves weighed all together.

_____

26. **Classifying Numbers** Which of the following numbers are written in scientific notation?

0.641×10^3 9.999×10^4

2×10^1 4.38×5^{10}

27. Explain the Error Polly's parents' car weighs about 3500 pounds. Samantha, Esther, and Polly each wrote the weight of the car in scientific notation. Polly wrote 35.0×10^2, Samantha wrote 0.35×10^4, and Esther wrote 3.5×10^4.

Which of these girls, if any, is correct?

_____

b. Explain the mistakes of those who got the question wrong.

_____

_____

_____

28. Justify Reasoning If you were a biologist counting very large numbers of cells as part of your research, give several reasons why you might prefer to record your cell counts in scientific notation instead of standard notation.

_____

_____

_____

H.O.T. FOCUS ON HIGHER ORDER THINKING

29. Draw Conclusions Which measurement would be least likely to be written in scientific notation: number of stars in a galaxy, number of grains of sand on a beach, speed of a car, or population of a country? Explain your reasoning.

_____

_____

30. Analyze Relationships Compare the two numbers to find which is greater. Explain how you can compare them without writing them in standard notation first.

$$4.5 \times 10^6 \qquad 2.1 \times 10^8$$

_____

_____

31. Communicate Mathematical Ideas To determine whether a number is written in scientific notation, what test can you apply to the first factor, and what test can you apply to the second factor?

_____

_____

Scientific Notation with Negative Powers of 10

FL 8.EE.1.3

Use numbers expressed in the form of a single digit times an integer power of 10 to estimate very large or very small quantities, ...

ESSENTIAL QUESTION

How can you use scientific notation to express very small quantities?

EXPLORE ACTIVITY   FL 8.EE.1.3

Animated Math
my.hrw.com

Negative Powers of 10

You can use what you know about writing very large numbers in scientific notation to write very small numbers in scientific notation.

A typical human hair has a diameter of 0.000025 meter. Write this number in scientific notation.

A Notice how the decimal point moves in the list below. Complete the list.

2.345×10^0	$= 2.345$	It moves one place to the right with each increasing power of 10.
2.345×10^1	$= 23.45$	
2.345×10^2	$= 234.5$	
$2.345 \times 10^{\boxed{}}$	$= 2345.$	

2.345×10^0	$= 2.345$	It moves one place to the left with each decreasing power of 10.
2.345×10^{-1}	$= 0.2345$	
2.345×10^{-2}	$= 0.02345$	
$2.345 \times 10^{\boxed{}}$	$= 0.002345$	

B Move the decimal point in 0.000025 to the right as many places as necessary to find a number that is greater than or equal to 1 and

less than 10. What number did you find? _____

C Divide 0.000025 by your answer to **B**. _____

Write your answer as a power of 10. _____

D Combine your answers to **B** and **C** to represent 0.000025 in

scientific notation. _____

Reflect

1. When you move the decimal point, how can you know whether you are increasing or decreasing the number?

_____

2. Explain how the two steps of moving the decimal and multiplying by a power of 10 leave the value of the original number unchanged.

_____

Writing a Number in Scientific Notation

To write a number less than 1 in scientific notation, move the decimal point right and use a negative exponent.

Writing Small Quantities in Scientific Notation		
When the number is between 0 and 1, use a negative exponent.	$0.0783 = 7.83 \times 10^{-2}$	*The decimal point moves 2 places to the right.*

EXAMPLE 1

The average size of an atom is about 0.00000003 centimeter across. Write the average size of an atom in scientific notation.

Move the decimal point as many places as necessary to find a number that is greater than or equal to 1 and less than 10.

STEP 1 Place the decimal point.   3.0

STEP 2 Count the number of places you moved the decimal point.   8

STEP 3 Multiply 3.0 times a power of 10. 3.0×10^{-8}

Since 0.00000003 is less than 1, you moved the decimal point to the right and the exponent on 10 is negative.

The average size of an atom in scientific notation is 3.0×10^{-8}.

Reflect

3. **Critical Thinking** When you write a number that is less than 1 in scientific notation, how does the power of 10 differ from when you write a number greater than 1 in scientific notation?

_____

YOUR TURN

Write each number in scientific notation.

4. 0.0000829   5. 0.000000302

_____   _____

6. A typical red blood cell in human blood has a diameter of approximately 0.000007 meter. Write this diameter

in scientific notation. _____

Writing a Number in Standard Notation

To translate between scientific notation and standard notation with very small numbers, you can move the decimal point the number of places indicated by the exponent on the power of 10. When the exponent is negative, move the decimal point to the left.

Math On the Spot
my.hrw.com

EXAMPLE 2   **FL**   8.EE.1.3

Platelets are one component of human blood. A typical platelet has a diameter of approximately 2.33×10^{-6} meter. Write 2.33×10^{-6} in standard notation.

STEP 1   Use the exponent of the power of 10 to see   6 places
how many places to move the decimal point.

STEP 2   Place the decimal point. Since you are going to   0.0 0 0 0 0 2 3 3
write a number less than 2.33, move the decimal
point to the *left*. Add placeholder zeros if necessary.

The number 2.33×10^{-6} in standard notation is 0.00000233.

> **Math Talk**
> **Mathematical Practices**
>
> Describe the two factors that multiply together to form a number written in scientific notation.

Reflect

7. Justify Reasoning Explain whether 0.9×10^{-5} is written in scientific notation. If not, write the number correctly in scientific notation.

_____

_____

_____

8. Which number is larger, 2×10^{-3} or 3×10^{-2}? Explain.

_____

YOUR TURN

Write each number in standard notation.

9. 1.045×10^{-6} **10.** 9.9×10^{-5}

_____   _____

11. Jeremy measured the length of an ant as 1×10^{-2} meter. Write this length in standard notation.

_____

Personal Math Trainer
Online Assessment and Intervention
my.hrw.com

Guided Practice

Write each number in scientific notation. (Explore Activity and Example 1)

1. 0.000487
Hint: Move the decimal right 4 places.

_____

2. 0.000028
Hint: Move the decimal right 5 places.

_____

3. 0.000059

_____

4. 0.0417

_____

5. Picoplankton can be as small as 0.00002 centimeter.

_____

6. The average mass of a grain of sand on a beach is about 0.000015 gram.

_____

Write each number in standard notation. (Example 2)

7. 2×10^{-5}
Hint: Move the decimal left 5 places.

_____

8. 3.582×10^{-6}
Hint: Move the decimal left 6 places.

_____

9. 8.3×10^{-4}

_____

10. 2.97×10^{-2}

_____

11. 9.06×10^{-5}

_____

12. 4×10^{-5}

_____

13. The average length of a dust mite is approximately 0.0001 meter. Write this number in scientific notation. (Example 1)

_____

14. The mass of a proton is about 1.7×10^{-24} gram. Write this number in standard notation. (Example 2)

_____

ESSENTIAL QUESTION CHECK-IN

15. Describe how to write 0.0000672 in scientific notation.

_____

_____

_____

10.3 Independent Practice

FL 8.EE.1.3

Personal
Math Trainer

Online
Assessment and
Intervention

my.hrw.com

Use the table for problems 16–21. Write the diameter of the fibers in scientific notation.

Average Diameter of Natural Fibers	
Animal	**Fiber Diameter (cm)**
Vicuña	0.0008
Angora rabbit	0.0013
Alpaca	0.00277
Angora goat	0.0045
Llama	0.0035
Orb web spider	0.015

16. Alpaca

_____

17. Angora rabbit

_____

18. Llama

_____

19. Angora goat

_____

20. Orb web spider

_____

21. Vicuña

_____

22. Make a Conjecture Which measurement would be least likely to be written in scientific notation: the thickness of a dog hair, the radius of a period on this page, the ounces in a cup of milk? Explain your reasoning.

_____

_____

23. Multiple Representations Convert the length 7 centimeters to meters. Compare the numerical values when both numbers are written in scientific notation.

_____

_____

_____

_____

24. Draw Conclusions A graphing calculator displays 1.89×10^{12} as 1.89E12. How do you think it would display 1.89×10^{-12}? What does the E stand for?

_____

_____

25. Communicate Mathematical Ideas When a number is written in scientific notation, how can you tell right away whether or not it is greater than or equal to 1?

_____

_____

_____

26. The volume of a drop of a certain liquid is 0.000047 liter. Write the volume of the drop of liquid in scientific notation.

_____

27. Justify Reasoning If you were asked to express the weight in ounces of a ladybug in scientific notation, would the exponent of the 10 be positive or negative? Justify your response.

_____

_____

Physical Science The table shows the length of the radii of several very small or very large items. Complete the table.

	Item	Radius in Meters (Standard Notation)	Radius in Meters (Scientific Notation)
28.	The Moon	1,740,000	
29.	Atom of silver		1.25×10^{-10}
30.	Atlantic wolfish egg	0.0028	
31.	Jupiter		7.149×10^7
32.	Atom of aluminum	0.000000000182	
33.	Mars		3.397×10^6

34. List the items in the table in order from the smallest to the largest.

_____

_____

 FOCUS ON HIGHER ORDER THINKING

Work Area

35. Analyze Relationships Write the following diameters from least to greatest.
1.5×10^{-2} m 1.2×10^2 m 5.85×10^{-3} m 2.3×10^{-2} m 9.6×10^{-1} m

_____

_____

36. Critique Reasoning Jerod's friend Al had the following homework problem:

Express 5.6×10^{-7} in standard form.

Al wrote 56,000,000. How can Jerod explain Al's error and how to correct it?

_____

_____

_____

37. Make a Conjecture Two numbers are written in scientific notation. The number with a positive exponent is divided by the number with a negative exponent. Describe the result. Explain your answer.

_____

_____

_____

10.4 Operations with Scientific Notation

FL 8.EE.1.4

Perform operations . . . in scientific notation. . . . choose units of appropriate size for measurements . . . . Interpret scientific notation . . . generated by technology.

ESSENTIAL QUESTION

How do you add, subtract, multiply, and divide using scientific notation?

Adding and Subtracting with Scientific Notation

Numbers in scientific notation can be added and subtracted, either directly or by rewriting them in standard form.

Math On the Spot
my.hrw.com

EXAMPLE 1   **FL** 8.EE.1.4

The table below shows the population of the three largest countries in North America in 2011. Find the total population of these countries.

Country	United States	Canada	Mexico
Population	3.1×10^8	3.38×10^7	1.1×10^8

Method 1:

STEP 1 First, write each population with the same power of 10.

United States: 3.1×10^8

Canada: 0.338×10^8

Mexico: 1.1×10^8

STEP 2 Add the multipliers for each population.

$3.1 + 0.338 + 1.1 = 4.538$

STEP 3 Write the final answer in scientific notation: 4.538×10^8.

Method 2:

STEP 1 First, write each number in standard notation.

United States: 310,000,000

Canada: 33,800,000

Mexico: 110,000,000

STEP 2 Find the sum of the numbers in standard notation.

$310,000,000 + 33,800,000 + 110,000,000 = 453,800,000$

STEP 3 Write the answer in scientific notation: 4.538×10^8.

Personal Math Trainer
Online Assessment and Intervention

my.hrw.com

Math On the Spot

my.hrw.com

Math Talk
Mathematical Practices

Could you write 2.025×10^{14} in standard notation to do the division? Would this be a good way to solve the problem?

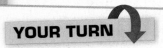

YOUR TURN

1. Using the population table above, how many more people live in Mexico than in Canada? Write your answer in scientific notation.

_____

Multiplying and Dividing with Scientific Notation

Numbers in scientific notation can be multiplied and divided directly by using properties of exponents.

EXAMPLE 2 *Problem Solving* **FL 8.EE.1.4**

When the Sun makes an orbit around the center of the Milky Way, it travels 2.025×10^{14} kilometers. The orbit takes 225 million years. At what rate does the Sun travel? Write your answer in scientific notation.

 Analyze Information

The answer is the number of kilometers per year that the Sun travels around the Milky Way.

 Formulate a Plan

Set up a division problem using Rate $= \frac{\text{Distance}}{\text{Time}}$ to represent the situation.

 Solve

STEP 1 Substitute the values from the problem into the Rate formula.

$$\text{Rate} = \frac{2.025 \times 10^{14} \text{ kilometers}}{225{,}000{,}000 \text{ years}}$$

STEP 2 Write the expression for rate with years in scientific notation.

$$\text{Rate} = \frac{2.025 \times 10^{14} \text{ kilometers}}{2.25 \times 10^8 \text{ years}} \qquad 225 \text{ million} = 2.25 \times 10^8$$

STEP 3 Find the quotient by dividing the decimals and using the laws of exponents.

$2.025 \div 2.25 = 0.9$ *Divide the multipliers.*

$\frac{10^{14}}{10^8} = 10^{14-8} = 10^6$ *Divide the powers of 10.*

STEP 4 Combine the answers to write the rate in scientific notation.

$$\text{Rate} = 0.9 \times 10^6 = 9.0 \times 10^5 \text{ km per year}$$

 Justify and Evaluate

Check your answer using multiplication.

$900{,}000 \times 225{,}000{,}000 = 202{,}500{,}000{,}000{,}000$, or 2.025×10^{14}. The answer is correct.

YOUR TURN

2. Light travels at a speed of 1.86×10^5 miles per second. It takes light from the Sun about 4.8×10^3 seconds to reach Saturn. Find the approximate distance from the Sun to Saturn. Write your answer

   in scientific notation. _____

3. Light travels at the speed of 1.17×10^7 miles per minute. Pluto's average distance from the Sun is 3,670,000,000 miles. On average, how long does it take sunlight to reach Pluto? Write your answer in scientific

   notation. _____

Scientific Notation on a Calculator

On many scientific calculators, you can enter numbers in scientific notation by using a function labeled "ee" or "EE". Usually, the letter "E" takes the place of "$\times 10$". So, the number 4.1×10^9 would appear as 4.1E9 on the calculator.

Math On the Spot

my.hrw.com

EXAMPLE 3 Real World   FL   8.EE.1.4

The table shows the approximate areas for three continents given in square meters. What is the total area of these three continents? Write the answer in scientific notation using more appropriate units.

Continent	Asia	Africa	Europe
Area (m²)	4.4×10^{13}	3.02×10^{13}	1.04×10^{13}

Find $4.4 \times 10^{13} + 3.02 \times 10^{13} + 1.04 \times 10^{13}$.

Enter 4.4E13 + 3.02E13 + 1.04E13 on your calculator.

Write the results from your calculator: 8.46E13.

Write this number in scientific notation: 8.46×10^{13} m².

Square kilometers is more appropriate: 8.46×10^7 km².

> Because 1 km = 1,000 m, 1 km² = 1,000² m², or 10^6 m². Divide by 10^6.

YOUR TURN

Write each number using calculator notation.

4. 7.5×10^5 5. 3×10^{-7} 6. 2.7×10^{13}

   _____   _____   _____

Write each number using scientific notation.

7. 4.5E−1   8. 5.6E12   9. 6.98E−8

   _____   _____   _____

Guided Practice

Add or subtract. Write your answer in scientific notation. (Example 1)

1. $4.2 \times 10^6 + 2.25 \times 10^5 + 2.8 \times 10^6$

$4.2 \times 10^6 + \boxed{} \times 10^{\boxed{}} + 2.8 \times 10^6$

$4.2 + \boxed{} + \boxed{}$

$\boxed{} \times 10^{\boxed{}}$

2. $8.5 \times 10^3 - 5.3 \times 10^3 - 1.0 \times 10^2$

$8.5 \times 10^3 - 5.3 \times 10^3 - \boxed{} \times 10^{\boxed{}}$

$\boxed{} - \boxed{} - \boxed{}$

$\boxed{} \times 10^{\boxed{}}$

3. $1.25 \times 10^2 + 0.50 \times 10^2 + 3.25 \times 10^2$

_____

4. $6.2 \times 10^5 - 2.6 \times 10^4 - 1.9 \times 10^2$

_____

Multiply or divide. Write your answer in scientific notation. (Example 2)

5. $\left(1.8 \times 10^9\right)\left(6.7 \times 10^{12}\right)$ _____

6. $\dfrac{3.46 \times 10^{17}}{2 \times 10^9}$ _____

7. $\left(5 \times 10^{12}\right)\left(3.38 \times 10^6\right)$ _____

8. $\dfrac{8.4 \times 10^{21}}{4.2 \times 10^{14}}$ _____

Write each number using calculator notation. (Example 3)

9. 3.6×10^{11}

_____

10. 7.25×10^{-5}

_____

11. 8×10^{-1}

_____

Write each number using scientific notation. (Example 3)

12. 7.6E−4

_____

13. 1.2E16

_____

14. 9E1

_____

? ESSENTIAL QUESTION CHECK-IN

15. How do you add, subtract, multiply, and divide numbers written in scientific notation?

_____

_____

_____

_____

_____

10.4 Independent Practice

FL 8.EE.1.4

16. An adult blue whale can eat 4.0×10^7 krill in a day. At that rate, how many krill can an adult blue whale eat in 3.65×10^2 days?

_____

17. A newborn baby has about 26,000,000,000 cells. An adult has about 4.94×10^{13} cells. How many times as many cells does an adult have than a newborn? Write your answer in scientific notation.

_____

Represent Real-World Problems The table shows the number of tons of waste generated and recovered (recycled) in 2010.

	Paper	Glass	Plastics
Tons generated	7.131×10^7	1.153×10^7	3.104×10^7
Tons recovered	4.457×10^7	0.313×10^7	0.255×10^7

18. What is the total amount of paper, glass, and plastic waste generated?

_____

_____

19. What is the total amount of paper, glass, and plastic waste recovered?

_____

20. What is the total amount of paper, glass, and plastic waste **not** recovered?

_____

21. Which type of waste has the lowest recovery ratio?

_____

Social Studies **The table shows the approximate populations of three countries.**

Country	China	France	Australia
Population	1.3×10^9	6.48×10^7	2.15×10^7

22. How many more people live in France than in Australia?

_____

23. The area of Australia is 2.95×10^6 square miles. What is the approximate average number of people per square mile in Australia?

_____

_____

24. How many times greater is the population of China than the population of France? Write your answer in standard notation.

_____

_____

25. Mia is 7.01568×10^6 minutes old. Convert her age to more appropriate units using years, months, and days. Assume each month to have 30.5 days.

_____

_____

26. Courtney takes 2.4×10^4 steps during her a long-distance run. Each step covers an average of 810 mm. What total distance (in mm) did Courtney cover during her run? Write your answer in scientific notation. Then convert the distance to the more appropriate unit kilometers. Write that answer in standard form.

_____

27. Social Studies The U.S. public debt as of October 2010 was $\$9.06 \times 10^{12}$. What was the average U.S. public debt per American if the population in 2010 was 3.08×10^8 people?

_____

 FOCUS ON HIGHER ORDER THINKING

28. Communicate Mathematical Ideas How is multiplying and dividing numbers in scientific notation different from adding and subtracting numbers in scientific notation?

_____

_____

_____

_____

_____

29. Explain the Error A student found the product of 8×10^6 and 5×10^9 to be 4×10^{15}. What is the error? What is the correct product?

_____

_____

30. Communicate Mathematical Ideas Describe a procedure that can be used to simplify $\dfrac{(4.87 \times 10^{12}) - (7 \times 10^{10})}{(3 \times 10^7) + (6.1 \times 10^8)}$. Write the expression in scientific notation in simplified form.

_____

_____

_____

_____

_____

_____

_____

Work Area

320 Unit 5

Ready to Go On?

Personal Math Trainer
Online Assessment and Intervention
⊙ my.hrw.com

10.1 Integer Exponents

Find the value of each power.

1. 3^{-4} _____

2. 35^0 _____

3. 4^4 _____

Use the properties of exponents to write an equivalent expression.

4. $8^3 \cdot 8^7$ _____

5. $\dfrac{12^6}{12^2}$ _____

6. $(10^3)^5$ _____

10.2 Scientific Notation with Positive Powers of 10

Convert each number to scientific notation or standard notation.

7. 2,000 _____

8. 91,007,500 _____

9. 1.0395×10^9 _____

10. 4×10^2 _____

10.3 Scientific Notation with Negative Powers of 10

Convert each number to scientific notation or standard notation.

11. 0.02 _____

12. 0.000701 _____

13. 8.9×10^{-5} _____

14. 4.41×10^{-2} _____

10.4 Operations with Scientific Notation

Perform the operation. Write your answer in scientific notation.

15. $7 \times 10^6 - 5.3 \times 10^6$ _____

16. $3.4 \times 10^4 + 7.1 \times 10^5$ _____

17. $(2 \times 10^4)(5.4 \times 10^6)$ _____

18. $\dfrac{7.86 \times 10^9}{3 \times 10^4}$ _____

19. Neptune's average distance from the Sun is 4.503×10^9 km. Mercury's average distance from the Sun is 5.791×10^7 km. About how many times farther from the Sun is Neptune than Mercury? Write your answer in scientific notation.

_____

? ESSENTIAL QUESTION

20. How is scientific notation used in the real world?

_____

_____

_____

Selected Response

1. Which of the following is equivalent to 6^{-3}?

(A) 216

(C) $-\frac{1}{216}$

(B) $\frac{1}{216}$

(D) -216

2. About 786,700,000 passengers traveled by plane in the United States in 2010. What is this number written in scientific notation?

(A) $7{,}867 \times 10^5$ passengers

(B) 7.867×10^2 passengers

(C) 7.867×10^8 passengers

(D) 7.867×10^9 passengers

3. In 2011, the population of Mali was about 1.584×10^7 people. What is this number written in standard notation?

(A) 1.584 people

(B) 1,584 people

(C) 15,840,000 people

(D) 158,400,000 people

4. The square root of a number is between 7 and 8. Which could be the number?

(A) 72

(C) 51

(B) 83

(D) 66

5. Each entry-level account executive in a large company makes an annual salary of 3.48×10^4. If there are 5.2×10^2 account executives in the company, how much do they make in all?

(A) 6.69×10^1

(B) 3.428×10^4

(C) 3.532×10^4

(D) 1.8096×10^7

6. Place the numbers in order from least to greatest.

$0.24, 4 \times 10^{-2}, 0.042, 2 \times 10^{-4}, 0.004$

(A) $2 \times 10^{-4}, 4 \times 10^{-2}, 0.004, 0.042, 0.24$

(B) $0.004, 2 \times 10^{-4}, 0.042, 4 \times 10^{-2}, 0.24$

(C) $0.004, 2 \times 10^{-4}, 4 \times 10^{-2}, 0.042, 0.24$

(D) $2 \times 10^{-4}, 0.004, 4 \times 10^{-2}, 0.042, 0.24$

7. Guillermo is $5\frac{5}{6}$ feet tall. What is this number of feet written as a decimal?

(A) 5.7 feet

(C) 5.83 feet

(B) $5.\overline{7}$ feet

(D) $5.8\overline{3}$ feet

8. A human hair has a width of about 6.5×10^{-5} meter. What is this width written in standard notation?

(A) 0.00000065 meter

(B) 0.0000065 meter

(C) 0.000065 meter

(D) 0.00065 meter

Mini-Task

9. Consider the following numbers: 7000, 700, 70, 0.7, 0.07, 0.007

a. Write the numbers in scientific notation.

_____

_____

b. Look for a pattern in the given list and the list in scientific notation. Which numbers are missing from the lists?

_____

c. Make a conjecture about the missing numbers.

_____

_____

MODULE 9 Real Numbers

? ESSENTIAL QUESTION

How can you use real numbers to solve real-world problems?

EXAMPLE 1

Write $0.\overline{81}$ as a fraction in simplest form.

$$x = 0.\overline{81}$$
$$100x = 81.\overline{81}$$
$$\underline{-x \quad -0.\overline{81}}$$
$$99x = 81$$
$$x = \frac{81}{99}$$
$$x = \frac{9}{11}$$

EXAMPLE 2

Solve each equation for *x*.

A $x^2 = 289$

$x = \pm\sqrt{289}$

$x = \pm 17$

The solutions are 17 and -17.

B $x^3 = 1{,}000$

$x = \sqrt[3]{1{,}000}$

$x = 10$

The solution is 10.

EXAMPLE 3

Write all names that apply to each number.

A $5.\overline{4}$
rational, real

$5.\overline{4}$ is a repeating decimal.

B $\frac{8}{4}$
whole, integer, rational, real

$\frac{8}{4} = 2$

C $\sqrt{13}$
irrational, real

13 is a whole number that is not a perfect square.

EXAMPLE 4

Order 6, 2π, and √38 from least to greatest.

2π is approximately equal to 2 × 3.14, or 6.28.

√38 is approximately 6.15 based on the following reasoning.

$$\sqrt{36} < \sqrt{38} < \sqrt{49} \qquad 6 < \sqrt{38} < 7 \qquad 6.1^2 = 37.21 \qquad 6.2^2 = 38.44$$

From least to greatest, the numbers are 6, √38, and 2π.

EXERCISES

Find the two square roots of each number. If the number is not a perfect square, approximate the values to the nearest 0.05.
(Lesson 9.1)

1. 16 _____

2. $\frac{4}{25}$ _____

3. 225 _____

4. $\frac{1}{49}$ _____

5. $\sqrt{10}$ _____

6. $\sqrt{18}$ _____

Write each decimal as a fraction in simplest form. (Lesson 9.1)

7. $0.\overline{5}$ _____

8. $0.\overline{63}$ _____

9. $0.2\overline{14}$ _____

Solve each equation for x. (Lesson 9.1)

10. $x^2 = 361$

11. $x^3 = 1{,}728$

12. $x^2 = \frac{49}{121}$

_____

_____

_____

Write all names that apply to each number. (Lesson 9.2)

13. $\frac{2}{3}$

14. $-\sqrt{100}$

_____

_____

15. $\frac{15}{5}$

16. $\sqrt{21}$

_____

_____

Compare. Write <, >, or =. (Lesson 9.3)

17. $\sqrt{7} + 5$ ◯ $7 + \sqrt{5}$

18. $6 + \sqrt{8}$ ◯ $\sqrt{6} + 8$

19. $\sqrt{4} - 2$ ◯ $4 - \sqrt{2}$

Order the numbers from least to greatest. (Lesson 9.3)

20. $\sqrt{81}, \frac{72}{7}, 8.9$ _____

21. $\sqrt{7}, 2.55, \frac{7}{3}$ _____

Exponents and Scientific Notation

? ESSENTIAL QUESTION

How can you use scientific notation to solve real-world problems?

EXAMPLE 1

Write each measurement in scientific notation.

A The diameter of Earth at the equator is approximately 12,700 kilometers.

Move the decimal point in 12,700 four places to the left: 1.2 7 0 0.

$12{,}700 = 1.27 \times 10^4$

B The diameter of a human hair is approximately 0.00254 centimeters.

Move the decimal point in 0.00254 three places to the right: 0.0 0 2.5 4

$0.00254 = 2.54 \times 10^{-3}$

EXAMPLE 2

Find the quotient: $\dfrac{2.4 \times 10^7}{9.6 \times 10^3}$

Divide the multipliers: $2.4 \div 9.6 = 0.25$

Divide the powers of ten: $\dfrac{10^7}{10^3} = 10^{7-3} = 10^4$

Combine the answers and write the product in scientific notation.

$0.25 \times 10^4 = 0.25 \times (10 \times 10^3) = (0.25 \times 10) \times 10^3 = 2.5 \times 10^3$

EXERCISES

Write each number in scientific notation. (Lessons 10.2, 10.3)

1. 25,500,000 _____

2. 0.00734 _____

Write each number in standard notation. (Lessons 10.2, 10.3)

3. 5.23×10^4 _____

4. 1.33×10^{-5} _____

Simplify each expression. (Lessons 10.1, 10.4)

5. $(9 - 7)^3 \cdot 5^0 + (8 + 3)^2$ _____

6. $\dfrac{(4 + 2)^2}{[(9 - 3)^3]^2}$ _____

7. $3.2 \times 10^5 + 1.25 \times 10^4 + 2.9 \times 10^5$

8. $(2{,}600)(3.24 \times 10^4)$

_____

_____

1. **CAREERS IN MATH** **Astronomer** An astronomer is studying Proxima Centauri, which is the closest star to our Sun. Proxima Centauri is 39,900,000,000,000,000 meters away.

   a. Write this distance in scientific notation.

   _____

   b. Light travels at a speed of 3.0×10^8 m/s (meters per second). How can you use this information to calculate the time in seconds it takes for light from Proxima Centauri to reach Earth? How many seconds does it take? Write your answer in scientific notation.

   _____

   _____

   c. Knowing that 1 year $= 3.1536 \times 10^7$ seconds, how many years does it take for light to travel from Proxima Centauri to Earth? Write your answer in standard notation. Round your answer to two decimal places.

   _____

2. Cory is making a poster of common geometric shapes. He draws a square with a side of length 4^3 cm, an equilateral triangle with a height of $\sqrt{200}$ cm, a circle with a circumference of 8π cm, a rectangle with length $\frac{122}{5}$ cm, and a parallelogram with base 3.14 cm.

   a. Which of these numbers are irrational?

   _____

   b. Write the numbers in this problem in order from least to greatest. Approximate π as 3.14.

   _____

   c. Explain why 3.14 is rational, but π is not.

   _____

   _____

   _____

Assessment Readiness

Personal Math Trainer

Online Assessment and Intervention

my.hrw.com

Selected Response

1. A square on a large calendar has an area of 4,220 square millimeters. Between which two integers is the length of one side of the square?

- Ⓐ between 20 and 21 millimeters
- Ⓑ between 64 and 65 millimeters
- Ⓒ between 204 and 205 millimeters
- Ⓓ between 649 and 650 millimeters

2. Which of the following numbers is rational but **not** an integer?

- Ⓐ −9   Ⓒ 0
- Ⓑ −4.3   Ⓓ 3

3. Which statement is false?

- Ⓐ No integers are irrational numbers.
- Ⓑ All whole numbers are integers.
- Ⓒ All rational numbers are real numbers.
- Ⓓ All integers are whole numbers.

4. In 2011, the population of Laos was about 6.586×10^6 people. What is this number written in standard notation?

- Ⓐ 6,586 people
- Ⓑ 658,600 people
- Ⓒ 6,586,000 people
- Ⓓ 65,860,000 people

5. Which of the following is **not** true?

- Ⓐ $\sqrt{16} + 4 > \sqrt{4} + 5$
- Ⓑ $4\pi > 12$
- Ⓒ $\sqrt{18} + 2 < \frac{15}{2}$
- Ⓓ $6 - \sqrt{35} < 0$

6. Which number is between $\sqrt{50}$ and $\frac{5\pi}{2}$?

- Ⓐ $\frac{22}{3}$ Ⓒ 6
- Ⓑ $2\sqrt{8}$ Ⓓ $\pi + 3$

7. Which number is indicated on the number line?

- Ⓐ $\pi + 4$ Ⓒ $\sqrt{14} + 4$
- Ⓑ $\frac{152}{20}$ Ⓓ $7.\overline{8}$

8. Which of the following is the number 5.03×10^{-5} written in standard form?

- Ⓐ 503,000
- Ⓑ 50,300,000
- Ⓒ 0.00503
- Ⓓ 0.0000503

9. Which correctly describes the relationship between supplementary angles?

- Ⓐ They have the same angle measure.
- Ⓑ The sum of their angle measures is 90 degrees.
- Ⓒ The sum of their angle measures is 180 degrees.
- Ⓓ The sum of their angle measures is 360 degrees.

10. A quarter weighs about 0.025 pounds. What is this weight written in scientific notation?

- Ⓐ 2.5×10^{-2} pounds
- Ⓑ 2.5×10^{1} pounds
- Ⓒ 2.5×10^{-1} pounds
- Ⓓ 2.5×10^{2} pounds

11. Which fraction is equivalent to $0.\overline{45}$?

   (A) $\frac{4}{9}$ (C) $\frac{4}{5}$

   (B) $\frac{5}{9}$ (D) $\frac{5}{11}$

12. What is the value of x if $x^2 = \frac{36}{81}$?

   (A) $\frac{2}{3}$ (C) $\frac{4}{9}$

   (B) $\pm\frac{2}{3}$ (D) $\pm\frac{4}{9}$

13. What is $\frac{[(9-2)^2]^4}{(4+3)^5}$ written in simplest form?

   (A) 7

   (B) 21

   (C) 49

   (D) 343

14. The total land area on Earth is about 6×10^7 square miles. The land area of Australia is about 3×10^6 square miles. About how many times larger is the land area on Earth than the land area of Australia?

   (A) 2

   (B) 10

   (C) 20

   (D) 60

15. Ricardo rolls a standard number cube 48 times. What is the best prediction for the number of times he will roll an even number that is greater than 2?

   (A) 4   (C) 24

   (B) 16   (D) 32

16. What is the value of the expression $(2.3 \times 10^7)(1.4 \times 10^{-2})$ written in scientific notation?

   (A) 3.7×10^{-14}

   (B) 3.7×10^5

   (C) 0.322×10^6

   (D) 3.22×10^5

17. What is the value of $\sqrt[3]{64}$?

   (A) 2

   (B) 4

   (C) 8

   (D) 16

Mini-Task

18. Amanda says that a human fingernail has a thickness of about 4.2×10^{-4} meter. Justin says that a human fingernail has a thickness of about 0.42 millimeter.

   a. What is the width in meters written in standard notation?

   _____

   b. Do Justin's and Amanda's measurements agree? Explain.

   _____

   _____

   _____

   _____

   c. Explain why Justin's estimate of the thickness of a human fingernail is more appropriate than Amanda's estimate.

   _____

   _____

   _____

   _____

   _____

   _____

Proportional and Nonproportional Relationships and Functions

CAREERS IN MATH

Cost Estimator A cost estimator determines the cost of a product or project, which helps businesses decide whether or not to manufacture a product or build a structure. Cost estimators analyze the costs of labor, materials, and use of equipment, among other things. Cost estimators use math when they assemble and analyze data. If you are interested in a career as a cost estimator, you should study these mathematical subjects:

- Algebra
- Trigonometry
- Calculus

Research other careers that require analyzing costs.

Unit 6 Performance Task

At the end of the unit, check out how **cost estimators** use math.

Vocabulary Preview

Use the puzzle to preview key vocabulary from this unit. Unscramble the circled letters within the found words to answer the riddle at the bottom of the page.

```
D  I  N  T  F  O  K  F  Z  Y  X  I  R  H  Ⓛ
T  I  D  Ⓞ  N  O  T  N  I  R  A  V  Z  B  I
U  U  R  Z  I  E  K  N  M  C  J  E  H  Z  N
Ⓟ  N  X  E  V  T  T  H  W  C  V  W  S  E  E
T  A  E  B  U  E  C  E  K  Q  O  P  D  U  A
U  I  V  A  Ⓡ  N  P  Ⓝ  M  K  Q  W  N  Z  R
Ⓞ  X  G  C  B  O  I  Q  U  M  Y  X  P  L  E
C  P  E  B  Ⓛ  K  B  T  J  F  H  L  A  K  Q
J  Ⓟ  V  S  L  Q  M  J  Ⓡ  G  H  R  U  N  U
T  E  F  N  I  Z  B  M  C  A  D  A  X  A  Ⓐ
T  T  O  S  V  D  T  H  W  B  T  D  B  E  T
K  O  O  I  I  E  Y  W  U  O  Q  E  P  K  I
P  G  T  G  L  S  O  J  Q  R  F  D  I  Q  Ⓞ
D  T  A  M  H  Q  T  S  T  A  J  Q  X  O  N
B  Ⓘ  V  A  R  I  A  T  E  D  A  Ⓣ  A  Y  N
```

- The *y*-coordinate of the point where the graph crosses the *y*-axis. (Lesson 12.2)
- A rule that assigns exactly one output to each input. (Lesson 14.1)
- The result after applying the function machine's rule. (Lesson 14.1)
- A rate in which the second quantity in the comparison is one unit. (Lesson 11.3)
- The ratio of change in rise to the corresponding change in run on a graph. (Lesson 11.2)
- A set of data that is made up of two paired variables. (Lesson 13.3)
- An equation whose solutions form a straight line on a coordinate plane. (Lesson 12.1)

Q: How much of the money earned does a professional sports team pay its star athlete?

A: An ___ ___ ___ ___ ___ ___ – ___ ___ ___ ___ ___ ___ ___ ___!

Proportional Relationships

? ESSENTIAL QUESTION

How can you use proportional relationships to solve real-world problems?

Real-World Video

Speedboats can travel at fast rates while sailboats travel more slowly. If you graphed distance versus time for both types of boats, you could tell by the steepness of the graph which boat was faster.

my.hrw.com

GO DIGITAL
my.hrw.com

my.hrw.com

Go digital with your write-in student edition, accessible on any device.

Math On the Spot

Scan with your smart phone to jump directly to the online edition, video tutor, and more.

Animated Math

Interactively explore key concepts to see how math works.

Personal Math Trainer

Get immediate feedback and help as you work through practice sets.

Are YOU Ready?

Complete these exercises to review skills you will need for this module.

Personal Math Trainer

Online Assessment and Intervention

⏻ my.hrw.com

Write Fractions as Decimals

EXAMPLE $\dfrac{1.7}{2.5} = ?$

Multiply the numerator and the denominator by a power of 10 so that the denominator is a whole number.

$\dfrac{1.7 \times 10}{2.5 \times 10} = \dfrac{17}{25}$

Write the fraction as a division problem. Write a decimal point and zeros in the dividend.
Place a decimal point in the quotient.
Divide as with whole numbers.

$$\begin{array}{r} 0.68 \\ 25\overline{)17.00} \\ -15\,0 \\ \hline 2\,00 \\ -2\,00 \\ \hline 0 \end{array}$$

Write each fraction as a decimal.

1. $\dfrac{3}{8}$ _____

2. $\dfrac{0.3}{0.4}$ _____

3. $\dfrac{0.13}{0.2}$ _____

4. $\dfrac{0.39}{0.75}$ _____

5. $\dfrac{4}{5}$ _____

6. $\dfrac{0.1}{2}$ _____

7. $\dfrac{3.5}{14}$ _____

8. $\dfrac{7}{14}$ _____

9. $\dfrac{0.3}{10}$ _____

Solve Proportions

EXAMPLE $\dfrac{5}{7} = \dfrac{x}{14}$

$\dfrac{5 \times 2}{7 \times 2} = \dfrac{x}{14}$ $7 \times 2 = 14$, so multiply the numerator and denominator by 2.

$\dfrac{10}{14} = \dfrac{x}{14}$ $5 \times 2 = 10$

$x = 10$

Solve each proportion for x.

10. $\dfrac{20}{18} = \dfrac{10}{x}$ _____

11. $\dfrac{x}{12} = \dfrac{30}{72}$ _____

12. $\dfrac{x}{4} = \dfrac{4}{16}$ _____

13. $\dfrac{11}{x} = \dfrac{132}{120}$ _____

14. $\dfrac{36}{48} = \dfrac{x}{4}$ _____

15. $\dfrac{x}{9} = \dfrac{21}{27}$ _____

16. $\dfrac{24}{16} = \dfrac{x}{2}$ _____

17. $\dfrac{30}{15} = \dfrac{6}{x}$ _____

18. $\dfrac{3}{x} = \dfrac{18}{36}$ _____

Reading Start-Up

Visualize Vocabulary

Use the ✔ words to complete the diagram.

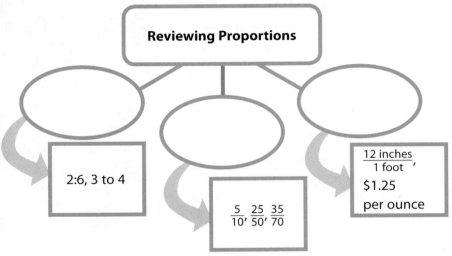

Reviewing Proportions

2:6, 3 to 4

$\frac{5}{10}, \frac{25}{50}, \frac{35}{70}$

$\frac{12 \text{ inches}}{1 \text{ foot}}$,
$1.25
per ounce

Understand Vocabulary

Match the term on the left to the definition on the right.

1. unit rate

2. constant of proportionality

3. proportional relationship

A. A constant ratio of two variables related proportionally.

B. A rate in which the second quantity in the comparison is one unit.

C. A relationship between two quantities in which the ratio of one quantity to the other quantity is constant.

Active Reading

Key-Term Fold Before beginning the module, create a key-term fold to help you learn the vocabulary in this module. Write the highlighted vocabulary words on one side of the flap. Write the definition for each word on the other side of the flap. Use the key-term fold to quiz yourself on the definitions used in this module.

Unpacking the Standards

Understanding the standards and the vocabulary terms in the standards will help you know exactly what you are expected to learn in this module.

 FL 8.EE.2.5

Graph proportional relationships, interpreting the unit rate as the slope of the graph. Compare two different proportional relationships represented in different ways.

Key Vocabulary

proportional relationship
(relación proporcional)
A relationship between two quantities in which the ratio of one quantity to the other quantity is constant.

slope *(pendiente)*
A measure of the steepness of a line on a graph; the rise divided by the run.

unit rate *(tasa unitaria)*
A rate in which the second quantity in the comparison is one unit.

What It Means to You

You will use data from a table and a graph to apply your understanding of rates to analyzing real-world situations.

UNPACKING EXAMPLE 8.EE.2.5

The table shows the volume of water released by Hoover Dam over a certain period of time. Use the data to make a graph. Find the slope of the line and explain what it shows.

Water Released from Hoover Dam	
Time (s)	Volume of water (m³)
5	75,000
10	150,000
15	225,000
20	300,000

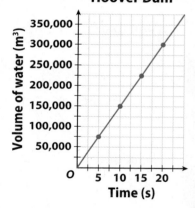

Water Released from Hoover Dam

The slope of the line is 15,000. This means that for every second that passed, 15,000 m³ of water was released from Hoover Dam.

Suppose another dam releases water over the same period of time at a rate of 180,000 m³ per minute. How do the two rates compare?

180,000 m³ per minute is equal to 3,000 m³ per second. This rate is one fifth the rate released by the Hoover Dam over the same time period.

Visit **my.hrw.com** to see all **Florida Math Standards** unpacked.

my.hrw.com

Representing Proportional Relationships

 FL 8.EE.2.6

...derive the equation $y = mx$ for a line through the origin... *Also 8.F.2.4*

ESSENTIAL QUESTION

How can you use tables, graphs, and equations to represent proportional situations?

EXPLORE ACTIVITY   FL Prep for 8.EE.2.6

Representing Proportional Relationships with Tables

In 1870, the French writer Jules Verne published *20,000 Leagues Under the Sea*, one of the most popular science fiction novels ever written. One definition of a *league* is a unit of measure equaling 3 miles.

A Complete the table.

Distance (leagues)	1	2	6		20,000
Distance (miles)	3			36	

B What relationships do you see among the numbers in the table?

_____

_____

C For each column of the table, find the ratio of the distance in miles to the distance in leagues. Write each ratio in simplest form.

$\dfrac{3}{1} = \boxed{}$ $\dfrac{\boxed{}}{2} = \boxed{}$ $\dfrac{\boxed{}}{6} = \boxed{}$ $\dfrac{36}{\boxed{}} = \boxed{}$ $\dfrac{\boxed{}}{20,000} = \boxed{}$

D What do you notice about the ratios? _____

Reflect

1. If you know the distance between two points in leagues, how can you

find the distance in miles? _____

2. If you know the distance between two points in miles, how can you find

the distance in leagues? _____

Representing Proportional Relationships with Equations

The ratio of the distance in miles to the distance in leagues is constant. This relationship is said to be *proportional*. A **proportional relationship** is a relationship between two quantities in which the ratio of one quantity to the other quantity is constant.

A proportional relationship can be described by an equation of the form $y = kx$, where k is a number called the **constant of proportionality**.

Sometimes it is useful to use another form of the equation, $k = \frac{y}{x}$.

EXAMPLE 1

 FL 8.EE.2.6

Meghan earns \$12 an hour at her part-time job. Show that the relationship between the amount she earned and the number of hours she worked is a proportional relationship. Then write an equation for the relationship.

STEP 1 Make a table relating amount earned to number of hours.

> For every hour Meghan works, she earns \$12. So, for 8 hours of work, she earns $8 \times \$12 = \$96$.

Number of hours	1	2	4	8
Amount earned ($)	12	24	48	96

STEP 2 For each number of hours, write the relationship of the amount earned and the number of hours as a ratio in simplest form.

$\frac{\text{amount earned}}{\text{number of hours}}$ $\quad \frac{12}{1} = \frac{12}{1} \quad\quad \frac{24}{2} = \frac{12}{1} \quad\quad \frac{48}{4} = \frac{12}{1} \quad\quad \frac{96}{8} = \frac{12}{1}$

Since the ratios for the two quantities are all equal to $\frac{12}{1}$, the relationship is proportional.

STEP 3 Write an equation.

> First tell what the variables represent.

Let x represent the number of hours.
Let y represent the amount earned.

Use the ratio as the constant of proportionality in the equation $y = kx$.

The equation is $y = \frac{12}{1}x$ or $y = 12x$.

Math Talk
Mathematical Practices

Describe two real-world quantities with a proportional relationship that can be described by the equation $y = 25x$.

YOUR TURN

3. Fifteen bicycles are produced each hour at the Speedy Bike Works. Show that the relationship between the number of bikes produced and the number of hours is a proportional relationship. Then write an equation for the relationship.

_____

Representing Proportional Relationships with Graphs

You can represent a proportional relationship with a graph. The graph will be a line that passes through the origin (0, 0). The graph shows the relationship between distance measured in miles to distance measured in leagues.

EXAMPLE 2

FL 8.EE.2.6

The graph shows the relationship between the weight of an object on the Moon and its weight on Earth. Write an equation for this relationship.

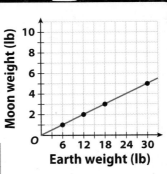

STEP 1 Use the points on the graph to make a table.

Earth weight (lb)	6	12	18	30
Moon weight (lb)	1	2	3	5

STEP 2 Find the constant of proportionality.

$\dfrac{\text{Moon weight}}{\text{Earth weight}}$ $\dfrac{1}{6} = \dfrac{1}{6}$ $\dfrac{2}{12} = \dfrac{1}{6}$ $\dfrac{3}{18} = \dfrac{1}{6}$ $\dfrac{5}{30} = \dfrac{1}{6}$

The constant of proportionality is $\dfrac{1}{6}$.

STEP 3 Write an equation.

Let x represent weight on Earth.

Let y represent weight on the Moon.

The equation is $y = \dfrac{1}{6}x$.   *Replace k with $\dfrac{1}{6}$ in $y = kx$.*

YOUR TURN

The graph shows the relationship between the amount of time that a backpacker hikes and the distance traveled.

4. What does the point (5, 6) represent?

_____

5. What is the equation of the relationship?

_____

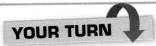

Personal Math Trainer

Online Assessment and Intervention

my.hrw.com

1. Vocabulary A proportional relationship is a relationship between two quantities in which the ratio of one quantity to the other quantity

| is / is not | constant.

2. Vocabulary When writing an equation of a proportional relationship in the form $y = kx$, k represents the _____.

3. Write an equation that describes the proportional relationship between the number of days and the number of weeks in a given length of time. (Explore Activity and Example 1)

a. Complete the table.

Time (weeks)	1	2	4		10
Time (days)	7			56	

b. Let x represent _____.

Let y represent _____.

The equation that describes the relationship is _____.

Each table or graph represents a proportional relationship. Write an equation that describes the relationship. (Example 1 and Example 2)

4. Physical Science The relationship between the numbers of oxygen atoms and hydrogen atoms in water

Oxygen atoms	2	5		120
Hydrogen atoms	4		34	

_____

5.

Map of Iowa

_____

6. If you know the equation of a proportional relationship, how can you draw the graph of the equation?

_____

_____

11.1 Independent Practice

FL 8.EE.2.6, 8.F.2.4

Personal Math Trainer

Online Assessment and Intervention

my.hrw.com

The table shows the relationship between temperatures measured on the Celsius and Fahrenheit scales.

Celsius temperature	0	10	20	30	40	50
Fahrenheit temperature	32	50	68	86	104	122

7. Is the relationship between the temperature scales proportional? Why or why not?

_____

_____

8. Describe the graph of the Celsius-Fahrenheit relationship.

_____

_____

9. Analyze Relationships Ralph opened a savings account with a deposit of $100. Every month after that, he deposited $20 more.

a. Why is the relationship described not proportional?

_____

_____

b. How could the situation be changed to make the situation proportional?

_____

_____

10. Represent Real-World Problems Describe a real-world situation that can be modeled by the equation $y = \frac{1}{20}x$. Be sure to describe what each variable represents.

_____

_____

Look for a Pattern The variables x and y are related proportionally.

11. When $x = 8$, $y = 20$. Find y when $x = 42$. _____

12. When $x = 12$, $y = 8$. Find x when $y = 12$. _____

13. The graph shows the relationship between the distance that a snail crawls and the time that it crawls.

Snail Crawling

a. Use the points on the graph to make a table.

Distance (in.)					
Time (min)					

b. Write the equation for the relationship and tell what each variable represents.

_____

_____

c. How long does it take the snail to crawl 85 inches? _____

H.O.T. FOCUS ON HIGHER ORDER THINKING

14. Communicate Mathematical Ideas Explain why all of the graphs in this lesson show the first quadrant but omit the other three quadrants.

_____

_____

_____

_____

15. Analyze Relationships Complete the table.

Length of side of square	1	2	3	4	5
Perimeter of square					
Area of square					

a. Are the length of a side of a square and the perimeter of the square related proportionally? Why or why not?

_____

_____

b. Are the length of a side of a square and the area of the square related proportionally? Why or why not?

_____

_____

16. Make a Conjecture A table shows a proportional relationship where k is the constant of proportionality. The rows are then switched. How does the new constant of proportionality relate to the original one?

_____

Rate of Change and Slope

FL 8.F.2.4

...Determine the rate of change...of the function from...two (x, y) values, including reading these from a table or from a graph....

ESSENTIAL QUESTION

How do you find a rate of change or a slope?

Investigating Rates of Change

A **rate of change** is a ratio of the amount of change in the dependent variable, or *output*, to the amount of change in the independent variable, or *input*.

EXAMPLE 1

FL 8.F.2.4

Eve keeps a record of the number of lawns she has mowed and the money she has earned. Tell whether the rates of change are constant or variable.

	Day 1	Day 2	Day 3	Day 4
Number of lawns	1	3	6	8
Amount earned ($)	15	45	90	120

STEP 1 Identify the input and output variables.

Input variable: number of lawns   Output variable: amount earned

STEP 2 Find the rates of change.

Day 1 to Day 2: $\dfrac{\text{change in \$}}{\text{change in lawns}} = \dfrac{45 - 15}{3 - 1} = \dfrac{30}{2} = 15$

Day 2 to Day 3: $\dfrac{\text{change in \$}}{\text{change in lawns}} = \dfrac{90 - 45}{6 - 3} = \dfrac{45}{3} = 15$

Day 3 to Day 4: $\dfrac{\text{change in \$}}{\text{change in lawns}} = \dfrac{120 - 90}{8 - 6} = \dfrac{30}{2} = 15$

The rates of change are constant: $15 per lawn.

Math Talk
Mathematical Practices

Would you expect the rates of change of a car's speed during a drive through a city to be constant or variable? Explain.

YOUR TURN

1. The table shows the approximate height of a football after it is kicked. Tell whether the rates of change are constant or variable.

Find the rates of change:

_____

The rates of change are [**constant / variable**].

Time (s)	Height (ft)
0	0
0.5	18
1.5	31
2	26

Personal Math Trainer

Online Assessment and Intervention

⊙ my.hrw.com

Math On the Spot

⊙ my.hrw.com

Using Graphs to Find Rates of Change

You can also use a graph to find rates of change.

The graph shows the distance Nathan bicycled over time. What is Nathan's rate of change?

A Find the rate of change from 1 hour to 2 hours.

$$\frac{\text{change in distance}}{\text{change in time}} = \frac{30 - \boxed{}}{2 - 1} = \frac{\boxed{}}{1} = \boxed{} \text{ miles per hour}$$

B Find the rate of change from 1 hour to 4 hours.

$$\frac{\text{change in distance}}{\text{change in time}} = \frac{60 - \boxed{}}{4 - \boxed{}} = \frac{\boxed{}}{\boxed{}} = \boxed{} \text{ miles per hour}$$

C Find the rate of change from 2 hour to 4 hours.

$$\frac{\text{change in distance}}{\text{change in time}} = \frac{60 - \boxed{}}{4 - \boxed{}} = \frac{\boxed{}}{\boxed{}} = \boxed{} \text{ miles per hour}$$

D Recall that the graph of a proportional relationship is a line through the origin. Explain whether the relationship between Nathan's time and distance is a proportional relationship.

_____

_____

Reflect

2. **Make a Conjecture** Does a proportional relationship have a constant rate of change?

_____

3. Does it matter what interval you use when you find the rate of change of a proportional relationship? Explain.

_____

_____

Calculating Slope *m*

When the rate of change of a relationship is constant, any segment of its graph has the same steepness. The constant rate of change is called the *slope* of the line.

Slope Formula

The **slope** of a line is the ratio of the change in *y*-values (rise) for a segment of the graph to the corresponding change in *x*-values (run).

$$m = \frac{y_2 - y_1}{x_2 - x_1}$$

EXAMPLE 2

FL 8.F.2.4

Find *m*, the slope of the line.

STEP 1 Choose two points on the line.
$P_1(x_1, y_1) = (-3, 2)$ $P_2(x_2, y_2) = (-6, 4)$

STEP 2 Find the change in *y*-values (rise = $y_2 - y_1$) and the change in *x*-values (run = $x_2 - x_1$) as you move from one point to the other.

$$\begin{aligned}
\textbf{rise} &= y_2 - y_1 & \textbf{run} &= x_2 - x_1 \\
&= 4 - 2 & &= -6 - (-3) \\
&= 2 & &= -3
\end{aligned}$$

> If you move up or right, the change is positive. If you move down or left, the change is negative.

STEP 3 $m = \dfrac{\text{rise}}{\text{run}} = \dfrac{y_2 - y_1}{x_2 - x_1}$

$$= \frac{2}{-3}$$

$$= -\frac{2}{3}$$

My Notes

YOUR TURN

4. The graph shows the rate at which water is leaking from a tank. The slope of the line gives the leaking rate in gallons per minute. Find the slope of the line.

Rise = _____   Run = _____

Slope = _____

Personal
Math Trainer

Online Assessment
and Intervention

my.hrw.com

Guided Practice

Tell whether the rates of change are constant or variable. (Example 1)

1. building measurements _____

Feet	3	12	27	75
Yards	1	4	9	25

2. computers sold _____

Week	2	4	9	20
Number Sold	6	12	25	60

3. distance an object falls _____

Distance (ft)	16	64	144	256
Time (s)	1	2	3	4

4. cost of sweaters _____

Number	2	4	7	9
Cost ($)	38	76	133	171

Erica walks to her friend Philip's house. The graph shows Erica's distance from home over time. (Explore Activity)

5. Find the rate of change from 1 minute to 2 minutes.

$$\frac{\text{change in distance}}{\text{change in time}} = \frac{400 - \boxed{}}{2 - \boxed{}} = \frac{\boxed{}}{\boxed{}} = \boxed{} \text{ ft per min}$$

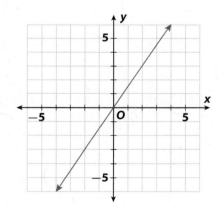

6. Find the rate of change from 1 minute to 4 minutes. _____

Find the slope of each line. (Example 2)

7.

slope = _____

8.

slope = _____

? ESSENTIAL QUESTION CHECK-IN

9. If you know two points on a line, how can you find the rate of change of the variables being graphed?

_____

_____

_____

Guided Practice

Tell whether the rates of change are constant or variable. (Example 1)

1. building measurements _____

Feet	3	12	27	75
Yards	1	4	9	25

2. computers sold _____

Week	2	4	9	20
Number Sold	6	12	25	60

3. distance an object falls _____

Distance (ft)	16	64	144	256
Time (s)	1	2	3	4

4. cost of sweaters _____

Number	2	4	7	9
Cost ($)	38	76	133	171

Erica walks to her friend Philip's house. The graph shows Erica's distance from home over time. (Explore Activity)

5. Find the rate of change from 1 minute to 2 minutes.

$$\frac{\text{change in distance}}{\text{change in time}} = \frac{400 - \boxed{}}{2 - \boxed{}} = \frac{\boxed{}}{\boxed{}} = \boxed{} \text{ ft per min}$$

6. Find the rate of change from 1 minute to 4 minutes. _____

Find the slope of each line. (Example 2)

7.

slope = _____

8.

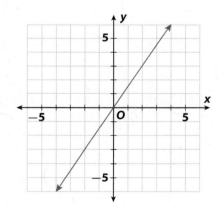

slope = _____

? ESSENTIAL QUESTION CHECK-IN

9. If you know two points on a line, how can you find the rate of change of the variables being graphed?

_____

_____

_____

11.2 Independent Practice

FL 8.F.2.4

10. Rectangle *EFGH* is graphed on a coordinate plane with vertices at *E*(−3, 5), *F*(6, 2), *G*(4, −4), and *H*(−5, −1).

a. Find the slopes of each side.

_____

b. What do you notice about the slopes of opposite sides?

_____

c. What do you notice about the slopes of adjacent sides?

_____

11. A bicyclist started riding at 8:00 A.M. The diagram below shows the distance the bicyclist had traveled at different times. What was the bicyclist's average rate of speed in miles per hour?

8:00 A.M. ← 4.5 miles → **8:18** A.M. ← 7.5 miles → **8:48** A.M.

_____

12. Multistep A line passes through (6, 3), (8, 4), and (*n*, −2). Find the value of *n*.

_____

13. A large container holds 5 gallons of water. It begins leaking at a constant rate. After 10 minutes, the container has 3 gallons of water left.

a. At what rate is the water leaking?

_____

b. After how many minutes will the container be empty?

_____

14. Critique Reasoning Billy found the slope of the line through the points (2, 5) and (−2, −5) using the equation $\frac{2-(-2)}{5-(-5)}=\frac{2}{5}$. What mistake did he make?

_____

_____

15. Multiple Representations Graph parallelogram *ABCD* on a coordinate plane with vertices at *A*(3, 4), *B*(6, 1), *C*(0, −2), and *D*(−3, 1).

   a. Find the slope of each side.

   _____

   _____

   b. What do you notice about the slopes?

   _____

   _____

   c. Draw another parallelogram on the coordinate plane. Do the slopes have the same characteristics?

   _____

H.O.T.   FOCUS ON HIGHER ORDER THINKING

Work Are

16. Communicate Mathematical Ideas Ben and Phoebe are finding the slope of a line. Ben chose two points on the line and used them to find the slope. Phoebe used two different points to find the slope. Did they get the same answer? Explain.

_____

_____

_____

17. Analyze Relationships Two lines pass through the origin. The lines have slopes that are opposites. Compare and contrast the lines.

_____

_____

_____

_____

18. Reason Abstractly What is the slope of the *x*-axis? Explain.

_____

_____

_____

Interpreting the Unit Rate as Slope

FL 8.EE.2.5

Graph proportional relationships, interpreting the unit rate as the slope of the graph. Compare two different proportional relationships represented in different ways.
Also 8.F.1.2, 8.F.2.4

ESSENTIAL QUESTION

How do you interpret the unit rate as slope?

EXPLORE ACTIVITY FL 8.EE.2.5, 8.F.2.4

Relating the Unit Rate to Slope

A rate is a comparison of two quantities that have different units, such as miles and hours. A **unit rate** is a rate in which the second quantity in the comparison is one unit.

A storm is raging on Misty Mountain. The graph shows the constant rate of change of the snow level on the mountain.

A Find the slope of the graph using the points (1, 2) and (5, 10). Remember that the slope is the constant rate of change.

Misty Mountain Storm

(graph: Snowfall (in.) vs. Time (h))

B Find the unit rate of snowfall in inches per hour. Explain your method.

_____

_____

C Compare the slope of the graph and the unit rate of change in the snow level. What do you notice?

_____

D Which unique point on this graph gives you the slope of the graph and the unit rate of change in the snow level? Explain how you found the point.

_____

_____

_____

_____

Graphing Proportional Relationships

You can use a table and a graph to find the unit rate and slope that describe a real-world proportional relationship. The constant of proportionality for a proportional relationship is the same as the slope.

EXAMPLE 1

Every 3 seconds, 4 cubic feet of water pass over a dam. Draw a graph of the situation. Find the unit rate of this proportional relationship.

STEP 1 Make a table.

Time (s)	3	6	9	12	15
Volume (ft³)	4	8	12	16	20

STEP 2 Draw a graph.

STEP 3 Find the slope.

$$\text{slope} = \frac{\text{rise}}{\text{run}} = \frac{8}{6}$$

$$= \frac{4}{3}$$

Water Over the Dam

Math Talk

Mathematical Practices

In a proportional relationship, how are the constant of proportionality, the unit rate, and the slope of the graph of the relationship related?

The unit rate of water passing over the dam and the slope of the graph of the relationship are equal, $\frac{4}{3}$ cubic feet per second.

Reflect

1. **What If?** Without referring to the graph, how do you know that the point $\left(1, \frac{4}{3}\right)$ is on the graph?

_____

_____

YOUR TURN

2. Tomas rides his bike at a steady rate of 2 miles every 10 minutes. Graph the situation. Find the unit rate of this proportional relationship.

_____

_____

_____

Tomas's Ride

Using Slopes to Compare Unit Rates

You can compare proportional relationships presented in different ways.

Math On the Spot

my.hrw.com

EXAMPLE 2   FL 8.EE.2.5, 8.F.1.2

The equation $y = 2.75x$ represents the rate, in barrels per hour, that oil is pumped from Well A. The graph represents the rate that oil is pumped from Well B. Which well pumped oil at a faster rate?

Well B Pumping Rate

STEP 1 Use the equation $y = 2.75x$ to make a table for Well A's pumping rate, in barrels per hour.

Time (h)	1	2	3	4
Quantity (barrels)	2.75	5.5	8.25	11

STEP 2 Use the table to find the slope of the graph of Well A.

$$\text{slope} = \text{unit rate} = \frac{5.5 - 2.75}{2 - 1} = \frac{2.75}{1} = \textbf{2.75 barrels/hour}$$

STEP 3 Use the graph to find the slope of the graph of Well B.

$$\text{slope} = \text{unit rate} = \frac{\text{rise}}{\text{run}} = \frac{10}{4} = \textbf{2.5 barrels/hour}$$

STEP 4 Compare the unit rates.

$2.75 > 2.5$, so Well A's rate, 2.75 barrels/hour, is faster.

Reflect

3. Describe the relationships among the slope of the graph of Well A's rate, the equation representing Well A's rate, and the constant of proportionality.

_____

_____

YOUR TURN

4. The equation $y = 375x$ represents the relationship between x, the time that a plane flies in hours, and y, the distance the plane flies in miles for Plane A. The table represents the relationship for Plane B. Find the slope of the graph for each plane and the plane's rate of speed. Determine which plane is flying at a faster rate of speed.

Time (h)	1	2	3	4
Distance (mi)	425	850	1275	1700

_____

Personal Math Trainer

Online Assessment and Intervention

my.hrw.com

Give the slope of the graph and the unit rate. (Explore Activity and Example 1)

1. Jorge: 5 miles every 6 hours

Jorge

2. Akiko

Time (h)	4	8	12	16
Distance (mi)	5	10	15	20

Akiko

_____

_____

3. The equation $y = 0.5x$ represents the distance Henry hikes, in miles, over time, in hours. The graph represents the rate that Clark hikes. Determine which hiker is faster. Explain. (Example 2)

Clark

_____

_____

_____

Write an equation relating the variables in each table. (Example 2)

4.

Time (x)	1	2	4	6
Distance (y)	15	30	60	90

5.

Time (x)	16	32	48	64
Distance (y)	6	12	18	24

_____

_____

? ESSENTIAL QUESTION CHECK-IN

6. Describe methods you can use to show a proportional relationship between two variables, x and y. For each method, explain how you can find the unit rate and the slope.

_____

_____

_____

_____

11.3 Independent Practice

 FL 8.EE.2.5, 8.F.1.2, 8.F.2.4

Personal Math Trainer

Online Assessment and Intervention

my.hrw.com

7. A Canadian goose migrated at a steady rate of 3 miles every 4 minutes.

a. Fill in the table to describe the relationship.

Time (min)	4	8			20
Distance (mi)			9	12	

b. Graph the relationship.

Migration Flight

c. Find the slope of the graph and describe what it means in the context of this problem.

_____

_____

_____

_____

8. **Vocabulary** A unit rate is a rate in which the

| **first quantity / second quantity** | in the comparison is one unit.

9. The table and the graph represent the rate at which two machines are bottling milk in gallons per second.

Machine 1

Time (s)	1	2	3	4
Amount (gal)	0.6	1.2	1.8	2.4

Machine 2

a. Determine the slope and unit rate of each machine.

_____

_____

b. Determine which machine is working at a faster rate.

_____

10. **Cycling** The equation $y = \frac{1}{9}x$ represents the distance y, in kilometers, that Patrick traveled in x minutes while training for the cycling portion of a triathlon. The table shows the distance y Jennifer traveled in x minutes in her training. Who has the faster training rate?

Time (min)	40	64	80	96
Distance (km)	5	8	10	12

_____

_____

_____

H.O.T. FOCUS ON HIGHER ORDER THINKING

Work Area

11. **Analyze Relationships** There is a proportional relationship between minutes and dollars per minute, shown on a graph of printing expenses. The graph passes through the point (1, 4.75). What is the slope of the graph? What is the unit rate? Explain.

_____

_____

_____

12. **Draw Conclusions** Two cars start at the same time and travel at different constant rates. A graph for Car A passes through the point (0.5, 27.5), and a graph for Car B passes through (4, 240). Both graphs show distance in miles and time in hours. Which car is traveling faster? Explain.

_____

_____

_____

_____

13. **Critical Thinking** The table shows the rate at which water is being pumped into a swimming pool.

Time (min)	2	5	7	12
Amount (gal)	36	90	126	216

Use the unit rate and the amount of water pumped after 12 minutes to find how much water will have been pumped into the pool after $13\frac{1}{2}$ minutes. Explain your reasoning.

_____

_____

_____

_____

Ready to Go On?

Personal Math Trainer

Online Assessment and Intervention

⏲ my.hrw.com

11.1 Representing Proportional Relationships

1. Find the constant of proportionality for the table of values.

x	2	3	4	5
y	3	4.5	6	7.5

_____

2. Phil is riding his bike. He rides 25 miles in 2 hours, 37.5 miles in 3 hours, and 50 miles in 4 hours. Find the constant of proportionality and write an equation to describe the situation.

_____

11.2 Rate of Change and Slope

Find the slope of each line.

3.

_____

4.

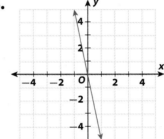

_____

11.3 Interpreting the Unit Rate as Slope

5. The distance Train A travels is represented by $d = 70t$, where d is the distance in kilometers and t is the time in hours. The distance Train B travels at various times is shown in the table. What is the unit rate of each train? Which train is going faster?

Time (hours)	Distance (km)
2	150
4	300
5	375

_____

_____

? **ESSENTIAL QUESTION**

6. What is the relationship among proportional relationships, lines, rates of change, and slope?

_____

_____

Selected Response

1. Which of the following is equivalent to 5^{-1}?

(A) 4

(C) $-\frac{1}{5}$

(B) $\frac{1}{5}$

(D) -5

2. Prasert earns $9 an hour. Which table represents this proportional relationship?

(A)

Hours	4	6	8
Earnings ($)	36	54	72

(B)

Hours	4	6	8
Earnings ($)	36	45	54

(C)

Hours	2	3	4
Earnings ($)	9	18	27

(D)

Hours	2	3	4
Earnings ($)	18	27	54

3. A factory produces widgets at a constant rate. After 4 hours, 3,120 widgets have been produced. At what rate are the widgets being produced?

(A) 630 widgets per hour

(B) 708 widgets per hour

(C) 780 widgets per hour

(D) 1,365 widgets per hour

4. A full lake begins dropping at a constant rate. After 4 weeks it has dropped 3 feet. What is the unit rate of change in the lake's level compared to its full level?

(A) 0.75 feet per week

(B) 1.33 feet per week

(C) −0.75 feet per week

(D) −1.33 feet per week

5. What is the slope of the line below?

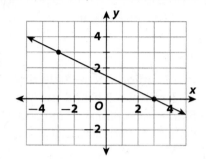

(A) −2

(C) $\frac{1}{2}$

(B) $-\frac{1}{2}$

(D) 2

6. Jim earns $41.25 in 5 hours. Susan earns $30.00 in 4 hours. Pierre's hourly rate is less than Jim's, but more than Susan's. What is his hourly rate?

(A) $6.50

(C) $7.35

(B) $7.75

(D) $8.25

Mini-Task

7. Joelle can read 3 pages in 4 minutes, 4.5 pages in 6 minutes, and 6 pages in 8 minutes.

a. Make a table of the data.

Minutes			
Pages			

b. Use the values in the table to find the unit rate.

_____

c. Graph the relationship between minutes and pages read.

Nonproportional Relationships

? ESSENTIAL QUESTION

How can you use non-proportional relationships to solve real-world problems?

Real-World Video

The distance a car can travel on a tank of gas or a full battery charge in an electric car depends on factors such as fuel capacity and the car's efficiency. This is described by a nonproportional relationship.

my.hrw.com

GO DIGITAL

my.hrw.com

my.hrw.com

Go digital with your write-in student edition, accessible on any device.

Math On the Spot

Scan with your smart phone to jump directly to the online edition, video tutor, and more.

Animated Math

Interactively explore key concepts to see how math works.

Personal Math Trainer

Get immediate feedback and help as you work through practice sets.

Are YOU Ready?

Complete these exercises to review skills you will need for this module.

Integer Operations

EXAMPLE

$$-7 - (-4) = -7 + 4$$

$$|-7| - |4|$$

$$7 - 4, \text{ or } 3$$

$$= -3$$

To subtract an integer, add its opposite.

The signs are different, so find the difference of the absolute values.

Use the sign of the number with the greater absolute value.

Find each difference.

1. $3 - (-5)$ _____

2. $-4 - 5$ _____

3. $6 - 10$ _____

4. $-5 - (-3)$ _____

5. $8 - (-8)$ _____

6. $9 - 5$ _____

7. $-3 - 9$ _____

8. $0 - (-6)$ _____

9. $12 - (-9)$ _____

10. $-6 - (-4)$ _____

11. $-7 - 10$ _____

12. $5 - 14$ _____

Graph Ordered Pairs (First Quadrant)

EXAMPLE

To graph a point at (6, 2), start at the origin.

Move 6 units right.

Then move 2 units up.

Graph point A(6, 2).

Graph each point on the coordinate grid.

13. B (0, 5)

14. C (8, 0)

15. D (5, 7)

16. E (2, 3)

Reading Start-Up

Visualize Vocabulary

Use the ✔ words to complete the diagram. You can put more than one word in each box.

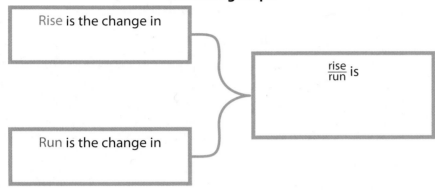

Reviewing Slope

Rise is the change in _____

Run is the change in _____

$\frac{rise}{run}$ is _____

Vocabulary

Review Words

   ordered pair *(par ordenado)*

   proportional relationship *(relación proporcional)*

✔ rate of change *(tasa de cambio)*

✔ slope *(pendiente)*

✔ *x*-coordinate *(coordenada x)*

✔ *y*-coordinate *(coordenada y)*

Preview Words

   linear equation *(ecuación lineal)*

   slope-intercept form of an equation *(forma de pendiente-intersección)*

   y-intercept *(intersección con el eje y)*

Understand Vocabulary

Complete the sentences using the preview words.

1. The *y*-coordinate of the point where a graph of a line crosses the *y*-axis is the _____.

2. A _____ is an equation whose solutions form a straight line on a coordinate plane.

3. A linear equation written in the form $y = mx + b$ is the

   _____.

Active Reading

Booklet Before beginning the module, create a booklet to help you learn the concepts. Write the main idea of each lesson on each page of the booklet. As you study each lesson, write important details that support the main idea, such as vocabulary and formulas. Refer to your finished booklet as you work on assignments and study for tests.

Unpacking the Standards

Understanding the standards and the vocabulary terms in the standards will help you know exactly what you are expected to learn in this module.

Interpret the equation $y = mx + b$ as defining a linear function whose graph is a straight line.

Key Vocabulary

slope *(pendiente)*
A measure of the steepness of a line on a graph; the rise divided by the run.

y-intercept *(intersección con el eje y)*
The y-coordinate of the point where the graph of a line crosses the y-axis.

What It Means to You

You will identify the slope and the y-intercept of a line by looking at its equation and use them to graph the line.

UNPACKING EXAMPLE 8.F.1.3

Graph $y = 3x - 2$ using the slope and the y-intercept.

$$y = mx + b$$

slope y-intercept

The slope m is 3, and the y-intercept is -2.

Plot the point $(0, -2)$. Use the slope $3 = \frac{3}{1}$ to find another point by moving *up* 3 and to the *right* 1. Draw the line through the points.

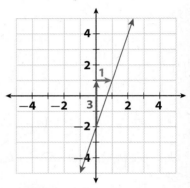

Give examples of functions that are not linear.

Key Vocabulary

function *(función)*
An input-output relationship that has exactly one output for each input.

linear function *(función lineal)*
A function whose graph is a straight line.

What It Means to You

You will distinguish linear relationships from nonlinear relationships by looking at graphs.

UNPACKING EXAMPLE 8.F.1.3

Which relationship is linear and which is nonlinear?

$P = 4s$

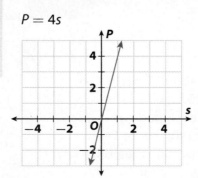

$P = 4s$ is linear because its graph is a line.

$A = s^2$

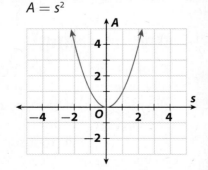

$A = s^2$ is not linear because its graph is not a line.

Visit **my.hrw.com** to see all **Florida Math Standards** unpacked.

my.hrw.com

Representing Linear Nonproportional Relationships

 FL 8.F.1.3

Interpret the equation $y = mx + b$ as defining a linear function, whose graph is a straight line; ...

ESSENTIAL QUESTION

How can you use tables, graphs, and equations to represent linear nonproportional situations?

Representing Linear Relationships Using Tables

You can use an equation to describe the relationship between two quantities in a real-world situation. You can use a table to show some values that make the equation true.

Math On the Spot
my.hrw.com

EXAMPLE 1

FL Prep for 8.F.1.3

The equation $y = 3x + 2$ gives the total charge, y, for one person to rent a pair of shoes and bowl x games at Baxter Bowling Lanes based on the prices shown. Make a table of values for this situation.

STEP 1 Choose several values for x that make sense in context.

x (number of games)	1	2	3	4
y (total cost in dollars)				

STEP 2 Use the equation $y = 3x + 2$ to find y for each value of x.

x (number of games)	1	2	3	4
y (total cost in dollars)	5	8	11	14

Substitute 1 for x:
$y = 3(1) + 2 = 5$.

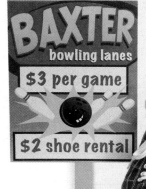

BAXTER bowling lanes

$3 per game

$2 shoe rental

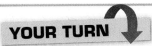

YOUR TURN

1. Francisco makes $12 per hour doing part-time work on Saturdays. He spends $4 on transportation to and from work. The equation $y = 12x - 4$ gives his earnings y, after transportation costs, for working x hours. Make a table of values for this situation.

x (number of hours)				
y (earnings in dollars)				

Personal Math Trainer

Online Assessment and Intervention

my.hrw.com

Examining Linear Relationships

Recall that a proportional relationship is a relationship between two quantities in which the ratio of one quantity to the other quantity is constant. The graph of a proportional relationship is a line through the origin. Relationships can have a constant rate of change but not be proportional.

The entrance fee for Mountain World theme park is $20. Visitors purchase additional $2 tickets for rides, games, and food. The equation $y = 2x + 20$ gives the total cost, y, to visit the park, including purchasing x tickets.

STEP 1 Complete the table.

x (number of tickets)	0	2	4	6	8
y (total cost in dollars)	20				

STEP 2 Plot the ordered pairs from the table. Describe the shape of the graph.

_____

STEP 3 Find the rate of change between each point and the next. Is the rate constant?

_____

STEP 4 Calculate $\frac{y}{x}$ for the values in the table. Explain why the relationship between number of tickets and total cost is not proportional.

_____

_____

_____

Theme Park Costs

Cost ($)

Number of tickets

Reflect

2. **Analyze Relationships** Would it make sense to add more points to the graph from $x = 0$ to $x = 10$? Would it make sense to connect the points with a line? Explain.

_____

_____

_____

_____

Representing Linear Relationships Using Graphs

A **linear equation** is an equation whose solutions are ordered pairs that form a line when graphed on a coordinate plane. Linear equations can be written in the form $y = mx + b$. When $b \neq 0$, the relationship between x and y is *nonproportional*.

Math On the Spot
my.hrw.com

 EXAMPLE 2 FL 8.F.1.3

The diameter of a Douglas fir tree is currently 10 inches when measured at chest height. Over the next 50 years, the diameter is expected to increase by an average growth rate of $\frac{2}{5}$ inch per year. The equation $y = \frac{2}{5}x + 10$ gives y, the diameter of the tree in inches, after x years. Draw a graph of the equation. Describe the relationship.

STEP 1 Make a table. Choose several values for x that make sense in context. To make calculations easier, choose multiples of 5.

x (years)	0	10	20	30	50
y (diameter in inches)	10	14	18	22	30

STEP 2 Plot the ordered pairs from the table. Then draw a line connecting the points to represent all the possible solutions.

STEP 3 The relationship is linear but nonproportional. The graph is a line but it does not go through the origin.

Fir Tree Growth

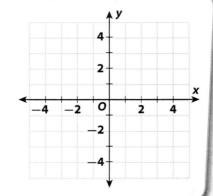

YOUR TURN

3. Make a table and graph the solutions of the equation $y = -2x + 1$.

x	−1	0	1	2
y				

Personal Math Trainer
Online Assessment and Intervention
my.hrw.com

My Notes

Make a table of values for each equation. (Example 1)

1. $y = 2x + 5$

x	−2	−1	0	1	2
y					

2. $y = \frac{3}{8}x - 5$

x	−8	0	8		
y					

Explain why each relationship is not proportional. (Explore Activity)

3.

x	0	2	4	6	8
y	3	7	11	15	19

First calculate $\frac{y}{x}$ for the values in the table.

_____

_____

_____

4.

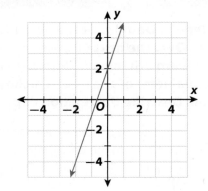

_____

_____

Complete the table for the equation. Then use the table to graph the equation. (Example 2)

5. $y = x - 1$

x	−2	−1	0	1	2
y					

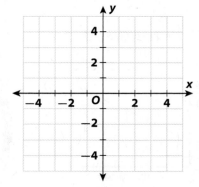

? ESSENTIAL QUESTION CHECK-IN

6. How can you choose values for x when making a table of values representing a real world situation?

_____

_____

_____

12.1 Independent Practice

FL 8.F.1.3

Personal
Math Trainer

Online
Assessment and
Intervention

my.hrw.com

State whether the graph of each linear relationship is a solid line or a set of unconnected points. Explain your reasoning.

7. The relationship between the number of $4 lunches you buy with a $100 school lunch card and the money remaining on the card

_____
_____
_____
_____

8. The relationship between time and the distance remaining on a 3-mile walk for someone walking at a steady rate of 2 miles per hour

_____
_____
_____
_____

9. Analyze Relationships Simone paid $12 for an initial year's subscription to a magazine. The renewal rate is $8 per year. This situation can be represented by the equation $y = 8x + 12$, where x represents the number of years the subscription is renewed and y represents the total cost.

a. Make a table of values for this situation.

b. Draw a graph to represent the situation. Include a title and axis labels.

c. Explain why this relationship is not proportional.

_____
_____
_____
_____

d. Does it make sense to connect the points on the graph with a solid line? Explain.

_____
_____
_____

(graph grid with y-axis labeled 8, 16, 24, 32, 40, 48, 56 and x-axis labeled 2, 4, 6, 8, 10, 12, 14, origin O)

10. Analyze Relationships A proportional relationship is a linear relationship because the rate of change is constant (and equal to the constant of proportionality). What is required of a proportional relationship that is *not* required of a general linear relationship?

_____

_____

11. Communicate Mathematical Ideas Explain how you can identify a linear non-proportional relationship from a table, a graph, and an equation.

_____

_____

_____

Work Area

12. Critique Reasoning George observes that for every increase of 1 in the value of x, there is an increase of 60 in the corresponding value of y. He claims that the relationship represented by the table is proportional. Critique George's reasoning.

x	1	2	3	4	5
y	90	150	210	270	330

_____

_____

_____

_____

_____

13. Make a Conjecture Two parallel lines are graphed on a coordinate plane. How many of the lines could represent proportional relationships? Explain.

_____

_____

_____

_____

_____

_____

Determining Slope and *y*-intercept

FL 8.EE.2.6
...; derive the equation
$y = mx$ for a line through
the origin and the equation
$y = mx + b$ for a line
intercepting the vertical axis
at *b*. Also 8.F.2.4

ESSENTIAL QUESTION

How can you determine the slope and the *y*-intercept of a line?

EXPLORE ACTIVITY 1   FL 8.EE.2.6

Investigating Slope and *y*-intercept

The graph of every nonvertical line crosses the *y*-axis. The **y-intercept** is the *y*-coordinate of the point where the graph intersects the *y*-axis. The *x*-coordinate of this point is always 0.

The graph represents the linear equation $y = -\frac{2}{3}x + 4.$

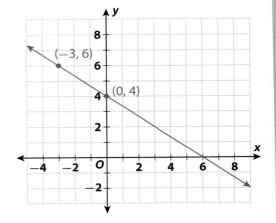

STEP 1 Find the slope of the line using the points (0, 4) and (−3, 6).

$$m = \frac{6 - \boxed{}}{\boxed{} - 0} = \frac{\boxed{}}{\boxed{}} = \boxed{}$$

STEP 2 The line also contains the point (6, 0). What is the slope using (0, 4) and (6, 0)? Using (−3, 6) and (6, 0). What do you notice?

_____

STEP 3 Compare your answers in Steps 1 and 2 with the equation of the graphed line.

_____

_____

STEP 3 Find the value of *y* when *x* = 0 using the equation $y = -\frac{2}{3}x + 4.$ Describe the point on the graph that corresponds to this solution.

_____

STEP 5 Compare your answer in Step 3 with the equation of the line.

_____

_____

Determining Rate of Change and Initial Value

The linear equation shown is written in the **slope-intercept form of an equation**. Its graph is a line with **slope** m and **y-intercept** b.

$$y = mx + b$$

slope → m b ← y-intercept

A linear relationship has a constant rate of change. You can find the **rate of change** m and the **initial value** b for a linear situation from a table of values.

EXAMPLE 1

FL   8.F.2.4

A phone salesperson is paid a minimum weekly salary and a commission for each phone sold, as shown in the table. Confirm that the relationship is linear and give the constant rate of change and the initial value.

STEP 1 Confirm that the rate of change is constant.

$$\frac{\text{change in income}}{\text{change in phones sold}} = \frac{630-480}{20-10} = \frac{150}{10} = \textbf{15}$$

$$\frac{\text{change in income}}{\text{change in phones sold}} = \frac{780-630}{30-20} = \frac{150}{10} = \textbf{15}$$

$$\frac{\text{change in income}}{\text{change in phones sold}} = \frac{930-780}{40-30} = \frac{150}{10} = \textbf{15}$$

Number of Phones Sold	Weekly Income ($)
10	$480
20	$630
30	$780
40	$930

The rate of change is a constant, **15**.

The salesperson receives a $15 commission for each phone sold.

STEP 2 Find the initial value when the number of phones sold is 0.

−10 −10

Number of phones sold	0	10	20
Weekly income ($)	330	480	630

−150 −150

Work backward from $x = 10$ to $x = 0$ to find the initial value.

The initial value is $330. The salesperson receives a salary of $330 each week before commissions.

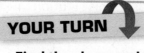

Math Talk

Mathematical Practices

How do you use the rate of change to work backward to find the initial value?

YOUR TURN

Find the slope and y-intercept of the line represented by each table.

1.

x	2	4	6	8
y	22	32	42	52

2.

x	1	2	3	4
y	8	15	22	29

Deriving the Slope-intercept Form of an Equation

In the following Explore Activity, you will derive the slope-intercept form of an equation.

STEP 1 Let L be a line with slope m and y-intercept b. Circle the point that must be on the line. Justify your choice.

$(b, 0)$ $(0, b)$ $(0, m)$ $(m, 0)$

_____

_____

STEP 2 Recall that slope is the ratio of change in y to change in x. Complete the equation for the slope m of the line using the y-intercept $(0, b)$ and another point (x, y) on the line.

$$m = \frac{y - \boxed{}}{\boxed{} - 0}$$

STEP 3 In an equation of a line, we often want y by itself on one side of the equation. Solve the equation from Step 2 for y.

$$m = \frac{y - b}{x}$$ *Simplify the denominator.*

$$m \cdot \boxed{} = \frac{y - b}{x} \cdot \boxed{}$$ *Multiply both sides of the equation by _____.*

$$m\boxed{} = y - b$$

$$mx + \boxed{} = y - b + \boxed{}$$ *Add _____ to both sides of the equation.*

$$mx + \boxed{} = y$$

$$y = mx + \boxed{}$$ *Write the equation with y on the left side.*

Reflect

3. **Critical Thinking** Write the equation of a line with slope m that passes through the origin. Explain your reasoning.

_____

_____

_____

Find the slope and *y*-intercept of the line in each graph. (Explore Activity 1)

1.

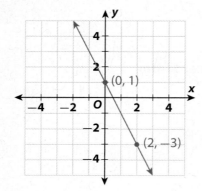

slope *m* = _____ *y*-intercept *b* = _____

2.

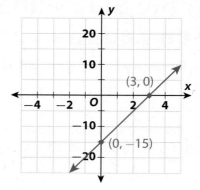

slope *m* = _____ *y*-intercept *b* = _____

3.

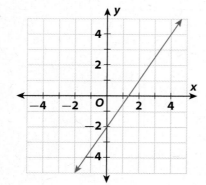

slope *m* = _____ *y*-intercept *b* = _____

4.

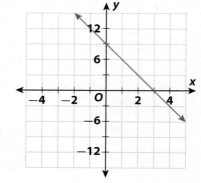

slope *m* = _____ *y*-intercept *b* = _____

Find the slope and *y*-intercept of the line represented by each table. (Example 1)

5.

x	0	2	4	6	8
y	1	7	13	19	25

slope *m* = _____ *y*-intercept *b* = _____

6.

x	0	5	10	15	20
y	140	120	100	80	60

slope *m* = _____ *y*-intercept *b* = _____

? ESSENTIAL QUESTION CHECK-IN

7. How can you determine the slope and the *y*-intercept of a line from a graph?

_____

_____

_____

12.2 Independent Practice

FL 8.EE.2.6, 8.F.2.4

Personal
Math Trainer

Online
Assessment and
Intervention

my.hrw.com

8. Some carpet cleaning costs are shown in the table. The relationship is linear. Find and interpret the rate of change and the initial value for this situation.

Rooms cleaned	1	2	3	4
Cost ($)	125	175	225	275

_____

_____

_____

9. Make Predictions The total cost to pay for parking at a state park for the day and rent a paddleboat are shown.

a. Find the cost to park for a day and the hourly rate to rent a paddleboat.

_____

b. What will Lin pay if she rents a paddleboat for 3.5 hours and splits the total cost with a friend? Explain.

_____

_____

Number of Hours	Cost ($)
1	$17
2	$29
3	$41
4	$53

10. Multi-Step Raymond's parents will pay for him to take sailboard lessons during the summer. He can take half-hour group lessons or half-hour private lessons. The relationship between cost and number of lessons is linear.

Lessons	1	2	3	4
Group ($)	55	85	115	145
Private ($)	75	125	175	225

a. Find the rate of change and the initial value for the group lessons.

_____

_____

b. Find the rate of change and the initial value for the private lessons.

_____

_____

c. Compare and contrast the rates of change and the initial values.

_____

_____

_____

Vocabulary Explain why each relationship is not linear.

11.

x	1	2	3	4
y	4.5	6.5	8.5	11.5

_____

_____

12.

x	3	5	7	9
y	140	126	110	92

_____

_____

13. **Communicate Mathematical Ideas** Describe the procedure you performed to derive the slope-intercept form of a linear equation.

_____

_____

_____

FOCUS ON HIGHER ORDER THINKING

Work Area

14. **Critique Reasoning** Your teacher asked your class to describe a real-world situation in which a *y*-intercept is 100 and the slope is 5. Your partner gave the following description: *My younger brother originally had 100 small building blocks, but he has lost 5 of them every month since.*

   a. What mistake did your partner make?

   _____

   _____

   b. Describe a real-world situation that does match the situation.

   _____

   _____

15. **Justify Reasoning** John has a job parking cars. He earns a fixed weekly salary of $300 plus a fee of $5 for each car he parks. His potential earnings for a week are shown in the graph. At what point does John begin to earn more from fees than his fixed salary? Justify your answer.

_____

_____

_____

Graphing Linear Nonproportional Relationships Using Slope and *y*-intercept

FL 8.F.2.4

... Interpret the rate of change and initial value of a linear function in terms of the situation it models, and in terms of its graph.... *Also 8.F.1.3*

ESSENTIAL QUESTION

How can you graph a line using the slope and *y*-intercept?

Using Slope-intercept Form to Graph a Line

Recall that $y = mx + b$ is the slope-intercept form of the equation of a line. In this form, it is easy to see the slope *m* and the *y*-intercept *b*. So you can use this form to quickly graph a line by plotting the point $(0, b)$ and using the slope to find a second point.

Math On the Spot

🔘 my.hrw.com

EXAMPLE 1

FL 8.F.1.3

Animated Math

🔘 my.hrw.com

A Graph $y = \frac{2}{3}x - 1$.

STEP 1 The *y*-intercept is $b = -1$. Plot the point that contains the *y*-intercept: $(0, -1)$.

STEP 2 The slope is $m = \frac{2}{3}$. Use the slope to find a second point. From $(0, -1)$, count *up* 2 and *right* 3. The new point is $(3, 1)$.

STEP 3 Draw a line through the points.

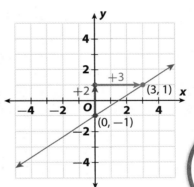

Math Talk
Mathematical Practices

Is a line with a positive slope always steeper than a line with a negative slope? Explain.

B Graph $y = -\frac{5}{2}x + 3$.

STEP 1 The *y*-intercept is $b = 3$. Plot the point that contains the *y*-intercept: $(0, 3)$.

STEP 2 The slope is $m = -\frac{5}{2}$. Use the slope to find a second point. From $(0, 3)$, count *down* 5 and *right* 2, or *up* 5 and *left* 2. The new point is $(2, -2)$ or $(-2, 8)$.

STEP 3 Draw a line through the points.

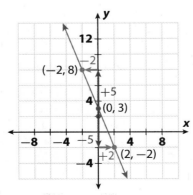

Note that the line passes through all three points: $(-2, 8)$, $(0, 3)$, and $(2, -2)$.

Reflect

1. **Draw Conclusions** How can you use the slope of a line to predict the way the line will be slanted? Explain.

_____

_____

YOUR TURN

Graph each equation.

2. $y = \frac{1}{2}x + 1$

3. $y = -3x + 4$

Analyzing a Graph

Many real-world situations can be represented by linear relationships. You can use graphs of linear relationships to visualize situations and solve problems.

EXAMPLE 2 Real World

FL 8.F.2.4

Ken has a weekly goal of burning 2400 calories by taking brisk walks. The equation $y = -300x + 2400$ represents the number of calories y Ken has left to burn after x hours of walking which burns 300 calories per hour.

A Graph the equation $y = -300x + 2400$.

STEP 1 Write the slope as a fraction.

$$m = \frac{-300}{1} = \frac{-600}{2} = \frac{-900}{3}$$

Using the slope as $\frac{-900}{3}$ helps in drawing a more accurate graph.

STEP 2 Plot the point for the y-intercept: (0, 2400).

STEP 3 Use the slope to locate a second point.

From (0, 2400), count *down* 900 and *right* 3.

The new point is (3, 1500).

STEP 4 Draw a line through the two points.

B After how many hours of walking will Ken have 600 calories left to burn? After how many hours will he reach his weekly goal?

STEP 1 Locate 600 calories on the *y*-axis. Read across and down to the *x*-axis.

Ken will have 600 calories left to burn after 6 hours.

STEP 2 Ken will reach his weekly goal when the number of calories left to burn is 0. Because every point on the *x*-axis has a *y*-value of 0, find the point where the line crosses the *x*-axis.

Ken will reach his goal after 8 hours of brisk walking.

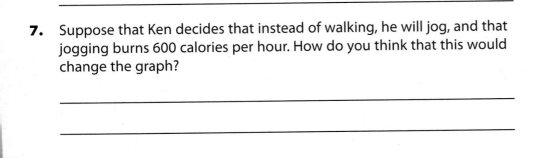

YOUR TURN

What If? Ken decides to modify his exercise plans from Example 2 by slowing the speed at which he walks. The equation for the modified plan is $y = -200x + 2400$.

4. Graph the equation.

5. How does the graph of the new equation compare with the graph in Example 2?

_____

_____

_____

Math Talk
Mathematical Practices

What do the slope and the *y*-intercept of the line represent in this situation?

6. Will Ken have to exercise more or less to meet his goal? Explain.

_____

_____

_____

7. Suppose that Ken decides that instead of walking, he will jog, and that jogging burns 600 calories per hour. How do you think that this would change the graph?

_____

_____

_____

Personal Math Trainer

Online Assessment and Intervention

my.hrw.com

Graph each equation using the slope and the *y*-intercept. (Example 1)

1. $y = \frac{1}{2}x - 3$

slope = _____ *y*-intercept = _____

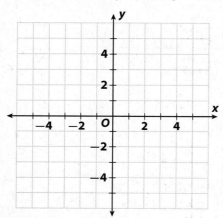

2. $y = -3x + 2$

slope = _____ *y*-intercept = _____

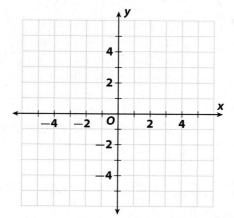

3. A friend gives you two baseball cards for your birthday. Afterward, you begin collecting them. You buy the same number of cards once each week. The equation $y = 4x + 2$ describes the number of cards, *y*, you have after *x* weeks. (Example 2)

  a. Find and interpret the slope and the *y*-intercept of the line that represents this situation. Graph $y = 4x + 2$. Include axis labels.

    _____

    _____

  b. Discuss which points on the line do not make sense in this situation. Then plot three more points on the line that do make sense.

    _____

    _____

    _____

? ESSENTIAL QUESTION CHECK-IN

4. Why might someone choose to use the *y*-intercept and the slope to graph a line?

_____

_____

_____

_____

12.3 Independent Practice

 FL 8.F.1.3, 8.F.2.4

Personal Math Trainer

Online Assessment and Intervention

⏻ my.hrw.com

5. Science A spring stretches in relation to the weight hanging from it according to the equation $y = 0.75x + 0.25$ where x is the weight in pounds and y is the length of the spring in inches.

a. Graph the equation. Include axis labels.

b. Interpret the slope and the y-intercept of the line.

_____

_____

_____

_____

_____

c. How long will the spring be if a 2-pound weight is hung on it? Will the length double if you double the weight? Explain

_____

Look for a Pattern **Identify the coordinates of four points on the line with each given slope and y-intercept.**

6. slope $= 5$, y-intercept $= -1$

_____

7. slope $= -1$, y-intercept $= 8$

_____

8. slope $= 0.2$, y-intercept $= 0.3$

_____

9. slope $= 1.5$, y-intercept $= -3$

_____

10. slope $= -\frac{1}{2}$, y-intercept $= 4$

_____

11. slope $= \frac{2}{3}$, y-intercept $= -5$

_____

12. A music school charges a registration fee in addition to a fee per lesson. Music lessons last 0.5 hour. The equation $y = 40x + 30$ represents the total cost y of x lessons. Find and interpret the slope and y-intercept of the line that represents this situation. Then find four points on the line.

_____

_____

13. A public pool charges a membership fee and a fee for each visit. The equation $y = 3x + 50$ represents the cost y for x visits.

   a. After locating the y-intercept on the coordinate plane shown, can you move up three gridlines and right one gridline to find a second point? Explain.

   _____

   _____

   _____

   b. Graph the equation $y = 3x + 50$. Include axis labels. Then interpret the slope and y-intercept.

   _____

   _____

   c. How many visits to the pool can a member get for $200?

   _____

 FOCUS ON HIGHER ORDER THINKING

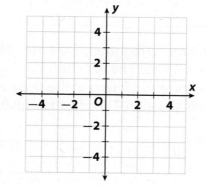

Work Area

14. Explain the Error A student says that the slope of the line for the equation $y = 20 - 15x$ is 20 and the y-intercept is 15. Find and correct the error.

_____

_____

_____

15. Critical Thinking Suppose you know the slope of a linear relationship and a point that its graph passes through. Can you graph the line even if the point provided does *not* represent the y-intercept? Explain.

_____

_____

_____

16. Make a Conjecture Graph the lines $y = 3x$, $y = 3x - 3$, and $y = 3x + 3$. What do you notice about the lines? Make a conjecture based on your observation.

_____

_____

_____

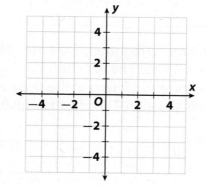

Proportional and Nonproportional Situations

FL 8.F.1.2

Compare properties of two functions each represented in a different way (algebraically, graphically, numerically in tables, or by verbal descriptions). *Also 8.F.1.3, 8.F.2.4*

? ESSENTIAL QUESTION

How can you distinguish between proportional and nonproportional situations?

Math On the Spot
my.hrw.com

Distinguish Between Proportional and Nonproportional Situations Using a Graph

If a relationship is nonlinear, it is nonproportional. If it is linear, it may be either proportional or nonproportional. When the graph of the linear relationship contains the origin, the relationship is proportional.

EXAMPLE 1 Real World

FL 8.F.1.3

The graph shows the sales tax charged based on the amount spent at a video game store in a particular city. Does the graph show a linear relationship? Is the relationship proportional or nonproportional?

The graph shows a linear proportional relationship because it is a line that contains the origin.

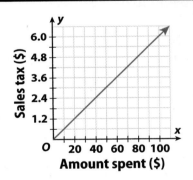

Math Talk
Mathematical Practices

What do the slope and the *y*-intercept of the graph represent in this situation?

YOUR TURN

Determine if each of the following graphs represents a proportional or nonproportional relationship.

1.

2.

Personal
Math Trainer

Online Assessment and Intervention

my.hrw.com

Math On the Spot

my.hrw.com

Animated Math

my.hrw.com

Distinguish Between Proportional and Nonproportional Situations Using an Equation

If an equation is not a linear equation, it represents a nonproportional relationship. A linear equation of the form $y = mx + b$ may represent either a proportional ($b = 0$) or nonproportional ($b \neq 0$) relationship.

EXAMPLE 2   **FL** 8.F.2.4

The number of years since Keith graduated from middle school can be represented by the equation $y = a - 14$, where y is the number of years and a is his age. Is the relationship between the number of years since Keith graduated and his age proportional or nonproportional?

$$y = a - 14$$

The equation is in the form $y = mx + b$, with a being used as the variable instead of x. The value of m is 1, and the value of b is -14. Since b is not 0, the relationship between the number of years since Keith graduated and his age is nonproportional.

Reflect

3. **Communicate Mathematical Ideas** In a proportional relationship, the ratio $\frac{y}{x}$ is constant. Show that this ratio is not constant for the equation $y = a - 14$.

_____

_____

4. **What If?** Suppose another equation represents Keith's age in months y given his age in years a. Is this relationship proportional? Explain.

_____

_____

YOUR TURN

Personal Math Trainer

Online Assessment and Intervention

my.hrw.com

Determine if each of the following equations represents a proportional or nonproportional relationship.

5. $d = 65t$

_____

6. $p = 0.1s + 2000$

_____

7. $n = 450 - 3p$

_____

8. $36 = 12d$

_____

Distinguish Between Proportional and Nonproportional Situations Using a Table

Math On the Spot
my.hrw.com

If there is not a constant rate of change in the data displayed in a table, then the table represents a nonlinear nonproportional relationship.

A linear relationship represented by a table is a proportional relationship when the quotient of each pair of numbers is constant. Otherwise, the linear relationship is nonproportional.

EXAMPLE 3

FL 8.F.2.4

The values in the table represent the numbers of U.S. dollars three tourists traded for Mexican pesos. The relationship is linear. Is the relationship proportional or nonproportional?

U.S. Dollars Traded	Mexican Pesos Received
130	1,690
255	3,315
505	6,565

$$\frac{1,690}{130} = \frac{169}{13} = 13$$

$$\frac{3,315}{255} = \frac{221}{17} = 13$$

Simplify the ratios to compare the pesos received to the dollars traded.

$$\frac{6,565}{505} = \frac{1313}{101} = 13$$

The ratio of pesos received to dollars traded is constant at 13 Mexican pesos per U.S. dollar. This is a proportional relationship.

Animated Math
my.hrw.com

Math Talk
Mathematical Practices

How could you confirm that the values in the table have a linear relationship?

YOUR TURN

Determine if the linear relationship represented by each table is a proportional or nonproportional relationship.

9.

x	y
2	30
8	90
14	150

10.

x	y
5	1
40	8
65	13

Personal Math Trainer
Online Assessment and Intervention
my.hrw.com

Comparing Proportional and Nonproportional Situations

You can use what you have learned about proportional and nonproportional relationships to compare similar real-world situations that are given using different representations.

EXAMPLE 4   FL   8.F.1.2

A **A laser tag league has the choice of two arenas for a tournament. In both cases, x is the number of hours and y is the total charge. Compare and contrast these two situations.**

Arena A

$y = 225x$

Arena B

- **Arena A's** equation has the form $y = mx + b$, where $b = 0$. So, Arena A's charges are a proportional relationship. The hourly rate, $225, is greater than Arena B's, but there is no additional fee.

- **Arena B's** graph is a line that does not include the origin. So, Arena B's charges are a nonproportional relationship. Arena B has a $50 initial fee but its hourly rate, $200, is lower.

B **Jessika is remodeling and has the choice of two painters. In both cases, x is the number of hours and y is the total charge. Compare and contrast these two situations.**

Painter A

$y = \$45x$

Painter B

x	0	1	2	3
y	20	55	90	125

Painter A's equation has the form $y = mx + b$, where $b = 0$. So, Painter A's charges are proportional. The hourly rate, $45, is greater than Painter B's, but there is no additional fee.

Painter B's table is a nonproportional relationship because the ratio of y to x is not constant. Because the table contains the ordered pair (0, 20), Painter B charges an initial fee of $20, but the hourly rate, $35, is less than Painter A's.

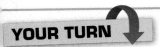

YOUR TURN

11. Compare and contrast the following two situations.

Personal Math Trainer

Online Assessment and Intervention

Test-Prep Center A	Test-Prep Center B
The cost for Test-Prep Center A is given by $c = 20h$, where c is the cost in dollars and h is the number of hours you attend.	Test-Prep Center B charges \$25 per hour to attend, but you have a \$100 coupon that you can use to reduce the cost.

_____

_____

_____

_____

Guided Practice

Determine if each relationship is a proportional or nonproportional situation. Explain your reasoning. (Example 1, Example 2, Example 4)

1.

Look at the origin.

_____

_____

2.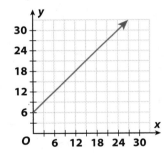

_____

_____

3. $q = 2p + \frac{1}{2}$

Compare the equation with $y = mx + b$.

_____

_____

_____

4. $v = \frac{1}{10}u$

_____

_____

_____

Lesson 12.4 **381**

The tables represent linear relationships. Determine if each relationship is a proportional or nonproportional situation. (Example 3, Example 4)

5.

x	y
3	12
9	36
21	84

Find the quotient of y and x.

_____

_____

_____

6.

x	y
22	4
46	8
58	10

_____

_____

_____

7. The values in the table represent the numbers of households that watched three TV shows and the ratings of the shows. The relationship is linear. Describe the relationship in other ways. (Example 4)

Number of Households that Watched TV Show	TV Show Rating
15,000,000	12
20,000,000	16
25,000,000	20

_____

_____

_____

_____

? ESSENTIAL QUESTION CHECK-IN

8. How are using graphs, equations, and tables similar when distinguishing between proportional and nonproportional linear relationships?

_____

_____

_____

12.4 Independent Practice

 FL 8.F.1.2, 8.F.1.3, 8.F.2.4

9. The graph shows the weight of a cross-country team's beverage cooler based on how much sports drink it contains.

a. Is the relationship proportional or nonproportional? Explain.

_____

_____

b. Identify and interpret the slope and the *y*-intercept.

_____

_____

In 10–11, tell if the relationship between a rider's height above the first floor and the time since the rider stepped on the elevator or escalator is proportional or nonproportional. Explain your reasoning.

height above floor

height above floor

10. The elevator paused for 10 seconds after you stepped on before beginning to rise at a constant rate of 8 feet per second.

_____

_____

_____

11. Your height, *h*, in feet above the first floor on the escalator is given by $h = 0.75t$, where *t* is the time in seconds.

_____

12. Analyze Relationships Compare and contrast the two graphs.

Graph A

$y = \frac{1}{3}x$

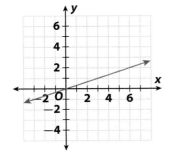

Graph B

$y = \sqrt{x}$

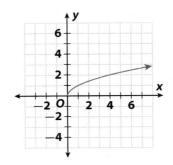

_____

_____

13. Represent Real-World Problems Describe a real-world situation where the relationship is linear and nonproportional.

_____

_____

Work Area

14. Mathematical Reasoning Suppose you know the slope of a linear relationship and one of the points that its graph passes through. How can you determine if the relationship is proportional or nonproportional?

_____

_____

_____

15. Multiple Representations An entrant at a science fair has included information about temperature conversion in various forms, as shown. The variables F, C, and K represent temperatures in degrees Fahrenheit, degrees Celsius, and Kelvin, respectively.

Equation A $F = \frac{9}{5}C + 32$	Table C	
	Degrees Celsius	**kelvins**
	8	281.15
Equation B	15	288.15
$K = C + 273.15$	36	309.15

a. Is the relationship between kelvins and degrees Celsius proportional? Justify your answer in two different ways.

_____

_____

_____

_____

b. Is the relationship between degrees Celsius and degrees Fahrenheit proportional? Why or why not?

_____

_____

_____

_____

Ready to Go On?

12.1 Representing Linear Nonproportional Relationships

1. Complete the table using the equation $y = 3x + 2$.

x	−1	0	1	2	3
y					

12.2 Determining Slope and *y*-intercept

2. Find the slope and *y*-intercept of the line in the graph.

_____

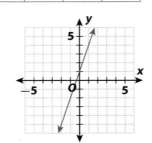

12.3 Graphing Linear Nonproportional Relationships

3. Graph the equation $y = 2x - 3$ using slope and *y*-intercept.

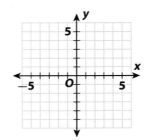

12.4 Proportional and Nonproportional Situations

4. Does the table represent a proportional or a nonproportional linear relationship?

x	1	2	3	4	5
y	4	8	12	16	20

_____

5. Does the graph in Exercise 2 represent a proportional or a nonproportional linear relationship? _____

6. Does the graph in Exercise 3 represent a proportional or a nonproportional relationship? _____

? ESSENTIAL QUESTION

7. How can you identify a linear nonproportional relationship from a table, a graph, and an equation?

_____

_____

MODULE 12 MIXED REVIEW

Assessment Readiness

Personal
Math Trainer

Online
Assessment and
Intervention

my.hrw.com

Selected Response

1. The table below represents which equation?

x	−1	0	1	2
y	−10	−6	−2	2

Ⓐ $y = -x - 10$ Ⓒ $y = 4x - 6$

Ⓑ $y = -6x$ Ⓓ $y = -4x + 2$

2. The graph of which equation is shown below?

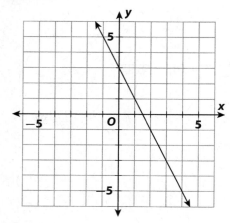

Ⓐ $y = -2x + 3$ Ⓒ $y = 2x + 3$

Ⓑ $y = -2x + 1.5$ Ⓓ $y = 2x + 1.5$

3. The table below represents a linear relationship.

x	2	3	4	5
y	4	7	10	13

What is the y-intercept?

Ⓐ −4 Ⓒ 2

Ⓑ −2 Ⓓ 3

4. Which equation represents a nonproportional relationship?

Ⓐ $y = 3x + 0$ Ⓒ $y = 3x + 5$

Ⓑ $y = -3x$ Ⓓ $y = \frac{1}{3}x$

5. The table shows a proportional relationship. What is the missing y-value?

x	4	10	12
y	6	15	?

Ⓐ 16 Ⓒ 18

Ⓑ 20 Ⓓ 24

6. What is 0.00000598 written in scientific notation?

Ⓐ 5.98×10^{-6} Ⓒ 59.8×10^{-6}

Ⓑ 5.98×10^{-5} Ⓓ 59.8×10^{-7}

Mini-Task

7. The graph shows a linear relationship.

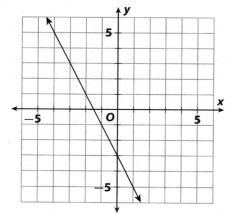

a. Is the relationship proportional or nonproportional?

_____

b. What is the slope of the line?

_____

c. What is the y-intercept of the line?

_____

d. What is the equation of the line?

_____

Writing Linear Equations

 ESSENTIAL QUESTION

How can you use linear equations to solve real-world problems?

Real-World Video

Linear equations can be used to describe many situations related to shopping. If a store advertised four books for $32.00, you could write and solve a linear equation to find the price of each book.

my.hrw.com

GO DIGITAL

my.hrw.com

 my.hrw.com

Go digital with your write-in student edition, accessible on any device.

 Math On the Spot

Scan with your smart phone to jump directly to the online edition, video tutor, and more.

 Animated Math

Interactively explore key concepts to see how math works.

 Personal Math Trainer

Get immediate feedback and help as you work through practice sets.

Are YOU Ready?

Complete these exercises to review skills you will need for this module.

Personal Math Trainer

Online Assessment and Intervention

my.hrw.com

Write Fractions as Decimals

EXAMPLE $\frac{0.5}{0.8} = ?$ Multiply the numerator and the denominator by a power of 10 so that the denominator is a whole number.

$\frac{0.5 \times 10}{0.8 \times 10} = \frac{5}{8}$

$$\begin{array}{r} 0.625 \\ 8\overline{)5.000} \\ -48 \\ \hline 20 \\ -16 \\ \hline 40 \\ -40 \\ \hline 0 \end{array}$$

Write the fraction as a division problem.
Write a decimal point and zeros in the dividend.
Place a decimal point in the quotient.
Divide as with whole numbers.

Write each fraction as a decimal.

1. $\frac{3}{8}$ _____

2. $\frac{0.3}{0.4}$ _____

3. $\frac{0.13}{0.2}$ _____

4. $\frac{0.39}{0.75}$ _____

Inverse Operations

EXAMPLE

$$5n = 20$$
$$\frac{5n}{5} = \frac{20}{5}$$
$$n = 4$$

n is multiplied by 5.
To solve the equation, use the inverse operation, division.

$$k + 7 = 9$$
$$k + 7 - 7 = 9 - 7$$
$$k = 2$$

7 is added to k.
To solve the equation, use the inverse operation, subtraction.

Solve each equation using the inverse operation.

5. $7p = 28$ _____

6. $h - 13 = 5$ _____

7. $\frac{y}{3} = -6$ _____

8. $b + 9 = 21$ _____

9. $c - 8 = -8$ _____

10. $3n = -12$ _____

11. $-16 = m + 7$ _____

12. $\frac{t}{-5} = -5$ _____

Reading Start-Up

Visualize Vocabulary

Use the ✔ words to complete the diagram. You can put more than one word in each bubble.

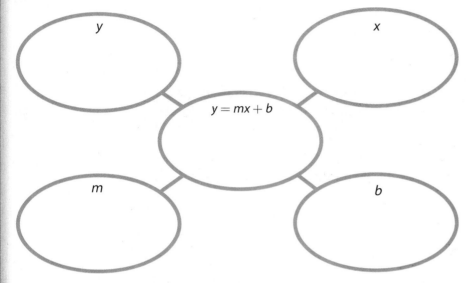

y

x

$y = mx + b$

m

b

Understand Vocabulary

Complete the sentences using the preview words.

1. A set of data that is made up of two paired variables

   is _____.

2. When the rate of change varies from point to point, the relationship

   is a _____.

Active Reading

Tri-Fold Before beginning the module, create a tri-fold to help you learn the concepts and vocabulary in this module. Fold the paper into three sections. Label the columns "What I Know," "What I Need to Know," and "What I Learned." Complete the first two columns before you read. After studying the module, complete the third column.

Unpacking the Standards

Understanding the standards and the vocabulary terms in the standards will help you know exactly what you are expected to learn in this module.

FL 8.F.2.4

Construct a function to model a linear relationship between two quantities. Determine the rate of change and initial value of the function from a description of a relationship.... Interpret the rate of change and initial value of a linear function in terms of the situation it models, and in terms of its graph or a table of values.

Key Vocabulary

rate of change *(tasa de cambio)*
A ratio that compares the amount of change in a dependent variable to the amount of change in an independent variable.

What It Means to You

You will learn how to write an equation based on a situation that models a linear relationship.

UNPACKING EXAMPLE 8.F.2.4

In 2006 the fare for a taxicab was an initial charge of $2.50 plus $0.30 per mile. Write an equation in slope-intercept form that can be used to calculate the total fare.

The constant charge is $2.50.
The rate of change is $0.30 per mile.

The input variable, x, is the number of miles driven.
So $0.3x$ is the cost for the miles driven.

The equation for the total fare, y, is as follows:

$$y = 0.3x + 2.5$$

FL 8.SP.1.3

Use the equation of a linear model to solve problems in the context of bivariate measurement data, interpreting the slope and intercept.

Key Vocabulary

bivariate data *(datos bivariados)*
A set of data that is made up of two paired variables.

Visit **my.hrw.com** to see all **Florida Math Standards** unpacked.

my.hrw.com

What It Means to You

You will see how to use a linear relationship between sets of data to make predictions.

UNPACKING EXAMPLE 8.SP.1.3

The graph shows the temperatures in degrees Celsius inside the earth at certain depths in kilometers. Use the graph to write an equation and find the temperature at a depth of 12 km.

The initial temperature is 20°C.
It increases at a rate of 10°C/km.

The equation is $t = 10d + 20$.
At a depth of 12 km, the temperature is 140°C.

Temperature Inside Earth

Writing Linear Equations from Situations and Graphs

FL 8.F.2.4

Construct a function to model a linear relationship between two quantities. Determine the rate of change and initial value.... Interpret the rate of change and initial value....

ESSENTIAL QUESTION

How do you write an equation to model a linear relationship given a graph or a description?

EXPLORE ACTIVITY   FL 8.F.2.4

Writing an Equation in Slope-Intercept Form

Greta makes clay mugs and bowls as gifts at the Crafty Studio. She pays a membership fee of $15 a month and an equipment fee of $3.00 an hour to use the potter's wheel, table, and kiln. Write an equation in the form $y = mx + b$ that Greta can use to calculate her monthly costs.

A What is the input variable, x, for this situation?

_____

What is the output variable, y, for this situation?

_____

B During April, Greta does not use the equipment at all. What will be her number of hours (x) for April? _____

What will be her cost (y) for April? _____

What will be the y-intercept, b, in the equation? _____

Math Talk
Mathematical Practices

What change could the studio make that would make a difference to the y-intercept of the equation?

C Greta spends 8 hours in May for a cost of $15 + 8($3) = _____.

In June, she spends 11 hours for a cost of _____.

From May to June, the change in x-values is _____.

From May to June, the change in y-values is _____.

What will be the slope, m, in the equation? _____

D Use the values for m and b to write an equation for Greta's costs in the form $y = mx + b$: _____

Math On the Spot
⊙ my.hrw.com

Writing an Equation from a Graph

You can use information presented in a graph to write an equation in slope-intercept form.

EXAMPLE 1 Real World

FL 8.F.2.4

A video club charges a one-time membership fee plus a rental fee for each DVD borrowed. Use the graph to write an equation in slope-intercept form to represent the amount spent, *y*, on *x* DVD rentals.

Video Club Costs

STEP 1 Choose two points on the graph, (x_1, y_1) and (x_2, y_2), to find the slope.

$m = \dfrac{y_2 - y_1}{x_2 - x_1}$ Find the change in y-values over the change in x-values.

$m = \dfrac{18 - 8}{8 - 0}$ Substitute $(0, 8)$ for (x_1, y_1) and $(8, 18)$ for (x_2, y_2).

$m = \dfrac{10}{8} = 1.25$ Simplify.

STEP 2 Read the *y*-intercept from the graph.

The *y*-intercept is 8.

STEP 3 Use your slope and *y*-intercept values to write an equation in slope-intercept form.

$y = mx + b$ Slope-intercept form

$y = 1.25x + 8$ Substitute 1.25 for m and 8 for y.

Math Talk
Mathematical Practices

If the graph of an equation is a line that goes through the origin, what is the value of the *y*-intercept?

Reflect

1. What does the value of the slope represent in this context?

_____

2. Describe the meaning of the *y*-intercept.

_____

YOUR TURN

3. The cash register subtracts $2.50 from a $25 Coffee Café gift card for every medium coffee the customer buys. Use the graph to write an equation in slope-intercept form to represent this situation.

_____

Amount on Gift Card

Personal Math Trainer
Online Assessment and Intervention
⊙ my.hrw.com

Writing an Equation from a Description

You can use information from a description of a linear relationship to find the slope and *y*-intercept and to write an equation.

EXAMPLE 2   **FL** 8.F.2.4

The rent charged for space in an office building is a linear relationship related to the size of the space rented. Write an equation in slope-intercept form for the rent at West Main Street Office Rentals.

West Main St. Office Rentals
Offices for rent at convenient locations.
Monthly Rates:
600 square feet for **$750**
900 square feet for **$1150**

My Notes

STEP 1 Identify the input and output variables.

The input variable is the square footage of floor space.

The output variable is the monthly rent.

STEP 2 Write the information given in the problem as ordered pairs.

The rent for 600 square feet of floor space is $750: (600, 750)

The rent for 900 square feet of floor space is $1150: (900, 1150)

STEP 3 Find the slope.

$$m = \frac{y_2 - y_1}{x_2 - x_1} = \frac{1150 - 750}{900 - 600} = \frac{400}{300} = \frac{4}{3}$$

STEP 4 Find the *y*-intercept. Use the slope and one of the ordered pairs.

$y = mx + b$ Slope-intercept form

$750 = \frac{4}{3} \cdot 600 + b$ Substitute for y, m, and x.

$750 = 800 + b$ Multiply.

$-50 = b$ Subtract 800 from both sides.

STEP 5 Substitute the slope and *y*-intercept.

$y = mx + b$ Slope-intercept form

$y = \frac{4}{3}x - 50$ Substitute $\frac{4}{3}$ for m and -50 for b.

Reflect

4. Without graphing, tell whether the graph of this equation rises or falls from left to right. What does the sign of the slope mean in this context?

_____

_____

_____

YOUR TURN

5. Hari's weekly allowance varies depending on the number of chores he does. He received $16 in allowance the week he did 12 chores, and $14 in allowance the week he did 8 chores. Write an equation for his allowance in slope-intercept form. _____

Guided Practice

1. Li is making beaded necklaces. For each necklace, she uses 27 spacers, plus 5 beads per inch of necklace length. Write an equation to find how many beads Li needs for each necklace. (Explore Activity)

   a. input variable: _____

   b. output variable: _____

   c. equation: _____

2. Kate is planning a trip to the beach. She estimates her average speed to graph her expected progress on the trip. Write an equation in slope-intercept form that represents the situation. (Example 1)

   Choose two points on the graph to find the slope.

   $m = \dfrac{y_2 - y_1}{x_2 - x_1} =$ _____

   Read the y-intercept from the graph: $b =$ _____

   Use your slope and y-intercept values to write an equation in slope-intercept form. _____

   My Beach Trip

   (graph: vertical axis labeled "Distance to beach (mi)" with values 100, 200, 300; horizontal axis labeled "Driving time (h)" with values 1 2 3 4 5 6; line from (0, 300) decreasing to (5, 0))

3. At 59 °F, crickets chirp at a rate of 76 times per minute, and at 65 °F, they chirp 100 times per minute. Write an equation in slope-intercept form that represents the situation. (Example 2)

   Input variable: _____   Output variable: _____

   $m = \dfrac{y_2 - y_1}{x_2 - x_1} =$ _____ Use the slope and one of the ordered

   pairs in $y = mx + b$ to find b. _____ = _____ · _____ + b; _____ = b

   Write an equation in slope-intercept form. _____

? ESSENTIAL QUESTION CHECK-IN

4. Explain what m and b in the equation $y = mx + b$ tell you about the graph of the line with that equation.

   _____

   _____

13.1 Independent Practice

  8.F.2.4

Personal Math Trainer

Online Assessment and Intervention

my.hrw.com

5. A dragonfly can beat its wings 30 times per second. Write an equation in slope-intercept form that shows the relationship between flying time in seconds and the number of times the dragonfly beats its wings.

_____

6. A balloon is released from the top of a platform that is 50 meters tall. The balloon rises at the rate of 4 meters per second. Write an equation in slope-intercept form that tells the height of the balloon above the ground after a given number of seconds.

_____

The graph shows a scuba diver's ascent over time.

7. Use the graph to find the slope of the line. Tell what the slope means in this context.

_____

_____

8. Identify the y-intercept. Tell what the y-intercept means in this context.

_____

Scuba Diver's Ascent

9. Write an equation in slope-intercept form that represents the diver's depth over time.

_____

10. The formula for converting Celsius temperatures to Fahrenheit temperatures is a linear equation. Water freezes at $0\,°C$, or $32\,°F$, and it boils at $100\,°C$, or $212\,°F$. Find the slope and y-intercept for a graph that gives degrees Celsius on the horizontal axis and degrees Fahrenheit on the vertical axis. Then write an equation in slope-intercept form that converts degrees Celsius into degrees Fahrenheit.

_____

_____

11. The cost of renting a sailboat at a lake is $20 per hour plus $12 for lifejackets. Write an equation in slope-intercept form that can be used to calculate the total amount you would pay for using this sailboat.

_____

The graph shows the activity in a savings account.

12. What was the amount of the initial deposit that started this savings account?

_____

13. Find the slope and *y*-intercept of the graphed line.

_____

14. Write an equation in slope-intercept form for the activity in this savings account.

_____

15. Explain the meaning of the slope in this graph.

_____

_____

H.O.T. FOCUS ON HIGHER ORDER THINKING

Work Area

16. **Communicate Mathematical Ideas** Explain how you decide which part of a problem will be represented by the variable *x*, and which part will be represented by the variable *y* in a graph of the situation.

_____

_____

_____

_____

17. **Represent Real-World Problems** Describe what would be true about the rate of change in a situation that could *not* be represented by a graphed line and an equation in the form $y = mx + b$.

_____

_____

_____

18. **Draw Conclusions** Must *m*, in the equation $y = mx + b$, always be a positive number? Explain.

_____

_____

_____

Writing Linear Equations from a Table

FL 8.F.2.4
Construct a function to model a linear relationship between two quantities. Determine the rate of change and initial value.... Interpret the rate of change and initial value....

ESSENTIAL QUESTION

How do you write an equation to model a linear relationship given a table?

Graphing from a Table to Write an Equation

You can use information from a table to draw a graph of a linear relationship and to write an equation for the graphed line.

Math On the Spot
my.hrw.com

EXAMPLE 1 **FL 8.F.2.4**

The table shows the temperature of a fish tank during an experiment. Graph the data, and find the slope and *y*-intercept from the graph. Then write the equation for the graph in slope-intercept form.

Time (h)	0	1	2	3	4	5
Temperature (°F)	82	80	78	76	74	72

STEP 1 Graph the ordered pairs from the table (time, temperature).

STEP 2 Draw a line through the points.

STEP 3 Choose two points on the graph to find the slope: for example, choose (0, 82) and (1, 80).

Tank Temperature

$m = \dfrac{y_2 - y_1}{x_2 - x_1}$ *Use the slope formula.*

$m = \dfrac{80 - 82}{1 - 0}$ *Substitute (0, 82) for (x_1, y_1) and (1, 80) for (x_2, y_2).*

$m = \dfrac{-2}{1} = -2$ *Simplify.*

STEP 4 Read the *y*-intercept from the graph.

$b = 82$

Math Talk
Mathematical Practices

Which variable in the equation $y = mx + b$ shows the initial temperature of the fish tank at the beginning of the experiment?

STEP 5 Use these slope and *y*-intercept values to write an equation in slope-intercept form.

$y = mx + b$
$y = -2x + 82$

1. The table shows the volume of water released by Hoover Dam over a certain period of time. Graph the data, and find the slope and *y*-intercept from the graph. Then write the equation for the graph in slope-intercept form.

Water Released from Hoover Dam

Time (s)	Volume of water (m³)
5	75,000
10	150,000
15	225,000
20	300,000

Math Talk

Mathematical Practices

Which variable in the equation $y = mx + b$ tells you the volume of water released every second from Hoover Dam?

Math On the Spot

⏻ my.hrw.com

Writing an Equation from a Table

The information from a table can also help you to write the equation that represents a given situation without drawing the graph.

Animated Math

⏻ my.hrw.com

EXAMPLE 2

Elizabeth's cell phone plan lets her choose how many minutes are included each month. The table shows the plan's monthly cost *y* for a given number of included minutes *x*. Write an equation in slope-intercept form to represent the situation.

Minutes included, *x*	100	200	300	400	500
Cost of plan ($), *y*	14	20	26	32	38

STEP 1 Notice that the change in cost is the same for each increase of 100 minutes. So, the relationship is linear. Choose any two ordered pairs from the table to find the slope.

$$m = \frac{y_2 - y_1}{x_2 - x_1} = \frac{(20 - 14)}{(200 - 100)} = \frac{6}{100} = 0.06$$

STEP 2 Find the *y*-intercept. Use the slope and any point from the table.

$y = mx + b$	Slope-intercept form
$14 = 0.06 \cdot 100 + b$	Substitute for *y*, *m*, and *x*.
$14 = 6 + b$	Multiply.
$8 = b$	Subtract 6 from both sides.

STEP 3 Substitute the slope and *y*-intercept.

$y = mx + b$	Slope-intercept form
$y = 0.06x + 8$	Substitute 0.06 for *m* and 8 for *b*.

Reflect

2. What is the base price for the cell phone plan, regardless of how many minutes are included? What is the cost per minute? Explain.

_____

_____

_____

_____

_____

3. **What If?** Elizabeth's cell phone company changes the cost of her plan as shown below. Write an equation in slope-intercept form to represent the situation. How did the plan change?

Minutes included, x	100	200	300	400	500
Cost of plan ($), y	30	35	40	45	50

_____

_____

Math Talk
Mathematical Practices

Explain the meaning of the slope and y-intercept of the equation.

YOUR TURN

4. A salesperson receives a weekly salary plus a commission for each computer sold. The table shows the total pay, p, and the number of computers sold, n. Write an equation in slope-intercept form to represent this situation.

Number of computers sold, n	4	6	8	10	12
Total pay ($), p	550	700	850	1000	1150

_____

5. To rent a van, a moving company charges $40.00 plus $0.50 per mile. The table shows the total cost, c, and the number of miles driven, d. Write an equation in slope-intercept form to represent this situation.

Number of miles driven, d	10	20	30	40	50
Total cost ($), c	45	50	55	60	65

_____

Personal Math Trainer

Online Assessment and Intervention

my.hrw.com

1. Jaime purchased a $20 bus pass. Each time he rides the bus, a certain amount is deducted from the pass. The table shows the amount, y, left on his pass after x rides. Graph the data, and find the slope and y-intercept from the graph or from the table. Then write the equation for the graph in slope-intercept form. (Example 1)

Number of rides, x	0	4	8	12	16
Amount left on pass ($), y	20	15	10	5	0

Bus Pass Balance

_____

The table shows the temperature (y) at different altitudes (x). This is a linear relationship. (Example 2)

Altitude (ft), x	0	2,000	4,000	6,000	8,000	10,000	12,000
Temperature (°F), y	59	51	43	35	27	19	11

2. Find the slope for this relationship.

_____

3. Find the y-intercept for this relationship.

_____

4. Write an equation in slope-intercept form that represents this relationship.

_____

5. Use your equation to determine the temperature at an altitude of 5000 feet.

_____

ESSENTIAL QUESTION CHECK-IN

6. Describe how you can use the information in a table showing a linear relationship to find the slope and y-intercept for the equation.

_____

_____

_____

13.2 Independent Practice

Personal Math Trainer

Online Assessment and Intervention

⊙ my.hrw.com

7. The table shows the costs of a large cheese pizza with toppings at a local pizzeria. Graph the data, and find the slope and *y*-intercept from the graph. Then write the equation for the graph in slope-intercept form.

Number of toppings, *t*	0	1	2	3	4	5
Total cost ($), *C*	8	10	12	14	16	18

Cost of Large Pizza

_____

8. The table shows how much an air-conditioning repair company charges for different numbers of hours of work. Graph the data, and find the slope and *y*-intercept from the graph. Then write the equation for the graph in slope-intercept form.

Number of hours (h), *t*	0	1	2	3	4	5
Amount charged ($), *A*	50	100	150	200	250	300

_____

9. A friend gave Ms. Morris a gift card for a local car wash. The table shows the linear relationship of how the value left on the card relates to the number of car washes.

Number of car washes, *x*	0	8	12
Amount left on card ($), *y*	30	18	12

a. Write an equation that shows the number of dollars left on the card.

_____

b. Explain the meaning of the negative slope in this situation.

_____

_____

c. What is the maximum value of *x* that makes sense in this context? Explain.

_____

The tables show linear relationships between *x* and *y*. Write an equation in slope-intercept form for each relationship.

10.

x	−2	−1	0	2
y	−1	0	1	3

11.

x	−4	1	0	6
y	14	4	6	−6

_____

12. Finance Desiree starts a savings account with $125.00. Every month, she deposits $53.50.

a. Complete the table to model the situation.

Month, x					
Amount in Savings ($), y					

b. Write an equation in slope-intercept form that shows how much money Desiree has in her savings account after x months.

_____

c. Use the equation to find how much money Desiree will have in savings after 11 months.

_____

13. Monty documented the amount of rain his farm received on a monthly basis, as shown in the table.

Month, x	1	2	3	4	5
Rainfall (in.), y	5	3	4.5	1	7

a. Is the relationship linear? Why or why not?

_____

_____

b. Can an equation be written to describe the amount of rain? Explain.

_____

 FOCUS ON HIGHER ORDER THINKING

Work Area

14. Analyze Relationships If you have a table that shows a linear relationship, when can you read the value for b, in $y = mx + b$, directly from the table without drawing a graph or doing any calculations? Explain.

_____

_____

15. What If? Jaíme graphed linear data given in the form (cost, number). The y-intercept was 0. Jayla graphed the same data given in the form (number, cost). What was the y-intercept of her graph? Explain.

_____

_____

_____

Linear Relationships and Bivariate Data

FL 8.SP.1.1

Construct and interpret scatter plots for bivariate measurement data... . Describe patterns such as... linear association, and nonlinear association. *Also 8.SP.1.2, 8.SP.1.3*

ESSENTIAL QUESTION

How can you contrast linear and nonlinear sets of bivariate data?

Finding the Equation of a Linear Relationship

You can use the points on a graph of a linear relationship to write an equation for the relationship. The equation of a linear relationship is $y = mx + b$, where m is the rate of change, or slope, and b is the value of y when x is 0.

Math On the Spot
⏻ my.hrw.com

EXAMPLE 1

FL 8.SP.1.2

A handrail runs alongside a stairway. As the horizontal distance from the bottom of the stairway changes, the height of the handrail changes. Show that the relationship is linear, and then find the equation for the relationship.

Animated Math
⏻ my.hrw.com

STEP 1 Show that the relationship is linear.

All of the points (5, 7), (10, 11), (15, 15), (20, 19), and (25, 23) lie on the same line, so the relationship is linear.

Math Talk
Mathematical Practices

What does the slope of the equation represent in this situation? What does the y-intercept represent?

STEP 2 Write the equation of the linear relationship.

Choose two points to find the slope.

(5, 7) and (25, 23)

$m = \dfrac{23 - 7}{25 - 5}$

$= \dfrac{16}{20}$

$= 0.8$

Choose a point and use the slope to substitute values for x, y, and m.

$y = mx + b$

$7 = 0.8(5) + b$

$7 = 4 + b$

$3 = b$

The equation of the linear relationship is $y = 0.8x + 3$.

YOUR TURN

Find the equation of each linear relationship.

1.

Cost ($) vs Time (min)

2.

Hours (x)	Number of units (y)
2	480
15	3,600
24	5,760
30	7,200
48	11,520
55	13,200

Making Predictions

You can use an equation of a linear relationship to predict a value between data points that you already know.

EXAMPLE 2 Real World   FL 8.SP.1.3

The graph shows the cost for taxi rides of different distances. Predict the cost of a taxi ride that covers a distance of 6.5 miles.

Cost ($) vs Distance (mi)

STEP 1 Write the equation of the linear relationship.

(2, 7) and (6, 15)   Select two points.

$m = \dfrac{15 - 7}{6 - 2}$ Calculate the rate of change.

$= \dfrac{8}{4}$ Simplify.

$= 2$

$y = mx + b$

$15 = 2(6) + b$ Fill in values for x, y, and m.

$15 = 12 + b$ Simplify.

$3 = b$ Solve for b.

The equation of the linear relationship is $y = 2x + 3$.

You can check your equation using another point on the graph. Try (8, 19). Substituting gives $19 = 2(8) + 3$. The right side simplifies to 19, so $19 = 19$. ✓

STEP 2 Use your equation from Step 1 to predict the cost of a 6.5-mile taxi ride.

$y = 2x + 3$

$y = 2(6.5) + 3$ Substitute $x = 6.5$.

$y = 16$ Solve for y.

A taxi ride that covers a distance of 6.5 miles will cost $16.

Reflect

3. **What If?** Suppose a regulation changes the cost of the taxi ride to $1.80 per mile, plus a fee of $4.30. How does the price of the 6.5 mile ride compare to the original price?

_____

_____

4. How can you use a graph of a linear relationship to predict an unknown value of y for a given value of x within the region of the graph?

_____

_____

_____

5. How can you use a table of linear data to predict a value?

_____

_____

_____

YOUR TURN

Paulina's income from a job that pays her a fixed amount per hour is shown in the graph. Use the graph to find the predicted value.

6. Income earned for working 2 hours

   _____

7. Income earned for working 3.25 hours

   _____

8. Total income earned for working for five 8-hour days all at the standard rate _____

Personal Math Trainer

Online Assessment and Intervention

my.hrw.com

Contrasting Linear and Nonlinear Data

Bivariate data is a set of data that is made up of two paired variables. If the relationship between the variables is linear, then the rate of change (slope) is constant. If the graph shows a **nonlinear relationship**, then the rate of change varies between pairs of points.

Andrew has two options in which to invest $200. Option A earns simple interest of 5%, while Option B earns interest of 5% compounded annually. The table shows the amount of the investment for both options over 20 years. Graph the data and describe the differences between the two graphs.

Year, x	Option A Total ($)	Option B Total ($)
0	200.00	200.00
5	250.00	255.26
10	300.00	325.78
15	350.00	415.79
20	400.00	530.66

STEP 1 Graph the data from the table for Options A and B on the same coordinate grid.

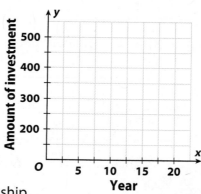

STEP 2 Find the rate of change between pairs of points for Option A and classify the relationship.

Option A	Rate of Change
(0, 200) and (5, 250)	$m = \dfrac{250 - 200}{5 - 0} = \underline{\hspace{1cm}}$
(5, 250) and (10, 300)	
(10, 300) and (15, 350)	

The rate of change between the data values is _____, so

the graph of Option A shows a _____ relationship.

Find the rate of change between pairs of points for Option B and classify the relationship.

Option B	Rate of Change
(0, 200) and (5, 255.26)	$m = \dfrac{252.26 - 200}{5 - 0} \approx$ _____
(5, 255.26) and (10, 325.78)	
(10, 325.78) and (15, 415.79)	

The rate of change between the data values is _____,

so the graph of Option B shows a _____ relationship.

Reflect

9. Why are the graphs drawn as lines or curves and not discrete points?

_____

_____

_____

_____

10. Can you determine by viewing the graph if the data have a linear or nonlinear relationship? Explain.

_____

_____

_____

_____

11. **Draw Conclusions** Find the differences in the account balances to the nearest dollar at 5 year intervals for Option B. How does the length of time that money is in an account affect the advantage that compound interest has over simple interest?

_____

_____

_____

Use the following graphs to find the equation of the linear relationship. (Example 1)

1.

_____

2.

_____

3. The graph shows the relationship between the number of hours a kayak is rented and the total cost of the rental. Write an equation of the relationship. Then use the equation to predict the cost of a rental that lasts 5.5 hours. (Example 2)

_____

Does each of the following graphs represent a linear relationship? Why or why not? (Explore Activity)

4.

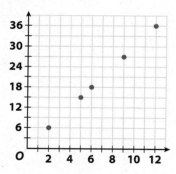

_____

_____

5.

_____

_____

? ESSENTIAL QUESTION CHECK-IN

6. How can you tell if a set of bivariate data shows a linear relationship?

_____

_____

13.3 Independent Practice

 FL 8.SP.1.1, 8.SP.1.2, 8.SP.1.3

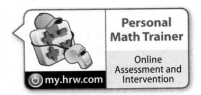

Personal Math Trainer

Online Assessment and Intervention

my.hrw.com

Does each of the following tables represent a linear relationship? Why or why not?

7.

Number of boxes	Weight (kg)
3	15
9	45
21	105

8.

Day	Height (cm)
5	30
8	76.8
14	235.2

_____

_____

_____

_____

Explain whether or not you think each relationship is linear.

9. the cost of equal-priced DVDs and the number purchased

_____

10. the height of a person and the person's age

_____

11. the area of a square quilt and its side length

_____

_____

12. the number of miles to the next service station and the number of kilometers

_____

_____

13. Multistep The Mars Rover travels 0.75 feet in 6 seconds. Add the point to the graph. Then determine whether the relationship between distance and time is linear, and if so, predict the distance that the Mars Rover would travel in 1 minute.

_____

_____

_____

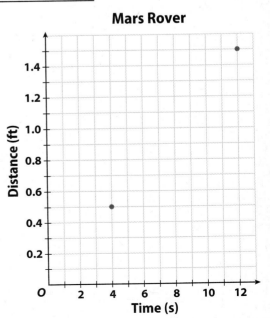

Mars Rover

14. Make a Conjecture Zefram analyzed a linear relationship, found that the slope-intercept equation was $y = 3.5x + 16$, and made a prediction for the value of y for a given value of x. He realized that he made an error calculating the y-intercept and that it was actually 12. Can he just subtract 4 from his prediction if he knows that the slope is correct? Explain.

_____

_____

H.O.T. **FOCUS ON HIGHER ORDER THINKING**

15. Communicate Mathematical Ideas The table shows a linear relationship. How can you predict the value of y when $x = 6$ without finding the equation of the relationship?

x	y
4	38
8	76
12	114

_____

_____

_____

16. Critique Reasoning Louis says that if the differences between the values of x are constant between all the points on a graph, then the relationship is linear. Do you agree? Explain.

_____

_____

_____

17. Make a Conjecture Suppose you know the slope of a linear relationship and one of the points that its graph passes through. How could you predict another point that falls on the graph of the line?

_____

_____

_____

18. Explain the Error Thomas used (7, 17.5) and (18, 45) from a graph to find the equation of a linear relationship as shown. What was his mistake?

$$m = \frac{45 - 7}{18 - 17.5} = \frac{38}{0.5} = 79$$

$$y = 79x + b$$

$$45 = 79 \cdot 18 + b$$

$$45 = 1422 + b, \text{ so } b = -1377$$

The equation is $y = 79x - 1377$.

_____

Ready to Go On?

Personal Math Trainer

Online Assessment and Intervention

my.hrw.com

13.1 Writing Linear Equations from Situations and Graphs

Write the equation of each line in slope-intercept form.

1.

_____

2.

_____

13.2 Writing Linear Equations from a Table

Write the equation of each linear relationship in slope-intercept form.

3.

x	0	100	200	300
y	1.5	36.5	71.5	106.5

_____

4.

x	25	35	45	55
y	94	88	82	76

_____

13.3 Linear Relationships and Bivariate Data

Write the equation of the line that connects each set of data points.

5.

_____

6.

_____

? ESSENTIAL QUESTION

7. Write a real-world situation that can be represented by a linear relationship.

_____

_____

MODULE 13 MIXED REVIEW

Assessment Readiness

Personal
Math Trainer

my.hrw.com

Online
Assessment and
Intervention

Selected Response

1. An hourglass is turned over with the top part filled with sand. After 3 minutes, there are 855 mL of sand in the top half. After 10 minutes, there are 750 mL of sand in the top half. Which equation represents this situation?

  Ⓐ $y = 285x$

  Ⓑ $y = -10.5x + 900$

  Ⓒ $y = -15x + 900$

  Ⓓ $y = 75x$

2. Which graph shows a linear relationship?

Ⓐ

Ⓑ

Ⓒ

Ⓓ
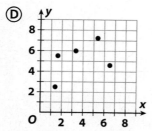

3. What are the slope and y-intercept of the relationship shown in the table?

x	10,000	20,000	30,000
y	2,500	3,000	3,500

  Ⓐ slope = 0.05, y-intercept = 1,500

  Ⓑ slope = 0.5, y-intercept = 1,500

  Ⓒ slope = 0.05, y-intercept = 2,000

  Ⓓ slope = 0.5, y-intercept = 2,000

4. Which is the sum of $3.15 \times 10^7 + 9.3 \times 10^6$? Write your answer in scientific notation.

  Ⓐ 4.08×10^7

  Ⓑ 4.08×10^6

  Ⓒ 0.408×10^8

  Ⓓ 40.8×10^6

Mini-Task

5. Franklin's faucet was leaking, so he put a bucket underneath to catch the water. After a while, Franklin started keeping track of how much water was in the bucket. His data is in the table below.

Hours	2	3	4	5
Quarts	5	6.5	8	9.5

  a. Is the relationship linear or nonlinear?

  _____

  b. Write the equation for the relationship.

  _____

  c. Predict how much water will be in the bucket after 14 hours if Franklin doesn't stop the leak.

  _____

Functions

ESSENTIAL QUESTION

How can you use functions to solve real-world problems?

Real-World Video

Computerized machines can assist doctors in surgeries such as laser vision correction. Each action the surgeon takes results in one end action by the machine. In math, functions also have a one-in-one-out relationship.

my.hrw.com

GO DIGITAL

my.hrw.com

my.hrw.com

Go digital with your write-in student edition, accessible on any device.

Math On the Spot

Scan with your smart phone to jump directly to the online edition, video tutor, and more.

Animated Math

Interactively explore key concepts to see how math works.

Personal Math Trainer

Get immediate feedback and help as you work through practice sets.

Are YOU Ready?

Complete these exercises to review skills you will need for this module.

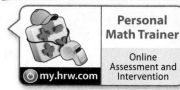

Personal Math Trainer

Online Assessment and Intervention

my.hrw.com

Evaluate Expressions

EXAMPLE   Evaluate $3x - 5$ for $x = -2$.

$$3x - 5 = 3(-2) - 5$$ Substitute the given value of x for x.

$$= -6 - 5$$ Multiply.

$$= -11$$ Subtract.

Evaluate each expression for the given value of x.

1. $2x + 3$ for $x = 3$ _____

2. $-4x + 7$ for $x = -1$ _____

3. $1.5x - 2.5$ for $x = 3$ _____

4. $0.4x + 6.1$ for $x = -5$ _____

5. $\frac{2}{3}x - 12$ for $x = 18$ _____

6. $-\frac{5}{8}x + 10$ for $x = -8$ _____

Connect Words and Equations

EXAMPLE   Erik's earnings equal 9 dollars per hour.   Define the variables used in the situation.

e = earnings; h = hours   Identify the operation involved. "Per" indicates multiplication.

multiplication

$e = 9 \times h$ Write the equation.

Define the variables for each situation. Then write an equation.

7. Jana's age plus 5 equals her sister's age.

_____

8. Andrew's class has 3 more students than Lauren's class.

_____

9. The bank is 50 feet shorter than the firehouse.

_____

10. The pencils were divided into 6 groups of 2.

_____

Reading Start-Up

Visualize Vocabulary

Use the ✔ words to complete the diagram. You can put more than one word in each section of the diagram.

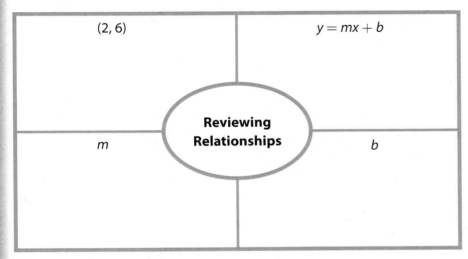

(2, 6)	$y = mx + b$
m	*b*

Reviewing Relationships

Understand Vocabulary

Complete the sentences using the preview words.

1. A rule that assigns exactly one output to each input

    is a _____.

2. The value that is put into a function is the _____.

3. The result after applying the function machine's rule is

    the _____.

Active Reading

Double-Door Fold Create a double-door fold to help you understand the concepts in this module. Label one flap "Proportional Functions" and the other flap "Non-proportional Functions." As you study each lesson, write important ideas under the appropriate flap. Include any sample problems that will help you remember the concepts when you look back at your notes.

Unpacking the Standards

Understanding the standards and the vocabulary terms in the standards will help you know exactly what you are expected to learn in this module.

 FL 8.F.1.1

Understand that a function is a rule that assigns to each input exactly one output. The graph of a function is the set of ordered pairs consisting of an input and the corresponding output.

Key Vocabulary

function *(función)*
An input-output relationship that has exactly one output for each input.

What It Means to You

You will identify sets of ordered pairs that are functions. A function is a rule that assigns exactly one output to each input.

UNPACKING EXAMPLE 8.F.1.1

Does the following table of inputs and outputs represent a function?

Yes, it is a function because each number in the input column is assigned to only one number in the output column.

Input	Output
14	110
20	130
22	120
30	110

The graph of the function is the set of ordered pairs (14, 110), (20, 130), (22, 120), and (30, 110).

 FL 8.F.1.2

Compare properties of two functions each represented in a different way (algebraically, graphically, numerically in tables, or by verbal descriptions).

What It Means to You

You will learn to identify and compare functions expressed as equations and tables.

UNPACKING EXAMPLE 8.F.1.2

A spider descends a 20-foot drainpipe at a rate of 2.5 feet per minute. Another spider descends a drainpipe as shown in the table. Find and compare the rates of change and initial values of the linear functions in terms of the situations they model.

Spider #1: $f(x) = -2.5x + 20$

Spider #2:

Time (min)	0	1	2
Height (ft)	32	29	26

For Spider #1, the rate of change is -2.5, and the initial value is 20. For Spider #2, the rate of change is -3, and the initial value is 32.

Spider #2 started at 32 feet, which is 12 feet higher than Spider #1. Spider #1 is descending at 2.5 feet per minute, which is 0.5 foot per minute slower than Spider #2.

Visit **my.hrw.com** to see all **Florida Math Standards** unpacked.

my.hrw.com

Identifying and Representing Functions

FL 8.F.1.1
Understand that a function is a rule that assigns to each input exactly one output. The graph of a function is the set of ordered pairs consisting of an input and the corresponding output.

ESSENTIAL QUESTION

How can you identify and represent functions?

  EXPLORE ACTIVITY Real World   FL 8.F.1.1

Understanding Relationships

Carlos needs to buy some new pencils from the school supply store at his school. Carlos asks his classmates if they know how much pencils cost. Angela says she bought 2 pencils for $0.50. Paige bought 3 pencils for $0.75, and Spencer bought 4 pencils for $1.00.

Carlos thinks about the rule for the price of a pencil as a machine. When he puts the number of pencils he wants to buy into the machine, the machine applies a rule and tells him the total cost of that number of pencils.

Input   **Output**

	Number of Pencils	Rule	Total Cost
i.	2	?	
ii.	3	?	
iii.	4	?	
iv.	x		
v.	12		

A Use the prices in the problem to fill in total cost in rows **i–iii** of the table.

B Describe any patterns you see. Use your pattern to determine the cost of 1 pencil.

_____

_____

_____

C Use the pattern you identified to write the rule applied by the machine. Write the rule as an algebraic expression and fill in rule column row **iv** of the table.

D Carlos wants to buy 12 pencils. Use your rule to fill in row **v** of the table to show how much Carlos will pay for 12 pencils.

Reflect

1. How did you decide what operation to use in your rule?

_____

_____

2. **What If?** Carlos decides to buy erasers in a package. There are 6 pencil-top erasers in 2 packages of erasers.

a. Write a rule in words for the number of packages Carlos needs to buy to get *x* erasers. Then write the rule as an algebraic expression.

_____

_____

b. How many packages does Carlos need to buy to get 18 erasers?

_____

Math On the Spot

my.hrw.com

Identifying Functions from Mapping Diagrams

A **function** assigns exactly one output to each input. The value that is put into a function is the **input**. The result is the **output**.

A mapping diagram can be used to represent a relationship between input values and output values. A mapping diagram represents a function if each input value is paired with only one output value.

EXAMPLE 1

FL 8.F.1.1

Determine whether each relationship is a function.

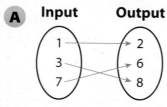

Since each input value is paired with only one output value, the relationship is a function.

Determine whether each relationship is a function.

B Since 2 is paired with more than one output value (both 4 and 5), the relationship is not a function.

Reflect

3. Is it possible for a function to have more than one input value but only one output value? Provide an illustration to support your answer.

_____

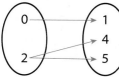
Determine whether each relationship is a function. Explain.

4.

_____

_____

_____

5.

_____

_____

_____

Personal Math Trainer
Online Assessment and Intervention
⏻ my.hrw.com

Math Talk
Mathematical Practices

What is always true about a mapping diagram that represents a function?

Identifying Functions from Tables

Relationships between input values and output values can also be represented using tables. The values in the first column are the input values. The values in the second column are the output values. The relationship represents a function if each input value is paired with only one output value.

Math On the Spot
⏻ my.hrw.com

EXAMPLE 2 FL 8.F.1.1

My Notes

Determine whether each relationship is a function.

A

Input	Output
5	7
10	6
15	15
20	2
25	15

Since 15 is a repeated output value, one output value is paired with two input values. If this occurs in a relationship, the relationship can still be a function.

Since each input value is paired with only one output value, the relationship is a function.

Determine whether each relationship is a function.

B

Input	Output
1	10
5	8
4	6
1	4
7	2

> Since 1 is a repeated input value, one input value is paired with two output values. Look back at the rule for functions. Is this relationship a function?

Since the input value 1 is paired with more than one output value (both 10 and 4), the relationship is not a function.

Reflect

6. What is always true about the numbers in the first column of a table that represents a function? Why must this be true?

_____

_____

_____

_____

_____

YOUR TURN

Determine whether each relationship is a function. Explain

7.

Input	Output
53	53
24	24
32	32
17	17
45	45

8.

Input	Output
14	52
8	21
27	16
36	25
8	34

_____   _____

_____   _____

_____   _____

_____   _____

Personal Math Trainer

Online Assessment and Intervention

my.hrw.com

Identifying Functions from Graphs

Graphs can be used to display relationships between two sets of numbers. Each point on a graph represents an ordered pair. The first coordinate in each ordered pair is the input value. The second coordinate is the output value. The graph represents a function if each input value is paired with only one output value.

Math On the Spot
my.hrw.com

EXAMPLE 3 FL 8.F.1.1

The graph shows the relationship between the number of hours students spent studying for an exam and the exam grades. Is the relationship represented by the graph a function?

The input values are the number of hours spent studying by each student. The output values are the exam grades. The points represent the following ordered pairs:

Hours Studied and Exam Grade

(1, 70)	(2, 70)	(2, 85)	(3, 75)	(5, 80)
(6, 82)	(7, 88)	(9, 90)	(9, 95)	(12, 98)

Notice that 2 is paired with both 70 and 85, and 9 is paired with both 90 and 95. Therefore, since these input values are paired with more than one output value, the relationship is not a function.

Reflect

9. Many real-world relationships are functions. For example, the amount of money made at a car wash is a function of the number of cars washed. Give another example of a real-world function.

_____

_____

10. The graph shows the relationship between the heights and weights of the members of a basketball team. Is the relationship represented by the graph a function? Explain.

_____

_____

_____

Heights and Weights of Team Members

Personal Math Trainer
Online Assessment and Intervention
my.hrw.com

Complete each table. In the row with *x* as the input, write a rule as an algebraic expression for the output. Then complete the last row of the table using the rule. (Explore Activity)

1.

Input	Output
Tickets	Cost ($)
2	40
5	100
7	140
x	
10	

2.

Input	Output
Minutes	Pages
2	1
10	5
20	10
x	
30	

3.

Input	Output
Muffins	Cost ($)
1	2.25
3	6.75
6	13.50
x	
12	

Determine whether each relationship is a function. (Examples 1 and 2)

4.

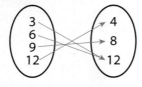

_____

_____

_____

5.

Input	Output
3	20
4	25
5	30
4	35
6	40

_____

_____

_____

6. The graph shows the relationship between the weights of 5 packages and the shipping charge for each package. Is the relationship represented by the graph a function? Explain.

_____

_____

Weights and Shipping Costs

? ESSENTIAL QUESTION CHECK-IN

7. What are four different ways of representing functions? How can you tell if a relationship is a function?

_____

_____

14.1 Independent Practice

FL 8.F.1.1

Personal Math Trainer

Online Assessment and Intervention

my.hrw.com

Determine whether each relationship represented by the ordered pairs is a function. Explain.

8. (2, 2), (3, 1), (5, 7), (8, 0), (9, 1)

_____

_____

_____

9. (0, 4), (5, 1), (2, 8), (6, 3), (5, 9)

_____

_____

_____

10. Draw Conclusions Joaquin receives $0.40 per pound for 1 to 99 pounds of aluminum cans he recycles. He receives $0.50 per pound if he recycles more than 100 pounds. Is the amount of money Joaquin receives a function of the weight of the cans he recycles? Explain your reasoning.

_____

_____

_____

11. A biologist tracked the growth of a strain of bacteria, as shown in the graph.

a. Explain why the relationship represented by the graph is a function.

_____

_____

_____

Bacteria B

b. What If? Suppose there was the same number of bacteria for two consecutive hours. Would the graph still represent a function? Explain.

_____

12. Multiple Representations Give an example of a function in everyday life, and represent it as a graph, a table, and a set of ordered pairs. Describe how you know it is a function.

_____

x				
y				

The graph shows the relationship between the weights of six wedges of cheese and the price of each wedge.

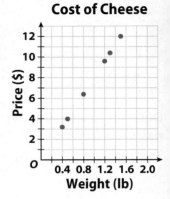

Cost of Cheese

13. Is the relationship represented by the graph a function? Justify your reasoning. Use the words "input" and "output" in your explanation, and connect them to the context represented by the graph.

_____

_____

14. **Analyze Relationships** Suppose the weights and prices of additional wedges of cheese were plotted on the graph. Might that change your answer to question 13? Explain your reasoning.

_____

_____

_____

_____

H.O.T. FOCUS ON HIGHER ORDER THINKING

Work Area

15. **Justify Reasoning** A mapping diagram represents a relationship that contains three different input values and four different output values. Is the relationship a function? Explain your reasoning.

_____

_____

_____

_____

16. **Communicate Mathematical Ideas** An onion farmer is hiring workers to help harvest the onions. He knows that the number of days it will take to harvest the onions is a function of the number of workers he hires. Explain the use of the word "function" in this context.

_____

_____

_____

_____

_____

_____

FL 8.F.1.3

Interpret the equation $y = mx + b$ as defining a linear function, whose graph is a straight line; give examples of functions that are not linear.
Also 8.F.1.1

ESSENTIAL QUESTION

What are some characteristics that you can use to describe functions?

EXPLORE ACTIVITY   FL 8.F.1.1

Investigating a Constant Rate of Change

The U.S. Department of Agriculture defines heavy rain as rain that falls at a rate of 1.5 centimeters per hour.

A The table shows the total amount of rain that falls in various amounts of time during a heavy rain. Complete the table.

Time (h)	0	1	2	3	4	5
Total Amount of Rain (cm)	0	1.5				

B Plot the ordered pairs from the table on the coordinate plane at the right.

C How much rain falls in 3.5 hours? _____

D Plot the point corresponding to 3.5 hours of heavy rain.

E What do you notice about all of the points you plotted?

_____

F Is the total amount of rain that falls a function of the number of hours that rain has been falling? Why or why not?

_____

_____

Heavy Rainfall

Reflect

1. Suppose you continued to plot points for times between those in the table, such as 1.2 hours or 4.5 hours. What can you say about the locations of these points?

_____

_____

Graphing Linear Functions

The relationship you investigated in the previous activity can be represented by the equation $y = 1.5x$, where x is the time and y is the total amount of rain. The graph of the relationship is a line, so the equation is a **linear equation**. Since there is exactly one value of y for each value of x, the relationship is a function. It is a **linear function** because its graph is a nonvertical line.

EXAMPLE 1

 FL 8.F.1.3

The temperature at dawn was 8 °F and increased steadily 2 °F every hour. The equation $y = 2x + 8$ gives the temperature y after x hours. State whether the relationship between the time and the temperature is proportional or nonproportional. Then graph the function.

STEP 1 Compare the equation with the general linear equation $y = mx + b$. $y = 2x + 8$ is in the form $y = mx + b$, with $m = 2$ and $b = 8$. Therefore, the equation is a linear equation. Since $b \neq 0$, the relationship is nonproportional.

STEP 2 Choose several values for the input x. Substitute these values for x in the equation to find the output y.

x	2x + 8	y	(x, y)
0	2(0) + 8	8	(0, 8)
2	2(2) + 8	12	(2, 12)
4	2(4) + 8	16	(4, 16)
6	2(6) + 8	20	(6, 20)

STEP 3 Graph the ordered pairs. Then draw a line through the points to represent the solutions of the function.

Temperatures

YOUR TURN

2. State whether the relationship between x and y in $y = 0.5x$ is proportional or nonproportional. Then graph the function.

_____

Determining Whether a Function is Linear

The linear equation in Example 1 has the form $y = mx + b$, where m and b are real numbers. Every equation in the form $y = mx + b$ is a linear equation. The linear equations represent linear functions. Equations that cannot be written in this form are not linear equations, and therefore are not linear functions.

EXAMPLE 2

FL 8.F.1.3

A square tile has a side length of x inches. The equation $y = x^2$ gives the area of the tile in square inches. Determine whether the relationship between x and y is linear and, if so, if it is proportional.

STEP 1 Choose several values for the input x. Substitute these values for x in the equation to find the output y.

STEP 2 Graph the ordered pairs.

x	x^2	y	(x, y)
1	1^2	1	$(1, 1)$
2	2^2	4	$(2, 4)$
3	3^2	9	$(3, 9)$
4	4^2	16	$(4, 16)$

STEP 3 Identify the shape of the graph. The points suggest a curve, not a line. Draw a curve through the points to represent the solutions of the function.

STEP 4 Describe the relationship between x and y.

The graph is not a line so the relationship is not linear.

Only a linear relationship can be proportional, so the relationship is not proportional.

Math Talk
Mathematical Practices

How can you use the numbers in the table to decide whether or not the relationship between x and y is linear?

YOUR TURN

3. A soda machine makes $\frac{2}{3}$ gallon of soda every minute. The total amount y that the machine makes in x minutes is given by the equation $y = \frac{2}{3}x$. Determine whether the relationship between x and y is linear and, if so, if it is proportional.

Time (min), x	0	3		9
Amount (gal), y			4	

Making Soda

Plot the ordered pairs from the table. Then graph the function represented by the ordered pairs and tell whether the function is linear or nonlinear. (Examples 1 and 2)

1. $y = 5 - 2x$

Input, x	−1	1	3	5
Output, y				

2. $y = 2 - x^2$

Input, x	−2	−1	0	1	2
Output, y					

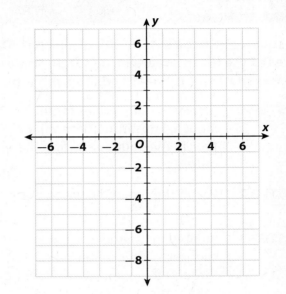

_____

_____

Explain whether each equation is a linear equation. (Example 2)

3. $y = x^2 - 1$

_____

_____

_____

_____

4. $y = 1 - x$

_____

_____

_____

_____

? ESSENTIAL QUESTION CHECK-IN

5. Explain how you can use a table of values, an equation, and a graph to determine whether a function represents a proportional relationship.

_____

_____

_____

14.2 Independent Practice

FL 8.F.1.1, 8.F.1.3

Personal
Math Trainer

Online
Assessment and
Intervention
my.hrw.com

6. State whether the relationship between x and y in $y = 4x - 5$ is proportional or nonproportional. Then graph the function.

_____

7. The Fortaleza telescope in Brazil is a radio telescope. Its shape can be approximated with the equation $y = 0.013x^2$. Is the relationship between x and y linear? Is it proportional? Explain.

_____

_____

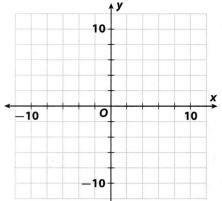

8. Kiley spent $20 on rides and snacks at the state fair. If x is the amount she spent on rides, and y is the amount she spent on snacks, the total amount she spent can be represented by the equation $x + y = 20$. Is the relationship between x and y linear? Is it proportional? Explain.

_____

_____

_____

9. **Represent Real-World Problems** The drill team is buying new uniforms. The table shows y, the total cost in dollars, and x, the number of uniforms purchased.

Number of uniforms, x	1	3	5	9
Total cost ($), y	60	180	300	540

a. Use the data to draw a graph. Is the relationship between x and y linear? Explain.

_____

b. Use your graph to predict the cost of purchasing 12 uniforms.

_____

Drill Team Uniforms

10. Marta, a whale calf in an aquarium, is fed a special milk formula. Her handler uses a graph to track the number of gallons of formula y the calf drinks in x hours. Is the relationship between x and y linear? Is it proportional? Explain.

_____

_____

Marta's Feedings

11. Critique Reasoning A student claims that the equation $y = 7$ is not a linear equation because it does not have the form $y = mx + b$. Do you agree or disagree? Why?

_____

_____

_____

12. Make a Prediction Let x represent the number of hours you read a book and y represent the total number of pages you have read. You have already read 70 pages and can read 30 pages per hour. Write an equation relating x hours and y pages you read. Then predict the total number of pages you will have read after another 3 hours.

_____

H.O.T. FOCUS ON HIGHER ORDER THINKING

Work Area

13. Draw Conclusions Rebecca draws a graph of a real-world relationship that turns out to be a set of unconnected points. Can the relationship be linear? Can it be proportional? Explain your reasoning.

_____

_____

_____

14. Communicate Mathematical Ideas Write a real-world problem involving a proportional relationship. Explain how you know the relationship is proportional.

_____

_____

_____

_____

15. Justify Reasoning Show that the equation $y + 3 = 3(2x + 1)$ is linear and that it represents a proportional relationship between x and y.

_____

_____

_____

_____

_____

LESSON
14.3 Comparing Functions

FL **8.F.1.2**
Compare properties of two functions each represented in a different way (algebraically, graphically, numerically in tables, or by verbal descriptions). *Also 8.EE.2.5, 8.F.2.4*

ESSENTIAL QUESTION

How can you use tables, graphs, and equations to compare functions?

Comparing a Table and an Equation

To compare a function written as an equation and another function represented by a table, find the equation for the function in the table.

 EXAMPLE 1 *Real World*

 FL **8.F.1.2, 8.F.2.4**

Math On the Spot
my.hrw.com

Josh and Maggie buy MP3 files from different music services. The monthly cost, _y_ dollars, for _x_ songs is linear. The cost of Josh's service is $y = 0.50x + 10$. The cost of Maggie's service is shown below.

Monthly Cost of MP3s at Maggie's Music Service					
Songs, _x_	5	10	15	20	25
Cost ($), _y_	4.95	9.90	14.85	19.80	24.75

A Write an equation to represent the monthly cost of Maggie's service.

STEP 1 Choose any two ordered pairs from the table to find the slope.

$$m = \frac{y_2 - y_1}{x_2 - x_1} = \frac{9.90 - 4.95}{10 - 5} = \frac{4.95}{5} = 0.99$$

The points (5, 4.95) and (10, 9.90) were used.

STEP 2 Find the _y_-intercept. Use the slope and any point.

$y = mx + b$ Slope-intercept form.

$4.95 = 0.99 \cdot 5 + b$ Substitute for _y_, _m_, and _x_.

$0 = b$

STEP 3 Substitute the slope and _y_-intercept.

$y = 0.99x + 0$ or $y = 0.99x$ Substitute 0.99 for _m_ and 0 for _y_.

> **Math Talk**
> Mathematical Practices
>
> Describe each service's cost in words using the meanings of the slopes and _y_-intercepts.

B Which service is cheaper when 30 songs are downloaded?

Josh's service: Maggie's service:

$y = 0.50 \times 30 + 10$ $y = 0.99 \times 30$

$y = 25$ $y = 29.7$

Josh's service is cheaper.

YOUR TURN

1. Quentin is choosing between buying books at the bookstore or buying online versions of the books for his tablet. The cost, y dollars, of ordering books online for x books is $y = 6.95x + 1.50$. The cost of buying the books at the bookstore is shown in the table. Which method of buying books is more expensive if Quentin wants to buy 6 books?

Cost of Books at the Bookstore					
Books, x	1	2	3	4	5
Cost (\$), y	7.50	15.00	22.50	30.00	37.50

_____

EXPLORE ACTIVITY 1   **FL** 8.F.1.2, 8.EE.2.5

Comparing a Table and a Graph

The table and graph show how many words Morgan and Brian typed correctly on a typing test. For both students, the relationship between words typed correctly and time is linear.

Brian's Typing Test

Morgan's Typing Test					
Time (min)	2	4	6	8	10
Words	30	60	90	120	150

A Find Morgan's unit rate.

_____

B Find Brian's unit rate.

_____

C Which student types more correct words per minute?

_____

Reflect

2. Katie types 17 correct words per minute. Explain how a graph of Katie's test results would compare to Morgan's and Brian's.

_____

_____

Comparing a Graph and a Description

Jamal wants to buy a new game system that costs $200. He does not have enough money to buy it today, so he compares layaway plans at different stores.

The plan at Store A is shown on the graph.

Store B requires an initial payment of $60 and weekly payments of $20 until the balance is paid in full.

Layaway Plan

(Graph: y-axis labeled "Balance owed ($)" with marks at 40, 80, 120, 160; x-axis labeled "Number of weeks" with marks at 2, 4, 6, 8, 10)

A Write an equation in slope-intercept form for Store A's layaway plan. Let x represent number of weeks and y represent balance owed.

_____

B Write an equation in slope-intercept form for Store B's layaway plan. Let x represent number of weeks and y represent balance owed.

_____

C Sketch a graph of the plan at Store B on the same grid as Store A.

D How can you use the graphs to tell which plan requires the greater down payment? How can you use the equations?

_____

_____

_____

E How can you use the graphs to tell which plan requires the greater weekly payment?

_____

_____

_____

F Which plan allows Jamal to pay for the game system faster? Explain.

_____

_____

Doctors have two methods of calculating maximum heart rate. With the first method, maximum heart rate, *y*, in beats per minute is $y = 220 - x$, where *x* is the person's age. Maximum heart rate with the second method is shown in the table. (Example 1)

Age, *x*	20	30	40	50	60
Heart rate (bpm), *y*	194	187	180	173	166

1. Which method gives the greater maximum heart rate for a 70-year-old?

_____

2. Are heart rate and age proportional or nonproportional for each method?

_____

Aisha runs a tutoring business. With Plan 1, students may choose to pay $15 per hour. With Plan 2, they may follow the plan shown on the graph. (Explore Activity 1 and 2)

Tutoring Fees

3. Describe the plan shown on the graph.

_____

4. Sketch a graph showing the $15 per hour option.

5. What does the intersection of the two graphs mean?

_____

6. Which plan is cheaper for 10 hours of tutoring?

_____

7. Are cost and time proportional or nonproportional for each plan?

_____

_____

? ESSENTIAL QUESTION CHECK-IN

8. When using tables, graphs, and equations to compare functions, why do you find the equations for tables and graphs?

_____

_____

Name_____ Class_____ Date_____

14.3 Independent Practice

FL 8.EE.2.5, 8.F.1.2, 8.F.2.4

Personal Math Trainer

Online Assessment and Intervention

my.hrw.com

The table and graph show the miles driven and gas used for two scooters.

Scooter A	
Distance (mi), x	Gas used (gal), y
150	2
300	4
450	6
600	8
750	10

Scooter B

9. Which scooter uses fewer gallons of gas when 1350 miles are driven?

_____

10. Are gas used and miles proportional or nonproportional for each scooter?

_____

A cell phone company offers two texting plans to its customers. The monthly cost, y dollars, of one plan is $y = 0.10x + 5$, where x is the number of texts. The cost of the other plan is shown in the table.

Number of texts, x	100	200	300	400	500
Cost ($), y	20	25	30	35	40

11. Which plan is cheaper for under 200 texts? _____

12. The graph of the first plan does not pass through the origin. What does this indicate?

_____

_____

13. Brianna wants to buy a digital camera for a photography class. One store offers the camera for $50 down and a payment plan of $20 per month. The payment plan for a second store is described by $y = 15x + 80$, where y is the total cost in dollars and x is the number of months. Which camera is cheaper when the camera is paid off in 12 months? Explain.

_____

_____

14. The French club and soccer team are washing cars to earn money. The amount earned, y dollars, for washing x cars is a linear function. Which group makes the most money per car? Explain.

French Club	
Number of cars, x	Amount earned ($), y
2	10
4	20
6	30
8	40
10	50

Soccer Team

_____

_____

_____

H.O.T.   **FOCUS ON HIGHER ORDER THINKING**

Work Area

15. Draw Conclusions Gym A charges $60 a month plus $5 per visit. The monthly cost at Gym B is represented by $y = 5x + 40$, where x is the number of visits per month. What conclusion can you draw about the monthly costs of the gyms?

_____

_____

_____

16. Justify Reasoning Why will the value of y for the function $y = 5x + 1$ always be greater than that for the function $y = 4x + 2$ when $x > 1$?

_____

_____

_____

17. Analyze Relationships The equations of two functions are $y = -21x + 9$ and $y = -24x + 8$. Which function is changing more quickly? Explain.

_____

_____

_____

_____

FL 8.F.2.5

Describe qualitatively the functional relationship between two quantities by analyzing a graph … . Sketch a graph that exhibits the qualitative features of a function that has been described verbally.

ESSENTIAL QUESTION

How can you describe a relationship given a graph and sketch a graph given a description?

EXPLORE ACTIVITY 1 FL 8.F.2.5

Interpreting Graphs

A roller coaster park is open from May to October each year. The graph shows the number of park visitors over its season.

Park Visitors

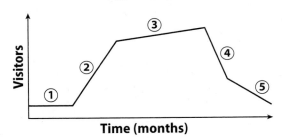

A Segment 1 shows that attendance during the opening weeks of the park's season stayed constant. Describe what Segment 2 shows.

_____

B Based on the time frame, give a possible explanation for the change in attendance represented by Segment 2.

_____

C Which segments of the graph show decreasing attendance? Give a possible explanation.

_____

_____

Reflect

1. Explain how the slope of each segment of the graph is related to whether attendance increases or decreases.

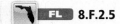
Matching Graphs to Situations

Grace, Jet, and Mike are studying 100 words for a spelling bee.

- Grace started by learning how to spell many words each day, but then learned fewer and fewer words each day.
- Jet learned how to spell the same number of words each day.
- Mike started by learning how to spell only a few words each day, but then learned a greater number of words each day.

_____   _____   _____

A Describe the progress represented by Graph A.

_____

_____

Math Talk
Mathematical Practices

Tell whether each graph is linear or nonlinear and proportional or nonproportional.

B Describe the progress represented by Graph B.

_____

_____

_____

C Describe the progress represented by Graph C.

_____

_____

_____

D Determine which graph represents each student's study progress and write the students' names under the appropriate graphs.

Reflect

2. What would it mean if one of the graphs slanted downward?

_____

Sketching a Graph for a Situation

Mrs. Sutton provides free math tutoring to her students every day after school. No one comes to tutoring sessions during the first week of school. Over the next two weeks, use of the tutoring service gradually increases.

A Sketch a graph showing the number of students who use the tutoring service over the first three weeks of school.

B Mrs. Sutton's students are told that they will have a math test at the end of the fifth week of school. How do you think this will affect the number of students who come to tutoring?

_____

_____

C Considering your answer to **B**, sketch a graph showing the number of students who might use the tutoring service over the first six weeks of school.

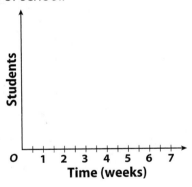

Reflect

3. If Mrs. Sutton offers bonus credit to students who come to tutoring, how might this affect the number of students?

_____

4. How would your answer to Question 3 affect the graph?

_____

_____

In a lab environment, colonies of bacteria follow a predictable pattern of growth. The graph shows this growth over time. (Explore Activity 1)

Bacterial Growth Curve

1. What is happening to the population during Phase 2?

   _____

   _____

2. What is happening to the population during Phase 4?

   _____

   _____

The graphs give the speeds of three people who are riding snowmobiles. Tell which graph corresponds to each situation. (Explore Activity 2)

Graph 1

Graph 2

Graph 3

3. Chip begins his ride slowly but then stops to talk with some friends. After a few minutes, he continues his ride, gradually increasing his speed.

   _____

4. Linda steadily increases her speed through most of her ride. Then she slows down as she nears some trees.

   _____

5. Paulo stood at the top of a diving board. He walked to the end of the board, and then dove forward into the water. He plunged down below the surface, then swam straight forward while underwater. Finally, he swam forward and upward to the surface of the water. Draw a graph to represent Paulo's elevation at different distances from the edge of the pool. (Explore Activity 3)

Paulo's elevation

14.4 Independent Practice

FL 8.F.2.5

Personal Math Trainer

Online Assessment and Intervention

my.hrw.com

Tell which graph corresponds to each situation below.

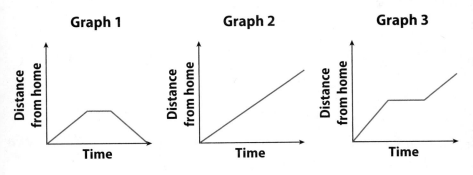

Graph 1   Graph 2   Graph 3

6. Arnold started from home and walked to a friend's house. He stayed with his friend for a while and then walked to another friend's house farther from home.

_____

7. Francisco started from home and walked to the store. After shopping, he walked back home.

_____

8. Celia walks to the library at a steady pace without stopping.

_____

Regina rented a motor scooter. The graph shows how far away she is from the rental site after each half hour of riding.

9. Represent Real-World Problems Use the graph to describe Regina's trip. You can start the description like this: "Regina left the rental shop and rode for an hour…"

_____

_____

_____

_____

_____

Distance from Rental Site

10. Analyze Relationships Determine during which half hour Regina covered the greatest distance.

_____

The data in the table shows the speed of a ride at an amusement park at different times one afternoon.

Time	3:20	3:21	3:22	3:23	3:24	3:25
Speed (mi/h)	0	14	41	62	8	0

11. Sketch a graph that shows the speed of the ride over time.

12. Between which times is the ride's speed increasing the fastest?

_____

13. Between which times is the ride's speed decreasing the fastest?

_____

H.O.T. FOCUS ON HIGHER ORDER THINKING

A woodland area on an island contains a population of foxes. The graph describes the changes in the population over time.

14. **Justify Reasoning** What is happening to the fox population before time t? Explain your reasoning.

_____

_____

_____

_____

Fox Population

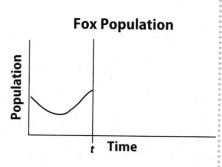

15. **What If?** Suppose at time t, a conservation organization moves a large group of foxes to the island. Sketch a graph to show how this action might affect the population on the island after time t.

16. **Make a Prediction** At some point after time t, a forest fire destroys part of the woodland area on the island. Describe how your graph from problem 15 might change.

Fox Population

_____

_____

_____

Ready to Go On?

Personal Math Trainer
Online Assessment and Intervention
⏻ my.hrw.com

14.1 Identifying and Representing Functions

Determine whether each relationship is a function.

1.
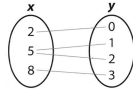

x	y
2	0
5	1
8	2
	3

2.

Input, x	Output, y
−1	6
3	5
6	5

3. (2, 5), (7, 2), (−3, 4), (2, 9), (1, 1)

_____ _____ _____

14.2 Describing Functions

Determine whether each situation is linear or nonlinear, and proportional or nonproportional.

4. Joanna is paid $14 per hour.

5. Alberto started out bench pressing 50 pounds. He then added 5 pounds every week.

_____ _____

14.3 Comparing Functions

6. Which function is changing more quickly? Explain.

_____

_____

_____

Function 1

Function 2	
Input, x	Output, y
2	11
3	6.5
4	2

14.4 Analyzing Graphs

7. Describe a graph that shows Sam running at a constant rate.

_____

? ESSENTIAL QUESTION

8. How can you use functions to solve real-world problems?

_____

Selected Response

1. Which table shows a proportional function?

(A)

x	0	5	10
y	3	15	30

(B)

x	0	5	10
y	10	20	30

(C)

x	0	5	10
y	0	50	100

(D)

x	0	5	10
y	10	5	0

2. What is the slope and *y*-intercept of the function shown in the table?

x	1	4	7
y	6	12	18

(A) $m = -2; b = -4$

(B) $m = -2; b = 4$

(C) $m = 2; b = 4$

(D) $m = 4; b = 2$

3. The table below shows some input and output values of a function.

Input	4	5	6	7
Output	14	17.5		24.5

What is the missing output value?

(A) 20

(B) 21

(C) 22

(D) 23

4. Tom walked to school at a steady pace, met his sister, and they walked home at a steady pace. Describe the graph relating Tom's distance from home to time.

(A) V-shaped

(B) upside down V-shaped

(C) Straight line sloping up

(D) Straight line sloping down

Mini-Task

5. Linear functions can be used to find the price of a building based on its floor area. Below are two of these functions.

$y = 40x + 15{,}000$

Floor Area (ft²)	400	700	1,000
Price ($1,000s)	32	56	80

a. Find and compare the slopes.

_____

_____

_____

b. Find and compare the *y*-intercepts.

_____

_____

_____

c. Describe each function as proportional or nonproportional.

_____

_____

_____

MODULE 11 ## Proportional Relationships

? **ESSENTIAL QUESTION**

How can you use proportional relationships to solve real-world problems?

EXAMPLE 1

Write an equation that represents the proportional relationship shown in the graph.

Use the points on the graph to make a table.

Bracelets sold	3	4	5	6
Profit ($)	9	12	15	18

Let x represent the number of bracelets sold.

Let y represent the profit.

The equation is $y = 3x$.

EXAMPLE 2

Find the slope of the line.

$\text{slope} = \dfrac{\text{rise}}{\text{run}}$

$\quad = \dfrac{3}{-4}$

$\quad = -\dfrac{3}{4}$

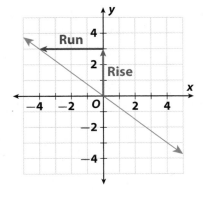

EXERCISES

1. The table represents a proportional relationship. Write an equation that describes the relationship. Then graph the relationship represented by the data. (Lessons 11.1, 11.2, 11.3)

Time (x)	6	8	10	12
Distance (y)	3	4	5	6

_____

Find the slope and the unit rate represented on each graph. (Lessons 11.2, 11.3)

2.

3.

 MODULE 12
Nonproportional Relationships

Key Vocabulary
linear equation
   (ecuación lineal)
slope-intercept form of an
   equation _(forma de
   pendiente-intersección)_
y-intercept
   (intersección con el eje y)

? ESSENTIAL QUESTION

How can you use nonproportional relationships to solve real-world problems?

EXAMPLE 1

Jai is saving to buy his mother a birthday gift. Each week, he saves $5. He started with $25. The equation $y = 5x + 25$ gives the total Jai has saved, y, after x weeks. Draw a graph of the equation. Then describe the relationship.

Use the equation to make a table. Then, graph the ordered pairs from the table, and draw a line through the points.

x (weeks)	0	1	2	3	4
y (savings in dollars)	25	30	35	40	45

The relationship is linear but nonproportional.

446 Unit 6

EXAMPLE 2

Graph $y = -\frac{1}{2}x - 2.$

The slope is $\frac{-1}{2}$, or $-\frac{1}{2}$.

The y-intercept is -2.

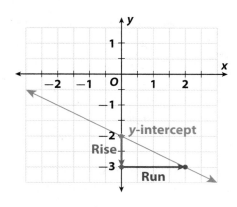

EXERCISES

Complete each table. Explain whether the relationship between x and y is proportional or nonproportional and whether it is linear. (Lesson 12.1)

1. $y = 10x - 4$

x	0	2		6	
y	−4		36		

2. $y = -\frac{3}{2}x$

x	0		2	
y		−1.5		−4.5

_____

_____

3. Find the slope and y-intercept for the linear relationship shown in the table. Graph the line. Is the relationship proportional or nonproportional? (Lessons 12.2, 12.4)

x	−4	−1	0	1
y	−4	2	4	6

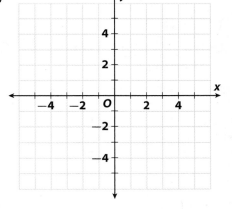

slope _____

y-intercept _____

The relationship is _____.

4. Tom's Taxis charges a fixed rate of $4 per ride plus $0.50 per mile. Carla's Cabs does not charge a fixed rate but charges $1.00 per mile. (Lessons 12.3)

a. Write an equation that represents the cost of Tom's Taxis. _____

b. Write an equation that represents the cost of Carla's cabs. _____

c. Steve calculated that for the distance he needs to travel, Tom's Taxis will charge the same amount as Carla's Cabs. Graph both equations. How far is Steve going to travel and how much will he pay?

_____

_____

MODULE 13 Writing Linear Equations

Key Vocabulary
bivariate data (*datos bivariados*)
nonlinear relationship (*relación no lineal*)

? ESSENTIAL QUESTION

How can you use linear equations to solve real-world problems?

EXAMPLE 1

Jose is renting a backhoe for a construction job. The rental charge for a month is based on the number of days in the month and a set charge per month. In September, which has 30 days, Jose paid $700. In August, which has 31 days, he paid $715. Write an equation in slope-intercept form that represents this situation.

$(x_1, y_1), (x_2, y_2) \rightarrow (30, 700), (31, 715)$	Write the information given as ordered pairs.
$m = \dfrac{y_2 - y_1}{x_2 - x_1} = \dfrac{715 - 700}{31 - 30} = 15$	Find the slope.
$y = mx + b$	Slope-intercept form
$715 = 15(31) + b$	Substitute for y, m, and x to find b.
$250 = b$	Solve for b.
$y = 15x + 250$	Write the equation.

EXAMPLE 2

Determine if the graph shown represents a linear or nonlinear relationship.

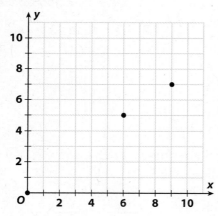

Points	Rate of Change
$(0, 0)$ and $(6, 5)$	$m = \dfrac{5 - 0}{6 - 0} = \dfrac{5}{6}$
$(6, 5)$ and $(9, 7)$	$m = \dfrac{7 - 5}{9 - 6} = \dfrac{2}{3}$
$(0, 0)$ and $(9, 7)$	$m = \dfrac{7 - 0}{9 - 0} = \dfrac{7}{9}$

The rates of change are not constant. The graph represents a nonlinear relationship.

EXERCISES

1. Ms. Thompson is grading math tests. She is giving everyone that took the test a 10-point bonus. Each correct answer is worth 5 points. Write an equation in slope-intercept form that represents the scores on the tests. (Lesson 13.1)

_____

The table shows a pay scale based on years of experience. (Lessons 13.1, 13.2)

Experience (years), x	0	2	4	6	8
Hourly pay ($), y	9	14	19	24	29

2. Find the slope for this relationship. _____

3. Find the y-intercept. _____

4. Write an equation in slope-intercept form that represents this

   relationship. _____

5. Graph the equation, and use it to predict the hourly pay of someone with 10 years of experience.

   _____

   _____

   _____

   _____

Does each of the following graphs represent a linear relationship? Why or why not? (Lesson 13.3)

6.

_____

_____

_____

7.

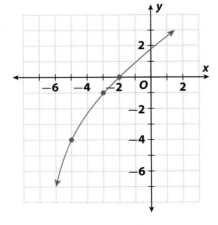

_____

_____

_____

? **ESSENTIAL QUESTION**

How can you use functions to solve real-world problems?

EXAMPLE 1

Determine whether each relationship is a function.

A

Input	Output
3	10
4	4
5	2
4	0
6	5

The relationship is not a function, because an input, 4, is paired with 2 different outputs, 4 and 0.

B

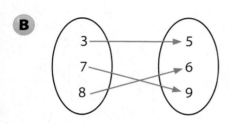

Since each input value is paired with only one output value, the relationship is a function.

EXAMPLE 2

Sally and Louis are on a long-distance bike ride. Sally bikes at a steady rate of 18 miles per hour. The distance *y* that Sally covers in *x* hours is given by the equation $y = 18x$. Louis's speed can be found by using the numbers in the table. Who will travel farther in 4 hours and by how much?

Louis's Biking Speed			
Time (h), *x*	3	5	7
Distance (mi), *y*	60	100	140

Each distance in the table is 20 times each number of hours. Louis's speed is 20 miles per hour, and his distance covered is represented by $y = 20x$.

Sally's ride: Louis's ride:

$y = 18x$ $y = 20x$

$y = 18(4)$ $y = 20(4)$

$y = 72$ $y = 80$

Sally will ride 72 miles in 4 hours. Louis will ride 80 miles in 4 hours. Louis will go 8 miles farther.

EXERCISES

Determine whether each relationship is a function. (Lesson 14.1)

1.

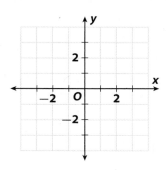

2.

Input	Output
−1	8
0	4
1	8
2	16

_____   _____

Tell whether the function is linear or nonlinear. (Lesson 14.2)

3. $y = 5x + \dfrac{1}{2}$ _____

4. $y = x^2 + 3$ _____

5. Elaine has a choice of two health club memberships. The first membership option is to pay $500 now and then pay $150 per month. The second option is shown in the table. Elaine plans to go to the club for 12 months. Which option is cheaper? Explain. (Lesson 14.3)

Months, x	1	2	3
Total paid ($), y	215	430	645

_____

_____

_____

6. Jenny rode her bike around her neighborhood. Use the graph to describe Jenny's bike ride. (Lesson 14.4)

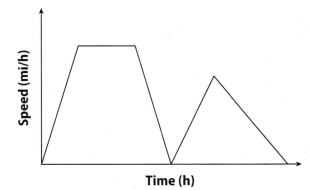

_____

_____

_____

_____

_____

_____

_____

_____

1. **CAREERS IN MATH** Cost Estimator To make MP3 players, a cost estimator determined it costs a company $1,500 per week for overhead and $45 for each MP3 player made.

a. Define a variable to represent the number of players made. Then write an equation to represent the company's total cost *c*.

_____

b. One week, the company spends $5460 making MP3 players. How many players were made that week? Show your work.

_____

_____

c. If the company sells MP3 players for $120, how much profit would it make if it sold 80 players in one week? Explain how you found your answer.

_____

2. The temperature in Portland was 56 °F at 9 a.m. and increased 2° per hour during the day. For the same day in San Francisco, the temperature *y* in degrees Fahrenheit for *x* hours after 9 a.m. was recorded in the table shown.

x	0	1	2	3	4	5	6	7
y	66	65.5	65	64.5	64	63.5	63	62.5

a. For each city, write an equation in slope-intercept form for the temperature as a function of hours after 9 a.m.

_____

_____

_____

b. What does the slope and *y*-intercept represent in the equation for each city?

_____

_____

_____

c. Graph the relationships you found in part **a** in the grid provided.

d. Explain what the intersection point represents.

_____

_____

Selected Response

1. Rickie earns $7 an hour babysitting. Which table represents this proportional relationship?

Ⓐ
Hours	4	6	8
Earnings ($)	28	42	56

Ⓑ
Hours	4	6	8
Earnings ($)	28	35	42

Ⓒ
Hours	2	3	4
Earnings ($)	7	14	21

Ⓓ
Hours	2	3	4
Earnings ($)	14	21	42

2. Which of the relationships below is a function?

Ⓐ (6, 3), (5, 2), (6, 8), (0, 7)

Ⓑ (8, 2), (1, 7), (−1, 2), (1, 9)

Ⓒ (4, 3), (3, 0), (−1, 3), (2, 7)

Ⓓ (7, 1), (0, 0), (6, 2), (0, 4)

3. Which set best describes the numbers used on the scale for a standard thermometer?

Ⓐ whole numbers

Ⓑ rational numbers

Ⓒ real numbers

Ⓓ integers

4. Which term refers to slope?

Ⓐ rate of change

Ⓑ equation

Ⓒ y-intercept

Ⓓ coordinate

5. The graph of which equation is shown below?

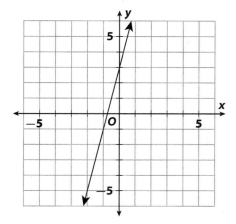

Ⓐ $y = 4x + 3$

Ⓑ $y = -4x - 0.75$

Ⓒ $y = -4x + 3$

Ⓓ $y = 4x - 0.75$

6. Which equation represents a nonproportional relationship?

Ⓐ $y = 5x$

Ⓑ $y = -5x$

Ⓒ $y = 5x + 3$

Ⓓ $y = -\frac{1}{5}x$

7. Which number is 7.0362×10^{-4} written in standard notation?

Ⓐ 0.000070362

Ⓑ 0.00070362

Ⓒ 7.0362

Ⓓ 7,036.2

8. Which term does not correctly describe the relationship shown in the table?

x	0	2	4
y	0	70	140

Ⓐ function

Ⓑ linear

Ⓒ proportional

Ⓓ nonproportional

9. As part of a science experiment, Greta measured the amount of water flowing from Container A to Container B. Container B had half a gallon of water in it to start the experiment. Greta found that the water was flowing at a rate of two gallons per hour. Which equation represents the amount of water in Container B?

Ⓐ $y = 2x$

Ⓑ $y = 0.5x$

Ⓒ $y = 2x + 0.5$

Ⓓ $y = 0.5x + 2$

10. Carl and Jeannine both work at appliance stores. Carl earns a weekly salary of $600 plus $40 for each appliance he sells. The equation $p = 50n + 550$ represents the amount of money Jeannine earns in a week, p ($), as a function of the number of appliances she sells, n. Which of the following statements is true?

Ⓐ Carl has a greater salary and a greater rate per appliance sold.

Ⓑ Jeannine has a greater salary and a greater rate per appliance sold.

Ⓒ Carl will earn more than Jeannine if they each sell 10 appliances in a given week.

Ⓓ Both Carl and Jeannine earn the same amount if they each sell 5 appliances in a given week.

Mini-Tasks

11. The table below represents a linear relationship.

x	2	3	4	5
y	14	17	20	23

a. Find the slope for this relationship.

_____

b. Find the y-intercept. Explain how you found it.

_____

_____

_____

_____

c. Write an equation in slope-intercept form that represents this relationship.

_____

Hot Tip! Estimate your answer before solving the problem. Use your estimate to check the reasonableness of your answer.

12. Jacy has a choice of cell phone plans. Plan A is to pay $260 for the phone and then pay $70 per month for service. Plan B is to get the phone for free and pay $82 per month for service.

a. Write an equation to represent the total cost, c, of Plan A for m months.

_____

b. Write an equation to represent the total cost, c, of Plan B for m months.

_____

c. If Jacy plans to keep the phone for 24 months, which plan is cheaper? Explain.

_____

_____

_____

Solving Equations and Systems of Equations

CAREERS IN MATH

Hydraulic Engineer A hydraulic engineer specializes in the behavior of fluids, mainly water. A hydraulic engineer applies the mathematics of fluid dynamics to the collection, transport, measurement, and regulation of water and other fluids.

If you are interested in a career in hydraulic engineering, you should study the following mathematical subjects:
- Algebra
- Geometry
- Trigonometry
- Probability and Statistics
- Calculus

Research other careers that require the understanding of the mathematics of fluid dynamics.

Unit 7 Performance Task

At the end of the unit, check out how **hydraulic engineers** use math.

Use the puzzle to preview key vocabulary from this unit. Unscramble the circled letters to answer the riddle at the bottom of the page.

1. FIACALRONT INFEOCIECTF

2. LCMADEI CINETFOEFIC

3. UQAOTENI

4. ROPWE

5. TNUSITBUOSIT DOHMTE

1. A number that is multiplied by the variable in an algebraic expression, where the number is a fraction. (Lesson 15.2)

2. A number that is multiplied by the variable in an algebraic expression, where the number is a decimal. (Lesson 15.2)

3. A mathematical statement that two expressions are equal. (Lesson 15.1)

4. A number that is formed by repeated multiplication of the same factor. Multiply by this to remove decimals from an unsolved equation. (Lesson 15.2)

5. A process used to solve systems of linear equations by solving an equation for one variable and then substituting the resulting expression for that variable into the other equation. (Lesson 16.2)

Q: What is the best time to divide a half dollar between two people?

A: at a ___ ___ ___ ___ ___ ___ ___ ___ ___ ___ ___ ___!

Solving Linear Equations

MODULE 15

ESSENTIAL QUESTION

How can you use equations with the variable on both sides to solve real-world problems?

Real-World Video

Some employees earn commission plus their salary when they make a sale. There may be options about their pay structure. They can find the best option by solving an equation with the variable on both sides.

my.hrw.com

GO DIGITAL
my.hrw.com

my.hrw.com

Go digital with your write-in student edition, accessible on any device.

Math On the Spot

Scan with your smart phone to jump directly to the online edition, video tutor, and more.

Animated Math

Interactively explore key concepts to see how math works.

Personal Math Trainer

Get immediate feedback and help as you work through practice sets.

Are YOU Ready?

Complete these exercises to review skills you will need for this module.

Personal Math Trainer

Online Assessment and Intervention

⏻ my.hrw.com

Find Common Denominators

EXAMPLE   Find the LCD of 3, 5, and 10.

3: 3, 6, 9, 12, 15, 18, 21, 24, 27, 30,…
5: 5, 10, 15, 20, 25, 30, 35,…
10: 10, 20, 30, 40, 50,…

List the multiples of each number. Choose the least multiple the lists have in common.
LCD(3, 5, 10) = 30

Find the LCD.

1. 8, 12 _____ **2.** 9, 12 _____ **3.** 15, 20 _____ **4.** 8, 10 _____

Multiply Decimals by Powers of 10

EXAMPLE 3.719×100

$3.719 \times 100 = 371.9$

Count the zeros in 100: 2 zeros
Move the decimal point 2 places to the right.

Find the product.

5. 0.683×100 **6.** $9.15 \times 1,000$ **7.** 0.005×100 **8.** $1,000 \times 1,000$

_____ _____ _____ _____

Connect Words and Equations

EXAMPLE   Two times a number decreased by 5 is −6.

Two times x decreased by 5 is −6.
2x − 5 is −6
2x − 5 = −6

Represent the unknown with a variable.
Times means multiplication. Decreased by means subtraction.
Place the equal sign.

Write an algebraic equation for the sentence.

9. The difference between three times a number and 7 is 14. _____

10. The quotient of five times a number and 7 is no more than 10. _____

11. 14 less than 3 times a number is 5 more than half of the number. _____

Reading Start-Up

Vocabulary

Review Words
- ✔ algebraic expression (*expresión algebraica*)
- coefficient (*coeficiente*)
- common denominator (*denominador común*)
- ✔ constant (*constante*)
- ✔ equation (*ecuación*)
- integers (*entero*)
- least common multiple (*mínimo común múltiplo*)
- operations (*operaciones*)
- solution (*solución*)
- ✔ variable (*variable*)

Visualize Vocabulary

Use the ✔ words to complete the bubble map. You may put more than one word in each oval.

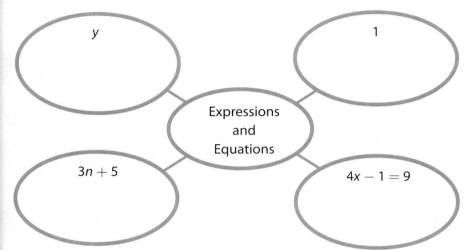

y

1

Expressions and Equations

$3n + 5$

$4x - 1 = 9$

Understand Vocabulary

Complete the sentences using the review words.

1. A value of the variable that makes an equation true is a _____.

2. The set of all whole numbers and their opposites are _____.

3. An _____ is an expression that contains at least one variable.

Active Reading

Layered Book Before beginning the module, create a layered book to help you learn the concepts in this module. At the top of the first flap, write the title of the book, "Solving Linear Equations." Then label each flap with one of the lesson titles in this module. As you study each lesson, write important ideas, such as vocabulary and formulas, under the appropriate flap.

Unpacking the Standards

Understanding the standards and the vocabulary terms in the standards will help you know exactly what you are expected to learn in this module.

 FL 8.EE.3.7a

Give examples of linear equations in one variable with one solution, infinitely many solutions, or no solutions. Show which of these possibilities is the case by successively transforming the given equation into simpler forms, until an equivalent equation of the form $x = a$, $a = a$, or $a = b$ results (where a and b are different numbers).

Key Vocabulary

linear equation in one variable
(ecuación lineal en una variable)
An equation that can be written in the form $ax = b$ where a and b are constants and $a \neq 0$.

What It Means to You

You will identify the number of solutions an equation has.

UNPACKING EXAMPLE 8.EE.3.7a

Your gym charges $50 per month. Find the number of months for which your costs will equal the cost of membership at each gym shown.

A: $40 per month plus $100 one-time fee
$50x = 40x + 100 \rightarrow x = 10$
Equal in 10 months → one solution

B: $50 per month plus $25 one-time fee
$50x = 50x + 25 \rightarrow 0 = 25$
Never equal → no solution

C: $40 per month plus $10 monthly garage fee
$50x = 40x + 10x \rightarrow x = x$
Equal for any number of months → infinitely many solutions

 FL 8.EE.3.7b

Solve linear equations with rational number coefficients, including equations whose solutions require expanding expressions using the distributive property and collecting like terms.

Key Vocabulary

solution *(solución)*
In an equation, the value for the variable that makes the equation true.

Visit **my.hrw.com** to see all **Florida Math Standards** unpacked.

ⓜ **my.hrw.com**

What It Means to You

You can write and solve an equation that has a variable on both sides of the equal sign.

UNPACKING EXAMPLE 8.EE.3.7b

Yellow Taxi has no pickup fee but charges $0.25 per mile. AAA Taxi charges $3 for pickup and $0.15 per mile. Find the number of miles for which the cost of the two taxis is the same.

$$0.25x = 3 + 0.15x$$
$$100(0.25x) = 100(3) + 100(0.15x)$$
$$25x = 300 + 15x$$
$$10x = 300$$
$$x = 30$$

The cost is the same for 30 miles.

Equations with the Variable on Both Sides

FL 8.EE.3.7

Solve linear equations in one variable. *Also 8.EE.3.7b*

ESSENTIAL QUESTION

How can you represent and solve equations with the variable on both sides?

EXPLORE ACTIVITY **FL** 8.EE.3.7, 8.EE.3.7b

Modeling an Equation with a Variable on Both Sides

Algebra tiles can model equations with a variable on both sides.

KEY

$\boxed{+} = 1$

$\boxed{-} = -1$

$\boxed{+} + \boxed{-} = 0$

$\boxed{+} = x$

Use algebra tiles to model and solve $x + 5 = 3x - 1$.

Model $x + 5$ on the left side of the mat and $3x - 1$ on the right side.
Remember that $3x - 1$ is the same as

$3x + $ _____ .

Remove one x-tile from both sides. This

represents subtracting _____ from both sides of the equation.

> **Math Talk**
> **Mathematical Practices**
>
> Why is a positive unit tile added to both sides in the third step?

Place one $+1$-tile on both sides. This

represents adding _____ to both sides of the equation. Remove zero pairs.

Separate each side into 2 equal groups.

One x-tile is equivalent to _____ $+1$-tiles.

The solution is _____ = _____ .

Reflect

1. How can you check the solution to $x + 5 = 3x - 1$ using algebra tiles?

_____

_____

Math On the Spot
🔘 my.hrw.com

Animated Math
🔘 my.hrw.com

Solving an Equation with the Variable on Both Sides

Equations with the variable on both sides can be used to compare costs of real-world situations. To solve these equations, use inverse operations to get the variable terms on one side of the equation.

EXAMPLE 1   FL   8.EE.3.7, 8.EE.3.7b

Andy's Rental Car charges an initial fee of $20 plus an additional $30 per day to rent a car. Buddy's Rental Car charges an initial fee of $36 plus an additional $28 per day. For what number of days is the total cost charged by the companies the same?

STEP 1 Write an expression representing the total cost of renting a car from Andy's Rental Car.

Initial fee	+	Cost for x days
20	+	30x

STEP 2 Write an expression representing the total cost of renting a car from Buddy's Rental Car.

Initial fee	+	Cost for x days
36	+	28x

STEP 3 Write an equation that can be solved to find the number of days for which the total cost charged by the companies would be the same.

Total cost at Andy's	=	Total cost at Buddy's
20 + 30x	=	36 + 28x

STEP 4 Solve the equation for x.

Math Talk
Mathematical Practices

When is it more economical to rent from Andy's Rental Car? When is it more economical to rent from Buddy's?

$$20 + 30x = 36 + 28x \qquad \textit{Write the equation.}$$
$$\underline{-28x -28x} \qquad \textit{Subtract 28x from both sides.}$$
$$20 + 2x = 36$$
$$\underline{-20 -20} \qquad \textit{Subtract 20 from both sides.}$$
$$2x = 16$$
$$\frac{2x}{2} = \frac{16}{2} \qquad \textit{Divide both sides by 2.}$$
$$x = 8$$

The total cost is the same if the rental is for 8 days.

2. A water tank holds 256 gallons but is leaking at a rate of 3 gallons per week. A second water tank holds 384 gallons but is leaking at a rate of 5 gallons per week. After how many weeks will the amount of water in the two tanks be the same?

_____

Personal Math Trainer
Online Assessment and Intervention
my.hrw.com

Writing a Real-World Situation from an Equation

As shown in Example 1, an equation with the variable on both sides can be used to represent a real-world situation. You can reverse this process by writing a real-world situation for a given equation.

Math On the Spot
my.hrw.com

EXAMPLE 2   FL 8.EE.3.7

Write a real-world situation that could be modeled by the equation 150 + 25x = 55x.

STEP 1 The left side of the equation consists of a constant plus a variable term. It could represent the total cost for doing a job where there is an initial fee plus an hourly charge.

STEP 2 The right side of the equation consists of a variable term. It could represent the cost for doing the same job based on an hourly charge only.

STEP 3 The equation 150 + 25x = 55x could be represented by this situation: A handyman charges $150 plus $25 per hour for house painting. A painter charges $55 per hour. How many hours would a job have to take for the handyman's fee and the painter's fee to be the same?

My Notes

3. Write a real-world situation that could be modeled by the equation $30x = 48 + 22x$.

_____
_____
_____
_____

Personal Math Trainer
Online Assessment and Intervention
my.hrw.com

Guided Practice

Use algebra tiles to model and solve each equation. (Explore Activity)

1. $x + 4 = -x - 4$ _____

2. $2 - 3x = -x - 8$ _____

3. At Silver Gym, membership is $25 per month, and personal training sessions are $30 each. At Fit Factor, membership is $65 per month, and personal training sessions are $20 each. In one month, how many personal training sessions would Sarah have to buy to make the total cost at the two gyms equal? (Example 1)

_____

4. Write a real-world situation that could be modeled by the equation $120 + 25x = 45x$. (Example 2)

_____

_____

_____

_____

5. Write a real-world situation that could be modeled by the equation $100 - 6x = 160 - 10x$. (Example 2)

_____

_____

_____

_____

_____

? ESSENTIAL QUESTION CHECK-IN

6. How can you solve an equation with the variable on both sides?

_____

_____

_____

_____

_____

Equations with Rational Numbers

FL   8.EE.3.7b
Solve linear equations with rational number coefficients, ... Also 8.EE.3.7

ESSENTIAL QUESTION

How can you solve equations with rational number coefficients and constants?

Solving an Equation that Involves Fractions

To solve an equation with the variable on both sides that involves fractions, start by eliminating the fractions from the equation.

Math On the Spot

my.hrw.com

EXAMPLE 1

FL   8.EE.3.7b, 8.EE.3.7

Solve $\frac{7}{10}n + \frac{3}{2} = \frac{3}{5}n + 2$.

$$10 = 10 \times 1$$
$$= 5 \times 2$$
$$= 2 \times 5$$

STEP 1 Determine the least common multiple of the denominators: LCM(**10**, **5**, **2**) = 10

STEP 2 Multiply both sides of the equation by the LCM.

$$10\left(\frac{7}{10}n + \frac{3}{2}\right) = 10\left(\frac{3}{5}n + 2\right)$$

$${}^1\cancel{10}\left(\frac{7}{\cancel{10}_1}n\right) + {}^5\cancel{10}\left(\frac{3}{\cancel{2}_1}\right) = {}^2\cancel{10}\left(\frac{3}{\cancel{5}_1}n\right) + 10(2)$$

$$7n + 15 = 6n + 20$$

STEP 3 Use inverse operations to solve the equation.

$$\begin{array}{rcl}
7n + 15 & = & 6n + 20 \\
\underline{-15} & & \underline{-15} \\
7n & = & 6n + 5 \\
\underline{-6n} & & \underline{-6n} \\
n & = & 5
\end{array}$$

Subtract 15 from both sides.

Subtract 6n from both sides.

Math Talk
Mathematical Practices

The constant on the right side, 2, is not a fraction. Why do you still need to multiply it by the LCM, 10?

Reflect

1. What is the advantage of multiplying both sides of the equation by the least common multiple of the denominators in the first step?

_____

2. **What If?** What happens in the first step if you multiply both sides by a common multiple of the denominators that is not the LCM?

_____

_____

Personal Math Trainer

Online Assessment and Intervention

⏻ my.hrw.com

Math On the Spot

⏻ my.hrw.com

YOUR TURN

Solve.

3. $\frac{1}{7}k - 6 = \frac{3}{7}k + 4$ _____

4. $\frac{5}{6}y + 1 = -\frac{1}{2}y + \frac{1}{4}$ _____

Solving an Equation that Involves Decimals

Solving an equation with the variable on both sides that involves decimals is similar to solving an equation with fractions. But instead of first multiplying both sides by the LCM, multiply by a power of 10 to eliminate the decimals.

EXAMPLE 2 *Real World* **FL** 8.EE.3.7, 8.EE.3.7b

Javier walks from his house to the zoo at a constant rate. After walking 0.75 mile, he meets his brother, Raul, and they continue walking at the same constant rate. When they arrive at the zoo, Javier has walked for 0.5 hour and Raul has walked for 0.2 hour. What is the rate in miles per hour at which the brothers walked to the zoo?

STEP 1 Write an equation for the distance from the brothers' house to the zoo, using the fact that distance equals rate times time. Let $r =$ the brothers' walking rate.

$$\underbrace{0.2r + 0.75}_{\text{distance to zoo}} = \underbrace{0.5r}_{\text{distance to zoo}}$$

STEP 2 Multiply both sides of the equation by $10^2 = 100$.

$$100(0.2r) + 100(0.75) = 100(0.5r)$$
$$20r + 75 = 50r$$

> Multiplying by 100 clears the equation of decimals. Multiplying by 10 does not: $10 \times 0.75 = 7.5$.

STEP 3 Use inverse operations to solve the equation.

$$
\begin{array}{ll}
20r + 75 = 50r & \text{Write the equation.} \\
\underline{-20r \qquad -20r} & \text{Subtract } 20r \text{ from both sides.} \\
75 = 30r & \\
\dfrac{75}{30} = \dfrac{30r}{30} & \text{Divide both sides by 30.} \\
2.5 = r &
\end{array}
$$

So, the brothers' constant rate of speed was 2.5 miles per hour.

5. Logan has two aquariums. One aquarium contains 1.3 cubic feet of water and the other contains 1.9 cubic feet of water. The water in the larger aquarium weighs 37.44 pounds more than the water in the smaller aquarium. Write an equation with a variable on both sides to represent the situation. Then find the weight of 1 cubic foot of water.

_____

Writing a Real-World Situation from an Equation

Real-world situations can often be represented by equations involving fractions and decimals. Fractions and decimals can represent quantities such as weight, volume, capacity, time, and temperature. Decimals can also be used to represent dollars and cents.

EXAMPLE 3 FL 8.EE.3.7

Write a real-world situation that can be modeled by the equation
$0.95x = 0.55x + 60.$

My Notes

The left side of the equation consists of a variable term. It could represent the total cost for *x* items.

The right side of the equation consists of a variable term plus a constant. It could represent the total cost for *x* items plus a flat fee.

The equation $0.95x = 0.55x + 60$ could be represented by this situation: Toony Tunes charges $0.95 for each song you download. Up With Downloads charges $0.55 for each song but also charges an annual membership fee of $60. How many songs must a customer download in a year so that the cost will be the same at both websites?

6. Write a real-world problem that can be modeled by the equation
$\frac{1}{3}x + 10 = \frac{3}{5}x$.

_____

_____

_____

_____

1. Sandy is upgrading her Internet service. Fast Internet charges $60 for installation and $50.45 per month. Quick Internet has free installation but charges $57.95 per month. (Example 2)

   a. Write an equation that can be used to find the number of months at which the Internet service would cost the same.

   _____

   b. Solve the equation.

   _____

Solve. (Examples 1 and 2)

2. $\frac{3}{4}n - 18 = \frac{1}{4}n - 4$

   _____

3. $6 + \frac{4}{5}b = \frac{9}{10}b$

   _____

4. $\frac{2}{11}m + 16 = 4 + \frac{6}{11}m$

   _____

5. $2.25t + 5 = 13.5t + 14$

   _____

6. $3.6w = 1.6w + 24$

   _____

7. $-0.75p - 2 = 0.25p$

   _____

8. Write a real-world problem that can be modeled by the equation $1.25x = 0.75x + 50$. (Example 3)

   _____

   _____

   _____

   _____

   _____

? ESSENTIAL QUESTION CHECK-IN

9. How does the method for solving equations with fractional or decimal coefficients and constants compare with the method for solving equations with integer coefficients and constants?

   _____

   _____

   _____

Equations with the Distributive Property

 FL 8.EE.3.7b
Solve linear equations with rational number coefficients, including equations whose solutions require expanding expressions using the distributive property and collecting like terms.

ESSENTIAL QUESTION

How do you use the Distributive Property to solve equations?

Using the Distributive Property

The Distributive Property can be useful in solving equations.

EXAMPLE 1

 FL 8.EE.3.7b

Math On the Spot
⊙ my.hrw.com

A Solve: $3(x - 5) + 1 = 2 + x$

STEP 1   Use the Distributive Property.

$3x - 15 + 1 = 2 + x$ *Distribute 3 to the terms within the parentheses.*

$3x - 14 = 2 + x$ *Simplify.*

STEP 2   Use inverse operations to solve the equation.

$$3x - 14 = 2 + x$$
$$\underline{-x \qquad\qquad -x}$$
$$2x - 14 = 2$$ *Subtract x from both sides.*
$$\underline{+14 \quad +14}$$
$$2x = 16$$ *Add 14 to both sides.*
$$x = 8$$ *Divide both sides by 2.*

B Solve: $5 - 7k = -4(k + 1) - 3$

STEP 1   Use the Distributive Property.

$5 - 7k = -4k - 4 - 3$ *Distribute −4 to the terms within the parentheses.*

$5 - 7k = -4k - 7$ *Simplify.*

STEP 2   Use inverse operations to solve the equation.

$$5 - 7k = -4k - 7$$
$$\underline{+4k \quad +4k}$$
$$5 - 3k = -7$$ *Add 4k to both sides.*
$$\underline{-5 \qquad -5}$$
$$-3k = -12$$ *Subtract 5 from both sides.*
$$k = 4$$ *Divide both sides by −3.*

Math Talk
Mathematical Practices

How can you rewrite $7 - (2a + 3) = 12$ without parentheses? Explain your answer.

YOUR TURN

Solve each equation.

1. $y - 5 = 3 - 9(y + 2)$ _____

2. $2(x - 7) - 10 = 12 - 4x$ _____

Using the Distributive Property on Both Sides

Some equations require the use of the Distributive Property on both sides.

EXAMPLE 2 FL 8.EE.3.7b

Solve: $\frac{3}{4}(x - 13) = -2(9 + x)$

Math Talk
Mathematical Practices

How can you eliminate fractions if there is a fraction being distributed on both sides of an equation?

STEP 1 Eliminate the fraction.

$\frac{3}{4}(x - 13) = -2(9 + x)$

$4 \times \frac{3}{4}(x - 13) = 4 \times [-2(9 + x)]$ Multiply both sides by 4.

$3(x - 13) = -8(9 + x)$

STEP 2 Use the Distributive Property.

$3x - 39 = -72 - 8x$ Distribute 3 and -8 to the terms within the parentheses.

STEP 3 Use inverse operations to solve the equation.

$$3x - 39 = -72 - 8x$$

$$\underline{+8x \qquad\qquad +8x}$$ Add $8x$ to both sides.

$$11x - 39 = -72$$

$$\underline{+39 \quad +39}$$ Add 39 to both sides.

$$11x = -33$$

$$\frac{11x}{11} = \frac{-33}{11}$$ Divide both sides by 11.

$$x = -3$$

YOUR TURN

Solve each equation.

3. $-4(-5 - b) = \frac{1}{3}(b + 16)$ _____

4. $\frac{3}{5}(t + 18) = -3(2 - t)$ _____

Solving a Real-World Problem Using the Distributive Property

Solving a real-world problem may involve using the Distributive Property.

EXAMPLE 3 Problem Solving
FL **8.EE.3.7b**

The Coleman family had their bill at a restaurant reduced by $7.50 because of a special discount. They left a tip of $8.90, which was 20% of the reduced amount. How much was their bill before the discount?

 Analyze Information

The answer is the amount before the discount.

 Formulate a Plan

Use an equation to find the amount before the discount.

Solve

STEP 1 Write the equation $0.2(x - 7.5) = 8.9$, where x is the amount of the Coleman family's bill before the discount.

STEP 2 Use the Distributive Property: $0.2x - 1.5 = 8.9$

STEP 3 Use inverse operations to solve the equation.

$$0.2x - 1.5 = 8.9$$
$$\underline{+ 1.5 \quad + 1.5}$$ Add 1.5 to both sides.
$$0.2x = 10.4$$

$$\frac{0.2x}{0.2} = \frac{10.4}{0.2}$$ Divide both sides by 0.2.

$$x = 52$$

The Coleman family's bill before the discount was $52.00.

Math Talk
Mathematical Practices
Why do you use 0.2 in Step 1?

 Justify and Evaluate

$52.00 - $7.50 = $44.50 and 0.2($44.50) = $8.90. This is the amount of the tip the Colemans left. The answer is reasonable.

 YOUR TURN

5. The Smiths spend 8% of their budget on entertainment. Their total budget this year is $2,000 more than last year, and this year they plan to spend $3,840 on entertainment. What was their total budget last year? _____

Solve each equation.

1. $4(x + 8) - 4 = 34 - 2x$ (Ex. 1)

$$\boxed{}x + \boxed{} - 4 = 34 - 2x$$

$$\boxed{}x + \boxed{} = 34 - 2x$$

$$\boxed{}x + \boxed{} = 34$$

$$\boxed{}x = \boxed{}$$

$$\frac{\boxed{}x}{\boxed{}} = \frac{\boxed{}}{\boxed{}}$$

$$x = \boxed{}$$

2. $\frac{2}{3}(9 + x) = -5(4 - x)$ (Ex. 2)

$$\boxed{} \times \frac{2}{3}(9 + x) = \boxed{} \times [-5(4 - x)]$$

$$\boxed{}(9 + x) = \boxed{}(4 - x)$$

$$\boxed{} + \boxed{}x = \boxed{} \bigcirc \boxed{} x$$

$$\boxed{} = \boxed{}$$

$$\frac{\boxed{}x}{\boxed{}} = \frac{\boxed{}}{\boxed{}}$$

$$x = \boxed{}$$

3. $-3(x + 4) + 15 = 6 - 4x$ (Ex. 1)

_____

4. $10 + 4x = 5(x - 6) + 33$ (Ex. 1)

_____

5. $x - 9 = 8(2x + 3) - 18$ (Ex. 1)

_____

6. $-6(x - 1) - 7 = -7x + 2$ (Ex. 1)

_____

7. $\frac{1}{10}(x + 11) = -2(8 - x)$ (Ex. 2)

_____

8. $-(4 - x) = \frac{3}{4}(x - 6)$ (Ex. 2)

_____

9. $-8(8 - x) = \frac{4}{5}(x + 10)$ (Ex. 2)

_____

10. $\frac{1}{2}(16 - x) = -12(x + 7)$ (Ex. 2)

_____

11. Sandra saves 12% of her salary for retirement. This year her salary was $3,000 more than in the previous year, and she saved $4,200. What was her salary in the previous year? (Example 3)

Write an equation. _____

Sandra's salary in the previous year was _____.

? ESSENTIAL QUESTION CHECK-IN

12. When solving an equation using the Distributive Property, if the numbers being distributed are fractions, what is your first step? Why?

_____

Equations with Many Solutions or No Solution

 FL   8.EE.3.7a

Give examples of linear equations ... with one solution, infinitely many solutions, or no solutions. Show which of these ... is the case by ... transforming the given equation into ... $x = a$, $a = a$, or $a = b$ ... .

ESSENTIAL QUESTION

How can you give examples of equations with a given number of solutions?

Determining the Number of Solutions

So far, when you solved a linear equation in one variable, you found one value of x that makes the equation a true statement. When you simplify some equations, you may find that they do not have one solution.

Math On the Spot

my.hrw.com

EXAMPLE 1

 FL   8.EE.3.7a

Use the properties of equality to simplify each equation. Tell whether the final equation is a true statement.

A $4x - 3 = 2x + 13$

$4x - 3 = 2x + 13$

$\underline{+3 = \quad +3}$ ⟶ Add 3 to both sides.

$4x = 2x + 16$

$\underline{-2x \quad -2x}$ ⟶ Subtract 2x from both sides.

$2x = 16$

$\dfrac{2x}{2} = \dfrac{16}{2}$ ⟶ Divide both sides by 2.

$x = 8$

The statement is true. There is one solution.

B $4x - 5 = 2(2x - 1) - 3$

$4x - 5 = 2(2x - 1) - 3$

$4x - 5 = 4x - 2 - 3$ ⟶ Distributive Property

$4x - 5 = 4x - 5$ ⟶ Simplify.

$\underline{-4x \qquad -4x}$ ⟶ Subtract 4x from both sides.

$-5 = -5$

The statement is true. There are many solutions.

My Notes

C $4x + 2 = 4x - 5$

$$4x + 2 = 4x - 5$$

$$\underline{-2 -2}$$ Subtract 2 from both sides.

$$4x = 4x - 7$$

$$\underline{-4x -4x}$$ Subtract $4x$ from both sides.

$$0 = -7$$

The statement is false. There is no solution.

Reflect

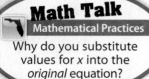
Math Talk

Mathematical Practices

Why do you substitute values for x into the *original* equation?

1. What happens when you substitute any value for x in the original equation in part B? In the original equation in part C?

_____

_____

Personal Math Trainer

Online Assessment and Intervention

my.hrw.com

YOUR TURN

Use the properties of equality to simplify each equation. Tell whether the final equation is a true statement.

2. $2x + 1 = 5x - 8$ **3.** $3(4x + 3) - 2 = 12x + 7$ **4.** $3x - 9 = 5 + 3x$

_____   _____   _____

Math On the Spot

my.hrw.com

Writing Equations with a Given Number of Solutions

When you simplify an equation using the properties of equality, you will find one of three results.

Result	What does this mean?	How many solutions?
$x = a$	When the value of x is a, the equation is a true statement.	1
$a = a$	Any value of x makes the equation a true statement.	Infinitely many
$a = b$, where $a \neq b$	There is no value of x that makes the equation a true statement.	0

You can use these results to write a linear equation that has a given number of solutions.

EXAMPLE 2

Write a linear equation in one variable that has no solution.

You can use the strategy of working backward:

STEP 1 Start with a false statement such as $3 = 5$. Add the same variable term to both sides.

$3 + x = 5 + x$ *Add x to both sides.*

STEP 2 Next, add the same constant to both sides and combine like terms on each side of the equation.

$10 + x = 12 + x$ *Add 7 to both sides.*

STEP 3 Verify that your equation has no solutions by using properties of equality to simplify your equation.

$$10 + x = 12 + x$$
$$\underline{ - x = - x}$$
$$10 = 12$$

Math Talk
Mathematical Practices

What type of statement do you start with to write an equation with infinitely many solutions? Give an example.

Reflect

5. Explain why the result of the process above is an equation with no solution.

_____

_____

_____

_____

YOUR TURN

Tell whether each equation has one, zero, or infinitely many solutions.

6. $6 + 3x = x - 8$ _____

7. $8x + 4 = 4(2x + 1)$ _____

Complete each equation so that it has the indicated number of solutions.

8. No solution: $3x + 1 = 3x +$ _____

9. Infinitely many: $2x - 4 = 2x -$ _____

Personal Math Trainer

Online Assessment and Intervention

my.hrw.com

Use the properties of equality to simplify each equation. Tell whether the final equation is a true statement. (Example 1)

1. $3x - 2 = 25 - 6x$

$$\underline{+\,6x} \qquad\qquad \underline{+\,6x}$$

$$\boxed{} - 2 = \boxed{}$$

$$\dfrac{\boxed{}}{} = \dfrac{\boxed{}}{}$$

$$\boxed{}\,x = \boxed{}$$

$$\dfrac{\boxed{}\,x}{\boxed{}} = \dfrac{\boxed{}}{\boxed{}}$$

$$x = \boxed{}$$

The statement is $\boxed{}$.

2. $2x - 4 = 2(x - 1) + 3$

$$2x - 4 = \boxed{} + 3$$

$$2x - 4 = 2x + \boxed{}$$

$$\dfrac{-\boxed{}}{} = \dfrac{-\boxed{}}{}$$

$$\boxed{} = \boxed{}$$

The statement is $\boxed{}$.

3. How many solutions are there to the equation in Exercise 2? (Example 1)   _____

4. After simplifying an equation, Juana gets $6 = 6$. Explain what this means. (Example 1)

_____

Write a linear equation in one variable that has infinitely many solutions. (Example 2)

5. Start with a _____ statement.

Add the _____ to both sides.

Add the _____ to both sides.

Combine _____ terms.

$$10 = \boxed{}$$

$$10 + x = \boxed{}$$

$$10 + x + 5 = \boxed{}$$

$$\boxed{} = \boxed{}$$

? ESSENTIAL QUESTION CHECK-IN

6. Give an example of an equation with an infinite number of solutions. Then make one change to the equation so that it has no solution.

_____

_____

15.4 Independent Practice

FL 8.EE.3.7a

Personal Math Trainer

Online Assessment and Intervention

my.hrw.com

Tell whether each equation has one, zero, or infinitely many solutions.

7. $-(2x + 2) - 1 = -x - (x + 3)$

_____

8. $-2(z + 3) - z = -z - 4(z + 2)$

_____

Create an equation with the indicated number of solutions.

9. No solution:

$3\left(x - \dfrac{4}{3}\right) = 3x + \boxed{}$

10. Infinitely many solutions:

$2(x - 1) + 6x = 4\left(\boxed{} - 1\right) + 2$

11. One solution of $x = -1$:

$5x - (x - 2) = 2x - \left(\boxed{}\right)$

12. Infinitely many solutions:

$-(x - 8) + 4x = 2\left(\boxed{}\right) + x$

13. Persevere in Problem Solving The Dig It Project is designing two gardens that have the same perimeter. One garden is a trapezoid whose nonparallel sides are equal. The other is a quadrilateral. Two possible designs are shown at the right.

$2x - 2$

$x + 1$ $x + 1$

x

a. Based on these designs, is there more than one value for x? Explain how you know this.

_____

_____

_____

_____

_____

$2x - 9$

x $x + 1$

$x + 8$

b. Why does your answer to part a make sense in this context?

_____

_____

_____

c. Suppose the Dig It Project wants the perimeter of each garden to be 60 meters. What is the value of x in this case? How did you find this?

_____

_____

14. Critique Reasoning Lisa says that the indicated angles cannot have the same measure. Marita disagrees and says she can prove that they can have the same measure. Who do you agree with? Justify your answer.

$(9x - 25 + x)°$ $(x + 50 + 2x - 12)°$

_____

_____

_____

_____

15. Represent Real-World Problems Adele opens an account with $100 and deposits $35 a month. Kent opens an account with $50 and also deposits $35 a month. Will they have the same amount in their accounts at any point? If so, in how many months and how much will be in each account? Explain.

_____

_____

_____

H.O.T. **FOCUS ON HIGHER ORDER THINKING**

Work Area

16. Communicate Mathematical Ideas Frank solved an equation and got the result $x = x$. Sarah solved the same equation and got $12 = 12$. Frank says that one of them is incorrect because you cannot get different results for the same equation. What would you say to Frank? If both results are indeed correct, explain how this happened.

_____

_____

_____

_____

17. Critique Reasoning Matt said $2x - 7 = 2(x - 7)$ has infinitely many solutions. Is he correct? Justify Matt's answer or show how he is incorrect.

_____

_____

_____

Ready to Go On?

15.1 Equations with the Variable on Both Sides

Solve.

1. $4a - 4 = 8 + a$ _____

2. $4x + 5 = x + 8$ _____

3. Hue is arranging chairs. She can form 6 rows of a given length with 3 chairs left over, or 8 rows of that same length if she gets 11 more chairs. Write and solve an equation to find how many chairs are in that row length.

_____

15.2 Equations with Rational Numbers

Solve.

4. $\frac{2}{3}n - \frac{2}{3} = \frac{n}{6} + \frac{4}{3}$ _____

5. $1.5d + 3.25 = 1 + 2.25d$ _____

6. Happy Paws charges $19.00 plus $1.50 per hour to keep a dog during the day. Woof Watchers charges $15.00 plus $2.75 per hour. Write and solve an equation to find for how many hours the total cost of the services is equal.

_____

15.3 Equations with the Distributive Property

Solve.

7. $14 + 5x = 3(-x + 3) - 11$ _____

8. $\frac{1}{4}(x - 7) = 1 + 3x$ _____

9. $-5(2x - 9) = 2(x - 8) - 11$ _____

10. $3(x + 5) = 2(3x + 12)$ _____

15.4 Equations with Many Solutions or No Solution

Tell whether each equation has one, zero, or infinitely many solutions.

11. $5(x - 3) + 6 = 5x - 9$ _____

12. $5(x - 3) + 6 = 5x - 10$ _____

13. $5(x - 3) + 6 = 4x + 3$ _____

MODULE 15 **MIXED REVIEW**

Assessment
Readiness

Personal Math Trainer

Online Assessment and Intervention

my.hrw.com

Selected Response

1. Two cars are traveling in the same direction. The first car is going 40 mi/h, and the second car is going 55 mi/h. The first car left 3 hours before the second car. Which equation could you solve to find how many hours it will take for the second car to catch up to the first car?

Ⓐ $55t + 3 = 40t$

Ⓑ $55t + 165 = 40t$

Ⓒ $40t + 3 = 55t$

Ⓓ $40t + 120 = 55t$

2. Which linear equation is represented by the table?

x	−2	1	3	6
y	7	4	2	−1

Ⓐ $y = -x + 5$ Ⓒ $y = x + 3$

Ⓑ $y = 2x - 1$ Ⓓ $y = -3x + 11$

3. Shawn's Rentals charges $27.50 per hour to rent a surfboard and a wetsuit. Darla's Surf Shop charges $23.25 per hour to rent a surfboard plus $17 extra for a wetsuit. For what total number of hours are the charges for Shawn's Rentals the same as the charges for Darla's Surf Shop?

Ⓐ 3   Ⓒ 5

Ⓑ 4   Ⓓ 6

4. Which of the following is irrational?

Ⓐ −8   Ⓒ $\sqrt{11}$

Ⓑ 4.63   Ⓓ $\frac{1}{3}$

5. Greg and Jane left a 15% tip after dinner. The amount of the tip was $9. Greg's dinner cost $24. Which equation can you use to find x, the cost of Jane's dinner?

Ⓐ $0.15x + 24 = 9$

Ⓑ $0.15(x + 24) = 9$

Ⓒ $15(x + 24) = 9$

Ⓓ $0.15x = 24 + 9$

6. For the equation $3(2x - 5) = 6x + k$, which value of k will create an equation with infinitely many solutions?

Ⓐ 15   Ⓒ 5

Ⓑ −5   Ⓓ −15

7. Which of the following is equivalent to 2^{-4}?

Ⓐ $\frac{1}{16}$ Ⓒ −2

Ⓑ $\frac{1}{8}$ Ⓓ −16

Mini-Task

8. Use the figures below for parts a and b.

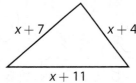

a. Both figures have the same perimeter. Solve for x.

_____

b. What is the perimeter of each figure?

_____

Solving Systems of Linear Equations

? ESSENTIAL QUESTION

How can you use systems of equations to solve real-world problems?

 my.hrw.com

Real-World Video

The distance contestants in a race travel over time can be modeled by a system of equations. Solving such a system can tell you when one contestant will overtake another who has a head start, as in a boating race or marathon.

GO DIGITAL

my.hrw.com

my.hrw.com

Go digital with your write-in student edition, accessible on any device.

Math On the Spot

Scan with your smart phone to jump directly to the online edition, video tutor, and more.

Animated Math

Interactively explore key concepts to see how math works.

Personal Math Trainer

Get immediate feedback and help as you work through practice sets.

Are YOU Ready?

Complete these exercises to review skills you will need for this module.

Simplify Algebraic Expressions

> **EXAMPLE** Simplify $5 - 4y + 2x - 6 + y$.
>
> $-4y + y + 2x - 6 + 5$ Group like terms.
>
> $-3y + 2x - 1$ Combine like terms.

Simplify.

1. $14x - 4x + 21$

_____

2. $-y - 4x + 4y$

_____

3. $5.5a - 1 + 21b + 3a$

_____

4. $2y - 3x + 6x - y$

_____

Graph Linear Equations

> **EXAMPLE** Graph $y = -\frac{1}{3}x + 2$.
>
> Step 1: Make a table of values.
>
> | x | $y = -\frac{1}{3}x + 2$ | (x, y) |
> |---|---|---|
> | 0 | $y = -\frac{1}{3}(0) + 2 = 2$ | $(0, 2)$ |
> | 3 | $y = -\frac{1}{3}(3) + 2 = 1$ | $(3, 1)$ |
>
> Step 2: Plot the points.
> Step 3: Connect the points with a line.
>
>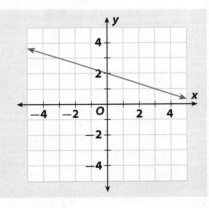

Graph each equation.

5. $y = 4x - 1$

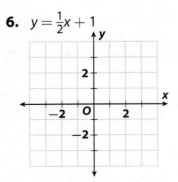

6. $y = \frac{1}{2}x + 1$

7. $y = -x$

Reading Start-Up

Visualize Vocabulary

Use the ✔ words to complete the graphic.

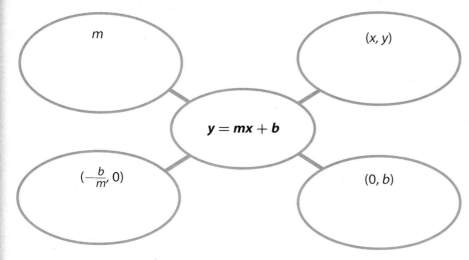

Understand Vocabulary

Complete the sentences using the preview words.

1. A _____ is any ordered pair

   that satisfies all the equations in a system.

2. A set of two or more equations that contain two or more variables is

   called a _____.

Vocabulary

Review Words

  linear equation *(ecuación lineal)*

✔ ordered pair *(par ordenado)*

✔ slope *(pendiente)*

  slope-intercept form *(forma pendiente intersección)*

  x-axis *(eje x)*

✔ *x*-intercept *(intersección con el eje x)*

  y-axis *(eje y)*

✔ *y*-intercept *(intersección con el eje y)*

Preview Words

  solution of a system of equations *(solución de un sistema de ecuaciones)*

  system of equations *(sistema de ecuaciones)*

Active Reading

Four-Corner Fold Before beginning the module, create a four-corner fold to help you organize what you learn about solving systems of equations. Use the categories "Solving by Graphing," "Solving by Substitution," "Solving by Elimination," and "Solving by Multiplication." As you study this module, note similarities and differences among the four methods. You can use your four-corner fold later to study for tests and complete assignments.

Unpacking the Standards

Understanding the standards and the vocabulary terms in the standards will help you know exactly what you are expected to learn in this module.

FL 8.EE.3.8a

Understand that solutions to a system of two linear equations in two variables correspond to points of intersection of their graphs, because points of intersection satisfy both equations simultaneously.

FL 8.EE.3.8b

Solve systems of two linear equations in two variables algebraically, and estimate solutions by graphing the equations. Solve simple cases by inspection.

Key Vocabulary

solution of a system of equations *(solución de un sistema de ecuaciones)* A set of values that make all equations in a system true.

system of equations *(sistema de ecuaciones)* A set of two or more equations that contain two or more variables.

Visit **my.hrw.com** to see all **Florida Math Standards** unpacked.

my.hrw.com

What It Means to You

You will understand that the points of intersection of two or more graphs represent the solution to a system of linear equations.

UNPACKING EXAMPLE 8.EE.3.8a, 8.EE.3.8b

Use the elimination method.

A.
$$-x = -1 + y$$
$$\underline{x + y = 4}$$
$$y = y + 3$$

This is never true, so the system has no solution.

The lines never intersect.

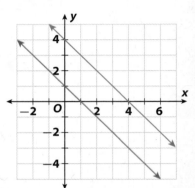

B.
$$2y + x = 1$$
$$y - 2 = x$$

Use the substitution method.

$$2y + (y - 2) = 1$$
$$3y - 2 = 1$$
$$y = 1$$
$$x = y - 2$$
$$x = 1 - 2$$
$$= -1$$

There is only one solution: $x = -1$, $y = 2$.

The lines intersect at a single point: $(-1, 2)$.

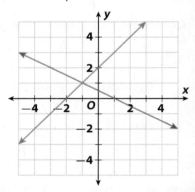

C.
$$3y - 6x = 3$$
$$y - 2x = 1$$

Use the multiplication method.

$$3y - 6x = 3$$
$$\frac{3y - 6x = 3}{0 = 0}$$

This is always true. So the system has infinitely many solutions.

The graphs overlap completely. They are the same line.

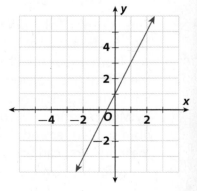

LESSON 16.1

Solving Systems of Linear Equations by Graphing

FL 8.EE.3.8a

Understand that solutions to a system of two linear equations in two variables correspond to points of intersection of their graphs, because points of intersection satisfy both equations simultaneously. *Also 8.EE.3.8, 8.EE.3.8c*

ESSENTIAL QUESTION

How can you solve a system of equations by graphing?

EXPLORE ACTIVITY
FL 8.EE.3.8a

> Slope-intercept form is $y = mx + b$, where m is the slope and b is the y-intercept.

Investigating Systems of Equations

You have learned several ways to graph a linear equation in slope-intercept form. For example, you can use the slope and y-intercept or you can find two points that satisfy the equation and connect them with a line.

A Graph the pair of equations together: $\begin{cases} y = 3x - 2 \\ y = -2x + 3 \end{cases}$.

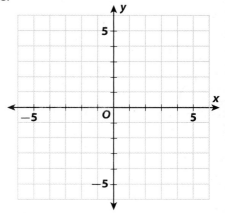

B Explain how to tell whether $(2, -1)$ is a solution of the equation $y = 3x - 2$ without using the graph.

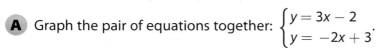

C Explain how to tell whether $(2, -1)$ is a solution of the equation $y = -2x + 3$ without using the graph.

D Use the graph to explain whether $(2, -1)$ is a solution of each equation.

E Determine if the point of intersection is a solution of both equations.

Point of intersection: $\left(\boxed{}, \boxed{} \right)$

$y = 3x - 2$

$\boxed{} = 3\boxed{} - 2$

$1 = \boxed{}$

$y = -2x + 3$

$\boxed{} = -2\boxed{} + 3$

$1 = \boxed{}$

The point of intersection **is / is not** the solution of both equations.

Solving Systems Graphically

An ordered pair (x, y) is a solution of an equation in two variables if substituting the x- and y-values into the equation results in a true statement. A **system of equations** is a set of equations that have the same variables. An ordered pair is a **solution of a system of equations** if it is a solution of every equation in the set.

Since the graph of an equation represents all ordered pairs that are solutions of the equation, if a point lies on the graphs of two equations, the point is a solution of both equations and is, therefore, a solution of the system.

EXAMPLE 1

FL 8.EE.3.8

Solve each system by graphing.

A $\begin{cases} y = -x + 4 \\ y = 3x \end{cases}$

STEP 1 Start by graphing each equation.

STEP 2 Find the point of intersection of the two lines. It appears to be $(1, 3)$. Check by substitution to determine if it is a solution to both equations.

$$y = -x + 4 \qquad y = 3x$$

$$3 \overset{?}{=} -(1) + 4 \qquad 3 \overset{?}{=} 3(1)$$

$$3 = 3 \checkmark \qquad 3 = 3 \checkmark$$

The solution of the system is $(1, 3)$.

B $\begin{cases} y = 3x - 3 \\ y = 3(x - 1) \end{cases}$

STEP 1 Start by graphing each equation.

STEP 2 Identify any ordered pairs that are solutions of both equations.

The graphs of the equations are the same line. So, every ordered pair that is a solution of one equation is also a solution of the other equation. The system has infinitely many solutions.

My Notes

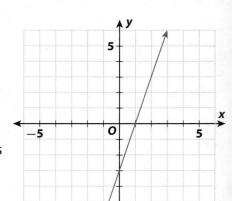

Reflect

1. A system of linear equations has infinitely many solutions. Does that mean any ordered pair in the coordinate plane is a solution?

   _____

   _____

2. Can you show algebraically that both equations in part B represent the same line? If so, explain how.

   _____

   _____

   _____

Solve each system by graphing. Check by substitution.

3. $\begin{cases} y = -x + 2 \\ y = -4x - 1 \end{cases}$ _____

   Check:

   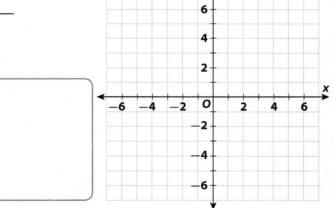

4. $\begin{cases} y = -2x + 5 \\ y = 3x \end{cases}$ _____

   Check:

Personal Math Trainer

Online Assessment and Intervention

⏻ my.hrw.com

Solving Problems Using Systems of Equations

When using graphs to solve a system of equations, it is best to rewrite both equations in slope-intercept form for ease of graphing.

To write an equation in slope-intercept form starting from $ax + by = c$:

$$ax + by = c$$

$$by = c - ax \qquad \text{Subtract } ax \text{ from both sides.}$$

$$y = \frac{c}{b} - \frac{ax}{b} \qquad \text{Divide both sides by } b.$$

$$y = -\frac{a}{b}x + \frac{c}{b} \qquad \text{Rearrange the equation.}$$

EXAMPLE 2 Real World **FL** 8.EE.3.8c, 8.EE.3.8

Keisha and her friends visit the concession stand at a football game. The stand charges \$2 for a hot dog and \$1 for a drink. The friends buy a total of 8 items for \$11. Tell how many hot dogs and how many drinks they bought.

STEP 1 Let x represent the number of hot dogs they bought and let y represent the number of drinks they bought.

Write an equation representing the **number of items they purchased.**

Number of hot dogs	+	Number of drinks	=	Total items
x	+	y	=	8

Write an equation representing the **money spent on the items.**

Cost of 1 hot dog times number of hot dogs	+	Cost of 1 drink times number of drinks	=	Total cost
$2x$	+	$1y$	=	11

STEP 2 Write the equations in slope-intercept form. Then graph.

$$x + y = 8$$
$$y = 8 - x$$
$$y = -x + 8$$

$$2x + 1y = 11$$
$$1y = 11 - 2x$$
$$y = -2x + 11$$

Graph the equations $y = -x + 8$ and $y = -2x + 11$.

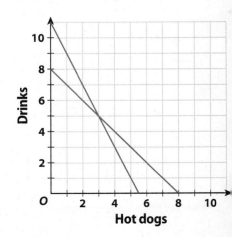

STEP 3 Use the graph to identify the solution of the system of equations. Check your answer by substituting the ordered pair into both equations.

Apparent solution: (3, 5)
Check:

$$x + y = 8 \qquad 2x + y = 11$$
$$3 + 5 \overset{?}{=} 8 \qquad 2(3) + 5 \overset{?}{=} 11$$
$$8 = 8 \checkmark \qquad 11 = 11 \checkmark$$

The point (3, 5) is a solution of both equations.

STEP 4 Interpret the solution in the original context.

Keisha and her friends bought 3 hot dogs and 5 drinks.

Reflect

5. **Conjecture** Why do you think the graph is limited to the first quadrant?

_____

_____

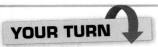 **YOUR TURN**

6. During school vacation, Marquis wants to go bowling and to play laser tag. He wants to play 6 total games but needs to figure out how many of each he can play if he spends exactly $20. Each game of bowling is $2 and each game of laser tag is $4.

a. Let x represent the number of games Marquis bowls and let y represent the number of games of laser tag Marquis plays. Write a system of equations that describes the situation. Then write the equations in slope-intercept form.

_____

_____

b. Graph the solutions of both equations.

c. How many games of bowling and how many games of laser tag will Marquis play?

_____

_____

_____

Guided Practice

Solve each system by graphing. (Example 1)

1. $\begin{cases} y = 3x - 4 \\ y = x + 2 \end{cases}$ _____

2. $\begin{cases} x - 3y = 2 \\ -3x + 9y = -6 \end{cases}$ _____

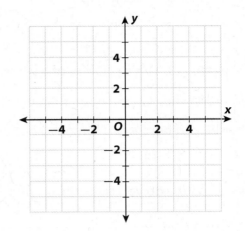

3. Mrs. Morales wrote a test with 15 questions covering spelling and vocabulary. Spelling questions (*x*) are worth 5 points and vocabulary questions (*y*) are worth 10 points. The maximum number of points possible on the test is 100. (Example 2)

a. Write an equation in slope-intercept form to represent the number of questions on the test.

_____

b. Write an equation in slope-intercept form to represent the total number of points on the test.

_____

c. Graph the solutions of both equations.

d. Use your graph to tell how many of each question type are on the test.

_____

? ESSENTIAL QUESTION CHECK-IN

4. When you graph a system of linear equations, why does the intersection of the two lines represent the solution of the system?

_____

_____

_____

16.1 Independent Practice

 FL 8.EE.3.8, 8.EE.3.8a, 8.EE.3.8c

5. Vocabulary A _____ is a set of equations that have the same variables.

6. Eight friends started a business. They will wear either a baseball cap or a shirt imprinted with their logo while working. They want to spend exactly $36 on the shirts and caps. Shirts cost $6 each and caps cost $3 each.

   a. Write a system of equations to describe the situation. Let x represent the number of shirts and let y represent the number of caps.

   _____

   _____

   b. Graph the system. What is the solution and what does it represent?

   Business Logo Wear

   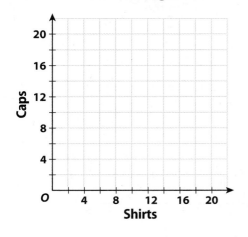

   _____

   _____

   _____

   _____

7. Multistep The table shows the cost for bowling at two bowling alleys.

	Shoe Rental Fee	Cost per Game
Bowl-o-Rama	$2.00	$2.50
Bowling Pinz	$4.00	$2.00

   a. Write a system of equations, with one equation describing the cost to bowl at Bowl-o-Rama and the other describing the cost to bowl at Bowling Pinz. For each equation, let x represent the number of games played and let y represent the total cost.

   _____

   _____

   b. Graph the system. What is the solution and what does it represent?

   Cost of Bowling

   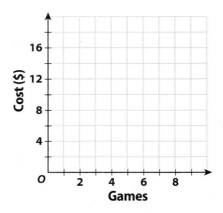

   _____

   _____

   _____

   _____

8. **Multi-Step** Jeremy runs 7 miles per week and increases his distance by 1 mile each week. Tony runs 3 miles per week and increases his distance by 2 miles each week. In how many weeks will Jeremy and Tony be running the same distance? What will that distance be?

_____

9. **Critical Thinking** Write a real-world situation that could be represented by the system of equations shown below.

$$\begin{cases} y = 4x + 10 \\ y = 3x + 15 \end{cases}$$

_____

_____

_____

 FOCUS ON HIGHER ORDER THINKING

Work Area

10. **Multistep** The table shows two options provided by a high-speed Internet provider.

	Setup Fee ($)	Cost per Month ($)
Option 1	50	30
Option 2	No setup fee	$40

a. In how many months will the total cost of both options be the same? What will that cost be?

_____

b. If you plan to cancel your Internet service after 9 months, which is the cheaper option? Explain.

_____

_____

_____

11. **Draw Conclusions** How many solutions does the system formed by $x - y = 3$ and $ay - ax + 3a = 0$ have for a nonzero number a? Explain.

_____

_____

_____

_____

Solving Systems by Substitution

 FL 8.EE.3.8b

Solve systems of two linear equations in two variables algebraically, and estimate solutions by graphing the equations. ... *Also 8.EE.3.8c*

ESSENTIAL QUESTION

How do you use substitution to solve a system of linear equations?

Solving a Linear System by Substitution

The **substitution method** is used to solve systems of linear equations by solving an equation for one variable and then substituting the resulting expression for that variable into the other equation. The steps for this method are as follows:

1. Solve one of the equations for one of its variables.

2. Substitute the expression from step 1 into the other equation and solve for the other variable.

3. Substitute the value from step 2 into either original equation and solve to find the value of the variable in step 1.

Math On the Spot
my.hrw.com

EXAMPLE 1

 FL 8.EE.3.8b

My Notes

Solve the system of linear equations by substitution. Check your answer.

$$\begin{cases} -3x + y = 1 \\ 4x + y = 8 \end{cases}$$

STEP 1 Solve an equation for one variable.

$-3x + y = 1$ *Select one of the equations.*

$y = 3x + 1$ *Solve for the variable y. Isolate y on one side.*

STEP 2 Substitute the expression for y in the other equation and solve.

$4x + (3x + 1) = 8$ *Substitute the expression for the variable y.*

$7x + 1 = 8$ *Combine like terms.*

$7x = 7$ *Subtract 1 from each side.*

$x = 1$ *Divide each side by 7.*

STEP 3 Substitute the value of x you found into one of the equations and solve for the other variable, y.

$-3(1) + y = 1$ *Substitute the value of x into the first equation.*

$-3 + y = 1$ *Simplify.*

$y = 4$ *Add 3 to each side.*

So, (1, 4) is the solution of the system.

STEP 4 Check the solution by graphing.

$-3x + y = 1$ $4x + y = 8$

x-intercept: $-\frac{1}{3}$ x-intercept: 2

y-intercept: 1 y-intercept: 8

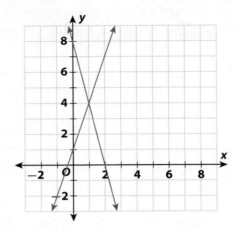

The point of intersection is (1, 4).

Reflect

1. Is it more efficient to solve $-3x + y = 1$ for x? Why or why not?

_____

_____

2. Is there another way to solve the system?

_____

_____

3. What is another way to check your solution?

_____

_____

Personal Math Trainer

Online Assessment and Intervention

my.hrw.com

YOUR TURN

Solve each system of linear equations by substitution.

4. $\begin{cases} 3x + y = 11 \\ -2x + y = 1 \end{cases}$

5. $\begin{cases} 2x - 3y = -24 \\ x + 6y = 18 \end{cases}$

6. $\begin{cases} x - 2y = 5 \\ 3x - 5y = 8 \end{cases}$

_____   _____   _____

Using a Graph to Estimate the Solution of a System

You can use a graph to estimate the solution of a system of equations before solving the system algebraically.

EXAMPLE 2

FL   8.EE.3.8b

Solve the system $\begin{cases} x - 4y = 4 \\ 2x - 3y = -3 \end{cases}$.

STEP 1   Sketch a graph of each equation by substituting values for x and generating values of y.

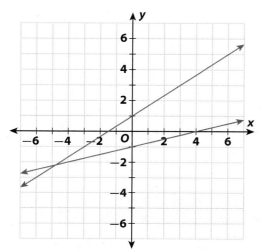

STEP 2   Find the intersection of the lines. The lines appear to intersect near $(-5, -2)$.

Math Talk
Mathematical Practices

In Step 2, how can you tell that $(-5, -2)$ is not the solution?

STEP 3   Solve the system algebraically.

Solve $x - 4y = 4$ for x.   Substitute to find y.   Substitute to find x.

$x - 4y = 4$

$\qquad x = 4 + 4y$

$2(4 + 4y) - 3y = -3$ $x = 4 + 4y$

$8 + 8y - 3y = -3$ $= 4 + 4\left(-\dfrac{11}{5}\right)$

$8 + 5y = -3$ $= \dfrac{20 - 44}{5}$

$5y = -11$ $= -\dfrac{24}{5}$

$y = -\dfrac{11}{5}$

The solution is $\left(-\dfrac{24}{5}, -\dfrac{11}{5}\right)$.

STEP 4   Use the estimate you made using the graph to judge the reasonableness of your solution.

$-\dfrac{24}{5}$ is close to the estimate of -5, and $-\dfrac{11}{5}$ is close to the estimate of -2, so the solution seems reasonable.

YOUR TURN

7. Estimate the solution of the system $\begin{cases} x + y = 4 \\ 2x - y = 6 \end{cases}$ by sketching a graph of each linear function. Then solve the system algebraically. Use your estimate to judge the reasonableness of your solution.

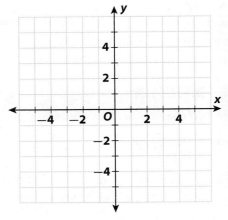

The estimated solution is _____.

The algebraic solution is _____.

The solution | is/is not | reasonable because

_____

_____

Solving Problems with Systems of Equations

EXAMPLE 3 Real World   FL 8.EE.3.8c

As part of Class Day, the eighth grade is doing a treasure hunt. Each team is given the following riddle and map. At what point is the treasure located?

There's pirate treasure to be found. So search on the island, all around. Draw a line through *A* and *B*. Then another through *C* and *D*. Dance a jig, "X" marks the spot. Where the lines intersect, that's the treasure's plot!

STEP 1 Give the coordinates of each point and find the slope of the line through each pair of points.

A: $(-2, -1)$ C: $(-1, 4)$

B: $(2, 5)$ D: $(1, -4)$

Slope: Slope:

$\dfrac{5 - (-1)}{2 - (-2)} = \dfrac{6}{4}$ $\dfrac{-4 - 4}{1 - (-1)} = \dfrac{-8}{2}$

$\qquad\qquad = \dfrac{3}{2}$ $\qquad\qquad = -4$

STEP 2 Write equations in slope-intercept form describing the line through points A and B and the line through points C and D.

Line through A and B:

Use the slope and a point to find b.

$5 = \left(\frac{3}{2}\right)2 + b$

$b = 2$

The equation is $y = \frac{3}{2}x + 2$.

Line through C and D:

Use the slope and a point to find b.

$4 = -4(-1) + b$

$b = 0$

The equation is $y = -4x$.

STEP 3 Solve the system algebraically.

Substitute $\frac{3}{2}x + 2$ for y in $y = -4x$ to find x.

$\frac{3}{2}x + 2 = -4x$

$\frac{11}{2}x = -2$

$x = -\frac{4}{11}$

Substitute to find x.

$y = -4\left(-\frac{4}{11}\right) = \frac{16}{11}$

The solution is $\left(-\frac{4}{11}, \frac{16}{11}\right)$.

YOUR TURN

8. Ace Car Rental rents cars for x dollars per day plus y dollars for each mile driven. Carlos rented a car for 4 days, drove it 160 miles, and spent $120. Vanessa rented a car for 1 day, drove it 240 miles, and spent $80. Write equations to represent Carlos's expenses and Vanessa's expenses. Then solve the system and tell what each number represents.

_____

_____

_____

_____

_____

Personal Math Trainer

Online Assessment and Intervention

🔘 my.hrw.com

Solve each system of linear equations by substitution. (Example 1)

1. $\begin{cases} 3x - 2y = 9 \\ y = 2x - 7 \end{cases}$ _____

2. $\begin{cases} y = x - 4 \\ 2x + y = 5 \end{cases}$ _____

3. $\begin{cases} x + 4y = 6 \\ y = -x + 3 \end{cases}$ _____

4. $\begin{cases} x + 2y = 6 \\ x - y = 3 \end{cases}$ _____

Solve each system. Estimate the solution first. (Example 2)

5. $\begin{cases} 6x + y = 4 \\ x - 4y = 19 \end{cases}$

Estimate _____

Solution _____

6. $\begin{cases} x + 2y = 8 \\ 3x + 2y = 6 \end{cases}$

Estimate _____

Solution _____

7. $\begin{cases} 3x + y = 4 \\ 5x - y = 22 \end{cases}$

Estimate _____

Solution _____

8. $\begin{cases} 2x + 7y = 2 \\ x + y = -1 \end{cases}$

Estimate _____

Solution _____

9. Adult tickets to Space City amusement park cost x dollars. Children's tickets cost y dollars. The Henson family bought 3 adult and 1 child tickets for $163. The Garcia family bought 2 adult and 3 child tickets for $174. (Example 3)

   a. Write equations to represent the Hensons' cost and the Garcias' cost.

   Hensons' cost: _____   Garcias' cost: _____

   b. Solve the system.

   adult ticket price: _____   child ticket price: _____

? ESSENTIAL QUESTION CHECK-IN

10. How can you decide which variable to solve for first when you are solving a linear system by substitution?

_____

_____

_____

16.2 Independent Practice

 FL 8.EE.3.8b, 8.EE.3.8c

Personal Math Trainer

Online Assessment and Intervention

my.hrw.com

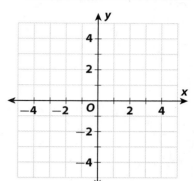

11. **Check for Reasonableness** Zach solves the system $\begin{cases} x + y = -3 \\ x - y = 1 \end{cases}$ and finds the solution $(1, -2)$. Use a graph to explain whether Zach's solution is reasonable.

_____

_____

12. **Represent Real-World Problems** Angelo bought apples and bananas at the fruit stand. He bought 20 pieces of fruit and spent $11.50. Apples cost $0.50 and bananas cost $0.75 each.

a. Write a system of equations to model the problem. (Hint: One equation will represent the number of pieces of fruit. A second equation will represent the money spent on the fruit.)

_____

b. Solve the system algebraically. Tell how many apples and bananas Angelo bought.

_____

Apples $0.50
Bananas $0.75

13. **Represent Real-World Problems** A jar contains n nickels and d dimes. There is a total of 200 coins in the jar. The value of the coins is $14.00. How many nickels and how many dimes are in the jar?

_____

14. **Multistep** The graph shows a triangle formed by the x-axis, the line $3x - 2y = 0$, and the line $x + 2y = 10$. Follow these steps to find the area of the triangle.

a. Find the coordinates of point A by solving the system $\begin{cases} 3x - 2y = 0 \\ x + 2y = 10 \end{cases}$.

Point A: _____

b. Use the coordinates of point A to find the height of the triangle.

height: _____

c. What is the length of the base of the triangle?

base: _____

d. What is the area of the triangle? _____

15. Jed is graphing the design for a kite on a coordinate grid. The four vertices of the kite are at $A\left(-\frac{4}{3}, \frac{2}{3}\right)$, $B\left(\frac{14}{3}, -\frac{4}{3}\right)$, $C\left(\frac{14}{3}, -\frac{16}{3}\right)$, and $D\left(\frac{2}{3}, -\frac{16}{3}\right)$. One kite strut will connect points A and C. The other will connect points B and D. Find the point where the struts cross.

_____

Work Area

16. Analyze Relationships Consider the system $\begin{cases} 6x - 3y = 15 \\ x + 3y = -8 \end{cases}$. Describe three different substitution methods that can be used to solve this system. Then solve the system.

_____

_____

_____

_____

_____

_____

17. Communicate Mathematical Ideas Explain the advantages, if any, that solving a system of linear equations by substitution has over solving the same system by graphing.

_____

_____

_____

_____

18. Persevere in Problem Solving Create a system of equations of the form $\begin{cases} Ax + By = C \\ Dx + Ey = F \end{cases}$ that has $(7, -2)$ as its solution. Explain how you found the system.

_____

_____

_____

_____

Solving Systems by Elimination

FL 8.EE.3.8b

Solve systems of two linear equations in two variables algebraically, ... *Also* *8.EE.3.8c*

ESSENTIAL QUESTION

How do you solve a system of linear equations by adding or subtracting?

Solving a Linear System by Adding

The **elimination method** is another method used to solve a system of linear equations. In this method, one variable is *eliminated* by adding or subtracting the two equations of the system to obtain a single equation in one variable. The steps for this method are as follows:

1. Add or subtract the equations to eliminate one variable.

2. Solve the resulting equation for the other variable.

3. Substitute the value into either original equation to find the value of the eliminated variable.

Math On the Spot
⏻ my.hrw.com

EXAMPLE 1

FL 8.EE.3.8b

Solve the system of equations by adding. Check your answer.

$$\begin{cases} 2x - 3y = 12 \\ x + 3y = 6 \end{cases}$$

My Notes

STEP 1   Add the equations.

$$\begin{aligned} 2x - 3y &= 12 \\ + x + 3y &= 6 \\ \hline 3x + 0 &= 18 \end{aligned}$$

   Write the equations so that like terms are aligned.
   Notice that the terms −3y and 3y are opposites.
   Add to eliminate the variable y.

$$3x = 18$$ Simplify and solve for x.

$$\frac{3x}{3} = \frac{18}{3}$$ Divide each side by 3.

$$x = 6$$ Simplify.

STEP 2   Substitute the solution into one of the original equations and solve for y.

$$x + 3y = 6$$ Use the second equation.

$$6 + 3y = 6$$ Substitute 6 for the variable x.

$$3y = 0$$ Subtract 6 from each side.

$$y = 0$$ Divide each side by 3 and simplify.

STEP 3 Write the solution as an ordered pair: (6, 0)

STEP 4 Check the solution by graphing.

$2x - 3y = 12$ $x + 3y = 6$

x-intercept: 6   *x*-intercept: 6

y-intercept: −4   *y*-intercept: 2

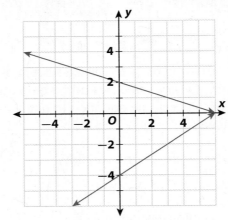

The point of intersection is (6, 0).

Math Talk

Mathematical Practices

Is it better to check a solution by graphing or by substituting the values in the original equations?

Reflect

1. Can this linear system be solved by subtracting one of the original equations from the other? Why or why not?

_____

_____

_____

2. What is another way to check your solution?

_____

_____

_____

Personal Math Trainer

Online Assessment and Intervention

my.hrw.com

YOUR TURN

Solve each system of equations by adding. Check your answers.

3. $\begin{cases} x + y = -1 \\ x - y = 7 \end{cases}$

4. $\begin{cases} 2x + 2y = -2 \\ 3x - 2y = 12 \end{cases}$

5. $\begin{cases} 6x + 5y = 4 \\ -6x + 7y = 20 \end{cases}$

_____   _____   _____

Solving a Linear System by Subtracting

If both equations contain the same x- or y-term, you can solve by subtracting.

EXAMPLE 2

 FL 8.EE.3.8b

Solve the system of equations by subtracting. Check your answer.

$$\begin{cases} 3x + 3y = 6 \\ 3x - y = -6 \end{cases}$$

STEP 1   Subtract the equations.

$$\begin{array}{l} 3x + 3y = 6 \\ \underline{-(3x - y\ = -6)} \\ \quad 0 + 4y = 12 \\ \qquad\quad 4y = 12 \\ \qquad\quad\ y = 3 \end{array}$$

   Write the equations so that like terms are aligned.

   Notice that both equations contain the term $3x$.

   Subtract to eliminate the variable x.

   Simplify and solve for y.

   Divide each side by 4 and simplify.

STEP 2   Substitute the solution into one of the original equations and solve for x.

$$3x - y = -6$$ Use the second equation.

$$3x - 3 = -6$$ Substitute 3 for the variable y.

$$3x = -3$$ Add 3 to each side.

$$x = -1$$ Divide each side by 3 and simplify.

STEP 3   Write the solution as an ordered pair: $(-1, 3)$

STEP 4   Check the solution by graphing.

$$3x + 3y = 6 \qquad 3x - y = -6$$

x-intercept: 2 x-intercept: -2

y-intercept: 2 y-intercept: 6

The point of intersection is $(-1, 3)$.

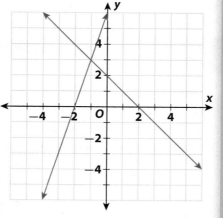

Reflect

6. What would happen if you added the original equations?

_____

_____

My Notes

7. How can you decide whether to add or subtract to eliminate a variable in a linear system? Explain your reasoning.

_____

_____

_____

_____

YOUR TURN

Solve each system of equations by subtracting. Check your answers.

8. $\begin{cases} 6x - 3y = 6 \\ 6x + 8y = -16 \end{cases}$

9. $\begin{cases} 4x + 3y = 19 \\ 6x + 3y = 33 \end{cases}$

10. $\begin{cases} 2x + 6y = 17 \\ 2x - 10y = 9 \end{cases}$

_____   _____   _____

Solving Problems with Systems of Equations

Many real-world situations can be modeled and solved with a system of equations.

EXAMPLE 3 Real World   **FL** 8.EE.3.8c

The Polar Bear Club wants to buy snowshoes and camp stoves. The club will spend $554.50 to buy them at Top Sports and $602.00 to buy them at Outdoor Explorer, before taxes, but Top Sports is farther away. How many of each item does the club intend to buy?

	Snowshoes	Camp Stoves
Top Sports	$79.50 per pair	$39.25
Outdoor Explorer	$89.00 per pair	$39.25

STEP 1 Choose variables and write a system of equations.
Let x represent the number of pairs of snowshoes.
Let y represent the number of camp stoves.

Top Sports cost: $79.50x + 39.25y = 554.50$
Outdoor Explorer cost: $89.00x + 39.25y = 602.00$

STEP 2 Subtract the equations.

$$79.50x + 39.25y = 554.50$$
$$-(89.00x + 39.25y = 602.00)$$

Both equations contain the term 39.25y.

$$-9.50x + 0 \quad\quad = -47.50$$ Subtract to eliminate the variable y.

$$-9.50x = -47.50$$ Simplify and solve for x.

$$\frac{-9.50x}{-9.50} = \frac{-47.50}{-9.50}$$ Divide each side by −9.50.

$$x = 5$$ Simplify.

STEP 3 Substitute the solution into one of the original equations and solve for y.

$$79.50x + 39.25y = 554.50$$ Use the first equation.

$$79.50(5) + 39.25y = 554.50$$ Substitute 5 for the variable x.

$$397.50 + 39.25y = 554.50$$ Multiply.

$$39.25y = 157.00$$ Subtract 397.50 from each side.

$$\frac{39.25y}{39.25} = \frac{157.00}{39.25}$$ Divide each side by 39.25.

$$y = 4$$ Simplify.

STEP 4 Write the solution as an ordered pair: (5, 4)

The club intends to buy 5 pairs of snowshoes and 4 camp stoves.

YOUR TURN

11. At the county fair, the Baxter family bought 6 hot dogs and 4 juice drinks for $16.70. The Farley family bought 3 hot dogs and 4 juice drinks for $10.85. Find the price of a hot dog and the price of a juice drink.

_____

_____

Personal Math Trainer

Online Assessment and Intervention

my.hrw.com

Guided Practice

1. Solve the system $\begin{cases} 4x + 3y = 1 \\ x - 3y = -11 \end{cases}$ by adding. (Example 1)

STEP 1 Add the equations.

$$4x + 3y = 1$$

Write the equations so that like terms are aligned.

$$+ \quad \underline{x - 3y = -11}$$

$$5x + \boxed{} = \boxed{}$$

Add to eliminate the variable $\boxed{}$.

$$5x = \boxed{}$$

Simplify and solve for x.

$$x = \boxed{}$$

Divide both sides by $\boxed{}$ and simplify.

STEP 2 Substitute into one of the original equations and solve for *y*.

$$y = \boxed{} \qquad \text{So,} \boxed{} \text{ is the solution of the system.}$$

Solve each system of equations by adding or subtracting. (Examples 1, 2)

2. $\begin{cases} x + 2y = -2 \\ -3x + 2y = -10 \end{cases}$

3. $\begin{cases} 3x + y = 23 \\ 3x - 2y = 8 \end{cases}$

4. $\begin{cases} -4x - 5y = 7 \\ 3x + 5y = -14 \end{cases}$

5. $\begin{cases} x - 2y = -19 \\ 5x + 2y = 1 \end{cases}$

6. $\begin{cases} 3x + 4y = 18 \\ -2x + 4y = 8 \end{cases}$

7. $\begin{cases} -5x + 7y = 11 \\ -5x + 3y = 19 \end{cases}$

8. The Green River Freeway has a minimum and a maximum speed limit. Tony drove for 2 hours at the minimum speed limit and 3.5 hours at the maximum limit, a distance of 355 miles. Rae drove 2 hours at the minimum speed limit and 3 hours at the maximum limit, a distance of 320 miles. What are the two speed limits? (Example 3)

   a. Write equations to represent Tony's distance and Rae's distance.

   Tony: _____ Rae: _____

   b. Solve the system.

   minimum speed limit: _____ maximum speed limit: _____

? ESSENTIAL QUESTION CHECK-IN

9. Can you use addition or subtraction to solve any system? Explain.

_____

_____

16.3 Independent Practice

Personal
Math Trainer

Online
Assessment and
Intervention

my.hrw.com

10. **Represent Real-World Problems** Marta bought new fish for her home aquarium. She bought 3 guppies and 2 platies for a total of $13.95. Hank also bought guppies and platies for his aquarium. He bought 3 guppies and 4 platies for a total of $18.33. Find the price of a guppy and the price of a platy.

_____

11. **Represent Real-World Problems** The rule for the number of fish in a home aquarium is 1 gallon of water for each inch of fish length. Marta's aquarium holds 13 gallons and Hank's aquarium holds 17 gallons. Based on the number of fish they bought in Exercise 10, how long is a guppy and how long is a platy?

_____

12. Line m passes through the points (6, 1) and (2, −3). Line n passes through the points (2, 3) and (5, −6). Find the point of intersection of these lines.

_____

13. **Represent Real-World Problems** Two cars got an oil change at the same auto shop. The shop charges customers for each quart of oil plus a flat fee for labor. The oil change for one car required 5 quarts of oil and cost $22.45. The oil change for the other car required 7 quarts of oil and cost $25.45. How much is the labor fee and how much is each quart of oil?

_____

14. **Represent Real-World Problems** A sales manager noticed that the number of units sold for two T-shirt styles, style A and style B, was the same during June and July. In June, total sales were $2779 for the two styles, with A selling for $15.95 per shirt and B selling for $22.95 per shirt. In July, total sales for the two styles were $2385.10, with A selling at the same price and B selling at a discount of 22% off the June price. How many T-shirts of each style were sold in June and July combined?

_____

_____

15. **Represent Real-World Problems** Adult tickets to a basketball game cost $5. Student tickets cost $1. A total of $2,874 was collected on the sale of 1,246 tickets. How many of each type of ticket were sold?

_____

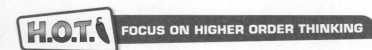
16. Communicate Mathematical Ideas Is it possible to solve the system $\begin{cases} 3x - 2y = 10 \\ x + 2y = 6 \end{cases}$ by using substitution? If so, explain how. Which method, substitution or elimination, is more efficient? Why?

_____

_____

_____

_____

_____

_____

_____

17. Jenny used substitution to solve the system $\begin{cases} 2x + y = 8 \\ x - y = 1 \end{cases}$. Her solution is shown below.

Step 1 $y = -2x + 8$ Solve the first equation for y.

Step 2 $2x + (-2x + 8) = 8$ Substitute the value of y in an original equation.

Step 3 $2x - 2x + 8 = 8$ Use the Distributive Property.

Step 4 $8 = 8$ Simplify.

a. Explain the Error Explain the error Jenny made. Describe how to correct it.

_____

_____

_____

_____

b. Communicate Mathematical Ideas Would adding the equations have been a better method for solving the system? If so, explain why.

_____

_____

_____

_____

LESSON 16.4
Solving Systems by Elimination with Multiplication

FL 8.EE.3.8b

Solve systems of two linear equations in two variables algebraically, ... *Also 8.EE.3.8c*

ESSENTIAL QUESTION

How do you solve a system of linear equations by multiplying?

Solving a System by Multiplying and Adding

In some linear systems, neither variable can be eliminated by adding or subtracting the equations directly. In systems like these, you need to multiply one of the equations by a constant so that adding or subtracting the equations will eliminate one variable. The steps for this method are as follows:

1. Decide which variable to eliminate.

2. Multiply one equation by a constant so that adding or subtracting will eliminate that variable.

3. Solve the system using the elimination method.

EXAMPLE 1

FL 8.EE.3.8b

Solve the system of equations by multiplying and adding.

$$\begin{cases} 2x + 10y = 2 \\ 3x - 5y = -17 \end{cases}$$

STEP 1 The coefficient of *y* in the first equation, 10, is 2 times the coefficient of *y*, 5, in the second equation. Also, the *y*-term in the first equation is being added, while the *y*-term in the second equation is being subtracted. To eliminate the *y*-terms, multiply the second equation by 2 and add this new equation to the first equation.

$2(3x - 5y = -17)$ Multiply each term in the second equation by 2 to get opposite coefficients for the y-terms.

$6x - 10y = -34$ Simplify.

$$\begin{aligned} 6x - 10y &= -34 \\ + \ 2x + 10y &= 2 \\ \hline 8x + 0y &= -32 \end{aligned}$$

Add the first equation to the new equation.

Add to eliminate the variable y.

$8x = -32$ Simplify and solve for x.

$\dfrac{8x}{8} = \dfrac{-32}{8}$ Divide each side by 8.

$x = -4$ Simplify.

My Notes

Lesson 16.4 **515**

STEP 2 Substitute the solution into one of the original equations and solve for y.

$2x + 10y = 2$ *Use the first equation.*

$2(-4) + 10y = 2$ *Substitute −4 for the variable x.*

$-8 + 10y = 2$ *Simplify.*

$10y = 10$ *Add 8 to each side.*

$y = 1$ *Divide each side by 10 and simplify.*

STEP 3 Write the solution as an ordered pair: $(-4, 1)$

STEP 4 Check your answer algebraically.

Substitute −4 for x and 1 for y in the original system.

$$\begin{cases} 2x + 10y = 2 \rightarrow 2(-4) + 10(1) = -8 + 10 = 2 \ \checkmark \\ 3x - 5y = -17 \rightarrow 3(-4) - 5(1) = -12 - 5 = -17 \ \checkmark \end{cases}$$

The solution is correct.

Math Talk
Mathematical Practices

When you check your answer algebraically, why do you substitute your values for x and y into the original system? Explain.

Reflect

1. How can you solve this linear system by subtracting? Which is more efficient, adding or subtracting? Explain your reasoning.

   _____

   _____

   _____

2. Can this linear system be solved by adding or subtracting without multiplying? Why or why not?

   _____

   _____

3. What would you need to multiply the second equation by to eliminate x by adding? Why might you choose to eliminate y instead of x?

   _____

   _____

Personal Math Trainer

Online Assessment and Intervention

⏻ my.hrw.com

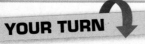

YOUR TURN

Solve each system of equations by multiplying and adding.

4. $\begin{cases} 5x + 2y = -10 \\ 3x + 6y = 66 \end{cases}$

5. $\begin{cases} 4x + 2y = 6 \\ 3x - y = -8 \end{cases}$

6. $\begin{cases} -6x + 9y = -12 \\ 2x + y = 0 \end{cases}$

   _____   _____   _____

Solving a System by Multiplying and Subtracting

You can solve some systems of equations by multiplying one equation by a constant and then subtracting.

Math On the Spot
my.hrw.com

EXAMPLE 2

 FL 8.EE.3.8b

Solve the system of equations by multiplying and subtracting.

$$\begin{cases} 6x + 5y = 7 \\ 2x - 4y = -26 \end{cases}$$

STEP 1 Multiply the second equation by 3 and subtract this new equation from the first equation.

$3(2x - 4y) = -26$ Multiply each term in the second equation by 3 to get the same coefficients for the x-terms.

$6x - 12y = -78$ Simplify.

$$\begin{aligned} 6x + 5y &= 7 \\ -(6x - 12y &= -78) \end{aligned}$$ Subtract the new equation from the first equation.

$0x + 17y = 85$ Subtract to eliminate the variable x.

$17y = 85$ Simplify and solve for y.

$\dfrac{17y}{17} = \dfrac{85}{17}$ Divide each side by 17.

$y = 5$ Simplify.

STEP 2 Substitute the solution into one of the original equations and solve for x.

$6x + 5y = 7$ Use the first equation.

$6x + 5(5) = 7$ Substitute 5 for the variable y.

$6x + 25 = 7$ Simplify.

$6x = -18$ Subtract 25 from each side.

$x = -3$ Divide each side by 6 and simplify.

STEP 3 Write the solution as an ordered pair: $(-3, 5)$

STEP 4 Check your answer algebraically.
Substitute -3 for x and 5 for y in the original system.

$$\begin{cases} 6x + 5y = 7 \rightarrow 6(-3) + 5(5) = -18 + 25 = 7 \checkmark \\ 2x - 4y = -26 \rightarrow 2(-3) - 4(5) = -6 - 20 = -26 \checkmark \end{cases}$$

The solution is correct.

Personal Math Trainer

Online Assessment and Intervention

my.hrw.com

Math On the Spot

my.hrw.com

My Notes

....
....
....
....
....
....
....
....
....
....
....
....
....
....
....
....

YOUR TURN

Solve each system of equations by multiplying and subtracting.

7. $\begin{cases} 3x - 7y = 2 \\ 6x - 9y = 9 \end{cases}$

_____

8. $\begin{cases} -3x + y = 11 \\ 2x + 3y = -11 \end{cases}$

_____

9. $\begin{cases} 9x + y = 9 \\ 3x - 2y = -11 \end{cases}$

_____

Solving Problems with Systems of Equations

Many real-world situations can be modeled with a system of equations.

EXAMPLE 3 Problem Solving

FL 8.EE.3.8c

The Simon family attended a concert and visited an art museum. Concert tickets were $24.75 for adults and $16.00 for children, for a total cost of $138.25. Museum tickets were $8.25 for adults and $4.50 for children, for a total cost of $42.75. How many adults and how many children are in the Simon family?

 Analyze Information

The answer is the number of adults and children.

 Formulate a Plan

Solve a system to find the number of adults and children.

 Solve

STEP 1 Choose variables and write a system of equations. Let x represent the number of adults. Let y represent the number of children.

Concert cost: $24.75x + 16.00y = 138.25$
Museum cost: $8.25x + 4.50y = 42.75$

STEP 2 Multiply both equations by 100 to eliminate the decimals.

$100(24.75x + 16.00y = 138.25) \rightarrow 2{,}475x + 1{,}600y = 13{,}825$

$100(8.25x + 4.50y = 42.75) \rightarrow 825x + 450y = 4{,}275$

Multiply the second equation by 3 and subtract this new equation from the first equation.

$$3(825x + 450y = 4,275)$$ Multiply each term in the second equation by 3 to get the same coefficients for the x-terms.

$$2,475x + 1,350y = 12,825$$ Simplify.

$$\begin{array}{r} 2,475x + 1,600y = 13,825 \\ -(2,475x + 1,350y = 12,825) \\ \hline \end{array}$$ Subtract the new equation from the first equation.

$$0x + 250y = 1,000$$ Subtract to eliminate the variable x.

$$250y = 1,000$$ Simplify and solve for y.

$$\frac{250y}{250} = \frac{1,000}{250}$$ Divide each side by 250.

$$y = 4$$ Simplify.

STEP 4 Substitute the solution into one of the original equations and solve for x.

$$8.25x + 4.50y = 42.75$$ Use the second equation.

$$8.25x + 4.50(4) = 42.75$$ Substitute 4 for the variable y.

$$8.25x + 18 = 42.75$$ Simplify.

$$8.25x = 24.75$$ Subtract 18 from each side.

$$x = 3$$ Divide each side by 8.25 and simplify.

STEP 5 Write the solution as an ordered pair: (3, 4).
There are 3 adults and 4 children in the family.

Justify and Evaluate

Substituting $x = 3$ and $y = 4$ into the original equations results in true statements. The answer is correct.

YOUR TURN

10. Contestants in the Run-and-Bike-a-thon run for a specified length of time, then bike for a specified length of time. Jason ran at an average speed of 5.2 mi/h and biked at an average speed of 20.6 mi/h, going a total of 14.2 miles. Seth ran at an average speed of 10.4 mi/h and biked at an average speed of 18.4 mi/h, going a total of 17 miles. For how long do contestants run and for how long do they bike?

_____

_____

Personal Math Trainer

Online Assessment and Intervention

⊕ my.hrw.com

1. Solve the system $\begin{cases} 3x - y = 8 \\ -2x + 4y = -12 \end{cases}$ by multiplying and adding. (Example 1)

STEP 1 Multiply the first equation by 4. Add to the second equation.

$4(3x - y = 8)$ Multiply each term in the first equation by 4 to get opposite coefficients for the y-terms.

$\boxed{}x - \boxed{}y = \boxed{}$ Simplify.

$\underline{+ \ (-2x) \ + \ \ 4y \ \ = -12}$ Add the second equation to the new equation.

$10x = \boxed{}$ Add to eliminate the variable $\boxed{}$.

$x = \boxed{}$ Divide both sides by $\boxed{}$ and simplify.

STEP 2 Substitute into one of the original equations and solve for y.

$y = \boxed{}$ So, $\boxed{}$ is the solution of the system.

Solve each system of equations by multiplying first. (Examples 1, 2)

2. $\begin{cases} x + 4y = 2 \\ 2x + 5y = 7 \end{cases}$ _____

3. $\begin{cases} 3x + y = -1 \\ 2x + 3y = 18 \end{cases}$ _____

4. $\begin{cases} 2x + 8y = 21 \\ 6x - 4y = 14 \end{cases}$ _____

5. $\begin{cases} 2x + y = 3 \\ -x + 3y = -12 \end{cases}$ _____

6. $\begin{cases} 6x + 5y = 19 \\ 2x + 3y = 5 \end{cases}$ _____

7. $\begin{cases} 2x + 5y = 16 \\ -4x + 3y = 20 \end{cases}$ _____

8. Bryce spent $5.26 on some apples priced at $0.64 each and some pears priced at $0.45 each. At another store he could have bought the same number of apples at $0.32 each and the same number of pears at $0.39 each, for a total cost of $3.62. How many apples and how many pears did Bryce buy? (Example 3)

   a. Write equations to represent Bryce's expenditures at each store.

   First store: _____

   Second store: _____

   b. Solve the system.

   Number of apples: _____

   Number of pears: _____

? ESSENTIAL QUESTION CHECK-IN

9. When solving a system by multiplying and then adding or subtracting, how do you decide whether to add or subtract?

   _____

   _____

16.4 Independent Practice

FL 8.EE.3.8b, 8.EE.3.8c

Personal Math Trainer

Online Assessment and Intervention

my.hrw.com

10. Explain the Error Gwen used elimination with multiplication to solve the system $\begin{cases} 2x + 6y = 3 \\ x - 3y = -1 \end{cases}$. Her work to find x is shown. Explain her error. Then solve the system.

$$2(x - 3y) = -1$$
$$2x - 6y = -1$$
$$\underline{+2x + 6y = 3}$$
$$4x + 0y = 2$$
$$x = \frac{1}{2}$$

11. Represent Real-World Problems At Raging River Sports, polyester-fill sleeping bags sell for $79. Down-fill sleeping bags sell for $149. In one week the store sold 14 sleeping bags for $1,456.

Sleeping Bags

Nylon Down-filled, 35° $149

Flannel-lined Polyester-filled, 40° $79

a. Let x represent the number of polyester-fill bags sold and let y represent the number of down-fill bags sold. Write a system of equations you can solve to find the number of each type sold.

b. Explain how you can solve the system for y by multiplying and subtracting.

c. Explain how you can solve the system for y using substitution.

d. How many of each type of bag were sold?

12. Twice a number plus twice a second number is 310. The difference between the numbers is 55. Find the numbers by writing and solving a system of equations. Explain how you solved the system.

13. Represent Real-World Problems A farm stand sells apple pies and jars of applesauce. The table shows the number of apples needed to make a pie and a jar of applesauce. Yesterday, the farm picked 169 Granny Smith apples and 95 Red Delicious apples. How many pies and jars of applesauce can the farm make if every apple is used?

Type of apple	Granny Smith	Red Delicious
Needed for a pie	5	3
Needed for a jar of applesauce	4	2

_____

H.O.T. FOCUS ON HIGHER ORDER THINKING

Work Area

14. Make a Conjecture Lena tried to solve a system of linear equations algebraically and in the process found the equation $5 = 9$. Lena thought something was wrong, so she graphed the equations and found that they were parallel lines. Explain what Lena's graph and equation could mean.

_____

_____

_____

_____

_____

15. Consider the system $\begin{cases} 2x + 3y = 6 \\ 3x + 7y = -1 \end{cases}$.

a. Communicate Mathematical Ideas Describe how to solve the system by multiplying the first equation by a constant and subtracting. Why would this method be less than ideal?

_____

_____

_____

b. Draw Conclusions Is it possible to solve the system by multiplying both equations by integer constants? If so, explain how.

_____

_____

_____

c. Use your answer from part b to solve the system.

_____

Solving Special Systems

FL 8.EE.3.8b

Solve systems of two linear equations in two variables algebraically, ... Solve simple cases by inspection. *Also 8.EE.3.8c*

ESSENTIAL QUESTION

How do you solve systems with no solution or infinitely many solutions?

EXPLORE ACTIVITY   FL 8.EE.3.8b

Solving Special Systems by Graphing

As with equations, some systems may have no solution or infinitely many solutions. One way to tell how many solutions a system has is by inspecting its graph.

Use the graph to solve each system of linear equations.

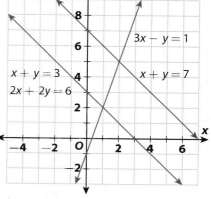

$3x - y = 1$

$x + y = 3$

$2x + 2y = 6$

$x + y = 7$

 A $\begin{cases} x + y = 7 \\ 2x + 2y = 6 \end{cases}$

Is there a point of intersection? Explain.

_____

_____

Does this linear system have a solution? Use the graph to explain.

_____

_____

B $\begin{cases} 2x + 2y = 6 \\ x + y = 3 \end{cases}$

Is there a point of intersection? Explain.

_____

Does this linear system have a solution? Use the graph to explain.

_____

_____

Reflect

1. Use the graph to identify two lines that represent a linear system with exactly one solution. What are the equations of the lines? Explain your reasoning.

_____

2. If each equation in a system of two linear equations is represented by a different line when graphed, what is the greatest number of solutions the system can have? Explain your reasoning.

_____

_____

3. Identify the three possible numbers of solutions for a system of linear equations. Explain when each type of solution occurs.

_____

_____

_____

Math On the Spot

my.hrw.com

Solving Special Systems Algebraically

As with equations, if you solve a system of equations with no solution, you get a false statement, and if you solve a system with infinitely many solutions, you get a true statement.

EXAMPLE 1

 FL 8.EE.3.8b

My Notes

A Solve the system of linear equations by substitution.

$$\begin{cases} x - y = -2 \\ -x + y = \ \ 4 \end{cases}$$

STEP 1 Solve $x - y = -2$ for x:
$$x = y - 2$$

STEP 2 Substitute the resulting expression into the other equation and solve.

$$-(y - 2) + y = 4 \qquad \text{Substitute the expression for the variable } x.$$

$$2 = 4 \qquad \text{Simplify.}$$

STEP 3 Interpret the solution. The result is the false statement $2 = 4$, which means there is no solution.

STEP 4 Graph the equations to check your answer. The graphs do not intersect, so there is no solution.

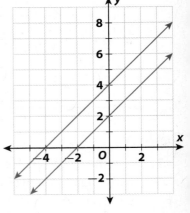

B Solve the system of linear equations by elimination.

$$\begin{cases} 2x + y = -2 \\ 4x + 2y = -4 \end{cases}$$

Math Talk
Mathematical Practices

What solution do you get when you solve the system in part B by substitution? Does this result change the number of solutions? Explain.

STEP 1 Multiply the first equation by -2.

$$-2(2x + y = -2) \rightarrow -4x + (-2y) = 4$$

STEP 2 Add the new equation from Step 1 to the original second equation.

$$\begin{array}{r} -4x + (-2y) = 4 \\ +\underline{4x + 2y = -4} \\ 0x + 0y = 0 \\ 0 = 0 \end{array}$$

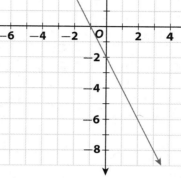

STEP 3 Interpret the solution. The result is the statement $0 = 0$, which is always true. This means that the system has infinitely many solutions.

STEP 4 Graph the equations to check your answer. The graphs are the same line, so there are infinitely many solutions.

Reflect

4. If x represents a variable and a and b represent constants so that $a \neq b$, interpret what each result means when solving a system of equations.

$x = a$ _____

$a = b$ _____

$a = a$ _____

5. In part B, can you tell without solving that the system has infinitely many solutions? If so, how?

_____

_____

_____

YOUR TURN

Solve each system. Tell how many solutions each system has.

6. $\begin{cases} 4x - 6y = 9 \\ -2x + 3y = 4 \end{cases}$

_____

_____

7. $\begin{cases} x + 2y = 6 \\ 2x - 3y = 26 \end{cases}$

_____

_____

8. $\begin{cases} 12x - 8y = -4 \\ -3x + 2y = 1 \end{cases}$

_____

_____

Personal
Math Trainer

Online Assessment and Intervention

🔵 my.hrw.com

1. Use the graph to solve each system of linear equations. (Explore Activity)

   A. $\begin{cases} 4x - 2y = -6 \\ 2x - y = 4 \end{cases}$
   B. $\begin{cases} 4x - 2y = -6 \\ x + y = 6 \end{cases}$
   C. $\begin{cases} 2x - y = 4 \\ 6x - 3y = 12 \end{cases}$

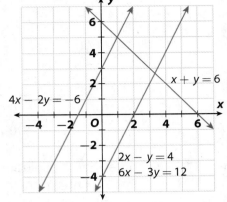

STEP 1 Decide if the graphs of the equations in each system intersect, are parallel, or are the same line.

System A: The graphs _____ .

System B: The graphs _____ .

System C: The graphs _____ .

STEP 2 Decide how many points the graphs have in common.

Intersecting lines have _____ point(s) in common.

Parallel lines have _____ point(s) in common.

The same lines have _____ point(s) in common.

STEP 3 Solve each system.

System A has _____ points in common, so it has _____ solution.

System B has _____ point in common. That point is the solution, _____ .

System C has _____ points in common. _____ ordered pairs on the line will make both equations true.

Solve each system. Tell how many solutions each system has. (Example 1)

2. $\begin{cases} x - 3y = 4 \\ -5x + 15y = -20 \end{cases}$

3. $\begin{cases} 6x + 2y = -4 \\ 3x + y = 4 \end{cases}$

4. $\begin{cases} 6x - 2y = -10 \\ 3x + 4y = -25 \end{cases}$

_____   _____   _____

? ESSENTIAL QUESTION CHECK-IN

5. When you solve a system of equations algebraically, how can you tell whether the system has zero, one, or an infinite number of solutions?

_____

_____

_____

_____

16.5 Independent Practice

FL 8.EE.3.8b, 8.EE.3.8c

Solve each system by graphing. Check your answer algebraically.

6. $\begin{cases} -2x + 6y = 12 \\ x - 3y = 3 \end{cases}$

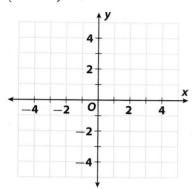

7. $\begin{cases} 15x + 5y = 5 \\ 3x + y = 1 \end{cases}$

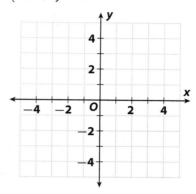

Solution: _____

Solution: _____

For Exs. 8–14, state the number of solutions for each system of linear equations.

8. a system whose graphs have the same slope but different y-intercepts

_____

9. a system whose graphs have the same y-intercepts but different slopes

_____

10. a system whose graphs have the same y-intercepts and the same slopes

_____

11. a system whose graphs have different y-intercepts and different slopes

_____

12. the system $\begin{cases} y = 2 \\ y = -3 \end{cases}$ _____

13. the system $\begin{cases} x = 2 \\ y = -3 \end{cases}$ _____

14. the system whose graphs were drawn using these tables of values:

Equation 1

x	0	1	2	3
y	1	3	5	7

Equation 2

x	0	1	2	3
y	3	5	7	9

_____

15. Draw Conclusions The graph of a linear system appears in a textbook. You can see that the lines do not intersect on the graph, but also they do not appear to be parallel. Can you conclude that the system has no solution? Explain.

_____

_____

_____

16. Represent Real-World Problems Two school groups go to a roller skating rink. One group pays $243 for 36 admissions and 21 skate rentals. The other group pays $81 for 12 admissions and 7 skate rentals. Let x represent the cost of admission and let y represent the cost of a skate rental. Is there enough information to find values for x and y? Explain.

_____

17. Represent Real-World Problems Juan and Tory are practicing for a track meet. They start their practice runs at the same point, but Tory starts 1 minute after Juan. Both run at a speed of 704 feet per minute. Does Tory catch up to Juan? Explain.

_____

_____

_____

H.O.T. FOCUS ON HIGHER ORDER THINKING

Work Area

18. Justify Reasoning A linear system with no solution consists of the equation $y = 4x - 3$ and a second equation of the form $y = mx + b$. What can you say about the values of m and b? Explain your reasoning.

_____

_____

_____

_____

_____

19. Justify Reasoning A linear system with infinitely many solutions consists of the equation $3x + 5 = 8$ and a second equation of the form $Ax + By = C$. What can you say about the values of A, B, and C? Explain your reasoning.

_____

_____

_____

_____

20. Draw Conclusions Both the points $(2, -2)$ and $(4, -4)$ are solutions of a system of linear equations. What conclusions can you make about the equations and their graphs?

_____

_____

Ready to Go On?

Personal Math Trainer

Online Assessment and Intervention

⏻ my.hrw.com

16.1 Solving Systems of Linear Equations by Graphing

Solve each system by graphing.

1. $\begin{cases} y = x - 1 \\ y = 2x - 3 \end{cases}$

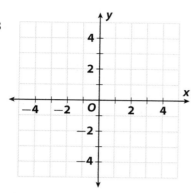

2. $\begin{cases} x + 2y = 1 \\ -x + y = 2 \end{cases}$

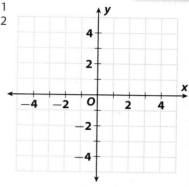

16.2 Solving Systems by Substitution

Solve each system of equations by substitution.

3. $\begin{cases} y = 2x \\ x + y = -9 \end{cases}$ _____

4. $\begin{cases} 3x - 2y = 11 \\ x + 2y = 9 \end{cases}$ _____

16.3 Solving Systems by Elimination

Solve each system of equations by adding or subtracting.

5. $\begin{cases} 3x + y = 9 \\ 2x + y = 5 \end{cases}$ _____

6. $\begin{cases} -x - 2y = 4 \\ 3x + 2y = 4 \end{cases}$ _____

16.4 Solving Systems by Elimination with Multiplication

Solve each system of equations by multiplying first.

7. $\begin{cases} x + 3y = -2 \\ 3x + 4y = -1 \end{cases}$ _____

8. $\begin{cases} 2x + 8y = 22 \\ 3x - 2y = 5 \end{cases}$ _____

16.5 Solving Special Systems

Solve each system. Tell how many solutions each system has.

9. $\begin{cases} -2x + 8y = 5 \\ x - 4y = -3 \end{cases}$ _____

10. $\begin{cases} 6x + 18y = -12 \\ x + 3y = -2 \end{cases}$ _____

❓ ESSENTIAL QUESTION

11. What are the possible solutions to a system of linear equations, and what do they represent graphically?

_____

_____

Personal
Math Trainer

Online
Assessment and
Intervention

my.hrw.com

Selected Response

1. The graph of which equation is shown?

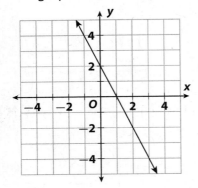

(A) $y = -2x + 2$ (C) $y = 2x + 2$

(B) $y = -x + 2$ (D) $y = 2x + 1$

2. Which best describes the solutions to the system $\begin{cases} x + y = -4 \\ -2x - 2y = 0 \end{cases}$?

(A) one solution   (C) infinitely many

(B) no solution   (D) (0, 0)

3. Which of the following represents 0.000056023 written in scientific notation?

(A) 5.6023×10^5 (C) 5.6023×10^{-4}

(B) 5.6023×10^4 (D) 5.6023×10^{-5}

4. Which is the solution to $\begin{cases} 2x - y = 1 \\ 4x + y = 11 \end{cases}$?

(A) (2, 3)   (C) (−2, 3)

(B) (3, 2)   (D) (3, −2)

5. Which expression can you substitute in the indicated equation to solve $\begin{cases} 3x - y = 5 \\ x + 2y = 4 \end{cases}$?

(A) $2y - 4$ for x in $3x - y = 5$

(B) $4 - x$ for y in $3x - y = 5$

(C) $3x - 5$ for y in $3x - y = 5$

(D) $3x - 5$ for y in $x + 2y = 4$

6. What is the solution to the system of linear equations shown on the graph?

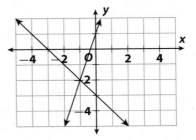

(A) −1   (C) (−1, −2)

(B) −2   (D) (−2, −1)

7. Which step could you use to start solving $\begin{cases} x - 6y = 8 \\ 2x - 5y = 3 \end{cases}$?

(A) Add $2x - 5y = 3$ to $x - 6y = 8$.

(B) Multiply $x - 6y = 8$ by 2 and add it to $2x - 5y = 3$.

(C) Multiply $x - 6y = 8$ by 2 and subtract it from $2x - 5y = 3$.

(D) Substitute $x = 6y - 8$ for x in $2x - 5y = 3$.

Mini-Task

8. A hot-air balloon begins rising from the ground at 4 meters per second at the same time as a parachutist's chute opens at a height of 200 meters. The parachutist descends at 6 meters per second.

a. Define the variables and write a system that represents the situation.

_____

_____

b. Find the solution. What does it mean?

_____

_____

Study Guide Review

MODULE 15 Solving Linear Equations

How can you use equations with variables on both sides to solve real-world problems?

EXAMPLE 1

A tutor gives students a choice of how to pay: a base rate of $20 plus $8 per hour, or a set rate of $13 per hour. Find the number of hours of tutoring for which the cost is the same for either choice.

Plan 1 cost: $20 + 8x$ Plan 2 cost: $13x$

$$20 + 8x = 13x \qquad \textit{Write the equation.}$$
$$\underline{-8x \quad\;\; -8x} \qquad \textit{Subtract 8x from both sides.}$$
$$20 = 5x \qquad \textit{Divide both sides by 5.}$$
$$x = 4$$

The cost is the same for 4 hours of tutoring.

EXAMPLE 2

Solve $-2.4(3x + 5) = 0.8(x + 3.5)$.

$$-2.4(3x + 5) = 0.8(x + 3.5)$$

$$10(-2.4)(3x + 5) = 10(0.8)(x + 3.5) \qquad \textit{Multiply each side by 10 to clear some decimals.}$$

$$-24(3x + 5) = 8(x + 3.5)$$

$$-24(3x) - 24(5) = 8(x) + 8(3.5) \qquad \textit{Apply the Distributive Property.}$$

$$-72x - 120 = 8x + 28$$

$$\underline{-8x \qquad\quad -8x} \qquad \textit{Subtract 8x from both sides of the equation.}$$

$$-80x - 120 = 28$$

$$\underline{+ 120 \quad + 120} \qquad \textit{Add 120 to both sides of the equation.}$$

$$-80x = 148$$

$$\frac{-80x}{-80} = \frac{148}{-80} \qquad \textit{Divide both sides of the equation by -80.}$$

$$x = -1.85$$

EXAMPLE 3

Solve $4(3x - 6) = 2(6x - 5)$.

$$4(3x - 6) = 2(6x - 5)$$

$12x - 24 = \quad 12x - 10$	Apply the Distributive Property.
$\underline{-12x} \qquad \underline{\quad -12x}$	Subtract $8x$ from both sides of the equation.
$-24 = -10$	The statement is false.

There is no value of x that makes a true statement. Therefore, this equation has no solution.

EXERCISES

Solve. (Lessons 15.1, 15.2, 15.3, 15.4)

1. $13.02 - 6y = 8y$ _____

2. $\frac{1}{5}x + 5 = 19 - \frac{1}{2}x$ _____

3. $7.3t + 22 = 2.1t - 22.2$ _____

4. $1.4 + \frac{2}{5}e = \frac{3}{15}e - 0.8$ _____

5. $5(x - 4) = 2(x + 5)$ _____

6. $-7(3 + t) = 4(2t + 6)$ _____

7. $\frac{3}{4}(x + 8) = \frac{1}{3}(x + 27)$ _____

8. $3(4x - 8) = \frac{1}{5}(35x + 30)$ _____

9. $-1.6(2y + 15) = -1.2(2y - 10)$

10. $9(4a - 2) = 12(3a + 8)$

_____

_____

11. $6(x - \frac{1}{3}) = -2(x + 23)$

12. $8(p - 0.25) = 4(2p - 0.5)$

_____

_____

13. Write a real-world situation that could be modeled by the equation $650 + 10m = 60m + 400$. (Lesson 15.1)

_____

_____

_____

_____

Key Vocabulary
solution of a system of equations *(solución de un sistema de ecuaciones)*
system of equations *(sistema de ecuaciones)*

? ESSENTIAL QUESTION

How can you use systems of equations to solve real-world problems?

EXAMPLE 1 Solve the system of equations by substitution.

$$\begin{cases} 3x + y = 7 \\ x + y = 3 \end{cases}$$

Step 1 Solve an equation for one variable.

$$3x + y = 7$$
$$y = -3x + 7$$

Step 2 Substitute the expression for y in the other equation and solve.

$$x + y = 3$$
$$x + (-3x + 7) = 3$$
$$-2x + 7 = 3$$
$$-2x = -4$$
$$x = 2$$

Step 3 Substitute the value of x into one of the equations and solve for the other variable, y.

$$x + y = 3$$
$$2 + y = 3$$
$$y = 1$$

(2, 1) is the solution of the system.

EXAMPLE 2 Solve the system of equations by elimination.

$$\begin{cases} x + y = 8 \\ 2x - 3y = 1 \end{cases}$$

Step 1 Multiply the first equation by 3 and add this new equation to the second equation.

$$3(x + y = 8) = 3x + 3y = 24$$
$$3x + 3y = 24$$
$$\underline{2x - 3y = 1}$$
$$5x + 0y = 25$$
$$5x = 25$$
$$x = 5$$

Step 2 Substitute the solution into one of the original equations and solve for y.

$$x + y = 8$$
$$5 + y = 8$$
$$y = 3$$

(5, 3) is the solution of the system.

EXERCISES

Solve each system of linear equations. (Lessons 8.1, 8.2, 8.3, 8.4, and 8.5)

14. $\begin{cases} x + y = -2 \\ 2x - y = 5 \end{cases}$

15. $\begin{cases} y = 2x + 1 \\ x + 2y = 17 \end{cases}$

16. $\begin{cases} y = -2x - 3 \\ 2x + y = 9 \end{cases}$

_____

_____

_____

17. $\begin{cases} y = 5 - x \\ 2x + 2y = 10 \end{cases}$

18. $\begin{cases} 2x - y = 26 \\ 3x - 2y = 42 \end{cases}$

19. $\begin{cases} 2x + 3y = 11 \\ 5x - 2y = 18 \end{cases}$

_____

_____

_____

20. Last week Andrew bought 3 pounds of zucchini and 2 pounds of tomatoes for $7.05 at a farm stand. This week he bought 4 pounds of zucchini and 3 pounds of tomatoes, at the same prices, for $9.83. What is the cost of 1 pound of zucchini and 1 pound of tomatoes at the farm stand?

_____

Unit 3 Performance Tasks

1. **CAREERS IN MATH** Hydraulic Engineer A hydraulic engineer is studying the pressure in a particular fluid. The pressure is equal to the atmospheric pressure 101 kN/m plus 8 kN/m for every meter below the surface, where kN/m is kilonewtons per meter, a unit of pressure.

a. Write an expression for the pressure at a depth of d_1 meters below the liquid surface.

_____

b. Write and solve an equation to find the depth at which the pressure is 200 kN/m.

_____

c. The hydraulic engineer alters the density of the fluid so that the pressure at depth d_2 below the surface is atmospheric pressure 101 kN/m plus 9 kN/m for every meter below the surface. Write an expression for the pressure at depth d_2.

_____

d. If the pressure at depth d_1 in the first fluid is equal to the pressure at depth d_2 in the second fluid, what is the relationship between d_1 and d_2? Explain how you found your answer.

_____

_____

_____

Selected Response

1. Ricardo and John start swimming from the same location. Ricardo starts 15 seconds before John and swims at a rate of 3 feet per second. John swims at a rate of 4 feet per second in the same direction as Ricardo. Which equation could you solve to find how long it will take John to catch up with Ricardo?

- Ⓐ $4t + 3 = 3t$
- Ⓑ $4t + 60 = 3t$
- Ⓒ $3t + 3 = 4t$
- Ⓓ $3t + 45 = 4t$

2. Gina and Rhonda work for different real estate agencies. Gina earns a monthly salary of $5,000 plus a 6% commission on her sales. Rhonda earns a monthly salary of $6,500 plus a 4% commission on her sales. How much must each sell to earn the same amount in a month?

- Ⓐ $1,500
- Ⓒ $75,000
- Ⓑ $15,000
- Ⓓ $750,000

3. What is the slope of the line?

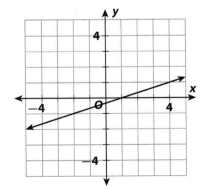

- Ⓐ -3
- Ⓒ $\frac{1}{3}$
- Ⓑ $-\frac{1}{3}$
- Ⓓ 3

4. What is the solution of the system of equations?
$$\begin{cases} y = 2x - 3 \\ 5x + y = 11 \end{cases}$$

- Ⓐ $(2, 1)$
- Ⓑ $(1, 2)$
- Ⓒ $(3, -4)$
- Ⓓ $(1, -1)$

5. Alana is having a party. She bought 3 rolls of streamers and 2 packages of balloons for $10.00. She realized she needed more supplies and went back to the store and bought 2 more rolls of streamers and 1 more package of balloons for $6.25. How much did each roll of streamers and each package of balloons cost?

- Ⓐ streamers: $3.00, balloons: $2.00
- Ⓑ streamers: $2.00, balloons: $1.00
- Ⓒ streamers: $1.25, balloons: $2.50
- Ⓓ streamers: $2.50, balloons: $1.25

6. The triangle and the rectangle have the same perimeter.

Find the value of x.

- Ⓐ 2
- Ⓑ 10
- Ⓒ 18
- Ⓓ 24

7. What is the solution of the equation
$8(3x + 4) = 2(12x - 8)$?

Ⓐ $x = -2$

Ⓑ $x = 2$

Ⓒ no solution

Ⓓ infinitely many solutions

8. A square wall tile has an area of 58,800 square millimeters. Between which two measurements is the length of one side?

Ⓐ between 24 and 25 millimeters

Ⓑ between 76 and 77 millimeters

Ⓒ between 242 and 243 millimeters

Ⓓ between 766 and 767 millimeters

Mini-Tasks

9. Lily and Alex went to a Mexican restaurant. Lily paid $9 for 2 tacos and 3 enchiladas, and Alex paid $12.50 for 3 tacos and 4 enchiladas.

a. Write a system of equations that represents this situation.

_____

_____

b. Use the system of equations to find how much the restaurant charges for a taco and for an enchilada.

_____

c. Describe the method you used to solve the system of equations.

_____

_____

_____

_____

Solutions of a system of two equations must make both equations true. Check solutions in both equations.

10. Use the system of equations to answer the questions below.

$$\begin{cases} 4x + 2y = -8 \\ 2x + y = 4 \end{cases}$$

a. Graph the equations on the grid.

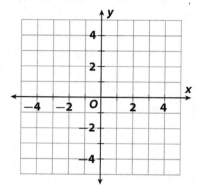

b. How many solutions does the system of equations have? Explain your answer.

_____

_____

11. Isaac wants to join a gym. He checked out the membership fees at two gyms.

Gym A charges a new member fee of $65 and $20 per month.

Gym B charges a new member fee of $25 and $35 per month, but Isaac will get a discount of 20% on the monthly fee.

a. Write an equation you can use to find the number of months for which the total costs at the gyms are the same.

_____

b. Solve the equation to find the number of months for which the total costs of the gyms are the same.

_____

_____

_____

Transformational Geometry

MODULE 17
Transformations and Congruence
FL 8.G.1.1, 8.G.1.2, 8.G.1.3

MODULE 18
Transformations and Similarity
FL 8.G.1.3, 8.G.1.4

CAREERS IN MATH

Contractor A contractor is engaged in the construction, repair, and dismantling of structures such as buildings, bridges, and roads. Contractors use math when researching and implementing building codes, making measurements and scaling models, and in financial management.

If you are interested in a career as a contractor, you should study the following mathematical subjects:
- Business Math
- Geometry
- Algebra
- Trigonometry

Research other careers that require the use of business math and scaling.

Unit 8 Performance Task

At the end of the unit, check out how **contractors** use math.

Vocabulary Preview

Use the puzzle to preview key vocabulary from this unit. Unscramble the circled letters within found words to answer the riddle at the bottom of the page.

```
W T C F V A F I L I T U G N S
M U J L O C Z H B R S D E O W
F E Q V H B T E A N T P X I A
M Y J G B O G N P K G G B T Q
N X L H A A S E V Z R U B C W
L O X D M L A G R H H L R U A
G P I I A E M X K V A K X D K
B D E T N E M E G R A L N E A
W R I E C A N R E Y M A T R P
P O G L K E R O T A T I O N R
N Z Y E A C L R O V Z S P I U
U Y T J N T Q F N B X G G C J
O N E R Z I I P E I Y F A B W
I F V U C M S O G R P Q K B W
C Q T U I C C U N L N T L D Y
```

The input of a transformation. (Lesson 17.1)

A transformation that flips a figure across a line. (Lesson 17.2)

A transformation that slides a figure along a straight line. (Lesson 17.1)

A transformation that turns a figure around a given point. (Lesson 17.3)

The product of a figure made larger by dilation. (Lesson 18.1)

The product of a figure made smaller by dilation. (Lesson 18.1)

Scaled replicas that change the size but not the shape of a figure. (Lesson 18.1)

Q: What do you call an angle that's broken?

A: A __ __ __ __ __ __ __ __ __ __ __ !

Transformations and Congruence

MODULE 17

ESSENTIAL QUESTION

How can you use transformations and congruence to solve real-world problems?

Real-World Video

When a marching band lines up and marches across the field, they are modeling a translation. As they march, they maintain size and orientation. A translation is one type of transformation.

⏻ my.hrw.com

GO DIGITAL

my.hrw.com

my.hrw.com

Go digital with your write-in student edition, accessible on any device.

Math On the Spot

Scan with your smart phone to jump directly to the online edition, video tutor, and more.

X²

Animated Math

Interactively explore key concepts to see how math works.

Personal Math Trainer

Get immediate feedback and help as you work through practice sets.

Are YOU Ready?

Complete these exercises to review skills you will need for this module.

Personal Math Trainer

Online Assessment and Intervention

my.hrw.com

Integer Operations

EXAMPLE

$-3 - (-6) = -3 + 6$

$= |-3| - |6|$

$= 3$

To subtract an integer, add its opposite. The signs are different, so find the difference of the absolute values: $6 - 3 = 3$. Use the sign of the number with the greater absolute value.

Find each difference.

1. $5 - (-9)$

_____

2. $-6 - 8$

_____

3. $2 - 9$

_____

4. $-10 - (-6)$

_____

5. $3 - (-11)$

_____

6. $12 - 7$

_____

7. $-4 - 11$

_____

8. $0 - (-12)$

_____

Measure Angles

EXAMPLE

$m\angle JKL = 70°$

Place the center point of the protractor on the angle's vertex.

Align one ray with the base of the protractor.

Read the angle measure where the other ray intersects the semicircle.

Use a protractor to measure each angle.

9.

_____

10.

_____

11.

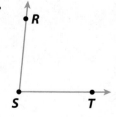

_____

Reading Start-Up

Visualize Vocabulary

Use the ✔ words to complete the graphic organizer. You will put one word in each oval.

Types of Quadrilaterals

A quadrilateral in which all sides are congruent and opposite sides are parallel.

A quadrilateral in which opposite sides are parallel and congruent.

A quadrilateral in which two sides are parallel.

Vocabulary

Review Words

coordinate plane *(plano cartesiano)*

✔ parallelogram *(paralelogramo)*

quadrilateral *(cuadrilátero)*

✔ rhombus *(rombo)*

✔ trapezoid *(trapecio)*

Preview Words

center of rotation *(centro de rotación)*

congruent *(congruente)*

image *(imagen)*

line of reflection *(línea de reflexión)*

preimage *(imagen original)*

reflection *(reflexión)*

rotation *(rotación)*

transformation *(transformación)*

translation *(traslación)*

Understand Vocabulary

Match the term on the left to the correct expression on the right.

1. transformation

A. A function that describes a change in the position, size, or shape of a figure.

2. reflection

B. A function that slides a figure along a straight line.

3. translation

C. A transformation that flips a figure across a line.

Active Reading

Booklet Before beginning the module, create a booklet to help you learn the concepts in this module. Write the main idea of each lesson on each page of the booklet. As you study each lesson, write important details that support the main idea, such as vocabulary and formulas. Refer to your finished booklet as you work on assignments and study for tests.

MODULE 17
Unpacking the Standards

Understanding the standards and the vocabulary terms in the standards will help you know exactly what you are expected to learn in this module.

FL 8.G.1.2

Understand that a two-dimensional figure is congruent to another if the second can be obtained from the first by a sequence of rotations, reflections, and translations; given two congruent figures, describe a sequence that exhibits the congruence between them.

What It Means to You

You will identify a rotation, a reflection, a translation, and a sequence of transformations, and understand that the image has the same shape and size as the preimage.

UNPACKING EXAMPLE 8.G.1.2

The figure shows triangle *ABC* and its image after three different transformations. Identify and describe the translation, the reflection, and the rotation of triangle *ABC*.

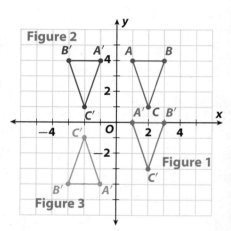

Figure 1 is a translation 4 units down. Figure 2 is a reflection across the *y*-axis. Figure 3 is a rotation of 180°.

FL 8.G.1.3

Describe the effect of dilations, translations, rotations, and reflections on two-dimensional figures using coordinates.

What It Means to You

You can use an algebraic representation to translate, reflect, or rotate a two-dimensional figure.

UNPACKING EXAMPLE 8.G.1.3

Rectangle *RSTU* with vertices $(-4, 1)$, $(-1, 1)$, $(-1, -3)$, and $(-4, -3)$ is reflected across the *y*-axis. Find the coordinates of the image.

The rule to reflect across the *y*-axis is to change the sign of the *x*-coordinate.

Coordinates	Reflect across the *y*-axis $(-x, y)$	Coordinates of image
$(-4, 1)$, $(-1, 1)$, $(-1, -3)$, $(-4, -3)$	$(-(-4), 1)$, $(-(-1), 1)$, $(-(-1), -3)$, $(-(-4), -3)$	$(4, 1)$, $(1, 1)$, $(1, -3)$, $(4, -3)$

The coordinates of the image are $(4, 1)$, $(1, 1)$, $(1, -3)$, and $(4, -3)$.

Visit **my.hrw.com** to see all **Florida Math Standards** unpacked.

my.hrw.com

LESSON 17.1 Properties of Translations

FL 8.G.1.1
Verify experimentally the properties of . . . translations. Also 8.G.1.1a, 8.G.1.1b, 8.G.1.1c, 8.G.1.3

ESSENTIAL QUESTION

How do you describe the properties of translation and their effect on the congruence and orientation of figures?

EXPLORE ACTIVITY 1

 FL 8.G.1.1

Exploring Translations

You learned that a function is a rule that assigns exactly one output to each input. A **transformation** is a function that describes a change in the position, size, or shape of a figure. The input of a transformation is the **preimage**, and the output of a transformation is the **image**.

A **translation** is a transformation that slides a figure along a straight line.

The triangle shown on the grid is the preimage (input). The arrow shows the motion of a translation and how point A is translated to point A′.

A Trace triangle *ABC* onto a piece of paper. Cut out your traced triangle.

B Slide your triangle along the arrow to model the translation that maps point *A* to point *A′*.

C The image of the translation is the triangle produced by the translation. Sketch the image of the translation.

D The vertices of the image are labeled using prime notation. For example, the image of *A* is *A′*. Label the images of points *B* and *C*.

E Describe the motion modeled by the translation.

Move _____ units right and _____ units down.

F Check that the motion you described in part **E** is the same motion that maps point *A* onto *A′*, point *B* onto *B′*, and point *C* onto *C′*.

Reflect

1. How is the orientation of the triangle affected by the translation?

Properties of Translations

Use trapezoid *TRAP* to investigate the properties of translations.

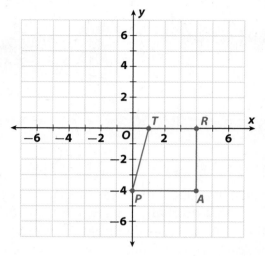

A Trace the trapezoid onto a piece of paper. Cut out your traced trapezoid.

B Place your trapezoid on top of the trapezoid in the figure. Then translate your trapezoid 5 units to the left and 3 units up. Sketch the image of the translation by tracing your trapezoid in this new location. Label the vertices of the image *T′*, *R′*, *A′*, and *P′*.

C Use a ruler to measure the sides of trapezoid *TRAP* in centimeters.

TR = _____   RA = _____   AP = _____   TP = _____

D Use a ruler to measure the sides of trapezoid *T′R′A′P′* in centimeters.

T′R′ = _____   R′A′ = _____   A′P′ = _____   T′P′ = _____

E What do you notice about the lengths of corresponding sides of the two figures?

_____

F Use a protractor to measure the angles of trapezoid *TRAP*.

m∠T = _____   m∠R = _____   m∠A = _____   m∠P = _____

G Use a protractor to measure the angles of trapezoid *T′R′A′P′*.

m∠T′ = _____   m∠R′ = _____   m∠A′ = _____   m∠P′ = _____

H What do you notice about the measures of corresponding angles of the two figures?

_____

I Which sides of trapezoid *TRAP* are parallel? How do you know?

_____

Which sides of trapezoid *T′R′A′P′* are parallel? _____

What do you notice? _____

_____

Reflect

2. Make a Conjecture Use your results from parts **E**, **H**, and **I** to make a conjecture about translations.

_____

_____

3. Two figures that have the same size and shape are called *congruent*. What can you say about translations and congruence?

_____

Graphing Translations

To translate a figure in the coordinate plane, translate each of its vertices. Then connect the vertices to form the image.

Math On the Spot
my.hrw.com

EXAMPLE 1

FL 8.G.1.3

The figure shows triangle *XYZ*. Graph the image of the triangle after a translation of 4 units to the right and 1 unit up.

STEP 1 Translate point *X*.

Count right 4 units and up 1 unit and plot point *X′*.

STEP 2 Translate point *Y*.

Count right 4 units and up 1 unit and plot point *Y′*.

STEP 3 Translate point *Z*.

Count right 4 units and up 1 unit and plot point *Z′*.

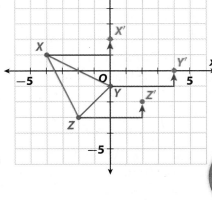

STEP 4 Connect *X′*, *Y′*, and *Z′* to form triangle *X′Y′Z′*.

Each vertex is moved 4 units right and 1 unit up.

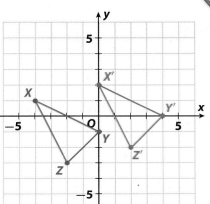

Math Talk
Mathematical Practices

Is the image congruent to the preimage? How do you know?

YOUR TURN

4. The figure shows parallelogram *ABCD*. Graph the image of the parallelogram after a translation of 5 units to the left and 2 units down.

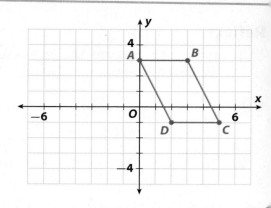

Guided Practice

1. **Vocabulary** A _____ is a change in the position, size, or shape of a figure.

2. **Vocabulary** When you perform a transformation of a figure on the coordinate plane, the input of the transformation is called

   the _____, and the output of the transformation is

   called the _____.

3. Joni translates a right triangle 2 units down and 4 units to the right. How does the orientation of the image of the triangle compare with the orientation of the preimage? (Explore Activity 1)

   _____

4. Rashid drew rectangle *PQRS* on a coordinate plane. He then translated the rectangle 3 units up and 3 units to the left and labeled the image *P'Q'R'S'*. How do rectangle *PQRS* and rectangle *P'Q'R'S'* compare? (Explore Activity 2)

   _____

5. The figure shows trapezoid *WXYZ*. Graph the image of the trapezoid after a translation of 4 units up and 2 units to the left. (Example 1)

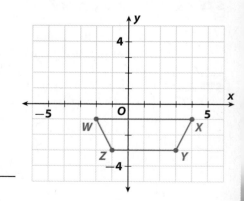

? ESSENTIAL QUESTION CHECK-IN

6. What are the properties of translations?

   _____

   _____

17.1 Independent Practice

Personal Math Trainer

Online Assessment and Intervention

my.hrw.com

7. The figure shows triangle *DEF*.

  a. Graph the image of the triangle after the translation that maps point *D* to point *D′*.

  b. How would you describe the translation?

  _____

  _____

  c. How does the image of triangle *DEF* compare with the preimage?

  _____

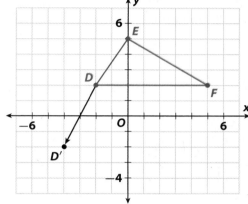

8. a. Graph quadrilateral *KLMN* with vertices *K*(−3, 2), *L*(2, 2), *M*(0, −3), and *N*(−4, 0) on the coordinate grid.

  b. On the same coordinate grid, graph the image of quadrilateral *KLMN* after a translation of 3 units to the right and 4 units up.

  c. Which side of the image is congruent to side $\overline{LM}$?

  _____

  Name three other pairs of congruent sides.

  _____

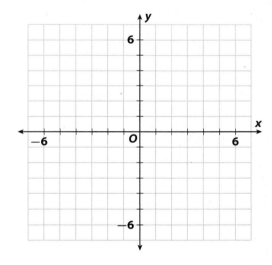

Draw the image of the figure after each translation.

9. 4 units left and 2 units down

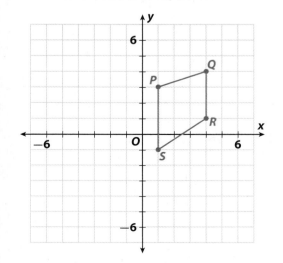

10. 5 units right and 3 units up

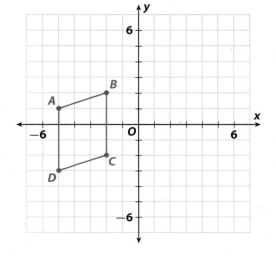

11. The figure shows the ascent of a hot air balloon. How would you describe the translation?

_____

_____

12. Critical Thinking Is it possible that the orientation of a figure could change after it is translated? Explain.

_____

_____

_____

13. a. Multistep Graph triangle XYZ with vertices $X(-2, -5)$, $Y(2, -2)$, and $Z(4, -4)$ on the coordinate grid.

b. On the same coordinate grid, graph and label triangle $X'Y'Z'$, the image of triangle XYZ after a translation of 3 units to the left and 6 units up.

c. Now graph and label triangle $X''Y''Z''$, the image of triangle $X'Y'Z'$ after a translation of 1 unit to the left and 2 units down.

d. Analyze Relationships How would you describe the translation that maps triangle XYZ onto triangle $X''Y''Z''$?

_____

_____

14. Critical Thinking The figure shows rectangle $P'Q'R'S'$, the image of rectangle $PQRS$ after a translation of 5 units to the right and 7 units up. Graph and label the preimage $PQRS$.

15. Communicate Mathematical Ideas Explain why the image of a figure after a translation is congruent to its preimage.

_____

_____

_____

_____

_____

FL 8.G.1.1
Verify experimentally
the properties
of ... reflections. . . .
Also 8.G.1.1a, 8.G.1.1b,
8.G.1.1c, 8.G.1.3

ESSENTIAL QUESTION

How do you describe the properties of reflection and their effect on the congruence and orientation of figures?

EXPLORE ACTIVITY 1   **FL** 8.G.1.1

Exploring Reflections

A **reflection** is a transformation that flips a figure across a line. The line is called the **line of reflection**. Each point and its image are the same distance from the line of reflection.

The triangle shown on the grid is the preimage. You will explore reflections across the *x*- and *y*-axes.

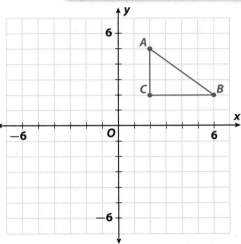

A Trace triangle *ABC* and the *x*- and *y*-axes onto a piece of paper.

B Fold your paper along the *x*-axis and trace the image of the triangle on the opposite side of the *x*-axis. Unfold your paper and label the vertices of the image *A'*, *B'*, and *C'*.

C What is the line of reflection for this transformation?

_____

D Find the perpendicular distance from each point to the line of reflection.

    Point *A* _____   Point *B* _____   Point *C* _____

E Find the perpendicular distance from each point to the line of reflection.

    Point *A'* _____   Point *B'* _____   Point *C'* _____

F What do you notice about the distances you found in **D** and **E**?

_____

Reflect

1. Fold your paper from **A** along the *y*-axis and trace the image of triangle *ABC* on the opposite side. Label the vertices of the image *A''*, *B''*, and *C''*. What is the line of reflection for this transformation? _____

2. How does each image in your drawings compare with its preimage?

_____

Properties of Reflections

Use trapezoid _TRAP_ to investigate the properties of reflections.

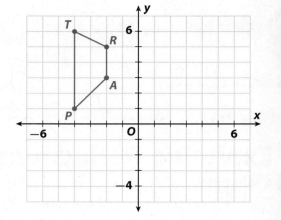

A Trace the trapezoid onto a piece of paper. Cut out your traced trapezoid.

B Place your trapezoid on top of the trapezoid in the figure. Then reflect your trapezoid across the _y_-axis. Sketch the image of the reflection by tracing your trapezoid in this new location. Label the vertices of the image _T′_, _R′_, _A′_, and _P′_.

C Use a ruler to measure the sides of trapezoid _TRAP_ in centimeters.

_TR_ = _____   _RA_ = _____   _AP_ = _____   _TP_ = _____

D Use a ruler to measure the sides of trapezoid _T′R′A′P′_ in centimeters.

_T′R′_ = _____   _R′A′_ = _____   _A′P′_ = _____   _T′P′_ = _____

E What do you notice about the lengths of corresponding sides of the two figures?

_____

F Use a protractor to measure the angles of trapezoid _TRAP_.

_m∠T_ = _____   _m∠R_ = _____   _m∠A_ = _____   _m∠P_ = _____

G Use a protractor to measure the angles of trapezoid _T′R′A′P′_.

_m∠T′_ = _____   _m∠R′_ = _____   _m∠A′_ = _____   _m∠P′_ = _____

H What do you notice about the measures of corresponding angles of the two figures?

_____

I Which sides of trapezoid _TRAP_ are parallel? _____

Which sides of trapezoid _T′R′A′P′_ are parallel? _____
What do you notice?

_____

_____

Reflect

3. **Make a Conjecture** Use your results from , , and to make a conjecture about reflections.

_____

_____

_____

Math Talk
Mathematical Practices

What can you say about reflections and congruence?

Graphing Reflections

To reflect a figure across a line of reflection, reflect each of its vertices. Then connect the vertices to form the image. Remember that each point and its image are the same distance from the line of reflection.

Math On the Spot
my.hrw.com

EXAMPLE 1

FL 8.G.1.3

The figure shows triangle _XYZ_. Graph the image of the triangle after a reflection across the _x_-axis.

My Notes

STEP 1 Reflect point _X_.

Point _X_ is 3 units below the _x_-axis. Count 3 units above the _x_-axis and plot point _X′_.

STEP 2 Reflect point _Y_.

Point _Y_ is 1 unit below the _x_-axis. Count 1 unit above the _x_-axis and plot point _Y′_.

STEP 3 Reflect point _Z_.

Point _Z_ is 5 units below the _x_-axis. Count 5 units above the _x_-axis and plot point _Z′_.

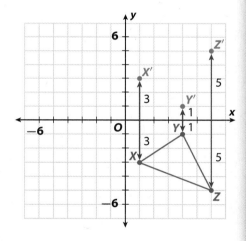

STEP 4 Connect _X′_, _Y′_, and _Z′_ to form triangle _X′Y′Z′_.

Each vertex of the image is the same distance from the _x_-axis as the corresponding vertex in the original figure.

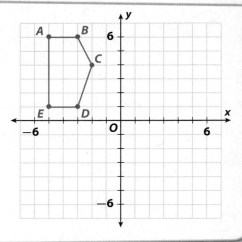

YOUR TURN

4. The figure shows pentagon *ABCDE*. Graph the image of the pentagon after a reflection across the *y*-axis.

Guided Practice

1. Vocabulary A reflection is a transformation that flips a figure across

a line called the _____.

2. The figure shows trapezoid *ABCD*. (Explore Activities 1 and 2 and Example 1)

   a. Graph the image of the trapezoid after a reflection across the *x*-axis. Label the vertices of the image.

   b. How do trapezoid *ABCD* and trapezoid *A'B'C'D'* compare?

   _____

   c. What If? Suppose you reflected trapezoid *ABCD* across the *y*-axis. How would the orientation of the image of the trapezoid compare with the orientation of the preimage?

   _____

   _____

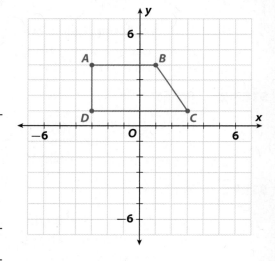

_____

_____

❓ ESSENTIAL QUESTION CHECK-IN

3. What are the properties of reflections?

_____

_____

17.2 Independent Practice

 FL 8.G.1.1, 8.G.1.3

Personal Math Trainer

Online Assessment and Intervention

my.hrw.com

The graph shows four right triangles. Use the graph for Exercises 4–7.

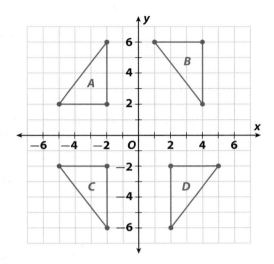

4. Which two triangles are reflections of each other across the *x*-axis?

_____

5. For which two triangles is the line of reflection the *y*-axis?

_____

6. Which triangle is a translation of triangle *C*? How would you describe the translation?

_____

_____

7. Which triangles are congruent? How do you know?

_____

_____

_____

_____

_____

8. a. Graph quadrilateral *WXYZ* with vertices *W*(−2, −2), *X*(3, 1), *Y*(5, −1), and *Z*(4, −6) on the coordinate grid.

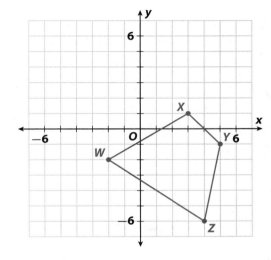

b. On the same coordinate grid, graph quadrilateral *W′X′Y′Z′*, the image of quadrilateral *WXYZ* after a reflection across the *x*-axis.

c. Which side of the image is congruent to side $\overline{YZ}$?

_____

Name three other pairs of congruent sides.

_____

_____

d. Which angle of the image is congruent to ∠*X*?

_____

Name three other pairs of congruent angles.

_____

_____

9. Critical Thinking Is it possible that the image of a point after a reflection could be the same point as the preimage? Explain.

_____

_____

10. a. Graph the image of the figure shown after a reflection across the *y*-axis.

b. On the same coordinate grid, graph the image of the figure you drew in part **a** after a reflection across the *x*-axis.

c. Make a Conjecture What other sequence of transformations would produce the same final image from the original preimage? Check your answer by performing the transformations. Then make a conjecture that generalizes your findings.

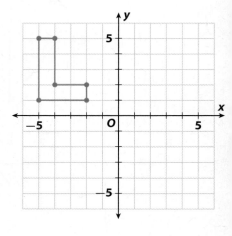

_____

_____

_____

_____

_____

_____

11. a. Graph triangle *DEF* with vertices *D*(2, 6), *E*(5, 6), and *F*(5, 1) on the coordinate grid.

b. Next graph triangle *D′E′F′*, the image of triangle *DEF* after a reflection across the *y*-axis.

c. On the same coordinate grid, graph triangle *D″E″F″*, the image of triangle *D′E′F′* after a translation of 7 units down and 2 units to the right.

d. Analyze Relationships Find a different sequence of transformations that will transform triangle *DEF* to triangle *D″E″F″*.

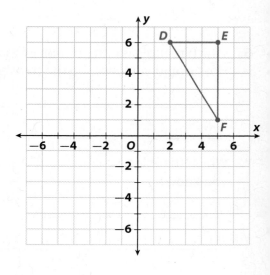

_____

_____

_____

_____

LESSON 17.3 Properties of Rotations

FL 8.G.1.1
Verify experimentally the properties of rotations.... .
Also 8.G.1.1a, 8.G.1.1b, 8.G.1.1c, 8.G.1.3

ESSENTIAL QUESTION

How do you describe the properties of rotation and their effect on the congruence and orientation of figures?

EXPLORE ACTIVITY 1   FL 8.G.1.1

Exploring Rotations

A **rotation** is a transformation that turns a figure around a given point called the **center of rotation**. The image has the same size and shape as the preimage.

The triangle shown on the grid is the preimage. You will use the origin as the center of rotation.

A Trace triangle *ABC* onto a piece of paper. Cut out your traced triangle.

B Rotate your triangle 90° counterclockwise about the origin. The side of the triangle that lies along the *x*-axis should now lie along the *y*-axis.

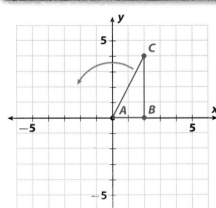

C Sketch the image of the rotation. Label the images of points *A*, *B*, and *C* as *A'*, *B'*, and *C'*.

D Describe the motion modeled by the rotation.

Rotate _____ degrees _____ about the origin.

E Check that the motion you described in **D** is the same motion that maps point *A* onto *A'*, point *B* onto *B'*, and point *C* onto *C'*.

Reflect

1. **Communicate Mathematical Ideas** How are the size and the orientation of the triangle affected by the rotation?

_____

_____

_____

2. Rotate triangle *ABC* 90° clockwise about the origin. Sketch the result on the coordinate grid above. Label the image vertices *A''*, *B''*, and *C''*.

Properties of Rotations

Use trapezoid *TRAP* to investigate the properties of rotations.

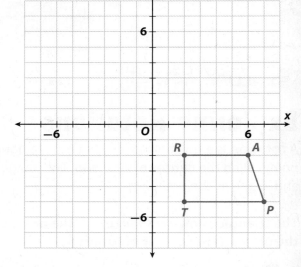

A Trace the trapezoid onto a piece of paper. Include the portion of the *x*- and *y*-axes bordering the third quadrant. Cut out your tracing.

B Place your trapezoid and axes on top of those in the figure. Then use the axes to help rotate your trapezoid 180° counterclockwise about the origin. Sketch the image of the rotation of your trapezoid in this new location. Label the vertices of the image *T′*, *R′*, *A′*, and *P′*.

C Use a ruler to measure the sides of trapezoid *TRAP* in centimeters.

$TR =$ _____ $RA =$ _____

$AP =$ _____ $TP =$ _____

D Use a ruler to measure the sides of trapezoid *T′R′A′P′* in centimeters.

$T′R′ =$ _____ $R′A′ =$ _____

$A′P′ =$ _____ $T′P′ =$ _____

E What do you notice about the lengths of corresponding sides of the two figures?

_____

F Use a protractor to measure the angles of trapezoid *TRAP*.

$m\angle T =$ _____ $m\angle R =$ _____ $m\angle A =$ _____ $m\angle P =$ _____

G Use a protractor to measure the angles of trapezoid *T′R′A′P′*.

$m\angle T′ =$ _____ $m\angle R′ =$ _____ $m\angle A′ =$ _____ $m\angle P′ =$ _____

H What do you notice about the measures of corresponding angles of the two figures?

_____

I Which sides of trapezoid *TRAP* are parallel? _____

Which sides of trapezoid *T′R′A′P′* are parallel? _____

What do you notice? _____

_____

Reflect

3. **Make a Conjecture** Use your results from **E**, **H**, and **I** to make a conjecture about rotations.

_____

_____

4. Place your tracing back in its original position. Then perform a 180° _clockwise_ rotation about the origin. Compare the result with the result of the transformation in **B**.

_____

_____

Graphing Rotations

To rotate a figure in the coordinate plane, rotate each of its vertices. Then connect the vertices to form the image.

Math On the Spot
⏻ my.hrw.com

Animated Math
⏻ my.hrw.com

EXAMPLE 1

FL 8.G.1.3

The figure shows triangle _ABC_. Graph the image of triangle _ABC_ after a rotation of 90° clockwise.

STEP 1 Rotate the figure clockwise from the y-axis to the x-axis. Point A will still be at (0, 0).

Point B is 2 units to the left of the y-axis, so point B′ is 2 units above the x-axis.

Point C is 2 units to the right of the y-axis, so point C′ is 2 units below the x-axis.

STEP 2 Connect A′, B′, and C′ to form the image triangle A′B′C′.

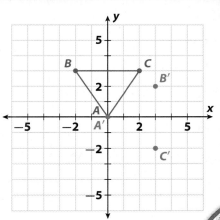

Math Talk
Mathematical Practices

How is the orientation of the triangle affected by the rotation?

Reflect

5. Is the image congruent to the preimage? How do you know?

_____

_____

_____

_____

YOUR TURN

Graph the image of quadrilateral *ABCD* after each rotation.

6. 180°

7. 270° clockwise

8. Find the coordinates of Point *C* after a 90° counterclockwise rotation followed by a 180° rotation.

_____

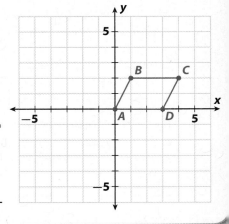

Guided Practice

1. **Vocabulary** A rotation is a transformation that turns a figure around a

   given _____ called the center of rotation.

Siobhan rotates a right triangle 90° counterclockwise about the origin.

2. How does the orientation of the image of the triangle compare with the orientation of the preimage? (Explore Activity 1)

   _____

3. Is the image of the triangle congruent to the preimage? (Explore Activity 2)

   _____

Draw the image of the figure after the given rotation about the origin. (Example 1)

4. 90° counterclockwise

5. 180°

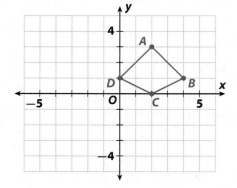

? ESSENTIAL QUESTION CHECK-IN

6. What are the properties of rotations?

   _____

17.3 Independent Practice

FL 8.G.1.1, 8.G.1.3

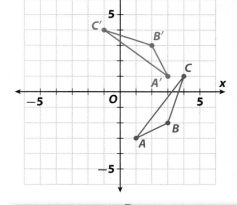

Personal Math Trainer

Online Assessment and Intervention

my.hrw.com

7. The figure shows triangle *ABC* and a rotation of the triangle about the origin.

   a. How would you describe the rotation?

   _____

   _____

   b. What are the coordinates of the image?

   _____ , _____ , _____

8. The graph shows a figure and its image after a transformation.

   a. How would you describe this as a rotation?

   _____

   _____

   b. Can you describe this as a transformation other than a rotation? Explain.

   _____

   _____

9. What type of rotation will preserve the orientation of the H-shaped figure in the grid?

   _____

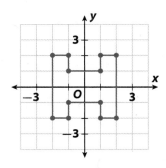

10. A point with coordinates $(-2, -3)$ is rotated 90° clockwise about the origin. What are the coordinates of its image?

   _____

Complete the table with rotations of 180° or 90°. Include the direction of rotation for rotations of 90°.

	Shape in quadrant	Image in quadrant	Rotation
11.	I	IV	
12.	III	I	
13.	IV	III	

Draw the image of the figure after the given rotation about the origin.

14. 180°

15. 270° counterclockwise

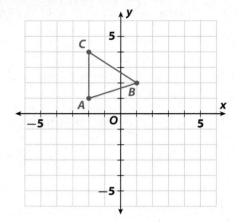

16. Is there a rotation for which the orientation of the image is always the same as that of the preimage? If so, what?

_____

 FOCUS ON HIGHER ORDER THINKING

Work Area

17. Problem Solving Lucas is playing a game where he has to rotate a figure for it to fit in an open space. Every time he clicks a button, the figure rotates 90 degrees clockwise. How many times does he need to click the button so that each figure returns to its original orientation?

Figure A _____

Figure B _____

Figure C _____

18. Make a Conjecture Triangle *ABC* is reflected across the *y*-axis to form the image *A'B'C'*. Triangle *A'B'C'* is then reflected across the *x*-axis to form the image *A"B"C"*. What type of rotation can be used to describe the relationship between triangle *A"B"C"* and triangle *ABC*?

_____

19. Communicate Mathematical Ideas Point *A* is on the *y*-axis. Describe all possible locations of image *A'* for rotations of 90°, 180°, and 270°. Include the origin as a possible location for *A*.

_____

_____

_____

_____

Algebraic Representations of Transformations

FL 8.G.1.3
Describe the effect of ...,
translations, rotations,
and reflections on two-
dimensional figures using
coordinates.

ESSENTIAL QUESTION

How can you describe the effect of a translation, rotation, or reflection on coordinates using an algebraic representation?

Algebraic Representations of Translations

The rules shown in the table describe how coordinates change when a figure is translated up, down, right, and left on the coordinate plane.

Math On the Spot
my.hrw.com

Translations	
Right a units	Add a to the x-coordinate: $(x, y) \rightarrow (x + a, y)$
Left a units	Subtract a from the x-coordinate: $(x, y) \rightarrow (x - a, y)$
Up b units	Add b to the y-coordinate: $(x, y) \rightarrow (x, y + b)$
Down b units	Subtract b from the y-coordinate: $(x, y) \rightarrow (x, y - b)$

EXAMPLE 1

FL 8.G.1.3

Triangle XYZ has vertices $X(0, 0)$, $Y(2, 3)$, and $Z(4, -1)$. Find the vertices of triangle $X'Y'Z'$ after a translation of 3 units to the right and 1 unit down. Then graph the triangle and its image.

Add 3 to the x-coordinate of each vertex and subtract 1 from the y-coordinate of each vertex.

STEP 1 Apply the rule to find the vertices of the image.

Vertices of △XYZ	Rule: $(x + 3, y - 1)$	Vertices of △$X'Y'Z'$
$X(0, 0)$	$(0 + 3, 0 - 1)$	$X'(3, -1)$
$Y(2, 3)$	$(2 + 3, 3 - 1)$	$Y'(5, 2)$
$Z(4, -1)$	$(4 + 3, -1 - 1)$	$Z'(7, -2)$

STEP 2 Graph triangle XYZ and its image.

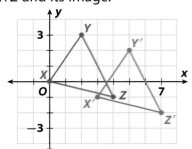

Math Talk
Mathematical Practices

When you translate a figure to the left or right, which coordinate do you change?

YOUR TURN

1. A rectangle has vertices at (0, −2), (0, 3), (3, −2), and (3, 3). What are the coordinates of the vertices of the image after the translation $(x, y) \rightarrow (x − 6, y − 3)$? Describe the translation.

_____

_____

Algebraic Representations of Reflections

The signs of the coordinates of a figure change when the figure is reflected across the *x*-axis and *y*-axis. The table shows the rules for changing the signs of the coordinates after a reflection.

Reflections	
Across the *x*-axis	Multiply each *y*-coordinate by −1: $(x, y) \rightarrow (x, −y)$
Across the *y*-axis	Multiply each *x*-coordinate by −1: $(x, y) \rightarrow (−x, y)$

EXAMPLE 2

FL 8.G.1.3

Rectangle *RSTU* has vertices R(−4, −1), S(−1, −1), T(−1, −3), and U(−4, −3). Find the vertices of rectangle *R′S′T′U′* after a reflection across the *y*-axis. Then graph the rectangle and its image.

Multiply the x-coordinate of each vertex by

STEP 1 Apply the rule to find the vertices of the image.

Vertices of *RSTU*	Rule: $(−1 \cdot x, y)$	Vertices of *R′S′T′U′*
R(−4, −1)	(−1 · (−4), −1)	R′(4, −1)
S(−1, −1)	(−1 · (−1), −1)	S′(1, −1)
T(−1, −3)	(−1 · (−1), −3)	T′(1, −3)
U(−4, −3)	(−1 · (−4), −3)	U′(4, −3)

STEP 2 Graph rectangle *RSTU* and its image.

My Notes

YOUR TURN

2. Triangle *ABC* has vertices *A*(−2, 6), *B*(0, 5), and *C*(3, −1). Find the vertices of triangle *A'B'C'* after a reflection across the *x*-axis.

_____

Algebraic Representations of Rotations

When points are rotated about the origin, the coordinates of the image can be found using the rules shown in the table.

Rotations	
90° clockwise	Multiply each *x*-coordinate by −1; then switch the *x*- and *y*-coordinates: $(x, y) \rightarrow (y, -x)$
90° counterclockwise	Multiply each *y*-coordinate by −1; then switch the *x*- and *y*-coordinates: $(x, y) \rightarrow (-y, x)$
180°	Multiply both coordinates by −1: $(x, y) \rightarrow (-x, -y)$

EXAMPLE 3   FL   8.G.1.3

Quadrilateral *ABCD* has vertices at *A*(−4, 2), *B*(−3, 4), *C*(2, 3), and *D*(0, 0). Find the vertices of quadrilateral *A'B'C'D'* after a 90° clockwise rotation. Then graph the quadrilateral and its image.

> Multiply the *x*-coordinate of each vertex by −1, and then switch the *x*- and *y*-coordinates.

STEP 1 Apply the rule to find the vertices of the image.

Vertices of *ABCD*	Rule: (*y*, −*x*)	Vertices of *A'B'C'D'*
A(−4, 2)	(2, −1 · (−4))	*A'*(2, 4)
B(−3, 4)	(4, −1 · (−3))	*B'*(4, 3)
C(2, 3)	(3, −1 · 2)	*C'*(3, −2)
D(0, 0)	(0, −1 · 0)	*D'*(0, 0)

STEP 2 Graph the quadrilateral and its image.

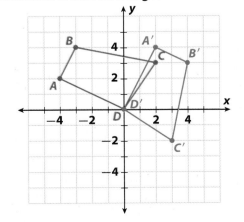

Reflect

3. **Communicate Mathematical Ideas** How would you find the vertices of an image if a figure were rotated 270° clockwise? Explain.

_____

_____

_____

YOUR TURN

4. A triangle has vertices at $J(-2, -4)$, $K(1, 5)$, and $L(2, 2)$. What are the coordinates of the vertices of the image after the triangle is rotated 90° counterclockwise?

_____

Guided Practice

1. Triangle XYZ has vertices $X(-3, -2)$, $Y(-1, 0)$, and $Z(1, -6)$. Find the vertices of triangle $X'Y'Z'$ after a translation of 6 units to the right. Then graph the triangle and its image. (Example 1)

   _____

2. Describe what happens to the x- and y-coordinates after a point is reflected across the x-axis. (Example 2)

   _____

   _____

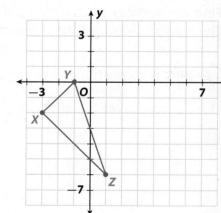

3. Use the rule $(x, y) \rightarrow (y, -x)$ to graph the image of the triangle at right. Then describe the transformation. (Example 3)

   _____

   _____

? ESSENTIAL QUESTION CHECK-IN

4. How do the x- and y-coordinates change when a figure is translated right a units and down b units?

   _____

   _____

17.4 Independent Practice

FL 8.G.1.3

Personal
Math Trainer

Online
Assessment and
Intervention

my.hrw.com

**Write an algebraic rule to describe each transformation.
Then describe the transformation.**

5.

_____

_____

6.

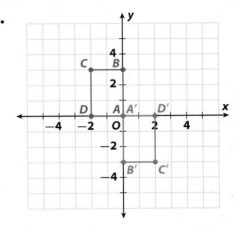

_____

_____

7. Triangle XYZ has vertices $X(6, -2.3)$, $Y(7.5, 5)$, and $Z(8, 4)$. When translated, X' has coordinates $(2.8, -1.3)$. Write a rule to describe this transformation. Then find the coordinates of Y' and Z'.

_____

8. Point L has coordinates $(3, -5)$. The coordinates of point L' after a reflection are $(-3, -5)$. Without graphing, tell which axis point L was reflected across. Explain your answer.

_____

_____

_____

9. Use the rule $(x, y) \rightarrow (x - 2, y - 4)$ to graph the image of the rectangle. Then describe the transformation.

_____

_____

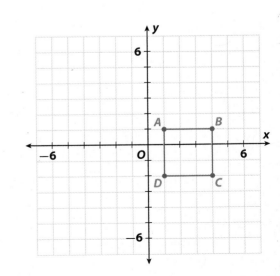

10. Parallelogram $ABCD$ has vertices $A(-2, -5\frac{1}{2})$, $B(-4, -5\frac{1}{2})$, $C(-3, -2)$, and $D(-1, -2)$. Find the vertices of parallelogram $A'B'C'D'$ after a translation of $2\frac{1}{2}$ units down.

_____

_____

11. Alexandra drew the logo shown on half-inch graph paper. Write a rule that describes the translation Alexandra used to create the shadow on the letter A.

_____

12. Kite *KLMN* has vertices at *K*(1, 3), *L*(2, 4), *M*(3, 3), and *N*(2, 0). After the kite is rotated, *K'* has coordinates (−3, 1). Describe the rotation, and include a rule in your description. Then find the coordinates of *L'*, *M'*, and *N'*.

_____

_____

H.O.T. FOCUS ON HIGHER ORDER THINKING

13. Make a Conjecture Graph the triangle with vertices (−3, 4), (3, 4), and (−5, −5). Use the transformation (*y*, *x*) to graph its image.

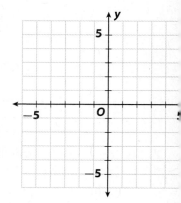

   a. Which vertex of the image has the same coordinates as a vertex of the original figure? Explain why this is true.

   _____

   _____

   b. What is the equation of a line through the origin and this point?

   _____

   c. Describe the transformation of the triangle.

   _____

14. Critical Thinking Mitchell says the point (0, 0) does not change when reflected across the *x*- or *y*-axis or when rotated about the origin. Do you agree with Mitchell? Explain why or why not.

_____

_____

_____

15. Analyze Relationships Triangle *ABC* with vertices *A*(−2, −2), *B*(−3, 1), and *C*(1, 1) is translated by $(x, y) \rightarrow (x − 1, y + 3)$. Then the image, triangle *A'B'C'*, is translated by $(x, y) \rightarrow (x + 4, y − 1)$, resulting in *A"B"C"*.

   a. Find the coordinates for the vertices of triangle *A"B"C"*.

   _____

   b. Write a rule for one translation that maps triangle *ABC* to triangle *A"B"C"*.

   _____

Work Area

17.5 Congruent Figures

FL 8.G.1.2

Understand that a two-dimensional figure is congruent to another if the second can be obtained from the first by a sequence of rotations, reflections, and translations; given two congruent figures, describe a sequence that exhibits the congruence between them.

ESSENTIAL QUESTION What is the connection between transformations and figures that have the same shape and size?

EXPLORE ACTIVITY FL 8.G.1.2

Combining Transformations

Apply the indicated series of transformations to the triangle. Each transformation is applied to the image of the previous transformation, not the original figure. Label each image with the letter of the transformation applied.

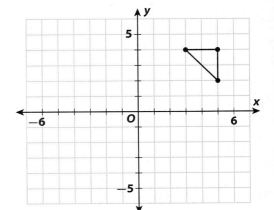

A Reflection across the x-axis

B $(x, y) \rightarrow (x - 3, y)$

C Reflection across the y-axis

D $(x, y) \rightarrow (x, y + 4)$

E Rotation 90° clockwise around the origin

F Compare the size and shape of the final image to that of the original figure.

_____

_____

Reflect

1. Which transformation(s) change the orientation of figures? Which do not?

_____

2. **Make a Conjecture** Two figures have the same size and shape. What does this indicate about the figures?

_____

_____

_____

Congruent Figures

Recall that segments and their images have the same length and angles and their images have the same measure under a translation, reflection, or rotation. Two figures are said to be **congruent** if one can be obtained from the other by a sequence of translations, reflections, and rotations. Congruent figures have the same size and shape.

When you are told that two figures are congruent, there must be a sequence of translations, reflections, and/or rotations that transforms one into the other.

EXAMPLE 1

  FL 8.G.1.2

A Identify a sequence of transformations that will transform figure *A* into figure *B*.

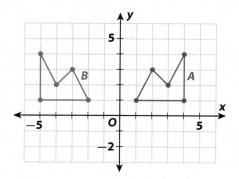

To transform figure *A* into figure *B*, you need to reflect it over the *y*-axis and translate one unit to the left. A sequence of transformations that will accomplish this is $(x, y) \rightarrow (-x, y)$ and $(x, y) \rightarrow (x - 1, y)$.

B Identify a sequence of transformations that will transform figure *B* into figure *C*.

Math Talk

Mathematical Practices

How do you know that the sequence of transformations in Parts B and C must include a rotation?

Any sequence of transformations that changes figure *B* into figure *C* will need to include a rotation. A 90° counterclockwise rotation around the origin would result in the figure being oriented as figure *C*.

However, the rotated figure would be 2 units below and 1 unit to the left of where figure *C* is. You would need to translate the rotated figure up 2 units and right 1 unit.

The sequence of transformations is a 90° counterclockwise rotation about the origin, $(x, y) \rightarrow (-y, x)$, followed by $(x, y) \rightarrow (x + 1, y + 2)$.

C Identify a sequence of transformations that will transform figure *D* into figure *E*.

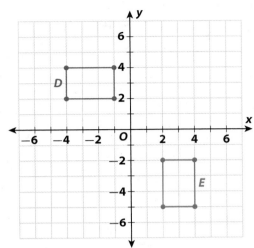

A sequence of transformations that changes figure *D* to figure *E* will need to include a rotation. A 90° clockwise rotation around the origin would result in the figure being oriented as figure *E*.

However, the rotated figure would be 6 units above where figure *E* is. You would need to translate the rotated figure down 6 units.

The sequence of transformations is a 90° clockwise rotation about the origin, $(x, y) \rightarrow (y, -x)$, followed by $(x, y) \rightarrow (x, y - 6)$.

YOUR TURN

3. Identify a sequence of transformations that will transform figure *A* into figure *B*.

_____

_____

_____

Personal Math Trainer

Online Assessment and Intervention

⏻ my.hrw.com

1. Apply the indicated series of transformations to the rectangle. Each transformation is applied to the image of the previous transformation, not the original figure. Label each image with the letter of the transformation applied. *(Explore Activity)*

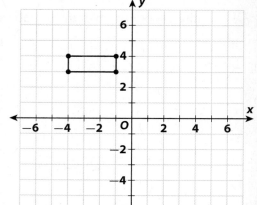

   a. Reflection across the *y*-axis

   b. Rotation 90° clockwise around the origin

   c. $(x, y) \rightarrow (x - 2, y)$

   d. Rotation 90° counterclockwise around the origin

   e. $(x, y) \rightarrow (x - 7, y - 2)$

Identify a sequence of transformations that will transform figure A into figure C. *(Example 1)*

2. What transformation is used to transform figure *A* into figure *B*?

_____

_____

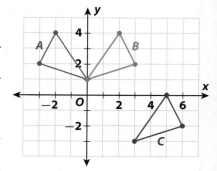

3. What transformation is used to transform figure *B* into figure *C*?

_____

_____

4. What sequence of transformations is used to transform figure *A* into figure *C*? Express the transformations algebraically.

_____

_____

5. **Vocabulary** What does it mean for two figures to be congruent?

_____

_____

6. After a sequence of translations, reflections, and rotations, what is true about the first figure and the final figure?

_____

_____

17.5 Independent Practice

 FL 8.G.1.2

Personal Math Trainer

Online Assessment and Intervention

my.hrw.com

For each given figure A, graph figures B and C using the given sequence of transformations. State whether figures A and C have the same or different orientation.

7.

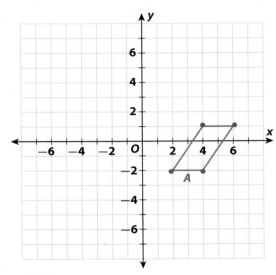

Figure B: a translation of 1 unit to the right and 3 units up

Figure C: a 90° clockwise rotation around the origin

_____

8.

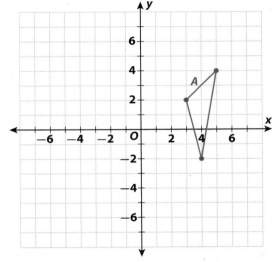

Figure B: a reflection across the y-axis

Figure C: a 180° rotation around the origin

_____

9.

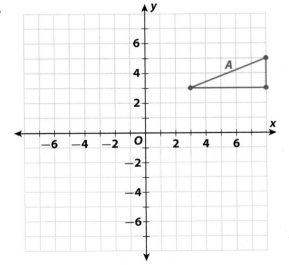

Figure B: a reflection across the y-axis

Figure C: a translation 2 units down

_____

10.

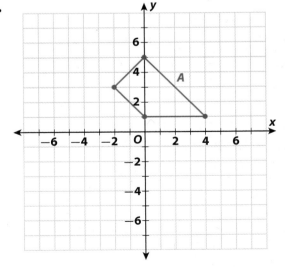

Figure B: a translation 2 units up

Figure C: a rotation of 180° around the origin

_____

11. Represent Real-World Problems A city planner wanted to place the new town library at site *A*. The mayor thought that it would be better at site *B*. What transformations were applied to the building at site *A* to relocate the building to site *B*? Did the mayor change the size or orientation of the library?

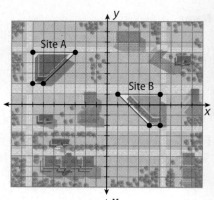

_____

_____

_____

12. Persevere in Problem Solving Find a sequence of three transformations that can be used to obtain figure *D* from figure *A*. Graph the figures *B* and *C* that are created by the transformations.

_____

_____

_____

_____

  FOCUS ON HIGHER ORDER THINKING

Work Area

13. Counterexamples The Commutative Properties for Addition and Multiplication state that the order of two numbers being added or multiplied does not change the sum or product. Are translations and rotations commutative? If not, give a counterexample.

_____

_____

_____

_____

_____

14. Multiple Representations For each representation, describe a possible sequence of transformations.

a. $(x, y) \rightarrow (-x - 2, y + 1)$

_____

_____

b. $(x, y) \rightarrow (y, -x - 3)$

_____

_____

Ready to Go On?

17.1–17.3 Properties of Translations, Reflections, and Rotations

1. Graph the image of triangle *ABC* after a translation of 6 units to the right and 4 units down. Label the vertices of the image *A'*, *B'*, and *C'*.

2. On the same coordinate grid, graph the image of triangle *ABC* after a reflection across the *x*-axis. Label the vertices of the image *A"*, *B"*, and *C"*.

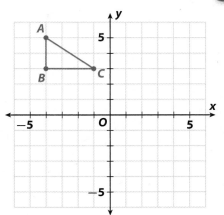

3. Graph the image of *HIJK* after it is rotated 180° about the origin. Label the vertices of the image *H'I'J'K'*.

17.4 Algebraic Representations of Transformations

4. A triangle has vertices at (2, 3), (−2, 2), and (−3, 5). What are the coordinates of the vertices of the image after the translation $(x, y) \rightarrow (x + 4, y - 3)$?

_____

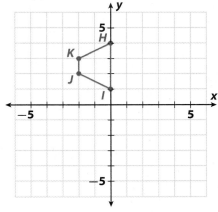

17.5 Congruent Figures

5. **Vocabulary** Translations, reflections, and rotations produce a figure

   that is _____ to the original figure.

6. Use the coordinate grid for Exercise 3. Reflect *H'I'J'K'* over the *y*-axis, then rotate it 180° about the origin. Label the new figure *H"I"J"K"*.

? **ESSENTIAL QUESTION**

7. How can you use transformations to solve real-world problems?

   _____

   _____

MODULE 17 **MIXED REVIEW**

Assessment Readiness

Personal
Math Trainer

Online
Assessment and
Intervention

⏻ **my.hrw.com**

Selected Response

1. What would be the orientation of the figure L after a translation of 8 units to the right and 3 units up?

Ⓐ

Ⓒ

Ⓑ

Ⓓ

2. Figure A is reflected over the y-axis and then lowered 6 units. Which sequence describes these transformations?

Ⓐ $(x, y) \rightarrow (x, -y)$ and $(x, y) \rightarrow (x, y - 6)$

Ⓑ $(x, y) \rightarrow (-x, y)$ and $(x, y) \rightarrow (x, y - 6)$

Ⓒ $(x, y) \rightarrow (x, -y)$ and $(x, y) \rightarrow (x - 6, y)$

Ⓓ $(x, y) \rightarrow (-x, y)$ and $(x, y) \rightarrow (x - 6, y)$

3. What quadrant would the triangle be in after a rotation of 90° counterclockwise about the origin?

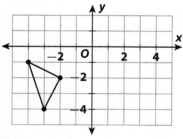

Ⓐ I   Ⓑ II   Ⓒ III   Ⓓ IV

4. Which rational number is greater than $-3\frac{1}{3}$ but less than $-\frac{4}{5}$?

Ⓐ -0.4 Ⓒ -0.19

Ⓑ $-\frac{9}{7}$ Ⓓ $-\frac{22}{5}$

5. Which of the following is **not** true of a trapezoid that has been reflected across the x-axis?

Ⓐ The new trapezoid is the same size as the original trapezoid.

Ⓑ The new trapezoid is the same shape as the original trapezoid.

Ⓒ The new trapezoid is in the same orientation as the original trapezoid.

Ⓓ The x-coordinates of the new trapezoid are the same as the x-coordinates of the original trapezoid.

6. A triangle with coordinates (6, 4), (2, −1), and (−3, 5) is translated 4 units left and rotated 180° about the origin. What are the coordinates of its image?

Ⓐ (2, 4), (−2, −1), (−7, 5)

Ⓑ (4, 6), (−1, 2), (5, −3)

Ⓒ (4, −2), (−1, 2), (5, 7)

Ⓓ (−2, −4), (2, 1), (7, −5)

Mini-Task

7. A rectangle with vertices (3, −2), (3, −4), (7, −2), (7, −4) is reflected across the x-axis and then rotated 90° counterclockwise.

   a. In what quadrant does the image lie?

   _____

   b. What are the vertices of the image?

   _____

   c. What other transformations produce the same image?

   _____

   _____

Transformations and Similarity

MODULE

18

? **ESSENTIAL QUESTION**

How can you use dilations and similarity to solve real-world problems?

Real-World Video

To plan a mural, the artist first makes a smaller drawing showing what the mural will look like. Then the image is enlarged by a scale factor on the mural canvas. This enlargement is called a dilation.

⏻ my.hrw.com

GO DIGITAL
my.hrw.com

my.hrw.com

Go digital with your write-in student edition, accessible on any device.

Math On the Spot

Scan with your smart phone to jump directly to the online edition, video tutor, and more.

Animated Math

Interactively explore key concepts to see how math works.

Personal Math Trainer

Get immediate feedback and help as you work through practice sets.

Are YOU Ready?

Complete these exercises to review skills you will need for this module.

Personal Math Trainer

Online Assessment and Intervention

my.hrw.com

Simplify Ratios

EXAMPLE $\frac{35}{21} = \frac{35 \div 7}{21 \div 7}$ To write a ratio in simplest form, find the greatest common factor of the numerator and denominator.

$= \frac{5}{3}$ Divide the numerator and denominator by the GCF.

Write each ratio in simplest form.

1. $\frac{6}{15}$ _____   **2.** $\frac{8}{20}$ _____   **3.** $\frac{30}{18}$ _____   **4.** $\frac{36}{30}$ _____

Multiply with Fractions and Decimals

EXAMPLE $2\frac{3}{5} \times 20$

$= \frac{13 \times 20}{5 \times 1}$ Write numbers as fractions and multiply.

$= \frac{13 \times \overset{4}{\cancel{20}}}{\underset{1}{\cancel{5}} \times 1}$ Simplify.

$= 52$

Multiply as you would with whole numbers.

$$\begin{array}{r} 68 \\ \times 4.5 \\ \hline 340 \\ +272 \\ \hline 306.0 \end{array}$$

Place the decimal point in the answer based on the total number of decimal places in the two factors.

Multiply.

5. $60 \times \frac{25}{100}$ **6.** 3.5×40 **7.** 4.4×44 **8.** $24 \times \frac{8}{9}$

_____   _____   _____   _____

Graph Ordered Pairs (First Quadrant)

EXAMPLE

Graph the point A(4, 3.5).
Start at the origin.
Move 4 units right.
Then move 3.5 units up.
Graph point A(4, 3.5).

Graph each point on the coordinate grid above.

9. B (9, 0)   **10.** C (2, 7)   **11.** D (0, 4.5)   **12.** E (6, 2.5)

Reading Start-Up

Visualize Vocabulary

Use the ✔ words to complete the graphic organizer. You will put one word in each rectangle.

```
┌─────────────────────┐        ┌─────────────────────┐
│  The four regions    │        │  The point where the │
│  on a coordinate     │        │  axes intersect to   │
│  plane.              │        │  form the            │
│                      │        │  coordinate plane.   │
└─────────────────────┘        └─────────────────────┘
           \                            /
            ┌─────────────────────────┐
            │    Reviewing the        │
            │    Coordinate Plane     │
            └─────────────────────────┘
           /                            \
┌─────────────────────┐        ┌─────────────────────┐
│  The horizontal      │        │  The vertical axis   │
│  axis of a coordinate│        │  of a coordinate     │
│  plane.              │        │  plane.              │
└─────────────────────┘        └─────────────────────┘
```

Understand Vocabulary

Complete the sentences using the preview words.

1. A figure larger than the original, produced through dilation, is

an _____.

2. A figure smaller than the original, produced through dilation, is

a _____.

Vocabulary

Review Words

coordinate plane *(plano cartesiano)*

image *(imagen)*

✔ origin *(origen)*

preimage *(imagen original)*

✔ quadrants *(cuadrante)*

ratio *(razón)*

scale *(escala)*

✔ x-axis *(eje x)*

✔ y-axis *(eje y)*

Preview Words

center of dilation *(centro de dilatación)*

dilation *(dilatación)*

enlargement *(agrandamiento)*

reduction *(reducción)*

scale factor *(factor de escala)*

similar *(similar)*

Active Reading

Key-Term Fold Before beginning the module, create a key-term fold to help you learn the vocabulary in this module. Write the highlighted vocabulary words on one side of the flap. Write the definition for each word on the other side of the flap. Use the key-term fold to quiz yourself on the definitions used in this module.

MODULE 18
Unpacking the Standards

Understanding the standards and the vocabulary terms in the standards will help you know exactly what you are expected to learn in this module.

FL 8.G.1.3

Describe the effect of dilations, translations, rotations, and reflections on two-dimensional figures using coordinates.

What It Means to You

You will use an algebraic representation to describe a dilation.

UNPACKING EXAMPLE 8.G.1.3

The blue square *ABCD* is the preimage. Write two algebraic representations, one for the dilation to the green square and one for the dilation to the purple square.

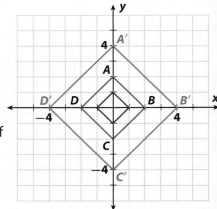

The coordinates of the vertices of the original image are multiplied by 2 for the green square.

Green square: $(x, y) \rightarrow (2x, 2y)$

The coordinates of the vertices of the original image are multiplied by $\frac{1}{2}$ for the purple square.

Purple square: $(x, y) \rightarrow \left(\frac{1}{2}x, \frac{1}{2}y\right)$

FL 8.G.1.4

Understand that a two-dimensional figure is similar to another if the second can be obtained from the first by a sequence of rotations, reflections, translations, and dilations; given two similar two-dimensional figures, describe a sequence that exhibits the similarity between them.

What It Means to You

You will describe a sequence of transformations between two similar figures.

UNPACKING EXAMPLE 8.G.1.4

Identify a sequence of two transformations that will transform figure *A* into figure *B*.

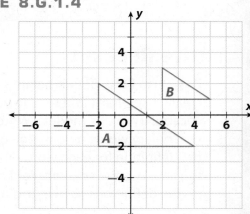

Dilate with center at the origin by a scale factor of $\frac{1}{2}$.

Then translate right 3 units and up 2 units.

LESSON 18.1 Properties of Dilations

FL 8.G.1.4
Understand that a two-dimensional figure is similar to another if the second can be obtained from the first by a sequence of ... dilations; ... Also 8.G.1.3

ESSENTIAL QUESTION

How do you describe the properties of dilations?

EXPLORE ACTIVITY 1 (Real World) FL 8.G.1.4

Exploring Dilations

The missions that placed 12 astronauts on the moon were controlled at the Johnson Space Center in Houston. The toy models at the right are scaled-down replicas of the Saturn V rocket that powered the moon flights. Each replica is a transformation called a **dilation**. Unlike the other transformations you have studied—translations, rotations, and reflections—dilations change the size (but not the shape) of a figure.

Every dilation has a fixed point called the **center of dilation** located where the lines connecting corresponding parts of figures intersect.

Triangle R'S'T' is a dilation of triangle RST. Point C is the center of dilation.

A Use a ruler to measure segments $\overline{CR}$, $\overline{CR'}$, $\overline{CS}$, $\overline{CS'}$, $\overline{CT}$, and $\overline{CT'}$ to the nearest millimeter. Record the measurements and ratios in the table.

CR'	CR	$\frac{CR'}{CR}$	CS'	CS	$\frac{CS'}{CS}$	CT'	CT	$\frac{CT'}{CT}$

B Write a conjecture based on the ratios in the table.

_____

C Measure and record the corresponding side lengths of the triangles.

R'S'	RS	$\frac{R'S'}{RS}$	S'T'	ST	$\frac{S'T'}{ST}$	R'T'	RT	$\frac{R'T'}{RT}$

D Write a conjecture based on the ratios in the table.

_____

E Measure the corresponding angles and describe your results.

_____

Center of dilation

Reflect

1. Two figures that have the same shape but different sizes are called *similar*. Are triangles *RST* and *R'S'T'* similar? Why or why not?

_____

_____

2. Compare the orientation of a figure with the orientation of its dilation.

_____

EXPLORE ACTIVITY 2 **FL** 8.G.1.3

Exploring Dilations on a Coordinate Plane

In this activity you will explore how the coordinates of a figure on a coordinate plane are affected by a dilation.

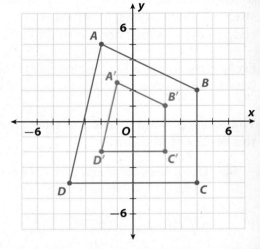

A Complete the table. Record the *x*- and *y*-coordinates of the points in the two figures and the ratios of the *x*-coordinates and the *y*-coordinates.

Vertex	x	y	Vertex	x	y	Ratio of x-coordinates (A'B'C'D' ÷ ABCD)	Ratio of y-coordinates (A'B'C'D' ÷ ABCD)
A'			A				
B'			B				
C'			C				
D'			D				

B Write a conjecture about the ratios of the coordinates of a dilation image to the coordinates of the original figure.

_____

_____

Reflect

3. In Explore Activity 1, triangle $R'S'T'$ was larger than triangle RST. How is the relationship between quadrilateral $A'B'C'D'$ and quadrilateral $ABCD$ different?

_____

Finding a Scale Factor

As you have seen in the two activities, a dilation can produce a larger figure (an **enlargement**) or a smaller figure (a **reduction**). The **scale factor** describes how much the figure is enlarged or reduced. The scale factor is the ratio of a length of the image to the corresponding length on the original figure.

In Explore Activity 1, the side lengths of triangle $R'S'T'$ were twice the length of those of triangle RST, so the scale factor was 2. In Explore Activity 2, the side lengths of quadrilateral $A'B'C'D'$ were half those of quadrilateral $ABCD$, so the scale factor was 0.5.

EXAMPLE 1   FL   8.G.1.4

An art supply store sells several sizes of drawing triangles. All are dilations of a single basic triangle. The basic triangle and one of its dilations are shown on the grid. Find the scale factor of the dilation.

STEP 1   Use the coordinates to find the lengths of the sides of each triangle.

Triangle ABC: $AC = 2$ $CB = 3$

Triangle $A'B'C'$: $A'C' = 4$ $C'B' = 6$

Since the scale factor is the same for all corresponding sides, you can record just two pairs of side lengths. Use one pair as a check on the other.

STEP 2   Find the ratios of the corresponding sides.

$\frac{A'C'}{AC} = \frac{4}{2} = 2$ $\frac{C'B'}{CB} = \frac{6}{3} = 2$

The scale factor of the dilation is 2.

Reflect

4. Is the dilation an enlargement or a reduction? How can you tell?

_____

_____

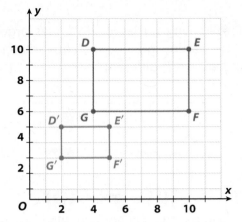

YOUR TURN

5. Find the scale factor of the dilation.

_____

_____

Math Talk

Mathematical Practices

Which scale factors lead to enlargements? Which scale factors lead to reductions?

Guided Practice

Use triangles *ABC* and *A'B'C'* for 1–5. (Explore Activities 1 and 2, Example 1)

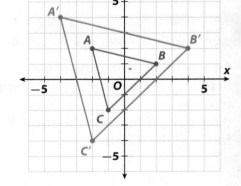

1. For each pair of corresponding vertices, find the ratio of the *x*-coordinates and the ratio of the *y*-coordinates.

   ratio of *x*-coordinates = _____

   ratio of *y*-coordinates = _____

2. I know that triangle *A'B'C'* is a dilation of triangle *ABC* because the ratios of the corresponding

   x-coordinates are _____ and the ratios of the

   corresponding *y*-coordinates are _____.

3. The ratio of the lengths of the corresponding sides of triangle *A'B'C'* and

   triangle *ABC* equals _____.

4. The corresponding angles of triangle *ABC* and triangle *A'B'C'*

   are _____.

5. The scale factor of the dilation is _____.

❓ ESSENTIAL QUESTION CHECK-IN

6. How can you find the scale factor of a dilation?

   _____

   _____

18.1 Independent Practice

 FL 8.G.1.3, 8.G.1.4

For 7–11, tell whether one figure is a dilation of the other or not. Explain your reasoning.

7. Quadrilateral *MNPQ* has side lengths of 15 mm, 24 mm, 21 mm, and 18 mm. Quadrilateral *M'N'P'Q'* has side lengths of 5 mm, 8 mm, 7 mm, and 4 mm.

_____

_____

_____

8. Triangle *RST* has angles measuring 38° and 75°. Triangle *R'S'T'* has angles measuring 67° and 38°. The sides are proportional.

_____

_____

_____

9. Two triangles, Triangle 1 and Triangle 2, are similar.

_____

_____

10. Quadrilateral *MNPQ* is the same shape but a different size than quadrilateral *M'N'P'Q*.

_____

_____

_____

_____

_____

11. On a coordinate plane, triangle *UVW* has coordinates *U*(20, −12), *V*(8, 6), and *W*(−24, −4). Triangle *U'V'W'* has coordinates *U'*(15, −9), *V'*(6, 4.5), and *W'*(−18, −3).

_____

_____

_____

_____

_____

_____

Complete the table by writing "same" or "changed" to compare the image with the original figure in the given transformation.

	Image Compared to Original Figure		
	Orientation	Size	Shape
12. Translation			
13. Reflection			
14. Rotation			
15. Dilation			

16. Describe the image of a dilation with a scale factor of 1.

_____

_____

Identify the scale factor used in each dilation.

17.

_____

18.

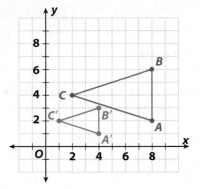

_____

Work Area

19. **Critical Thinking** Explain how you can find the center of dilation of a triangle and its dilation.

_____

_____

_____

20. **Make a Conjecture**

   a. A square on the coordinate plane has vertices at (−2, 2), (2, 2), (2, −2), and (−2, −2). A dilation of the square has vertices at (−4, 4), (4, 4), (4, −4), and (−4, −4). Find the scale factor and the perimeter of each square.

   _____

   _____

   b. A square on the coordinate plane has vertices at (−3, 3), (3, 3), (3, −3), and (−3, −3). A dilation of the square has vertices at (−6, 6), (6, 6), (6, −6), and (−6, −6). Find the scale factor and the perimeter of each square.

   _____

   _____

   c. Make a conjecture about the relationship of the scale factor to the perimeter of a square and its image.

   _____

   _____

Algebraic Representations of Dilations

FL 8.G.1.3
Describe the effect of dilations, ... on two-dimensional figures using coordinates.

ESSENTIAL QUESTION

How can you describe the effect of a dilation on coordinates using an algebraic representation?

EXPLORE ACTIVITY 1 FL 8.G.1.3

Graphing Enlargements

When a dilation in the coordinate plane has the origin as the center of dilation, you can find points on the dilated image by multiplying the x- and y-coordinates of the original figure by the scale factor. For scale factor k, the algebraic representation of the dilation is $(x, y) \rightarrow (kx, ky)$. For enlargements, $k > 1$.

The figure shown on the grid is the preimage. The center of dilation is the origin.

A List the coordinates of the vertices of the preimage in the first column of the table.

Preimage (x, y)	Image (3x, 3y)
(2, 2)	(6, 6)

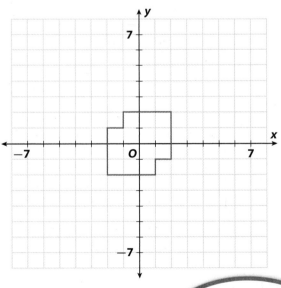

B What is the scale factor for the dilation? _____

C Apply the dilation to the preimage and write the coordinates of the vertices of the image in the second column of the table.

D Sketch the image after the dilation on the coordinate grid.

Math Talk
Mathematical Practices
What effect would the dilation $(x, y) \rightarrow (4x, 4y)$ have on the radius of a circle?

Reflect

1. How does the dilation affect the length of line segments?

_____

_____

2. How does the dilation affect angle measures?

_____

EXPLORE ACTIVITY 2 FL 8.G.1.3

Graphing Reductions

For scale factors between 0 and 1, the image is smaller than the preimage. This is called a reduction.

The arrow shown is the preimage. The center of dilation is the origin.

A List the coordinates of the vertices of the preimage in the first column of the table.

B What is the scale factor for the dilation? _____

C Apply the dilation to the preimage and write the coordinates of the vertices of the image in the second column of the table.

Preimage (x, y)	Image $\left(\frac{1}{2}x, \frac{1}{2}y\right)$

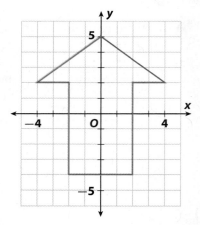

D Sketch the image after the dilation on the coordinate grid.

Reflect

3. How does the dilation affect the length of line segments?

_____

4. How would a dilation with scale factor 1 affect the preimage?

_____

Center of Dilation Outside the Image

The center of dilation can be inside *or* outside the original image and the dilated image. The center of dilation can be anywhere on the coordinate plane as long as the lines that connect each pair of corresponding vertices between the original and dilated image intersect at the center of dilation.

EXAMPLE 1

 FL 8.G.1.3

Graph the image of △ABC after a dilation with the origin as its center and a scale factor of 3. What are the vertices of the image?

STEP 1 Multiply each coordinate of the vertices of △ABC by 3 to find the vertices of the dilated image.

$$△ABC \ (x, y) \rightarrow (3x, 3y) \ △A'B'C'$$

$$A(1, 1) \rightarrow A'(1 \cdot 3, 1 \cdot 3) \rightarrow A'(3, 3)$$

$$B(3, 1) \rightarrow B'(3 \cdot 3, 1 \cdot 3) \rightarrow B'(9, 3)$$

$$C(1, 3) \rightarrow C'(1 \cdot 3, 3 \cdot 3) \rightarrow C'(3, 9)$$

The vertices of the dilated image are $A'(3, 3)$, $B'(9, 3)$, and $C'(3, 9)$.

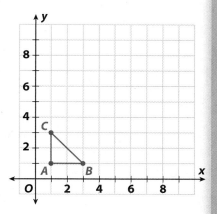

STEP 2 Graph the dilated image.

Math Talk
Mathematical Practices

Describe how you can check graphically that you have drawn the image triangle correctly.

YOUR TURN

5. Graph the image of △XYZ after a dilation with a scale factor of $\frac{1}{3}$ and the origin as its center. Then write an algebraic rule to describe the dilation.

_____

Personal Math Trainer

Online Assessment and Intervention

my.hrw.com

1. The grid shows a diamond-shaped preimage. Write the coordinates of the vertices of the preimage in the first column of the table. Then apply the dilation $(x, y) \rightarrow \left(\frac{3}{2}x, \frac{3}{2}y\right)$ and write the coordinates of the vertices of the image in the second column. Sketch the image of the figure after the dilation. (Explore Activities 1 and 2)

Preimage	Image
(2, 0)	(3, 0)

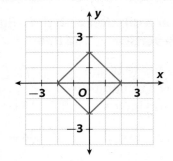

Graph the image of each figure after a dilation with the origin as its center and the given scale factor. Then write an algebraic rule to describe the dilation. (Example 1)

2. scale factor of 1.5

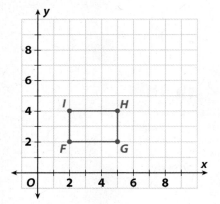

_____

3. scale factor of $\frac{1}{3}$

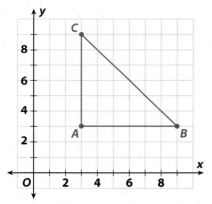

_____

? ESSENTIAL QUESTION CHECK-IN

4. A dilation of $(x, y) \rightarrow (kx, ky)$ when $0 < k < 1$ has what effect on the figure? What is the effect on the figure when $k > 1$?

_____

_____

_____

18.2 Independent Practice

FL 8.G.1.3

Personal Math Trainer

Online Assessment and Intervention

my.hrw.com

5. The blue square is the preimage. Write two algebraic representations, one for the dilation to the green square and one for the dilation to the purple square.

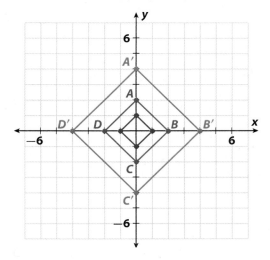

_____

_____

6. Critical Thinking A triangle has vertices $A(-5, -4)$, $B(2, 6)$, and $C(4, -3)$. The center of dilation is the origin and $(x, y) \rightarrow (3x, 3y)$. What are the vertices of the dilated image?

_____

_____

7. Critical Thinking $M'N'O'P'$ has vertices at $M'(3, 4)$, $N'(6, 4)$, $O'(6, 7)$, and $P'(3, 7)$. The center of dilation is the origin. $MNOP$ has vertices at $M(4.5, 6)$, $N(9, 6)$, $O'(9, 10.5)$, and $P'(4.5, 10.5)$. What is the algebraic representation of this dilation?

_____

8. Critical Thinking A dilation with center $(0,0)$ and scale factor k is applied to a polygon. What dilation can you apply to the image to return it to the original preimage?

_____

9. Represent Real-World Problems The blueprints for a new house are scaled so that $\frac{1}{4}$ inch equals 1 foot. The blueprint is the preimage and the house is the dilated image. The blueprints are plotted on a coordinate plane.

a. What is the scale factor in terms of inches to inches?

_____

b. One inch on the blueprint represents how many inches in the actual house? How many feet?

_____

c. Write the algebraic representation of the dilation from the blueprint to the house.

_____

d. A rectangular room has coordinates $Q(2, 2)$, $R(7, 2)$, $S(7, 5)$, and $T(2, 5)$ on the blueprint. The homeowner wants this room to be 25% larger. What are the coordinates of the new room?

_____

_____

e. What are the dimensions of the new room, in inches, on the blueprint? What will the dimensions of the new room be, in feet, in the new house?

_____

_____

_____

10. Write the algebraic representation of the dilation shown.

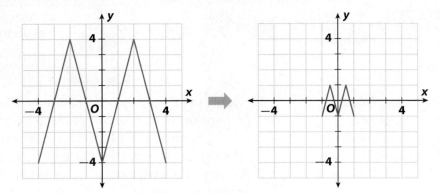

_____

Work Area

11. Critique Reasoning The set for a school play needs a replica of a historic building painted on a backdrop that is 20 feet long and 16 feet high. The actual building measures 400 feet long and 320 feet high. A stage crewmember writes $(x, y) \rightarrow \left(\frac{1}{12}x, \frac{1}{12}y\right)$ to represent the dilation. Is the crewmember's calculation correct if the painted replica is to cover the entire backdrop? Explain.

_____

_____

12. Communicate Mathematical Ideas Explain what each of these algebraic transformations does to a figure.

a. $(x, y) \rightarrow (y, -x)$ _____

b. $(x, y) \rightarrow (-x, -y)$ _____

c. $(x, y) \rightarrow (x, 2y)$ _____

_____

d. $(x, y) \rightarrow \left(\frac{2}{3}x, y\right)$ _____

_____

e. $(x, y) \rightarrow (0.5x, 1.5y)$ _____

_____

13. Communicate Mathematical Ideas Triangle *ABC* has coordinates $A(1, 5)$, $B(-2, 1)$, and $C(-2, 4)$. Sketch triangle *ABC* and $A'B'C'$ for the dilation $(x, y) \rightarrow (-2x, -2y)$. What is the effect of a negative scale factor?

_____

_____

FL 8.G.1.4

Understand that a ... figure is similar to another if the second can be obtained ... by a sequence of rotations, reflections, translations, and dilations; given two similar ... figures, describe a sequence that exhibits the similarity between them.

ESSENTIAL QUESTION

What is the connection between transformations and similar figures?

EXPLORE ACTIVITY FL 8.G.1.4

Combining Transformations with Dilations

When creating an animation, figures need to be translated, reflected, rotated, and sometimes dilated. As an example of this, apply the indicated sequence of transformations to the rectangle. Each transformation is applied to the image of the previous transformation, not to the original figure. Label each image with the letter of the transformation applied.

A $(x, y) \rightarrow (x + 7, y - 2)$

B $(x, y) \rightarrow (x, -y)$

C rotation 90° clockwise around the origin

D $(x, y) \rightarrow (x + 5, y + 3)$

E $(x, y) \rightarrow (3x, 3y)$

F List the coordinates of the vertices of rectangle *E*.

_____

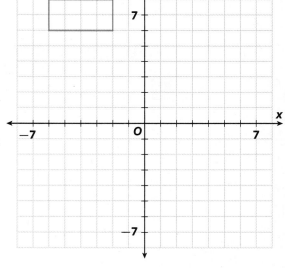

G Compare the following attributes of rectangle *E* to those of the original figure.

Shape	
Size	
Angle Measures	

EXPLORE ACTIVITY *(cont'd)*

Reflect

1. Which transformation represents the dilation? How can you tell?

_____

_____

2. A sequence of transformations containing a single dilation is applied to a figure. Are the original figure and its final image congruent? Explain.

_____

_____

Math On the Spot

my.hrw.com

Similar Figures

Two figures are **similar** if one can be obtained from the other by a sequence of translations, reflections, rotations, and dilations. Similar figures have the same shape but may be different sizes.

When you are told that two figures are similar, there must be a sequence of translations, reflections, rotations, and/or dilations that can transform one to the other.

EXAMPLE 1

 FL 8.G.1.4

A Identify a sequence of transformations that will transform figure *A* into figure *B*. Tell whether the figures are congruent. Tell whether they are similar.

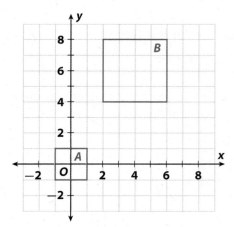

My Notes

Both figures are squares whose orientations are the same, so no reflection or rotation is needed. Figure *B* has sides twice as long as figure *A*, so a dilation with a scale factor of 2 is needed. Figure *B* is moved to the right and above figure *A*, so a translation is needed. A sequence of transformations that will accomplish this is a dilation by a scale factor of 2 centered at the origin followed by the translation $(x, y) \rightarrow (x + 4, y + 6)$. The figures are not congruent, but they are similar.

B Identify a sequence of transformations that will transform figure *C* into figure *D*. Include a reflection. Tell whether the figures are congruent. Tell whether they are similar.

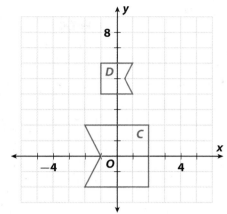

The orientation of figure *D* is reversed from that of figure *C*, so a reflection over the *y*-axis is needed. Figure *D* has sides that are half as long as figure *C*, so a dilation with a scale factor of $\frac{1}{2}$ is needed. Figure *D* is moved above figure *C*, so a translation is needed. A sequence of transformations that will accomplish this is a dilation by a scale factor of $\frac{1}{2}$ centered at the origin, followed by the reflection $(x, y) \rightarrow (-x, y)$, followed by the translation $(x, y) \rightarrow (x, y + 5)$. The figures are not congruent, but they are similar.

Math Talk
Mathematical Practices
A figure and its image have different sizes and orientations. What do you know about the sequence of transformations that generated the image?

C Identify a sequence of transformations that will transform figure *C* into figure *D*. Include a rotation.

The orientation of figure *D* is reversed from that of figure *C*, so a rotation of 180° is needed. Figure *D* has sides that are half as long as figure *C*, so a dilation with a scale factor of $\frac{1}{2}$ is needed. Figure *D* is moved above figure *C*, so a translation is needed. A sequence of transformations that will accomplish this is a rotation of 180° about the origin, followed by a dilation by a scale factor of $\frac{1}{2}$ centered at the origin, followed by the translation $(x, y) \rightarrow (x, y + 5)$.

YOUR TURN

3. Look again at the Explore Activity. Start with the original figure. Create a new sequence of transformations that will yield figure *E*, the final image. Your transformations do not need to produce the images in the same order in which they originally appeared.

_____

_____

_____

Personal Math Trainer

Online Assessment and Intervention

⊙ my.hrw.com

1. Apply the indicated sequence of transformations to the square. Apply each transformation to the image of the previous transformation. Label each image with the letter of the transformation applied.
(Explore Activity)

   A $(x, y) \rightarrow (-x, y)$

   B Rotate the square 180° around the origin.

   C $(x, y) \rightarrow (x - 5, y - 6)$

   D $(x, y) \rightarrow (\frac{1}{2}x, \frac{1}{2}y)$

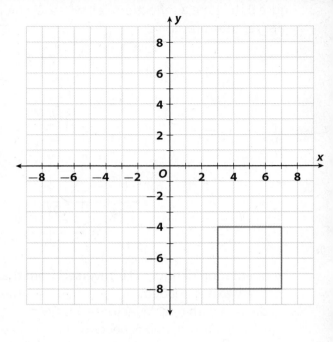

Identify a sequence of two transformations that will transform figure A into the given figure. (Example 1)

2. figure B

   _____

   _____

3. figure C

   _____

   _____

4. figure D

   _____

   _____

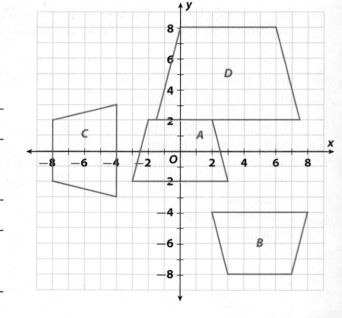

5. If two figures are similar but not congruent, what do you know about the sequence of transformations used to create one from the other?

   _____

   _____

18.3 Independent Practice

 FL 8.G.1.4

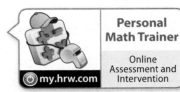

Personal
Math Trainer

Online
Assessment and
Intervention
my.hrw.com

6. A designer creates a drawing of a triangular sign on centimeter grid paper for a new business. The drawing has sides measuring 6 cm, 8 cm, and 10 cm, and angles measuring 37°, 53°, and 90°. To create the actual sign shown, the drawing must be dilated using a scale factor of 40.

a. Find the lengths of the sides of the actual sign.

_____

b. Find the angle measures of the actual sign.

_____

c. The drawing has the hypotenuse on the bottom. The business owner would like it on the top. Describe two transformations that will do this.

_____

_____

d. The shorter leg of the drawing is currently on the left. The business owner wants it to remain on the left after the hypotenuse goes to the top. Which transformation in part c will accomplish this?

_____

In Exercises 7–10, the transformation of a figure into its image is described. Describe the transformations that will transform the image back into the original figure. Then write them algebraically.

7. The figure is reflected across the *x*-axis and dilated by a scale factor of 3.

_____

_____

8. The figure is dilated by a scale factor of 0.5 and translated 6 units left and 3 units up.

_____

_____

9. The figure is dilated by a scale factor of 5 and rotated 90° clockwise.

_____

_____

10. The figure is reflected across the *y*-axis and dilated by a scale factor of 4.

_____

_____

Work Area

11. **Draw Conclusions** A figure undergoes a sequence of transformations that include dilations. The figure and its final image are congruent. Explain how this can happen.

_____

_____

_____

12. **Multistep** As with geometric figures, graphs can be transformed through translations, reflections, rotations, and dilations. The equation $y = x$ is graphed at the right. Describe how the graph is changed through each of the following transformations.

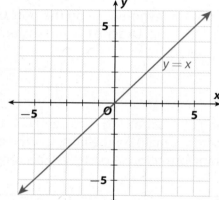

a. a dilation by a scale factor of 4, producing the graph of the equation $y = 4x$

_____

_____

_____

b. a translation producing the graph of the equation $y = x - 3$.

_____

_____

c. a reflection across the *y*-axis

_____

_____

13. **Justify Reasoning** The graph of the line $y = x$ is dilated by a scale factor of 3 and then translated up 5 units. Is this the same as translating the graph up 5 units and then dilating by a scale factor of 3? Explain. How are the new graphs related?

_____

_____

Ready to Go On?

Personal Math Trainer
Online Assessment and Intervention

my.hrw.com

18.1 Properties of Dilations

Determine whether one figure is a dilation of the other. Justify your answer.

1. Triangle *XYZ* has angles measuring 54° and 29°. Triangle *X'Y'Z'* has angles measuring 29° and 92°.

_____

2. Quadrilateral *DEFG* has sides measuring 16 m, 28 m, 24 m, and 20 m. Quadrilateral *D'E'F'G'* has sides measuring 20 m, 35 m, 30 m, and 25 m.

_____

_____

18.2 Algebraic Representations of Dilations

Dilate each figure with the origin as the center of dilation.

3. $(x, y) \rightarrow (0.8x, 0.8y)$

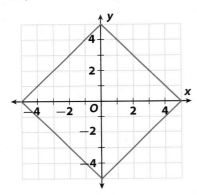

4. $(x, y) \rightarrow (2.5x, 2.5y)$

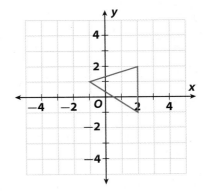

18.3 Similar Figures

5. Describe what happens to a figure when the given sequence of transformations is applied to it: $(x, y) \rightarrow (-x, y)$; $(x, y) \rightarrow (0.5x, 0.5y)$; $(x, y) \rightarrow (x - 2, y + 2)$

_____

_____

? ESSENTIAL QUESTION

6. How can you use dilations to solve real-world problems?

_____

Assessment Readiness

Personal
Math Trainer

Online
Assessment and
Intervention

my.hrw.com

Selected Response

1. A rectangle has vertices (6, 4), (2, 4), (6, −2), and (2, −2). What are the coordinates of the vertices of the image after a dilation with the origin as its center and a scale factor of 1.5?

- Ⓐ (9, 6), (3, 6), (9, −3), (3, −3)
- Ⓑ (3, 2), (1, 2), (3, −1), (1, −1)
- Ⓒ (12, 8), (4, 8), (12, −4), (4, −4)
- Ⓓ (15, 10), (5, 10), (15, −5), (5, −5)

2. Which represents the dilation shown where the black figure is the preimage?

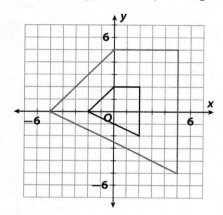

- Ⓐ $(x, y) \rightarrow (1.5x, 1.5y)$
- Ⓑ $(x, y) \rightarrow (2.5x, 2.5y)$
- Ⓒ $(x, y) \rightarrow (3x, 3y)$
- Ⓓ $(x, y) \rightarrow (6x, 6y)$

3. Identify the sequence of transformations that will reflect a figure over the *x*-axis and then dilate it by a scale factor of 3.

- Ⓐ $(x, y) \rightarrow (−x, y); (x, y) \rightarrow (3x, 3y)$
- Ⓑ $(x, y) \rightarrow (−x, y); (x, y) \rightarrow (x, 3y)$
- Ⓒ $(x, y) \rightarrow (x, −y); (x, y) \rightarrow (3x, y)$
- Ⓓ $(x, y) \rightarrow (x, −y); (x, y) \rightarrow (3x, 3y)$

4. Solve $−a + 7 = 2a − 8$.

- Ⓐ $a = −3$
- Ⓒ $a = 5$
- Ⓑ $a = −\frac{1}{3}$
- Ⓓ $a = 15$

5. Which equation does **not** represent a line with an *x*-intercept of 3?

- Ⓐ $y = −2x + 6$
- Ⓒ $y = \frac{2}{3}x − 2$
- Ⓑ $y = −\frac{1}{3}x + 1$
- Ⓓ $y = 3x − 1$

Mini-Task

6. The square is dilated under the dilation $(x, y) \rightarrow (0.25x, 0.25y)$.

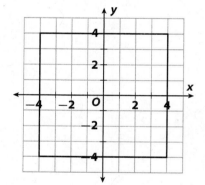

a. Graph the image. What are the coordinates?

_____

b. What is the length of a side of the image?

_____

c. What are the perimeter and area of the preimage?

_____

d. What are the perimeter and area of the image?

_____

Study Guide Review

Transformations and Congruence

Key Vocabulary

center of rotation *(centro de rotación)*

congruent *(congruente)*

image *(imagen)*

line of reflection *(línea de reflexión)*

preimage *(imagen original)*

reflection *(reflexión)*

rotation *(rotación)*

transformation *(transformación)*

translation *(traslación)*

? ESSENTIAL QUESTION

How can you use transformations and congruence to solve real-world problems?

EXAMPLE

Translate triangle *XYZ* left 4 units and down 2 units. Graph the image and label the vertices.

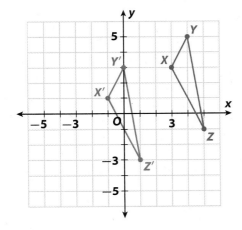

Translate the vertices by subtracting 4 from each *x*-coordinate and 2 from each *y*-coordinate. The new vertices are $X'(-1, 1)$, $Y'(0, 3)$, and $Z'(1, -3)$.

Connect the vertices to draw triangle $X'Y'Z'$.

EXERCISES

Perform the transformation shown. (Lessons 17.1, 17.2, 17.3)

1. Reflection over the *x*-axis

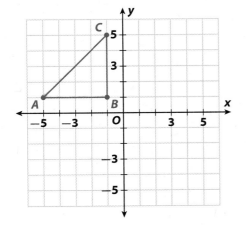

2. Translation 5 units right

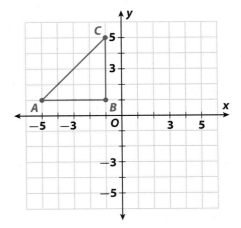

3. Rotation 90° counterclockwise about the origin

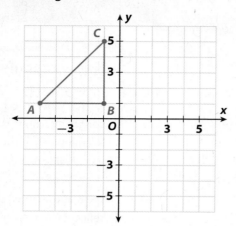

4. Translation 4 units right and 4 units down

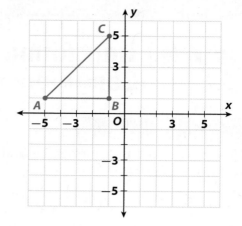

5. Quadrilateral *ABCD* with vertices *A*(4, 4), *B*(5, 1), *C*(5, −1) and *D*(4, −2) is translated left 2 units and down 3 units. Graph the preimage and the image. (Lesson 17.4)

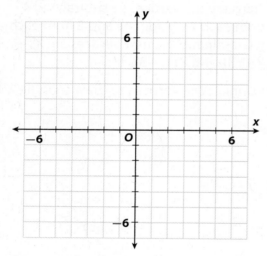

6. Triangle *ABC* with vertices *A*(1, 2), *B*(1, 4), and *C*(3, 3) is translated by $(x, y) \rightarrow (x - 4, y)$, and the result is reflected by $(x, y) \rightarrow (x, -y)$. Graph the preimage and the image. (Lesson 17.5)

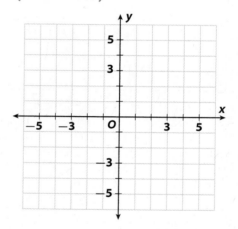

7. Triangle *RST* has vertices at (−8, 2), (−4, 0), and (−12, 8). Find the vertices after the triangle has been reflected over the *y*-axis. (Lesson 17.4)

_____

8. Triangle *XYZ* has vertices at (3, 7), (9, 14), and (12, −1). Find the vertices after the triangle has been rotated 180° about the origin. (Lesson 17.4)

_____

9. Triangle *MNP* has its vertices located at (−1, −4), (−2, −5), and (−3, −3). Find the vertices after the triangle has been reflected by $(x, y) \rightarrow (x, -y)$ and translated by $(x, y) \rightarrow (x + 6, y)$. (Lesson 17.5)

_____

Transformations and Similarity

Key Vocabulary

center of dilation *(centro de dilatación)*

dilation *(dilatación)*

enlargement *(agrandamiento)*

reduction *(reducción)*

scale factor *(factor de escala)*

similar *(semejantes)*

? ESSENTIAL QUESTION

How can you use dilations, similarity, and proportionality to solve real-world problems?

EXAMPLE

Dilate triangle *ABC* with the origin as the center of dilation and scale factor $\frac{1}{2}$. Graph the dilated image.

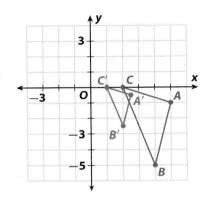

Multiply each coordinate of the vertices of *ABC* by $\frac{1}{2}$ to find the vertices of the dilated image.

$$A(5, -1) \to A'\left(5 \cdot \frac{1}{2}, -1 \cdot \frac{1}{2}\right) \to A'\left(2\frac{1}{2}, -\frac{1}{2}\right)$$

$$B(4, -5) \to B'\left(4 \cdot \frac{1}{2}, -5 \cdot \frac{1}{2}\right) \to B'\left(2, -2\frac{1}{2}\right)$$

$$C(2, 0) \to C'\left(2 \cdot \frac{1}{2}, 0 \cdot \frac{1}{2}\right) \to C'(1, 0)$$

EXERCISES

1. For each pair of corresponding vertices, find the ratio of the *x*-coordinates and the ratio of the *y*-coordinates. (Lesson 18.1)

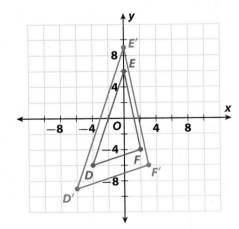

Ratio of *x*-coordinates: _____

Ratio of *y*-coordinates: _____

What is the scale factor of the dilation? _____

2. Rectangle *WXYZ* has vertices at $(-2, -1)$, $(-2, 1)$, $(2, -1)$, and $(2, 1)$. It is first dilated by $(x, y) \to (2x, 2y)$, and then translated by $(x, y) \to (x, y + 3)$. (Lesson 18.3)

a. What are the vertices of the image? _____

b. Are the preimage and image congruent? Are they similar? Explain.

_____

_____

Dilate each figure with the origin as the center of the dilation. List the vertices of the dilated figure then graph the figure. (Lesson 18.2)

3. $(x, y) \rightarrow \left(\frac{1}{4}x, \frac{1}{4}y \right)$

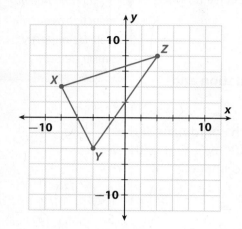

4. $(x, y) \rightarrow (2x, 2y)$

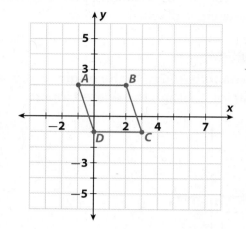

Unit 8 Performance Tasks

1. **CAREERS IN MATH** Contractor Fernando is expanding his dog's play yard. The original yard has a fence represented by rectangle *LMNO* on the coordinate plane. Fernando hires a contractor to construct a new fence that should enclose 6 times as much area as the current fence. The shape of the fence must remain the same. The contractor constructs the fence shown by rectangle *L'M'N'O'*.

   a. Did the contractor increase the area by the amount Fernando wanted? Explain.

   _____

   _____

   b. Does the new fence maintain the shape of the old fence? How do you know?

   _____

   _____

2. A sail for a sailboat is represented by a triangle on the coordinate plane with vertices (0, 0), (5, 0), and (5, 4). The triangle is dilated by a scale factor of 1.5 with the origin as the center of dilation. Find the coordinates of the dilated triangle. Are the triangles similar? Explain.

   _____

   _____

UNIT 8 MIXED REVIEW

Assessment Readiness

Personal
Math Trainer

Online
Assessment and
Intervention

my.hrw.com

Selected Response

1. What would be the orientation of the figure below after a reflection over the *x*-axis?

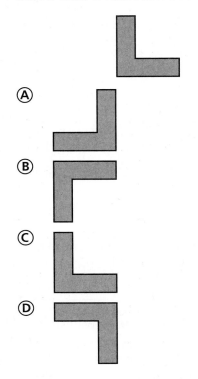

Ⓐ

Ⓑ

Ⓒ

Ⓓ

2. A triangle with coordinates (4, 2), (0, −3), and (−5, 3) is translated 5 units right and rotated 180° about the origin. What are the coordinates of its image?

Ⓐ (9, 2), (−1, −2), (5, −7)

Ⓑ (−10, 3), (−1, 2), (−5, −3)

Ⓒ (2, −1), (−3, −5), (3, −10)

Ⓓ (−9, −2), (−5, 3), (0, −3)

3. Quadrilateral *LMNP* has sides measuring 16, 28, 12, and 32. Which could be the side lengths of a dilation of *LMNP*?

Ⓐ 24, 40, 18, 90

Ⓑ 32, 60, 24, 65

Ⓒ 20, 35, 15, 40

Ⓓ 40, 70, 30, 75

4. The table below represents which equation?

x	−1	0	1	2
y	1	−2	−5	−8

Ⓐ $y = x + 2$

Ⓑ $y = -x$

Ⓒ $y = 3x + 6$

Ⓓ $y = -3x - 2$

5. Which of the following is **not** true of a trapezoid that has been translated 8 units down?

Ⓐ The new trapezoid is the same size as the original trapezoid.

Ⓑ The new trapezoid is the same shape as the original trapezoid.

Ⓒ The new trapezoid is in the same orientation as the original trapezoid.

Ⓓ The *y*-coordinates of the new trapezoid are the same as the *y*-coordinates of the original trapezoid.

6. Which represents a reduction?

Ⓐ $(x, y) \rightarrow (0.9x, 0.9y)$

Ⓑ $(x, y) \rightarrow (1.4x, 1.4y)$

Ⓒ $(x, y) \rightarrow (0.7x, 0.3y)$

Ⓓ $(x, y) \rightarrow (2.5x, 2.5y)$

7. Which is the solution for $4(x + 1) = 2(3x - 2)$?

Ⓐ $x = -4$

Ⓑ $x = -1$

Ⓒ $x = 0$

Ⓓ $x = 4$

8. A rectangle has vertices (8, 6), (4, 6), (8, −4), and (4, −4). What are the coordinates after dilating from the origin by a scale factor of 1.5?

Ⓐ (9, 6), (3, 6), (9, −3), (3, −3)

Ⓑ (10, 8), (5, 8), (10, −5), (5, −5)

Ⓒ (16, 12), (8, 12), (16, −8), (8, −8)

Ⓓ (12, 9), (6, 9), (12, −6), (6, −6)

Make sure you look at all answer choices before making your decision. Try substituting each answer choice into the problem if you are unsure of the answer.

9. Two apples plus four bananas cost $2.00. An apple costs twice as much as a banana. Using the equations $2a + 4b = 2.00$ and $a = 2b$, where a is the cost of one apple and b is the cost of one banana, what are a and b?

Ⓐ $a = \$0.25$; $b = \$0.25$

Ⓑ $a = \$0.25$; $b = \$0.50$

Ⓒ $a = \$0.50$; $b = \$0.25$

Ⓓ $a = \$0.50$; $b = \$0.50$

10. Which statement is false?

Ⓐ No integers are irrational numbers.

Ⓑ All whole numbers are integers.

Ⓒ No real numbers are rational numbers.

Ⓓ All integers greater than or equal to 0 are whole numbers.

11. Consider the system of equations $3x + 4y = 2$ and $2x - 4y = 8$. Which is its solution?

Ⓐ $x = -1, y = -2$

Ⓑ $x = 1, y = 2$

Ⓒ $x = -2, y = 1$

Ⓓ $x = 2, y = -1$

Mini-Tasks

12. A triangle with vertices (−2, −3), (−4, 0), and (0, 0) is congruent to a second triangle located in quadrant I with two of its vertices at (3, 2) and (1, 5).

a. Graph the two triangles on the same coordinate grid.

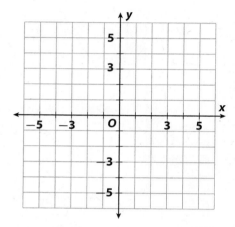

b. What are the coordinates of the third vertex of the second triangle?

_____

13. Tamiko is planning a stone wall shaped like a triangle, with vertices at (−1, −2), (2, 2), and (−2, 2) on a coordinate grid. She plans to add a second wall, in the same shape, enclosing the first wall, with the origin as the center of dilation. The vertices of the second wall are (−3, −6), (6, 6), and (−6, 6).

a. What scale factor did Tamiko use for the second wall?

_____

b. Are the two walls similar? Explain.

_____

_____

_____

_____

Measurement Geometry

CAREERS IN MATH

Hydrologist A hydrologist is a scientist who studies and solves water-related issues. A hydrologist might work to prevent or clean up polluted water sources, locate water supplies for urban or rural needs, or control flooding and erosion. A hydrologist uses math to assess water resources and mathematical models to understand water systems, as well as statistics to analyze phenomena such as rainfall patterns. If you are interested in a career as a hydrologist, you should study the following mathematical subjects:

- Algebra
- Trigonometry
- Calculus
- Statistics

Research other careers that require creating and using mathematical models to understand physical phenomena.

Unit 9 Performance Task

At the end of the unit, check out how **hydrologists** use math.

Vocabulary Preview

Use the puzzle to preview key vocabulary from this unit. Unscramble the circled letters to answer the riddle at the bottom of the page.

Across

1. The angle formed by two sides of a triangle (2 words) (Lesson 19.2)

5. A three-dimensional figure that has two congruent circular bases. (Lesson 21.1)

6. A three-dimensional figure with all points the same distance from the center. (Lesson 21.3)

Down

2. The line that intersects two or more lines. (Lesson 19.1)

3. The side opposite the right angle in a right triangle. (Lesson 20.1)

4. Figures with the same shape but not necessarily the same size. (Lesson 19.3)

5. A three-dimensional figure that has one vertex and one circular base. (Lesson 21.2)

Q: What do you call an angle that is adorable?

A: __ _____ _____!

Angle Relationships in Parallel Lines and Triangles

? ESSENTIAL QUESTION

How can you use angle relationships in parallel lines and triangles to solve real-world problems?

my.hrw.com

Real-World Video

Many cities are designed on a grid with parallel streets. If another street runs across the parallel lines, it is a transversal. Special relationships exist between parallel lines and transversals.

GO DIGITAL
my.hrw.com

my.hrw.com

Go digital with your write-in student edition, accessible on any device.

Math On the Spot

Scan with your smart phone to jump directly to the online edition, video tutor, and more.

Animated Math

Interactively explore key concepts to see how math works.

Personal Math Trainer

Get immediate feedback and help as you work through practice sets.

Are YOU Ready?

Complete these exercises to review skills you will need for this module.

Personal
Math Trainer

Online
Assessment and
Intervention

my.hrw.com

Solve Two-Step Equations

EXAMPLE	$7x + 9 = 30$	Write the equation.
	$7x + 9 - 9 = 30 - 9$	Subtract 9 from both sides.
	$7x = 21$	Simplify.
	$\frac{7x}{7} = \frac{21}{7}$	Divide both sides by 7.
	$x = 3$	Simplify.

Solve for *x*.

1. $6x + 10 = 46$ **2.** $7x - 6 = 36$ **3.** $3x + 26 = 59$ **4.** $2x + 5 = -25$

_____   _____   _____   _____

5. $6x - 7 = 41$ **6.** $\frac{1}{2}x + 9 = 30$ **7.** $\frac{1}{3}x - 7 = 15$ **8.** $0.5x - 0.6 = 8.4$

_____   _____   _____   _____

Name Angles

EXAMPLE

Use three points of an angle, including the vertex, to name the angle. Write the vertex between the other two points: $\angle JKL$ or $\angle LKJ$. You can also use just the vertex letter to name the angle if there is no danger of confusing the angle with another. This is also $\angle K$.

Give two names for the angle formed by the dashed rays.

9. _____   **10.** _____   **11.** _____

Reading Start-Up

Visualize Vocabulary

Use the ✔ words to complete the graphic. You can put more than one word in each section of the triangle.

Reviewing Angles

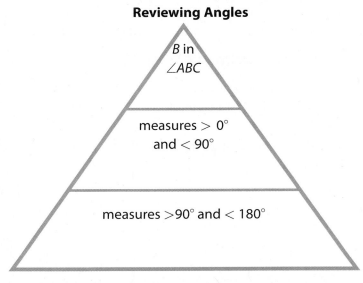

B in
∠*ABC*

measures > 0°
and < 90°

measures >90° and < 180°

Understand Vocabulary

Complete the sentences using preview words.

1. A line that intersects two or more lines is a _____.

2. Figures with the same shape but not necessarily the same size
   are _____.

3. An _____ is an angle formed by one side of
   the triangle and the extension of an adjacent side.

Active Reading

Pyramid Before beginning the module, create a pyramid to help you organize what you learn. Label each side with one of the lesson titles from this module. As you study each lesson, write important ideas like vocabulary, properties, and formulas on the appropriate side.

Unpacking the Standards

Understanding the standards and the vocabulary terms in the standards will help you know exactly what you are expected to learn in this module.

 FL 8.G.1.5

Use informal arguments to establish facts about the angle sum and exterior angle of triangles, about the angles created when parallel lines are cut by a transversal, and the angle-angle criterion for similarity of triangles.

Key Vocabulary

transversal *(transversal)*
A line that intersects two or more lines.

What It Means to You

You will learn about the special angle relationships formed when parallel lines are intersected by a third line called a transversal.

UNPACKING EXAMPLE 8.G.1.5

Which angles formed by the transversal and the parallel lines seem to be congruent?

It appears that the angles below are congruent.

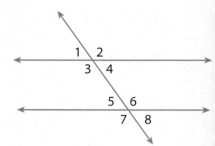

$\angle 1 \cong \angle 4 \cong \angle 5 \cong \angle 8$

$\angle 2 \cong \angle 3 \cong \angle 6 \cong \angle 7$

 FL 8.G.1.5

Use informal arguments to establish facts about the angle sum and exterior angle of triangles, about the angles created when parallel lines are cut by a transversal, and the angle-angle criterion for similarity of triangles.

What It Means to You

You will use the angle-angle criterion to determine similarity of two triangles.

UNPACKING EXAMPLE 8.G.1.5

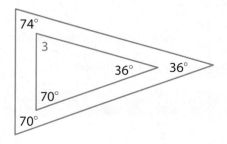

Explain whether the triangles are similar.

Two angles in the large triangle are congruent to two angles in the smaller triangle, so the third pair of angles must also be congruent, which makes the triangles similar.

$70° + 36° + m\angle 3 = 180°$

$m\angle 3 = 74°$

Parallel Lines Cut by a Transversal

FL 8.G.1.5

Use informal arguments to establish facts about... the angles created when parallel lines are cut by a transversal....

ESSENTIAL QUESTION

What can you conclude about the angles formed by parallel lines that are cut by a transversal?

EXPLORE ACTIVITY 1   FL 8.G.1.5

Parallel Lines and Transversals

A **transversal** is a line that intersects two lines in the same plane at two different points. Transversal t and lines a and b form eight angles.

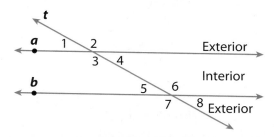

Angle Pairs Formed by a Transversal	
Term	**Example**
Corresponding angles lie on the same side of the transversal t, on the same side of lines a and b.	$\angle 1$ and $\angle 5$
Alternate interior angles are nonadjacent angles that lie on opposite sides of the transversal t, between lines a and b.	$\angle 3$ and $\angle 6$
Alternate exterior angles lie on opposite sides of the transversal t, outside lines a and b.	$\angle 1$ and $\angle 8$
Same-side interior angles lie on the same side of the transversal t, between lines a and b.	$\angle 3$ and $\angle 5$

Use geometry software to explore the angles formed when a transversal intersects parallel lines.

A Construct a line and label two points on the line A and B.

B Create point C not on $\overleftrightarrow{AB}$. Then construct a line parallel to $\overleftrightarrow{AB}$ through point C. Create another point on this line and label it D.

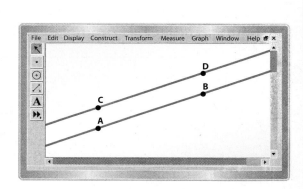

C Create two points outside the two parallel lines and label them *E* and *F*. Construct transversal $\overleftrightarrow{EF}$. Label the points of intersection *G* and *H*.

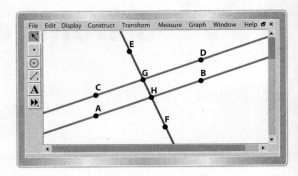

D Measure the angles formed by the parallel lines and the transversal. Write the angle measures in the table below.

E Drag point *E* or point *F* to a different position. Record the new angle measures in the table.

Angle	∠CGE	∠DGE	∠CGH	∠DGH	∠AHG	∠BHG	∠AHF	∠BHF
Measure								
Measure								

Reflect

Make a Conjecture Identify the pairs of angles in the diagram. Then make a conjecture about their angle measures. Drag a point in the diagram to confirm your conjecture.

1. corresponding angles

   _____

   _____

   _____

2. alternate interior angles

   _____

   _____

3. alternate exterior angles

   _____

   _____

4. same-side interior angles

   _____

   _____

Justifying Angle Relationships

You can use tracing paper to informally justify your conclusions from the first Explore Activity.

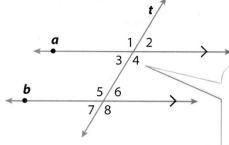

Lines *a* and *b* are parallel. (The black arrows on the diagram indicate parallel lines.)

> Recall that vertical angles are the opposite angles formed by two intersecting lines. ∠1 and ∠4 are vertical angles.

A Trace the diagram onto tracing paper.

B Position the tracing paper over the original diagram so that ∠1 on the tracing is over ∠5 on the original diagram. Compare the two angles. Do they appear to be congruent?

_____

_____

Math Talk
Mathematical Practices
What do you notice about the special angle pairs formed by the transversal?

C Use the tracing paper to compare all eight angles in the diagram to each other. List all of the congruent angle pairs.

_____

_____

_____

Finding Unknown Angle Measures

You can find any unknown angle measure when two parallel lines are cut by a transversal if you are given at least one other angle measure.

Math On the Spot
⊙ my.hrw.com

EXAMPLE 1   FL 8.G.1.5

A **Find m∠2 when m∠7 = 125°.**

∠2 is congruent to ∠7 because they are alternate exterior angles.

Therefore, m∠2 = 125°.

B **Find m∠VWZ.**

∠VWZ is supplementary to ∠YVW because they are same-side interior angles.
m∠VWZ + m∠YVW = 180°

Animated Math
⊙ my.hrw.com

From the previous page, m∠VWZ + m∠YVW = 180°, m∠VWZ = 3x°, and m∠YVW = 6x°.

$$m\angle VWZ + m\angle YVW = 180°$$

$$3x° + 6x° = 180°$$ Replace m∠VWZ with 3x° and m∠YVW with 6x°.

$$9x = 180$$ Combine like terms.

$$\frac{9x}{9} = \frac{180}{9}$$ Divide both sides by 9.

$$x = 20$$ Simplify.

$$m\angle VWZ = 3x° = (3 \cdot 20)° = 60°$$

Personal Math Trainer

Online Assessment and Intervention

my.hrw.com

YOUR TURN

Find each angle measure.

5. m∠GDE = _____

6. m∠BEF = _____

7. m∠CDG = _____

Guided Practice

Use the figure for Exercises 1–4. (Explore Activity 1 and Example 1)

1. ∠UVY and _____ are a pair of corresponding angles.

2. ∠WVY and ∠VWT are _____ angles.

3. Find m∠SVW. _____

4. Find m∠VWT. _____

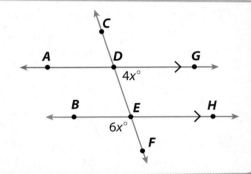

5. **Vocabulary** When two parallel lines are cut by a transversal,

_____ angles are supplementary. (Explore Activity 1)

? ESSENTIAL QUESTION CHECK-IN

6. What can you conclude about the interior angles formed when two parallel lines are cut by a transversal?

_____

_____

19.1 Independent Practice

 FL 8.G.1.5

Vocabulary Use the figure for Exercises 7–10.

7. Name all pairs of corresponding angles.

_____

8. Name both pairs of alternate exterior angles.

_____

9. Name the relationship between ∠3 and ∠6.

_____

10. Name the relationship between ∠4 and ∠6.

_____

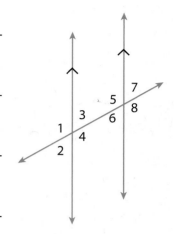

Find each angle measure.

11. m∠AGE when m∠FHD = 30° _____

12. m∠AGH when m∠CHF = 150° _____

13. m∠CHF when m∠BGE = 110° _____

14. m∠CHG when m∠HGA = 120° _____

15. m∠BGH = _____

16. m∠GHD = _____

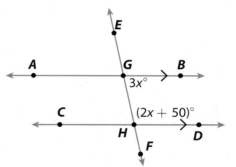

17. The Cross Country Bike Trail follows a straight line where it crosses 350th and 360th Streets. The two streets are parallel to each other. What is the measure of the larger angle formed at the intersection of the bike trail and 360th Street? Explain.

_____

_____

_____

18. **Critical Thinking** How many different angles would be formed by a transversal intersecting three parallel lines? How many different angle measures would there be?

_____

_____

19. Communicate Mathematical Ideas In the diagram at the right, suppose m∠6 = 125°. Explain how to find the measures of each of the other seven numbered angles.

_____

_____

_____

_____

_____

_____

H.O.T. FOCUS ON HIGHER ORDER THINKING

20. Draw Conclusions In a diagram showing two parallel lines cut by a transversal, the measures of two same-side interior angles are both given as $3x°$. Without writing and solving an equation, can you determine the measures of both angles? Explain. Then write and solve an equation to find the measures.

_____

_____

_____

21. Make a Conjecture Draw two parallel lines and a transversal. Choose one of the eight angles that are formed. How many of the other seven angles are congruent to the angle you selected? How many of the other seven angles are supplementary to your angle? Will your answer change if you select a different angle?

_____

22. Critique Reasoning In the diagram at the right, ∠2, ∠3, ∠5, and ∠8 are all congruent, and ∠1, ∠4, ∠6, and ∠7 are all congruent. Aiden says that this is enough information to conclude that the diagram shows two parallel lines cut by a transversal. Is he correct? Justify your answer.

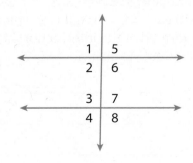

_____

_____

_____

_____

_____

Work Area

LESSON 19.2 Angle Theorems for Triangles

FL 8.G.1.5

Use informal arguments to establish facts about the angle sum and exterior angle of triangles.... *Also 8.EE.3.7, 8.EE.3.7b*

ESSENTIAL QUESTION

What can you conclude about the measures of the angles of a triangle?

EXPLORE ACTIVITY 1 FL 8.G.1.5

Sum of the Angle Measures in a Triangle

There is a special relationship between the measures of the interior angles of a triangle.

A Draw a triangle and cut it out. Label the angles *A*, *B*, and *C*.

B Tear off each "corner" of the triangle. Each corner includes the vertex of one angle of the triangle.

C Arrange the vertices of the triangle around a point so that none of your corners overlap and there are no gaps between them.

D What do you notice about how the angles fit together around a point?

_____

E What is the measure of a straight angle? _____

F Describe the relationship among the measures of the angles of △*ABC*.

_____

The Triangle Sum Theorem states that for △*ABC*, m∠*A* + m∠*B* + m∠*C* = _____.

Reflect

1. **Justify Reasoning** Can a triangle have two right angles? Explain.

_____

_____

_____

2. **Analyze Relationships** Describe the relationship between the two acute angles in a right triangle. Explain your reasoning.

_____

_____

_____

Justifying the Triangle Sum Theorem

You can use your knowledge of parallel lines intersected by a transversal to informally justify the Triangle Sum Theorem.

Follow the steps to informally prove the Triangle Sum Theorem. You should draw each step on your own paper. The figures below are provided for you to check your work.

A Draw a triangle and label the angles as ∠1, ∠2, and ∠3 as shown.

B Draw line *a* through the base of the triangle.

C The Parallel Postulate states that through a point not on a line ℓ, there is exactly one line parallel to line ℓ. Draw line *b* parallel to line *a*, through the vertex opposite the base of the triangle.

D Extend each of the non-base sides of the triangle to form transversal *s* and transversal *t*. Transversals *s* and *t* intersect parallel lines *a* and *b*.

E Label the angles formed by line *b* and the transversals as ∠4 and ∠5.

F Because ∠4 and _____ are alternate interior

angles, they are _____.

Label ∠4 with the number of the angle to which it is congruent.

G Because ∠5 and _____ are alternate interior angles,

they are _____.

Label ∠5 with the number of the angle to which it is congruent.

H The three angles that lie along line *b* at the vertex of the triangle are ∠1, ∠4, and ∠5. Notice that these three angles lie along a line.

So, m∠1 + m∠2 + m∠5 = _____.

Because angles 2 and 4 are congruent and angles 3 and 5 are congruent, you can substitute m∠2 for m∠4 and m∠3 for m∠5 in the equation above.

So, m∠1 + m∠2 + m∠3 = _____.

This shows that the sum of the angle measures in a triangle is

always _____.

Reflect

3. Analyze Relationships How can you use the fact that $m\angle 4 + m\angle 1 + m\angle 5 = 180°$ to show that $m\angle 2 + m\angle 1 + m\angle 3 = 180°$?

_____

_____

_____

Finding Missing Angle Measures in Triangles

If you know the measures of two angles in a triangle, you can use the Triangle Sum Theorem to find the measure of the third angle.

EXAMPLE 1   FL   8.EE.3.7

Find the missing angle measure.

STEP 1 Write the Triangle Sum Theorem for this triangle.

$m\angle D + m\angle E + m\angle F = 180°$

STEP 2 Substitute the given angle measures.

$55° + m\angle E + 100° = 180°$

STEP 3 Solve the equation for $m\angle E$.

$55° + m\angle E + 100° = 180°$

$155° + m\angle E = 180°$ Simplify.

$\underline{-155°} \qquad \underline{-155°}$ Subtract 155° from both sides.

$m\angle E = \quad 25°$

So, $m\angle E = 25°$.

My Notes

YOUR TURN

Find the missing angle measure.

4.

$m\angle K = $ _____

5.

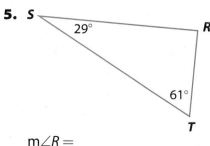

$m\angle R = $ _____

Personal Math Trainer

Online Assessment and Intervention

my.hrw.com

Exterior Angles and Remote Interior Angles

An **interior angle** of a triangle is formed by two sides of the triangle. An **exterior angle** is formed by one side of the triangle and the extension of an adjacent side. Each exterior angle has two remote interior angles. A **remote interior angle** is an interior angle that is not adjacent to the exterior angle.

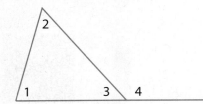

- ∠1, ∠2, and ∠3 are interior angles.

- ∠4 is an exterior angle.

- ∠1 and ∠2 are remote interior angles to ∠4.

There is a special relationship between the measure of an exterior angle and the measures of its remote interior angles.

A Extend the base of the triangle and label the exterior angle as ∠4.

B The Triangle Sum Theorem states:

m∠1 + m∠2 + m∠3 = _____.

C ∠3 and ∠4 form a _____,

so m∠3 + m∠4 = _____.

D Use the equations in **B** and **C** to complete the following equation:

m∠1 + m∠2 + _____ = _____ + m∠4

E Use properties of equality to simplify the equation in **D** :

_____

The Exterior Angle Theorem states that the measure of an _____ angle

is equal to the sum of its _____ angles.

Reflect

6. Sketch a triangle and draw all of its exterior angles. How many exterior angles does a triangle have at each vertex?

_____

7. How many total exterior angles does a triangle have?

_____

Using the Exterior Angle Theorem

You can use the Exterior Angle Theorem to find the measures of the interior angles of a triangle.

EXAMPLE 2

FL 8.EE.3.7b

Find m∠A and m∠B.

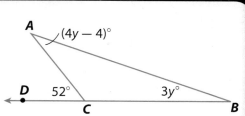

STEP 1 Write the Exterior Angle Theorem as it applies to this triangle.

$$m\angle A + m\angle B = m\angle ACD$$

STEP 2 Substitute the given angle measures.

$$(4y - 4)° + 3y° = 52°$$

STEP 3 Solve the equation for y.

$$(4y - 4)° + 3y° = 52°$$

$4y° - 4° + 3y° = 52°$ *Remove parentheses.*

$7y° - 4° = 52°$ *Simplify.*

$\underline{\quad +4° \quad\quad +4°\quad}$ *Add 4° to both sides.*

$7y° = 56°$ *Simplify.*

$\dfrac{7y°}{7} = \dfrac{56°}{7}$ *Divide both sides by 7.*

$y = 8$ *Simplify.*

Math Talk
Mathematical Practices

Describe two ways to find m∠ACB.

STEP 4 Use the value of y to find m∠A and m∠B.

m∠A = 4y − 4   m∠B = 3y

= 4(8) − 4   = 3(8)

= 32 − 4   = 24

= 28

So, m∠A = 28° and m∠B = 24°.

YOUR TURN

8. Find m∠M and m∠N.

m∠M = _____

m∠N = _____

Personal Math Trainer

Online Assessment and Intervention

⏱ my.hrw.com

Find each missing angle measure. (Explore Activity 1 and Example 1)

1.

$m\angle M = \underline{\hspace{3cm}}$

2.

$m\angle Q = \underline{\hspace{3cm}}$

Use the Triangle Sum Theorem to find the measure of each angle in degrees. (Explore Activity 2 and Example 1)

3.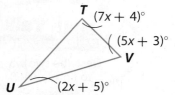

$m\angle T = \underline{\hspace{2cm}}$, $m\angle U = \underline{\hspace{2cm}}$,

$m\angle V = \underline{\hspace{2cm}}$

4.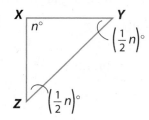

$m\angle X = \underline{\hspace{2cm}}$, $m\angle Y = \underline{\hspace{2cm}}$,

$m\angle Z = \underline{\hspace{2cm}}$

Use the Exterior Angle Theorem to find the measure of each angle in degrees. (Explore Activity 3 and Example 2)

5.

$m\angle C = \underline{\hspace{2cm}}$, $m\angle D = \underline{\hspace{2cm}}$,

$m\angle DEC = \underline{\hspace{2cm}}$

6.

$m\angle L = \underline{\hspace{2cm}}$, $m\angle M = \underline{\hspace{2cm}}$,

$m\angle LKM = \underline{\hspace{2cm}}$

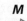 **ESSENTIAL QUESTION CHECK-IN**

7. Describe the relationships among the measures of the angles of a triangle.

_____

_____

_____

19.2 Independent Practice

 FL 8.EE.3.7, 8.EE.3.7b, 8.G.1.5

Find the measure of each angle.

8.

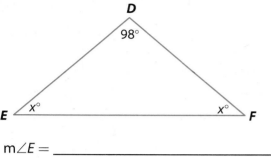

m∠E = _____

m∠F = _____

9.

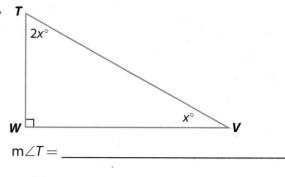

m∠T = _____

m∠V = _____

10.

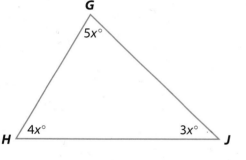

m∠G = _____

m∠H = _____

m∠J = _____

11.

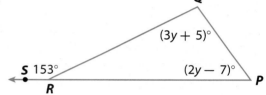

m∠Q = _____

m∠P = _____

m∠QRP = _____

12.

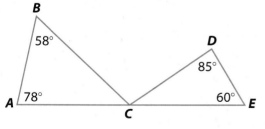

m∠ACB = _____

m∠BCD = _____

m∠DCE = _____

13.

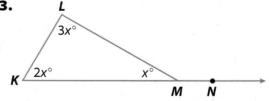

m∠K = _____

m∠L = _____

m∠KML = _____

m∠LMN = _____

14. Multistep The second angle in a triangle is five times as large as the first. The third angle is two-thirds as large as the first. Find the angle measures. _____

15. Analyze Relationships Can a triangle have two obtuse angles? Explain.

_____

_____

_____

_____

H.O.T. FOCUS ON HIGHER ORDER THINKING

Work Area

16. Critical Thinking Explain how you can use the Triangle Sum Theorem to find the measures of the angles of an equilateral triangle.

_____

_____

_____

_____

17. a. Draw Conclusions Find the sum of the measures of the angles in quadrilateral *ABCD*. (Hint: Draw diagonal $\overline{AC}$. How can you use the figures you have formed to find the sum?)

Sum = _____

b. Make a Conjecture Write a "Quadrilateral Sum Theorem." Explain why you think it is true.

_____

_____

_____

_____

_____

18. Communicate Mathematical Ideas Describe two ways that an exterior angle of a triangle is related to one or more of the interior angles.

_____

_____

_____

_____

LESSON
19.3

Angle-Angle Similarity

FL 8.G.1.5

Use informal arguments to establish facts about . . . the angle-angle criterion for similarity of triangles. *Also 8.EE.2.6, 8.EE.3.7*

ESSENTIAL QUESTION

How can you determine when two triangles are similar?

EXPLORE ACTIVITY 1   FL 8.G.1.5

Discovering Angle-Angle Similarity

Similar figures have the same shape but may have different sizes. Two triangles are **similar** if their corresponding angles are congruent and the lengths of their corresponding sides are proportional.

A Use your protractor and a straightedge to draw a triangle. Make one angle measure 45° and another angle measure 60°.

B Compare your triangle to those drawn by your classmates. How are the triangles the same?

_____

How are they different?

_____

C Use the Triangle Sum Theorem to find the measure of the third angle of your triangle.

_____

Reflect

1. If two angles in one triangle are congruent to two angles in another triangle, what do you know about the third pair of angles?

_____

2. **Make a Conjecture** Are two pairs of congruent angles enough information to conclude that two triangles are similar? Explain.

_____

_____

_____

Using the AA Similarity Postulate

Angle-Angle (AA) Similarity Postulate

If two angles of one triangle are congruent to two angles of another triangle, then the triangles are similar.

EXAMPLE 1

FL 8.G.1.5

Explain whether the triangles are similar.

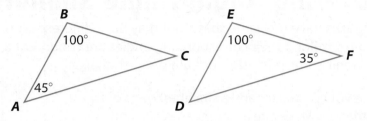

The figure shows only one pair of congruent angles. Find the measure of the third angle in each triangle.

$$45° + 100° + m\angle C = 180° \qquad 100° + 35° + m\angle D = 180°$$

$$145° + m\angle C = 180° \qquad 135° + m\angle D = 180°$$

$$145° + m\angle C - 145° = 180° - 145° \qquad 135° + m\angle D - 135° = 180° - 135°$$

$$m\angle C = 35° \qquad\qquad m\angle D = 45°$$

Math Talk
Mathematical Practices

Are all right triangles similar? Why or why not?

Because two angles in one triangle are congruent to two angles in the other triangle, the triangles are similar.

YOUR TURN

3. **Explain whether the triangles are similar.**

_____

_____

_____

Finding Missing Measures in Similar Triangles

Because corresponding angles are congruent and corresponding sides are proportional in similar triangles, you can use similar triangles to solve real-world problems.

Math On the Spot
my.hrw.com

EXAMPLE 2 Real World
FL 8.EE.3.7

While playing tennis, Matt is 12 meters from the net, which is 0.9 meter high. He needs to hit the ball so that it just clears the net and lands 6 meters beyond the base of the net. At what height should Matt hit the tennis ball?

Both triangles contain ∠A and a right angle, so △ABC and △ADE are similar.

In similar triangles, corresponding side lengths are proportional.

$$\frac{AD}{AB} = \frac{DE}{BC} \longrightarrow \frac{6+12}{6} = \frac{h}{0.9}$$ Substitute the lengths from the figure.

$$0.9 \times \frac{18}{6} = \frac{h}{0.9} \times 0.9$$ Use properties of equality to get h by itself.

$$0.9 \times 3 = h$$ Simplify.

$$2.7 = h$$ Multiply.

Matt should hit the ball at a height of 2.7 meters.

Reflect

4. **What If?** Suppose you set up a proportion so that each ratio compares parts of one triangle, as shown below.

height of △ABC ⟶ $\frac{BC}{AB}$ = $\frac{DE}{AD}$ ⟵ height of △ADE
base of △ABC ⟶ ⟵ base of △ADE

Show that this proportion leads to the same value for h as in Example 2.

YOUR TURN

5. Rosie is building a wheelchair ramp that is 24 feet long and 2 feet high. She needs to install a vertical support piece 8 feet from the end of the ramp. What is the length of the support piece in inches?

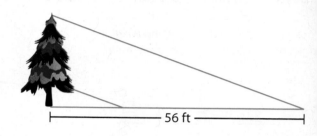

h ft

8 ft

24 ft

2 ft

_____

6. The lower cable meets the tree at a height of 6 feet and extends out 16 feet from the base of the tree. If the triangles are similar, how tall is the tree?

56 ft

_____

EXPLORE ACTIVITY 2   FL   8.EE.2.6

Using Similar Triangles to Explain Slope

You can use similar triangles to show that the slope of a line is constant.

A Draw a line ℓ that is not a horizontal line. Label four points on the line as *A*, *B*, *C*, and *D*.

You need to show that the slope between points *A* and *B* is the same as the slope between points *C* and *D*.

B Draw the rise and run for the slope between points A and B. Label the intersection as point E. Draw the rise and run for the slope between points C and D. Label the intersection as point F.

C Write expressions for the slope between A and B and between C and D.

Slope between A and B: $\dfrac{BE}{\boxed{}}$ Slope between C and D: $\dfrac{\boxed{}}{CF}$

D Extend $\overleftrightarrow{AE}$ and $\overleftrightarrow{CF}$ across your drawing. $\overleftrightarrow{AE}$ and $\overleftrightarrow{CF}$ are both horizontal lines, so they are parallel.

Line ℓ is a _____ that intersects parallel lines.

E Complete the following statements:

$\angle BAE$ and _____ are corresponding angles and are _____.

$\angle BEA$ and _____ are right angles and are _____.

F By Angle–Angle Similarity, $\triangle ABE$ and _____ are similar triangles.

G Use the fact that the lengths of corresponding sides of similar triangles are proportional to complete the following ratios: $\dfrac{BE}{DF} = \dfrac{\boxed{}}{CF}$

H Recall that you can also write the proportion so that the ratios compare parts of the same triangle: $\dfrac{\boxed{}}{AE} = \dfrac{DF}{\boxed{}}$.

I The proportion you wrote in step **H** shows that the ratios you wrote in **C** are equal. So, the slope of line ℓ is constant.

Reflect

7. What If? Suppose that you label two other points on line ℓ as G and H. Would the slope between these two points be different than the slope you found in the Explore Activity? Explain.

_____

_____

_____

1. Explain whether the triangles are similar. Label the angle measures in the figure. (Explore Activity 1 and Example 1)

△ABC has angle measures _____ and △DEF has angle

measures _____. Because _____ in one

triangle are congruent to _____ in the other triangle, the

triangles are _____.

2. A flagpole casts a shadow 23.5 feet long. At the same time of day, Mrs. Gilbert, who is 5.5 feet tall, casts a shadow that is 7.5 feet long. How tall in feet is the flagpole? Round your answer to the nearest tenth. (Example 2)

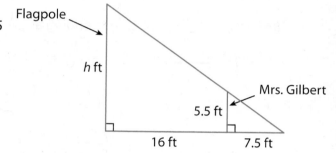

$$\frac{5.5}{\boxed{}} = \frac{h}{\boxed{}}$$

$h =$ _____ feet

3. Two transversals intersect two parallel lines as shown. Explain whether △ABC and △DEC are similar. (Example 1)

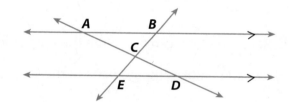

∠BAC and ∠EDC are _____ since they are _____.

∠ABC and ∠DEC are _____ since they are _____.

By _____, △ABC and △DEC are _____.

4. How can you determine when two triangles are similar?

_____

_____

_____

19.3 Independent Practice

FL 8.EE.2.6, 8.EE.3.7, 8.G.1.5

Personal
Math Trainer

Online
Assessment and
Intervention

my.hrw.com

Use the diagrams for Exercises 5–7.

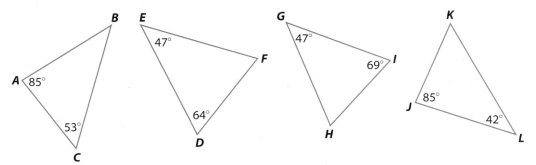

5. Find the missing angle measures in the triangles.

_____

6. Which triangles are similar?

_____

7. **Analyze Relationships** Determine which angles are congruent to the
angles in △ABC.

_____

8. **Multistep** A tree casts a shadow that is 20 feet long. Frank is 6 feet tall,
and while standing next to the tree he casts a shadow that is 4 feet long.

a. How tall is the tree? _____

b. How much taller is the tree than Frank? _____

9. **Represent Real-World Problems** Sheila is climbing on a ladder that
is attached against the side of a jungle gym wall. She is 5 feet off the
ground and 3 feet from the base of the ladder, which is 15 feet from the
wall. Draw a diagram to help you solve the problem. How high up the
wall is the top of the ladder?

_____

10. **Justify Reasoning** Are two equilateral triangles always similar? Explain.

_____

_____

_____

11. Critique Reasoning Ryan calculated the missing measure in the diagram shown. What was his mistake?

$$\frac{3.4}{6.5} = \frac{h}{19.5}$$

$$19.5 \times \frac{3.4}{6.5} = \frac{h}{19.5} \times 19.5$$

$$\frac{66.3}{6.5} = h$$

$$10.2 \text{ cm} = h$$

_____

_____

_____

Work Area

12. Communicate Mathematical Ideas For a pair of triangular earrings, how can you tell if they are similar? How can you tell if they are congruent?

_____

_____

_____

_____

13. Critical Thinking When does it make sense to use similar triangles to measure the height and length of objects in real life?

_____

_____

_____

14. Justify Reasoning Two right triangles on a coordinate plane are similar but not congruent. Each of the legs of both triangles are extended by 1 unit, creating two new right triangles. Are the resulting triangles similar? Explain using an example.

_____

_____

_____

_____

_____

_____

Ready to Go On?

19.1 Parallel Lines Cut by a Transversal

In the figure, line $p \parallel$ line q. Find the measure of each angle if m$\angle 8 = 115°$.

1. m$\angle 7 =$ _____

2. m$\angle 6 =$ _____

3. m$\angle 1 =$ _____

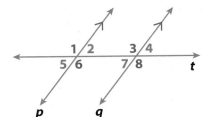

19.2 Angle Theorems for Triangles

Find the measure of each angle.

4. m$\angle A =$ _____

5. m$\angle B =$ _____

6. m$\angle BCA =$ _____

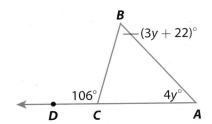

19.3 Angle-Angle Similarity

Triangle *FEG* is similar to triangle *IHJ*. Find the missing values.

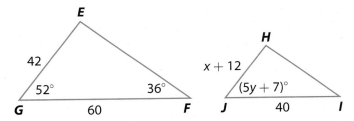

7. $x =$ _____

8. $y =$ _____

9. m$\angle H =$ _____

? ESSENTIAL QUESTION

10. How can you use similar triangles to solve real-world problems?

_____

_____

Personal
Math Trainer

Online
Assessment and
Intervention

my.hrw.com

Selected Response

Use the figure for Exercises 1 and 2.

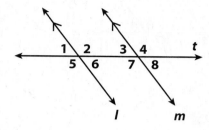

1. Which angle pair is a pair of alternate exterior angles?

ⓐ ∠5 and ∠6

ⓒ ∠5 and ∠4

ⓑ ∠6 and ∠7

ⓓ ∠5 and ∠2

2. Which of the following angles is **not** congruent to ∠3?

ⓐ ∠1

ⓒ ∠6

ⓑ ∠2

ⓓ ∠8

3. The measures, in degrees, of the three angles of a triangle are given by $2x + 1$, $3x - 3$, and $9x$. What is the measure of the smallest angle?

ⓐ 13°

ⓒ 36°

ⓑ 27°

ⓓ 117°

4. Which is a possible measure of ∠DCA in the triangle below?

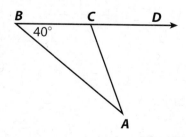

ⓐ 36°

ⓒ 40°

ⓑ 38°

ⓓ 70°

5. Kaylee wrote in her dinosaur report that the Jurassic period was 1.75×10^8 years ago. What is this number written in standard form?

ⓐ 1,750,000

ⓑ 17,500,000

ⓒ 175,000,000

ⓓ 17,500,000,000

6. Given that y is proportional to x, what linear equation can you write if y is 16 when x is 20?

ⓐ $y = 20x$

ⓒ $y = \frac{4}{5}x$

ⓑ $y = \frac{5}{4}x$

ⓓ $y = 0.6x$

Mini-Task

7. Two transversals intersect two parallel lines as shown.

a. What is the value of x?

_____

b. What is the measure of ∠LMN?

_____

c. What is the measure of ∠KLM?

_____

d. Which two triangles are similar? How do you know?

_____

_____

_____

The Pythagorean Theorem

MODULE **20**

?

ESSENTIAL QUESTION

How can you use the Pythagorean Theorem to solve real-world problems?

LESSON 20.1

The Pythagorean Theorem

 FL 8.G.2.6, 8.G.2.7

LESSON 20.2

Converse of the Pythagorean Theorem

 FL 8.G.2.6

LESSON 20.3

Distance Between Two Points

 FL 8.G.2.8

Real-World Video

The sizes of televisions are usually described by the length of the diagonal of the screen. To find this length of the diagonal of a rectangle, you can use the Pythagorean Theorem.

⏻ my.hrw.com

GO DIGITAL

my.hrw.com

my.hrw.com

Go digital with your write-in student edition, accessible on any device.

Math On the Spot

Scan with your smart phone to jump directly to the online edition, video tutor, and more.

Animated Math

Interactively explore key concepts to see how math works.

Personal Math Trainer

Get immediate feedback and help as you work through practice sets.

635

Are YOU Ready?

Complete these exercises to review skills you will need for this module.

Find the Square of a Number

EXAMPLE   Find the square of 2.7.

$$\begin{array}{r} 2.7 \\ \times\, 2.7 \\ \hline 189 \\ 54 \\ \hline 7.29 \end{array}$$

Multiply the number by itself.

So, $2.7^2 = 7.29$.

Find the square of each number.

1. 5 _____

2. 16 _____

3. −11 _____

4. $\frac{2}{7}$ _____

Order of Operations

EXAMPLE

$\sqrt{(5-2)^2 + (8-4)^2}$ First, operate within parentheses.

$\sqrt{(3)^2 + (4)^2}$ Next, simplify exponents.

$\sqrt{9 + 16}$ Then add and subtract left to right.

$\sqrt{25}$ Finally, take the square root.

5

Evaluate each expression.

5. $\sqrt{(6+2)^2 + (3+3)^2}$ _____

6. $\sqrt{(9-4)^2 + (5+7)^2}$ _____

7. $\sqrt{(10-6)^2 + (15-12)^2}$ _____

8. $\sqrt{(6+9)^2 + (10-2)^2}$ _____

Simplify Numerical Expressions

EXAMPLE $\frac{1}{2}(2.5)^2(4) = \frac{1}{2}(6.25)(4)$ Simplify the exponent.

$= 12.5$ Multiply from left to right.

Simplify each expression.

9. $5(8)(10)$ _____

10. $\frac{1}{2}(6)(12)$ _____

11. $\frac{1}{3}(3)(12)$ _____

12. $\frac{1}{2}(8)^2(4)$ _____

13. $\frac{1}{4}(10)^2(15)$ _____

14. $\frac{1}{3}(9)^2(6)$ _____

Reading Start-Up

Visualize Vocabulary

Use the ✔ words to complete the graphic.

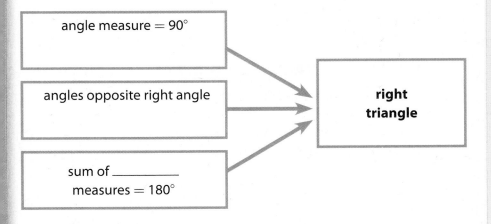

| angle measure = 90° |
| angles opposite right angle |
| sum of _____ measures = 180° |

→ **right triangle**

Understand Vocabulary

Match the term on the left to the correct expression on the right.

1. hypotenuse

2. theorem

3. legs

A. An idea that has been demonstrated as true.

B. The two sides that form the right angle of a right triangle.

C. The side opposite the right angle in a right triangle.

Vocabulary

Review Words
✔ acute angles (*ángulos agudos*)
✔ angles (*ángulos*)
  area (*área*)
  ordered pair (*par ordenado*)
✔ right angle (*ángulo recto*)
✔ right triangle (*triángulo recto*)
  square root (*raíz cuadrada*)
  x-coordinate (*coordenada x*)
  y-coordinate (*coordenada y*)

Preview Words
  hypotenuse (*hipotenusa*)
  legs (*catetos*)
  theorem (*teorema*)
  vertex (*vértice*)

Active Reading

Booklet Before beginning the module, create a booklet to help you learn about the Pythagorean Theorem. Write the main idea of each lesson on each page of the booklet. As you study each lesson, write important details that support the main idea, such as vocabulary and formulas. Refer to your finished booklet as you work on assignments and study for tests.

Unpacking the Standards

Understanding the standards and the vocabulary terms in the standards will help you know exactly what you are expected to learn in this module.

 FL 8.G.2.7

Apply the Pythagorean Theorem to determine unknown side lengths in right triangles in real-world and mathematical problems in two and three dimensions.

Key Vocabulary

Pythagorean Theorem
(Teorema de Pitágoras)
In a right triangle, the square of the length of the hypotenuse is equal to the sum of the squares of the lengths of the legs.

What It Means to You

You will find a missing length in a right triangle, or use side lengths to see whether a triangle is a right triangle.

UNPACKING EXAMPLE 8.G.2.7

Mark and Sarah start walking at the same point, but Mark walks 50 feet north while Sarah walks 75 feet east. How far apart are Mark and Sarah when they stop?

$$a^2 + b^2 = c^2$$ Pythagorean Theorem

$$50^2 + 75^2 = c^2$$ Substitute.

$$2500 + 5625 = c^2$$

$$8125 = c^2$$

$$90.1 \approx c$$

Mark and Sarah are approximately 90.1 feet apart.

 FL 8.G.2.8

Apply the Pythagorean Theorem to find the distance between two points in a coordinate system.

Key Vocabulary

coordinate plane
(plano cartesiano)
A plane formed by the intersection of a horizontal number line called the *x*-axis and a vertical number line called the *y*-axis.

What It Means to You

You can use the Pythagorean Theorem to find the distance between two points.

UNPACKING EXAMPLE 8.G.2.8

Find the distance between points *A* and *B*.

$$(AC)^2 + (BC)^2 = (AB)^2$$

$$(4 - 1)^2 + (6 - 2)^2 = (AB)^2$$

$$3^2 + 4^2 = (AB)^2$$

$$9 + 16 = (AB)^2$$

$$25 = (AB)^2$$

$$5 = AB$$

The distance is 5 units.

 Visit **my.hrw.com** to see all **Florida Math Standards** unpacked.

my.hrw.com

The Pythagorean Theorem

 FL 8.G.2.7

Apply the Pythagorean Theorem to determine unknown side lengths in right triangles in real-world and mathematical problems in two and three dimensions. *Also 8.G.2.6*

ESSENTIAL QUESTION

How can you prove the Pythagorean Theorem and use it to solve problems?

EXPLORE ACTIVITY FL 8.G.2.6

Proving the Pythagorean Theorem

In a right triangle, the two sides that form the right angle are the **legs**. The side opposite the right angle is the **hypotenuse**.

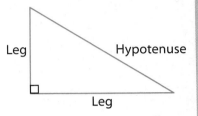

The Pythagorean Theorem

In a right triangle, the sum of the squares of the lengths of the legs is equal to the square of the length of the hypotenuse.

If a and b are legs and c is the hypotenuse, $a^2 + b^2 = c^2$.

A Draw a right triangle on a piece of paper and cut it out. Make one leg shorter than the other.

B Trace your triangle onto another piece of paper four times, arranging them as shown. For each triangle, label the shorter leg a, the longer leg b, and the hypotenuse c.

C What is the area of the unshaded square?

_____

Label the unshaded square with its area.

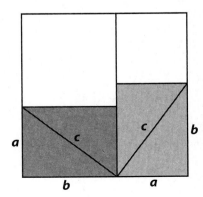

D Trace your original triangle onto a piece of paper four times again, arranging them as shown. Draw a line outlining a larger square that is the same size as the figure you made in **B**.

E What is the area of the unshaded square at the top right of the figure in **D**? at the top left?

_____

Label the unshaded squares with their areas.

F What is the total area of the unshaded regions in **D**?

_____

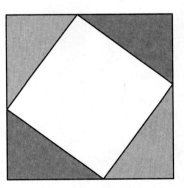

Reflect

1. Explain whether the figures in Ⓑ and Ⓓ have the same area.

_____

2. Explain whether the unshaded regions of the figures in Ⓑ and Ⓓ have the same area.

_____

_____

_____

3. **Analyze Relationships** Write an equation relating the area of the unshaded region in step Ⓑ to the unshaded region in Ⓓ.

_____

Using the Pythagorean Theorem

You can use the Pythagorean Theorem to find the length of a side of a right triangle when you know the lengths of the other two sides.

EXAMPLE 1 FL **8.G.2.7**

Find the length of the missing side.

Ⓐ

7 in.

24 in.

$$a^2 + b^2 = c^2$$

$$24^2 + 7^2 = c^2$$ Substitute into the formula.

$$576 + 49 = c^2$$ Simplify.

$$625 = c^2$$ Add.

$$25 = c$$ Take the square root of both sides.

The length of the hypotenuse is 25 inches.

Math Talk
Mathematical Practices

If you are given the length of the hypotenuse and one leg, does it matter whether you solve for a or b? Explain.

Ⓑ

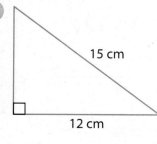

15 cm

12 cm

$$a^2 + b^2 = c^2$$

$$a^2 + 12^2 = 15^2$$ Substitute into the formula.

$$a^2 + 144 = 225$$ Simplify.

$$a^2 = 81$$ Use properties of equality to get a^2 by itself.

$$a = 9$$ Take the square root of both sides.

The length of the leg is 9 centimeters.

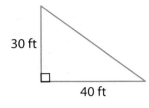
Find the length of the missing side.

4.
30 ft
40 ft

_____

5.
41 in.
40 in.

_____

Pythagorean Theorem in Three Dimensions

You can use the Pythagorean Theorem to solve problems in three dimensions.

EXAMPLE 2 Real World

FL 8.G.2.7

A box used for shipping narrow copper tubes measures 6 inches by 6 inches by 20 inches. What is the length of the longest tube that will fit in the box, given that the length of the tube must be a whole number of inches?

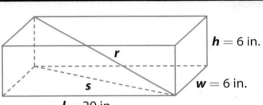

$h = 6$ in.

r

$w = 6$ in.

s

$l = 20$ in.

STEP 1 You want to find r, the length from a bottom corner to the opposite top corner. First, find s, the length of the diagonal across the bottom of the box.

$w^2 + l^2 = s^2$

$6^2 + 20^2 = s^2$ Substitute into the formula.

$36 + 400 = s^2$ Simplify.

$436 = s^2$ Add.

STEP 2 Use your expression for s to find r.

$h^2 + s^2 = r^2$

$6^2 + 436 = r^2$ Substitute into the formula.

$472 = r^2$ Add.

$\sqrt{472} = r$ Take the square root of both sides.

$21.7 \approx r$ Use a calculator to round to the nearest tenth.

The length of the longest tube that will fit in the box is 21 inches.

Math Talk
Mathematical Practices

Looking at Step 2, why did the calculations in Step 1 stop before taking the square root of both sides of the final equation?

YOUR TURN

6. Tina ordered a replacement part for her desk. It was shipped in a box that measures 4 in. by 4 in. by 14 in. What is the greatest length in whole inches that the part could have been?

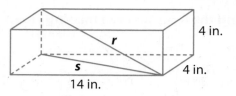

4 in.

4 in.

14 in.

r

s

Guided Practice

1. Find the length of the missing side of the triangle. (Explore Activity 1 and Example 1)

$$a^2 + b^2 = c^2 \rightarrow 24^2 + \boxed{} = c^2 \rightarrow \boxed{} = c^2$$

The length of the hypotenuse is $\boxed{}$ feet.

10 ft

24 ft

2. Mr. Woo wants to ship a fishing rod that is 42 inches long to his son. He has a box with the dimensions shown. (Example 2)

$h = 10$ in.

$w = 10$ in.

$l = 40$ in.

a. Find the square of the length of the diagonal across the bottom of the box.

_____

b. Find the length from a bottom corner to the opposite top corner to the nearest tenth. Will the fishing rod fit?

_____

? ESSENTIAL QUESTION CHECK-IN

3. State the Pythagorean Theorem and tell how you can use it to solve problems.

_____

_____

_____

_____

20.1 Independent Practice

 FL 8.G.2.6, 8.G.2.7

Personal Math Trainer

Online Assessment and Intervention

my.hrw.com

Find the length of the missing side of each triangle. Round your answers to the nearest tenth.

4.

8 cm

4 cm

_____

5.

14 in.

8 in.

_____

6. The diagonal of a rectangular big-screen TV screen measures 152 cm. The length measures 132 cm. What is the height of the screen?   _____

7. Dylan has a square piece of metal that measures 10 inches on each side. He cuts the metal along the diagonal, forming two right triangles. What is the length of the hypotenuse of each right triangle to the nearest tenth of an inch?   _____

8. **Represent Real-World Problems** A painter has a 24-foot ladder that he is using to paint a house. For safety reasons, the ladder must be placed at least 8 feet from the base of the side of the house. To the nearest tenth of a foot, how high can the ladder safely reach?   _____

9. What is the longest flagpole (in whole feet) that could be shipped in a box that measures 2 ft by 2 ft by 12 ft? _____

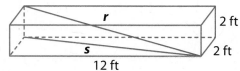
r

s

12 ft

2 ft

2 ft

10. **Sports** American football fields measure 100 yards long between the end zones, and are $53\frac{1}{3}$ yards wide. Is the length of the diagonal across this field more or less than 120 yards? Explain.

_____

11. **Justify Reasoning** A tree struck by lightning broke at a point 12 ft above the ground as shown. What was the height of the tree to the nearest tenth of a foot? Explain your reasoning.

12 ft

39 ft

_____

_____

_____

12. Multistep Main Street and Washington Avenue meet at a right angle. A large park begins at this corner. Joe's school lies at the opposite corner of the park. Usually Joe walks 1.2 miles along Main Street and then 0.9 miles up Washington Avenue to get to school. Today he walked in a straight path across the park and returned home along the same path. What is the difference in distance between the two round trips? Explain.

_____

_____

_____

13. Analyze Relationships An isosceles right triangle is a right triangle with congruent legs. If the length of each leg is represented by x, what algebraic expression can be used to represent the length of the hypotenuse? Explain your reasoning.

_____

_____

14. Persevere in Problem Solving A square hamburger is centered on a circular bun. Both the bun and the burger have an area of 16 square inches.

a. How far, to the nearest hundredth of an inch, does each corner of the burger stick out from the bun? Explain.

_____

_____

_____

_____

_____

b. How far does each bun stick out from the center of each side of the burger?

_____

c. Are the distances in part **a** and part **b** equal? If not, which sticks out more, the burger or the bun? Explain.

_____

_____

_____

Converse of the Pythagorean Theorem

FL 8.G.2.6
Explain a proof of the Pythagorean Theorem and its converse.

ESSENTIAL QUESTION

How can you test the converse of the Pythagorean Theorem and use it to solve problems?

EXPLORE ACTIVITY FL 8.G.2.6

Testing the Converse of the Pythagorean Theorem

The Pythagorean Theorem states that if a triangle is a right triangle, then $a^2 + b^2 = c^2$.

The *converse* of the Pythagorean Theorem states that if $a^2 + b^2 = c^2$, then the triangle is a right triangle.

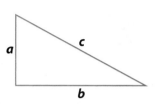

Decide whether the converse of the Pythagorean Theorem is true.

A Verify that the following sets of lengths make the equation $a^2 + b^2 = c^2$ true. Record your results in the table.

a	b	c	Is $a^2 + b^2 = c^2$ true?	Makes a right triangle?
3	4	5		
5	12	13		
7	24	25		
8	15	17		
20	21	29		

B For each set of lengths in the table, cut strips of grid paper with a width of one square and lengths that correspond to the values of a, b, and c.

C For each set of lengths, use the strips of grid paper to try to form a right triangle. An example using the first set of lengths is shown. Record your findings in the table.

Reflect

1. **Draw Conclusions** Based on your observations, explain whether you think the converse of the Pythagorean Theorem is true.

_____

_____

Identifying a Right Triangle

The converse of the Pythagorean Theorem gives you a way to tell if a triangle is a right triangle when you know the side lengths.

EXAMPLE 1

 FL 8.G.2.6

Tell whether each triangle with the given side lengths is a right triangle.

A 9 inches, 40 inches, and 41 inches

Let $a = 9$, $b = 40$, and $c = 41$.

$$a^2 + b^2 = c^2$$

$$9^2 + 40^2 \overset{?}{=} 41^2 \qquad \text{Substitute into the formula.}$$

$$81 + 1600 \overset{?}{=} 1681 \qquad \text{Simpify.}$$

$$1681 = 1681 \qquad \text{Add.}$$

Since $9^2 + 40^2 = 41^2$, the triangle is a right triangle by the converse of the Pythagorean Theorem.

B 8 meters, 10 meters, and 12 meters

Let $a = 8$, $b = 10$, and $c = 12$.

$$a^2 + b^2 = c^2$$

$$8^2 + 10^2 \overset{?}{=} 12^2 \qquad \text{Substitute into the formula.}$$

$$64 + 100 \overset{?}{=} 144 \qquad \text{Simpify.}$$

$$164 \neq 144 \qquad \text{Add.}$$

Since $8^2 + 10^2 \neq 12^2$, the triangle is not a right triangle by the converse of the Pythagorean Theorem.

YOUR TURN

Tell whether each triangle with the given side lengths is a right triangle.

2. 14 cm, 23 cm, and 25 cm

3. 16 in., 30 in., and 34 in.

_____

_____

4. 27 ft, 36 ft, 45 ft

5. 11 mm, 18 mm, 21 mm

_____

_____

Using the Converse of the Pythagorean Theorem

You can use the converse of the Pythagorean Theorem to solve real-world problems.

Math On the Spot
⊙ my.hrw.com

EXAMPLE 2   **FL** 8.G.2.6

Katya is buying edging for a triangular flower garden she plans to build in her backyard. If the lengths of the three pieces of edging that she purchases are 13 feet, 10 feet, and 7 feet, will the flower garden be in the shape of a right triangle?

Use the converse of the Pythagorean Theorem. Remember to use the longest length for c.

Let $a = 7$, $b = 10$, and $c = 13$.

$$a^2 + b^2 = c^2$$

$$7^2 + 10^2 \overset{?}{=} 13^2 \qquad \text{Substitute into the formula.}$$

$$49 + 100 \overset{?}{=} 169 \qquad \text{Simpify.}$$

$$149 \neq 169 \qquad \text{Add.}$$

Since $7^2 + 10^2 \neq 13^2$, the garden will not be in the shape of a right triangle.

> **Math Talk**
> **Mathematical Practices**
>
> To what length, to the nearest tenth, can Katya trim the longest piece of edging to form a right triangle?

YOUR TURN

6. A blueprint for a new triangular playground shows that the sides measure 480 ft, 140 ft, and 500 ft. Is the playground in the shape of a right triangle? Explain.

_____

_____

7. A triangular piece of glass has sides that measure 18 in., 19 in., and 25 in. Is the piece of glass in the shape of a right triangle? Explain.

_____

8. A corner of a fenced yard forms a right angle. Can you place a 12 foot long board across the corner to form a right triangle for which the leg lengths are whole numbers? Explain.

_____

_____

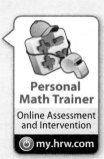
Personal Math Trainer
Online Assessment and Intervention
⊙ my.hrw.com

1. Lashandra used grid paper to construct the triangle shown. (Explore Activity)

   a. What are the lengths of the sides of Lashandra's triangle?

   _____units, _____units, _____units

   b. Use the converse of the Pythagorean Theorem
   to determine whether the triangle is a right triangle.

   $$a^2 + b^2 = c^2$$

   The triangle that Lashandra constructed is / is not a right triangle.

2. A triangle has side lengths 9 cm, 12 cm, and 16 cm. Tell whether the triangle
   is a right triangle. (Example 1)

   Let $a =$ _____ , $b =$ _____ , and $c =$ _____ .

   $$a^2 + b^2 = c^2$$

   By the converse of the Pythagorean Theorem, the triangle is / is not
   a right triangle.

3. The marketing team at a new electronics company is designing a logo that
   contains a circle and a triangle. On one design, the triangle's side lengths are
   2.5 in., 6 in., and 6.5 in. Is the triangle a right triangle? Explain. (Example 2)

   _____

? ESSENTIAL QUESTION CHECK-IN

4. How can you use the converse of the Pythagorean Theorem
   to tell if a triangle is a right triangle?

   _____

   _____

20.2 Independent Practice

 FL 8.G.2.6

Personal
Math Trainer

Online
Assessment and
Intervention

my.hrw.com

Tell whether each triangle with the given side lengths is a right triangle.

5. 11 cm, 60 cm, 61 cm

_____

6. 5 ft, 12 ft, 15 ft

_____

7. 9 in., 15 in., 17 in.

_____

8. 15 m, 36 m, 39 m

_____

9. 20 mm, 30 mm, 40 mm

_____

10. 20 cm, 48 cm, 52 cm

_____

11. 18.5 ft, 6 ft, 17.5 ft

_____

12. 2 mi, 1.5 mi, 2.5 mi

_____

13. 35 in., 45 in., 55 in.

_____

14. 25 cm, 14 cm, 23 cm

_____

15. The emblem on a college banner consists of the face of a tiger inside a triangle. The lengths of the sides of the triangle are 13 cm, 14 cm, and 15 cm. Is the triangle a right triangle? Explain.

_____

16. Kerry has a large triangular piece of fabric that she wants to attach to the ceiling in her bedroom. The sides of the piece of fabric measure 4.8 ft, 6.4 ft, and 8 ft. Is the fabric in the shape of a right triangle? Explain.

_____

17. A mosaic consists of triangular tiles. The smallest tiles have side lengths 6 cm, 10 cm, and 12 cm. Are these tiles in the shape of right triangles? Explain.

_____

18. History In ancient Egypt, surveyors made right angles by stretching a rope with evenly spaced knots as shown. Explain why the rope forms a right angle.

_____

_____

_____

19. Justify Reasoning Yoshi has two identical triangular boards as shown. Can he use these two boards to form a rectangle? Explain.

1 m

0.7

1.25 m 1.25 m

0.75 m 1 m

_____

_____

_____

20. Critique Reasoning Shoshanna says that a triangle with side lengths 17 m, 8 m, and 15 m is not a right triangle because $17^2 + 8^2 = 353$, $15^2 = 225$, and $353 \neq 225$. Is she correct? Explain.

_____

_____

H.O.T. FOCUS ON HIGHER ORDER THINKING

Work Area

21. Make a Conjecture Diondre says that he can take any right triangle and make a new right triangle just by doubling the side lengths. Is Diondre's conjecture true? Test his conjecture using three different right triangles.

_____

_____

_____

_____

22. Draw Conclusions A diagonal of a parallelogram measures 37 inches. The sides measure 35 inches and 1 foot. Is the parallelogram a rectangle? Explain your reasoning.

_____

_____

_____

_____

23. Represent Real-World Problems A soccer coach is marking the lines for a soccer field on a large recreation field. The dimensions of the field are to be 90 yards by 48 yards. Describe a procedure she could use to confirm that the sides of the field meet at right angles.

_____

_____

_____

_____

Distance Between Two Points

FL 8.G.2.8

Apply the Pythagorean Theorem to find the distance between two points in a coordinate system.

ESSENTIAL QUESTION

How can you use the Pythagorean Theorem to find the distance between two points on a coordinate plane?

Pythagorean Theorem in the Coordinate Plane

EXAMPLE 1
FL 8.G.2.8

Math On the Spot
my.hrw.com

The figure shows a right triangle. Approximate the length of the hypotenuse to the nearest tenth using a calculator.

STEP 1   Find the length of each leg.

The length of the vertical leg is 4 units.

The length of the horizontal leg is 2 units.

STEP 2   Let $a = 4$ and $b = 2$. Let c represent the length of the hypotenuse. Use the Pythagorean Theorem to find c.

$$a^2 + b^2 = c^2$$

$$4^2 + 2^2 = c^2 \quad \text{Substitute into the formula.}$$

$$20 = c^2 \quad \text{Add.}$$

$$\sqrt{20} = c \quad \text{Take the square root of both sides.}$$

$$\sqrt{20} \approx 4.5 \quad \text{Use a calculator and round to the nearest tenth.}$$

STEP 3   Check for reasonablenes by finding perfect squares close to 20.

$\sqrt{20}$ is between $\sqrt{16}$ and $\sqrt{25}$, or $\sqrt{16} < \sqrt{20} < \sqrt{25}$.

Simplifying gives $4 < \sqrt{20} < 5$.

Since 4.5 is between 4 and 5, the answer is reasonable.

The hypotenuse is about 4.5 units long.

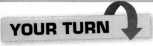
YOUR TURN

1. Approximate the length of the hypotenuse to the nearest tenth using a calculator.

_____

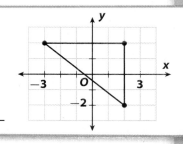
Personal Math Trainer

Online Assessment and Intervention

my.hrw.com

Finding the Distance Between Any Two Points

The Pythagorean Theorem can be used to find the distance between any two points (x_1, y_1) and (x_2, y_2) in the coordinate plane. The resulting expression is called the Distance Formula.

> ## Distance Formula
>
> In a coordinate plane, the distance d between two points (x_1, y_1) and (x_2, y_2) is
> $$d = \sqrt{(x_2 - x_1)^2 + (y_2 - y_1)^2}.$$

Use the Pythagorean Theorem to derive the Distance Formula.

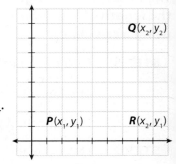

A To find the distance between points P and Q, draw segment $\overline{PQ}$ and label its length d. Then draw horizontal segment $\overline{PR}$ and vertical segment $\overline{QR}$. Label the lengths of these segments a and b. Triangle

PQR is a _____ triangle, with hypotenuse _____.

B Since $\overline{PR}$ is a horizontal segment, its length, a, is the difference between its x-coordinates. Therefore, $a = x_2 -$ _____.

C Since $\overline{QR}$ is a vertical segment, its length, b, is the difference between its y-coordinates. Therefore, $b = y_2 -$ _____.

D Use the Pythagorean Theorem to find d, the length of segment $\overline{PQ}$. Substitute the expressions from **B** and **C** for a and b.

$$d^2 = a^2 + b^2$$

$$d = \sqrt{a^2 + b^2}$$

$$d = \sqrt{\left(\bigcirc - \bigcirc\right)^2 + \left(\bigcirc - \bigcirc\right)^2}$$

> **Math Talk**
> **Mathematical Practices**
>
> What do $x_2 - x_1$ and $y_2 - y_1$ represent in terms of the Pythagorean Theorem?

Reflect

2. Why are the coordinates of point R the ordered pair (x_2, y_1)?

_____

_____

_____

Finding the Distance Between Two Points

The Pythagorean Theorem can be used to find the distance between two points in a real-world situation. You can do this by using a coordinate grid that overlays a diagram of the real-world situation.

EXAMPLE 2 FL 8.G.2.8

Francesca wants to find the distance between her house on one side of a lake and the beach on the other side. She marks off a third point forming a right triangle, as shown. The distances in the diagram are measured in meters.

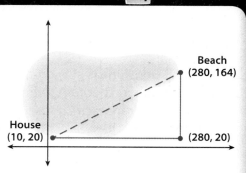
Beach (280, 164)
House (10, 20)
(280, 20)

Use the Pythagorean Theorem to find the straight-line distance from Francesca's house to the beach.

STEP 1 Find the length of the horizontal leg.

The length of the horizontal leg is the absolute value of the difference between the *x*-coordinates of the points (280, 20) and (10, 20).

$$|280 - 10| = 270$$

The length of the horizontal leg is 270 meters.

STEP 2 Find the length of the vertical leg.

The length of the vertical leg is the absolute value of the difference between the *y*-coordinates of the points (280, 164) and (280, 20).

$$|164 - 20| = 144$$

The length of the vertical leg is 144 meters.

STEP 3 Let $a = 270$ and $b = 144$. Let c represent the length of the hypotenuse. Use the Pythagorean Theorem to find c.

$$a^2 + b^2 = c^2$$

$270^2 + 144^2 = c^2$ Substitute into the formula.

$72,900 + 20,736 = c^2$ Simplify.

$93,636 = c^2$ Add.

$\sqrt{93,636} = c$ Take the square root of both sides.

$306 = c$ Simplify.

The distance from Francesca's house to the beach is 306 meters.

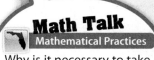
Math Talk
Mathematical Practices

Why is it necessary to take the absolute value of the coordinates when finding the length of a segment?

Reflect

3. Show how you could use the Distance Formula to find the distance from Francesca's house to the beach.

_____

_____

_____

YOUR TURN

4. Camp Sunshine is also on the lake. Use the Pythagorean Theorem to find the distance between Francesca's house and Camp Sunshine to the nearest tenth of a meter.

_____

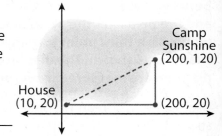

Camp Sunshine (200, 120)

House (10, 20)

(200, 20)

Guided Practice

1. Approximate the length of the hypotenuse of the right triangle to the nearest tenth using a calculator. (Example 1) _____

2. Find the distance between the points (3, 7) and (15, 12) on the coordinate plane. (Explore Activity) _____

3. A plane leaves an airport and flies due north. Two minutes later, a second plane leaves the same airport flying due east. The flight plan shows the coordinates of the two planes 10 minutes later. The distances in the graph are measured in miles. Use the Pythagorean Theorem to find the distance shown between the two planes.

(Example 2) _____

(1, 80)

Airport (1, 1)

(68, 1)

? ESSENTIAL QUESTION CHECK-IN

4. Describe two ways to find the distance between two points on a coordinate plane.

_____

_____

_____

20.3 Independent Practice

FL 8.G.2.8

5. A metal worker traced a triangular piece of sheet metal on a coordinate plane, as shown. The units represent inches. What is the length of the longest side of the metal triangle? Approximate the length to the nearest tenth of an inch using a calculator. Check that your answer is reasonable.

_____

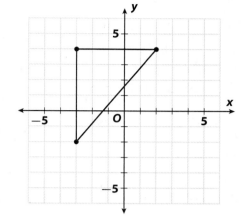

6. When a coordinate grid is superimposed on a map of Harrisburg, the high school is located at (17, 21) and the town park is located at (28, 13). If each unit represents 1 mile, how many miles apart are the high school and the town park? Round your answer to the nearest tenth.

_____

7. The coordinates of the vertices of a rectangle are given by $R(-3, -4)$, $E(-3, 4)$, $C(4, 4)$, and $T(4, -4)$. Plot these points on the coordinate plane at the right and connect them to draw the rectangle. Then connect points E and T to form diagonal $\overline{ET}$.

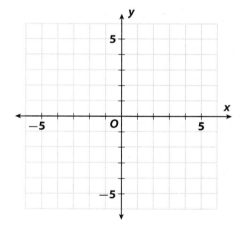

a. Use the Pythagorean Theorem to find the exact length of $\overline{ET}$.

_____

b. How can you use the Distance Formula to find the length of $\overline{ET}$? Show that the Distance Formula gives the same answer.

_____

_____

_____

_____

_____

_____

8. Multistep The locations of three ships are represented on a coordinate grid by the following points: $P(-2, 5)$, $Q(-7, -5)$, and $R(2, -3)$. Which ships are farthest apart?

_____

9. Make a Conjecture Find as many points as you can that are 5 units from the origin. Make a conjecture about the shape formed if all the points 5 units from the origin were connected.

_____

_____

_____

10. Justify Reasoning The graph shows the location of a motion detector that has a maximum range of 34 feet. A peacock at point P displays its tail feathers. Will the motion detector sense this motion? Explain.

_____

_____

H.O.T. FOCUS ON HIGHER ORDER THINKING

Work Area

11. Persevere in Problem Solving One leg of an isosceles right triangle has endpoints (1, 1) and (6, 1). The other leg passes through the point (6, 2). Draw the triangle on the coordinate plane. Then show how you can use the Distance Formula to find the length of the hypotenuse. Round your answer to the nearest tenth.

_____

_____

_____

12. Represent Real-World Problems The figure shows a representation of a football field. The units represent yards. A sports analyst marks the locations of the football from where it was thrown (point A) and where it was caught (point B). Explain how you can use the Pythagorean Theorem to find the distance the ball was thrown. Then find the distance.

A (40, 26)

B (75, 14)

_____

_____

_____

_____

_____

Ready to Go On?

Personal Math Trainer
Online Assessment and Intervention
⏻ my.hrw.com

20.1 The Pythagorean Theorem

Find the length of the missing side.

1.

35 m

21 m

_____

2.

16 ft

30 ft

_____

20.2 Converse of the Pythagorean Theorem

Tell whether each triangle with the given side lengths is a right triangle.

3. 11, 60, 61 _____

4. 9, 37, 40 _____

5. 15, 35, 38 _____

6. 28, 45, 53 _____

7. Keelie has a triangular-shaped card. The lengths of its sides are 4.5 cm, 6 cm, and 7.5 cm. Is the card a right triangle?   _____

20.3 Distance Between Two Points

Find the distance between the given points. Round to the nearest tenth.

8. A and B _____

9. B and C _____

10. A and C _____

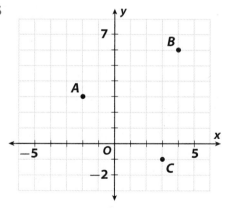

❓ ESSENTIAL QUESTION

11. How can you use the Pythagorean Theorem to solve real-world problems?

_____

_____

_____

Selected Response

1. What is the missing length of the side?

89 ft

80 ft

Ⓐ 9 ft   Ⓒ 39 ft

Ⓑ 30 ft   Ⓓ 120 ft

2. Which relation does **not** represent a function?

Ⓐ (0, 8), (3, 8), (1, 6)

Ⓑ (4, 2), (6, 1), (8, 9)

Ⓒ (1, 20), (2, 23), (9, 26)

Ⓓ (0, 3), (2, 3), (2, 0)

3. Two sides of a right triangle have lengths of 72 cm and 97 cm. The third side is **not** the hypotenuse. How long is the third side?

Ⓐ 25 cm   Ⓒ 65 cm

Ⓑ 45 cm   Ⓓ 121 cm

4. To the nearest tenth, what is the distance between point F and point G?

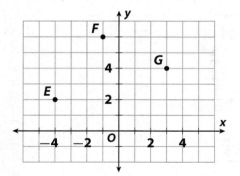

Ⓐ 4.5 units   Ⓒ 7.3 units

Ⓑ 5.0 units   Ⓓ 20 units

5. A flagpole is 53 feet tall. A rope is tied to the top of the flagpole and secured to the ground 28 feet from the base of the flagpole. What is the length of the rope?

Ⓐ 25 feet   Ⓒ 53 feet

Ⓑ 45 feet   Ⓓ 60 feet

6. Which set of lengths are **not** the side lengths of a right triangle?

Ⓐ 36, 77, 85   Ⓒ 27, 120, 123

Ⓑ 20, 99, 101   Ⓓ 24, 33, 42

7. A triangle has one right angle. What could the measures of the other two angles be?

Ⓐ 25° and 65°   Ⓒ 55° and 125°

Ⓑ 30° and 15°   Ⓓ 90° and 100°

Mini-Task

8. A fallen tree is shown on the coordinate grid below. Each unit represents 1 meter.

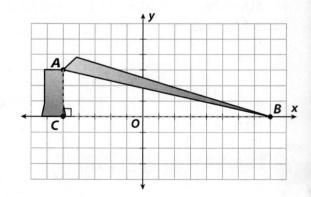

a. What is the distance from A to B?

_____

b. What was the height of the tree before it fell?

_____

Volume

MODULE

21

 ESSENTIAL QUESTION

How can you use volume to solve real-world problems?

Ⓞ my.hrw.com

Real-World Video

Many foods are in the shape of cylinders, cones, and spheres. To find out how much of the food you are eating, you can use formulas for volume.

GO DIGITAL
my.hrw.com

my.hrw.com
Go digital with your write-in student edition, accessible on any device.

Math On the Spot
Scan with your smart phone to jump directly to the online edition, video tutor, and more.

Animated Math
Interactively explore key concepts to see how math works.

Personal Math Trainer
Get immediate feedback and help as you work through practice sets.

659

Are YOU Ready?

Complete these exercises to review skills you will need for this module.

Exponents

EXAMPLE
$6^3 = 6 \times 6 \times 6$ Multiply the base (6) by itself the number of times indicated by the exponent (3).

$= 36 \times 6$ Find the product of the first two terms.

$= 216$ Find the product of all the terms.

Evaluate each exponential expression.

1. 11^2 _____ **2.** 2^5 _____ **3.** $\left(\frac{1}{5}\right)^3$ _____ **4.** $(0.3)^2$ _____

5. 2.1^3 _____ **6.** 0.1^3 _____ **7.** $\left(\frac{9.6}{3}\right)^2$ _____ **8.** 100^3 _____

Round Decimals

EXAMPLE
Round 43.2685 to the underlined place.

$43.2685 \rightarrow 43.27$

The digit to be rounded: 6
The digit to its right is 8.
8 is *5 or greater,* so round *up.*
The rounded number is 43.27.

Round to the underlined place.

9. 2.3_7_4 _____ **10.** 12_6_.399 _____ **11.** 13._9_577 _____ **12.** 42.6_9_0 _____

13. 134._9_5 _____ **14.** 2._0_486 _____ **15.** 63.6_3_52 _____ **16.** 98._9_499 _____

Simplify Numerical Expressions

EXAMPLE
$\frac{1}{3}(3.14)(4)^2(3) = \frac{1}{3}(3.14)(16)(3)$ Simplify the exponent.

$= 50.24$ Multiply from left to right.

Simplify each expression.

17. $3.14(5)^2(10)$ _____ **18.** $\frac{1}{3}(3.14)(3)^2(5)$ _____ **19.** $\frac{4}{3}(3.14)(3)^3$ _____

20. $\frac{4}{3}(3.14)(6)^3$ _____ **21.** $3.14(4)^2(9)$ _____ **22.** $\frac{1}{3}(3.14)(9)^2\left(\frac{2}{3}\right)$ _____

Reading Start-Up

Visualize Vocabulary

Use the ✔ words to complete the empty columns in the chart. You may use words more than once.

Shape	Distance Around	Attributes	Associated Review Words
circle		r, d	
square		90° corner, sides	
rectangle		90° corner, sides	

Vocabulary

Review Words
  area *(área)*
  base *(base, en numeración)*
✔ circumference *(circunferencia)*
✔ diameter *(diámetro)*
  height *(altura)*
✔ length *(longitud)*
✔ perimeter *(perímetro)*
✔ radius *(radio)*
✔ right angle *(ángulo recto)*
✔ width *(ancho)*

Preview Words
  cone *(cono)*
  cylinder *(cilindro)*
  sphere *(esfera)*

Understand Vocabulary

Complete the sentences using the preview words.

1. A three-dimensional figure that has one vertex and one circular

   base is a _____.

2. A three-dimensional figure with all points the same distance

   from the center is a _____.

3. A three-dimensional figure that has two congruent circular bases

   is a _____.

Active Reading

Three-Panel Flip Chart Before beginning the module, create a three-panel flip chart to help you organize what you learn. Label each flap with one of the lesson titles from this module. As you study each lesson, write important ideas like vocabulary, properties, and formulas under the appropriate flap.

Unpacking the Standards

Understanding the standards and the vocabulary terms in the standards will help you know exactly what you are expected to learn in this module.

 FL 8.G.3.9

Know the formulas for the volumes of cones, cylinders, and spheres and use them to solve real-world and mathematical problems.

Key Vocabulary

volume *(volumen)*
The number of cubic units needed to fill a given space.

cylinder *(cilindro)*
A three-dimensional figure with two parallel, congruent circular bases connected by a curved lateral surface.

What It Means to You

You will learn the formula for the volume of a cylinder.

UNPACKING EXAMPLE 8.G.3.9

The Asano Taiko Company of Japan built the world's largest drum in 2000. The drum's diameter is 4.8 meters, and its height is 4.95 meters. Estimate the volume of the drum.

$d = 4.8 \approx 5$ $V = (\pi r^2)h$ *Volume of a cylinder*

$h = 4.95 \approx 5$ $\approx (3)(2.5)^2 \cdot 5$ *Use 3 for π.*

$r = \frac{d}{2} \approx \frac{5}{2} = 2.5$ $= (3)(6.25)(5)$

$\qquad\qquad\qquad = 18.75 \cdot 5$

$\qquad\qquad\qquad = 93.75 \approx 94$

The volume of the drum is approximately 94 m³.

 FL 8.G.3.9

Know the formulas for the volumes of cones, cylinders, and spheres and use them to solve real-world and mathematical problems.

Key Vocabulary

cone *(cono)*
A three-dimensional figure with one vertex and one circular base.

sphere *(esfera)*
A three-dimensional figure with all points the same distance from the center.

What It Means to You

You will learn formulas for the volume of a cone and a sphere.

UNPACKING EXAMPLE 8.G.3.9

6 in.

2 in.

Find the volume of the cone. Use 3.14 for π.

$B = \pi(2^2) = 4\pi$ in²

$V = \frac{1}{3} \cdot 4\pi \cdot 6$ $V = \frac{1}{3}Bh$

$V = 8\pi$ *Use 3.14 for π.*

$\quad \approx 25.1$ in³

The volume of the cone is approximately 25.1 in³.

The volume of a sphere with the same radius is $V = \frac{4}{3}\pi r^3 \approx \frac{4}{3}(3)(2)^3 = 32$ in³.

21.1 Volume of Cylinders

FL 8.G.3.9

Know the formulas for the volumes of...cylinders...and use them to solve real-world and mathematical problems.

ESSENTIAL QUESTION

How do you find the volume of a cylinder?

EXPLORE ACTIVITY FL 8.G.3.9

Modeling the Volume of a Cylinder

A **cylinder** is a three-dimensional figure that has two congruent circular bases that lie in parallel planes. The volume of any three-dimensional figure is the number of cubic units needed to fill the space taken up by the solid figure.

One cube represents one cubic unit of volume. You can develop the formula for the volume of a cylinder using an empty soup can or other cylindrical container. First, remove one of the bases.

A Arrange centimeter cubes in a single layer at the bottom of the cylinder. Fit as many cubes into the layer as possible. How many cubes are in this layer?

_____

B To find how many layers of cubes fit in the cylinder, make a stack of cubes along the inside of the cylinder. How many layers fit in the cylinder?

_____

C How can you use what you know to find the approximate number of cubes that would fit in the cylinder?

_____

_____

Reflect

1. Make a Conjecture Suppose you know the area of the base of a cylinder and the height of the cylinder. How can you find the cylinder's volume?

_____

2. Let the area of the base of a cylinder be B and the height of the cylinder be h. Write a formula for the cylinder's volume V. _____

Math On the Spot

my.hrw.com

Finding the Volume of a Cylinder Using a Formula

Finding volumes of cylinders is similar to finding volumes of prisms. You find the volume V of both a prism and a cylinder by multiplying the height h by the area of the base B, so $V = Bh$.

The base of a cylinder is a circle, so for a cylinder, $B = \pi r^2$.

Volume of a Cylinder	
The volume V of a cylinder with radius r is the area of the base B times the height h.	
$V = Bh$ or $V = \pi r^2 h$	

EXAMPLE 1

FL 8.G.3.9

Find the volume of each cylinder. Round your answers to the nearest tenth if necessary. Use 3.14 for π.

A

10 in.

3 in.

$V = \pi r^2 h$

$\approx 3.14 \cdot 3^2 \cdot 10$ Substitute.

$\approx 3.14 \cdot 9 \cdot 10$ Simplify.

≈ 282.6 Multiply.

The volume is about 282.6 in³.

B

6.4 cm   13 cm

Since the diameter is 6.4 cm, the radius is 3.2 cm.

$V = \pi r^2 h$

$\approx 3.14 \cdot 3.2^2 \cdot 13$ Substitute.

$\approx 3.14 \cdot 10.24 \cdot 13$ Simplify.

≈ 418 Multiply.

> Recall that the diameter of a circle is twice the radius, so $2r = d$ and $r = \frac{d}{2}$.

The volume is about 418 cm³.

Reflect

3. **What If?** If you want a formula for the volume of a cylinder that involves the diameter d instead of the radius r, how can you rewrite it?

_____

Animated Math

my.hrw.com

My Notes

YOUR TURN

Find the volume of each cylinder. Round your answers to the nearest tenth if necessary. Use 3.14 for π.

4. 6 in. 10 in.

5. 4 ft 12 ft

Personal Math Trainer
Online Assessment and Intervention
⟳ my.hrw.com

Finding the Volume of a Cylinder in a Real-World Context

The Longhorn Band at the University of Texas at Austin has one of the world's largest bass drums, known as Big Bertha.

Math On the Spot
⟳ my.hrw.com

EXAMPLE 2

FL 8.G.3.9

Big Bertha has a diameter of 8 feet and is 4.5 feet deep. Find the volume of the drum to the nearest tenth. Use 3.14 for π.

STEP 1 Find the radius of the drum.

$$r = \frac{d}{2} = \frac{8}{2} = 4 \text{ ft}$$

STEP 2 Find the volume of the drum.

$V = \pi r^2 h$

$\approx 3.14 \cdot 4^2 \cdot 4.5$ Substitute.

$\approx 3.14 \cdot 16 \cdot 4.5$ Simplify the exponent.

≈ 226.08 Multiply.

The volume of the drum is about 226.1 ft³.

YOUR TURN

6. A drum company advertises a snare drum that is 4 inches high and 12 inches in diameter. Find the volume of the drum to the nearest tenth. Use 3.14 for π.

Personal Math Trainer
Online Assessment and Intervention
⟳ my.hrw.com

Lesson 21.1 **665**

1. **Vocabulary** Describe the bases of a cylinder. (Explore Activity)

   _____

2. Figure 1 shows a view from above of inch cubes on the bottom of a cylinder. Figure 2 shows the highest stack of cubes that will fit inside the cylinder. Estimate the volume of the cylinder. Explain your reasoning. (Explore Activity)

   _____

   _____

   _____

Figure 1   Figure 2

3. Find the volume of the cylinder to the nearest tenth. Use 3.14 for π. (Example 1)

   $V = \pi r^2 h$

   $V = \pi \cdot \boxed{}^2 \cdot \boxed{}$

   $\approx 3.14 \cdot \boxed{} \cdot \boxed{}$

   $\approx \boxed{}$

6 m

15 m

   The volume of the cylinder is approximately _____ m³.

4. A Japanese odaiko is a very large drum that is made by hollowing out a section of a tree trunk. A museum in Takayama City has three odaikos of similar size carved from a single tree trunk. The largest measures about 2.7 meters in both diameter and length, and weighs about 4.5 metric tons. Using the volume formula for a cylinder, approximate the volume of the drum to the nearest tenth. (Example 2)

   The radius of the drum is about _____ m.

   The volume of the drum is about _____ m³.

? ESSENTIAL QUESTION CHECK-IN

5. How do you find the volume of a cylinder? Describe which measurements of a cylinder you need to know.

   _____

   _____

   _____

21.1 Independent Practice

 FL 8.G.3.9

Personal Math Trainer

Online Assessment and Intervention

my.hrw.com

Find the volume of each figure. Round your answers to the nearest tenth if necessary. Use 3.14 for π.

6.
1.5 cm
11 cm

_____

7.
4 in.   24 in.

_____

8.
5 m   16 m

_____

9.
10 in.
12 in.

_____

10. A cylinder has a radius of 4 centimeters and a height of 40 centimeters.

_____

11. A cylinder has a radius of 8 meters and a height of 4 meters.

_____

Round your answer to the nearest tenth, if necessary. Use 3.14 for π.

12. The cylindrical Giant Ocean Tank at the New England Aquarium in Boston is 24 feet deep and has a radius of 18.8 feet. Find the volume of the tank.

_____

13. A standard-size bass drum has a diameter of 22 inches and is 18 inches deep. Find the volume of this drum.

_____

14. Grain is stored in cylindrical structures called silos. Find the volume of a silo with a diameter of 11.1 feet and a height of 20 feet.

_____

15. The Frank Erwin Center, or "The Drum," at the University of Texas in Austin can be approximated by a cylinder that is 120 meters in diameter and 30 meters in height. Find its volume.

_____

16. A barrel of crude oil contains about 5.61 cubic feet of oil. How many barrels of oil are contained in 1 mile (5280 feet) of a pipeline that has an inside diameter of 6 inches and is completely filled with oil? How much is "1 mile" of oil in this pipeline worth at a price of $100 per barrel?

_____

17. A pan for baking French bread is shaped like half a cylinder. It is 12 inches long and 3.5 inches in diameter. What is the volume of uncooked dough that would fill this pan?

3.5 in.

12 in.

_____

H.O.T.   FOCUS ON HIGHER ORDER THINKING

18. Explain the Error A student said the volume of a cylinder with a 3-inch diameter is two times the volume of a cylinder with the same height and a 1.5-inch radius. What is the error?

_____

_____

_____

Work Area

19. Communicate Mathematical Ideas Explain how you can find the height of a cylinder if you know the diameter and the volume. Include an example with your explanation.

_____

_____

_____

_____

_____

20. Analyze Relationships Cylinder A has a radius of 6 centimeters. Cylinder B has the same height and a radius half as long as cylinder A. What fraction of the volume of cylinder A is the volume of cylinder B? Explain.

_____

_____

_____

21.2 Volume of Cones

FL 8.G.3.9

Know the formulas for the volumes of cones…and use them to solve real-world and mathematical problems.

ESSENTIAL QUESTION

How do you find the volume of a cone?

EXPLORE ACTIVITY FL 8.G.3.9

Modeling the Volume of a Cone

A **cone** is a three-dimensional figure that has one vertex and one circular base.

To explore the volume of a cone, Sandi does an experiment with a cone and a cylinder that have congruent bases and heights. She fills the cone with popcorn kernels and then pours the kernels into the cylinder. She repeats this until the cylinder is full.

Sandi finds that it takes **3 cones** to fill the volume of the cylinder.

STEP 1 What is the formula for the volume V of a cylinder with base area B and height h? _____

STEP 2 What is the area of the base of the cone? _____

STEP 3 Sandi found that, when the bases and height are the same,

_____ times $V_{cone} = V_{cylinder}$.

STEP 4 How does the volume of the cone compare to the volume of the cylinder?

Volume of the cone: $V_{cone} = \dfrac{\Box}{\Box} \cdot V_{cylinder}$

Reflect

1. Use the conclusion from this experiment to write a formula for the volume of a cone in terms of the height and the radius. Explain.

   _____

2. How do you think the formula for the volume of a cone is similar to the formula for the volume of a pyramid?

   _____

Math On the Spot

my.hrw.com

Finding the Volume of a Cone Using a Formula

The formulas for the volume of a prism and the volume of a cylinder are the same: multiply the height h by the area of the base B, so $V = Bh$.

In the **Explore Activity**, you saw that the volume of a cone is one third the volume of a cylinder with the same base and height.

Volume of a Cone

The volume V of a cone with radius r is one third the area of the base B times the height h.	
$V = \frac{1}{3} Bh$ or $V = \frac{1}{3} \pi r^2 h$	

My Notes

EXAMPLE 1

FL 8.G.3.9

Find the volume of each cone. Round your answers to the nearest tenth. Use 3.14 for π.

A

8 in.

2 in.

$V = \frac{1}{3} \pi r^2 h$

$\approx \frac{1}{3} \cdot 3.14 \cdot 2^2 \cdot 8$ Substitute.

$\approx \frac{1}{3} \cdot 3.14 \cdot 4 \cdot 8$ Simplify.

≈ 33.5 Multiply.

The volume is about 33.5 in³.

B Since the diameter is 8 ft, the radius is 4 ft.

9 ft

8 ft

$V = \frac{1}{3} \pi r^2 h$

$\approx \frac{1}{3} \cdot 3.14 \cdot 4^2 \cdot 9$ Substitute.

$\approx \frac{1}{3} \cdot 3.14 \cdot 16 \cdot 9$ Simplify.

≈ 150.7 Multiply.

The volume is about 150.7 ft³.

Reflect

3. How can you rewrite the formula for the volume of a cone using the diameter d instead of the radius r? _____

YOUR TURN

Find the volume of each cone. Round your answers to the nearest tenth. Use 3.14 for π.

4.
15 cm
16 cm

5.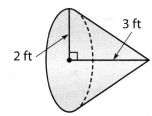
3 ft
2 ft

_____

_____

Finding the Volume of a Volcano

The mountain created by a volcano is often cone–shaped.

Math On the Spot

⏱ my.hrw.com

EXAMPLE 2

FL 8.G.3.9

For her geography project, Karen built a clay model of a volcano in the shape of a cone. Her model has a diameter of 12 inches and a height of 8 inches. Find the volume of clay in her model to the nearest tenth. Use 3.14 for π.

STEP 1 Find the radius.

$r = \dfrac{12}{2} = 6$ in.

STEP 2 Find the volume of clay.

$V = \frac{1}{3}\pi r^2 h$

$\approx \frac{1}{3} \cdot 3.14 \cdot 6^2 \cdot 8$ Substitute.

$\approx \frac{1}{3} \cdot 3.14 \cdot 36 \cdot 8$ Simplify.

≈ 301.44 Multiply.

The volume of the clay is about 301.4 in³.

YOUR TURN

6. The cone of the volcano Parícutin in Mexico had a height of 410 meters and a diameter of 424 meters. Approximate the volume of the cone.

_____

1. The area of the base of a cylinder is 45 square inches and its height is 10 inches. A cone has the same area for its base and the same height. What is the volume of the cone? (Explore Activity)

$$V_{cylinder} = Bh = \boxed{} \cdot \boxed{} = \boxed{}$$

$$V_{cone} = \frac{1}{3} V_{cylinder}$$

$$= \frac{1}{3} \boxed{}$$

$$= \boxed{}$$

The volume of the cone is _____ in³.

2. A cone and a cylinder have congruent height and bases. The volume of the cone is 18 m³. What is the volume of the cylinder? Explain. (Explore Activity)

_____

_____

_____

_____

_____

Find the volume of each cone. Round your answer to the nearest tenth if necessary. Use 3.14 for π. (Example 1)

3.

7 ft

6 ft

_____

4.

100 in.

33 in.

_____

5. Gretchen made a paper cone to hold a gift for a friend. The paper cone was 15 inches high and had a radius of 3 inches. Find the volume of the paper cone to the nearest tenth. Use 3.14 for π. (Example 2)

_____

6. A cone-shaped building is commonly used to store sand. What would be the volume of a cone-shaped building with a diameter of 50 meters and a height of 20 meters? Round your answer to the nearest tenth. Use 3.14 for π. (Example 2)

_____

? ESSENTIAL QUESTION CHECK-IN

7. How do you find the volume of a cone?

_____

_____

_____

21.2 Independent Practice

  8.G.3.9

Personal Math Trainer

Online Assessment and Intervention

my.hrw.com

Find the volume of each cone. Round your answers to the nearest tenth if necessary. Use 3.14 for π.

8.

7 mm

8 mm

_____

9.

6 in.

2 in.

_____

10. A cone has a diameter of 6 centimeters and a height of 11.5 centimeters.

_____

11. A cone has a radius of 3 meters and a height of 10 meters.

_____

Round your answers to the nearest tenth if necessary. Use 3.14 for π.

12. Antonio is making mini waffle cones. Each waffle cone is 3 inches high and has a radius of $\frac{3}{4}$ inch. What is the volume of a waffle cone?

_____

13. A snack bar sells popcorn in cone-shaped containers. One container has a diameter of 8 inches and a height of 10 inches. How many cubic inches of popcorn does the container hold?

_____

14. A volcanic cone has a diameter of 300 meters and a height of 150 meters. What is the volume of the cone?

_____

15. Multistep Orange traffic cones come in a variety of sizes. Approximate the volume, in cubic inches, of a traffic cone that has a height of 2 feet and a diameter of 10 inches. Use 3.14 for π.

_____

Find the missing measure for each cone. Round your answers to the nearest tenth if necessary. Use 3.14 for π.

16. radius = _____

height = 6 in.

volume = 100.48 in³

17. diameter = 6 cm

height = _____

volume = 56.52 cm³

18. The diameter of a cone-shaped container is 4 inches, and its height is 6 inches. How much greater is the volume of a cylinder-shaped container with the same diameter and height? Round your answer to the nearest hundredth. Use 3.14 for π.

_____

FOCUS ON HIGHER ORDER THINKING

19. Alex wants to know the volume of sand in an hourglass. When all the sand is in the bottom, he stands a ruler up beside the hourglass and estimates the height of the cone of sand.

    a. What else does he need to measure to find the volume of sand?

    _____

    _____

    b. Make a Conjecture If the volume of sand is increasing at a constant rate, is the height increasing at a constant rate? Explain.

    _____

    _____

    _____

20. Problem Solving The diameter of a cone is x cm, the height is 18 cm, and the volume is 301.44 cm³. What is x? Use 3.14 for π.

_____

21. Analyze Relationships A cone has a radius of 1 foot and a height of 2 feet. How many cones of liquid would it take to fill a cylinder with a diameter of 2 feet and a height of 2 feet? Explain.

_____

_____

_____

22. Critique Reasoning Herb knows that the volume of a cone is one third that of a cylinder with the same base and height. He reasons that a cone with the same height as a given cylinder but 3 times the radius should therefore have the same volume as the cylinder, since $\frac{1}{3} \cdot 3 = 1$. Is Herb correct? Explain.

_____

_____

_____

_____

_____

LESSON
21.3 Volume of Spheres

FL 8.G.3.9
Know the formulas for the volumes of...spheres and use them to solve real-world and mathematical problems.

ESSENTIAL QUESTION

How do you find the volume of a sphere?

EXPLORE ACTIVITY FL 8.G.3.9

Modeling the Volume of a Sphere

A **sphere** is a three-dimensional figure with all points the same distance from the center. The **radius** of a sphere is the distance from the center to any point on the sphere.

You have seen that a cone fills $\frac{1}{3}$ of a cylinder of the same radius and height h. If you were to do a similar experiment with a sphere of the same radius, you would find that a sphere fills $\frac{2}{3}$ of the cylinder. The cylinder's height is equal to twice the radius of the sphere.

  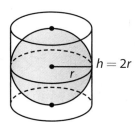

STEP 1 Write the formula $V = Bh$ for each shape. Use $B = \pi r^2$ and substitute the fractions you know for the cone and sphere.

Cylinder	**Cone**	**Sphere**
$V = \pi r^2 h$	$V = \frac{1}{3}\pi r^2 h$	$V = \frac{2}{3}\pi r^2 h$

STEP 2 Notice that a sphere always has a height equal to twice the radius. Substitute $2r$ for h.

$$V = \frac{2}{3}\pi r^2 (2r)$$

STEP 3 Simplify this formula for the volume of a sphere.

$$V = \boxed{}\,\pi r^3$$

Reflect

1. **Analyze Relationships** A cone has a radius of r and a height of $2r$. A sphere has a radius of r. Compare the volume of the sphere and cone.

_____

_____

_____

Finding the Volume of a Sphere Using a Formula

The Explore Activity illustrates a formula for the volume of a sphere with radius *r*.

> ### Volume of a Sphere
>
> The volume *V* of a sphere is $\frac{4}{3}\pi$ times the cube of the radius *r*.
>
> $V = \frac{4}{3}\pi r^3$
>
>

EXAMPLE 1

 FL 8.G.3.9

Find the volume of each sphere. Round your answers to the nearest tenth if necessary. Use 3.14 for π.

A

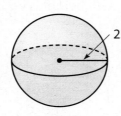

2.1 cm

$V = \frac{4}{3}\pi r^3$

$\approx \frac{4}{3} \cdot 3.14 \cdot 2.1^3$ Substitute.

$\approx \frac{4}{3} \cdot 3.14 \cdot 9.26$ Simplify.

≈ 38.8 Multiply.

The volume is about 38.8 cm³.

B

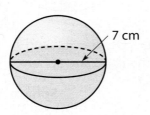

7 cm

Since the diameter is 7 cm, the radius is 3.5 cm.

$V = \frac{4}{3}\pi r^3$

$\approx \frac{4}{3} \cdot 3.14 \cdot 3.5^3$ Substitute.

$\approx \frac{4}{3} \cdot 3.14 \cdot 42.9$ Simplify.

≈ 179.6 Multiply.

The volume is about 179.6 cm³.

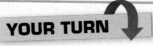
YOUR TURN

Find the volume of each sphere. Round your answers to the nearest tenth. Use 3.14 for π.

2. A sphere has a radius of 10 centimeters. _____

3. A sphere has a diameter of 3.4 meters. _____

Finding the Volume of a Sphere in a Real-World Context

Many sports, including golf and tennis, use a ball that is spherical in shape.

EXAMPLE 2   FL 8.G.3.9

Soccer balls come in several different sizes. One soccer ball has a diameter of 22 centimeters. What is the volume of this soccer ball? Round your answer to the nearest tenth. Use 3.14 for π.

STEP 1 Find the radius.

$r = \frac{d}{2} = 11$ cm

STEP 2 Find the volume of the soccer ball.

$V = \frac{4}{3}\pi r^3$

$\approx \frac{4}{3} \cdot 3.14 \cdot 11^3$ Substitute.

$\approx \frac{4}{3} \cdot 3.14 \cdot 1331$ Simplify.

≈ 5572.4533 Multiply.

The volume of the soccer ball is about 5572.5 cm³.

Reflect

4. What is the volume of the soccer ball in terms of π, to the nearest whole number multiple? Explain your answer.

_____

_____

5. **Analyze Relationships** The diameter of a basketball is about 1.1 times that of a soccer ball. The diameter of a tennis ball is about 0.3 times that of a soccer ball. How do the volumes of these balls compare to that of a soccer ball? Explain.

_____

_____

_____

YOUR TURN

6. Val measures the diameter of a ball as 12 inches. How many cubic inches of air does this ball hold, to the nearest tenth? Use 3.14 for π.

_____

1. **Vocabulary** A sphere is a three-dimensional figure with all points

   _____ from the center. (Explore Activity)

2. **Vocabulary** The _____ is the distance from the center
   of a sphere to a point on the sphere. (Explore Activity)

**Find the volume of each sphere. Round your answers to the nearest tenth
if necessary. Use 3.14 for π.** (Example 1)

3.

1 in.

_____

4.

20 cm

_____

5. A sphere has a radius of 1.5 feet. _____

6. A sphere has a diameter of 2 yards. _____

7. A baseball has a diameter of 2.9 inches. Find the volume of the baseball. Round
   your answer to the nearest tenth if necessary. Use 3.14 for π. (Example 2) _____

8. A basketball has a radius of 4.7 inches. What is its volume to the nearest
   cubic inch? Use 3.14 for π. (Example 2) _____

9. A company is deciding whether to package a ball
   in a cubic box or a cylindrical box. In either case,
   the ball will touch the bottom, top, and sides.
   (Explore Activity)

   a. What portion of the space inside the cylindrical
   box is empty? Explain.

   _____

   b. Find an expression for the volume of the cubic box. _____

   c. About what portion of the space inside the cubic box is empty? Explain.

   _____

   _____

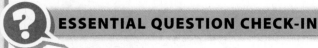

ESSENTIAL QUESTION CHECK-IN

10. Explain the steps you use to find the volume of a sphere.

    _____

21.3 Independent Practice

 FL 8.G.3.9

Personal Math Trainer

Online Assessment and Intervention

my.hrw.com

Find the volume of each sphere. Round your answers to the nearest tenth if necessary. Use 3.14 for π.

11. radius of 3.1 meters _____

12. diameter of 18 inches _____

13. $r = 6$ in. _____

14. $d = 36$ m _____

15.

11 cm

_____

16.

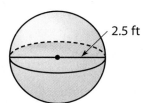

2.5 ft

_____

The eggs of birds and other animals come in many different shapes and sizes. Eggs often have a shape that is nearly spherical. When this is true, you can use the formula for a sphere to find their volume.

17. The green turtle lays eggs that are approximately spherical with an average diameter of 4.5 centimeters. Each turtle lays an average of 113 eggs at one time. Find the total volume of these eggs, to the nearest cubic centimeter.

_____

18. Hummingbirds lay eggs that are nearly spherical and about 1 centimeter in diameter. Find the volume of an egg. Round your answer to the nearest tenth.

_____

19. Fossilized spherical eggs of dinosaurs called titanosaurid sauropods were found in Patagonia. These eggs were 15 centimeters in diameter. Find the volume of an egg. Round your answer to the nearest tenth.

_____

20. **Persevere in Problem Solving** An ostrich egg has about the same volume as a sphere with a diameter of 5 inches. If the eggshell is about $\frac{1}{12}$ inch thick, find the volume of just the shell, not including the interior of the egg. Round your answer to the nearest tenth.

_____

21. **Multistep** Write the steps you would use to find a formula for the volume of the figure at right. Then write the formula.

_____

_____

_____

_____

_____

_____

_____

_____

_____

_____

22. Critical Thinking Explain what happens to the volume of a sphere if you double the radius.

_____

23. Multistep A cylindrical can of tennis balls holds a stack of three balls so that they touch the can at the top, bottom, and sides. The radius of each ball is 1.25 inches. Find the volume inside the can that is not taken up by the three tennis balls.

_____

H.O.T. FOCUS ON HIGHER ORDER THINKING

Work Area

24. Critique Reasoning A sphere has a radius of 4 inches, and a cube-shaped box has an edge length of 7.5 inches. J.D. says the box has a greater volume, so the sphere will fit in the box. Is he correct? Explain.

_____

_____

_____

25. Critical Thinking Which would hold the most water: a bowl in the shape of a hemisphere with radius r, a cylindrical glass with radius r and height r, or a cone-shaped drinking cup with radius r and height r? Explain.

_____

_____

_____

26. Analyze Relationships Hari has models of a sphere, a cylinder, and a cone. The sphere's diameter and the cylinder's height are the same, $2r$. The cylinder has radius r. The cone has diameter $2r$ and height $2r$. Compare the volumes of the cone and the sphere to the volume of the cylinder.

_____

_____

_____

27. A spherical helium balloon that is 8 feet in diameter can lift about 17 pounds. What does the diameter of a balloon need to be to lift a person who weighs 136 pounds? Explain.

_____

_____

_____

Ready to Go On?

Personal Math Trainer
Online Assessment and Intervention

⏻ my.hrw.com

21.1 Volume of Cylinders

Find the volume of each cylinder. Round your answers to the nearest tenth if necessary. Use 3.14 for π.

1. 6 ft

8 ft

_____

2. A can of juice has a radius of 4 inches and a height of 7 inches. What is the volume of the can?

_____

21.2 Volume of Cones

Find the volume of each cone. Round your answers to the nearest tenth if necessary. Use 3.14 for π.

3.

15 cm

6 cm _____

4.

20 in.

12 in. _____

21.3 Volume of Spheres

Find the volume of each sphere. Round your answers to the nearest tenth if necessary. Use 3.14 for π.

5.

3 ft

_____

6.

13 cm

_____

? ESSENTIAL QUESTION

7. What measurements do you need to know to find the volume of a cylinder? a cone? a sphere?

_____

_____

Personal
Math Trainer

Online
Assessment and
Intervention

my.hrw.com

Selected Response

1. The bed of a pickup truck measures 4 feet by 8 feet. To the nearest inch, what is the length of the longest thin metal bar that will lie flat in the bed?

Ⓐ 11 ft 3 in.   Ⓒ 8 ft 11 in.

Ⓑ 10 ft 0 in.   Ⓓ 8 ft 9 in.

2. Using 3.14 for π, what is the volume of the cylinder below to the nearest tenth?

11.4 yd

10.7 yd

Ⓐ 102 cubic yards

Ⓑ 347.6 cubic yards

Ⓒ 1,091.6 cubic yards

Ⓓ 4,366.4 cubic yards

3. Rhett made mini waffle cones for a birthday party. Each waffle cone was 3.5 inches high and had a radius of 0.8 inches. What is the volume of each cone to the nearest hundredth?

Ⓐ 1.70 cubic inches

Ⓑ 2.24 cubic inches

Ⓒ 2.34 cubic inches

Ⓓ 8.79 cubic inches

4. What is the volume of a cone that has a height of 17 meters and a base with a radius of 6 meters? Use 3.14 for π and round to the nearest tenth.

Ⓐ 204 cubic meters

Ⓑ 640.6 cubic meters

Ⓒ 2,562.2 cubic meters

Ⓓ 10,249 cubic meters

5. Using 3.14 for π, what is the volume of the sphere to the nearest tenth?

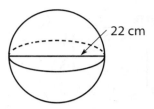

22 cm

Ⓐ 4,180 cubic centimeters

Ⓑ 5,572.5 cubic centimeters

Ⓒ 33,434.7 cubic centimeters

Ⓓ 44,579.6 cubic centimeters

Mini-Task

6. A diagram of a deodorant container is shown. It is made up of a cylinder and half of a sphere.

1.6 cm

6.2 cm

Use 3.14 for π and round answers to the nearest tenth.

a. What is the volume of the half sphere?

_____

b. What is the volume of the cylinder?

_____

c. What is the volume of the whole figure?

_____

MODULE 19 ## Angle Relationships in Parallel Lines and Triangles

? **ESSENTIAL QUESTION**

How can you solve real-world problems that involve angle relationships in parallel lines and triangles?

EXAMPLE 1
Find each angle measure when m∠6 = 81°.

A m∠5 = 180° − 81° = 99°

 5 and 6 are supplementary angles.

B m∠1 = 99°

 1 and 5 are corresponding angles.

C m∠3 = 180° − 81° = 99°

 3 and 6 are same-side interior angles.

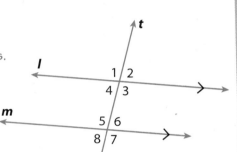

EXAMPLE 2
Are the triangles similar? Explain your answer.

$y = 180° - (67° + 35°)$

$y = 78°$

$x = 180° - (67° + 67°)$

$x = 46°$

The triangles are not similar, because they do not have 2 or more pairs of corresponding congruent angles.

EXERCISES

1. If m∠GHA = 106°, find the measures of the given angles.
   (Lesson 19.1)

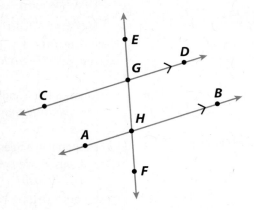

   m∠EGC = _____

   m∠EGD = _____

   m∠BHF = _____

   m∠HGD = _____

2. Find the measure of the missing angles. (Lesson 19.2)

   m∠JKL = _____

   m∠LKM = _____

3. Is the larger triangle similar to the smaller triangle?
   Explain your answer. (Lesson 19.3)

   _____

   _____

   _____

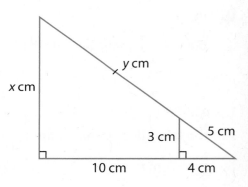

4. Find the value of x and y in the figure. (Lesson 19.3)

   _____

5. If m∠CJI = 132° and m∠EIH = 59°, find the measures of
   the given angles. (Lesson 19.1)

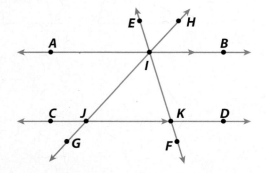

   m∠IKJ = _____

   m∠HIB = _____

   m∠EIJ = _____

   m∠AIK = _____

? **ESSENTIAL QUESTION**

How can you use the Pythagorean Theorem to solve real-world problems?

EXAMPLE 1

Find the missing side length.
Round your answer to the nearest tenth.

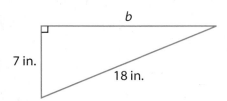

$a^2 + b^2 = c^2$

$7^2 + b^2 = 18^2$

$49 + b^2 = 324$

$b^2 = 275$

$b = \sqrt{275} \approx 16.6$

The length of the leg is about 16.6 inches.

EXAMPLE 2

Thomas drew a diagram to represent the location of his house, the school, and his friend Manuel's house. What is the distance from the school to Manuel's house? Round your answer to the nearest tenth.

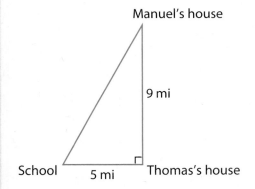

$a^2 + b^2 = c^2$

$5^2 + 9^2 = c^2$

$25 + 81 = c^2$

$c^2 = 106$

$c = \sqrt{106} \approx 10.3$

The distance from the school to Manuel's house is about 10.3 miles.

EXERCISES

Find the missing side lengths. Round your answers to the nearest hundredth. *(Lesson 20.1)*

1.

2.

_____

_____

3. Hye Sun has a modern coffee table whose top is a triangle with the following side lengths: 8 feet, 3 feet, and 5 feet. Is Hye Sun's coffee table top a right triangle? (Lesson 20.2)

_____

4. Find the length of each side of triangle *ABC*. If necessary, round your answers to the nearest hundredth. (Lesson 20.3)

$\overline{AB}$ _____

$\overline{BC}$ _____

$\overline{AC}$ _____

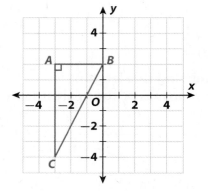

Volume

? ESSENTIAL QUESTION

How can you solve real-world problems that involve volume?

EXAMPLE 1

Find the volume of the cistern. Round your answer to the nearest hundredth.

$V = \pi r^2 h$

$\approx 3.14 \cdot 2.5^2 \cdot 7.5$

$\approx 3.14 \cdot 6.25 \cdot 7.5$

≈ 147.19

The cistern has a volume of approximately 147.19 cubic feet.

EXAMPLE 2

Find the volume of a sphere with a radius of 3.7 cm. Write your answer in terms of π and to the nearest hundredth.

$V = \frac{4}{3}\pi r^3$ $V = \frac{4}{3}\pi r^3$

$\approx \frac{4}{3} \cdot \pi \cdot 3.7^3$ $\approx \frac{4}{3} \cdot 3.14 \cdot 3.7^3$

$\approx \frac{4}{3} \cdot \pi \cdot 50.653$ $\approx \frac{4}{3} \cdot 3.14 \cdot 50.653$

$\approx 67.54\pi$ ≈ 212.07

The volume of the sphere is approximately 67.54π cm³, or 212.07 cm³.

EXERCISES

Find the volume of each figure. Round your answers to the nearest hundredth. (Lessons 21.1, 21.2, 21.3)

1.
12 mm
4 mm

_____

2.
34 in.
50 in.

_____

3. Find the volume of a ball with a radius of 1.68 inches.

_____

4.
10 cm

_____

5.
2.2 m
1.4 m

_____

6. A round above-ground swimming pool has a diameter of 15 ft and a height of 4.5 ft. What is the volume of the swimming pool?

_____

7.
0.8 in.
11.2 in.

_____

8.
10 yd
13.3 yd

_____

9. A paper cup in the shape of a cone has a height of 4.7 inches and a diameter of 3.6 inches. What is the volume of the paper cup?

_____

1. **CAREERS IN MATH**   **Hydrologist** A hydrologist needs to estimate the mass of water in an underground aquifer, which is roughly cylindrical in shape. The diameter of the aquifer is 65 meters, and its depth is 8 meters. One cubic meter of water has a mass of about 1000 kilograms.

   a. The aquifer is completely filled with water. What is the total mass of the water in the aquifer? Explain how you found your answer. Use 3.14 for π and round your answer to the nearest kilogram.

   _____

   _____

   _____

   b. Another cylindrical aquifer has a diameter of 70 meters and a depth of 9 meters. The mass of the water in it is 27×10^7 kilograms. Is the aquifer totally filled with water? Explain your reasoning.

   _____

   _____

   _____

2. From his home, Myles walked his dog north 5 blocks, east 2 blocks, and then stopped at a drinking fountain. He then walked north 3 more blocks and east 4 more blocks. It started to rain so he cut through a field and walked straight home.

   a. Draw a diagram of his path.

   _____

   b. How many blocks did Myles walk in all? How much longer was his walk before it started to rain than his walk home?

   _____

Selected Response

1. Which of the following angle pairs formed by a transversal that intersects two parallel lines are not congruent?

Ⓐ alternate interior angles

Ⓑ adjacent angles

Ⓒ corresponding angles

Ⓓ alternate exterior angles

2. The measures of the three angles of a triangle are given by $3x + 1$, $2x - 3$, and $9x$. What is the measure of the smallest angle?

Ⓐ 13°   Ⓒ 29°

Ⓑ 23°   Ⓓ 40°

3. Using 3.14 for π, what is the volume of the cylinder?

10 yd

8 yd

Ⓐ 200 cubic yards

Ⓑ 628 cubic yards

Ⓒ 1,256 cubic yards

Ⓓ 2,512 cubic yards

4. Which of the following is **not** true?

Ⓐ $\sqrt{36} + 2 > \sqrt{16} + 5$

Ⓑ $5\pi < 17$

Ⓒ $\sqrt{10} + 1 < \frac{9}{2}$

Ⓓ $5 - \sqrt{35} < 0$

5. A pole is 65 feet tall. A support wire is attached to the top of the pole and secured to the ground 33 feet from the base of the pole. Find the approximate length of the wire.

Ⓐ 32 feet   Ⓒ 56 feet

Ⓑ 73 feet   Ⓓ 60 feet

6. Using 3.14 for π, what is the volume of the sphere to the nearest tenth?

7 cm

Ⓐ 205.1 cm³

Ⓑ 1,077 cm³

Ⓒ 179.5 cm³

Ⓓ 4,308.1 cm³

7. Which set of lengths are **not** the side lengths of a right triangle?

Ⓐ 28, 45, 53   Ⓒ 36, 77, 85

Ⓑ 13, 84, 85   Ⓓ 16, 61, 65

8. Which statement describes the solution of a system of linear equations for two lines with different slopes and different y-intercepts?

Ⓐ one nonzero solution

Ⓑ infinitely many solutions

Ⓒ no solution

Ⓓ solution of 0

9. What is the side length of a cube that has a volume of 729 cubic inches?

Ⓐ 7 inches   Ⓒ 9 inches

Ⓑ 8 inches   Ⓓ 10 inches

10. What is the solution to the system of equations?

$$\begin{cases} x + 3y = 5 \\ 2x - y = -4 \end{cases}$$

Ⓐ no solution

Ⓑ infinitely many solutions

Ⓒ (2, 1)

Ⓓ (−1, 2)

Mini-Tasks

11. In the figure shown, m∠AGE = (5x − 7)°
and m∠BGH = (3x + 19)°.

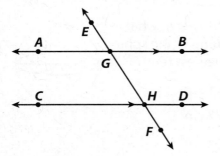

   a. Find the value of x. _____

   b. Find m∠AGE. _____

   c. Find m∠GHD. _____

12. Tom drew two right triangles as shown with
angle measures to the nearest whole unit.

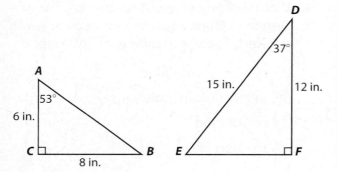

   a. Find the length of $\overline{AB}$ in triangle *ABC*.

   _____

   b. Find the length of $\overline{EF}$ in triangle *DEF*.

   _____

   c. Are the triangles similar? Explain your
answer.

   _____

   _____

   _____

   _____

   _____

Hot Tip!

**Read graphs and diagrams
carefully. Look at the labels for
important information.**

13. In the diagram, the figure at the top of the
cone is a hemisphere.

   a. What is the volume of the cone?
Round your answer to the nearest
hundredth.

   _____

   b. What is the volume of the hemisphere
on the top of the cone? Round your
answer to the nearest hundredth.

   _____

   c. What would be the radius of a sphere
with the same total volume as the figure?
Explain how you found your answer.

   _____

   _____

   _____

   _____

   _____

Statistics: Bivariate Data

MODULE 22

Scatter Plots

FL 8.SP.1.1, 8.SP.1.2, 8.SP.1.3

MODULE 23

Two-Way Tables

FL 8.SP.1.4

CAREERS IN MATH

Psychologist A psychologist investigates the physical, mental, emotional, and social aspects of human behavior. Psychologists use math to evaluate and interpret data about human activities and the human mind. They create and use mathematical models to predict behavior of humans, both individually and in groups.

If you are interested in a career in psychology, you should study the following mathematical subjects:

- Algebra
- Trigonometry
- Probability and Statistics
- Calculus

Research other careers that require the analysis of data and use of mathematical models.

Unit 10 Performance Task

At the end of the unit, check out how **psychologists** use math.

Vocabulary Preview

Use the puzzle to preview key vocabulary from this unit. Unscramble the circled letters within found words to answer the riddle at the bottom of the page.

A description of how sets of data are related. (Lesson 14.1)

A set of closely related data. (Lesson 14.1)

A data point that is very different from the rest of the data in the set. (Lesson 14.1)

A straight line that comes closest to the points on a scatter plot (2 words). (Lesson 14.2)

Using a trend line to predict a value between data points you already know. (Lesson 14.2)

A relative frequency found by dividing a row total or a column total by the grand total. (Lesson 15.2)

Q: Why doesn't Joe Average have any friends?

A: Because he's so ___ ___ ___ ___!

Scatter Plots

? ESSENTIAL QUESTION

How can you use scatter plots to solve real-world problems?

Real-World Video

An anthropologist measures dinosaur bones. To estimate a dinosaur's height based on the length of a bone, he can make a scatter plot comparing bone length and height of several dinosaurs.

my.hrw.com

GO DIGITAL
my.hrw.com

my.hrw.com

Go digital with your write-in student edition, accessible on any device.

Math On the Spot

Scan with your smart phone to jump directly to the online edition, video tutor, and more.

Animated Math

Interactively explore key concepts to see how math works.

Personal Math Trainer

Get immediate feedback and help as you work through practice sets.

Are YOU Ready?

Complete these exercises to review skills you will need for this module.

Personal
Math Trainer

Online
Assessment and
Intervention

my.hrw.com

Evaluate Expressions

> **EXAMPLE**   Evaluate $4x + 3$ for $x = 5$.
> $4x + 3 = 4(5) + 3$ Substitute the given value for x.
> $ = 20 + 3$ Multiply.
> $ = 23$ Add.

Evaluate each expression for the given value of x.

1. $6x - 5$ for $x = 4$

2. $-2x + 7$ for $x = 2$

3. $5x - 6$ for $x = 3$

4. $0.5x + 8.4$ for $x = -1$

5. $\frac{3}{4}x - 9$ for $x = -20$

6. $1.4x + 3.5$ for $x = -4$

Solve Two-Step Equations

> **EXAMPLE** $5x + 3 = -7$
> $\underline{-3 = -3}$ Subtract 3 from both sides.
> $5x = -10$
> $\dfrac{5x}{5} = \dfrac{-10}{5}$ Divide both sides by 5.
> $x = -2$

Solve for x.

7. $3x + 4 = 10$

8. $5x - 11 = 34$

9. $-2x + 5 = -9$

10. $8x + 13 = -11$

11. $4x - 7 = -27$

12. $\frac{1}{2}x + 16 = 39$

13. $\frac{2}{3}x - 16 = 12$

14. $0.5x - 1.5 = -6.5$

Reading Start-Up

Visualize Vocabulary

Use the ✔ words to complete the right column of the chart.

Reviewing Slope	
Mathematical Representation	**Review Word**
$y = mx + b$	
y	
m	
x	
b	

Understand Vocabulary

Match the term on the left to the correct expression on the right.

1. cluster

2. outlier

3. trend line

A. A data point that is very different from the rest of the data in a set

B. A straight line that comes closest to the points on a scatter plot.

C. A set of closely grouped data.

Vocabulary

Review Words
  bivariate data *(datos bivariados)*
  data *(datos)*
✔ linear equation *(ecuación lineal)*
✔ slope *(pendiente)*
✔ slope-intercept form of an equation *(forma pendiente-intersección)*
✔ *x*-coordinate *(coordenada x)*
✔ *y*-coordinate *(coordenada y)*
✔ *y*-intercept *(intersección con el eje y)*

Preview Words
  cluster *(agrupación)*
  outlier *(valor extremo)*
  scatter plot *(diagrama de dispersión)*
  trend line *(línea de tendencia)*

Active Reading

Two-Panel Flip Chart Create a two-panel flip chart, to help you understand the concepts in this module. Label each flap with the title of one of the lessons in the module. As you study each lesson, write important ideas under the appropriate flap. Include any sample problems or equations that will help you remember the concepts later when you look back at your notes.

Unpacking the Standards

Understanding the standards and the vocabulary terms in the standards will help you know exactly what you are expected to learn in this module.

FL 8.SP.1.1

Construct and interpret scatter plots for bivariate measurement data to investigate patterns of association between two quantities. Describe patterns such as clustering, outliers, positive or negative association, linear association, and nonlinear association.

What It Means to You

You will describe how the data in a scatter plot are related.

UNPACKING EXAMPLE 8.SP.1.1

The scatter plot shows Bob's height at various ages. Describe the type(s) of association between Bob's age and his height. Explain.

As Bob gets older, his height increases roughly along a straight line on the graph, so the association is positive and basically linear.

FL 8.SP.1.2

Know that straight lines are widely used to model relationships between two quantitative variables. For scatter plots that suggest a linear association, informally fit a straight line, and informally assess the model fit by judging the closeness of the data points to the line.

What It Means to You

You will use a trend line to show the relationship between two quantities.

UNPACKING EXAMPLE 8.SP.1.2

Joyce is training for a 10K race. For each of her training runs, she recorded the distance she ran and the time she ran. She made a scatter plot of her data and drew a trend line. Use the trend line to predict how long it would take Joyce to run 4.5 miles.

Distance (mi)	Time (min)
4	38
2	25
1	7
2	16
3	26
5	55
2	20
4	45
3	31

For a distance of 4.5 miles, the trend line shows a time of 45 minutes. So, it will take Joyce about 45 minutes to run 4.5 miles.

Visit **my.hrw.com** to see all **Florida Math Standards** unpacked.

my.hrw.com

LESSON
22.1 Scatter Plots and Association

 FL 8.SP.1.1

Construct and interpret
scatter plots.... Describe
patterns such as clustering,
outliers, positive or
negative association, linear
association, and nonlinear
association.

ESSENTIAL QUESTION

How can you construct and interpret scatter plots?

EXPLORE ACTIVITY 1   **FL** 8.SP.1.1

Making a Scatter Plot

Recall that a set of bivariate data involves two variables. Bivariate data are used to explore the relationship between two variables. You can graph bivariate data on a *scatter plot*. A **scatter plot** is a graph with points plotted to show the relationship between two sets of data.

The final question on a math test reads, "How many hours did you spend studying for this test?" The teacher records the number of hours each student studied and the grade the student received on the test.

Hours Spent Studying	Test Grade
0	75
0.5	80
1	80
1	85
1.5	85
1.5	95
2	90
3	100
4	90

A Make a prediction about the relationship between the number of hours spent studying and test grades.

_____

_____

_____

B Make a scatter plot. Graph hours spent studying as the independent variable and test grades as the dependent variable.

Reflect

1. What trend do you see in the data?

_____

_____

2. Justify Reasoning Do you think the grade associated with studying for 10 hours would follow this trend?

_____

_____

Interpreting Clusters and Outliers

A **cluster** is a set of closely grouped data. Data may cluster around a point or along a line. An **outlier** is a data point that is very different from the rest of the data in the set.

A scientist gathers information about the eruptions of Old Faithful, a geyser in Yellowstone National Park. She uses the data to create a scatter plot. The data show the length of time between eruptions (interval) and how long the eruption lasts (duration).

A Describe any clusters you see in the scatter plot.

_____

_____

B What do the clusters tell you about eruptions of Old Faithful?

_____

_____

C Describe any outliers you see in the scatter plot.

_____

_____

Math Talk
Mathematical Practices

If the point (20, 1) appeared on the scatter plot, would it be an outlier? Explain.

Reflect

3. Suppose the geyser erupts for 2.2 minutes after a 75-minute interval. Would this point lie in one of the clusters? Would it be an outlier? Explain your answer.

_____

_____

_____

4. Suppose the geyser erupts after an 80-minute interval. Give a range of possible duration times for which the point on the scatter plot would not be considered an outlier. Explain your reasoning.

_____

_____

Determining Association

Association describes how sets of data are related. A *positive* association means that both data sets increase together. A *negative* association means that as one data set increases, the other decreases. *No* association means that there is no relationship between the two data sets.

Positive association

Negative association

No association

Data that show a positive or negative association and lie basically along a line exhibit a *linear* association. Data that show a positive or negative association but do not lie basically along a line exhibit a *nonlinear* association.

EXAMPLE 1

FL   8.SP.1.1

Susan asked 20 people if they would buy a new product she developed at each of several prices. The scatter plot shows how many of the 20 said "yes" at a given price. Describe the association between price and the number of buyers.

As price increases, the number of buyers decreases. So, there is a negative association. Because the data points do not lie along a line, the association is nonlinear.

Animated Math
my.hrw.com

Math On the Spot
my.hrw.com

Reflect

5. **What If?** Based on the association shown in the scatter plot, what might happen if Susan increased the price to $14?

_____

YOUR TURN

6. The plot shows the reading level and height for 16 students in a district. Describe the association and give a possible reason for it.

_____

_____

_____

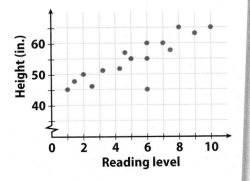

Personal Math Trainer

Online Assessment and Intervention

my.hrw.com

Bob recorded his height at different ages. The table below shows his data.

Age (years)	6	8	10	12	14
Height (inches)	45	50	55	61	63

1. Make a scatter plot of Bob's data. (Explore Activity 1)

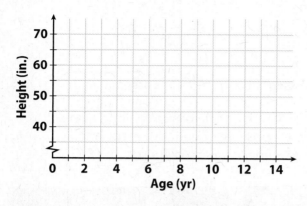

2. Describe the association between Bob's age and his height. Explain the association. (Example 1)

_____

_____

_____

3. The scatter plot shows the basketball shooting results for 14 players. Describe any clusters you see in the scatter plot. Identify any outliers. (Explore Activity 2)

_____

_____

_____

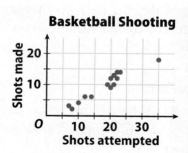

Basketball Shooting

? ESSENTIAL QUESTION CHECK-IN

4. Explain how you can make a scatter plot from a set of bivariate data.

_____

_____

_____

_____

22.1 Independent Practice

FL 8.SP.1.1

Sports Use the scatter plot for 5–8.

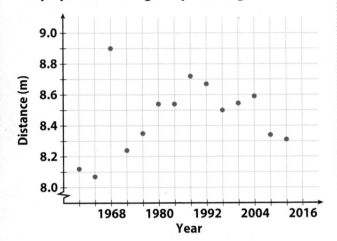

Olympic Men's Long Jump Winning Distances

5. Describe the association between the year and the distance jumped for the years 1960 to 1988.

_____

_____

_____

_____

6. Describe the association between the year and the distance jumped for the years after 1988.

_____

_____

_____

_____

_____

7. For the entire scatter plot, is the association between the year and the distance jumped linear or nonlinear?

_____

_____

_____

_____

_____

8. Identify the outlier and interpret its meaning.

_____

_____

_____

_____

9. **Communicate Mathematical Ideas** Compare a scatter plot that shows no association to one that shows negative association.

_____

_____

_____

_____

_____

_____

_____

_____

_____

For 10–11, describe a set of real-world bivariate data that the given scatter plot could represent. Define the variable represented on each axis.

10.

11.

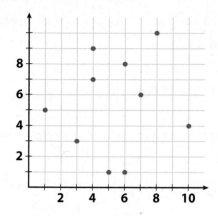

_____

_____

_____

_____

_____

_____

H.O.T. FOCUS ON HIGHER ORDER THINKING

Work Area

12. Multiple Representations Describe what you might see in a table of bivariate data that would lead you to conclude that the scatter plot of the data would show a cluster.

_____

_____

13. Justify Reasoning Is it possible for a scatter plot to have a positive or negative association that is not linear? Explain.

_____

_____

_____

14. Critical Thinking To try to increase profits, a theater owner increases the price of a ticket by $25 every month. Describe what a scatter plot might look like if x represents the number of months and y represents the profits. Explain your reasoning.

_____

_____

_____

_____

_____

702 Unit 10

Trend Lines and Predictions

FL 8.SP.1.3
Use the equation of a linear model to solve problems in the context of bivariate measurement data, interpreting the slope and intercept. *Also 8.SP.1.1, 8.SP.1.2*

ESSENTIAL QUESTION

How can you use a trend line to make a prediction from a scatter plot?

EXPLORE ACTIVITY 1   FL 8.SP.1.2, 8.SP.1.1

Drawing a Trend Line

When a scatter plot shows a linear association, you can use a line to model the relationship between the variables. A **trend line** is a straight line that comes closest to the points on a scatter plot.

Joyce is training for a 10K race. For some of her training runs, she records the distance she ran and how many minutes she ran.

A Make a scatter plot of Joyce's running data.

Distance (mi)	Time (min)
4	38
2	25
1	7
2	16
3	26
5	55
2	20
4	45
3	31

B To draw a trend line, use a straight edge to draw a line that has about the same number of points above and below it. Ignore any outliers.

C Use your trend line to predict how long it would take Joyce to run 4.5 miles.

_____

Reflect

1. How well does your trend line fit the data? Explain.

_____

_____

2. Do you think you can use a scatter plot that shows no association to make a prediction? Explain your answer.

_____

_____

Finding the Equation of a Trend Line

You can use two points on a trend line to write an equation in slope-intercept form for the trend line.

EXAMPLE 1   Real World   FL   8.SP.1.3

The scatter plot and trend line show the relationship between the number of chapters and the total number of pages for several books. Write an equation for the trend line.

STEP 1   Find the slope of the trend line. The line passes through points (5, 50) and (17, 170).

$m = \dfrac{y_2 - y_1}{x_2 - x_1}$ *Use the slope formula.*

$m = \dfrac{170 - 50}{17 - 5}$ *Substitute (5, 50) for (x_1, y_1) and (17, 170) for (x_2, y_2).*

$m = \dfrac{120}{12} = 10$ *Simplify.*

Math Talk
Mathematical Practices

Why are (5, 50) and (17, 170) the best points to use to draw the trend line?

STEP 2   Find the y-intercept of the trend line.

$y = mx + b$ *Slope-intercept form*

$50 = 10 \cdot 5 + b$ *Substitute 50 for y, 10 for m, and 5 for x.*

$50 = 50 + b$ *Simplify.*

$50 - 50 = 50 - 50 + b$ *Subtract 50 from both sides.*

$0 = b$ *Simplify.*

STEP 3   Use your slope and y-intercept values to write the equation.

$y = mx + b$ *Slope-intercept form*

$y = 10x + 0$ *Substitute 10 for m and 0 for y.*

The equation for the trend line is $y = 10x$.

Reflect

3. What type(s) of association does the scatter plot show?

_____

4. What is the meaning of the slope in this situation?

_____

5. What is the meaning of the *y*-intercept in this situation?

_____

6. The scatter plot and trend line show the relationship between the number of rainy days in a month and the number of umbrellas sold each month. Write an equation for the trend line.

_____

_____

Personal Math Trainer

Online Assessment and Intervention

my.hrw.com

EXPLORE ACTIVITY 2

Real World

FL 8.SP.1.3

Making Predictions

When you use a trend line or its equation to predict a value between data points that you already know, you *interpolate* the predicted value. When you make a prediction that is outside the data that you know, you *extrapolate* the predicted value.

Use the equation of the trend line in Example 1 to predict how many pages would be in a book with 26 chapters.

Is this prediction an example of interpolation or extrapolation? _____

$y = $ ⬚   *Write the equation for your trend line.*

$y = $ ⬚   *Substitute the number of chapters for x.*

$y = $ ⬚   *Simplify.*

I predict that a book with 26 chapters will have _____ pages.

Reflect

7. **Make a Prediction** Predict how many pages would be in a book with 14 chapters. Is this prediction an example of interpolation or extrapolation?

_____

8. Do you think that extrapolation or interpolation is more accurate? Explain.

_____

_____

_____

Guided Practice

Angela recorded the price of different weights of several bulk grains. She made a scatter plot of her data. Use the scatter plot for 1–4.

1. Draw a trend line for the scatter plot. (Explore Activity 1)

2. How do you know whether your trend line is a good fit for the data? (Explore Activity 1)

_____

_____

_____

3. Write an equation for your trend line. (Example 1) _____

4. Use the equation for your trend line to interpolate the price of 7 ounces and extrapolate the price of 50 ounces.

(Explore Activity 2) _____

? ESSENTIAL QUESTION CHECK-IN

5. A trend line passes through two points on a scatter plot. How can you use the trend line to make a prediction between or outside the given data points?

_____

_____

_____

22.2 Independent Practice

 FL 8.SP.1.1, 8.SP.1.2, 8.SP.1.3

Personal
Math Trainer

Online
Assessment and
Intervention

my.hrw.com

Use the data in the table for Exercises 6–10.

Apparent Temperature Due to Wind at 15 °F						
Wind speed (mi/h)	10	20	30	40	50	60
Wind chill (°F)	2.7	−2.3	−5.5	−7.9	−9.8	−11.4

Apparent Temperature Due to Wind at 15 °F

6. Make a scatter plot of the data and draw a trend line.

7. What type of association does the trend line show?

_____

8. Write an equation for your trend line. _____

9. **Make a Prediction** Use the trend line to predict the wind chill at these wind speeds.

   a. 36 mi/h _____   **b.** 100 mi/h _____

10. What is the meaning of the slope of the line?

_____

_____

Use the data in the table for Exercises 11–14.

Apparent Temperature Due to Humidity at a Room Temperature of 72 °F						
Humidity (%)	0	20	40	60	80	100
Apparent temperature (°F)	64	67	70	72	74	76

Apparent Temperature at a Room Temperature of 72 °F

11. Make a scatter plot of the data and draw a trend line.

12. Write an equation for your trend line.

_____

13. **Make a Prediction** Use the trend line to predict the apparent

    temperature at 70% humidity. _____

14. What is the meaning of the y-intercept of the line?

_____

15. Communicate Mathematical Ideas Is it possible to draw a trend line on a scatter plot that shows no association? Explain.

_____

_____

_____

16. Critique Reasoning Sam drew a trend line that had about the same number of data points above it as below it, but did not pass through any data points. He then picked two data points to write the equation for the line. Is this a correct way to write the equation? Explain.

_____

_____

_____

_____

17. Marlene wanted to find a relationship between the areas and populations of counties in Texas. She plotted x (area in square miles) and y (population) for two counties on a scatter plot:

Kent County (903, 808)   Edwards County (2118, 2002)

She concluded that the population of Texas counties is approximately equal to their area in square miles and drew a trend line through her points.

a. Critique Reasoning Do you agree with Marlene's method of creating a scatter plot and a trend line? Explain why or why not.

_____

_____

_____

b. Counterexamples Harris County has an area of 1778 square miles and a population of about 4.3 million people. Dallas County has an area of 908 square miles and a population of about 2.5 million people. What does this data show about Marlene's conjecture that the population of Texas counties is approximately equal to their area?

_____

_____

_____

_____

Ready to Go On?

Personal Math Trainer

Online Assessment and Intervention

ⓑ my.hrw.com

22.1 Scatter Plots and Association

An auto store is having a sale on motor oil. The chart shows the price per quart as the number of quarts purchased increases. Use the data for Exs. 1–2.

Number of quarts	1	2	3	4	5	6
Price per quart ($)	2	1.50	1.25	1.10	1	0.95

1. Use the given data to make a scatter plot.

2. Describe the association you see between the number of quarts purchased and the price per quart. Explain.

_____

_____

_____

22.2 Trend Lines and Predictions

The scatter plot below shows data comparing wind speed and wind chill for an air temperature of 20°F. Use the scatter plot for Exs. 3–5.

3. Draw a trend line for the scatter plot.

4. Write an equation for your trend line.

_____

5. Use your equation to predict the wind chill to the nearest degree for a wind speed of 60 mi/h.

_____

? **ESSENTIAL QUESTION**

6. How can you use scatter plots to solve real-world problems?

_____

_____

Selected Response

1. Which scatter plot could have a trend line whose equation is $y = 3x + 10$?

2. What type of association would you expect between a person's age and hair length?

Ⓐ linear Ⓒ none

Ⓑ negative Ⓓ positive

3. Which is **not** shown on the scatter plot?

Ⓐ cluster

Ⓑ negative association

Ⓒ outlier

Ⓓ positive association

4. A restaurant claims to have served 352,000,000 hamburgers. What is this number in scientific notation?

Ⓐ 3.52×10^6 Ⓒ 35.2×10^7

Ⓑ 3.52×10^8 Ⓓ 352×10^6

5. Which equation describes the relationship between x and y in the table?

x	−8	−4	0	4	8
y	2	1	0	−1	−2

Ⓐ $y = -4x$ Ⓒ $y = 4x$

Ⓑ $y = -\frac{1}{4}x$ Ⓓ $y = \frac{1}{4}x$

Mini-Task

6. Use the data in the table.

Temp (°F)	97	94	87	92	100	90
Pool visitors	370	315	205	135	365	240

a. Make a scatterplot of the data.

b. Which data point is an outlier?

_____

c. Predict the number of visitors on a day when the high temperature is 102 °F.

_____

Two-Way Tables

23

ESSENTIAL QUESTION

How can you use two-way frequency tables to solve real-world problems?

LESSON 23.1

Two-Way Frequency Tables

 FL 8.SP.1.4

LESSON 23.2

Two-Way Relative Frequency Tables

 FL 8.SP.1.4

Real-World Video

Two-way tables can help identify and compare probabilities for non-numerical data, such as the probability that girls will like one of two sports teams more than boys will.

⏻ my.hrw.com

GO DIGITAL
my.hrw.com

my.hrw.com

Go digital with your write-in student edition, accessible on any device.

Math On the Spot

Scan with your smart phone to jump directly to the online edition, video tutor, and more.

Animated Math

Interactively explore key concepts to see how math works.

Personal Math Trainer

Get immediate feedback and help as you work through practice sets.

Are YOU Ready?

Complete these exercises to review skills you will need for this module.

Personal Math Trainer

Online Assessment and Intervention

my.hrw.com

Simplify Fractions

EXAMPLE Simplify $\frac{18}{30}$.

$\dfrac{1, 2, 3, 6, 9, 18}{1, 2, 3, 5, 6, 10, 30}$

$\dfrac{18 \div 6}{30 \div 6} = \dfrac{3}{5}$

List all the factors of the numerator and denominator.

Find the greatest common factor (GCF). Divide the numerator and denominator by the GCF.

Write each fraction in simplest form.

1. $\frac{25}{30}$ _____

2. $\frac{27}{36}$ _____

3. $\frac{14}{16}$ _____

4. $\frac{15}{45}$ _____

5. $\frac{27}{63}$ _____

6. $\frac{45}{75}$ _____

7. $\frac{8}{27}$ _____

8. $\frac{16}{28}$ _____

Fractions, Decimals, Percents

EXAMPLE Write $\frac{13}{20}$ as a decimal and a percent.

$$\begin{array}{r} 0.65 \\ 20{\overline{)13.00}} \\ \underline{12\ 0} \\ 100 \\ \underline{-100} \\ 0 \end{array}$$

$0.65 = 65\%$

Write the fraction as a division problem. Write a decimal point and zeros in the dividend.
Place a decimal point in the quotient.

Write the decimal as a percent.

Write each fraction as a decimal and a percent.

9. $\frac{7}{8}$ _____

10. $\frac{4}{5}$ _____

11. $\frac{5}{4}$ _____

12. $\frac{3}{10}$ _____

13. $\frac{19}{20}$ _____

14. $\frac{7}{25}$ _____

Find the Percent of a Number

EXAMPLE 6.5% of $24 = ?$

$6.5\% = 0.065$

$$\begin{array}{r} 24 \\ \times\ 0.065 \\ \hline 1.56 \end{array}$$

Write the percent as a decimal.

Multiply.

Find each percent of a number.

15. 4% of 40 _____

16. 7% of 300 _____

17. 4.3% of 1,200 _____

18. 2.9% of 780 _____

19. 1.6% of 75.20 _____

20. 3.56% of 3,200 _____

Reading Start-Up

Visualize Vocabulary

Use the ✔ words to complete the chart.

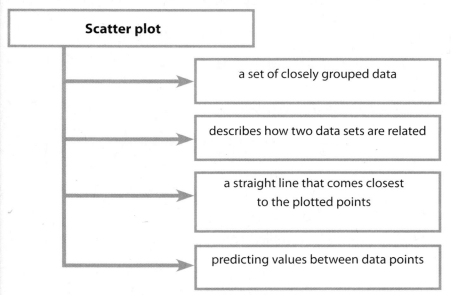

Scatter plot

→ a set of closely grouped data

→ describes how two data sets are related

→ a straight line that comes closest to the plotted points

→ predicting values between data points

Understand Vocabulary

Complete the sentences using preview words.

1. The _____ is the number of times an event occurs.

2. A _____ shows the frequencies of data that is categorized two ways.

3. _____ is the ratio of the number of times an event occurs to the total number of events.

Vocabulary

Review Words

✔ association *(asociación)*
✔ cluster *(grupo)*
  data *(datos)*
✔ interpolation *(interpolación)*
  extrapolation *(extrapolación)*
  outlier *(parte aislada)*
  scatter plot *(gráfico de dispersión)*
✔ trend line *(la línea de tendencia)*

Preview Words

conditional relative frequency *(frecuencia relativa condicional)*
frequency *(frecuencia)*
joint relative frequency *(frecuencia relativa conjunta)*
marginal relative frequency *(frecuencia relativa marginal)*
relative frequency *(frecuencia relativa)*
two-way table *(de dos vías mesa)*
two-way relative frequency table *(dos vías tabla de frecuencias relativas)*

Active Reading

Tri-Fold Before beginning the module, create a tri-fold to help you learn the concepts and vocabulary in this module. Fold the paper into three sections. Label the columns "What I Know," "What I Want to Know," and "What I Learned." Complete the first two columns before you read. After studying the module, complete the third column.

MODULE 23
Unpacking the Standards

Understanding the standards and the vocabulary terms in the standards will help you know exactly what you are expected to learn in this module.

 FL 8.SP.1.4

Understand that patterns of association can also be seen in bivariate categorical data by displaying frequencies and relative frequencies in a two-way table. Construct and interpret a two-way table summarizing data on two categorical variables collected from the same subjects.

Key Vocabulary

two-way table *(tabla de doble entrada)* A table that shows the frequencies of data categorized in two ways.

What It Means to You

You will use two-way tables to find relative frequencies.

UNPACKING EXAMPLE 8.SP.1.4

Soojinn counted the vehicles in the school parking lot and recorded the data in the two-way table shown.

	During School Day	After School Day	Total
Cars	36	14	50
Trucks	19	6	25
Total	55	20	75

What percent of the vehicles parked after school were trucks?

$$\frac{\text{trucks after school}}{\text{total vehicles after school}} = \frac{6}{20} = 0.3, \text{ or } 30\%$$

30% of the vehicles in the school parking lot after school were trucks.

 FL 8.SP.1.4

Understand … frequencies and relative frequencies in a two-way table. Construct and interpret a two-way table … . Use relative frequencies calculated for rows or columns to describe possible association between the two variables.

Key Vocabulary

conditional relative frequency *(frecuencia relativa condicional)* The ratio of a joint relative frequency to a related marginal relative frequency in a two-way table.

Visit **my.hrw.com** to see all **Florida Math Standards** unpacked.

my.hrw.com

What It Means to You

You will use two-way tables to find conditional relative frequencies.

UNPACKING EXAMPLE 8.SP.1.4

Soojinn determined the gender of the driver for each of the 55 vehicles parked in the school parking lot during the day.

	Male	Female	Total
Cars	8	25	33
Trucks	15	7	22
Total	23	32	55

What is the conditional relative frequency that a driver is female given that the vehicle is a car?

$$\frac{\text{female car drivers}}{\text{total cars}} = \frac{25}{33} \approx 0.758, \text{ or about } 76\%$$

There is a 76% likelihood that a driver is female given that the vehicle is a car.

LESSON
23.1
Two-Way Frequency Tables

FL 8.SP.1.4

Understand that patterns
... can be seen in bivariate
categorical data by
displaying frequencies in
a two-way table. Construct
and interpret a two-way
table .... Use relative
frequencies ... to describe
possible association ....

ESSENTIAL QUESTION

How can you construct and interpret two-way frequency tables?

EXPLORE ACTIVITY   **FL** 8.SP.1.4

Making a Two-Way Table

The **frequency** is the number of times an event occurs. A **two-way table** shows the frequencies of data that is categorized two ways. The rows indicate one categorization and the columns indicate another.

A poll of 120 town residents found that 40% own a bike. Of those who own a bike, 75% shop at the farmer's market. Of those who do not own a bike, 25% shop at the farmer's market.

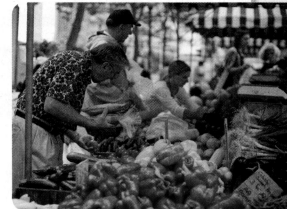

	Farmer's Market	No Farmer's Market	TOTAL
Bike			
No Bike			
TOTAL			

A Start in the bottom right cell of the table. Enter the total number of people polled.

B **Fill in the right column.** 40% of 120 people polled own a bike.

The remaining people polled do not own a bike.

C **Fill in the top row.** 75% of those who own a bike also shop at the market.

The remaining bike owners do not shop at the market.

D **Fill in the second row.** 25% of those who do not own a bike shop at the market.

The remaining people without bikes do not shop at the market.

E **Fill in the last row.** In each column, add the numbers in the first two rows to find the total number of people who shop at the farmer's market and who do not shop at the farmer's market.

Reflect

1. How can you check that your table is completed correctly?

_____

_____

Math On the Spot

🕐 my.hrw.com

Animated Math

🕐 my.hrw.com

Deciding Whether There Is an Association

Relative frequency is the ratio of the number of times an event occurs to the total number of events. In the Explore Activity, the relative frequency of bike owners who shop at the farmer's market is $\frac{36}{120} = 0.30 = 30\%$. You can use relative frequencies to decide if there is an association between two variables or events.

EXAMPLE 1 Real World FL 8.SP.1.4

Determine whether there is an association between the events.

A One hundred teens were polled about whether they are required to do chores and whether they have a curfew. Is there an association between having a curfew and having to do chores?

	Curfew	No Curfew	TOTAL
Chores	16	4	20
No Chores	16	64	80
TOTAL	32	68	100

Math Talk

Mathematical Practices

What is the difference between frequency and relative frequency?

STEP 1 **Find the relative frequency of having to do chores.**

Total who have to do chores $\rightarrow$
Total number of teens polled $\rightarrow$ $\frac{20}{100} = 0.20 = 20\%$

STEP 2 **Find the relative frequency of having to do chores among those who have a curfew.**

Number with a curfew who have chores $\rightarrow$
Total number with a curfew $\rightarrow$ $\frac{16}{32} = 0.50 = 50\%$

STEP 3 **Compare the relative frequencies.** Students who have a curfew are more likely to have to do chores than the general population. There is an association. The relative frequencies show that students who have a curfew are more likely to have to do chores than the general population of teens polled in the survey.

B Data from 200 flights were collected. The flights were categorized as domestic or international and late or not late. Is there an association between international flights and a flight being late?

	Late	Not Late	TOTAL
Domestic	30	120	150
International	10	40	50
TOTAL	40	160	200

STEP 1 **Find the relative frequency of a flight being late.**

Total flights that are late $\rightarrow$
Total number of flights $\rightarrow$ $\frac{40}{200} = 0.20 = 20\%$

STEP 2 **Find the relative frequency of a flight being late among international flights.**

Number of international flights that are late $\rightarrow$
Total number of international flights $\rightarrow$ $\frac{10}{50} = 0.20 = 20\%$

STEP 3 **Compare the relative frequencies.** International flights are no more likely to be late than flights in general. There is no association. The relative frequencies show that international flights are just as likely to be late as any other flight.

YOUR TURN

2. Data from 200 middle school and high school students were collected. Students were asked whether or not they had visited at least one national park. Is there an association between being a high school student and visiting a national park? Explain.

	Have Visited a National Park	Have NOT Visited a National Park	TOTAL
Middle School	25	55	80
High School	80	40	120
TOTAL	105	95	200

_____

_____

_____

_____

_____

_____

Personal Math Trainer

Online Assessment and Intervention

my.hrw.com

1. In a survey of 50 students, 60% said that they have a cat. Of the students who have a cat, 70% also have a dog. Of the students who do not have a cat, 75% have a dog. Complete the two-way table. (Explore Activity)

	Dog	No Dog	TOTAL
Cat			
No Cat			
TOTAL			

   a. Enter the total number of students surveyed in the bottom right cell of the table.

   b. Fill in right column.

   c. Fill in top row.

   d. Fill in second row.

   e. Fill in last row.

2. The results of a survey at a school are shown. Is there an association between being a boy and being left-handed? Explain. (Example 1)

	Left-handed	Right-handed	TOTAL
Boys	14	126	140
Girls	10	90	100
TOTAL	24	216	240

_____

_____

_____

? ESSENTIAL QUESTION CHECK-IN

3. Voters were polled to see whether they supported Smith or Jones. Can you construct a two-way table of the results? Why or why not?

_____

_____

_____

23.1 Independent Practice

 FL 8.SP.1.4

Personal Math Trainer

Online Assessment and Intervention

my.hrw.com

4. **Represent Real-World Problems** One hundred forty students were asked about their language classes. Out of 111 who take French, only 31 do not take Spanish. Twelve take neither French nor Spanish. Use this information to make a two-way table.

	Take French	Do NOT Take French	TOTAL
Take Spanish			
Do NOT Take Spanish			
TOTAL			

5. **Represent Real-World Problems** Seventh- and eighth-grade students were asked whether they preferred science or math.

a. Complete the two-way table.

	Prefer Science	Prefer Math	TOTAL
Seventh Grade		72	96
Eighth Grade	32		
TOTAL			176

b. Is there an association between being in eighth grade and preferring math? Explain.

_____

_____

_____

6. **Persevere in Problem Solving** The table gives partial information on the number of men and women who play in the four sections of the Metro Orchestra.

a. Complete the table.

	Strings	Brass	Woodwinds	Percussion	TOTAL
Men	13	7		5	33
Women			10		
TOTAL	55			9	98

b. Is there an association between being a woman and playing strings? Explain.

_____

_____

_____

Work Area

7. Multi-Step The two-way table below shows the results of a survey of Florida teenagers who were asked whether they preferred surfing or snorkeling.

a. To the right of the number in each cell, write the relative frequency of the number compared to the total for the *row* the number is in. Round to the nearest percent.

	Prefer Surfing	**Prefer Snorkeling**	**TOTAL**
Ages 13–15	52 _____ ; _____	78 _____ ; _____	130 100%
Ages 16–18	52 _____ ; _____	28 _____ ; _____	80 _____
TOTAL	104 _____ ; _____	106 _____ ; _____	210 _____

b. Explain the meaning of the relative frequency you wrote beside 28.

_____

_____

_____

c. To the right of each number you wrote in part a, write the relative frequency of each number compared to the total for the *column* the number is in. Are the relative frequencies the same? Why or why not?

_____

_____

_____

d. Explain the meaning of the relative frequency you wrote beside 28.

_____

_____

_____

Two-Way Relative Frequency Tables

Understand that patterns ... can be seen in bivariate categorical data by displaying frequencies in a two-way table. Construct and interpret a two-way table ... . Use relative frequencies calculated for rows or columns to describe possible association ... .

ESSENTIAL QUESTION

How can categorical data be organized and analyzed?

EXPLORE ACTIVITY 1   FL 8.SP.1.4

Creating a Relative Frequency Table

The frequency table below shows the results of a survey that Maria took at her school. She asked 50 randomly selected students whether they preferred dogs, cats, or other pets. Convert this table to a *relative frequency* table that uses decimals as well as one that uses percents.

Preferred Pet	Dog	Cat	Other	TOTAL
Frequency	22	15	13	50

A Divide the numbers in the frequency table by the total to obtain relative frequencies as decimals. Record the results in the table below.

Preferred Pet	Dog	Cat	Other	TOTAL
Relative Frequency	$\frac{22}{50} = 0.44$			

B Write the decimals as percents in the table below.

Preferred Pet	Dog	Cat	Other	TOTAL
Relative Frequency	44%			

Reflect

1. How can you check that you have correctly converted frequencies to relative frequencies?

_____

_____

2. Explain why the number in the Total column of a relative frequency table is always 1 or 100%.

_____

_____

Creating a Two-Way Frequency Table

In the previous Explore Activity, the categorical variable was pet preference, and the variable had three possible data values: dog, cat, and other. The frequency table listed the frequency for each value of that single variable. If you have two categorical variables whose values have been paired, you list the frequencies of the paired values in a **two-way frequency table.**

For her survey, Maria also recorded the gender of each student. The results are shown in the two-way frequency table below. Each entry is the frequency of students who prefer a certain pet *and* are a certain gender. For instance, 10 girls prefer dogs as pets. Complete the table.

Preferred Pet \\ Gender	Dog	Cat	Other	TOTAL
Girl	10	9	3	
Boy	12	6	10	
TOTAL				

A Find the total for each gender by adding the frequencies in each row.

B Find the total for each pet by adding the frequencies in each column.

C Find the grand total, which is the sum of the row totals as well as the sum of the column totals. Write this in the lower-right corner.

Reflect

3. Where have you seen the numbers in the Total row before?

_____

4. In terms of Maria's survey, what does the grand total represent?

_____

Creating a Two-Way Relative Frequency Table

You can obtain *relative* frequencies from a two-way frequency table:

- A **joint relative frequency** is found by dividing a frequency that is not in the Total row or the Total column by the grand total.
- A **marginal relative frequency** is found by dividing a row total or a column total by the grand total.

A **two-way relative frequency table** displays both joint relative frequencies and marginal relative frequencies.

Math Talk
Mathematical Practices

What is the relationship between joint relative frequency and marginal relative frequency?

Create a two-way relative frequency table for Maria's data.

A Divide each number in the two-way frequency table from the previous Explore Activity by the grand total. Write the quotients as decimals.

Preferred Pet \\ Gender	Dog	Cat	Other	TOTAL
Girl	$\frac{10}{50} = 0.2$			
Boy				
TOTAL	$\frac{22}{50} = 0.44$			$\frac{50}{50} = 1$

B Check by adding the joint relative frequencies in a row or column to see if the sum equals that row's or column's marginal relative frequency.

Girl row: $0.2 +$ _____ $+$ _____ $=$ _____

Boy row: _____ $+$ _____ $+$ _____ $=$ _____

Dog column: $0.2 +$ _____ $=$ _____

Cat column: _____ $+$ _____ $=$ _____

Other column: _____ $+$ _____ $=$ _____

Reflect

5. A joint relative frequency in a two-way relative frequency table tells you what portion of the entire data set falls into the intersection of a particular value of one variable and a particular value of the other variable. What is the joint relative frequency of students surveyed who are boys and prefer cats as pets?

   _____

6. A marginal relative frequency in a two-way relative frequency table tells you what portion of the entire data set represents a particular value of just one of the variables. What is the marginal relative frequency of students surveyed who are boys?

   _____

Calculating Conditional Relative Frequencies

One other type of relative frequency that you can obtain from a two-way frequency table is a *conditional relative frequency*. A **conditional relative frequency** is found by dividing a frequency that is not in the Total row or the Total column by the frequency's row total or column total.

EXAMPLE 1   FL 8.SP.1.4

From Maria's two-way frequency table you know that 22 students are girls and 15 students prefer cats. You also know that 9 students are girls who prefer cats. Use this to find each conditional relative frequency.

A Find the conditional relative frequency that a student surveyed prefers cats as pets, given that the student is a girl.

Divide the number of girls who prefer cats by the number of girls. Express your answer as a decimal and as a percent.

$\frac{9}{22} = 0.409$, or 40.9%

B Find the conditional relative frequency that a student surveyed is a girl, given that the student prefers cats as pets.

Divide the number of girls who prefer cats by the number of students who prefer cats. Express your answer as a decimal and as a percent.

$\frac{9}{15} = 0.6$, or 60%

Reflect

7. When calculating a conditional relative frequency, why do you divide by a row total or a column total and not by the grand total?

_____

_____

_____

_____

YOUR TURN

8. You can obtain conditional relative frequencies from a two-way relative frequency table. Find the conditional relative frequency that a student prefers cats as pets, given that the student is a girl.

_____

Finding Possible Associations Between Variables

You can use conditional relative frequency to see if there is an association between two variables.

EXAMPLE 2

FL 8.SP.1.4

Maria conducted her survey because she was interested in the question "Does gender influence what type of pet people prefer?" If there is no influence, then the distribution of gender within each subgroup of pet preference should roughly equal the distribution of gender within the whole group. Use the results of Maria's survey to investigate possible influences of gender on pet preference.

My Notes

STEP 1 Identify the percent of all students surveyed who are girls: 44%

STEP 2 Determine each conditional relative frequency.

Of the 22 students who prefer dogs as pets, 10 are girls.
Percent who are girls, given a preference for dogs as pets: 45%

Of the 15 students who prefer cats as pets, 9 are girls.
Percent who are girls, given a preference for cats as pets: 60%

Of the 13 students who prefer other pets. 3 are girls.
Percent who are girls, given a preference for other pets: 23%

STEP 3 Interpret the results by comparing each conditional relative frequency to the percent of all students surveyed who are girls.

The percent of girls among students who prefer dogs is close to 44%, so gender does not appear to influence preference for dogs.

The percent of girls among students who prefer cats is much greater than 44%, so girls are more likely than boys to prefer cats.

The percent of girls among students who prefer other pets is much less than 44%, so girls are less likely than boys to prefer other pets.

YOUR TURN

9. Suppose you analyzed the data by focusing on boys rather than girls. How would the percent in Step 1 change? How would the percents in Step 2 change? How would the conclusions in Step 3 change?

_____

_____

_____

1. In a class survey, students were asked to choose their favorite vacation destination. The results are displayed by gender in the two-way frequency table. (Explore Activities 1–3)

Preferred Pet / Gender	Seashore	Mountains	Other	TOTAL
Girl	7	3	2	
Boy	5	2	6	
TOTAL				

a. Find the total for each gender by adding the frequencies in each row. Write the row totals in the Total column.

b. Find the total for each preferred vacation spot by adding the frequencies in each column. Write the column totals in the Total row.

c. Write the grand total (the sum of the row totals and the column totals) in the lower-right corner of the table.

d. Create a two-way relative frequency table by dividing each number in the above table by the grand total. Write the quotients as decimals.

Preferred Pet / Gender	Seashore	Mountains	Other	TOTAL
Girl				
Boy				
TOTAL				

e. Use the table to find the joint relative frequency of students surveyed who are boys and who prefer vacationing in the mountains. _____

f. Use the table to find the marginal relative frequency of students surveyed who prefer vacationing at the seashore. _____

g. Find the conditional relative frequency that a student surveyed prefers vacationing in the mountains, given that the student is a girl. Interpret this result. (Examples 1–2)

_____

? ESSENTIAL QUESTION CHECK-IN

2. How can you use a two-way frequency table to learn more about its data?

_____

_____

23.2 Independent Practice

FL 8.SP.1.4

Personal Math Trainer

Online Assessment and Intervention

my.hrw.com

Stefan surveyed 75 of his classmates about their participation in school activities as well as whether they have a part-time job. The results are shown in the two-way frequency table. Use the table for Exercises 3–6.

Job \ Activity	Clubs Only	Sports Only	Both	Neither	TOTAL
Yes		12		9	51
No	5		10		
TOTAL	15	18			75

3. a. Complete the table.

    b. Explain how you found the correct data to enter in the table.

_____

_____

_____

_____

4. Create a two-way relative frequency table using decimals. Round to the nearest hundredth.

Job \ Activity	Clubs Only	Sports Only	Both	Neither	TOTAL
Yes					
No					
TOTAL					

5. Give each relative frequency as a percent.

    a. the joint relative frequency of students surveyed who participate in school clubs only and have part-time jobs _____

    b. the marginal frequency of students surveyed who do not have a part-time job _____

    c. the conditional relative frequency that a student surveyed participates in both school clubs and sports, given that the student has a part-time job _____

6. Discuss possible influences of having a part-time job on participation in school activities. Support your response with an analysis of the data.

_____

_____

_____

_____

H.O.T. FOCUS ON HIGHER ORDER THINKING

7. The head of quality control for a chair manufacturer collected data on the quality of two types of wood that the company grows on its tree farm. The table shows the acceptance and rejection data.

Accept/Reject Wood	Accepted	Rejected	TOTAL
White Oak	245	105	350
Redwood	140	110	250
TOTAL	385	215	600

a. Critique Reasoning To create a two-way relative frequency table for this data, the head of quality control divided each number in each row by the row total. Is this correct? Explain.

_____

_____

b. Draw Conclusions Are any of the data the head of quality control entered into the two-way relative frequency table correct? If so, which is and which isn't? Explain.

_____

_____

_____

_____

8. Analyze Relationships What is the difference between relative frequency and conditional relative frequency?

_____

_____

_____

Work Area

Ready to Go On?

Personal Math Trainer

Online Assessment and Intervention

my.hrw.com

23.1 Two-Way Frequency Tables

Martin collected data from students about whether they played a musical instrument. The table shows his results. Use the table for Exercises 1–4.

	Instrument	No Instrument	TOTAL
Boys	42	70	112
Girls	48		88
Total	90	110	200

1. Of the students surveyed, how many played an instrument? _____

2. How many girls surveyed did NOT play an instrument? _____

3. What is the relative frequency of a student playing an instrument? Write the answer as a percent. _____

4. What is the relative frequency of a boy playing an instrument? Write the answer as a decimal. _____

23.2 Two-Way Relative Frequency Tables

Students were asked how they traveled to school. The two-way relative frequency table shows the results. Use the table for Exercises 5–7. Write answers as decimals rounded to the nearest hundredth.

	Method			
School	Car	Bus	Other	TOTAL
Middle School	0.18	0.14	0.10	0.42
High School	0.38	0.12	0.08	0.58
TOTAL	0.56	0.26	0.18	1.00

5. What is the joint relative frequency of high school students who ride the bus? _____

6. What is the marginal relative frequency of students surveyed who are in middle school? _____

7. What is the conditional relative frequency that a student rides the bus, given that the student is in middle school? _____

? ESSENTIAL QUESTION

8. How can you use two-way tables to solve real-world problems?

_____

_____

Personal
Math Trainer

my.hrw.com

Online
Assessment and
Intervention

Selected Response

The table gives data on the length of time that teachers at Tenth Avenue School have taught. Use the table for Exercises 1–5.

	Fewer than 10 years	10 or more years	TOTAL
Male	9	6	15
Female	?	4	25
TOTAL	30	10	40

1. How many female teachers have taught for fewer than 10 years?

Ⓐ 4   Ⓒ 21

Ⓑ 9   Ⓓ 30

2. What is the relative frequency of teachers who have taught for 10 or more years?

Ⓐ 10%   Ⓒ 30%

Ⓑ 25%   Ⓓ 60%

3. What is the relative frequency of male teachers who have taught for fewer than 10 years?

Ⓐ 0.09   Ⓒ 0.6

Ⓑ 0.225   Ⓓ 1.50

4. What is the joint relative frequency of female teachers who have taught for more than 10 years?

Ⓐ 4%   Ⓒ 16%

Ⓑ 10%   Ⓓ 25%

5. What is the marginal relative frequency of teachers who are female?

Ⓐ 0.16   Ⓒ 0.4

Ⓑ 0.25   Ⓓ 0.625

6. A triangle has an exterior angle of $x°$. Which of the following represents the measure of the interior angle next to it?

Ⓐ $(180 - x)°$ Ⓒ $(90 - x)°$

Ⓑ $(x - 180)°$ Ⓓ $(x - 90)°$

7. What is the volume of a cone that has a diameter of 12 cm and a height of 4 cm? Use 3.14 for π and round to the nearest tenth.

Ⓐ 25.12 cm^3 Ⓒ 150.72 cm^3

Ⓑ 602.88 cm^3 Ⓓ 1,808.64 cm^3

Mini-Task

8. The table gives data on books read by members of the Summer Reading Club.

	Fewer than 25 books	25 or more books	TOTAL
Boys	7	21	28
Girls	9	27	36
TOTAL	16	48	64

a. Find the relative frequency of a club member reading fewer than 25 books.

_____

b. Find the relative frequency of a girl club member reading fewer than 25 books.

_____

c. Is there an association between being a girl and reading fewer than 25 books? Explain.

_____

_____

_____

_____

Study Guide Review

MODULE 22 ▶ Scatter Plots

Key Vocabulary
cluster *(agrupación)*
outlier *(valor extremo)*
scatter plot *(diagrama de dispersión)*
trend line *(línea de tendencia)*

? ESSENTIAL QUESTION

How can you use scatter plots to solve real-world problems?

EXAMPLE 1

As part of a research project, a researcher made a table of test scores and the number of hours of sleep a person got the night before the test. Make a scatter plot of the data. Does the data show a positive association, negative association, or no association?

Sleep (hours)	Test score
4	30
5	40
6	50
6	70
8	100
9	90
10	100

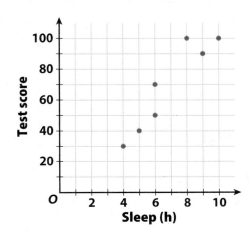

The data show a positive association. Generally, as the number of hours of sleep increases, so do the test scores.

EXAMPLE 2

Write an equation for a trend line of the data shown on the graph.

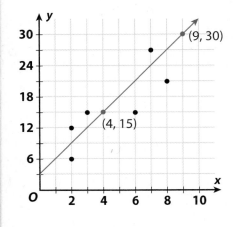

$m = \dfrac{30 - 15}{9 - 4} = 3$ Find the slope.

$15 = 3(4) + b$ Find the y-intercept.

$b = 3$

$y = 3x + 3$ Use the slope and y-intercept to write the equation.

EXERCISES

1. The table shows the income of 8 households, in thousands of dollars, and the number of televisions in each household. (Lesson 22.1)

Income ($1000)	20	20	30	30	40	60	70	90
Number of televisions	4	0	1	2	2	3	3	4

   a. Make a scatter plot of the data.

   b. Describe the association between income and number of televisions. Are any of the values outliers?

   _____

   _____

   _____

   _____

   _____

2. The scatter plot shows the relationship between the price of a product and the number of potential buyers. (Lesson 22.2)

   a. Draw a trend line for the scatter plot.

   b. Write an equation for your trend line.

   _____

   c. When the price of the product is $3.50, the number of potential buyers will be

   about _____.

   d. When the price of the product is $5.50, the number of potential buyers will be

   about _____.

MODULE 23 Two-Way Tables

? ESSENTIAL QUESTION

How can you use two-way tables to solve real-world problems?

EXAMPLE

A movie theater kept a record of patrons who bought tickets for a particular movie for two different times. The results are shown in the two-way frequency table. Create a two-way relative frequency table of these data.

	5:00 P.M. Showing	8:00 P.M. Showing	Total
Adults	22	39	61
Children	40	25	65
Total	62	64	126

Step 1: Divide each entry by the total number of patrons. Round to the nearest hundredth.

	5:00 P.M. Showing	8:00 P.M. Showing	Total
Adults	$\frac{22}{126} \approx 0.17$	$\frac{39}{126} \approx 0.31$	$\frac{61}{126} \approx 0.48$
Children	$\frac{40}{126} \approx 0.32$	$\frac{25}{126} \approx 0.20$	$\frac{65}{126} \approx 0.52$
Total	$\frac{62}{126} \approx 0.49$	$\frac{64}{126} \approx 0.51$	$\frac{126}{126} \approx 1.00$

Step 2: Convert decimals to percents.

	5:00 P.M. Showing	8:00 P.M. Showing	Total
Adults	17%	31%	48%
Children	32%	20%	52%
Total	49%	51%	100%

Key Vocabulary

conditional relative frequency (*frecuencia relativa condicional*)

frequency (*frecuencia*)

joint relative frequency (*frecuencia relativa común*)

marginal relative frequency (*frecuencia relativa marginal*)

relative frequency (*frecuencia relativa*)

two-way frequency table (*de dos vías frecuencia mesa*)

two-way relative frequency table (*dos vías tabla de frecuencias relativas*)

two-way table (*de dos vías mesa*)

EXERCISES

Use the tables in the Example to answer each question. (Lessons 23.1, 23.2)

1. What is the joint relative frequency of patrons who are adults and attended the 8:00 P.M. showing? _____

2. What is the marginal relative frequency of patrons who went to the 8:00 P.M. showing? _____

3. What is the conditional relative frequency that a patron is an adult, given that the patron attends the 8:00 P.M. showing? _____

1. **CAREERS IN MATH** Psychologist A psychologist gave a test to 15 women of different ages to measure their short-term memory. The test score scale goes from 0 to 24, and a higher score means that the participant has a better short-term memory. The scatter plot shows the results of this study.

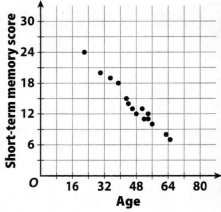

   a. Describe the pattern in the data. Is there a positive or negative correlation?

   _____

   _____

   b. Draw a line of best fit on the scatter plot and estimate its slope. Interpret the slope in the context of the problem.

   _____

   _____

   c. In another test, a 70-year-old woman scored 8. Does your line of best fit predict a higher or lower score? What may have happened?

   _____

   _____

2. Kalila has developed two different varieties of tomatoes, called Big Red and Sweet Summer, which she grows in her garden. When she harvests the tomatoes, she measures the diameters of each variety. The results are shown in the table.

	Diameter ≤ 2 in.	Diameter > 2 in.
Big Red	36	45
Sweet Summer	28	39

   a. Use the data to create a two-way frequency table.

	Diameter ≤ 2 in.	Diameter > 2 in.	Total
Big Red			
Sweet Summer			
Total			

   b. What is the relative frequency of a tomato having a diameter that is greater than two inches? Round to the nearest percent.   _____

   c. What is the relative frequency of a Big Red tomato having a diameter that is greater than two inches? Round to the nearest percent.   _____

   d. Is there an association between Big Red tomatoes and diameters that are greater than two inches? Explain.

   _____

   _____

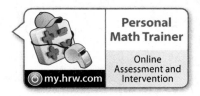
Selected Response

1. A local election conducted an exit poll of the age and gender of its voters. The results are shown in the two-way frequency table.

	18–62 years old	63 years and older	Total
Female	142	22	164
Male	126	15	141
Total	268	37	305

What percent of the voters were female and 18 to 62 years old?

- (A) 6.5%
- (B) 47%
- (C) 53%
- (D) 87%

2. What type of association is there between the speed of a car and the distance the car travels in a given time at that speed?

- (A) cluster
- (B) negative association
- (C) no association
- (D) positive association

3. Using 3.14 for π, what is the volume of the sphere to the nearest tenth?

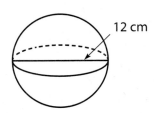

12 cm

- (A) 508.7 cubic centimeters
- (B) 678.2 cubic centimeters
- (C) 904.3 cubic centimeters
- (D) 2713 cubic centimeters

Read graphs and diagrams carefully. Look at the labels for important information.

4. Which scatter plot could have a trend line given by the equation $y = -4x + 70$?

5. A group of middle school students were asked whether they prefer communicating with their friends by text message or email. The results are shown in the two-way frequency table.

	Text Message	Email	Total
Female	28	16	44
Male	31	18	49
Total	59	34	93

What is the conditional relative frequency that a student prefers email, given that the student is female?

Ⓐ 17% Ⓒ 47%

Ⓑ 36% Ⓓ 64%

6. The vertices of a triangle are (11, 9), (7, 4), and (1, 11). What are the vertices after the triangle has been reflected over the *y*-axis?

Ⓐ (9, 11), (4, 7), (11, 1)

Ⓑ (11, −9), (7, −4), (1, −11)

Ⓒ (9, 11), (4, 7), (11, 1)

Ⓓ (−11, 9), (−7, 4), (−1, 11)

7. Which of the following is **not** shown on the scatter plot below?

Ⓐ cluster

Ⓑ negative association

Ⓒ outlier

Ⓓ positive association

Mini-Task

8. A scatter plot and trend line of the weight of a Chihuahua puppy versus age is shown.

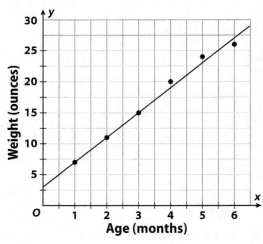

a. The trend line for these data is given by $y = 4x + 3$. What does the 3 represent in this context?

_____

_____

_____

b. If you use the trend line to predict the weight of the puppy after 60 months, the result is 243 ounces, or about 15 pounds. Is this a reasonable weight for the Chihuahua at 5 years old? Explain.

_____

_____

_____

_____

MODULE 1

LESSON 1.1

Your Turn

2. $10x - 4$ **3.** $-1.75x - 4.4$
5. $63k + 42m$ **6.** $0.6b - 3c$
7. $4e + 6f - 14g$ **9.** $2(x + 1)$
10. $3(x + 3)$ **11.** $5(x + 3)$
12. $4(x + 4)$

Guided Practice

1. Step 1: baseballs: $14 + 12n$,
tennis balls: $23 + 16n$; Step 2: $14 + 12n + 23 + 16n$, $14 + 23 + 12n + 16n$, $37 + 28n$, $37 + 28n$ **2.** 289
3. $0.5(12m) - 0.5(22n)$, $6m - 11n$
4. $\frac{2}{3}(18x) + \frac{2}{3}(6z) = 12x + 4z$
5. $2(x + 6)$ **6.** $12(x + 2)$
7. $7(x + 5)$

Independent Practice

9. $15(100 + 5d) + 20(50 + 7d) = 2{,}500 + 215d$ **11.** 3 and $x + 2$;
$3x + 6$ **13.** The area is the product of the length and width (6×9).
It is also the sum of the areas of the rectangles separated by the dashed line (6×5 and 6×4). So, $6(9) = 6(5) + 6(4)$.
15. $2x + 6$ **17.** $x^2 + 5x + 6$
19. (1) Think of 997 as $1{,}000 - 3$.
So, $8 \times 997 = 8(1{,}000 - 3)$. By the Distributive Property,
$8(1{,}000 - 3) = 8{,}000 - 24 = 7{,}976$. (2) Think of 997 as $900 + 90 + 7$. By the Distributive Property, $8(900 + 90 + 7) = 7{,}200 + 720 + 56 = 7{,}976$.

LESSON 1.2

Your Turn

1. $z = -13.9$ **2.** $r = 12.3$
3. $c = -12$ **5.** $x - 1.5 = 5.25$;
$x = 6.75$; the initial elevation of the plane is 6.75 miles.
6. $\frac{x}{3.5} = -1.2$; $x = -4.2$; \$4.20
7. $2.5x = 7.5$; $x = 3$; 3 hours

Guided Practice

1. Step 1: the number of degrees warmer the average temperature is in Nov. than in Jan., $x + (-13.4) = -1.7$ or $x - 13.4 = -1.7$; Step 2: 11.7°
2. Step 1: the number of days it takes the average temperature to decrease by 9 °F, $-1\frac{1}{2}x = -9$; Step 2: 6 days **3.** $x = -17$ **4.** $y = 1.4$
5. $z = -9$

Independent Practice

7. 29,028.87 ft
9. $28{,}251.31 - x = 11{,}194.21$;
$x = 17{,}057.1$; 17,057.1 ft
11. $26\frac{1}{2}$ ft/min
13. 18.8 °C warmer
15. $36\frac{1}{3}$ yards **17.** Sample answer: the elevation is the product of the rate and the time. **19.** (1) The elevations of the diver and the reef; both are below sea level. (2) The change in the plane's elevation; the plane is moving from a higher to a lower elevation.
21. Add the deposits and the withdrawals. Let x represent the amount of the initial deposit. Write and solve the equation $x + \text{deposits} - \text{withdrawals} = \$210.85$.

LESSON 1.3

Your Turn

4. $150 - 35x = 45$

Guided Practice

1.

2.

3. $6 + 9a = 78$ **4.** the solution; multiplied by 2; added to 2x; result

Independent Practice

7. three negative variable tiles and seven $+1$-tiles on one side of a line and 28 $+1$-tiles on the other side **9.** $1.25r + 6.75 = 31.75$
11. $\frac{1}{2}n + 45 = 172$ **13.** $500 - 20x = 220$ **15a.** $10 + 5c = 25$
b. 3 children **c.** They should choose Kimmi because she charges only \$25. If they chose Sandy, they would pay \$35.
17. Part of the equation is written in cents and part in dollars. All of the numbers in the equation should be written either in cents or in dollars.

LESSON 1.4

Your Turn

1. $x = 3$ **2.** $n = 3$
3. $a = -1$ **4.** $y = 1$
6. $3n + 10 = 37$; the triplets are 9 years old.
7. $\frac{n}{4} - 5 = 15$; the number is 80.
8. $-20 = \frac{5}{9}(x - 32)$; -4 °F
9. $120 - 4x = 92$; 7 incorrect answers

Guided Practice

1. one $+1$-tile from both sides; two equal groups **2.** 4 **3.** $2(18 + w) = 58$; the width is 11 inches
4. $1200 - 25x = 500$; 28 days

Independent Practice

7. $d = 9$ **9.** $k = 42$
11. $z = -190$ **13.** $n = -9$
15. $c = 9$ **17.** $t = -9$
19. 13 °F **21.** 12 years old
23. \$188 **25.** $x = 0.4$
27. $k = -180.44$ **29.** Sample answer: $\frac{x}{5} + 10 = 5$
31. The equation says that a number was divided by 4 and that 6 was then subtracted from the quotient, giving the result 2. So, working backward, first add 6 to 2, giving 8. Then multiply 8 by 4, giving $x = 32$. **33.** $w = \frac{P - 2\ell}{2}$

LESSON 2.1

Your Turn

4. $y \geq -2$

5. $x < 9$

6. $y > -6$

7. $t \geq -42$

8. $m \leq 9$; Tony can pay for no more than 9 months of his gym membership using this account.

Guided Practice

1. $2 \leq 5$ **2.** $2 > 1$ **3.** $0 > -11$
4. $2 \leq 16$ **5.** $n \geq 3$

6. $x < 4$

7. $y \geq -2$

8. $b > -5$

9a. $-4t \geq -80$
b. 20 or fewer hours
c. more than 20 hours

Independent Practice
11. $x > 50$

13. $q \leq 7$

15. $z < 8$ **17.** at most 16 in.
19. at most 7 in. **21.** at least 11 ft
23. $3\frac{1}{3}$ lb **25.** No; $1.25x \leq 3$; $x \leq$ 2.4 so 2.4 lb of onions is the most Florence can buy. $2.4 < 2.5$, so she cannot buy 2.5 lb. **27.** $x > 9$ for each inequality; in each case the number added to x is 9 less than the number on the right side of each inequality, so $x > 9$ is the solution.

LESSON 2.2

Your Turn
3. $1{,}240 + 45a \geq 6{,}000$
4. $6 + 3n \leq 40$

Guided Practice

1.

2.

3. \$7,000; \$1,250; 92; $1{,}250 + 92a \geq 7{,}000$ **4.** The solution of the problem; the solution multiplied by 7; 18 is subtracted from $7x$; the result can be no greater than 32.

Independent Practice
7. $3a + 28 > 200$; $a =$ possible amounts each friend earned
9. $4a - 25 \leq 75$; $a =$ the maximum amount each shirt can cost

10. $2{,}100 + 0.05s \geq 2{,}400$;
$s =$ the amount of her sales
13. $7 + 10c \leq 100$; $c =$ the number of CDs she buys **17.** $\leq$
19. $\leq$ **21.** $\geq$ **25.** $n > \frac{1}{n}$ if $n > 1$;
$n < \frac{1}{n}$ if $n < 1$; $n = \frac{1}{n}$ if $n = 1$

LESSON 2.3

Your Turn
1. $x > 2$ **2.** $h \geq 3$ **3.** $p \geq 6$; Joshua has to run at a steady pace of at least 6 mi/h. **4.** $v = 11$ **5.** $h = -3$; $h = -4$; $h = -5$

Guided Practice
1. Remove $4 + 1-$tiles from both sides, then divide each side into 3 equal groups; $x < 3$
2. $d < 9$

3. $b \geq 4$

4. $m = -10$ **5.** $y = \frac{1}{2}$; $y = 0$
6. $t \leq 1.25$;

Lizzy can spend from 0 to 1.25 h with each student. No; 1.5 h per student will exceed Lizzy's available time.

Independent Practice
9. $t \leq 10$ **11.** $m < 8$
13. $f < 140$ **15.** $g < -18$
17. $a \geq 16$ **19.** $7n - 25 \geq 65$;
$n \geq 12\frac{6}{7}$; Grace must wash at least 13 cars, because n must be a whole number.
21c. There is no number that satisfies both inequalities. **d.** The solution set is all numbers.

MODULE 3

LESSON 3.1

Your Turn

5. length: about 17.3 feet; width: about 13.3 feet; area: 230.1 square feet. **6.** The length is 22 feet, and the width is 10 feet. The area is 22 feet × 10 feet, or 220 square feet.

Guided Practice

1a. The wall is 30 feet long. **b.** 1.5 in. **2.** The length is 28 feet, and the width is 14 feet. The area is 28 feet × 14 feet, or 392 square feet. **3.** length: 25 meters; width: 15 meters; area: 375 square meters **4a.**

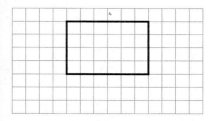

b. Length is 36 m and width is 24 m, using both scales.

Independent Practice

7. The scale drawing is 24 units by 15 units. **9.** Because the scale is 10 cm:1 mm and because 10 cm is longer than 1 mm, the drawing will be larger. **11a.** 6 toothpicks tall **b.** approximately 5 cotton swabs tall

LESSON 3.2

Guided Practice

1. a unique triangle
2. no triangle
3. a unique triangle
4. a unique triangle

Independent Practice

7. The side lengths proposed are 15, 21, and 37 ft, and 15 + 21 < 37. No such triangle can be created.
9. More than one triangle; two triangles can be created by connecting the top of the 2-in. segment with the dashed line, once in each spot where the arc intersects the dashed line. The triangles are different, but both have sides with lengths of 2 in. and $1\frac{1}{2}$ in., and a 45° angle not included between them.

LESSON 3.3

Guided Practice

1. triangle or equilateral triangle
2. rectangle
3. triangle
4. rainbow-shaped curve

Independent Practice

7. Circles or ovals
9a. It is a circle with a radius of 12 in.
b. The cross sections will still be circles, but their radii will decrease as the plane moves away from the sphere's center.
11. Sample answer: If you think of a building shaped like a rectangular prism, you can think of horizontal planes slicing the prism to form the different floors.

LESSON 3.4

Your Turn

5. Sample answer: ∠FGA and ∠AGC **6.** Sample answer: ∠FGE and ∠BGC **7.** Sample answer: ∠FGD and ∠DGC **8.** Sample answer: ∠BGC and ∠CGD **9.** 55° **10.** 54° + 3x = 180°, x = 42°, m∠JML = 3x = 126°

11. Sample answer: You can stop at the solution step where you find the value of 3x because the measure of ∠JML is equal to 3x.

Guided Practice

1. complementary **2.** adjacent **3.** vertical; 30° **4.** 50°, 30°, 2x; 80°; 100°; 100° **5.** 3x − 13, 58°, 45°; 45°, 15°; 15°; 45°; 32°

Independent Practice

7. Sample answer: ∠SUR and ∠QUR **9.** Sample answer: ∠TUS and ∠QUN **11.** m∠RUQ **13.** 96° **15.** 28° **17.** m∠A = 47°, m∠B = 43° **19.** 41 degrees, 33 minutes, 52 seconds **21.** Disagree; the sum of the measures of a pair of complementary angles is 90°. So, the measure of each angle must be less than 90°. But m∠A = 119°, and 119° > 90°.

MODULE 4

LESSON 4.1

Your Turn

3. about 34.54 cm **6.** about 2 hours

Guided Practice

1. 3.14(9); 28.26 **2.** 7; 44 **3.** 78.5 m **4.** 30.14 yd **5.** 47.1 in. **6.** 66; 66; 21; 21 + 4 = 25; 25; $11.25; $11.25 **7.** 0.5 yd; 1 yd **8.** 12.55 ft; 25.10 ft **9.** 1.7 in.; 10.68 in.

Independent Practice

11. 18.53 ft **13.** 110 in.
15. d = 18.8 ft; C ≈ 59.0 ft
17. r = 9 in.; C ≈ 56.52 in.
19. about 2,376 ft
21. about 0.14 mi
23. about $713.18
25. 12.56 feet **27.** Pool B; about 0.57 m or 1.84 ft

Selected Answers

LESSON 4.2

Your Turn
4. 314 ft^2

Guided Practice
1. 153.9 m^2 **2.** 452.2 mm^2
3. 314 yd^2 **4.** 200.96 in^2
5. 113.04 cm^2 **6.** 132.67 in^2 **7.** 4π
square units **8.** 36π square units
9. $\frac{\pi}{16}$ square units **10.** 16π yd

Independent Practice
13. 803.84 cm^2 **15.** 28.26 square
units **17.** 30.96 m^2 **19.** No; the
top of the large cake has an area
9 times that of the small cake. The
area of the top of the large cake
is 144π in^2 and that of the small
cake is 16π in^2. **21.** The 18-inch
pizza is a better deal because it
costs about 8¢ per square inch
while the 12-inch pizza costs
about 9¢ per square inch. **23.** No;
the combined area is $2\pi r^2$ while
the area of a circle with twice the
radius is $4\pi r^2$. **25.** $\frac{\pi (1.5)^2}{\pi (1.75)^2} =$
$\frac{2.25}{56.25} = \frac{1}{25}$ or 0.04 or 4%

LESSON 4.3

Your Turn
2. 51.5 ft^2 **3.** 139.25 m^2 **4.** $911.68

Guided Practice
1. rectangle; 4; 15; 15; 4; 15; 15; 34;
34 **2.** Method 1: Divide the figure
into a 12 by 9 rectangle and a 20
by 9 rectangle. Method 2: Divide
the figure into a 9 by 8 rectangle
and a 12 by 18 rectangle. The area
is 288 cm^2. **3.** $97.88

Independent Practice
5. 941.33 in^2
7. 30 square units

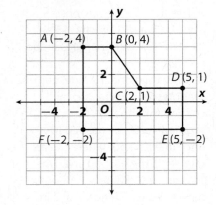

9. 60.56 cm^2 **11.** 5 ft; 32.5 ft^2 −
7.5 ft^2 = 25 ft^2; 25 ft^2 is area of
the square, so each side of the
square is 5 ft because 5 × 5 = 25
15a. 2,228 in^2 **b.** 3,016 in^2

LESSON 4.4

Your Turn
3. 69 in^2
4. 976 in^2

Guided Practice
1. 18 ft, 7 ft, 12 ft^2, (18 ft)(7 ft) +
2(12 ft^2), 150 ft^2 **2.** 37.5 m^2,
478 m^2, 6.25 m^2,
37.5 + 478 − 2(6.25), 503 m^2

Independent Practice
5. 3,720 tiles **7.** 66 ft^2
9. 3,264 in^2
11. No; they need 3 cans, which will
cost 3($6.79) = $20.37.
13. No; Ph doubles, and $2B$
quadruples. S more than doubles.
15. 138.2 in^2; 1,440 ft^2 of cardboard

LESSON 4.5

Your Turn
2. 1,848 m^3
5. 2,200 cm^3
7. 6,825 in^3

Guided Practice
1. 12 ft^2; (12 × 7) ft^3 = 84 ft^3
2. 30 m^2; (30 × 11) m^3 = 330 m^3
3. 288 ft^3; 72 ft^3; 360 ft^3
4. 40,000 ft^3
5. 385 cm^3

Independent Practice
7. 17.5 in^3
9. 384 ft^3
11. The units for volume are
incorrect; the volume is 300 cubic
inches.
13. 316.41 m^3
15. Triangular prism; you get 192 in^3
for the same price you would pay for
180 in^3 with the trapezoidal prism.
17. $V = 30(2.5) = 75$ cm^3; mass $\approx$
75(8.6) = 645g
19. Sample answers: (1) height
of trapezoid = 4 cm, base
lengths = 2 cm and 6 cm, height
of prism = 7.5 cm (2) height of
trapezoid = 2.5 cm, base
lengths = 1 cm and 7 cm, height of
prism = 12 cm

MODULE 5

LESSON 5.1

Your Turn

4. Yes; every employee had an equal chance of being selected. **5.** The question is biased since cats are suggested. **6.** The question is not biased. It does not lead people to pick a particular season.

Guided Practice

2. more; random **3.** less; biased **4.** Yes; Sample answer: What is your favorite color?

Independent Practice

9. It is biased because students who aren't in that class won't be selected. **11.** Yes; the sample is random. **13.** Jae's question is not biased since it does not suggest a type of art to students. **15a.** 60; a random sample **b.** 58%; it appears reasonable because Barbara used a random sample and surveyed a significant percent of the students.

LESSON 5.2

Your Turn

5. 420 damaged MP3s **6.** Sample answer: 6 is a little more than 10% of 50. 10% of 3,500 is 350, and 420 is a little more than that.

Guided Practice

1.

2.

3. 4; 7 **4.** 4; 11 **5.** 6.5 **6.** 280 **7.** 720 elk

Independent Practice

9. 48 people **11.** 240 puppies **13.** Yes, this seems reasonable because 25 is the median of the data. **17.** Kudrey needs to find the median and the lower and upper quartiles and plot those points. He assumed all quartiles would be equally long when each quartile represents an equal number of data values. **19.** a box plot

LESSON 5.3

Guided Practice

1. (1, 600); 20

2. 50; 51, 600

3. No, it has 4 defective batteries, or 20%. For the shipment, $\frac{50}{600}$, or about 8% of the batteries are defective.

Independent Practice

5. Shop A sells 100; Shop B sells 115; Shop C sells 140.

7. Shop A or Shop B; Both samples are large enough to produce a reasonably valid inference. Shop C's sample is too small.

9a. 49.8 palms **b.** about 3,187 palms

11. Sample answer: Roll two six-sided number cubes, with one cube representing the row and the other representing the column. Select the cell represented by the row and column shown on the cubes.

MODULE 6

LESSON 6.1

Your Turn

2. Dot plots for field hockey players and softball players have a similar spread. Center of the field hockey dot plot is less than the center for softball or basketball players. Dot plots for field hockey players and softball players have a similar spread.

3. median: 6 h, range: 10 h; If you remove the outliers, the range is 4 hours. The median is greater than the median for exercise. The range is less than the range for exercise.

Guided Practice

1. Class A: clustered around two areas; Class B: clustered in the middle **2.** Class A: two peaks at 4 and 13 mi; Class B: looks centered around 7 mi **3.** Class A: spread from 4 to 14 mi, a wide gap no data; Class B: spread from 3 to 9 mi **4.** The median for both dot plots is 6 miles. **5.** Range for Class A: 10 mi; range for Class B: 6 mi

Independent Practice

7. The dots have a relatively even spread, with a peak at 8 letters. **9.** The dots spread from 3 to 9 letters. **11.** AL: clustered in one small interval with an outlier to the left; VA: relatively uniform in height over the same interval **13.** AL: spreads from 1 to 12 days of rain, an outlier at 1; VA: spreads from 8 to 12 days of rain **15.** Group A: clustered to the left of size 9; Group B: clustered to the right of size 9 **17.** Group A: range with outlier = 6.5, without outlier = 2.5; Group B: range = 3 **19.** Yes; one group of five students could have the following number of pets: 1, 2, 3, 4, 5. Another group of five students could have the following number of pets: 1, 3, 3, 3, 5. For both groups of students, the median would be 3 and the range would be 4.

LESSON 6.2

Your Turn

3. Sample: The boxes have similar shapes, although Group B has a shorter box and shorter whiskers. Group B's median is greater than Group A's. Group B's shorter box means the middle 50% of the data are closer together than the middle 50% of Group A's.
4. Sample answer: The shape is similar to Store A's. The median is greater than Store A's and less than Store B's. The interquartile range is about the same as Store A's and longer than B's.

Guided Practice

1. 72; 88 **2.** 79 **3.** 16; 10
4. Volleyball players **5.** Hockey players **6.** Both groups

Independent Practice

9. Both cars have ranges of 45 in. Both cars have interquartile ranges of 25 in. **11.** Car A has less variability in the lowest quarter of its data and greater variability in the highest quarter of its data. The variability is reversed for Car B.
13. City A; $25

LESSON 6.3

Your Turn

1. About 1.1 times the MAD.
2. There is much more overlap between the two distributions.

Guided Practice

1. Class 1: 6, Class 2: 11; Class 1: 3, Class 2: 3 **2.** 1.67 **3.** Both distributions show longer

travel times for school A. The distribution of the medians shows less overlap, so is more convincing.

Independent Practice

5. Mean: 50 °F, MAD: 13 °F
7. 35 °F, 13 °F; the mean for City 2 must be 15 °F less than the mean for City 1, and the MAD must be the same.
9. The variation and overlap in the distributions make it hard to make any convincing comparison.
11. $1.75 \times$ range **13.** Ramon's; the larger the sample size, the less variability there should be in the distributions of the medians and means.

UNIT 4 Selected Answers

MODULE 7

LESSON 7.1

Your Turn

3. as likely as not; $\frac{1}{2}$ **4.** $\frac{1}{2}$ **5.** $\frac{1}{3}$
7. $\frac{7}{8}$ **8.** $\frac{1}{2}$

Guided Practice

1. 8; 5; 7; 1; 3; 2; 4; 6 **2.** impossible; 0 **3.** as likely as not; $\frac{1}{2}$ **4.** certain; 1 **5.** unlikely; close to 0 **6.** $\frac{2}{5}$ **7.** $\frac{1}{4}$ **8.** $\frac{5}{6}$ **9.** $\frac{2}{3}$ **10.** $\frac{4}{5}$ **11.** $\frac{12}{13}$

Independent Practice

13. $\frac{2}{13}$; The event can occur in 8 ways. There are 52 outcomes in the sample space. $\frac{8}{52} = \frac{2}{13}$
15. No, it is unlikely that she will have oatmeal for breakfast. **19a.** $\frac{8}{14} = \frac{4}{7}$
b. $8 - 1 = 7$ blue coins and $6 + 3 = 9$ red coins; $\frac{9}{16}$
c. $8 + 3 = 11$ blue coins and $6 - 1 = 5$ red coins; $\frac{5}{16}$ **21.** Yes; Because not selecting red means black will be selected, and vice versa. $P(\text{not black}) + P(\text{black}) = P(\text{not black}) + P(\text{not red}) = 1$.

LESSON 7.2

Your Turn

7. red: $\frac{1}{3}$, yellow: $\frac{7}{15}$, blue: $\frac{1}{5}$
8. Let 1 and 2 represent red, let 3 and 4 represent white, and let 5 and 6 represent blue. Toss the cube 50 times to determine the experimental probability for each color. Predict that the next ball released will be the color with the greatest experimental probability.

Guided Practice

1. A: $\frac{7}{20}$, 0.35, 35%; B: $\frac{7}{40}$, 0.175, 17.5%; C: $\frac{11}{40}$, 0.275, 27.5%; D: $\frac{1}{5}$, 0.2, 20%

2. Sample answer: Write "yes" on 6 cards and "no" on 4. Draw a card at random 50 times. Use the number of "yes" cards as her prediction.

Independent Practice

5. Sample answer: Compare the number of wins to the total number of trials; $\frac{1}{6}$.
7. Yes, because it is based on actual data of weather patterns.
9. $\frac{2}{5}$; 16 aces; $\frac{2}{5}$ of 40 is 16.
11. No; there were 40 heads in 100 trials; $P(\text{heads}) = \frac{40}{100}$.

LESSON 7.3

Your Turn

1. $\frac{60}{400} = \frac{3}{20} = 15\%$ **3.** $\frac{12}{75} = \frac{4}{25}$

Guided Practice

1. $\frac{50}{400} = \frac{1}{8}$

Independent Practice

5. $\frac{60}{400} = \frac{3}{20}$ **7.** 12; The total is the product of 3 page count choices and 4 color choices, which is 12. **13.** No, because coins are fair and the probabilities do not appear to be equally likely.

LESSON 7.4

Your Turn

1. 132 customers **3.** No; about 371 e-mails out of 12,372 will come back undelivered. The prediction is high. **4.** 84 customers; Yes, $107 > 84$, so more customers than normal bought two or more pairs.

Guided Practice

1. 15 times **2.** about 55 days **3.** No, about 1,009 candles out of 16,824 will be returned. The prediction is low. **4.** No, about 746 toys out of 24,850 will be

defective. The prediction is high. **5.** 39 times; The light-rail's claim is higher than the actual 85%. **6.** 900 students; The college's claim is close to the number actually accepted.

Independent Practice

9. Yes; 6th grade: $\frac{2}{100} = \frac{x}{250} \rightarrow x = 5$; 7th grade: $\frac{4}{100} = \frac{x}{200} \rightarrow x = 8$; 8th grade: $\frac{8}{100} = \frac{x}{150} \rightarrow x = 12$
11. 36 clients; more than would be expected on average **13.** He set up the fraction incorrectly; it should be $\frac{1}{3} = \frac{x}{180}$. **15.** 14,700 on-time flights

MODULE 8

LESSON 8.1

Your Turn

2. $\frac{1}{3}$ **3.** The total number of outcomes in the sample space is the denominator of the formula for theoretical probability.

Guided Practice

1.

	Basket A	Basket B
Total number of outcomes	16	20
Number of red balls	3	4
$P(\textbf{win}) = \dfrac{\text{number of red balls}}{\text{total number of outcomes}}$	$\frac{3}{16}$	$\frac{4}{20} = \frac{1}{5}$

2. Basket B **3.** odd, 6; sections, 11 **4.** even, 5; sections, 11 **5.** $\frac{2}{6} = \frac{1}{3}$ **6.** Sample answer: No, but it might be reasonably close.

Independent Practice

9. $\frac{2}{3}$, 0.67, 67% **11.** $\frac{1}{2}$, 0.50, 50% **13.** $\frac{3}{5}$, 0.60, 60% **15.** 9 represents the ways the event can occur; 13 represents the number of equally likely outcomes.

LESSON 8.2

Your Turn

3. $\frac{4}{12} = \frac{1}{3}$ **4.** $\frac{6}{12} = \frac{1}{2}$ **5.** $\frac{3}{8}$

Guided Practice

1.

	1	2	3	4	5	6
1	1	2	3	4	5	6
2	2	4	6	8	10	12
3	3	6	9	12	15	18
4	4	8	12	16	20	24
5	5	10	15	20	25	30
6	6	12	18	24	30	36

2. $\frac{15}{16}$ **3.** $\frac{23}{36}$

4.

Coin 1	H			T		
Coin 2	H		T		H		T
Coin 3	H	T	H	T	H	T	H	T
List:	HHH	HHT	HTH	HTT	THH	THT	TTH	TTT

5. 8 **6.** TTT **7.** $\frac{1}{8}$ **8.** 3; HTH, THH ; $\frac{3}{8}$

Independent Practice

11. $\frac{1}{2}$ **13.** $\frac{1}{10}$ **15.** $\frac{2}{9}$ **17.** Because there are 3 choices for the first item and 2 for the second, there are $3 \cdot 2 = 6$ possible outcomes. **19.** Neither

LESSON 8.3

Your Turn

1. about 167 times **2.** about 9 times **3.** more likely that he picks a marble of another color **4.** No

Guided Practice

1. $\frac{1}{3}, \frac{1}{3}, \frac{1}{3}, \frac{1}{3}$; 1, 3, 18, 6, 6 **2.** 50 people **3.** brown; $P(\text{hazel}) = \frac{9}{28}$, $P(\text{brown}) = \frac{10}{28}$, $P(\text{blue}) = \frac{7}{28}$, and $P(\text{green}) = \frac{2}{28}$. The event with the greatest probability is choosing a person with brown eyes.

Independent Practice

5. 15 white or gray marbles **7.** It is more likely that she draws 2 red cards. **9.** 500 times **11.** 45 days **17.** Yes, but only theoretically because in reality, nothing can occur 0.5 time.

LESSON 8.4

Guided Practice

1. years with a drought; years without a drought; 4

2.

Trial	Numbers generated	Drought years
1	10, 3, 5, 1	2
2	10, 4, 6, 5	0
3	3, 2, 10, 3	3
4	2, 10, 4, 4	1
5	7, 3, 6, 3	2

Trial	Numbers generated	Drought years
6	8, 4, 8, 5	0
7	6, 2, 2, 8	2
8	6, 5, 2, 4	1
9	2, 2, 3, 2	4
10	6, 3, 1, 5	2

3. 80%

Independent Practice

5. 1 trial **7.** 20%

LESSON 9.1

Your Turn
1. $0.\overline{45}$ 2. 0.125 3. $2.\overline{3}$ 4. $\frac{3}{25}$ 5. $\frac{19}{33}$

6. $1\frac{2}{5}$ 7. $x = \pm 14$ 8. $x = \pm\frac{3}{16}$
9. $x = 8$ 10. $x = \frac{4}{7}$

Guided Practice
1. 0.4 2. $0.\overline{8}$ 3. 3.75 4. 0.7
5. 2.375 6. $0.8\overline{3}$ 7. $\frac{27}{40}$ 8. $5\frac{3}{5}$ 9. $\frac{11}{25}$
10. $4.\overline{4}$; $0.\overline{4}$; 9; 4; $\frac{4}{9}$ 11. $26.\overline{26}$; $0.\overline{26}$;
99; 26; $\frac{26}{99}$ 12. $325.\overline{325}$; $0.\overline{325}$; 999;
325; $\frac{325}{999}$ 13. 144; ± 12 14. $\frac{25}{289}$; $\pm\frac{5}{17}$
15. 216; 6 16. 2.25 17. 1.75
18. 3.15

Independent Practice
21. $0.1\overline{6}$ 23. $98.\overline{6}$ innings
25. $26\frac{1}{5}$ mi 27. $\frac{101}{200}$ cent
29. His estimate is low because 15 is very close to 16, so $\sqrt{15}$ is very close to $\sqrt{16}$, or 4. A better estimate would be 3.8 or 3.9.
31. 3 feet
33. $\sqrt{\frac{4}{25}} = \frac{2}{5} = \frac{\sqrt{4}}{\sqrt{25}}$; $\sqrt{\frac{16}{81}} = \frac{4}{9} = \frac{\sqrt{16}}{\sqrt{81}}$;
$\sqrt{\frac{36}{49}} = \frac{6}{7} = \frac{\sqrt{36}}{\sqrt{49}}$; $\frac{\sqrt{a}}{\sqrt{b}} = \sqrt{\frac{a}{b}}$;
$\sqrt{a} \cdot \sqrt{b} = \sqrt{a \cdot b}$

LESSON 9.2

Your Turn
1. rational, real 2. irrational, real 3. False. Every integer is a rational number, but every rational number is not an integer. Rational numbers such as $\frac{3}{5}$ and $-\frac{5}{2}$ are not integers. 4. False. Real numbers are either rational or irrational numbers. Integers are rational numbers, so no integers are irrational numbers. 5. Real numbers; the amount can be any number greater than 0. 6. Real numbers; the number of seconds left can be any number less than 0.

Guided Practice
1. rational, real 2. whole, integer, rational, real 3. irrational, real
4. rational, real 5. whole, integer, rational, real 6. integer, rational, real 7. rational, real 8. integer, rational, real 9. True. Whole numbers are a subset of the set of rational numbers and can be written as a ratio of the whole number to 1. 10. True. Whole numbers are rational numbers. 11. Integers; the change can be a whole dollar amount and can be positive, negative, or zero. 12. Rational numbers; the ruler is marked every $\frac{1}{16}$th inch.

Independent Practice
15. whole, integer, rational, real 17. rational, real 19. whole, integer, rational, real 21. Integers; the scores are counting numbers, their opposites, and zero.
23. Whole; the diameter is $\frac{\pi}{\pi} =$ 1 mile. 25. rational number
27. Sample answer: If the calculator shows a terminating decimal, the number is rational. Otherwise, you cannot tell because you see only a few digits.

LESSON 9.3

Your Turn
3. $>$ 4. $<$ 5. $\sqrt{3}, \sqrt{5}, 2.5$

6. $\sqrt{75}, \pi^2, 10$

7. $3\frac{1}{2}$ mi, $3.\overline{45}$ mi, $\frac{10}{3}$ mi, $\sqrt{10}$ mi

Guided Practice
1. $<$ 2. $>$ 3. $<$ 4. $<$ 5. $>$
6. $<$ 7. $>$ 8. $>$ 9. 1.7; 1.8; 1.75; 6.28; 1.5; $\sqrt{3}$; 2π 10. $\left(1 + \frac{\pi}{2}\right)$ km, 2.5 km, $\frac{12}{5}$ km, $(\sqrt{17} - 2)$ km

Independent Practice
13. $\pi, \sqrt{10}, 3.5$ 15. $-3.75, \frac{9}{4}, \sqrt{8}, 3$
17a. $\sqrt{60} \approx 7.7.5, \frac{58}{8} = 7.25$, $7.\overline{3} \approx 7.33, 7\frac{3}{5} = 7.60$, so the average is 7.4825 km. b. They are nearly identical. $\sqrt{56}$ is approximately 7.4833...
19. Sample answer: $\sqrt{31}$
21a. between $\sqrt{7} \approx 2.65$ and $\sqrt{8} \approx 2.83$ b. between $\sqrt{9} = 3$ and $\sqrt{10} \approx 3.16$ 23. 2; rational numbers can have the same location, and irrational numbers can have the same location, but they cannot share a location.

MODULE 10

LESSON 10.1

Your Turn
6. 5 7. $63\frac{15}{16}$

Guided Practice
1. $\frac{1}{8}$ 2. $\frac{1}{36}$ 3. 1 4. 100 5. 625
6. $\frac{1}{32}$ 7. $\frac{1}{1024}$ 8. 1 9. $\frac{1}{1331}$ 10. 4^3
11. $2^2 \cdot 2^3 = 2^5$ 12. 6^2
13. $8^{12-9} = 8^3$ 14. 5^{12} 15. 7^{13}
16. 4; 6; 6; $(6 \cdot 6)$; 6^8 17. 3; 3; 3; $(3 \cdot 3 \cdot 3)$; 3^9 18. 1168 19. 343

Independent Practice
21. The exponents cannot be added because the bases are not the same.
23. Earth to Neptune; 22^3, or 10,648, times greater. 25. -3
27. 19 29. 10^3 kg, or 1000 kg
31. Both expressions equal x^5, so $x^7 \cdot x^{-2} = \frac{x^7}{x^2}$. When multiplying powers with the same base, you add exponents; $7 + (-2) = 5$. When dividing powers with

UNIT 5 Selected Answers *(cont'd)*

the same base, you subtract exponents; $7 - 2 = 5$. In cases like this, $x^n \cdot x^{-m} = \frac{x^n}{x^m}$.

33. 3^6; 3^3

35. No; $\frac{6^2}{36^2} = \frac{6 \cdot 6}{36 \cdot 36} = \frac{6 \cdot 6}{6 \cdot 6 \cdot 6 \cdot 6} = \frac{1}{6 \cdot 6} = \frac{1}{36}$

37. The number is 5.

LESSON 10.2

Your Turn

3. 6.4×10^3 **4.** 5.7×10^{11}
5. 9.461×10^{12} km **8.** 7,034,000,000
9. 236,000 **10.** 5,000,000 g

Guided Practice

1. 5.8927×10^4 **2.** 1.304×10^9
3. 6.73×10^6 **4.** 1.33×10^4
5. 9.77×10^{22} **6.** 3.84×10^5
7. 400,000 **8.** 1,849,900,00
9. 6,410 **10.** 84,560,00
11. 800,000 **12.** 90,000,000,000
13. 54,00 s **14.** 7,600,000 cans

Independent Practice

17. 2.2×10^5 lb **19.** 4×10^4 lb
21. 5×10^4 lb **23.** $108\frac{1}{3}$ hours or 108 hours and 20 minutes
25. 4.6×10^3 lb **27a.** None of the girls has the correct answer.
b. Polly and Samantha have the decimal in the wrong place; Esther miscounted the number of places the decimal moved. **29.** The speed of a car because it is likely to be less than 100. **31.** Is the first factor greater than 1 and less than 10? Is the second factor a power of 10?

LESSON 10.3

Your Turn

4. 8.29×10^{-5} **5.** 3.02×10^{-7}
6. 7×10^{-6} m **9.** 0.000001045
10. 0.000099 **11.** 0.01 m

Guided Practice

1. 4.87×10^{-4} **2.** 2.8×10^{-5}
3. 5.9×10^{-5} **4.** 4.17×10^{-2}
5. 2×10^{-5} **6.** 1.5×10^{-5}
7. 0.00002 **8.** 0.000003582
9. 0.00083 **10.** 0.0297
11. 0.0000906 **12.** 0.00004
13. 1×10^{-4}
14. 0.00000000000000000000000017

Independent Practice

17. 1.3×10^{-3} cm **19.** 4.5×10^{-3} cm **21.** 8×10^{-4} cm
23. 7 cm = 0.07 m, 7 cm = 7×10^0 cm; 0.07 m = 7×10^{-2} m
The first factors are the same; the exponents differ by 2. **25.** If the exponent on 10 is nonnegative, the number is greater than or equal to 1. **27.** Negative, because a ladybug would weigh less than 1 ounce. **29.** 0.000000000125
31. 71,490,000 **33.** 3,397,000
35. 5.85×10^{-3} m, 1.5×10^{-2} m, 2.3×10^{-2} m, 9.6×10^{-1} m, 1.2×10^2 m **37.** The result will be greater than the number with the positive exponent because the divisor is less than 1.

LESSON 10.4

Your Turn

1. 7.62×10^7 more people
2. 8.928×10^8 miles
3. 3.14×10^2 minutes **4.** 7.5E5
5. 3E–7 **6.** 2.7E13 **7.** 4.5×10^{-1}
8. 5.6×10^{12} **9.** 6.98×10^{-8}

Guided Practice

1. 0.225; 6; 0.225; 2.8; 7.225×10^6
2. 0.10; 3; 8.5; 5.3; 0.10; 3.1×10^3
3. 5×10^2 **4.** 5.9381×10^5
5. 1.206×10^{22} **6.** 1.73×10^8
7. 1.69×10^{19} **8.** 2×10^7
9. 3.6E11 **10.** 7.25E–5 **11.** 8E–1
12. 7.6×10^{-4} **13.** 1.2×10^{16}
14. 9×10^1

Independent Practice

17. about 1.9×10^3 as many
19. 5.025×10^7 tons **21.** Plastics
23. about 7 people per square mile **25.** 13 years, 3 months, 22.5 days **27.** $\$2.94 \times 10^4$, or $\$29,400$ per person. **29.** The student is off by a power of 10. The correct product is 40×10^{15}, or 4.0×10^{16}.

MODULE 11

LESSON 11.1

Your Turn

3. $y = 15x$ **4.** 6 miles hiked in 5 hours **5.** $y = \frac{6}{5}x$

Guided Practice

1. is **2.** constant of proportionality **3a.** The pairs (weeks, days) are (2, 14), (4, 28), (8, 56), (10, 70). **b.** the time in weeks; the time in days; $y = 7x$ **4.** The pairs (oxygen atoms, hydrogen atoms) are (5, 10), (17, 34), (120, 240); $y = 2x$ **5.** $y = 30x$

Independent Practice

7. No; the ratios of the numbers in each column are not equal. **9a.** Sample answer: The account had a balance of $100 to begin with. **b.** Sample answer: Have Ralph open the account with no money to begin with and then put $20 in every month. **11.** $y = 105$ **13a.** The pairs (distance, time) are (10, 1), (20, 2), (30, 3), (40, 4), (50, 5). **b.** $y = \frac{1}{10}x$, where y is the time in minutes and x is the distance in inches. **c.** 8.5 minutes **15.** For $S = 1$, $P = 4$ and $A = 1$; For $S = 2$, $P = 8$ and $A = 4$; For $S = 3$, $P = 12$ and $A = 9$; For $S = 4$, $P = 16$ and $A = 16$; For $S = 5$, $P = 20$ and $A = 25$. **a.** Yes. The ratio of the perimeter of a square to its side length is always 4. **b.** No. The ratio of the area of a square to its side length is not constant.

LESSON 11.2

Your Turn

1. 36, 13, −10; variable **4.** +3; +4; $\frac{3}{4}$

Guided Practice

1. constant **2.** variable **3.** variable **4.** constant **5.** 200; 1;

200; 1; 200 **6.** 200 ft per min **7.** −2 **8.** $\frac{3}{2}$

Independent Practice

11. 15 miles per hour **13a.** 1 gallon every 5 minutes, or 0.2 gal/min **b.** 25 minutes **15.**

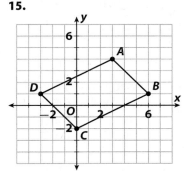

a. slope $\overline{AB} = -1$; slope $\overline{BC} = \frac{1}{2}$; slope $\overline{CD} = -1$; slope $\overline{DA} = \frac{1}{2}$ **b.** The slopes of the opposite sides are the same. **c.** Yes; opposite sides still have the same slope. **17.** Sample answer: One line has a positive slope and one has a negative slope. The lines are equally steep, but one slants upward left to right and the other slants downward left to right. The lines cross at the origin.

LESSON 11.3

Your Turn

2. His unit rate and the slope of a graph of the ride both equal $\frac{1}{5}$ mi/min.

Tomas's Ride

4. A: 375, 375 mi/h; B: 425, 425 mi/h; B is flying faster.

Guided Practice

1. slope = unit rate = $\frac{5}{6}$ mi/h **2.** slope = unit rate = $\frac{5}{4}$ mi/h **3.** Clark is faster. From the equation, Henry's rate is equal to 0.5, or $\frac{1}{2}$ mile per hour. Clark's rate is the slope of the line, which is $\frac{3}{2}$, or 1.5 miles per hour. **4.** $y = 15x$ **5.** $y = \frac{3}{8}x$

Independent Practice

7a. The pairs (time, distance) are (4, 3), (8, 6), (12, 9), (16, 12), (20, 15). **b.**

Migration Flight

c. $\frac{3}{4}$; The unit rate of migration of the goose and the slope of the graph both equal $\frac{3}{4}$ mi/min. **9a.** Machine 1: slope = unit rate = $\frac{0.6}{1}$ = 0.6 gal/s; Machine 2: slope = unit rate = $\frac{3}{4}$ = 0.75 gal/s **b.** Machine 2 is working at a faster rate since 0.75 > 0.6. **11.** slope = unit rate = 4.75. If the graph of a proportional relationship passes through the point (1, r), then r equals the slope and the unit rate, which is $4.75/min. **13.** 243 gallons; Sample answer: The unit rate is $\frac{36}{2}$ = 18 gal/min. So, $1\frac{1}{2}$ min after 12 min, an additional $18 \times 1\frac{1}{2}$ = 27 gal will be pumped in. The total is 216 + 27 = 243 gal.

MODULE 12

LESSON 12.1

Your Turn

1. Sample answer: (2, 20), (3, 32), (4, 44), (5, 56) **3.** (−1, 3), (0, 1), (1, −1), (2, −3)

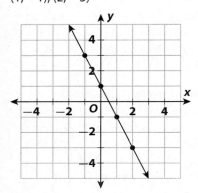

Guided Practice

1. (−2, 1), (−1, 3), (0, 5), (1, 7), (2, 9) **2.** (−8, −8), (0, −5), (8, −2), (16, 1), (24, 4) **3.** Undefined, 3.5, 2.75, 2.5, 2.375; The ratio $\frac{y}{x}$ is not constant. **4.** The graph is a line, but it does not pass through the origin. **5.** (−2, −3), (−1, −2), (0, −1), (1, 0), (2, 1)

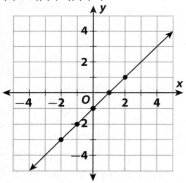

Independent Practice

7. Set of unconnected points; you cannot buy a fractional part of a lunch. **9a.** Sample answer: For (x, y) where x is number of years renewed and y is total cost in dollars: (0, 12), (1, 20), (2, 28), (3, 36), (4, 44)

b.

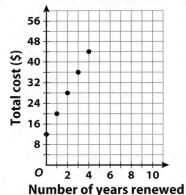

Magazine Subscription Costs

c. The graph does not include the origin. Also, the ratio of the total cost and number of years is not constant. **d.** No; the number of years must be a whole number, so total cost goes up in $8 increments. **11.** Sample answer: In a table, the ratios $\frac{y}{x}$ will not be equal; a graph will not pass through the origin; an equation will be in the form $y = mx + b$ where $b \neq 0$. **13.** At most one: A line representing a proportional relationship must pass through the origin. A line parallel to it cannot also pass through the origin.

LESSON 12.2

Your Turn

1. $m = 5$; $b = 12$ **2.** $m = 7$; $b = 1$

Guided Practice

1. −2; 1 **2.** 5; −15 **3.** $\frac{3}{2}$; −2 **4.** −3; 9 **5.** 3; 1 **6.** −4; 140

Independent Practice

9a. $5 to park; $12 per hour **b.** $23.50; (3.5 hours × $12 per hour + $5) ÷ 2 = $23.50 **11.** Rate of change is constant from 1 to 2 to 3, but not from 3 to 4. **13.** Express the slope m between a random point (x, y) on the line and the point (0, b) where the line crosses the y-axis. Then solve the equation for y.

15. After parking 61 cars; John earns a fixed weekly salary of $300 plus $5 for each car he parks. He earns the same in fees as his fixed salary for parking 300 ÷ 5 = 60 cars.

LESSON 12.3

Your Turn

2.

3.

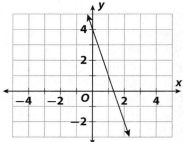

4.

5. The new graph has the same y-intercept but a slope of −200 instead of −300.

6. The calories left to burn will decrease more slowly with each hour of exercise, so it will take longer for Ken to meet his goal.

7. The y-intercept would not change, but the slope would become −600, which is much steeper. The line would intersect the x-axis when x = 4 hours.

Guided Practice

1. $\frac{1}{2}$; -3

2. -3; 2

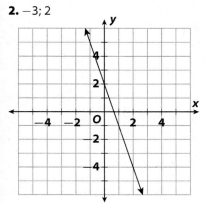

3a. Slope = 4; y-intercept = 2; you start with 2 cards and add 4 cards each week.

b. The points with coordinates that are not whole numbers; you will not buy part of a baseball card and you are buying only once a week.

Independent Practice

5a.

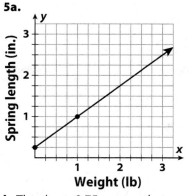

b. The slope, 0.75, means that the spring stretches by 0.75 inch with each additional pound of weight. The y-intercept, 0.25, is the unstretched length of the spring in inches. **c.** 1.75 inches; no; the length with a 4-pound weight is 3.25 in., not 3.5 in. **7.** (0, 8), (1, 7), (2, 6), (3, 5) **9.** (0, −3), (1, −1.5), (2, 0), (3, 1.5) **11.** (0, −5), (3, −3), (6, −1), (9, 1) **13a.** Yes; Since the horizontal and vertical gridlines each represent 25 units, moving up 3 gridlines and right 1 gridline represents a slope of $\frac{75}{25}$, or 3. **b.** $m = 3$ so $3 is the charge per visit; $b = 50$ so the membership fee is $50.

c. 50 visits **15.** Yes; plot the point and use the slope to find a second point. Then draw a line through the two points.

LESSON 12.4

Your Turn

1. nonproportional
2. proportional
5. proportional
6. nonproportional

7. nonproportional
8. nonproportional
9. nonproportional
10. proportional
11. Test-Prep Center A's charges are proportional, but B's are not. Center B offers a coupon for an initial credit, but its hourly rate, $25, is higher than Center A's hourly rate of $20. So, Center B will cost more in the long run.

Guided Practice

1. Proportional; the line includes the origin. **2.** Nonproportional; the line does not include the origin. **3.** Nonproportional; when the equation is written in the form $y = mx + b$, the value of b is not 0. **4.** Proportional; when the equation is written in the form $y = mx + b$, the value of b is 0. **5.** Proportional; the quotient of y and x is constant, 4, for every number pair. **6.** No; the quotient of y and x is not constant for every number pair. **7.** Sample answer: The rating is proportional to the number of households watching; the quotient of the rating and the number of households is always 0.0000008.

Independent Practice

9a. Nonproportional; the graph does not pass through the origin, so $b \neq 0$. **b.** $m = 0.5$, $b = 10$; each cup of sports drink weighs a half pound. The empty cooler weighs 10 pounds. **11.** Proportional; this equation has the form $y = mx + b$ where $b = 0$.

15a. No; from Equation B, the y-intercept is 273.15, not 0, so the graph does not include the origin. From Table C, the quotient of K and C is not constant.
b. No; Equation A is in the form $y = mx + b$, with F instead of y and C instead of x. The value of b is 32, not 0, so the relationship is not proportional.

Selected Answers

LESSON 13.1

Your Turn

3. $y = -2.5x + 25$ **5.** $y = 0.5x + 10$

Guided Practice

1a. the length of the necklace in inches **b.** the total number of beads in the necklace **c.** $y = 5x + 27$ **2.** $\frac{0 - 300}{5 - 0} = \frac{-300}{5} = -60$; 300; $y = -60x + 300$
3. temperature; chirps per minute; $\frac{100 - 76}{65 - 59} = \frac{24}{6} = 4$; $100 = 4 \cdot 65 + b$; -160; $y = 4x - 160$

Independent Practice

5. $y = 30x$ **7.** $m = 0.125$; the diver ascends at a rate of 0.125 m/s **9.** $y = 0.125x - 10$ **11.** $y = 20x + 12$ **13.** $m = 500$; $b = 1000$ **15.** The amount of money in the savings account increases by $500 each month. **17.** The rate of change would not be constant. Using different pairs of points in the slope formula would give different results.

LESSON 13.2

Your Turn

1. $m = 15,000$; $b = 0$; $y = 15,000x$

Water Released from Hoover Dam

4. $p = 75n + 250$ **5.** $c = 0.50d + 40$

Guided Practice

1. $m = -1.25$; $b = 20$; $y = -1.25x + 20$

Bus Pass Balance

2. $m = \frac{51 - 59}{2000 - 0} = \frac{-8}{2000} = -0.004$
3. $b = 59$ **4.** $y = -0.004x + 59$
5. $y = -0.004(5000) + 59 = 39°F$

Independent Practice

7. $m = 2$; $b = 8$; $C = 2t + 8$
9a. $y = -1.5x + 30$ **b.** The number of dollars left decreases as the number of car washes increases. **c.** 20; after 20 washes there is no money left on the card. **11.** $y = -2x + 6$ **13a.** No, the change between weeks is constant, but the change in the amount of rain is not constant. **b.** No; there is no apparent pattern in the table. **15.** 0; Jaíme's graph contained (0, 0). Since Jayla's data were the same, but with x and y switched, her graph also contained (0, 0).

LESSON 13.3

Your Turn

1. $y = 4x + 20$ **2.** $y = 240x$
6. $30 **7.** $48.75 **8.** $600

Guided Practice

1. $y = 30x$ **2.** $y = 2.5x + 2$ **3.** $y = 20x + 30$; $140 **4.** Yes, because the graph has a constant rate of change. **5.** No, because the graph does not have a constant rate of change.

Independent Practice

7. Yes, because the rate of change is constant. **9.** Linear; the rate of change is the cost of a DVD, which is constant. **11.** Not linear;

the rate of change in the area of a square increases as the side length increases. **13.** The relationship is linear; the equation of the linear relationship is $y = 0.125x$, so the Mars Rover would travel 7.5 feet in 60 seconds. **15.** Sample answer: Because $x = 6$ lies halfway between $x = 4$ and $x = 8$, so the y-value should lie halfway between the corresponding y-values. **17.** Find the equation of the linear relationship using the slope and given point, and then insert any x-value to find a y-value on the graph of the line.

LESSON 14.1

Your Turn

4. Function; each input value is paired with only one output value. **5.** Not a function; the input value is paired with more than one output value. **7.** Function; each input value is paired with only one output value. **8.** Not a function; the input value 8 is paired with more than one output value. **10.** Not a function; input values are paired with more than one output values; (70, 164) and (70, 174)

Guided Practice

1. $20x$; 200 **2.** $\frac{x}{2}$; 15 **3.** $2.25x$; 27.00 **4.** Function; each input value is paired with only one output value **5.** Not a function; the input value 4 is paired with more than one output value. **6.** Yes; each input value is paired with only one output value.

Independent Practice

9. Not a function; the input value 5 is paired with more than one output value. **11a.** There is only one number of bacteria for each number of hours, so each input is paired with only one output.

b. Yes. Each input value would still be paired with only one output value. **13.** Yes. Each input value (the weight) is paired with only one output value (the price). **15.** It does not represent a function. For the input values to be paired with all four output values, at least one of the input values would be paired with more than one output value.

LESSON 14.2

Your Turn
2. proportional
3. $(x, y) = (0, 0), (3, 2), (6, 4), (9, 6)$; linear; proportional

Making Soda

Guided Practice
1. $(-1, 7), (1, 3), (3, -1), (5, -5)$; linear

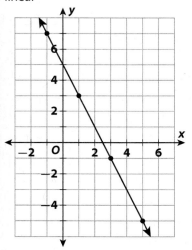

2. $(-2, -2), (-1, 1), (0, 2), (1, 1), (2, -2)$; nonlinear

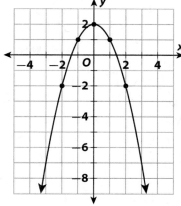

3. No; the equation cannot be written in the form $y = mx + b$, and the graph of the solutions is not a line. **4.** Yes; the equation can be written in the form $y = mx + b$, and the graph of the solutions is a line.

Independent Practice
7. No. The relationship is not linear because x is squared, so it will not be proportional. **9a.** Yes. The graph of the solutions lie in a line.

Drill Team Uniforms

b. $720
11. Disagree; the equation can be written in the form $y = mx + b$ where m is 0, and the graph of the solutions is a horizontal line. **13.** The relationship is linear if the points all lie on the same line, and proportional if it is linear and a line through the points passes through the origin. **15.** Applying the Distr. Prop gives $y + 3 = 6x + 3$, or $y = 6x$. This is in the form $y = mx + b$ with $b = 0$, so it is linear and proportional.

LESSON 14.3

Your Turn
1. Buying at the bookstore is more expensive.

Guided Practice
1. The second method (159 bpm vs. 150 bpm) gives the greater heart rate. **2.** Heart rate and age are nonproportional for each method. **3.** Students pay a $40 fee and $5 per hour.
4.

Tutoring Fees

5. With both plans, it costs $60 for 4 hours of tutoring. **6.** Plan 2 ($90 vs. $150) is cheaper for 10 hours of tutoring. **7.** Cost and time are proportional for Plan 1 and nonproportional for Plan 2.

Independent Practice
9. Scooter B (15 gallons vs. 18 gallons) uses fewer gallons of gas. **11.** the first plan **13.** The camera at the second store; the cost at the first store is $290 and the cost at the second store is $260. **15.** Since the rate per visit is the same, the monthly cost of Gym A is always more than Gym B. **17.** $y = -24x + 8$ is changing more quickly because even though -24 is less than -21, the absolute value of -24 is greater than the absolute value of -21.

LESSON 14.4

Guided Practice

1. The graph is increasing quickly. This shows a period of rapid growth.

2. The number of bacteria is decreasing.

3. Graph 2 **4.** Graph 3

5.

Independent Practice

7. Graph 1

9. Regina left the rental shop and rode for an hour. She took a half-hour rest and then started back. She changed her mind and continued for another half hour. She took a half-hour break and then returned to the rental shop.

11.

13. 3:23 to 3:24

15.

MODULE 15

LESSON 15.1

Your Turn

2. 64 weeks

Guided Practice

1. $x = -4$ **2.** $x = 5$ **3.** 4 personal training sessions

Independent Practice

7a. $12 + 5x = 18 + 3x$; $x = 3$; 3 hours **b.** Darlene's Dog Sitting; the cost would be $33, as opposed to $37 at Derrick's Dog Sitting. **9.** $3x - 2 = x + 10$; $x = 6$ **11.** $8x - 20 = x + 15$; $x = 5$ **13.** $9x + 3 = 7x + 19$; $x = 8$; 75 chairs **15.** $3x + 6 = 5x + 2$; $x = 2$; 6 laps

LESSON 15.2

Your Turn

3. $k = -35$ **4.** $y = -\frac{9}{16}$ **5.** $1.9x = 1.3x + 37.44$; 62.4 lb

Guided Practice

1a. $60 + 50.45x = 57.95x$ **b.** $x = 8$; 8 months **2.** $n = 28$ **3.** $b = 60$ **4.** $m = 33$ **5.** $t = -0.8$ **6.** $w = 12$ **7.** $p = -2$

Independent Practice

11. 60 tiles **13a.** 100 mi **b.** $80 **17.** $C = 1.8C + 32$; $-40°F = -40°C$ **19.** When you attempt to solve the equation, you eliminate the variable from both sides of the equation, leaving a false statement such as $-30 = 24$. Since the statement is false, the equation must not have a solution. **21.** No; his equation gives 3, 4, and 5 as the integers. The correct equation is $k + (k + 2) + (k + 4) = 4k$, which gives $k = 6$ and the integers 6, 8, 10.

LESSON 15.3

Your Turn

1. $y = -1$ **2.** $x = 6$ **3.** $b = -4$ **4.** $t = 7$ **5.** $46,000

Guided Practice

1. 4; 32; 4; 28; 6; 28; 6; 6; 6; 6; 6; 6; $x = 1$ **2.** 3; 3; 2; -15; 18; 2; -60; $+$; 15; -13; -78; -13; -78; -13; -13; $x = 6$ **3.** $x = 3$ **4.** $x = 7$ **5.** $x = -1$ **6.** $x = 3$ **7.** $x = 9$ **8.** $x = -2$ **9.** $x = 10$ **10.** $x = -8$ **11.** $0.12(x + 3,000) = 4,200$; $32,000

Independent Practice

13. a. $x + 14$ **b.** Joey's age in 5 years: $x + 5$; Martina's age in 5 years: $x + 19$ **c.** $3(x + 5) = x + 19$ **d.** Joey: 2 years old; Martina: 16 years old **15.** It is not necessary. In this case, distributing the fractions directly results in whole number coefficients and constants. **17.** Table first row: 0.25, $0.25x$; table second row: $100 - x$, 0.15, $0.15(100 - x)$; table third row: 0.19, 19 **a.** The milliliters of acid in the 25% solution plus the milliliters of acid in the 15% solution equals the milliliters of acid in the mixture. **b.** $0.25x + 0.15(100 - x) = 19$ **c.** The chemist used 40 ml of the 25% solution and 60 ml of the 15% solution. **19.** Use the Distributive Property to distribute both 3 and 2 inside the square parentheses on the left side. Combine like terms inside the square parentheses. Then use the Distributive Property again to distribute 5. Combine like terms on the left side and use inverse operations to solve the equation. $x = 1$

LESSON 15.4

Your Turn

2. True **3.** True **4.** False **6.** one solution **7.** infinitely many solutions **8.** Sample answer: 6; Any number except 1 will yield no solution. **9.** 4

Guided Practice

1. $9x$; 25; $+$; 2; $+$; 2; 9; 27; 9; 27; 9; 9; $x = 3$; true **2.** $2x - 2$; 1; $2x$; $2x$; $-4 = 1$; false **3.** none **4.** Any value of x will result in a true statement; infinitely many solutions **5.** true; same variable; same constant; like; 10; $10 + x$; $10 + x + 5$; $15 + x = 15 + x$

Independent Practice

7. $0 = 0$; infinitely many solutions **9.** Sample answer: 5 **11.** $x + 1$ **13. a.** Yes; because the perimeters are equal, you get the equation $(2x - 2) + (x + 1) + x + (x + 1) = (2x - 9) + (x + 1) + (x + 8) + x$, or $5x = 5x$. Since $5x = 5x$ is a true statement, there are an infinite number of values for x. **b.** The condition was that the two perimeters are to be equal. However, a specific number was not given, so there are an infinite number of possible perimeters. **c.** 12; Sample answer: I used the trapezoid and wrote the equation $(2x - 2) + (x + 1) + x + (x + 1) = 60$. Solving this gives $x = 12$. **15.** No; setting the expressions equal to each other and solving gives $100 + 35x = 50 + 35x$, or $100 = 50$, which is false. **17.** Matt is incorrect. He applied the Distributive Property to the right side incorrectly. Correctly simplified, the equation is $0 = -7$, which is false, meaning no solution.

LESSON 16.1

Your Turn

3. (−1, 3)

4. (1, 3)

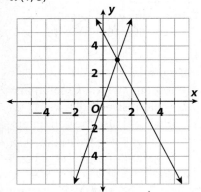

6a. $x + y = 6$ and $2x + 4y = 20$; $y = -x + 6$ and $y = -0.5x + 5$

b.

c. Marquis will bowl 2 games and play 4 games of laser tag.

Guided Practice

1. (3, 5)

2. infinitely many solutions

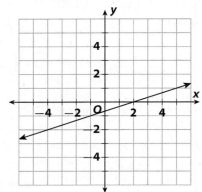

3a. $y = -x + 15$ **b.** $y = -0.5x + 10$

c.

d. 10 spelling questions and 5 vocabulary questions

Independent Practice

5. system of equations

7a. $y = 2.50x + 2$; $y = 2x + 4$

b. The solution is (4, 12). The cost at both alleys will be the same for 4 games bowled, $12.

Cost of Bowling

11. Infinitely many; Rearranging the left side of the 2nd equation and subtracting $3a$ from both sides gives $-ax + ay = -3a$. Dividing both sides by $-a$ gives $x - y = 3$. The equations describe the same line.

LESSON 16.2

Your Turn

4. (2, 5) **5.** (−6, 4) **6.** (−9, −7)

7.

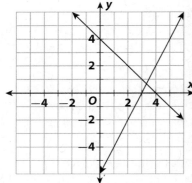

Estimate: (3, 1)
Solution: $\left(\frac{10}{3}, \frac{2}{3}\right)$
The solution is reasonable because $\frac{10}{3}$ is close to the estimate of 3 and $\frac{2}{3}$ is close to the estimate of 1.

8. Carlos: $4x + 160y = 120$
Vanessa: $x + 240y = 80$
(20, 0.25); 20 represents the cost per day: $20; 0.25 represents the cost per mile: $0.25

Guided Practice

1. (5, 3) **2.** (3, −1) **3.** (2, 1) **4.** (4, 1)
5. Estimate: (2, −5);
Solution: $\left(\frac{7}{5}, -\frac{22}{5}\right)$

6. Estimate: $(-1, 5)$;
Solution: $\left(-1, \frac{9}{2}\right)$
7. Estimate: $(3, -6)$;
Solution: $\left(\frac{13}{4}, -\frac{23}{4}\right)$
8. Estimate: $(-1, 1)$;
Solution: $\left(-\frac{3}{4}, \frac{1}{2}\right)$
9. a. Henson's cost: $3x + y = 163$;
Garcia's cost: $2x + 3y = 174$
b. adult ticket price: $45; child ticket price: $28

Independent Practice
11.

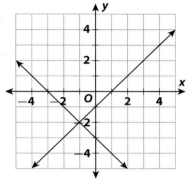

The graph shows that the x-coordinate of the solution is negative, so Zach's solution is not reasonable.
13. 120 nickels and 80 dimes
15. $\left(\frac{8}{3}, -\frac{10}{3}\right)$
17. The substitution method has the advantage of always giving an exact answer. Graphing produces an exact answer only if the solution is an ordered pair whose coordinates are integers.

LESSON 16.3

Your Turn
3. $(3, -4)$ **4.** $(2, -3)$ **5.** $(-1, 2)$
8. $(0, -2)$ **9.** $(7, -3)$ **10.** $\left(7, \frac{1}{2}\right)$
11. hot dog: $1.95; juice drink: $1.25

Guided Practice
1. Step 1: 0; -10; y; -10; -2; 5.
Step 2: 3; $(-2, 3)$ **2.** $(2, -2)$
3. $(6, 5)$ **4.** $(7, -7)$ **5.** $(-3, 8)$
6. $(2, 3)$ **7.** $(-5, -2)$
8. a. Tony: $2x + 3.5y = 355$;
Rae: $2x + 3y = 320$
b. Minimum speed limit: 55 mi/h; maximum speed limit: 70 mi/h

Independent Practice
11. Guppy: 3 inches; platy: 2 inches
13. Labor fee: $14.95; quart of oil: $1.50
15. 407 adult tickets; 839 student tickets
17. a. Jenny substituted her expression for y into the same equation she used to find y. She should substitute her expression into the other equation. **b.** Yes; adding the equations would have resulted in $3x = 9$, easily giving $x = 3$ after dividing each side by 3. Substitution requires many more steps.

LESSON 16.4

Your Turn
4. $(-8, 15)$ **5.** $(-1, 5)$ **6.** $\left(\frac{1}{2}, -1\right)$
7. $(3, 1)$ **8.** $(-4, -1)$
9. $\left(\frac{1}{3}, 6\right)$ **10.** Contestants run 0.75 hour and bike 0.5 hour.

Guided Practice
1. Step 1: 12; 4; 32; 20; y; 2; 10.
Step 2: -2; $(2, -2)$ **2.** $(6, -1)$
3. $(-3, 8)$ **4.** $\left(\frac{7}{2}, \frac{7}{4}\right)$ **5.** $(3, -3)$
6. $(4, -1)$ **7.** $(-2, 4)$
8. a. First store: $0.64x + 0.45y = 5.26$; second store: $0.32x + 0.39y = 3.62$ **b.** Number of apples: 4; number of pears: 6

Independent Practice
11. a. $\begin{cases} 79x + 149y = 1{,}456 \\ x + y = 14 \end{cases}$
b. Multiply the second equation by 79. Subtract the new equation from the first one and solve the resulting equation for y.
c. Solve the second equation for x. Substitute the expression for x in the first equation and solve the resulting equation for y.
d. 9 polyester-fill, 5 down-fill
13. 21 pies, 16 jars of applesauce
15. a. Multiply the first equation by 1.5 and subtract. This would be less than ideal because you would introduce decimals into the solution process. **b.** Yes; multiply the first equation by 3 and the

second equation by 2. Both x-term coefficients would be 6. Solve by eliminating the x-terms using subtraction. **c.** $(9, -4)$

LESSON 16.5

Your Turn
6. no solution **7.** $(10, -2)$; one solution **8.** infinitely many solutions

Guided Practice
1. Step 1: are parallel; intersect; are the same line Step 2: one; no; an infinite number of Step 3: no, no; 1, $(1, 5)$; an infinite number of, All
2. infinitely many solutions **3.** no solution **4.** $(-3, -4)$; one solution

Independent Practice
7.

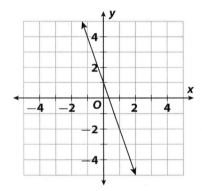

infinitely many solutions
9. one solution **11.** one solution
13. one solution
15. No; although the lines do not intersect on the graph, they intersect at a point that is not on the graph. To prove that a system has no solution, you must do so algebraically.
17. No; both Juan and Tory run at the same rate, so the lines representing the distances each has run are parallel. There is no solution to the system.
19. A, B, and C must all be the same multiple of 3, 5, and 8, respectively. The two equations represent a single line, so the coefficients and constants of one equation must be a multiple of the other.

Selected Answers

MODULE 17

LESSON 17.1

Your Turn

4.

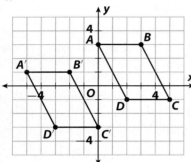

Guided Practice

1. transformation **2.** preimage; image **3.** The orientation will be the same. **4.** They are congruent.

5.

Independent Practice

7a.

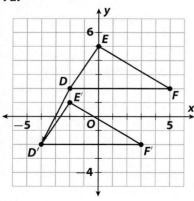

b. The translation moved the triangle 2 units to the left and 4 units down. **c.** They are congruent.

9.

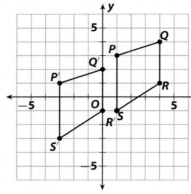

11. The hot air balloon was translated 4 units to the right and 5 units up.

13a.–c.

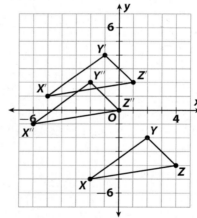

d. The original triangle was translated 4 units up and 4 units to the left.

LESSON 17.2

Your Turn

4.

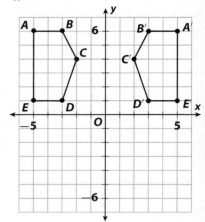

Guided Practice

1. line of reflection

2a.

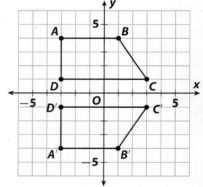

b. They are congruent. **c.** The orientation would be reversed horizontally: the figure from left to right in the preimage would match the figure from right to left in the image.

Independent Practice

5. *C* and *D* **7.** Sample answer: Since each triangle is either a reflection or translation of triangle *C*, they are all congruent. **9.** Yes; if the point lies on the line of reflection, then the image and the preimage will be the same point.

11a.–c.

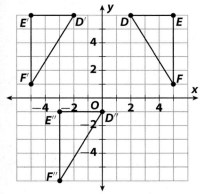

d. Sample answer: Translate triangle *DEF* 7 units down and 2 units to the left. Then reflect the image across the *y*-axis.

LESSON 17.3

Your Turn

6.–7.

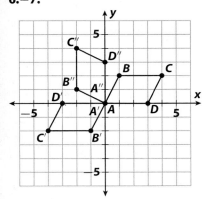

8. (2, −4)

Guided Practice

1. point **2.** The triangle is turned 90° to the left about vertex *E*.
3. Yes, the figures are congruent.
4.

5.

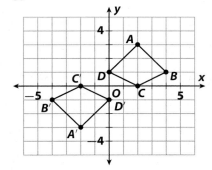

Independent Practice

7a. *ABC* was rotated 90° counterclockwise. **b.** *A*′ (3, 1); *B*′ (2, 3); *C*′ (−1, 4) **9.** 180° rotation
11. 90° clockwise **13.** 90° clockwise

15.

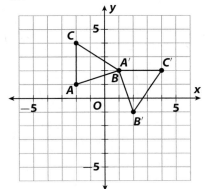

17. 2 times; 1 time; 4 times
19. Sample answer: If *A* is at the origin, then so is *A*′ for any rotation about the origin. Otherwise, *A*′ is on the *x*-axis for 90° and 270° rotations and on the *y*-axis for a 180° rotation.

LESSON 17.4

Your Turn

1. (−6, −5), (−6, 0), (−3, −5), and (−3, 0); the rectangle is translated 6 units to the left and 3 units down. **2.** *A*′(−2, −6), *B*′(0, −5), and *C*′(3, 1) **4.** *J*′(4, −2), *K*′(−5, 1), and *L*′(−2, 2)

Guided Practice

1. *X*′(3, −2), *Y*′(5, 0), and *Z*′(7, −6)

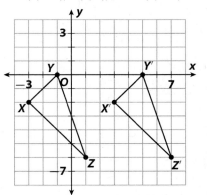

2. The *x*-coordinate remains the same, while the *y*-coordinate changes sign. **3.** The triangle is rotated 90° clockwise.

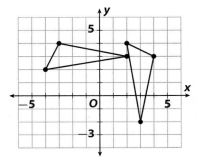

Independent Practice

5. (*x*, *y*) → (*x* + 5, *y* − 2); translation of 2 units to the left and 5 units down **7.** (*x*, *y*) → (*x* − 3.2, *y* + 1); *Y*′(4.3, 6), *Z*′(4.8, 5)
9. The rectangle is translated 2 units to the left and 4 units down.

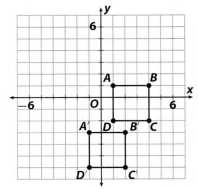

11. (*x*, *y*) → (*x* + 0.5, *y* − 0.25)
13a. (−5, −5); *x* and *y* are equal, so switching *x* and *y* has no effect on the coordinates. **b.** *y* = *x* **c.** The triangle is reflected across the line *y* = *x*.

Selected Answers

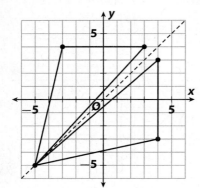

15a. $A''(1, 0)$, $B''(0, 3)$, and $C''(4, 3)$
b. $(x, y) \rightarrow (x + 3, y + 2)$

LESSON 17.5

Your Turn

3. Rotation 90° clockwise about the origin, translation 5 units down; $(x, y) \rightarrow (y, -x)$, $(x, y) \rightarrow (x, y - 5)$

Guided Practice

1.

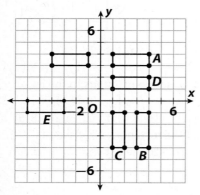

2. reflection across the y-axis
3. translation 3 units right and 4 units down
4. $(x, y) \rightarrow (-x, y)$, $(x, y) \rightarrow (x + 3, y - 4)$
5. The figures have the same size and the same shape.

Independent Practice

7.

Different orientation

9.

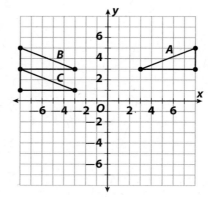

Different orientation

11. Sample answer: translation 2 units right and 4 units down, reflection across y-axis; size: no; orientation: yes

13. No; the point $(1, 2)$ translated 2 units to the right becomes $(3, 2)$, then rotated 90° clockwise about the origin, it becomes $(2, -3)$. The point $(1, 2)$ rotated 90° clockwise around the origin becomes $(2, -1)$, then translated 2 units to the right, it becomes $(4, -1)$, which is not the same.

MODULE 18

LESSON 18.1

Your Turn
5. The scale factor is 0.5.

Guided Practice
1. 2; 2 **2.** equal; equal **3.** 2
4. congruent **5.** 2

Independent Practice

7. No; the ratios of the lengths of the corresponding sides are not equal. **9.** Yes; a dilation produces an image similar to the original figure. **11.** Yes; each coordinate of triangle $U'V'W'$ is $\frac{3}{4}$ times the corresponding coordinate of triangle UVW. **13.** changed; same; same **15.** same; changed; same **17.** 3 **19.** Locate the corresponding vertices of the triangles, and draw lines connecting each pair. The lines will intersect at the center of dilation.

LESSON 18.2

Your Turn
5. $(x, y) \rightarrow \left(\frac{1}{3}x, \frac{1}{3}y\right)$

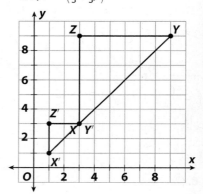

Guided Practice

1.

PreImage	Image
(2, 0)	(3, 0)
(0, 2)	(0, 3)
(−2, 0)	(−3, 0)
(0, −2)	(0, −3)

2.

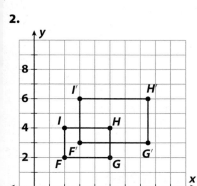

$(x, y) \rightarrow (1.5x, 1.5y)$

3.

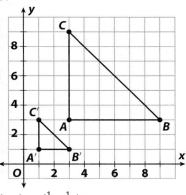

$(x, y) \rightarrow (\frac{1}{3}x, \frac{1}{3}y)$

Independent Practice
5. Green square: $(x, y) \rightarrow (2x, 2y)$; Purple square $(x, y) \rightarrow (\frac{1}{2}x, \frac{1}{2}y)$
7. $(x, y) \rightarrow (\frac{2}{3}x, \frac{2}{3}y)$ **9a.** The scale factor is 48. **b.** 48 inches or 4 feet **c.** $(x, y) \rightarrow (48x, 48y)$

d. $Q'(2.5, 2.5)$, $R'(8.75, 2.5)$, $S'(8.75, 6.25)$, and $T'(2.5, 6.25)$
e. Dimensions on blueprint: 6.25 in. by 3.75 in. Dimensions in house: 25 ft by 15 ft **11.** The crewmember's calculation is incorrect. The scale factor is $\frac{1}{20}$, not $\frac{1}{12}$. **13.** The figure is dilated by a factor of 2, but the orientation of the figure is rotated 180°.

LESSON 18.3

Your Turn
3. Sample answer: $(x, y) \rightarrow (x + 7, y - 12)$; rotation 90° counterclockwise about the origin; $(x, y) \rightarrow (x + 5, y + 3)$; $(x, y) \rightarrow (3x, 3y)$

Guided Practice
1.

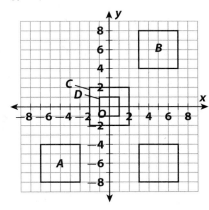

2. $(x, y) \rightarrow (x, -y)$; $(x, y) \rightarrow (x + 5, y - 6)$
3. $(x, y) \rightarrow (x, y + 6)$; rotate 90° counterclockwise
4. $(x, y) \rightarrow (1.5x, 1.5y)$; $(x, y) \rightarrow (x + 3, y + 5)$

Independent Practice
7. Dilate the image by a scale factor of $\frac{1}{3}$ and reflect it back across the x-axis; $(x, y) \rightarrow (\frac{1}{3}x, \frac{1}{3}y)$, $(x, y) \rightarrow (x, -y)$.
9. Rotate the image 90° counterclockwise and dilate it by a factor of $\frac{1}{5}$; $(x, y) \rightarrow (-y, x)$, $(x, y) \rightarrow (\frac{1}{5}x, \frac{1}{5}y)$.
11. There must be an even number of dilations and for each dilation applied to the figure, a dilation that has the opposite effect must be applied as well.
13. No; the first sequence results in $y = 3x + 5$, the second in $y = 3x + 15$. They are parallel lines.

UNIT 9 Selected Answers

MODULE 19

LESSON 19.1

Your Turn
5. 72° **6.** 108° **7.** 108°

Guided Practice
1. ∠VWZ **2.** alternate interior
3. 80° **4.** 100° **5.** same-side interior

Independent Practice
7. ∠1 and ∠5, ∠2 and ∠6, ∠3
and ∠7, ∠4 and ∠8 **9.** alternate
interior angles **11.** 30°
13. 110° **15.** 78° **17.** 132°; the
48° angle is supplementary to
the larger angle because the two
angles are same-side interior
angles. **19.** ∠6 and ∠2 are corr.,
so m∠2 = 125°. ∠6 and ∠3 are alt.
int., so m∠3 = 125°. ∠3 and ∠7
are corr., so m∠7 = 125°. ∠6 and
∠4 are same-side int., so m∠4 =
180° − 125°, or 55°. ∠4 and ∠8 are
corr., so m∠8 = 55°. ∠4 and ∠5
are alt. int., so m∠5 = 55°. ∠1 and
∠5 are corr., so m∠1 = 55°.
21. 3 angles; 4 angles; no

LESSON 19.2

Your Turn
4. 53° **5.** 90° **8.** 78°; 68°

Guided Practice
1. 71° **2.** 30° **3.** 88°; 29°; 63°
4. 90°; 45°; 45° **5.** 40°; 76°; 64°
6. 129°; 32°; 19°

Independent Practice
9. 60°; 30° **11.** 98°; 55°; 27°
13. 60°; 90°; 30°; 150° **15.** No; the
measure of an obtuse angle is
greater than 90°. If a triangle had
two obtuse angles, the sum of
their measures would be greater
than 180°, the sum of the angle
measures of a triangle. **17a.**
360° **b.** The sum of the angle
measures of a quadrilateral is 360°.

Sample answer: Any quadrilateral
can be divided into two triangles,
so the sum of its angle measures is
2 × 180° = 360°.

LESSON 19.3

Your Turn
3. The triangles are not similar
because only one angle is
congruent. The angle measures of
the triangles are 70°, 58°, and 52°
and 70°, 61°, and 49°. **5.** 8 inches
6. 21 ft

Guided Practice
1. 41°, 109°, and 30°; 41°, 109°,
and 30°; two angles; two angles;
similar **2.** 7.5; 23.5; 17.2
3. congruent; alternate interior
angles; congruent; alternate
interior angles; AA Similarity;
similar

Independent Practice
5. m∠B = 42°, m∠F = 69°, m∠H =
64°, m∠K = 53° **7.** ∠J ≅ ∠A,
∠L ≅ ∠B, and ∠K ≅ ∠C **9.** 25 feet
11. In the first line, Ryan should
have added 19.5 and 6.5 to get
a denominator of 26 for the
expression on the right side to get
the correct value of 13.6 cm for h.

MODULE 20

LESSON 20.1

Your Turn
4. 50 ft **5.** 9 in. **6.** $r = \sqrt{228}$, so
the greatest length is 15 in.

Guided Practice
1. 10^2, 676, 26 **2a.** 1700
2b. 41.2 in.; yes

Independent Practice
5. 11.5 in. **7.** 14.1 in. **9.** 12 feet
11. 52.8 ft; $12^2 + 39^2 = c^2$, so 144
+ 1521 = c^2, 1665 = c^2, and 40.8 ≈
c. Adding this to the height of the

bottom of the tree: 40.8 + 12 =
52.8 ft. **13.** $\sqrt{x^2 + x^2}$ (or $\sqrt{2x^2}$ or
$x\sqrt{2}$); if $a = x$ and $b = x$, then
$x^2 + x^2 = c^2$. Thus, $c = \sqrt{x^2 + x^2}$.

LESSON 20.2

Your Turn
2. not a right triangle **3.** right
triangle **4.** right triangle **5.** not
a right triangle **6.** Yes; $140^2 +$
$480^2 = 250,000$; $500^2 = 250,000$;
$250,000 = 250,000$ **7.** No; $18^2 +$
$19^2 = 685$, $25^2 = 625$, $685 \neq$
625 **8.** No; there are no pairs of
whole numbers whose squares
add to $12^2 = 144$.

Guided Practice
1a. 6; 8, 10 **b.** 6, 8, 10; 36, 64, 100;
100, 100; is **2.** 9, 12, 16; 9, 12, 16;
81, 144, 256; 225, 256; is not
3. Yes; $2.5^2 + 6^2 = 42.25$, $6.5^2 =$
42.25, $42.25 = 42.25$

Independent Practice
5. right triangle **7.** not a right
triangle **9.** not a right triangle
11. right triangle **13.** not a right
triangle **15.** No; $13^2 + 14^2 = 365$,
$15^2 = 225$, and $365 \neq 225$.
17. No; $6^2 + 10^2 = 136$, $12^2 = 144$,
and $136 \neq 144$. **19.** Yes; since
$0.75^2 + 1^2 = 1.25^2$, the triangles
are right triangles. Adjoining them
at their hypotenuses will form a
rectangle with sides 1 m and
0.75 m. **21.** Yes **23.** The diagonals
should measure $\sqrt{90^2 + 48^2} = 102$
yards if the sides of the field meet
at right angles.

LESSON 20.3

Your Turn
1. 6.4 units **4.** approximately
214.7 meters

Guided Practice
1. 5.8 units **2.** 13 units
3. 103.6 miles

Independent Practice

7a. $ET = \sqrt{113}$ units **b.** Let $(x_1, y_1) = (-3, 4)$ and $(x_2, y_2) = (4, -4)$. Substitute the coordinates into the Distance Formula and then simplify. **9.** (5, 0), (4, 3), (3, 4), (0, 5), (−3, 4), (−4, 3), (−5, 0), (−4, −3), (−3, −4), (0, −5), (3, −4), (4, −3); The points would form a circle.

11.

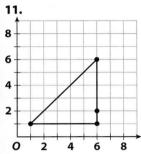

Let $(x_1, y_1) = (6, 6)$, and $(x_2, y_2) = (1, 1)$. Use the Distance Formula to show that hypotenuse = $\sqrt{50} \approx 7.1$.

LESSON 21.1

Your Turn

4. 471 in³ **5.** 602.9 ft³ **6.** 452.2 in³

Guided Practice

1. two congruent circles that lie in parallel planes **2.** Sample answer: 427 in³; there are 61 cubes on the bottom of the cylinder. The height is 7 cubes. $V = 61 \times 7 = 427$ in³ **3.** 6; 15; 36; 15; 1695.6; 1695.6 **4.** 1.35; 15.5

Independent Practice

7. 1205.8 in³ **9.** 942 in³ **11.** 803.8 m³ **13.** 6838.9 in³ **15.** 339,120 m³ **17.** 57.7 in³ **19.** Divide the diameter by 2 to find the radius. Substitute the volume and radius in $V = \pi r^2 h$ and solve for h.

LESSON 21.2

Your Turn

4. 942 cm³ **5.** 12.6 ft³ **6.** about 19,300,000 m³

Guided Practice

1. 45; 10; 450; 450; 150; 150 **2.** 54 m³; the volume of a cylinder is 3 times the volume of a cone with a congruent base and height. **3.** 65.9 ft³ **4.** 113,982 in³ **5.** 141.3 in³ **6.** 13,083.3 m³

Independent Practice

9. 25.1 in³ **11.** 94.2 m³ **13.** 167.5 in³ **15.** 628 in³ **17.** 6 cm **19a.** either the diameter or the radius of the base **b.** No; the cone is tapered from top to bottom. An equal volume of sand has a smaller radius and a greater height as the sand rises. **21.** Since the radius and height of the cones and cylinder are the same, it will take 3 cones to equal the volume of the cylinder.

LESSON 21.3

Your Turn

2. 4186.7 cm³ **3.** 20.6 m³ **6.** 904.3 in³

Guided Practice

1. the same distance **2.** radius **3.** 4.2 in³ **4.** 4,186.7 cm³ **5.** 14.1 ft³ **6.** 4.2 yd³ **7.** 12.8 in³ **8.** 435 in³ **9a.** $\frac{1}{3}$; the ball takes up $\frac{2}{3}$ of the space, so $\frac{1}{3}$ is empty. **b.** $(2r)^3 = 8r^3$ **c.** Almost $\frac{1}{2}$; the empty space is $8r^3 - \frac{4}{3}\pi r^3$, or about $3.81r^3$, and $\frac{3.81}{8} \approx 0.48$.

Independent Practice

11. 124.7 m³ **13.** 904.3 in³ **15.** 5572.5 cm³ **17.** 5389 cm³ **19.** 1766.3 cm³ **21.** Divide $V = \frac{4}{3}\pi r^3$ by 2 to find the volume of the hemisphere: $V = \frac{2}{3}\pi r^3$. Add the volume of the cylinder, $V = \pi r^2 h = \pi r^3$: $V = \frac{2}{3}\pi r^3 + \pi r^3 = \frac{5}{3}\pi r^3$. **23.** 12.3 in³ **25.** The cylindrical glass; the cylinder has a volume of πr^3, the hemisphere's volume is $\frac{2}{3}\pi r^3$, and the cone's volume is $\frac{1}{3}\pi r^3$. **27.** About 16 feet; 136 is 8 times 17, so the volume must be 8 times as big. Because $2^3 = 8$, this means the radius, and thus the diameter, must be twice as big.

MODULE **22**

LESSON 22.1

Your Turn

6. Positive and basically linear: older students would be taller and read at a higher level.

Guided Practice

1.

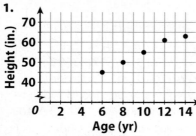

2. Positive and basically linear; the plot shows Bob's height increasing as he gets older. **3.** There is a cluster for 20–23 shots attempted and a lesser one for 7–14 shots attempted; (35, 18) is an outlier.

Independent Practice

5. A generally positive linear association: as the year increases, so does the winning distance. **7.** Nonlinear; the points generally rise up to 1988 and then fall from 1988 to 2012, so there is no overall linear pattern. **13.** Yes; for example, the points may appear to lie along a rising or falling curve, or may generally rise or fall, but not in a way that suggests a linear association.

LESSON 22.2

Your Turn

6. Sample answer: $y = \frac{9}{10}x$

Guided Practice

Answers for 1–4 may vary slightly.

1.

2. Most data points are close to the trend line, with about the same number of points above and below the line. **3.** $y = 0.09x$
4. $0.63; $4.50

Independent Practice

Answers for 6–14 may vary slightly.

7. negative; basically linear
9a. about $-6°F$ **b.** about $-22°F$
11.

13. about 73°F **17a.** No; two data points are not enough to create a scatter plot or trendline. A random sample of many counties should be used. **b.** Marlene's conjecture is incorrect. Harris and Dallas counties are counterexamples to Marlene's original conclusion.

MODULE **23**

LESSON 23.1

Your Turn

2. Yes; the relative frequency of visiting a park $= \frac{105}{200} = 0.525 = 52.5\%$; relative frequency of a high school student visiting a park $= \frac{80}{120} \approx 0.667 = 66.7\%$; $66.7\% > 52.5\%$, so being in high school improves the likelihood that a student has visited a national park.

Guided Practice

1.

	Dog	No Dog	TOTAL
Cat	21	9	30
No Cat	15	5	20
TOTAL	36	14	50

2. No; the relative frequency of being left-handed (10%) is the same as the relative frequency of being a left-handed boy (10%).

Independent Practice

5.a.

	Prefer Science	Prefer Math	TOTAL
Seventh Grade	24	72	96
Eighth Grade	32	48	80
TOTAL	56	120	176

b. No; the relative frequency of being an eighth-grader who prefers math $\left(\frac{48}{80} = 60\% \right)$ is less than the relative frequency of preferring math $\left(\frac{120}{176} \approx 68\% \right)$.

7.a.

	Prefer Surfing	Prefer Snorkeling	TOTAL
Ages 13–15	52 40%; 50%	78 60%; 74%	130 100%
Ages 16–18	52 65%; 50%	28 35%; 26%	80 100%
TOTAL	104 50%; 100%	106 50%; 100%	210 100%

b. It is the relative frequency of teenagers who are 16 to 18 years old and who prefer snorkeling to all 16- to 18-year-olds who were surveyed.

c. No; the total numbers in the last column (ages) are not the same as the total numbers in the last row (preferences), so the relative frequencies are different.

d. It is the relative frequency of teenagers who are 16 to 18 years old and who prefer snorkeling to all of those surveyed who prefer snorkeling.

LESSON 23. 2

Your Turn

8. $\frac{0.18}{0.44} \approx 0.409$, or 40.9%

9. Step1: 44% becomes 56%; Step 2: 45% becomes 55%, 60% becomes 40%, and 23% becomes 77%; Step 3: conclusions would not change.

Guided Practice

1. a-c. TOTAL row: 12, 5, 8, 25; TOTAL column: 12, 13, 25

d.

Gender \ Preferred Pet	Seashore	Mountains	Other	TOTAL
Girl	0.28	0.12	0.08	0.48
Boy	0.2	0.08	0.24	0.52
TOTAL	0.48	0.2	0.32	1.00

e. 0.08, or 8% **f.** 0.48, or 48%

g. 0.6, or 60%; girls are more likely than boys to prefer the mountains.

Independent Practice

3. a. first row: 10, 20; second row: 6, 3, 24; third row: 30, 12

b. Sample answer: I worked backward from the given data, using the fact that the sum of the entries in each row and each column must equal the total for that row or column.

5. a. 13% **b.** 32% **c.** about 40%

7. a. No; each data value should have been divided by the grand total, 600, not by the row total.

b. Yes, the data in the Total row and Total column are correct. These entries were created by dividing each entry by 600, the grand total, which results in the correct marginal relative frequency. The joint relative frequencies are incorrect.

Glossary/Glosario

ENGLISH	SPANISH	EXAMPLES
absolute value The distance of a number from zero on a number line; shown by | |.	**valor absoluto** Distancia a la que está un número de 0 en una recta numérica. El símbolo del valor absoluto es | |.	$\lvert -5 \rvert = 5$
accuracy The closeness of a given measurement or value to the actual measurement or value.	**exactitud** Cercanía de una medida o un valor a la medida o el valor real.	
acute angle An angle that measures greater than 0° and less than 90°.	**ángulo agudo** Ángulo que mide mas de 0° y menos de 90°.	
acute triangle A triangle with all angles measuring less than 90°.	**triángulo acutángulo** Triángulo en el que todos los ángulos miden menos de 90°.	
Addition Property of Equality The property that states that if you add the same number to both sides of an equation, the new equation will have the same solution.	**Propiedad de igualdad de la suma** Propiedad que establece que puedes sumar el mismo número a ambos lados de una ecuación y la nueva ecuación tendrá la misma solución.	$\begin{array}{rcr}14-6= & & 8 \\ +6 & & +6 \\ \hline 14 & = & 14\end{array}$
Addition Property of Opposites The property that states that the sum of a number and its opposite equals zero.	**Propiedad de la suma de los opuestos** Propiedad que establece que la suma de un número y su opuesto es cero.	$12+(-12)=0$
additive inverse The opposite of a number.	**inverso aditivo** El opuesto de un número.	The additive inverse of 5 is -5.
adjacent angles Angles in the same plane that have a common vertex and a common side.	**ángulos adyacentes** Ángulos en el mismo plano que comparten un vértice y un lado.	
algebraic expression An expression that contains at least one variable.	**expresión algebraica** Expresión que contiene al menos una variable.	$x+8$ $4(m-b)$
algebraic inequality An inequality that contains at least one variable.	**desigualdad algebraica** Desigualdad que contiene al menos una variable.	$x+3>10$ $5a>b+3$

ENGLISH	SPANISH	EXAMPLES
alternate exterior angles For two lines intersected by a transversal, a pair of angles that lie on opposite sides of the transversal and outside the other two lines.	**ángulos alternos externos** Dadas dos rectas cortadas por una transversal, par de ángulos no adyacentes ubicados en los lados opuestos de la transversal y fuera de las otras dos rectas.	$\angle 4$ and $\angle 5$ are alternate exterior angles.
alternate interior angles For two lines intersected by a transversal, a pair of nonadjacent angles that lie on opposite sides of the transversal and between the other two lines.	**ángulos alternos internos** Dadas dos rectas cortadas por una transversal, par de ángulos no adyacentes ubicados en los lados opuestos de la transversal y entre de las otras dos rectas.	$\angle 3$ and $\angle 6$ are alternate interior angles.
angle A figure formed by two rays with a common endpoint called the vertex.	**ángulo** Figura formada por dos rayos con un extremo común llamado vértice.	
angle bisector A line, segment, or ray that divides an angle into two congruent angles.	**bisectriz de un ángulo** Línea, segmento o rayo que divide un ángulo en dos ángulos congruentes.	$\overrightarrow{MP}$ is an angle bisector.
arc An unbroken part of a circle.	**arco** Parte continua de un círculo.	
area The number of square units needed to cover a given surface.	**área** El número de unidades cuadradas que se necesitan para cubrir una superficie dada.	
arithmetic sequence An ordered list of numbers in which the difference between consecutive terms is always the same.	**sucesión aritmética** Lista ordenada de números en la que la diferencia entre términos consecutivos es siempre la misma.	The sequence 2, 5, 8, 11, 14 … is an arithmetic sequence.
association A description of how data sets are related.	**asociación** Descripción de cómo se relaciona un conjunto de datos.	
Associative Property (of Addition) The property that states that for all real numbers a, b, and c, the sum is always the same, regardless of their grouping.	**Propiedad asociativa (de la suma)** Propiedad que establece que para todos los números reales a, b y c, la suma siempre es la misma sin importar cómo se agrupen.	$a + b + c = (a + b) + c = a + (b + c)$

Glossary/Glosario

ENGLISH	SPANISH	EXAMPLES
Associative Property (of Multiplication) The property that states that for all real numbers *a, b,* and *c,* their product is always the same, regardless of their grouping.	**Propiedad asociativa (de la multiplicación)** Propiedad que establece que para todos los números reales *a, b* y *c*, el producto siempre es el mismo, sin importar cómo se agrupen.	$a \cdot b \cdot c = (a \cdot b) \cdot c = a \cdot (b \cdot c)$

asymmetry Not identical on either side of a central line; not symmetrical.

asimetría Ocurre cuando dos lados separados por una línea central no son idénticos; falta de simetría.

The quadrilateral has asymmetry.

average The sum of a set of data divided by the number of items in the data set; also called *mean*.

promedio La suma de los elementos de un conjunto de datos dividida entre el número de elementos del conjunto. También se llama media.

Data set: 4, 6, 7, 8, 10

Average: $\frac{4+6+7+8+10}{5}$

$= \frac{35}{5} = 7$

back-to-back stem-and-leaf plot A stem-and-leaf plot that compares two sets of data by displaying one set of data to the left of the stem and the other to the right.

diagrama doble de tallo y hojas Diagrama de tallo y hojas que compara dos conjuntos de datos presentando uno de ellos a la izquierda del tallo y el otro a la derecha.

Data set A: 9, 12, 14, 16, 23, 27
Data set B: 6, 8, 10, 13, 15, 16, 21

Set A		Set B
9	0	6 8
6 4 2	1	0 3 5 6
7 3	2	1

Key: |2| 1 means 21
7 |2| means 27

bar graph A graph that uses vertical or horizontal bars to display data.

gráfica de barras Gráfica en la que se usan barras verticales u horizontales para presentar datos.

base When a number is raised to a power, the number that is used as a factor is the base.

base Cuando un número es elevado a una potencia, el número que se usa como factor es la base.

$3^5 = 3 \cdot 3 \cdot 3 \cdot 3 \cdot 3$; 3 is the base.

base (of a polygon or three-dimensional figure) A side of a polygon; a face of a three-dimensional figure by which the figure is measured or classified.

base (de un polígono o figura tridimensional) Lado de un polígono; cara de una figura tridimensional según la cual se mide o se clasifica la figura.

Bases of a cylinder

Bases of a prism

Base of a cone

Base of a pyramid

ENGLISH	SPANISH	EXAMPLES

biased question A question that leads people to give a certain answer.

pregunta tendenciosa pregunta que lleva a las personas a dar una respuesta determinada

---

biased sample A sample that does not fairly represent the population.

muestra no representativa Muestra que no representa adecuadamente la población.

---

binomial A polynomial with two terms.

binomio Polinomio con dos términos.

$x + y$
$2a^2 - 3$
$4m^3n^2 + 6mn^4$

---

bisect To divide into two congruent parts.

trazar una bisectriz Dividir en dos partes congruentes.

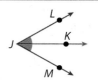

$\overrightarrow{JK}$ bisects $\angle LJM$.

---

bivariate data A set of data that is made of two paired variables.

datos bivariados Conjunto de datos compuesto de dos variables apareadas.

---

boundary line The set of points where the two sides of a two-variable linear inequality are equal.

línea de límite Conjunto de puntos donde los dos lados de una desigualdad lineal con dos variables son iguales.

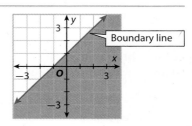

---

box-and-whisker plot A graph that shows how data are distributed by using the median, quartiles, least value, and greatest value; also called a *box plot*.

gráfica de mediana y rango Gráfica para demostrar la distribución de datos utilizando la mediana, los cuartiles y los valores menos y más grande; también llamado gráfica de caja.

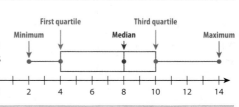

---

break (graph) A zigzag on a horizontal or vertical scale of a graph that indicates that some of the numbers on the scale have been omitted.

discontinuidad (gráfica) Zig-zag en la escala horizontal o vertical de una gráfica que indica la omisión de algunos de los números de la escala.

C

capacity The amount a container can hold when filled.

capacidad Cantidad que cabe en un recipiente cuando se llena.

A large milk container has a capacity of 1 gallon.

Celsius A metric scale for measuring temperature in which 0 °C is the freezing point of water and 100 °C is the boiling point of water; also called *centigrade*.

Celsius Escala métrica para medir la temperatura, en la que 0 °C es el punto de congelación del agua y 100 °C es el punto de ebullición. También se llama *centígrado*.

ENGLISH	SPANISH	EXAMPLES
center (of a circle) The point inside a circle that is the same distance from all the points on the circle.	**centro (de un círculo)** Punto interior de un círculo que se encuentra a la misma distancia de todos los puntos de la circunferencia.	
center of dilation The point of intersection of lines through each pair of corresponding vertices in a dilation.	**centro de una dilatación** Punto de intersección de las líneas que pasan a través de cada par de vértices correspondientes en una dilatación.	
center of rotation The point about which a figure is rotated.	**centro de una rotación** Punto alrededor del cual se hace girar una figura.	
central angle An angle formed by two radii with its vertex at the center of a circle.	**ángulo central de un círculo** Ángulo formado por dos radios cuyo vértice se encuentra en el centro de un círculo.	
certain (probability) Sure to happen; having a probability of 1.	**seguro (probabilidad)** Que con seguridad sucederá. Representa una probabilidad de 1.	
chord A segment with its endpoints on a circle.	**cuerda** Segmento de recta cuyos extremos forman parte de un círculo.	
circle The set of all points in a plane that are the same distance from a given point called the center.	**círculo** Conjunto de todos los puntos en un plano que se encuentran a la misma distancia de un punto dado llamado centro.	
circle graph A graph that uses sectors of a circle to compare parts to the whole and parts to other parts.	**gráfica circular** Gráfica que usa secciones de un círculo para comparar partes con el todo y con otras partes.	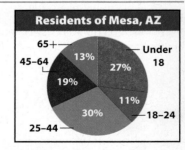
circuit A path in a graph that begins and ends at the same vertex.	**circuito** Una trayectoria en una gráfica que empieza y termina en el mismo vértice.	
circumference The distance around a circle.	**circunferencia** Distancia alrededor de un círculo.	

ENGLISH	SPANISH	EXAMPLES

clockwise A circular movement in the direction shown.

en el sentido de las manecillas del reloj Movimiento circular en la dirección que se indica.

---

cluster A set of closely grouped data.

agrupación Conjunto de datos bien agrupados.

---

clustering A condition that occurs when data points in a scatter plot are grouped more in one part of the graph than another.

arracimando Una condición que ocurre cuando los datos están apiñando en una parte de una diagrama de dispersión mas que en otras partes.

---

coefficient The number that is multiplied by the variable in an algebraic expression.

coeficiente Número que se multiplica por la variable en una expresión algebraica.

5 is the coefficient in 5*b*.

---

combination An arrangement of items or events in which order does not matter.

combinación Agrupación de objetos o sucesos en la que el orden no es importante.

For objects *A, B, C,* and *D,* there are 6 different combinations of 2 objects: *AB, AC, AD, BC, BD, CD.*

---

commission A fee paid to a person for making a sale.

comisión Pago que recibe una persona por realizar una venta.

---

commission rate The fee paid to a person who makes a sale expressed as a percent of the selling price.

tasa de comisión Pago que recibe una persona por hacer una venta, expresado como un porcentaje del precio de venta.

A commission rate of 5% on a sale of $10,000 results in a commission of $500.

---

common denominator A denominator that is the same in two or more fractions.

denominador común Denominador que es común a dos o más fracciones.

The common denominator of $\frac{5}{8}$ and $\frac{2}{8}$ is 8.

---

common difference In an arithmetic sequence, the nonzero constant difference of any term and the previous term.

diferencia común En una sucesión aritmética, diferencia constante distinta de cero entre cualquier término y el término anterior.

In the arithmetic sequence 3, 5, 7, 9, 11, …, the common difference is 2.

---

common factor A number that is a factor of two or more numbers.

factor común Número que es factor de dos o más números.

8 is a common factor of 16 and 40.

---

common multiple A number that is a multiple of each of two or more numbers.

múltiplo común Número que es múltiplo de dos o más números.

15 is a common multiple of 3 and 5.

---

common ratio The ratio each term is multiplied by to produce the next term in a geometric sequence.

razón común Razón por la que se multiplica cada término para obtener el siguiente término de una sucesión geométrica.

In the geometric sequence 32, 16, 8, 4, 2, …, the common ratio is $\frac{1}{2}$.

ENGLISH	SPANISH	EXAMPLES
Commutative Property (of Addition) The property that states that two or more numbers can be added in any order without changing the sum.	**Propiedad conmutativa (de la suma)** Propiedad que establece que sumar dos o más números en cualquier orden no altera la suma.	$8 + 20 = 20 + 8; a + b = b + a$
Commutative Property (of Multiplication) The property that states that two or more numbers can be multiplied in any order without changing the product.	**Propiedad conmutativa (de la multiplicación)** Propiedad que establece que multiplicar dos o más números en cualquier orden no altera el producto.	$6 \cdot 12 = 12 \cdot 6; a \cdot b = b \cdot a$
compatible numbers Numbers that are close to the given numbers that make estimation or mental calculation easier.	**números compatibles** Números que están cerca de los números dados y hacen más fácil la estimación o el cálculo mental.	To estimate $7,957 + 5,009$, use the compatible numbers 8,000 and 5,000: $8,000 + 5,000 = 13,000$
complement The set of all outcomes in the sample space that are not the event.	**complemento** La serie de resultados que no están en el suceso.	Experiment: rolling a number cube Sample space: {1, 2, 3, 4, 5, 6} Event: rolling a 1, 3, 4, or 6 Complement: rolling a 2 or 5
complementary angles Two angles whose measures add to 90°.	**ángulos complementarios** Dos ángulos cuyas medidas suman 90°.	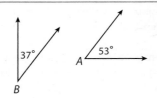 The complement of a 53° angle is a 37° angle.
composite figure A figure made up of simple geometric shapes.	**figura compuesta** Figura formada por figuras geométricas simples.	
composite number A number greater than 1 that has more than two whole-number factors.	**número compuesto** Número mayor que 1 que tiene más de dos factores que son números cabales.	4, 6, 8, and 9 are composite numbers.
compound event An event made up of two or more simple events.	**suceso compuesto** Suceso que consista de dos o más sucesos simples.	Rolling a 3 on a number cube and spinning a 2 on a spinner is a compound event.
compound inequality A combination of more than one inequality.	**desigualdad compuesta** Combinación de dos o más desigualdades.	$-2 \leq x < 10$
compound interest Interest earned or paid on principal and previously earned or paid interest.	**interés compuesto** Interés que se gana o se paga sobre el capital y los intereses previamente ganados o pagados.	If $100 is put into an account with an interest rate of 5% compounded monthly, then after 2 years, the account will have $100\left(1 + \frac{0.05}{12}\right)^{12 \cdot 2} =$ $110.49

ENGLISH	SPANISH	EXAMPLES
conditional relative frequency The ratio of a joint relative frequency to a related marginal relative frequency in a two-way table.	**frecuencia relativa condicional** Razón de una frecuencia relativa conjunta a una frecuencia relativa marginal en una tabla de doble entrada.	
cone A three-dimensional figure with one vertex and one circular base.	**cono** Figura tridimensional con un vértice y una base circular.	
congruence transformation A transformation that results in an image that is the same shape and the same size as the original figure.	**transformación de congruencia** Una transformación que resulta en una imagen que tiene la misma forma y el mismo tamaño como la figura original.	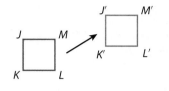
congruent Having the same size and shape; the symbol for congruent is ≅.	**congruentes** Que tienen la misma forma y el mismo tamaño expresado por ≅.	 $PQRS \cong WXYZ$
congruent angles Angles that have the same measure.	**ángulos congruentes** Ángulos que tienen la misma medida.	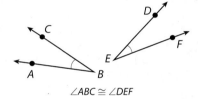 $\angle ABC \cong \angle DEF$
congruent figures See *congruent*.	**figuras congruentes** Vea *congruentes*.	
congruent segments Segments that have the same length.	**segmentos congruentes** Segmentos que tienen la misma longitud.	 $\overline{PQ} \cong \overline{SR}$
conjecture A statement believed to be true.	**conjetura** Enunciado que se supone verdadero.	
constant A value that does not change.	**constante** Valor que no cambia.	$3, 0, \pi$
constant of variation The constant k in direct and inverse variation equations.	**constante de variación** La constante k en ecuaciones de variación directa e inversa.	$y = 5x$ ↑ Constant of variation
continuous graph A graph made up of connected lines or curves.	**gráfica continua** Gráfica compuesta por líneas rectas *o* curvas conectadas.	

Glossary/Glosario

convenience sample A sample based on members of the population that are readily available.

muestra de conveniencia Una muestra basada en miembros de la población que están fácilmente disponibles.

conversion factor A fraction whose numerator and denominator represent the same quantity but use different units; the fraction is equal to 1 because the numerator and denominator are equal.

factor de conversión Fracción cuyo numerador y denominador representan la misma cantidad pero con unidades distintas; la fracción es igual a 1 porque el numerador y el denominador son iguales.

$\frac{24\text{ hours}}{1\text{ day}}$ and $\frac{1\text{ day}}{24\text{ hours}}$

coordinate One of the numbers of an ordered pair that locate a point on a coordinate graph.

coordenada Uno de los números de un par ordenado que ubica un punto en una gráfica de coordenadas.

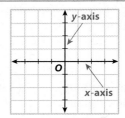

The coordinates of *B* are (−2, 3).

coordinate plane A plane formed by the intersection of a horizontal number line called the *x*-axis and a vertical number line called the *y*-axis.

plano cartesiano Plano formado por la intersección de una recta numérica horizontal llamada eje *x* y otra vertical llamada eje *y*.

correlation The description of the relationship between two data sets.

correlación Descripción de la relación entre dos conjuntos de datos.

Positive correlation

No correlation

Negative correlation

correspondence The relationship between two or more objects that are matched.

correspondencia La relación entre dos o más objetos que coinciden.

∠*A* and ∠*D* are corresponding angles.

$\overline{AB}$ and $\overline{DE}$ are corresponding sides.

corresponding angles (for lines) For two lines intersected by a transversal, a pair of angles that lie on the same side of the transversal and on the same sides of the other two lines.

ángulos correspondientes (en líneas) Dadas dos rectas cortadas por una transversal, el par de ángulos ubicados en el mismo lado de la transversal y en los mismos lados de las otras dos rectas.

∠1 and ∠3 are corresponding angles.

ENGLISH	SPANISH	EXAMPLES

corresponding angles (of polygons) Angles in the same relative position in polygons with an equal number of sides.

ángulos correspondientes (en polígonos) Ángulos en la misma posición formaron cuando una tercera línea interseca dos líneas.

$\angle A$ and $\angle D$ are corresponding angles.

---

corresponding sides Matching sides of two or more polygons.

lados correspondientes Lados que se ubican en la misma posición relativa en dos o más polígonos.

$\overline{AB}$ and $\overline{DE}$ are corresponding sides.

---

counterclockwise A circular movement in the direction shown.

en sentido contrario a las manecillas del reloj Movimiento circular en la dirección que se indica.

---

counterexample An example that proves that a conjecture or statement is false.

contraejemplo Ejemplo que demuestra que una conjetura o enunciado es falso.

---

cross section The intersection of a three-dimensional figure and a plane.

sección transversal Intersección de una figura tridimensional y un plano.

---

cube (geometric figure) A rectangular prism with six congruent square faces.

cubo (figura geométrica) Prisma rectangular con seis caras cuadradas congruentes.

---

cube (in numeration) A number raised to the third power.

cubo (en numeración) Número elevado a la tercera potencia.

$2^3 = 2 \cdot 2 \cdot 2 = 8$
8 is the cube of 2.

---

cube root A number, written as $\sqrt[3]{x}$, whose cube is x.

raíz cúbica Número, expresado como $\sqrt[3]{x}$, cuyo cubo es x.

$\sqrt[3]{8} = \sqrt[3]{2 \cdot 2 \cdot 2} = 2$
2 is the cube root of 8.

---

cumulative frequency The sum of successive data items.

frecuencia acumulativa La suma de datos sucesivos.

---

customary system of measurement The measurement system often used in the United States.

sistema usual de medidas El sistema de medidas que se usa comúnmente en Estados Unidos.

inches, feet, miles, ounces, pounds, tons, cups, quarts, gallons

---

cylinder A three-dimensional figure with two parallel, congruent circular bases connected by a curved lateral surface.

cilindro Figura tridimensional con dos bases circulares paralelas y congruentes, unidas por una superficie lateral curva.

decagon A polygon with ten sides.

decágono Polígono de diez lados.

deductive reasoning Using logic to show that a statement is true.

razonamiento deductivo Uso de la lógica para demostrar que un enunciado es verdadero.

degree The unit of measure for angles or temperature.

grado Unidad de medida para ángulos y temperaturas.

degree of a polynomial The highest power of the variable in a polynomial.

grado de un polinomio La potencia más alta de la variable en un polinomio.

The polynomial $4x^5 - 6x^2 + 7$ has degree 5.

denominator The bottom number of a fraction that tells how many equal parts are in the whole.

denominador Número que está abajo en una fracción y que indica en cuántas partes iguales se divide el entero.

In the fraction $\frac{2}{5}$, 5 is the denominator.

Density Property The property that states that between any two real numbers there is always another real number.

Propiedad de densidad Propiedad según la cual entre dos números reales cualesquiera siempre hay otro número real.

dependent events Events for which the outcome of one event affects the probability of the other.

sucesos dependientes Dos sucesos son dependientes si el resultado de uno afecta la probabilidad del otro.

A bag contains 3 red marbles and 2 blue marbles. Drawing a red marble and then drawing a blue marble without replacing the first marble is an example of dependent events.

dependent variable The output of a function; a variable whose value depends on the value of the input, or independent variable.

variable dependiente Salida de una función; variable cuyo valor depende del valor de la entrada, o variable independiente.

For $y = 2x + 1$, y is the dependent variable.
input: x output: y

diagonal A line segment that connects two nonadjacent vertices of a polygon.

diagonal Segmento de recta que une dos vértices no adyacentes de un polígono.

diameter A line segment that passes through the center of a circle and has endpoints on the circle, or the length of that segment.

diámetro Segmento de recta que pasa por el centro de un círculo y tiene sus extremos en la circunferencia, o bien la longitud de ese segmento.

dilation A transformation that enlarges or reduces a figure.

dilatación Transformación que agranda o reduce una figura.

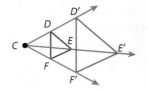

dimensions (geometry) The length, width, or height of a figure.

dimensiones (geometría) Longitud, ancho o altura de una figura.

---

dimensions (of a matrix) The number of horizontal rows and vertical columns in a matrix.

dimensiones (de una matriz) Número de filas y columnas que hay en una matriz.

---

direct variation A linear relationship between two variables, x and y, that can be written in the form $y = kx$, where k is a nonzero constant.

variación directa Relación lineal entre dos variables, x e y, que puede expresarse en la forma $y = kx$, donde k es una constante distinta de cero.

$y = 2x$

---

discount The amount by which the original price is reduced.

descuento Cantidad que se resta del precio original de un artículo.

---

discrete graph A graph made up of unconnected points.

gráfica discreta Gráfica compuesta de puntos no conectados.

Cost of Photo Printing

Cost ($)

Number of photos

---

disjoint events See *mutually exclusive*.

sucesos disjuntos Vea *mutuamente excluyentes*.

Distributive Property For all real numbers a, b, and c, $a(b + c) = ab + ac$, and $a(b - c) = ab - ac$.

Propiedad distributiva Dados los números reales a, b, y c, $a(b + c) = ab + ac$, y $a(b - c) = ab - ac$.

$5 \cdot 21 = 5(20 + 1) = (5 \cdot 20) + (5 \cdot 1)$

---

dividend The number to be divided in a division problem.

dividendo Número que se divide en un problema de división.

In $8 \div 4 = 2$, 8 is the dividend.

---

divisible Can be divided by a number without leaving a remainder.

divisible Que se puede dividir entre un número sin dejar residuo.

18 is divisible by 3.

Division Property of Equality The property that states that if you divide both sides of an equation by the same nonzero number, the new equation will have the same solution.

Propiedad de igualdad de la división Propiedad que establece que puedes dividir ambos lados de una ecuación entre el mismo número distinto de cero, y la nueva ecuación tendrá la misma solución.

---

divisor The number you are dividing by in a division problem.

divisor El número entre el que se divide en un problema de división.

In $8 \div 4 = 2$, 4 is the divisor.

---

dodecahedron A polyhedron with 12 faces.

dodecaedro Poliedro de 12 caras.

ENGLISH	SPANISH	EXAMPLES
domain The set of all possible input values of a function.	**dominio** Conjunto de todos los posibles valores de entrada de una función.	The domain of the function $y = x^2 + 1$ is all real numbers.
double-bar graph A bar graph that compares two related sets of data.	**gráfica de doble barra** Gráfica de barras que compara dos conjuntos de datos relacionados.	
double-line graph A line graph that shows how two related sets of data change over time.	**gráfica de doble línea** Gráfica lineal que muestra cómo cambian con el tiempo dos conjuntos de datos relacionados.	

edge The line segment along which two faces of a polyhedron intersect.	**arista** Segmento de recta donde se intersecan dos caras de un poliedro.	
endpoint A point at the end of a line segment or ray.	**extremo** Un punto ubicado al final de un segmento de recta o rayo.	
enlargement An increase in size of all dimensions in the same proportions.	**agrandamiento** Aumento de tamaño de todas las dimensiones en las mismas proporciones.	
entries (of a matrix) Individual entries in a matrix.	**elementos (de una matriz)** Entradas individuales de una matriz.	
equally likely Outcomes that have the same probability.	**resultados igualmente probables** Resultados que tienen la misma probabilidad de ocurrir.	When tossing a coin, the outcomes "heads" and "tails" are equally likely.
equation A mathematical sentence that shows that two expressions are equivalent.	**ecuación** Enunciado matemático que indica que dos expresiones son equivalentes.	$x + 4 = 7$ $6 + 1 = 10 - 3$

Glossary/Glosario

ENGLISH	SPANISH	EXAMPLES
equilateral triangle A triangle with three congruent sides.	**triángulo equilátero** Triángulo con tres lados congruentes.	
equivalent Having the same value.	**equivalentes** Que tienen el mismo valor.	
equivalent expressions Expressions that have the same value for all values of the variables.	**expresiones equivalentes** Las expresiones equivalentes tienen el mismo valor para todos los valores de las variables.	$4x + 5x$ and $9x$ are equivalent expressions.
equivalent fractions Fractions that name the same amount or part.	**fracciones equivalentes** Fracciones que representan la misma cantidad o parte.	$\frac{1}{2}$ and $\frac{2}{4}$ are equivalent fractions.
equivalent ratios Ratios that name the same comparison.	**razones equivalentes** Razones que representan la misma comparación.	$\frac{1}{2}$ and $\frac{2}{4}$ are equivalent ratios.
estimate (n) An answer that is close to the exact answer and is found by rounding or other methods. **(v)** To find such an answer.	**estimación** Una solución aproximada a la respuesta exacta que se halla mediante el redondeo u otros métodos. **estimar** Hallar una solución aproximada a la respuesta exacta.	500 is an estimate for the sum $98 + 287 + 104$.
evaluate To find the value of a numerical or algebraic expression.	**evaluar** Hallar el valor de una expresión numérica o algebraica.	Evaluate $2x + 7$ for $x = 3$. $2x + 7$ $2(3) + 7$ $6 + 7$ 13
event An outcome or set of outcomes of an experiment or situation.	**suceso** Un resultado o una serie de resultados de un experimento o una situación.	When rolling a number cube, the event "an odd number" consists of the outcomes 1, 3, and 5.
expanded form A number written as the sum of the values of its digits.	**forma desarrollada** Número escrito como suma de los valores de sus dígitos.	236,536 written in expanded form is $200,000 + 30,000 + 6,000 + 500 + 30 + 6$.
experiment (probability) In probability, any activity based on chance (such as tossing a coin).	**experimento (probabilidad)** En probabilidad, cualquier actividad basada en la posibilidad, como lanzar una moneda.	Tossing a coin 10 times and noting the number of "heads"
experimental probability The ratio of the number of times an event occurs to the total number of trials, or times that the activity is performed.	**probabilidad experimental** Razón del número de veces que ocurre un suceso al número total de pruebas o al número de que se realiza el experimento.	Kendra attempted 27 free throws and made 16 of them. Her experimental probability of making a free throw is $\frac{\text{number made}}{\text{number attempted}} = \frac{16}{27} \approx 0.59$.
exponent The number that indicates how many times the base is used as a factor.	**exponente** Número que indica cuántas veces se usa la base como factor.	$2^3 = 2 \times 2 \times 2 = 8$; 3 is the exponent.
exponential decay An exponential function of the form $f(x) = a \cdot r^x$ in which $0 < r < 1$.	**decremento exponencial** Función exponencial del tipo $f(x) = a \cdot r^x$ en la cual $0 < r < 1$.	

ENGLISH	SPANISH	EXAMPLES
exponential form A number written with a base and an exponent.	**forma exponencial** Se dice que un número está en forma exponencial cuando se escribe con una base y un exponente.	4^2 is the exponential form for $4 \cdot 4$.
exponential function A nonlinear function in which the variable is in the exponent.	**función exponencial** Función no lineal en la que la variable está en el exponente.	$f(x) = 4^x$
exponential growth An exponential function of the form $f(x) = a \cdot r^x$ in which $r > 1$.	**crecimiento exponencial** Función exponencial del tipo $f(x) = a \cdot r^x$ en la cual $r > 1$.	
expression A mathematical phrase that contains operations, numbers, and/or variables.	**expresión** Enunciado matemático que contiene operaciones, números y/o variables.	$6x + 1$
exterior angle (of a polygon) An angle formed by one side of a polygon and the extension of an adjacent side.	**ángulo extreno de un polígono** Ángulo formado por un lado de un polígono y la prolongación del lado adyacente.	

F

ENGLISH	SPANISH	EXAMPLES
face A flat surface of a polyhedron.	**cara** Superficie plana de un poliedro.	Face
factor A number that is multiplied by another number to get a product.	**factor** Número que se multiplica por otro para hallar un producto.	7 is a factor of 21 since $7 \cdot 3 = 21$.
factorial The product of all whole numbers except zero that are less than or equal to a number.	**factorial** El producto de todos los números cabales, excepto cero, que son menores que o iguales a un número.	4 factorial $= 4! = 4 \cdot 3 \cdot 2 \cdot 1$
Fahrenheit A temperature scale in which 32 °F is the freezing point of water and 212 °F is the boiling point of water.	**Fahrenheit** Escala de temperatura en la que 32° F es el punto de congelación del agua y 212° F es el punto de ebullición.	
fair When all outcomes of an experiment are equally likely, the experiment is said to be fair.	**justo** Se dice de un experimento donde todos los resultados posibles son igualmente probables.	When tossing a coin, heads and tails are equally likely, so it is a fair experiment.
Fibonacci sequence The infinite sequence of numbers (1, 1, 2, 3, 5, 8, 13,…); starting with the third term, each number is the sum of the two previous numbers; it is named after the thirteenth-century mathematician Leonardo Fibonacci.	**sucesión de Fibonacci** La sucesión infinita de números (1, 1, 2, 3, 5, 8, 13…); a partir del tercer término, cada número es la suma de los dos anteriores. Esta sucesión lleva el nombre de Leonardo Fibonacci, un matemático del siglo XIII.	1, 1, 2, 3, 5, 8, 13, …
first differences A sequence formed by subtracting each term of a sequence from the next term.	**primeras diferencias** Sucesión que se forma al restar cada término de una sucesión del término siguiente.	For the sequence 4, 7, 10, 13, 16, …, the first differences are all 3.

ENGLISH	SPANISH	EXAMPLES

first quartile The median of the lower half of a set of data; also called *lower quartile*.

primer cuartil La mediana de la mitad inferior de un conjunto de datos. También se llama *cuartil inferior*.

FOIL An acronym for the terms used when multiplying two binomials: the First, Outer, Inner, and Last terms.

FOIL Sigla en inglés de los términos que se usan al multiplicar dos binomios: los primeros, los externos, los internos y los últimos (First, Outer, Inner, Last).

$$(x + 2)(x - 3) = x^2 - 3x + 2x - 6$$
$$= x^2 - x - 6$$

---

formula A rule showing relationships among quantities.

fórmula Regla que muestra relaciones entre cantidades.

$A = \ell w$ is the formula for the area of a rectangle.

---

fractal A structure with repeating patterns containing shapes that are like the whole but are of different sizes throughout.

fractal Estructura con patrones repetidos que contiene figuras similares al patrón general pero de diferente tamaño.

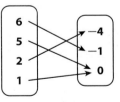

---

fraction A number in the form $\frac{a}{b}$, where $b \neq 0$.

fracción Número escrito en la forma $\frac{a}{b}$, donde $b \neq 0$.

$\frac{2}{3}$

---

frequency The number of times the value appears in the data set.

frecuencia Cantidad de veces que aparece el valor en un conjunto de datos.

Data set: 5, 6, 6, 7, 8, 9
The data value 6 has a frequency of 2.

---

frequency table A table that lists items together according to the number of times, or frequency, that the items occur.

tabla de frecuencia Una tabla en la que se organizan los datos de acuerdo con el número de veces que aparece cada valor (o la frecuencia).

Data set: 1, 1, 2, 2, 3, 5, 5, 5
Frequency table:

Data	Frequency
1	2
2	2
3	1

---

function An input-output relationship that has exactly one output for each input.

función Regla que relaciona dos candidates de forma que a cada valor de entrada corresponde exactamente un valor de salida.

---

function notation The notation used to describe a function.

notación de función Notación que se usa para describir una función.

Equation: $y = 2x$
Function notation: $f(x) = 2x$

---

function table A table of ordered pairs that represent solutions of a function.

tabla de función Tabla de pares ordenados que representan soluciones de una función.

x	3	4	5	6
y	7	9	11	13

Fundamental Counting Principle If one event has *m* possible outcomes and a second event has *n* possible outcomes after the first event has occurred, then there are *m · n* total possible outcomes for the two events.

Principio fundamental de conteo Si un suceso tiene *m* resultados posibles y otro suceso tiene *n* resultados posibles después de ocurrido el primer suceso, entonces hay *m · n* resultados posibles en total para los dos sucesos.

There are 4 colors of shirts and 3 colors of pants. There are 4 · 3 = 12 possible outfits.

geometric probability A form of theoretical probability determined by a ratio of geometric measures such as lengths, areas, or volumes.

probabilidad geométrica Método para calcular probabilidades basado en una medida geométrica como la longitud o el área.

The probability of the pointer landing on red is $\frac{80}{360}$, or $\frac{2}{9}$.

geometric sequence An ordered list of numbers that has a common ratio between consecutive terms.

sucesión geométrica Lista ordenada de números que tiene una razón común entre términos consecutivos.

The sequence 2, 4, 8, 16 . . . is a geometric sequence.

graph of an equation A graph of the set of ordered pairs that are solutions of the equation.

gráfica de una ecuación Gráfica del conjunto de pares ordenados que son soluciones de la ecuación.

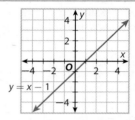

$y = x - 1$

great circle A circle on a sphere such that the plane containing the circle passes through the center of the sphere.

círculo máximo Círculo de una esfera tal que el plano que contiene el círculo pasa por el centro de la esfera.

Great circle

greatest common factor (GCF) The largest common factor of two or more given numbers.

máximo común divisor (MCD) El mayor de los factores comunes compartidos por dos o más números dados.

The GCF of 27 and 45 is 9.

height In a pyramid or cone, the perpendicular distance from the base to the opposite vertex.

altura En una pirámide o cono, la distancia perpendicular desde la base al vértice opuesto.

In a triangle or quadrilateral, the perpendicular distance from the base to the opposite vertex or side.

En un triángulo o cuadrilátero, la distancia perpendicular desde la base de la figura al vértice o lado opuesto.

In a prism or cylinder, the perpendicular distance between the bases.

En un prisma o cilindro, la distancia perpendicular entre las bases.

ENGLISH	SPANISH	EXAMPLES

hemisphere A half of a sphere.

hemisferio La mitad de una esfera.

---

heptagon A seven-sided polygon.

heptágono Polígono de siete lados.

---

hexagon A six-sided polygon.

hexágono Polígono de seis lados.

---

histogram A bar graph that shows the frequency of data within equal intervals.

histograma Gráfica de barras que muestra la frecuencia de los datos en intervalos iguales.

---

hypotenuse In a right triangle, the side opposite the right angle.

hipotenusa En un triángulo rectángulo, el lado opuesto al ángulo recto.

Hypotenuse

Identity Property (of One) The property that states that the product of 1 and any number is that number.

Propiedad de identidad (del uno) Propiedad que establece que el producto de 1 y cualquier número es ese número.

$$4 \cdot 1 = 4$$
$$-3 \cdot 1 = -3$$

Identity Property (of Zero) The property that states the sum of zero and any number is that number.

Propiedad de identidad (del cero) Propiedad que establece que la suma de cero y cualquier número es ese número.

$$4 + 0 = 4$$
$$-3 + 0 = -3$$

---

image A figure resulting from a transformation.

imagen Figura que resulta de una transformación.

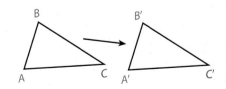

$A'B'C'$ is the image of ABC.

---

impossible (probability) Can never happen; having a probability of 0.

imposible (en probabilidad) Que no puede ocurrir. Suceso cuya probabilidad de ocurrir es 0.

Glossary/Glosario

ENGLISH	SPANISH	EXAMPLES
improper fraction A fraction in which the numerator is greater than or equal to the denominator.	**fracción impropia** Fracción cuyo numerador es mayor que o igual al denominador.	$\frac{17}{5}, \frac{3}{3}$
independent events Events for which the outcome of one event does not affect the probability of the other.	**sucesos independientes** Dos sucesos son independientes si el resultado de uno no afecta la probabilidad del otro.	A bag contains 3 red marbles and 2 blue marbles. Drawing a red marble, replacing it, and then drawing a blue marble is an example of independent events.
independent variable The input of a function; a variable whose value determines the value of the output, or dependent variable.	**variable independiente** Entrada de una función; variable cuyo valor determina el valor de la salida, o variable dependiente.	For $y = 2x + 1$, x is the independent variable. input: x output: y
indirect measurement The technique of using similar figures and proportions to find a measure.	**medición indirecta** La técnica de usar figuras semejantes y proporciones para hallar una medida.	
inductive reasoning Using a pattern to make a conclusion.	**razonamiento inductivo** Uso de un patrón para sacar una conclusión.	
inequality A mathematical sentence that shows the relationship between quantities that are not equivalent.	**desigualdad** Enunciado matemático que muestra una relación entre cantidades que no son equivalentes.	$5 < 8$ $5x + 2 \geq 12$
input The value substituted into an expression or function.	**valor de entrada** Valor que se usa para sustituir una variable en una expresión o función.	For the function $y = 6x$, the input 4 produces an output of 24.
inscribed angle An angle formed by two chords with its vertex on a circle.	**ángulo inscrito** Ángulo formado por dos cuerdas cuyo vértice está en un círculo.	
integers The set of whole numbers and their opposites.	**enteros** Conjunto de todos los números cabales y sus opuestos.	$\ldots -3, -2, -1, 0, 1, 2, 3, \ldots$
interest The amount of money charged for borrowing or using money.	**interés** Cantidad de dinero que se cobra por el préstamo o uso del dinero.	
interior angles Angles on the inner sides of two lines cut by a transversal.	**ángulos internos** Ángulos en los lados internos de dos líneas intersecadas por una transversal.	
interquartile range (IQR) The difference of the third (upper) and first (lower) quartiles in a data set, representing the middle half of the data.	**rango intercuartil (RIC)** Diferencia entre el tercer cuartil (superior) y el primer cuartil (inferior) de un conjunto de datos, que representa la mitad central de los datos.	 Interquartile range: $36 - 23 = 13$
intersecting lines Lines that cross at exactly one point.	**líneas secantes** Líneas que se cruzan en un solo punto.	

ENGLISH	SPANISH	EXAMPLES
interval The space between marked values on a number line or the scale of a graph.	**intervalo** El espacio entre los valores marcados en una recta numérica o en la escala de una gráfica.	
inverse operations Operations that undo each other: addition and subtraction, or multiplication and division.	**operaciones inversas** Operaciones que se cancelan mutuamente: suma y resta, o multiplicación y división.	Addition and subtraction are inverse operations: $5 + 3 = 8; 8 - 3 = 5$ Multiplication and division are inverse operations: $2 \cdot 3 = 6; 6 \div 3 = 2$
inverse variation A relationship in which one variable quantity increases as another variable quantity decreases; the product of the variables is a constant.	**variación inversa** Relación en la que una cantidad variable aumenta a medida que otra cantidad variable disminuye; el producto de las variables es una constante.	$xy = 7, y = \frac{7}{x}$
irrational number A number that cannot be expressed as a ratio of two integers or as a repeating or terminating decimal.	**número irracional** Número que no se puede expresar como una razón de dos enteros ni como un decimal periódico o finito.	$\sqrt{2}, \pi$
isolate the variable To get a variable alone on one side of an equation or inequality in order to solve the equation or inequality.	**despejar la variable** Dejar sola la variable en un lado de una ecuación o desigualdad para resolverla.	$\begin{array}{r} x + 7 = 22 \\ \underline{-7 \quad -7} \\ x \quad = 15 \end{array}$ $\begin{array}{r} \frac{12}{3} = \frac{3x}{3} \\ 4 = x \end{array}$
isometric drawing A representation of a three-dimensional figure that is drawn on a grid of equilateral triangles.	**dibujo isométrico** Representación de una figura tridimensional que se dibuja sobre una cuadrícula de triángulos equiláteros.	
isosceles triangle A triangle with at least two congruent sides.	**triángulo isósceles** Triángulo que tiene al menos dos lados congruentes.	

joint relative frequency The ratio of the frequency in a particular category divided by the total number of data values.	**frecuencia relativa conjunta** La razón de la frecuencia en una determinada categoría dividida entre el número total de valores.	

lateral area The sum of the areas of the lateral faces of a prism or pyramid, or the area of the lateral surface of a cylinder or cone.	**área lateral** Suma de las áreas de las caras laterales de un prisma o pirámide, o área de la superficie lateral de un cilindro o cono.	 Lateral area = area of the 5 rectangular faces

ENGLISH	SPANISH	EXAMPLES
lateral face In a prism or a pyramid, a face that is not a base.	**cara lateral** En un prisma o pirámide, una cara que no es la base.	

ENGLISH	SPANISH	EXAMPLES
lateral surface In a cylinder, the curved surface connecting the circular bases; in a cone, the curved surface that is not a base.	**superficie lateral** En un cilindro, superficie curva que une las bases circulares; en un cono, la superficie curva que no es la base.	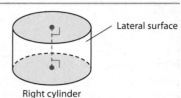
least common denominator (LCD) The least common multiple of two or more denominators.	**mínimo común denominador (mcd)** El mínimo común múltiplo más pequeño de dos o más denominadores.	The LCD of $\frac{3}{4}$ and $\frac{5}{6}$ is 12.
least common multiple (LCM) The smallest whole number, other than zero, that is a multiple of two or more given numbers.	**mínimo común múltiplo (mcm)** El menor de los números cabales, distinto de cero, que es múltiplo de dos o más números dados.	The LCM of 6 and 10 is 30.
legs In a right triangle, the sides that include the right angle; in an isosceles triangle, the pair of congruent sides.	**catetos** En un triángulo rectángulo, los lados adyacentes al ángulo recto. En un triángulo isósceles, el par de lados congruentes.	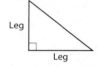
like fractions Fractions that have the same denominator.	**fracciones semejantes** Fracciones que tienen el mismo denominador.	$\frac{5}{12}$ and $\frac{7}{12}$ are like fractions.
like terms Terms that have the same variable raised to the same exponents.	**términos semejantes** Términos que contienen las mismas variables elevada a las mismas exponentes.	In the expression $3a^2 + 5b + 12a^2$, $3a^2$ and $12a^2$ are like terms.
line A straight path that has no thickness and extends forever.	**línea** Un trazo recto que no tiene grosor y se extiende infinitamente.	
line graph A graph that uses line segments to show how data changes.	**gráfica lineal** Gráfica que muestra cómo cambian los datos mediante segmentos de recta.	
line of best fit A straight line that comes closest to the points on a scatter plot.	**línea de mejor ajuste** La línea recta que más se aproxima a los puntos de un diagrama de dispersión.	

Glossary/Glosario

ENGLISH	SPANISH	EXAMPLES
line of reflection A line that a figure is flipped across to create a mirror image of the original figure.	**línea de reflexión** Línea sobre la cual se invierte una figura para crear una imagen reflejada de la figura original.	
line of symmetry A line that divides a figure into two congruent reflected halves.	**eje de simetría** Línea que divide una figura en dos mitades reflejas.	
line plot A number line with marks or dots that show frequency.	**diagrama de acumulación** Recta numérica con marcas o puntos que indican la frecuencia.	
line segment A part of a line consisting of two endpoints and all points between them.	**segmento de recta** Parte de una línea que consiste en dos extremos y todos los puntos entre éstos.	
line symmetry A figure has line symmetry if one half is a mirror image of the other half.	**simetría axial** Una figura tiene simetría axial si una de sus mitades es la imagen reflejada de la otra.	
linear equation An equation whose solutions form a straight line on a coordinate plane.	**ecuación lineal** Ecuación cuyas soluciones forman una línea recta en un plano cartesiano.	$y = 2x + 1$
linear function A function whose graph is a straight line.	**función lineal** Función cuya gráfica es una línea recta.	$y = x - 1$ 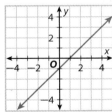
linear inequality A mathematical sentence using $<$, $>$, $\leq$, or $\geq$ whose graph is a region with a straight-line boundary.	**desigualdad lineal** Enunciado matemático en que se usan los símbolos $<$, $>$, $\leq$, o $\geq$ y cuya gráfica es una región con una línea de límite recta.	
linear relationship A relationship between two quantities in which one variable changes by a constant amount as the other variable changes by a constant amount.	**relación lineal** Relación entre dos cantidades en la cual una variable cambia según una cantidad constante y la otra variable también cambia según una cantidad constante.	
literal equation An equation that contains two or more variables.	**ecuación literal** Ecuación que contiene dos o más variables.	$d = rt$ $A = bh$

ENGLISH	SPANISH	EXAMPLES
lower quartile The median of the lower half of a set of data.	**cuartil inferior** La mediana de la mitad inferior de un conjunto de datos.	Lower half Upper half 18, (23,) 28, 29, 36, 42 ↑ Lower quartile

major arc An arc that is more than half of a circle.	**arco mayor** Arco que es más de la mitad de un círculo.	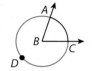 $\overset{\frown}{ADC}$ is a major arc of the circle.
marginal relative frequency The sum of the joint relative frequencies in a row or column of a two-way table.	**frecuencia relativa marginal** La suma de las frecuencias relativas conjuntas en una fila o columna de una tabla de doble entrada.	
matrix A rectangular arrangement of data enclosed in brackets.	**matriz** Arreglo rectangular de datos encerrado entre corchetes.	$\begin{bmatrix} 1 & 0 & 3 \\ -2 & 2 & -5 \\ 7 & -6 & 3 \end{bmatrix}$
mean The sum of a set of data divided by the number of items in the data set; also called *average*.	**media** La suma de todos los elementos de un conjunto de datos dividida entre el número de elementos del conjunto. También se llama promedio.	Data set: 4, 6, 7, 8, 10 Mean: $\frac{4+6+7+8+10}{5} = \frac{35}{5} = 7$
mean absolute deviation (MAD) The mean distance between each data value and the mean of the data set.	**desviación absoluta media (DAM)** Distancia media entre cada dato y la media del conjunto de datos.	
measure of center A measure used to describe the middle of a data set; the mean, median, and mode are measures of center. Also called *measure of central tendency*.	**medida de tendencia dominante** Medida que describe la parte media de un conjunto de datos; la media, la mediana y la moda son medidas de tendencia dominante.	
median The middle number, or the mean (average) of the two middle numbers, in an ordered set of data.	**mediana** El número intermedio o la media (el promedio) de los dos números intermedios en un conjunto ordenado de datos.	Data set: 4, 6, 7, 8, 10 Median: 7
metric system of measurement A decimal system of weights and measures that is used universally in science and commonly throughout the world.	**sistema métrico de medición** Sistema decimal de pesos y medidas empleado universalmente en las ciencias y de uso común en todo el mundo.	centimeters, meters, kilometers, grams, kilograms, milliliters, liters
midpoint The point that divides a line segment into two congruent line segments.	**punto medio** El punto que divide un segmento de recta en dos segmentos de recta congruentes.	 *B* is the midpoint of $\overline{AC}$.

Glossary/Glosario

ENGLISH	SPANISH	EXAMPLES
minor arc An arc that is less than half of a circle.	**arco menor** Arco que es menor que la mitad de un círculo.	$\overset{\frown}{AC}$ is the minor arc of the circle.
mixed number A number made up of a whole number that is not zero and a fraction.	**número mixto** Número compuesto por un número cabal distinto de cero y una fracción.	$4\frac{1}{8}$
mode The number or numbers that occur most frequently in a set of data; when all numbers occur with the same frequency, we say there is no mode.	**moda** Número o números más frecuentes en un conjunto de datos; si todos los números aparecen con la misma frecuencia, no hay moda.	Data set: 3, 5, 8, 8, 10 Mode: 8
monomial A number or a product of numbers and variables with exponents that are whole numbers.	**monomio** Un número o un producto de números y variables con exponentes que son números cabales.	$3x^2y^4$
multiple The product of any number and a nonzero whole number is a multiple of that number.	**múltiplo** El producto de cualquier número y un número cabal distinto de cero es un múltiplo de ese número.	
Multiplication Property of Equality The property that states that if you multiply both sides of an equation by the same number, the new equation will have the same solution.	**Propiedad de igualdad de la multiplicación** Propiedad que establece que puedes multiplicar ambos lados de una ecuación por el mismo número y la nueva ecuación tendrá la misma solución.	$3 \cdot 4 = 12$ $3 \cdot 4 \cdot 2 = 12 \cdot 2$ $24 = 24$
Multiplication Property of Zero The property that states that for all real numbers a, $a \cdot 0 = 0$ and $0 \cdot a = 0$.	**Propiedad de multiplicación del cero** Propiedad que establece que para todos los números reales a, $a \cdot 0 = 0$ y $0 \cdot a = 0$.	
multiplicative inverse A number times its multiplicative inverse is equal to 1; also called *reciprocal*.	**inverso multiplicativo** Un número multiplicado por su inverso multiplicativo es igual a 1. También se llama *recíproco*.	The multiplicative inverse of $\frac{4}{5}$ is $\frac{5}{4}$.
mutually exclusive Two events are mutually exclusive if they cannot occur in the same trial of an experiment.	**mutuamente excluyentes** Dos sucesos son mutuamente excluyentes cuando no pueden ocurrir en la misma prueba de un experimento.	When rolling a number cube once, rolling a 3 and rolling an even number are mutually exclusive events.

negative correlation Two data sets have a negative correlation if one set of data values increases while the other decreases.	**correlación negativa** Dos conjuntos de datos tienen correlación negativa si los valores de un conjunto aumentan a medida que los valores del otro conjunto disminuyen.	

ENGLISH	SPANISH	EXAMPLES
negative integer An integer less than zero.	**entero negativo** Entero menor que cero.	−2 is a negative integer.
net An arrangement of two-dimensional figures that can be folded to form a polyhedron.	**plantilla** Arreglo de figuras bidimensionales que se doblan para formar un poliedro.	
network A set of points and the line segments or arcs that connect the points.	**red** Conjunto de puntos y los segmentos de recta o arcos que los conectan.	
no correlation Two data sets have no correlation when there is no relationship between their data values.	**sin correlación** Caso en que los valores de dos conjuntos no muestran ninguna relación.	
nonlinear function A function whose graph is not a straight line.	**función no lineal** Función cuya gráfica no es una línea recta.	 $y = x^2 - 3$
nonlinear relationship A relationship between two variables in which the data do not increase or decrease together at the same rate.	**relación no lineal** Relación entre dos variables en la cual los datos no aumentan o disminuyen al mismo tiempo a una tasa constante.	
nonterminating decimal A decimal that never ends.	**decimal infinito** Decimal que nunca termina.	$0.\overline{3}$
numerator The top number of a fraction that tells how many parts of a whole are being considered.	**numerador** El número de arriba de una fracción; indica cuántas partes de un entero se consideran.	$\frac{4}{5}$ ← numerator
numerical expression An expression that contains only numbers and operations.	**expresión numérica** Expresión que incluye sólo números y operaciones.	$(2 \cdot 3) + 1$

obtuse angle An angle whose measure is greater than 90° but less than 180°.	**ángulo obtuso** Ángulo que mide más de 90° y menos de 180°.	
obtuse triangle A triangle containing one obtuse angle.	**triángulo obtusángulo** Triángulo que tiene un ángulo obtuso.	

ENGLISH	SPANISH	EXAMPLES

octagon An eight-sided polygon.

octágono Polígono de ocho lados.

---

odds A comparison of the number of ways an event can occur and the number of ways an event can *not* occur.

probabilidades Comparación del número de las maneras que puede ocurrir un suceso y el número de maneras que no puede ocurrir el suceso.

---

odds against The ratio of the number of unfavorable outcomes to the number of favorable outcomes.

probabilidades en contra Razón del número de resultados no favorables al número de resultados favorables.

The odds against rolling a 3 on a number cube are 5:1.

---

odds in favor The ratio of the number of favorable outcomes to the number of unfavorable outcomes.

probabilidades a favor Razón del número de resultados favorables al número de resultados no favorables.

The odds in favor of rolling a 3 on a number cube are 1:5.

---

opposites Two numbers that are an equal distance from zero on a number line; also called *additive inverse*.

opuestos Dos números que están a la misma distancia de cero en una recta numérica. También se llaman *inversos aditivos*.

5 and −5 are opposites.

---

order of operations A rule for evaluating expressions: First perform the operations in parentheses, then compute powers and roots, then perform all multiplication and division from left to right, and then perform all addition and subtraction from left to right.

orden de las operaciones Regla para evaluar expresiones: primero se hacen las operaciones entre paréntesis, luego se hallan las potencias y raíces, después todas las multiplicaciones y divisiones de izquierda a derecha, y por último, todas las sumas y restas de izquierda a derecha.

$4^2 + 8 \div 2$ Evaluate the power.
$16 + 8 \div 2$ Divide.
$16 + 4$ Add.
20

---

ordered pair A pair of numbers that can be used to locate a point on a coordinate plane.

par ordenado Par de números que sirven para ubicar un punto en un plano cartesiano.

The coordinates of B are $(-2, 3)$.

---

origin The point where the *x*-axis and *y*-axis intersect on the coordinate plane; (0, 0).

origen Punto de intersección entre el eje *x* y el eje *y* en un plano cartesiano: (0, 0).

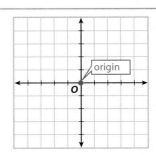

ENGLISH	SPANISH	EXAMPLES

orthogonal views A drawing that shows the top, bottom, front, back, and side views of a three-dimensional object.

vista ortogonal Un dibujo que muestra la vista superior, inferior, frontal, posterior y lateral de un objeto de tres dimensiones.

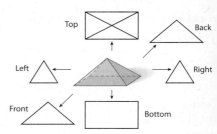

outcome (probability) A possible result of a probability experiment.

resultado (en probabilidad) Posible resultado de un experimento de probabilidad.

When rolling a number cube, the possible outcomes are 1, 2, 3, 4, 5, and 6.

outlier A value much greater or much less than the others in a data set.

valor extremo Un valor mucho mayor o menor que los demás valores de un conjunto de datos.

output The value that results from the substitution of a given input into an expression or function.

valor de salida Valor que resulta después de sustituir una variable por un valor de entrada determinado en una expresión o función.

For the function $y = 6x$, the input 4 produces an output of 24.

overestimate An estimate that is greater than the exact answer.

estimación alta Estimación mayor que la respuesta exacta.

100 is an overestimate for the sum $23 + 24 + 21 + 22$.

P

parabola The graph of a quadratic function.

parábola Gráfica de una función cuadrática.

parallel lines Lines in a plane that do not intersect.

líneas paralelas Líneas que se encuentran en el mismo plano pero que nunca se intersecan.

parallelogram A quadrilateral with two pairs of parallel sides.

paralelogramo Cuadrilátero con dos pares de lados paralelos.

pentagon A five-sided polygon.

pentágono Polígono de cinco lados.

percent A ratio comparing a number to 100.

porcentaje Razón que compara un número con el número 100.

$45\% = \frac{45}{100}$

percent change The amount stated as a percent that a number increases or decreases.

porcentaje de cambio Cantidad en que un número aumenta o disminuye, expresada como un porcentaje.

percent decrease A percent change describing a decrease in a quantity.

porcentaje de disminución Porcentaje de cambio en que una cantidad disminuye.

An item that costs $8 is marked down to $6. The amount of the decrease is $2, and the percent decrease is $\frac{2}{8} = 0.25 = 25\%$.

ENGLISH	SPANISH	EXAMPLES
percent increase A percent change describing an increase in a quantity.	**porcentaje de incremento** Porcentaje de cambio en que una cantidad aumenta.	The price of an item increases from \$8 to \$12. The amount of the increase is \$4, and the percent increase is $\frac{4}{8} = 0.5 = 50\%$.
perfect cube A cube of a whole number.	**cubo perfecto** El cubo de un número cabal.	$2^3 = 8$, so 8 is a perfect cube.
perfect square A square of a whole number.	**cuadrado perfecto** El cuadrado de un número cabal.	$5^2 = 25$, so 25 is a perfect square.
perimeter The distance around a polygon.	**perímetro** Distancia alrededor de un polígono.	18 ft 6 ft perimeter $= 18 + 6 + 18 + 6 = 48$ ft
permutation An arrangement of items or events in which order is important.	**permutación** Arreglo de objetos o sucesos en el que el orden es importante.	For objects A, B, and C, there are 6 different permutations: ABC, ACB, BAC, BCA, CAB, CBA.
perpendicular bisector A line that intersects a segment at its midpoint and is perpendicular to the segment.	**mediatriz** Línea que cruza un segmento en su punto medio y es perpendicular al segmento.	
perpendicular lines Lines that intersect to form right angles.	**líneas perpendiculares** Líneas que al intersecarse forman ángulos rectos.	
pi (π) The ratio of the circumference of a circle to the length of its diameter; $\pi \approx 3.14$ or $\frac{22}{7}$.	**pi** (π) Razón de la circunferencia de un círculo a la longitud de su diámetro; $\pi \approx 3.14$ ó $\frac{22}{7}$.	
plane A flat surface that has no thickness and extends forever.	**plano** Superficie plana que no tiene ningún grueso y que se extiende por siempre.	
point An exact location that has no size.	**punto** Ubicación exacta que no tiene ningún tamaño.	$P \bullet$
point-slope form The equation of a line in the form of $y - y_1 = m(x - x_1)$, where m is the slope and (x_1, y_1) is a specific point on the line.	**forma de punto y pendiente** Ecuación lineal del tipo $y - y_1 = m(x - x_1)$, donde m es la pendiente y (x_1, y_1) es un punto específico de la línea.	$y - 3 = 2(x - 3)$
polygon A closed plane figure formed by three or more line segments that intersect only at their endpoints (vertices).	**polígono** Figura plana cerrada, formada por tres o más segmentos de recta que se intersecan sólo en sus extremos (vértices).	

polyhedron A three-dimensional figure in which all the surfaces or faces are polygons.

poliedro Figura tridimensional cuyas superficies o caras tiene forma de polígonos.

---

polynomial One monomial or the sum or difference of monomials.

polinomio Un monomio o la suma o la diferencia de monomios.

$2x^2 + 3xy - 7y^2$

---

population The entire group of objects or individuals considered for a survey.

población Grupo completo de objetos o individuos que se desea estudiar.

In a survey about study habits of middle school students, the population is all middle school students.

---

positive correlation Two data sets have a positive correlation when their data values increase or decrease together.

correlación positiva Dos conjuntos de datos tienen una correlación positiva cuando los valores de ambos conjuntos aumentan o disminuyen al mismo tiempo.

---

positive integer An integer greater than zero.

entero positivo Entero mayor que cero.

2 is a positive integer.

---

power A number produced by raising a base to an exponent.

potencia Número que resulta al elevar una base a un exponente.

$2^3 = 8$, so 2 to the 3rd power is 8.

---

prediction Something you can reasonably expect to happen in the future.

predicción Algo que se puede razonablemente esperar suceder en el futuro.

---

preimage The original figure in a transformation.

imagen original Figura original en una transformación.

---

prime factorization A number written as the product of its prime factors.

factorización prima Un número escrito como el producto de sus factores primos.

$10 = 2 \cdot 5$,
$24 = 2^3 \cdot 3$

---

prime number A whole number greater than 1 that has exactly two factors, itself and 1.

número primo Número cabal mayor que 1 que sólo es divisible entre 1 y él mismo.

5 is prime because its only factors are 5 and 1.

---

principal The initial amount of money borrowed or saved.

principal Cantidad inicial de dinero depositada o recibida en préstamo.

---

principal square root The nonnegative square root of a number.

raíz cuadrada principal Raíz cuadrada no negativa de un número.

$\sqrt{25} = 5$; the principal square root of 25 is 5.

---

prism A polyhedron that has two congruent, polygon-shaped bases and other faces that are all parallelograms.

prisma Poliedro con dos bases congruentes con forma de polígono y caras con forma de paralelogramo.

---

probability A number from 0 to 1 (or 0% to 100%) that describes how likely an event is to occur.

probabilidad Un número entre 0 y 1 (ó 0% y 100%) que describe qué tan probable es un suceso.

A bag contains 3 red marbles and 4 blue marbles. The probability of randomly choosing a red marble is $\frac{3}{7}$.

Glossary/Glosario

ENGLISH	SPANISH	EXAMPLES
proper fraction A fraction in which the numerator is less than the denominator.	**fracción propia** Fracción en la que el numerador es menor que el denominador.	$\frac{3}{4}, \frac{1}{12}, \frac{7}{8}$
proportion An equation that states that two ratios are equivalent.	**proporción** Ecuación que establece que dos razones son equivalentes.	$\frac{2}{3} = \frac{4}{6}$
proportional relationship A relationship between two quantities in which the ratio of one quantity to the other quantity is constant.	**relación proporcional** Relación entre dos cantidades en que la razón de una cantidad a la otra es constante.	
protractor A tool for measuring angles.	**transportador** Instrumento para medir ángulos.	
pyramid A polyhedron with a polygon base and triangular sides that all meet at a common vertex.	**pirámide** Poliedro cuya base es un polígono; tiene caras triangulares que se juntan en un vértice común.	
Pythagorean Theorem In a right triangle, the square of the length of the hypotenuse is equal to the sum of the squares of the lengths of the legs.	**Teorema de Pitágoras** En un triángulo rectángulo, la suma de los cuadrados de los catetos es igual al cuadrado de la hipotenusa.	13 cm, 5 cm, 12 cm $5^2 + 12^2 = 13^2$ $25 + 144 = 169$
Pythagorean triple A set of three positive integers a, b, and c such that $a^2 + b^2 = c^2$.	**Tripleta de Pitágoras** Conjunto de tres números enteros positivos de cero a, b y c tal que $a^2 + b^2 = c^2$.	3, 4, 5 because $3^2 + 4^2 = 5^2$

Q

ENGLISH	SPANISH	EXAMPLES
quadrant The x- and y-axes divide the coordinate plane into four regions. Each region is called a quadrant.	**cuadrante** El eje x y el eje y dividen el plano cartesiano en cuatro regiones. Cada región recibe el nombre de cuadrante.	Quadrant II, Quadrant I, Quadrant III, Quadrant IV
quadratic function A function of the form $y = ax^2 + bx + c$, where $a \neq 0$.	**función cuadrática** Función del tipo $y = ax^2 + bx + c$, donde $a \neq 0$.	$y = x^2 - 6x + 8$
quadrilateral A four-sided polygon.	**cuadrilátero** Polígono de cuatro lados.	
quarterly Four times a year.	**trimestral** Cuatro veces al año.	

ENGLISH	SPANISH	EXAMPLES
quartile Three values, one of which is the median, that divide a data set into fourths.	**cuartil** Cada uno de tres valores, uno de los cuales es la mediana, que dividen en cuartos un conjunto de datos.	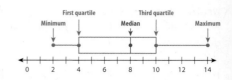
quotient The result when one number is divided by another.	**cociente** Resultado de dividir un número entre otro.	In $8 \div 4 = 2$, 2 is the quotient.

ENGLISH	SPANISH	EXAMPLES
radical symbol The symbol $\sqrt{}$ used to represent the nonnegative square root of a number.	**símbolo de radical** El símbolo $\sqrt{}$ con que se representa la raíz cuadrada no negativa de un número.	
radius A line segment with one endpoint at the center of the circle and the other endpoint on the circle, or the length of that segment.	**radio** Segmento de recta con un extremo en el centro de un círculo y el otro en la circunferencia, o bien se llama radio a la longitud de ese segmento.	
random numbers In a set of random numbers, each number has an equal chance of appearing.	**muestra aleatoria** Muestra en la que cada individuo u objeto de la población tiene la misma posibilidad de ser elegido.	
random sample A sample in which each individual or object in the entire population has an equal chance of being selected.	**números aleatorios** En un conjunto de números aleatorios, todos los números tienen la misma probabilidad de ser seleccionados.	
range (in statistics) The difference between the greatest and least values in a data set.	**rango (en estadística)** Diferencia entre los valores máximo y mínimo de un conjunto de datos.	Data set: 3, 5, 7, 7, 12 Range: $12 - 3 = 9$
range (of a function) The set of all possible output values of a function.	**rango (en una función)** El conjunto de todos los valores posibles de una función.	The range of $y = \lvert x \rvert$ is $y \geq 0$.
rate A ratio that compares two quantities measured in different units.	**tasa** Una razón que compara dos cantidades medidas en diferentes unidades.	The speed limit is 55 miles per hour or 55 mi/h.
rate of change A ratio that compares the amount of change in a dependent variable to the amount of change in an independent variable.	**tasa de cambio** Razón que compara la cantidad de cambio de la variable dependiente con la cantidad de cambio de la variable independiente.	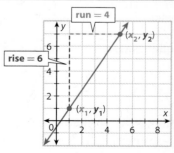 Rate of change $= \dfrac{\text{change in } y}{\text{change in } x} = \dfrac{6}{4} = \dfrac{3}{2}$

Glossary/Glosario

ENGLISH	SPANISH	EXAMPLES
rate of interest The percent charged or earned on an amount of money; see *simple interest*.	**tasa de interés** Porcentaje que se cobra por una cantidad de dinero prestada o que se gana por una cantidad de dinero ahorrada; ver *interés simple*.	
ratio A comparison of two quantities by division.	**razón** Comparación de dos cantidades mediante una división.	12 to 25, 12:25, $\frac{12}{25}$
rational number Any number that can be expressed as a ratio of two integers.	**número racional** Número que se puede escribir como una razón de dos enteros.	6 can be expressed as $\frac{6}{1}$. 0.5 can be expressed as $\frac{1}{2}$.
ray A part of a line that starts at one endpoint and extends forever in one direction.	**rayo** Parte de una línea que comienza en un extremo y se extiende de manera infinitamente en una dirección.	
real number A rational or irrational number.	**número real** Número racional o irracional.	
reciprocal One of two numbers whose product is 1; also called *multiplicative inverse*.	**recíproco** Uno de dos números cuyo producto es igual a 1. También se llama *inverso multiplicativo*.	The reciprocal of $\frac{2}{3}$ is $\frac{3}{2}$.
rectangle A parallelogram with four right angles.	**rectángulo** Paralelogramo con cuatro ángulos rectos.	
rectangular prism A polyhedron whose bases are rectangles and whose other faces are parallelograms.	**prisma rectangular** Poliedro cuyas bases son rectángulos y cuyas caras tienen forma de paralelogramo.	
reduction A decrease in the size of all dimensions.	**reducción** Disminución de tamaño en todas las dimensiones de una figura.	
reflection A transformation of a figure that flips the figure across a line.	**reflexión** Transformación que ocurre cuando se invierte una figura sobre una línea.	
regular polygon A polygon with congruent sides and angles.	**polígono regular** Polígono con lados y ángulos congruentes.	
regular pyramid A pyramid whose base is a regular polygon and whose lateral faces are all congruent.	**pirámide regular** Pirámide que tiene un polígono regular como base y caras laterales congruentes.	
relation A set of ordered pairs.	**relación** Conjunto de pares ordenados.	(0, 5), (0, 4), (2, 3), (4, 0)

ENGLISH	SPANISH	EXAMPLES
relative frequency The frequency of a specific data value divided by the total number of data values in the set.	**frecuencia relativa** La frecuencia de un valor dividido por el número total de los valores en el conjunto.	
relatively prime Two numbers are relatively prime if their greatest common factor (GCF) is 1.	**primo relativo** Dos números son primos relativos si su máximo común divisor (MCD) es 1.	8 and 15 are relatively prime.
remote interior angle An interior angle of a polygon that is not adjacent to the exterior angle.	**ángulo interno remoto** Ángulo interno de un polígono que no es adyacente al ángulo externo.	
repeating decimal A decimal in which one or more digits repeat infinitely.	**decimal periódico** Decimal en el que uno o más dígitos se repiten infinitamente.	$0.757575\ldots = 0.\overline{75}$
rhombus A parallelogram with all sides congruent.	**rombo** Paralelogramo en el que todos los lados son congruentes.	
right angle An angle that measures 90°.	**ángulo recto** Ángulo que mide exactamente 90°.	
right cone A cone in which a perpendicular line drawn from the base to the tip (vertex) passes through the center of the base.	**cono regular** Cono en el que una línea perpendicular trazada de la base a la punta (vértice) pasa por el centro de la base.	Right cone
right triangle A triangle containing a right angle.	**triángulo rectángulo** Triángulo que tiene un ángulo recto.	
rise The vertical change when the slope of a line is expressed as the ratio $\frac{\text{rise}}{\text{run}}$, or "rise over run."	**distancia vertical** El cambio vertical cuando la pendiente de una línea se expresa como la razón $\frac{\text{distancia vertical}}{\text{distancia horizontal}}$, o "distancia vertical sobre distancia horizontal".	For the points $(3, -1)$ and $(6, 5)$, the rise is $5 - (-1) = 6$.
rotation A transformation in which a figure is turned around a point.	**rotación** Transformación que ocurre cuando una figura gira alrededor de un punto.	
rotational symmetry A figure has rotational symmetry if it can be rotated less than 360° around a central point and coincide with the original figure.	**simetría de rotación** Ocurre cuando una figura gira menos de 360° alrededor de un punto central sin dejar de ser congruente con la figura original.	90°

ENGLISH	SPANISH	EXAMPLES
rounding Replacing a number with an estimate of that number to a given place value.	**redondear** Sustituir un número por una estimación de ese número hasta cierto valor posicional.	2,354 rounded to the nearest thousand is 2,000, and 2,354 rounded to the nearest 100 is 2,400.
run The horizontal change when the slope of a line is expressed as the ratio $\frac{rise}{run}$, or "rise over run."	**distancia horizontal** El cambio horizontal cuando la pendiente de una línea se expresa como la razón $\frac{distancia\ vertical}{distancia\ horizontal}$, o "distancia vertical sobre distancia horizontal".	For the points $(3, -1)$ and $(6, 5)$, the run is $6 - 3 = 3$.

S

sales tax A percent of the cost of an item that is charged by governments to raise money.	**impuesto sobre la venta** Porcentaje del costo de un artículo que los gobiernos cobran para recaudar fondos.	
same-side interior angles A pair of angles on the same side of a transversal and between two lines intersected by the transversal.	**ángulo internos del mismo lado** Dadas dos rectas cortadas por una transversal, par de ángulos ubicados en el mismo lado de la transversal y entre las dos rectas.	
sample A part of the population.	**muestra** Una parte de la población.	
sample space All possible outcomes of an experiment.	**espacio muestral** Conjunto de todos los resultados posibles de un experimento.	When rolling a number cube, the sample space is 1, 2, 3, 4, 5, 6.
scale The ratio between two sets of measurements.	**escala** La razón entre dos conjuntos de medidas.	1 cm : 5 mi
scale drawing A drawing that uses a scale to make an object smaller than (a reduction) or larger than (an enlargement) the real object.	**dibujo a escala** Dibujo en el que se usa una escala para que un objeto se vea menor (reducción) o mayor (agrandamiento) que el objeto real al que representa.	A blueprint is an example of a scale drawing.
scale factor The ratio used to enlarge or reduce similar figures.	**factor de escala** Razón empleada para agrandar o reducir figuras semejantes.	
scale model A proportional model of a three-dimensional object.	**modelo a escala** Modelo proporcional de un objeto tridimensional.	
scalene triangle A triangle with no congruent sides.	**triángulo escaleno** Triángulo que no tiene lados congruentes.	

ENGLISH	SPANISH	EXAMPLES

scatter plot A graph with points plotted to show a possible relationship between two sets of data.

diagrama de dispersión Gráfica de puntos que muestra una posible relación entre dos conjuntos de datos.

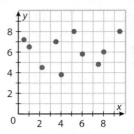

---

scientific notation A method of writing very large or very small numbers by using powers of 10.

notación científica Método que se usa para escribir números muy grandes o muy pequeños mediante potencias de 10.

$$12{,}560{,}000{,}000{,}000 = 1.256 \times 10^{13}$$

---

second quartile The median of a set of data.

segundo cuartil Mediana de un conjunto de datos.

Data set: 4, 6, 7, 8, 10
Second quartile: 7

---

sector A region enclosed by two radii and the arc joining their endpoints.

sector Región encerrada por dos radios y el arco que une sus extremos.

---

sector (data) A section of a circle graph representing part of the data set.

sector (datos) Sección de una gráfica circular que representa una parte del conjunto de datos.

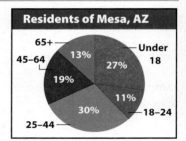

The circle graph has 5 sectors.

---

segment A part of a line between two endpoints.

segmento Parte de una línea entre dos extremos.

---

self-selected sample A sample in which members choose to be in the sample.

muestra auto-seleccionada Una muestra en la que los miembros eligen participar.

A store provides survey cards for customers who choose to fill them out.

---

sequence An ordered list of numbers.

sucesión Lista ordenada de números.

2, 4, 6, 8, 10, …

---

set A group of terms.

conjunto Un grupo de elementos.

---

side A line bounding a geometric figure; one of the faces forming the outside of an object.

lado Línea que delimita las figuras geométricas; una de las caras que forman la parte exterior de un objeto.

---

similar Figures with the same shape but not necessarily the same size.

semejantes Figuras que tienen la misma forma, pero no necesariamente el mismo tamaño.

Glossary/Glosario

ENGLISH	SPANISH	EXAMPLES
similarity transformation A transformation that results in an image that is the same shape, but not necessarily the same size, as the original figure.	**transformación de semejanza** Una transformación que resulta en una imagen que tiene la misma forma, pero no necesariamente el mismo tamaño como la figura original.	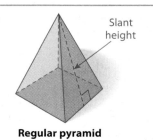
simple event An event consisting of only one outcome.	**suceso simple** Suceso que tiene sólo un resultado.	In the experiment of rolling a number cube, the event consisting of the outcome 3 is a simple event.
simple interest A fixed percent of the principal. It is found using the formula $I = Prt$, where P represents the principal, r the rate of interest, and t the time.	**interés simple** Un porcentaje fijo del capital. Se calcula con la fórmula $I = Cit$, donde C representa el capital, i, la tasa de interés y t, el tiempo.	$100 is put into an account with a simple interest rate of 5%. After 2 years, the account will have earned $I = 100 \cdot 0.05 \cdot 2 = \$10$.
simplest form A fraction in which the numerator and denominator have no common factors other than 1.	**mínima expresión** Una fracción está en su mínima expresión cuando el numerador y el denominador no tienen más factor común que 1.	Fraction: $\frac{8}{12}$ Simplest form: $\frac{2}{3}$
simplify To write a fraction or expression in simplest form.	**simplificar** Escribir una fracción o expresión numérica en su mínima expresión.	
simulation A model of an experiment, often one that would be too difficult or too time-consuming to actually perform.	**simulación** Representación de un experimento, por lo general, de uno cuya realización sería demasiado difícil o llevaría mucho tiempo.	
skew lines Lines that lie in different planes that are neither parallel nor intersecting.	**líneas oblicuas** Líneas que se encuentran en planos distintos, por eso no se intersecan ni son paralelas.	 $\overleftrightarrow{AB}$ and $\overleftrightarrow{CG}$ are skew lines.
slant height (of a regular pyramid) The distance from the vertex of a regular pyramid to the midpoint of an edge of the base.	**altura inclinada (de una pirámide)** Distancia desde el vértice de una pirámide hasta el punto medio de una arista de la base.	Slant height **Regular pyramid**
slant height (of a right cone) The distance from the vertex of a right cone to a point on the edge of the base.	**altura inclinada (de un cono recto)** Distancia desde el vértice de un cono recto hasta un punto en el borde de la base.	Slant height

ENGLISH	SPANISH	EXAMPLES

slope A measure of the steepness of a line on a graph; the rise divided by the run.

pendiente Medida de la inclinación de una línea en una gráfica. Razón de la distancia vertical a la distancia horizontal.

$$\text{Slope} = \frac{\text{rise}}{\text{run}} = \frac{3}{4}$$

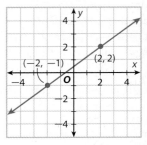

---

slope-intercept form A linear equation written in the form $y = mx + b$, where m represents slope and b represents the y-intercept.

forma de pendiente-intersección Ecuación lineal escrita en la forma $y = mx + b$, donde m es la pendiente y b es la intersección con el eje y.

$y = 6x - 3$

---

solid figure A three-dimensional figure.

cuerpo geométrico Figura tridimensional.

---

solution of an equation A value or values that make an equation true.

solución de una ecuación Valor o valores que hacen verdadera una ecuación.

Equation: $x + 2 = 6$
Solution: $x = 4$

---

solution of an inequality A value or values that make an inequality true.

solución de una desigualdad Valor o valores que hacen verdadera una desigualdad.

Inequality: $x + 3 \geq 10$
Solution: $x \geq 7$

---

solution of a system of equations A set of values that make all equations in a system true.

solución de un sistema de ecuaciones Conjunto de valores que hacen verdaderas todas las ecuaciones de un sistema.

System: $\begin{cases} x + y = -1 \\ -x + y = -3 \end{cases}$
Solution: $(1, -2)$

---

solution set The set of values that make a statement true.

conjunto solución Conjunto de valores que hacen verdadero un enunciado.

Inequality: $x + 3 \geq 5$
Solution set: $x \geq 2$

---

solve To find an answer or a solution.

resolver Hallar una respuesta o solución.

---

sphere A three-dimensional figure with all points the same distance from the center.

esfera Figura tridimensional en la que todos los puntos están a la misma distancia del centro.

---

square A rectangle with four congruent sides.

cuadrado Rectángulo con cuatro lados congruentes.

Glossary/Glosario

ENGLISH	SPANISH	EXAMPLES
square (numeration) A number raised to the second power.	**cuadrado (en numeración)** Número elevado a la segunda potencia.	In 5^2, the number 5 is squared.
square root A number that is multiplied by itself to form a product is called a square root of that product.	**raíz cuadrada** El número que se multiplica por sí mismo para formar un producto se denomina la raíz cuadrada de ese producto.	A square root of 16 is 4, because $4^2 = 4 \cdot 4 = 16$. Another square root of 16 is -4 because $(-4)^2 = (-4)(-4) = 16$.
stem-and-leaf plot A graph used to organize and display data so that the frequencies can be compared.	**diagrama de tallo y hojas** Gráfica que muestra y ordena los datos, y que sirve para comparar las frecuencias.	<table><tr><th>Stem</th><th>Leaves</th></tr><tr><td>3</td><td>2 3 4 4 7 9</td></tr><tr><td>4</td><td>0 1 5 7 7 7 8</td></tr><tr><td>5</td><td>1 2 2 3</td></tr></table> *Key: 3|2 means 3.2*
straight angle An angle that measures 180°.	**ángulo llano** Ángulo que mide exactamente 180°.	
subset A set contained within another set.	**subconjunto** Conjunto que pertenece a otro conjunto.	
substitute To replace a variable with a number or another expression in an algebraic expression.	**sustituir** Reemplazar una variable por un número u otra expresión en una expresión algebraica.	Substituting 3 for m in the expression $5m - 2$ gives $5(3) - 2 = 15 - 2 = 13$.
Subtraction Property of Equality The property that states that if you subtract the same number from both sides of an equation, the new equation will have the same solution.	**Propiedad de igualdad de la resta** Propiedad que establece que puedes restar el mismo número de ambos lados de una ecuación y la nueva ecuación tendrá la misma solución.	$$\begin{array}{r} 14 - 6 = 8 \\ \underline{-6 = -6} \\ 14 - 12 = 2 \end{array}$$
supplementary angles Two angles whose measures have a sum of 180°.	**ángulos suplementarios** Dos ángulos cuyas medidas suman 180°.	 30° 150°
surface area The sum of the areas of the faces, or surfaces, of a three-dimensional figure.	**área total** Suma de las áreas de las caras, o superficies, de una figura tridimensional.	 12 cm 6 cm 8 cm Surface area $= 2(8)(12) + 2(8)(6) + 2(12)(6) = 432 \text{ cm}^2$
system of equations A set of two or more equations that contain two or more variables.	**sistema de ecuaciones** Conjunto de dos o más ecuaciones que contienen dos o más variables.	$$\begin{cases} x + y = -1 \\ -x + y = -3 \end{cases}$$
systematic sample A sample of a population that has been selected using a pattern.	**muestra sistemática** Muestra de una población, que ha sido elegida mediante un patrón.	To conduct a phone survey, every tenth name is chosen from the phone book.

term (in an expression) A part of an expression that is added or subtracted.

término (en una expresión) Las partes de una expresión que se suman o se restan.

$$3x^2 \ + \ 6x \ - \ 8$$

Term   Term   Term

---

term (in a sequence) An element or number in a sequence.

término (en una sucesión) Elemento o número de una sucesión.

5 is the third term in the sequence
1, 3, 5, 7, 9, …

---

terminating decimal A decimal number that ends, or terminates.

decimal finito Decimal con un número determinado de posiciones decimales.

6.75

---

tessellation A repeating pattern of plane figures that completely cover a plane with no gaps or overlaps.

teselado Patrón repetido de figuras planas que cubren totalmente un plano sin superponerse ni dejar huecos.

---

theoretical probability The ratio of the number of ways an event can occur to the number of equally likely outcomes.

probabilidad teórica Razón del número de las maneras que puede ocurrir un suceso al numero total de resultados igualmente probables.

When rolling a number cube, the theoretical probability of rolling a 4 is $\frac{1}{6}$.

---

third quartile The median of the upper half of a set of data; also called *upper quartile*.

tercer cuartil La mediana de la mitad superior de un conjunto de datos. También se llama *cuartil superior*.

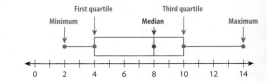

---

transformation A change in the size or position of a figure.

transformación Cambio en el tamaño o la posición de una figura.

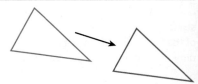

---

translation A movement (slide) of a figure along a straight line.

traslación Desplazamiento de una figura a lo largo de una línea recta.

---

transversal A line that intersects two or more lines.

transversal Línea que cruza dos o más líneas.

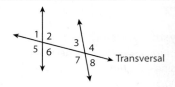

---

trapezoid A quadrilateral with exactly one pair of parallel sides.

trapecio Cuadrilátero con un par de lados paralelos.

tree diagram A branching diagram that shows all possible combinations or outcomes of an event.

diagrama de árbol Diagrama ramificado que muestra todas las posibles combinaciones o resultados de un suceso.

trend line A line on a scatter plot that helps show the correlation between data sets more clearly.

línea de tendencia Línea en un diagrama de dispersión que sirve para mostrar la correlación entre conjuntos de datos más claramente. *ver también* línea de mejor ajuste.

trial Each repetition or observation of an experiment.

prueba Una sola repetición u observación de un experimento.

When rolling a number cube, each roll is one trial.

Triangle Inequality Theorem The theorem that states that the sum of the lengths of any two sides of a triangle is greater than the length of the third side.

Teorema de desigualdad de triángulos El teorema dice que la suma de cualquier dos lados de un triangulo es mayor que la longitud del lado tercero.

Can form a triangle   Cannot form a triangle

Triangle Sum Theorem The theorem that states that the measures of the angles in a triangle add up to 180°.

Teorema de la suma del triángulo Teorema que establece que las medidas de los ángulos de un triángulo suman 180°.

triangular prism A polyhedron whose bases are triangles and whose other faces are parallelograms.

prisma triangular Poliedro cuyas bases son triángulos y cuyas demás caras tienen forma de paralelogramo.

trinomial A polynomial with three terms.

trinomio Polinomio con tres términos.

$4x^2 + 3xy - 5y^2$

two-way relative frequency table A two-way table that displays relative frequencies.

tabla de frecuencia relativa de doble entrada Una tabla de doble entrada que muestran las frecuencias relativas.

two-way table A table that displays two-variable data by organizing it into rows and columns.

tabla de doble entrada Una tabla que muestran los datos de dos variables por organizándolos en columnas y filas.

		Preference		
		Inside	**Outside**	*Total*
Pet	**Cats**	35	15	50
	Dogs	20	30	50
	Total	55	45	100

underestimate An estimate that is less than the exact answer.

estimación baja Estimación menor que la respuesta exacta.

ENGLISH	SPANISH	EXAMPLES
unit conversion The process of changing one unit of measure to another.	**conversión de unidades** Proceso que consiste en cambiar una unidad de medida por otra.	
unit conversion factor A fraction used in unit conversion in which the numerator and denominator represent the same amount but are in different units.	**factor de conversión de unidades** Fracción que se usa para la conversión de unidades, donde el numerador y el denominador representan la misma cantidad pero están en unidades distintas.	$\frac{60\ \text{min}}{1\ \text{h}}$ or $\frac{1\ \text{h}}{60\ \text{min}}$
unit price A unit rate used to compare prices.	**precio unitario** Tasa unitaria que sirve para comparar precios.	Cereal costs $0.23 per ounce.
unit rate A rate in which the second quantity in the comparison is one unit.	**tasa unitaria** Una tasa en la que la segunda cantidad de la comparación es la unidad.	10 cm per minute
upper quartile The median of the upper half of a set of data.	**cuartil superior** La mediana de la mitad superior de un conjunto de datos.	Lower half Upper half 18, 23, 28, 29, (36,) 42 ↑ Upper quartile

V

variability The spread of values in a set of data.	**variabilidad** Amplitud de los valores de un conjunto de datos.	The data set {1, 5, 7, 10, 25} has greater variability than the data set {8, 8, 9, 9, 9}.
variable A symbol used to represent a quantity that can change.	**variable** Símbolo que representa una cantidad que puede cambiar.	In the expression $2x + 3$, x is the variable.
Venn diagram A diagram that is used to show relationships between sets.	**diagrama de Venn** Diagrama que muestra las relaciones entre conjuntos.	Transformations / Rotations
vertex On an angle or polygon, the point where two sides intersect; on a polyhedron, the intersection of three or more faces; on a cone or pyramid, the top point.	**vértice** En un ángulo o polígono, el punto de intersección de dos lados; en un poliedro, el punto de intersección de tres o más caras; en un cono o pirámide, la punta.	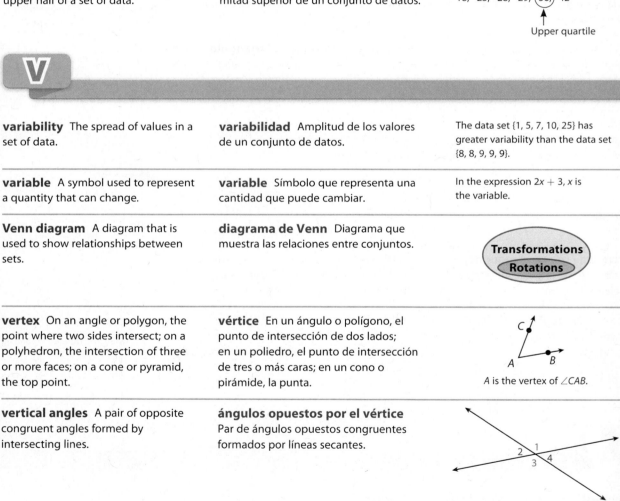 A is the vertex of $\angle CAB$.
vertical angles A pair of opposite congruent angles formed by intersecting lines.	**ángulos opuestos por el vértice** Par de ángulos opuestos congruentes formados por líneas secantes.	$\angle 1$ and $\angle 3$ are vertical angles.

Glossary/Glosario

ENGLISH	SPANISH	EXAMPLES

vertical line test A test used to determine whether a relation is a function. If any vertical line crosses the graph of a relation more than once, the relation is not a function.

prueba de la línea vertical Prueba utilizada para determinar si una relación es una función. Si una línea vertical corta la gráfica de una relación más de una vez, la relación no es una función.

Function   Not a function

---

volume The number of cubic units needed to fill a given space.

volumen Número de unidades cúbicas que se necesitan para llenar un espacio.

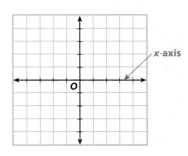

Volume $= 3 \cdot 4 \cdot 12 = 144$ ft^3

W

weighted average A mean that is calculated by multiplying each data value by a weight, and dividing the sum of these products by the sum of the weights.

promedio ponderado Promedio que se calcula por multiplicando cada valor de datos por un peso, y dividiendo la suma de estos productos por la suma de los pesos.

If the data values 0, 5, and 10 are assigned the weights 0.1, 0.2, and 0.7, respectively, the weighted average is:
$$\frac{0(0.1) + 5(0.2) + 10(0.7)}{0.1 + 0.2 + 0.7} = \frac{8}{1}$$

X

x-axis The horizontal axis on a coordinate plane.

eje x El eje horizontal del plano cartesiano.

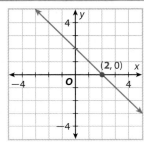

x-axis

---

x-coordinate The first number in an ordered pair; it tells the distance to move right or left from the origin (0, 0).

coordenada x El primer número de un par ordenado; indica la distancia que debes moverte hacia la izquierda o la derecha desde el origen, (0, 0).

5 is the *x*-coordinate in (5, 3).

---

x-intercept The *x*-coordinate of the point where the graph of a line crosses the *x*-axis.

intersección con el eje x Coordenada *x* del punto donde la gráfica de una línea cruza el eje *x*.

(2, 0)

The *x*-intercept is 2.

Glossary/Glosario

y-axis The vertical axis on a coordinate plane.

eje y El eje vertical del plano cartesiano.

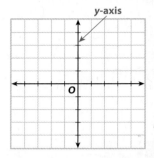

y-axis

y-coordinate The second number in an ordered pair; it tells the distance to move up or down from the origin (0, 0).

coordenada y El segundo número de un par ordenado; indica la distancia que debes avanzar hacia arriba o hacia abajo desde el origen, (0, 0).

3 is the y-coordinate in (5, 3).

y-intercept The y-coordinate of the point where the graph of a line crosses the y-axis.

intersección con el eje y Coordenada y del punto donde la gráfica de una línea cruza el eje y.

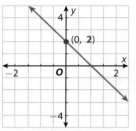

The y-intercept is 2.

zero pair A number and its opposite, which add to 0.

par nulo Un número y su opuesto, cuya suma es 0.

18 and −18

Index

Index

Index

ASSESSMENT REFERENCE SHEET

TABLE OF MEASURES

Length

1 inch = 2.54 centimeters

1 meter = 39.37 inches

1 mile = 5,280 feet

1 mile = 1,760 yards

1 mile = 1.609 kilometers

1 kilometer = 0.62 mile

Mass/Weight

1 pound = 16 ounces

1 pound = 0.454 kilograms

1 kilogram = 2.2 pounds

1 ton = 2,000 pounds

Capacity

1 cup = 8 fluid ounces

1 pint = 2 cups

1 quart = 2 pints

1 gallon = 4 quarts

1 gallon = 3.785 liters

1 liter = 0.264 gallons

1 liter = 1000 cubic centimeters

FORMULAS

Area

Parallelogram	$A = bh$
Circle	$A = \pi r^2$
Triangle	$A = \frac{1}{2} bh$

Volume

General Prisms	$V = Bh$
Cylinder	$V = \pi r^2 h$
Sphere	$V = \frac{4}{3} \pi r^3$
Cone	$V = \frac{1}{3} \pi r^2 h$

Circumference

Circle	$C = \pi d$ or $C = 2\pi r$

Other

Pythagorean Theorem	$a^2 + b^2 = c^2$